The Physiology and Biochemistry of
DROUGHT RESISTANCE
IN PLANTS

The Physiology and Biochemistry of
DROUGHT RESISTANCE IN PLANTS

Edited by

L. G. PALEG
and
D. ASPINALL

Department of Plant Physiology
Waite Agricultural Research Institute
The University of Adelaide, South Australia

1981

ACADEMIC PRESS
A Subsidiary of Harcourt Brace Jovanovich, Publishers
Sydney   New York   London   Toronto   San Francisco

Printed in Australia

National Library of Australia Cataloguing-in-Publication Data
Physiology and biochemistry of drought resistance in plants

   Bibliography
   Includes index
   ISBN 0 12 544380 3

   1. Plants—Drought resistance. 2. Plant Physiology.
   3. Botanical chemistry. I. Paleg, L. G. (Leslie Godell).
   II. Aspinall, D. (Donald).

581.1

Library of Congress Catalog Card Number: 80-70894

Contents

Preface   xi

List of Contributors   xiii

1. INTRODUCTION: THE HUMAN CONSEQUENCES OF DROUGHT AND CROP RESEARCH PRIORITIES FOR THEIR ALLEVIATION

L. D. SWINDALE AND F. R. BIDINGER

I.	The definition of drought	2
II.	Drought-susceptible areas	4
III.	Living with drought	4
IV.	Crop research needs for drought-susceptible areas	8
V.	Conclusion	13

2. MECHANISMS OF DROUGHT RESISTANCE

M. M. JONES, N. C. TURNER AND C. B. OSMOND

I.	Introduction	15
II.	Classification of drought resistance	16
III.	Drought escape	17
IV.	Drought tolerance at high tissue water potential	20
V.	Drought tolerance at low tissue water potential	24
VI.	Implications of different drought resistance mechanisms	35

3. WATER COLLECTION BY ROOTS

J. B. PASSIOURA

I.	Introduction	39
II.	Factors influencing the rate of water collection	40
III.	The amount of water collected	47

IV.   The efficiency with which the water is collected   51
V.   The pattern of water collection through time   51
VI.   Conclusions   53

4. WATER RELATIONS DURING DROUGHT

MERRILL R. KAUFMANN

I.   Introduction   55
II.   Water transport and redistribution   57
III. Water status of plant tissues   67

5. ION UPTAKE

M. G. PITMAN

I.   Introduction   71
II.   The uptake process   72
III. Interactions of water stress and the uptake process   74
IV.   Adaptations   91

6. SOLUTE ACCUMULATION AND REGULATION OF CELL WATER ACTIVITY

LESLEY J. BOROWITZKA

I.   Introduction   97
II.   Terms defined   99
III. Physicochemical aspects of solute accumulation   104

7. NITROGEN FIXATION

JANET I. SPRENT

I.   Introduction   131
II.   Legumes   132
III. Lichens   142

8. NITRATE REDUCTASE

S. K. SINHA AND D. J. D. NICHOLAS

I.	Introduction	145
II.	Properties of plant nitrate reductase	146
III.	Nitrate reductase, dry matter and yield	148
IV.	Regulation	150
V.	Effect of drought on nitrate reductase	155
VI.	Varietal effects	162
VII.	Relative effects of water deficit on nitrate reductase and related enzymes	164
VIII.	Evidence for inactivation	165
IX.	Analysis and integration	167
X.	Conclusions	168

9. BETAINES

R. G. WYN JONES AND R. STOREY

I.	Introduction	172
II.	Phytotaxonomic distribution of betaines	176
III.	Tissue distribution of betaines	190
IV.	Biosynthetic pathways	191
V.	Accumulation of betaines in stressed tissues	194
VI.	Possible physiological functions	200
VII.	Concluding discussion	204

10. PROLINE ACCUMULATION: PHYSIOLOGICAL ASPECTS

D. ASPINALL AND L. G. PALEG

I.	The response	206
II.	Consequences of proline accumulation	214
III.	Proline accumulation and stress resistance	219
IV.	Selection for proline accumulation	237
V.	Future prospects	240

11. PROLINE ACCUMULATION: BIOCHEMICAL ASPECTS

CECIL R. STEWART

I.   Introduction   243
II.   Proline metabolism   244
III. Effects of drought on proline metabolism   254
IV.   Conclusions   258

12. PROTEIN SYNTHESIS

J. DEREK BEWLEY

I.   Introduction   261
II.   Plants with a low tolerance of drought   262
III. Desiccation-tolerant plants   267
IV.   Tolerance of desiccation by seeds and its loss
      during seedling growth   275
V.   The relationship between desiccation tolerance,
      desiccation resistance and protein synthesis   281

13. PHOTOSYNTHESIS

P. E. KRIEDEMANN AND W. J. S. DOWNTON

I.   Introduction   283
II.   Comparative biochemistry and physiology of photosynthesis   284
III. Photosynthetic adjustments to water stress and implications
      for drought resistance   292
IV.   Summary   313

14. STOMATA AND STOMATAL MECHANISMS

T. A. MANSFIELD AND W. J. DAVIES

I.   Introduction   315
II.   First lines of defence   316
III. Second lines of defence   328
IV.   Natural and artificial strategies for improving efficiency
      of water use   341

15. ABSCISIC ACID AND OTHER HORMONES

B. V. MILBORROW

I.	Introduction	348
II.	Stress	349
III.	Metabolism	354
IV.	Solutes and permeability	373
V.	Effects on stomata	381
VI.	Conclusion	386

16. ULTRASTRUCTURAL CONSEQUENCES OF DROUGHT

ALEXANDRA POLJAKOFF-MAYBER

I.	Introduction	389
II.	Effect of water stress on the structure and function of the photosynthetic apparatus	390
III.	Changes induced by water stress in mitochondrial structure and function	394
IV.	Effect of water stress on protein synthesizing apparatus	397
V.	Changes occurring in the nucleus and cytoplasmic membranes due to water stress	399
VI.	General discussion	401

Appendix: Comparitive Systems of Measurement of Water Status	405
References	411
Author Index	467
Biological Index	481
Subject Index	485

Preface

Our aim in preparing this book was to present to higher degree and post-graduate research workers a comprehensive picture of the many recent changes in our knowledge of the metabolic consequences of drought. During the past fifteen years several areas of metabolism have been identified as being affected relatively early in the onset of a period of stress; for example, the conversion of polyribosomes to monosomes, accumulation of proline, accumulation of betaines, increase in abscisic acid levels and decrease in amounts of cytokinins. It has been speculated that many of these responses, together with the reaction of the enzyme nitrate reductase, may be involved in the resistance of the plant to stress. Thus we passed from a period of ignorance to a time in which proponents of a variety of processes, metabolic functions and biosynthetic pathways have promising and potentially important leads to explore.

We realized that a bringing together of these recent developments, all with a "drought resistance" orientation, would be useful. In a few of the areas covered, information about stress resistance *per se* is still sparse and speculative, but in each case an attempt has been made to base the speculation on the fundamental physiology or biochemistry of the plant during water stress. With each chapter providing a review as well as guidelines and suggestions for the future, we hope this book will serve not only as a reference, but as a starting point for biologists interested in particular plant processes or metabolic aspects of growth and development. Also, we hope the book will illustrate that fundamental questions of strong scientific import can be closely related to social needs and applied problems of great relevance. Some of the recent research findings may be of significance in future investigative programmes; some may be of use in the development of techniques for assessing and altering drought resistance — all are examples of the fruits of the union of basic scientific and mission-oriented research, a recent accomplishment in the long history of the field.

Generally our responses to the enumerated water requirements of various crops have been engineering responses. Almost 9,000 years ago, in Jericho, men were manipulating plant growth and development by moving water from its point of occurrence to agriculturally more desirable sites. More sophisticated engineering techniques have since expanded our water use and management capabilities, enabling us to progress from aquaducts to integrated, large-scale, inter-basin transfers such as the Snowy Mountains Scheme in Australia, the Rhône-Languedoc plan in southern France and the Californian river basin transfers. Such extensive projects change the geographic distribution of water, while the smaller, but equally innovative techniques, such as sprinklers and drippers, place the water in precise locations, at specified times and in predetermined amounts.

In contrast, during the history of agriculture, successful attempts to influence crop water requirements through an understanding of plants are conspicuously rare, and even unsuccessful attempts are scarce. It is our hope and expectation that the increase in knowledge of the metabolic consequences of drought will lead to a better understanding of the processes involved and eventually to techniques to increase the drought resistance of crop plants.

List of Contributors

Numbers in parentheses indicate the pages on which the authors' contributions begin.

D. ASPINALL (205), Department of Plant Physiology, Waite Agricultural Research Institute, The University of Adelaide, Glen Osmond, SA 5064, Australia.

J. D. BEWLEY (261), Department of Biology, University of Calgary, 2920 24th Ave NW, Calgary, Alberta T2N 1N4, Canada.

F. R. BIDINGER (1), International Crops Research Institute for the Semi-Arid Tropics, Patancheru PO, Andhra Pradesh 502324, India.

L. J. BOROWITZKA (97), Roche Institute of Marine Pharmacology, PO Box 255, Dee Why, NSW 2099, Australia.

W. J. DAVIES (315), Department of Biological Sciences, The University of Lancaster, Lancaster LA1 4YQ, England.

W. J. S. DOWNTON (283), Division of Horticultural Research, Commonwealth Scientific & Industrial Research Organization, Box 350 GPO, Adelaide, SA 5001, Australia.

M. M. JONES* (15), Division of Plant Industry, Commonwealth Scientific & Industrial Research Organization, PO Box 1600, Canberra, ACT 2601, Australia.

M. R. KAUFMANN (55), U.S. Department of Agriculture Forest Service, Rocky Mountain Forest & Range Experiment Station, 240 West Prospect St, Fort Collins, Colorado 80521, USA.

P. E. KRIEDEMANN‡ (283), Division of Irrigation Research, Commonwealth Scientific & Industrial Research Organization, Griffith, NSW 2680, Australia.

---

*Present address: Department of Primary Industry, Broughton St, Barton, ACT 2600, Australia.

‡Present address: Division of Soils, Commonwealth Scientific & Industrial Research Organization, Private Bag No. 2, Glen Osmond, SA 5064, Australia.

T. A. MANSFIELD (315), Department of Biological Sciences, The University of Lancaster, Lancaster LA1 4YQ, England.

B. V. MILBORROW (347), School of Biochemistry, University of New South Wales, PO Box 1, Kensington, NSW 2033, Australia.

D. J. D. NICHOLAS (145), Department of Agricultural Biochemistry, Waite Agricultural Research Institute, The University of Adelaide, Glen Osmond, SA 5064, Australia.

C. B. OSMOND (15), Research School of Biological Sciences, Australian National University, PO Box 475, Canberra City, ACT 2601, Australia.

L. G. PALEG (205), Department of Plant Physiology, Waite Agricultural Research Institute, The University of Adelaide, Glen Osmond, SA 5064, Australia.

J. B. PASSIOURA (39), Division of Plant Industry, Commonwealth Scientific & Industrial Research Organization, PO Box 1600, Canberra City, ACT 2601, Australia.

M. G. PITMAN (71), School of Biological Sciences, University of Sydney, NSW 2006, Australia.

A. POLJAKOFF-MAYBER (389), Department of Botany, Hebrew University, Jerusalem, Israel.

S. K. SINHA (145), Water Technology Centre, Indian Agricultural Research Institute, New Delhi 110012, India.

J. I. SPRENT (131), Department of Biological Science, University of Dundee, Dundee DD1 4HN, Scotland.

C. R. STEWART (243), Department of Botany & Plant Pathology, Iowa State University, Ames, Iowa 50010, USA.

R. STOREY* (171). School of Biological Sciences, University of Sydney, NSW 2006, Australia.

L. D. SWINDALE (1), International Crops Research Institute for the Semi-Arid Tropics, Patancheru PO, Andhra Pradesh 502324, India.

---

*Present address: Department of Agronomy, Waite Agricultural Research Institute, The University of Adelaide, Glen Osmond, SA 5064, Australia.

N. C. TURNER (15), Division of Plant Industry, Commonwealth Scientific & Industrial Research Organization, PO Box 1600, Canberra City, ACT 2601, Australia.

R. G. WYN JONES (171), Department of Biochemistry and Soil Science, University College of North Wales, Bangor, Gwynedd LL 57 2UW, Wales.

CHAPTER 1

Introduction: The Human Consequences of Drought and Crop Research Priorities for their Alleviation

L. D. SWINDALE AND F. R. BIDINGER

I.	The definition of drought	2
II.	Drought-susceptible areas	4
III.	Living with drought	4
	A. When crops fail	6
	B. Preventing crop failure	7
IV.	Crop research needs for drought-susceptible areas	8
	A. Research on crop and soil management techniques	9
	B. Breeding for drought resistance in crop plants	9
	C. Physiological and biochemical research on plant resistance to drought	11
V.	Conclusion	13

When drought is prolonged crops fail and people may starve.

Over the past few years there has been little serious drought in the world, but it is easy to recall the grim years of the early 1970s when severe droughts occurred in Asia and Africa in the latitudes just below the Tropic of Cancer. Many thousands of people and animals were affected and many lives were lost.

The effects of the drought in a large part of Western India were described in great detail by Subramanian (1975). In the state of Maharashtra, an area of 308,000 km², the rainfall was about 25% below the average in 1971 and about 40% below in 1972. Crop production suffered. Average production of all cereals and pulse crops for the 10 years prior to 1971–72 was 64,000 tonnes. Production dropped to 44,000 tonnes in 1971–72 and to 30,000 tonnes in 1972–73. In the Marathwada region, in the vicinity of Aurangabad, few crops survived to harvest in 1972–73, and there was an acute shortage of drinking water.

1

PHYSIOLOGY AND BIOCHEMISTRY
OF DROUGHT RESISTANCE
IN PLANTS

In the face of widespread crop failures, human and animal migration, and the very real threat of starvation, the Government of Maharashtra organized massive work-for-food programs in the rural areas of the state. At the peak, over 5 million people were employed on relief works, building roads, dams and canals. Subramanian claims that there were no deaths directly attributable to starvation in either year. Many critical and perceptive reporters visited the state and came away full of praise for the State's efforts. Wolf Ladejinsky, in the *Indian Economic and Political Weekly* (Bombay) of 17 February 1973, called the Maharashtra drought "a disaster of unprecedented dimension" and complimented the State Government for organizing relief and employment works on such a large scale. John Pilger, in the *New Statesman* (London) of 8 June 1973, commented, "the Herculean relief efforts of both the Indian and State Governments have undoubtedly prevented [the drought] from becoming a famine in the classic sense with people dying in their tracks."

The people of the Sahel were less fortunate. A drought of somewhat the same severity, but one year longer, in much the same years (1970–1974), fell heavily upon nations with rapidly increasing populations and poorly developed infrastructures undergoing profound socioeconomic changes. Cereal production decreased by about 30% in the region from Mauritania to Ethiopia, over the period of the drought (OECD, 1976), but decreased 90% in many places in 1973, the worst year (Oguntoyinbo & Richards, 1977; Faulkingham, 1977).

The migratory people of the Sahelian ecological zone were most affected. Thousands (OECD, 1976; Caldwell, 1977) and perhaps even hundreds of thousands (Seaman et al., 1974; Wood, 1977) of people and millions of animals died. The stock populations of Mauritania, Niger and Chad were reduced by at least 40% (OECD, 1976). Many more people and animals migrated, and many will not return (Boutrais, 1977; Toupet, 1977).

Drought years are common in the region. There is no evidence that major climatic changes have occurred (Bunting et al., 1976). Many of the scientific studies published following the disasters asserted that things could have been worse and were worse in a drought 60 years earlier. Certainly massive food aid from outside saved many lives from 1973 onwards, but it also produced a food preference shift towards mostly imported wheat and rice and away from locally grown and more drought-resistant sorghum and millet.

I. THE DEFINITION OF DROUGHT

Droughts do not need to be prolonged to affect crop yields. In fact, a "drought" or water stress for even one day will have some effect if the stress is large enough. If crops can be so easily affected by water stress, what constitutes drought? Linsley et al. (1959) defined drought as a sustained period of time without significant rainfall. This definition would probably fit most people's ideas of drought since it combines time and deficient rainfall. Katz and Glantz (1977) suggested that there were meteorological and agricultural definitions of drought. A meteorological drought could be defined as that time period when the amount of precipitation is less than some designated percentage of the long-term mean. An agricultural drought, on the other hand, could be defined in terms of seasonal vegetation development. Palmer (1964) commented that most American farmers do not call a dry spell a drought until the moisture shortage seriously affects the established economy. Morris (1974) took this idea substantially to its limit by defining a drought as "an unseasonally rapid rise in agricultural prices". This functional description may be abhorrent to the physical or biological scientist, but it has certain operational virtues for triggering government awareness of a need for action. There are, of course, many factors that would confound the use of such a definition, particularly in these times when aid intervention is a normal occurrence in times of serious drought. Thus, Figure 1 shows that the difference in rice prices between scarcity and non-scarcity areas during food shortage in urban Maharashtra in 1972–73 were substantially higher than the difference in wheat prices, because there were substantial inflows of wheat to

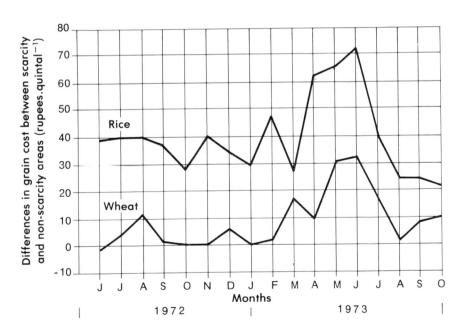

FIG. 1. Effect of grain imports on grain prices in areas of grain scarcity and non-scarcity in urban Maharashtra, 1972–73. (Data from Subramaniam, 1975.)

the scarcity areas from aid agencies. One must also take account of the fact that people in the drier regions expect to experience times of drought. Morris (1974) quoted an Indian report: "The district gazetteer states that in Kutch out of any decade two years will be famine years, five will be lean years and only three will be good years". One wonders why people continue to live in such areas if this is a true statement. The Indian Planning Commission has stated that the country should be prepared for conditions of drought over large areas once in 4 to 5 years.

II. DROUGHT-SUSCEPTIBLE AREAS

The frequency of drought tends to increase with the variability in rainfall, i.e. with decreasing annual rainfall. Ryan (1974), using an index developed by George et al. (1973), calculated the susceptibility to moderate or severe droughts in semi-arid tropical India during the monsoon (Fig. 2). The highest drought susceptibility (1 year in 3) occurs in arid areas like eastern Rajasthan, and the least (1 year in 6) in eastern Madhya Pradesh. For semi-arid India as a whole, the chance of drought by these standards is one year in four.

Arid areas tend to be most subject to drought, but they are less important areas for food crop production. Furthermore, arid areas generally have arid climates, whereas semi-arid and sub-humid areas experience a greater range. Table I illustrates the point for these regions in the United States. At the other end of the scale, in the more humid areas, moderate or more severe droughts may occur as frequently as one year in six.

Because of the high evapo-transpirative demand and the low water holding capacity of many of the soils, the tropical semi-arid regions are more drought susceptible than semi-arid areas of temperate regions. Approximately 600 million people live in semi-arid parts of the world. More than 80% of them live in the semi-arid tropics, and of these about 50% live in semi-arid, tropical India. They can grow few crops successfully in rainfed conditions, and they have few alternatives available when droughts come.

III. LIVING WITH DROUGHT

Drought susceptible areas are slow to develop because the farmers face too much uncertainty and risk. They under-invest in the agriculture that is their livelihood.

In areas too dry for crop production, nomads have learned to live with drought, but at their cost. Toynbee (1946) claims that nomadism and the domestication of animals were the responses of early hunters and agricultural peoples to the increasing desiccation that occurred with the waning of the ice in late Pleistocene times; but the environment in which they dwelt proved too harsh, and the nomads became an arrested civilization condemned, by their own choice, to exist on the edge of more successful civilizations.

Success, of course, is relative. Nations that are predominantly drought susceptible are all underdeveloped. To quote Subramanian (1975), "The primary reason for the backwardness of Maharashtra's agricultural economy is the very low coverage of cropped area under irrigation"; or Jodha (1975), "The process of pauperization [is] initiated and accentuated by recurrent droughts."

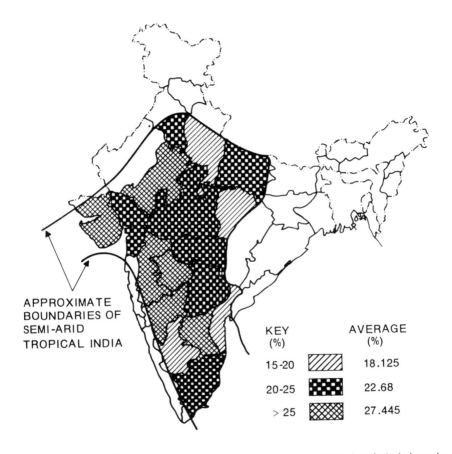

FIG. 2. Percentage failure of rains (occurrence of moderate or severe droughts) during rainy seasons in the Indian semi-arid tropics. Hatched areas indicate three frequency levels of rain failure. (After Ryan, 1974.)

A. WHEN CROPS FAIL

Jodha (1975, 1978) describes the adjustment mechanisms used by farmers in northwest India when crops fail due to drought. First, the farmer reduces his social consumption; that is, he will delay a family ceremony (a marriage) or make lesser inputs into annual festivals. He may also decide to sell off some non-productive assets. He will come to no permanent harm, nor will his family, and his productive resources will remain intact and available for use if conditions improve rapidly enough.

When the drought is severe the above measures are insufficient, and he must adjust in more drastic ways. The first recourse is to reduce the consumption of food. Table II shows that the greatest reduction tends to occur in the more expensive, protective foods (such as milk, sugar, meat and vegetables); cereals and pulse crops are the last to be given up. Obviously, a pronounced decline in the consumption of protective foods will seriously

TABLE I

Climatic variability at Jamestown, N. Dak., Fort Stanton, N. Mex., and Independence and Indio, Calif.[a]

Station	Length of record	Climatic type	Climatic distribution					
			Super humid	Humid	Moist sub-humid	Dry sub-humid	Semi arid	Arid
	Years		Years	Years	Years	Years	Years	Years
Jamestown, N. Dak	35	Dry sub-humid	0	1	15	13	5	1
Fort Stanton, N. Mex.	37	Semi-arid	0	1	1	5	25	5
Independence, Calif.	37	Arid	0	0	1	1	1	34
Indio, Calif.	36	Arid	0	0	0	0	0	36

[a]From Thornthwaite (1941).

TABLE II

Indexes of consumption expenditure by households in drought years relative to post-drought years in different areas (post-drought year situation = 100)[a]

Items of expenditure	Jodhpur (Rajasthan)			Barmer (Rajasthan)			Banas Kantha (Gujarat)		
	Small farms	Large farms	All households	Small farms	Large farms	All households	Small farms	Large farms	All households
Total food items	95	99	98	93	110	103	90	97	94
Protective foods	52	85	64	43	74	58	87	98	72
Clothing, fuel, etc.	79	85	84	84	83	85	72	76	69
Socio-religious ceremonies	23	56	36	69	50	52	63	18	66

[a]From Jodha (1978)

affect the farmer and his family. This is particularly likely where the cultural tradition is to deprive the children first (see, for example, Kloth, 1974). Faulkingham and Thorbahn (1975) have estimated, for an area of eastern Niger, that 25% of the children under the age of 5 died in the last Sahelian drought because of food deprivation.

When the farmer has reduced consumption as low as he dares, he disposes of his assets — first his animals, as he cannot work with them and he cannot feed them. Then he disposes of his farm implements and machinery. Assets disposed of may take several years to recover. In spite of the substantial governmental assistance provided to farmers in Maharashtra during the 1971–72 drought, farmers in some of the drier regions, such as Sholapur, had not fully replaced their lost animals in 1978.

The penultimate step is forced out-migration of families. In Gujarat and Rajasthan during the 1972 drought 40% or more families migrated from 50 to 243 km from home for periods of 100 to over 200 days (Jodha, 1978). During the same drought, the amount of out-migration in Maharashtra was very low, probably because the state government set up its relief works mostly in the rural areas, usually within 5 km of the villages. Seasonal migration for work, or in search of stock feed, is normal in transhumant societies, but in severe drought the migrating families may never return, as was true for the American Great Plains in the 1920s and for the Sahel in the 1970s.

The final act of adjustment and the most destructive is to sell one's land. No redress is possible and the seller is condemned to a landless life either in the rural labour force or in shanty towns on the fringes of cities. Clearly, it is wise for governments to bring in relief measures that will at least prevent starvation and distress sales of land.

B. PREVENTING CROP FAILURE

Not all droughts cause crops to fail. The farmer's ability to adjust to drought depends upon the nature and size of his farm, the production systems in use and the alternatives available. A small farm can adjust more rapidly than a large one; a mechanized farm can install drought-adapting practices more rapidly than a non-mechanized farm; a sole-commodity farm is less adaptable than one with mixed commodities.

When a farmer first perceives that his crop might fail his reaction may be to improve weed control or thin the stand. Both actions are designed to conserve water. In soils that crack, the creation of a dust mulch at the surface has the same effect.

If long-term weather forecasts are unsatisfactory, a farmer may defer side dressings of fertilizer. The crop can be ratooned to regrow when later rains fall, if the inflorescence has not yet developed.

If any water is available, a single life-saving application at flowering may allow a nearly full harvest. Kampen and Krantz (1977) found that a single application of 5 cm of water on maize at flowering doubled the yield on a rhodustalf soil. Under these circumstances, it may well be worthwhile for the farmer to hand-carry water from its source.

If the first crop fails, a second or even third may still be planted and survive in some areas. Near Hyderabad, India, in the middle of the semi-arid tropics, early season sorghum may be replaced by finger millet in mid-season, and even by cowpea or horsegram in the last month of the monsoon (AICRPDA, 1979). At Jodhpur, however, in a much drier region where pearl millet is the only suitable cereal, the farmer has no high-calorie alternative if that crop should fail.

Long-term adjustments to drought include the use of drought-tolerant indeterminate crops like pigeonpea (and sorghum to some extent) which will flower throughout the season but will set fruit only under low moisture stress. Intercropping of a cereal and pigeonpea or castor bean is a common practice in India to reduce the impact of drought.

More long-term solutions are to concentrate farming only upon those areas of the farm containing deeper soils, in dips and hollows, or close to the house or well, or, where soils are suitable, to fallow the land in the rainy season and grow food only on stored moisture in the dry season. One can tailor the crop to the amount of moisture in the soil profile at the commencement of cropping.

IV. CROP RESEARCH NEEDS FOR DROUGHT-SUSCEPTIBLE AREAS

Research is needed to reduce the chances of crop failure by improving crop and soil management, developing cultivars to resist drought and achieving a basic understanding of the effects of drought stress on plants. The emphasis must be on increasing the stability of cropping systems under conditions of drought, primarily in the dry years themselves.

Dry years, in addition to the immediate hardships they cause, have longer-term effects on the productivity of agricultural systems. Farmers forced to sell productive assets in a dry year cannot take advantage of subsequent, more favourable years until these assets have been rebuilt.

The alternative approach, maximizing production in favourable years to provide a buffer for the lean years, has limited applicability. The development of the level of knowledge and the capitalization required to achieve potential levels of production in favourable years is a long-term, and probably unrealistic, goal at present in drought-susceptible areas. In fact, even the relatively modest levels of inputs that would be recommended as part of a conservative strategy aimed at the dry years exceed the current level of inputs in many areas. In addition, storage facilities are inadequate to maintain large stocks of food.

A. RESEARCH ON CROP AND SOIL MANAGEMENT TECHNIQUES

The major short-term means for reducing the effects of drought are through improvements in crop and soil management in traditional agriculture. The productive potential of many drought-susceptible areas in the developing world is not being realized for a variety of reasons, technical, social and economic. Yet research has developed systems and methods capable of increasing production in these areas, and the basic principles of the useful technologies have been established (Charreau & Nicou, 1971a, 1971b, 1971c, 1971d; ICAR, 1972; ICRISAT, 1974, 1979). These basic principles include:

 (i) Land-water management systems to minimize the amount of run-off and soil erosion, and to maximize the amount of rainfall available for crop production;
 (ii) Crops or cropping systems adjusted to the duration and frequency of the expected seasonally available moisture period, and capable of utilizing as much of this moisture as possible in transpiration;
 (iii) Crop management recommendations (soil fertility, crop protection, plant population) designed to overcome non-moisture-based limitations to crop production;
 (iv) Cropping systems which reduce the risk of total failure through multiple or inter-cropping, or through alternative cropping patterns for different rainfall conditions.

Much research can be done on stress characteristics and phenomena in plants and crops, but it must be related to these principles of crop and soil management if it is to be useful to agriculture in drought-susceptible areas.

B. BREEDING FOR DROUGHT RESISTANCE IN CROP PLANTS

Success in breeding to improve the drought resistance of crop cultivars has been limited in the past by a lack of techniques, and a lack of knowledge of what conditions drought resistance in crop plants (Moss et al., 1974). The plant breeder attempting to improve the drought resistance of his material has three options, each of which has certain advantages, though none provides a complete answer.

1. Selecting for yield stability over dry sites and years

Standard multi-location testing procedures can be adapted to identify differences in response to stress among breeding lines by selecting sites or years in which moisture is the main yield determinant (Laing & Fischer, 1977). This procedure has the advantage of being easily integrated into an on-going breeding program and of utilizing performance in natural stress environments as the selection criteria. The major limitation is that it applies selection pressure for drought resistance at the final stage only of the breeding process, at which point genetic variability for resistance to stress may be limited, and differences among lines may be small and difficult to demonstrate.

2. Selecting directly for performance in controlled drought stress nurseries

This approach is based upon insect and disease resistance breeding strategy, in which test lines are exposed to a uniform, severe and repeatable pressure from the insect or disease organisms, permitting resistant lines to be identified with a high degree of certainty.

The development of field techniques for direct screening for drought resistance is more difficult than for screening for pest or disease resistance. The variabilities in timing, intensity and duration of stress are almost infinite, and screening methods can expose test lines to only a few combinations. A repeatable screen can only be established in seasons or locations in which the probability of natural rainfall is very low so that soil moisture can be controlled through irrigation. Even in these conditions, fluctuations in atmospheric conditions or chance rainfall will result in year to year differences. In spite of these problems, it is possible to obtain consistent differences among cultivars over years or tests (Fischer & Maurer, 1978), and the method is currently being used in plant breeding (O'Toole & Chang, 1979).

3. Selecting for physiological or biochemical characteristics directly related to field drought resistance

This is theoretically much more rapid and effective than selecting for yield and stability in natural stress environments or selecting directly for performance in controlled stress nurseries. It offers the possibility of working directly with a small number of characters (whose inheritance can perhaps be determined), rather than on a complex unknown like resistance. It also offers the possibility of carrying out at least the initial cycles of selection in the absence of actual stress; perhaps in controlled or partially controlled environments (such as glasshouses) where selection can be more efficient and progress more rapid.

There is much information in the literature to support these possibilities (Begg & Turner, 1976; Fischer & Turner, 1978; Hsaio, 1973). Several characteristics have received considerable attention; in particular, rooting patterns and root resistance (Hurd 1974; Passioura 1972), stomatal control of water loss (Jones, 1978), maintenance of leaf water potential (Blum, 1975; O'Toole & Moya, 1978), heat and desiccation tolerance (Sullivan & Ross, 1978), and changes in metabolites and hormones (Singh et al., 1972; Quarrie & Jones, 1977). Some experimental data is available to indicate for each of these characteristics that there is a relationship between characteristic and differential cultivar performance in at least some stress conditions. It is not difficult to understand how in certain stress situations each characteristic could contribute an advantage to the cultivar possessing it. What is lacking in nearly all cases, however, is the experimental evidence that breeding for a given characteristic will confer field drought resistance (as measured by growth or yield) upon the resulting cultivars. Without such evidence most plant breeders are unwilling to invest the necessary resources into breeding for physiological responses to stress.

C. PHYSIOLOGICAL AND BIOCHEMICAL RESEARCH ON PLANT RESISTANCE TO DROUGHT

Better understanding of how drought stress affects crop growth and development processes is fundamental. Research is needed to determine the procedures involved and to utilize this knowledge in breeding and agronomic research.

1. Understanding drought resistance in crop plants

There is much conjecture and argument in the literature about different mechanisms of resistance, each supported by evidence of varying quality. Many of the proposed mechanisms have not been critically evaluated (Moss et al., 1974). The stress conditions under which much of the research has been done have not been well defined (Hsaio, 1973). Too much of the work has been carried out under artificial stress conditions in which the plant response may not be representative of the crop response in field conditions (Begg & Turner, 1976), and in very few cases have there been comparative studies of mechanisms to evaluate the relative advantages afforded by one or the other.

2. Breeding for mechanisms of drought resistance

This entails evaluating the genetic variability for such mechanisms and demonstrating that incorporation of them into crop cultivars confers an advantage under stress. Physiologists and plant breeders must cooperate in this research. Incorporation of mechanisms of resistance is the appropriate test of the physiologist's hypothesis that a proposed character is, in fact, advantageous. If a mechanism does confer an advantage, selecting for it in a neutral genetic background should produce lines that will have an equivalent advantage.

3. Using physiological or biochemical responses to stress in breeding and in agronomic programs

The use of physiological or biochemical responses of plants to drought stress as criteria for the evaluation of breeding materials or soil and crop management practices will mean a much greater commitment of time and resources in data collection than is currently being made in either type of research. To a large degree, this cost will determine whether or not physiological or biochemical responses are accepted as selection or evaluation criteria.

A number of avenues are open for the improvement and simplification of techniques. The simplest is the development of scoring techniques by using visible changes in plants which correlate with internal physiological changes, such as leaf rolling and leaf water potential (O'Toole & Moya, 1978). A second is modification of existing equipment for measuring crop parameters to increase the number of measurements that can be made per unit time to the levels required for field screening. For example, a recent report describes modifications to a commercial pressure chamber to increase capacity to 60 readings .h^{-1}, and to a viscous flow porometer to read 200 leaves .h^{-1} (Fisher et al., 1977).

New technological developments obviously offer the most promise for field screening for differences in physiological response. Measurement of leaf or canopy temperatures using aerial infrared photographs have been used by several researchers (Blum, 1975; Blum et al., 1978) to rate large numbers of cultivars for drought resistance. Hopefully, similar advances can be made in procedures for analyses of changes in growth and biochemical processes as more is learned of their role in drought resistance.

V. CONCLUSION

Traditional agriculture in drought-susceptible countries has developed through experience over long periods of time; there has been selection for survival. Yields and returns are low but reasonably secure, although, unfortunately, today they fail to provide the minimum food requirements for expanding populations. Research should be directed at reducing the risk of loss in the bad years so that the farmer can invest more for the good years.

Agricultural research in these countries is generally concentrated upon increasing production in irrigated or dependable rainfall areas. The gap between the health and welfare of people in irrigated areas and in drought-susceptible areas has been growing. Research on drought-susceptible agriculture must be given higher priority if large food deficits are to be avoided. The potential for modern agriculture does exist.

CHAPTER 2

Mechanisms of Drought Resistance

M. M. JONES, N. C. TURNER AND C. B. OSMOND

I.	Introduction	15
II.	Classification of drought resistance	16
III.	Drought escape	17
IV.	Drought tolerance at high tissue water potential	20
	A. Maintenance of water uptake	20
	B. Reduction of water loss	21
V.	Drought tolerance at low tissue water potential	24
	A. Maintenance of turgor pressure	24
	B. Protoplasmic resistance	32
VI.	Implications of different drought resistance mechanisms	35

I. INTRODUCTION

"Drought" is defined in both the Concise Oxford Dictionary and Webster's New World Dictionary as "prolonged dry weather". This definition highlights the fact that drought is a meteorological term involving a rainfall deficit. The definition, however, is not precise as both "prolonged" and "dry" are relative terms, like drought, based on an expectation of rainfall. A drought in the world's wet tropics would constitute a flood in the arid zones. Similarly, a period of 2 weeks without significant rain may represent a drought to a lowland rice farmer in the Philippines, but would be proclaimed as abnormal rains by a nomadic grazier in the Sahel.

For a period of dry weather to affect a plant community, the rainfall deficit must lead to a soil water deficit and ultimately to a plant water deficit. The degree to which a rainfall deficit is translated into a soil water deficit depends on the rate of evaporation during the rain-free period, and on the physical and chemical characteristics of the soil. The degree to which a particular soil water deficit influences the plant again depends on the degree of aridity of the atmosphere. However, it also depends on a number of plant

15

PHYSIOLOGY AND BIOCHEMISTRY
OF DROUGHT RESISTANCE
IN PLANTS

characteristics that influence water uptake by the plant, the rate of transpiration and the response of the plant to the water deficit so generated. It is the degree to which the plant can withstand the rainfall deficit that constitutes its drought resistance. The characteristics that enable it to survive and grow through a rainfall deficit and soil-water depletion are the subject of this book, and in this chapter drought resistance will be defined and a simple classification of the various mechanisms of drought resistance in plants will be presented.

II. CLASSIFICATION OF DROUGHT RESISTANCE

Drought resistance is the generic term used to cover a range of mechanisms whereby plants withstand periods of dry weather. Three primary types of drought resistance have been identified (May & Milthorpe, 1962; Turner, 1979).

Drought escape: the ability of a plant to complete its life cycle before a serious plant water deficit develops.

Drought tolerance at high tissue water potential: the ability of a plant to endure periods of rainfall deficit while maintaining a high tissue water potential. Many reviewers (Levitt, 1972; Arnon, 1975; O'Toole & Chang, 1979), for convenience, simply refer to this as drought avoidance, although it must be recognized that plants with these mechanisms do not avoid drought but avoid tissue dehydration.

Drought tolerance at low tissue water potential: the ability of a plant to endure rainfall deficits at low tissue water potential.

This classification of types of drought resistance has been chosen because of its simplicity and because it uses drought as a meteorological term, thereby avoiding the confusion arising from equating "drought" with "plant water deficit". For a greatly amplified and subdivided system of defining drought resistance the reader is referred to Levitt (1972).

Within these three types of drought resistance there are a number of mechanisms that enable plants to resist drought. These are given in Table I, which is modified from a table presented by Turner (1979). This classification covers the mechanisms applicable in all plants: those in natural communities; those in loosely managed mixed communities such as improved grasslands and woodland; and those in highly manipulated and generally monospecific communities of agricultural crops.

With most agricultural crops the seed is the economic yield, and mechanisms that maintain productivity and increase reproductive efficiency under drought will be important (Turner, 1979). By contrast, in pasture systems mechanisms that maintain leaf production and plant persistence through periods of rainfall deficit will be more important (Turner & Begg, 1978). In tree crops persistence mechanisms override production mechanisms. Although reproductive gain is presumably the reward for plants which successfully compete in a natural community, ecologists studying the mechanisms of drought resistance in natural communities usually emphasize the ability of a plant to stay alive during periods of low water supply (Levitt et al., 1960). Plants may persist through periods of low water supply as green, potentially photosynthetically active plants but their productivity during this period will be low (Fischer & Turner, 1978). Thus, mechanisms of drought resistance that enable natural communities to stay alive and maintain their photosynthetic ability during severe water shortages may have little significance in an agricultural context in which productivity and yield are important.

III. DROUGHT ESCAPE

Heavy rain in a desert community enables the germination and growth of a range of plant species that quickly flower and set seed before the supply of water in the soil is depleted. Known as ephemerals, these drought escapers have long been considered to have no special physiological, biochemical or morphological mechanisms to cope with water deficits. Certainly they are

TABLE I
Mechanisms of drought resistance

Drought escape
    (a)   Rapid phenological development
    (b)   Developmental plasticity

Drought tolerance with high tissue water potential
    (a)   Maintenance of water uptake
        (i)   Increased rooting
        (ii)   Increased hydraulic conductance

    (b)   Reduction of water loss
        (i)   Reduction in epidermal conductance
        (ii)   Reduction in absorbed radiation
        (iii)   Reduction in evaporative surface

Drought tolerance with low tissue water potential
    (a)   Maintenance of turgor
        (i)   Solute accumulation
        (ii)   Increase in elasticity

    (b)   Desiccation tolerance
        (i)   Protoplasmic resistance

---

mesophytic, but the absence of special mechanisms of drought resistance is uncertain and warrants further investigation. Figure 1, which is reproduced from Walter and Stadelmann (1974), shows that ephemerals, particularly summer ephemerals, have values of osmotic potential as low as much more xerophytic, perennial desert shrubs that can tolerate drought at low water contents. Whether the low osmotic potentials represent an adaptation by the desert ephemeral to tolerate water deficits or are merely a result of tissue dehydration is not clear. Certainly changes in osmotic potential over a range of 4.0 MPa can be attributed to tissue dehydration (Kappen et al., 1972).

Mulroy and Rundel (1977) report a wide range of mechanisms of adaptation in summer and winter ephemerals, but these are primarily adaptations which prevent germination after light rain, and are adaptations to temperature rather than mechanisms of drought resistance. Thus, those ephemerals that grow as a result of winter rain have a rosette form and an anatomy typical of a C_3 pathway for photosynthesis, whereas those ephemerals that grow as a result of summer rains have an erect habit and a Kranz-type anatomy typical of a C_4 pathway of photosynthesis. These adaptations may be

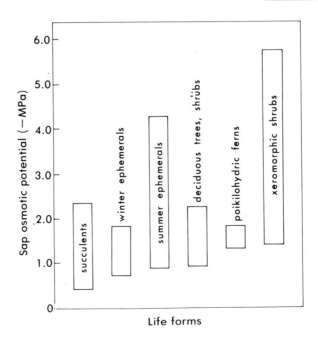

FIG. 1. Osmotic potential of expressed sap from vascular plants of different life form groups in an Arizonian desert. (After Walter and Stadelmann, 1974.)

significant in enabling maximum growth on a limited supply of water, and maximum water use efficiency under the particular temperature regime in which the growth occurs, but they are not mechanisms of drought resistance *per se*.

The two features of desert ephemerals that appear to be significant in drought resistance are rapid development and developmental plasticity. The desert annuals are characterized by an ability to produce flowers with a minimum of vegetative structure. If rainfall is limited they produce a small amount of vegetative growth, few flowers and few seeds; but if rainfall is plentiful they produce an abundance of vegetative growth, flowers and seeds (Mulroy & Rundel, 1977). To achieve the latter they frequently have an indeterminate habit. This is an important survival mechanism in that it enables the large amounts of seed produced in wet years to carry the species through prolonged drought periods.

Selection for rapid phenological development has undoubtedly been the most rewarding approach in breeding for drought resistance in crops. In small-grain cereals where this has been most widely studied, drought resistance was greater; that is, grain yields were affected less in those varieties of wheat and barley which flowered early than in those which flowered late (Chinoy, 1960; Derera et al., 1969; Fischer & Maurer, 1978). However, as May and Milthorpe (1962) pointed out, earliness is often negatively correlated with yield in years of adequate rainfall. Although some developmental plasticity exists in cereals (Turner, 1979; Fischer & Turner, 1978), the determinate habit of wheat and barley must limit the degree of plasticity. In years of high rainfall or under irrigated conditions, the early varieties cannot compensate for either the shorter time it takes to produce a flower or the contracted period, and hence smaller accumulation of photosynthates, between floral initiation and maturity.

Dryland wheat and barley are frequently grown under conditions in which the probability of drought increases as maturity approaches. Where the incidence of drought is greater at other times in the development of the plant, photoperiodic sensitivity can be adjusted by breeding and selection to minimize the chance of the plant experiencing drought at a yield-sensitive stage of development (O'Toole & Chang, 1979). In many crop species the stages most sensitive to water deficit are just prior to and around flowering (Salter & Goode, 1967).

Finally, it should be pointed out that drought escaping plants differ from plants that are drought tolerant only in the way in which they survive the dry period. Succulents tolerate drought at high tissue water contents by adaptations which effectively insulate them from their arid surroundings. Tight stomatal closure and an impermeable cuticle prevent water loss to the atmosphere, and suberization of the roots prevents water loss to the soil. In a similar manner, some drought escapers survive prolonged periods of dry weather as fleshy rhizomes insulated from the dry soil in which they live. The production by drought escapers of seeds that survive periods of dry weather at extremely low tissue water contents differs little in practice from the poikilohydric plants that survive similar dry periods with dehydrated leaves or stems.

IV. DROUGHT TOLERANCE AT HIGH TISSUE WATER POTENTIAL

Stated simply, the maintenance of a high tissue water potential during a period of high evaporative demand or a period of increasing soil water deficit can be associated with either a restricted water loss or the maintenance by the plant of its water supply. The mechanisms involved in each category are listed in Table I. Several of the mechanisms are dealt with in more detail elsewhere in this volume, but are briefly considered here for completeness.

A. MAINTENANCE OF WATER UPTAKE

1. Rooting patterns and density

In order to maintain water uptake as water is extracted from the soil, either a greater volume of soil can be tapped or the water within a particular volume of soil can be extracted to a greater extent. This would be achieved by roots growing deeper or, where low densities prevail, by an increase in root density. Certainly a characteristic of drought resistant species is that they have a large proportion of their total mass as roots and also a deep rooting habit. Perennial grasses and shrubs of dry regions usually have a greater proportion of dry matter in their roots than in their shoots, and in extreme cases 90% of the total dry matter is underground (Fischer & Turner, 1978).

A high root to shoot ratio does not in itself indicate a greater ability to absorb water: water deficits invariably increase the root to shoot ratio, but this may arise simply from a loss of shoot mass without loss of roots, or from a relatively greater loss of shoot than root dry weight. However, evidence for an absolute increase in root dry weight is available for several species (Turner, 1979). Even an absolute increase in root mass may not be of benefit if it merely increases the density of roots in a zone in which root density is already maximal. Finally, in perennials the high root to shoot ratio may simply represent accumulated dry matter. The high root biomass of cold winter desert perennials is well known (Caldwell et al., 1977), but related species from warm winter deserts have much lower root to shoot ratios. These differences are presumably the result of genetically controlled patterns of assimilate distribution, and Caldwell et al. (1977) established that 75% of all newly assimilated carbon was directed to the roots of these cold winter desert perennials, whether it was assimilated by the C_3 or C_4 photosynthetic pathways. The proportion of the root biomass which is active in water uptake in these plants has not been established, but root growth and water uptake proceed deep in the soil profile throughout summer (Fernandez & Caldwell, 1975).

2. Hydraulic conductance of plants

The roots may develop sufficiently to absorb adequate water from the soil to maintain water uptake, but for this to benefit the whole plant the hydraulic resistances within the plant must be low enough for the water to be freely available to the major metabolic centres in the shoot. The resistances to flow within the plant are usually sufficient to develop potentials in the leaf as low as -1.2 to -1.5 MPa on clear sunny days, even when soil water is freely available (e.g. Turner & Begg, 1973). It has generally been concluded that the major resistance to water flow occurs in the root (Kramer, 1969), but evidence for considerable resistances to flow in the stem and leaves has been obtained in several species (Dimond, 1966; Begg & Turner, 1970; Boyer, 1971; Boyer, 1974; Sheriff & Meidner, 1974). Variations in resistances to flow between species have been documented by Hellkvist et al. (1974), but the significance of these mechanisms in drought resistance has not been evaluated.

B. REDUCTION OF WATER LOSS

1. Change in epidermal conductance

The stomata, positioned in an impermeable epidermis and operating as regulatory valves between the wet leaf and the dry atmosphere, provide the principal mechanism for controlling the rate of water loss. However, the site of water loss is also the site of carbon gain by the plant, so that a reduction in water loss through stomatal control also results in a reduction in assimilation with consequent effects on productivity. Cowan and Farquhar (1977) and Cowan (1977) discussed strategies of stomatal control which make optimal the daily carbon gain per unit of water lost. However, on a long-term basis stomatal control of water loss is a mechanism for survival and not one that optimizes productivity, except in special circumstances (Turner, 1979). Secondly, to be effective in maintaining the internal water balance of the plant, the stomata must close firmly and water loss through the cuticle must be low. In some cases leaf water potential continues to decrease because of incomplete stomatal closure or water loss through the cuticle (see Kappen et al., 1972; Turner, 1975; Turner et al., 1978).

Succulents are the examples *par excellence* of epidermal control of tissue water potential. Szarek and Ting (1974) and Nobel (1977) showed that the stomata in two species of cacti are very sensitive to a lowered plant water potential and that cuticular loss is very slight once the stomata are closed. Thus, in drying soil the cactus isolates its wet interior from the dry atmosphere (Fig. 2). The water potential of *Opuntia basilaris* in wet soil varied between -0.2 and -0.5 MPa. When plant water potential fell to about -0.5 MPa the stomata closed and, thereafter, the plant water potential only slowly decreased to a stable value between -1.0 and -1.2 MPa, even though the soil water potential in the root zone decreased to lower than -4.0 MPa after 3 months without rain. Nobel (1977) also showed that stomatal closure occurred at a plant water potential of about -0.5 MPa in *Ferocactus*

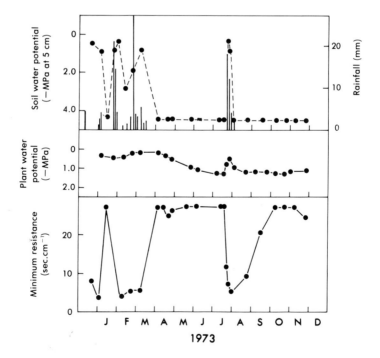

FIG. 2. Seasonal patterns of precipitation, soil and plant water potential and minimum epidermal resistance to water vapour exchange in *Opuntia basilaris*. (After Szarek and Ting, 1974.)

acanthodes and that, after 7 months without effective rain, when the soil in the root zone was about $-10\,$MPa, the plant water potential was still as high as $-0.6\,$MPa. Although the advantage of a high epidermal resistance for plant survival is evident, the importance of this mechanism in drought resistance of crops, where productivity is important, is less clear.

2. Change in radiation absorbed

A second mechanism for reducing water loss is a reduction in the amount of radiation absorbed. This can be achieved by leaf movements or changes in the reflectance characteristics of leaves. Begg and Torssell (1974) showed that *Stylosanthes humilis* leaves are aligned parallel to the incident radiation as plant water deficits increase. The wilting of leaves is a passive movement that is also effective in reducing the radiation load and as stomata close may counter excessive leaf temperatures which lower water use efficiency. Mooney et al. (1977) suggested that the steeply inclined leaves of *Atriplex hymenelytra* are efficient both in reducing the radiation absorbed in the middle of the day when temperature and vapour pressure deficit are maximal and in increasing the radiation absorbed in the cooler and more humid early morning and late afternoon. Table II shows calculations of leaf temperature and transpiration based on conditions experienced at noon in mid-summer at Death Valley, California. The values indicate that a leaf angle of 70° reduced the leaf temperature under extreme conditions by 2–3°C and this reduced transpiration by 8–12%. However, since photosynthesis saturated at lower light intensities, Mooney et al. (1977) concluded that the steep angle had little effect on photosynthesis.

Another way in which the radiation load of plants is reduced is by the production of hairs, surface wax or salt, all of which increase the reflectance

TABLE II

Calculated leaf temperatures and transpiration of *Atriplex hymenelytra* leaves showing the effect of leaf angle and absorptance. Calculations based on a characteristic mid-day summer environment in Death Valley, Calif. (air temp., 45°C; radiation, 1.5 cal.cm^{-2}.s^{-1}; dew point, 10°C) and the characteristic leaf (leaf area, 3.9 cm^2; stomatal conductance, 0.05 cm^2.s^{-1}) using the energy balance equation.[a]

Leaf category	Absorptance	Angle	Leaf temperature (°C)	Transpiration (μg.cm^{-2}.s^{-1})
Winter leaf	0.50	0°	50	3.5
Summer leaf	0.25	0°	45	2.7
Winter leaf	0.50	70°	47	3.0
Summer leaf	0.25	70°	43	2.5

[a]Data from Mooney et al (1977).

of the leaves. Water deficits or increasing aridity have been shown to increase the hairiness of wheat (Quarrie & Jones, 1977), sunflower (Turner, 1981) and *Encelia farinosa* (Ehleringer, 1976), and to increase salt crystallization on the leaf surfaces of *Atriplex hymenelytra* (Mooney et al., 1977). The influence of the increased reflectance resulting from salt crystallization and leaf dehydration on the leaf temperature and transpiration of *A. hymenelytra* is also shown in Table II. Halving leaf absorptance reduced leaf temperature by 5°C in horizontal leaves and 4°C in steeply inclined leaves, and it reduced transpiration by approximately 20% under simulated midday, hot desert, summer conditions. The decreased absorptance caused by increased hairiness, waxiness or salt crystals also reduced photosynthesis (Chatterton et al., 1975; Ehleringer, 1976; Mooney et al., 1977), but the reduced absorption of radiation due to changed leaf surface properties decreased transpiration more than photosynthesis and thereby increased water use efficiency (Chatterton et al., 1975; Mooney et al., 1977; Ehleringer, 1977).

3. Change in evaporative surface area

Finally, water loss may be reduced through a reduction in the area of evaporative surface. The dimorphic shrubs of the Mediterranean zone are perhaps the classic examples of this mechanism of drought resistance (Orshan, 1963; Evenari et al., 1971). The shedding of the large, thinner, winter leaves and the production of smaller, thicker leaves with the onset of the dry season clearly provides the plant with a smaller evaporative surface and aids its water economy. Although few species are able to produce a different set of leaves for the hot dry season, the leaf area of many desert species is reduced as water deficits develop (Evenari et al., 1971; Kozlowski, 1976). In many crop species the older leaves rapidly senesce and die, thereby reducing the rate of water loss and enabling the remaining leaves to maintain their water balance (McMichael et al., 1973; Constable & Hearn, 1978).

V. DROUGHT TOLERANCE AT LOW TISSUE WATER POTENTIAL

A. MAINTENANCE OF TURGOR PRESSURE

The maintenance of turgor pressure as the plant water potential declines is crucial for cell expansion, for growth and for many of the associated biochemical, physiological and morphological processes (Hsiao, 1973; Hsiao et al., 1976). The ability of tissues to maintain turgor pressure as water potentials decline in response to declining water contents is an important mechanism of drought resistance. Turgor maintenance is generally effective as a mechanism of drought resistance during decreases in relative water content of tissues to about 80%. In some cases the complete maintenance of turgor pressure has been observed, although generally only over a limited range of water potentials (summarized in Table III). In addition, there are examples of partial turgor maintenance (e.g. Cutler & Rains, 1978; Jones & Turner, 1978; Turner & Jones, 1980). Two processes may contribute to the maintenance of turgor pressure as water potentials decline: a low osmotic potential due to either a naturally high solute concentration or an accumulation of solutes, or a high tissue elasticity.

1. Solute accumulation (osmotic adjustment)

Although there are many examples of decreases in osmotic potential in response to the development of internal water deficits (Walter & Stadelmann, 1974), few studies have separated the component resulting from a *concentration* of solutes due to tissue dehydration from that due to an *accumulation* of solutes. This oversight may be responsible for the widespread notion that "protoplasmic tolerance" to increased solute concentration following tissue desiccation is an important component of drought resistance. It is probable that such processes are important in extreme examples of desiccation-tolerant resurrection plants discussed below. The importance of these processes in plants which withstand moderate tissue water deficits is not established. Hsiao et al. (1976) summarized this dilemma most lucidly:

> Walter and Stadelmann (1974) apparently interpreted the correlation between drought resistance and low ψ_S (osmotic potential) found within certain plant groups to mean the more resistant a plant (in a particular group) is to drought, the more likely it is to survive *in spite* of a low tissue ψ_S. Our interpretation, of course is that low ψ_S is *beneficial* under drought and that the less resistant species were not able to lower their ψ_S by osmotic adjustment (our italics).

TABLE III
Examples of full maintenance of turgor pressure in dehydrating tissue.[a]

Tissue	Species	Water potential range ($-MPa$)	Reference
Leaf	Wheat (fully expanded)	0–1.3	Morgan (1977)
	Wheat (expanding)	1.7–4.0	Munns et al. (1979)
	Sorghum	1.0–1.6	Hsiao et al. (1976)
	Sugar beet	0.6–0.8	Biscoe (1972)
	Apple	1.8–2.6	Goode and Higgs (1973)
	Orchard grass	1.2–2.0	Gavande and Taylor (1967)
Apex	Wheat	1.8–4.2	Munns et al. (1979)
Hypocotyl	Soybean	0.4–0.9	Meyer and Boyer (1972)
Root	Pea	0.3–0.8	Greacen and Oh (1972)

[a]From Turner and Jones (1980).

Two aspects of solute accumulation should be distinguished. First, many species such as summer ephemerals and xeromorphic shrubs (Fig. 1), and halophytes, accumulate high concentrations of solutes whether or not they are subject to water stress, and they should be able to maintain turgor and normal cellular function at low tissue water potential. Second, other species with naturally low solute concentration have the capacity to accumulate additional solutes in response to water stress and to achieve some measure of "osmotic adjustment".

Most measurements of the osmotic potential response to declining tissue water content have been made with photosynthetic tissues. Studies on mesophytic crop plants indicate that the capacity of fully expanded leaves to accumulate solutes at moderate water potentials is limited. For example, in fully expanded sorghum leaves the decrease in osmotic potential is restricted to -0.6 MPa at full turgor (relative water content $\simeq 100\%$, leaf water potential $\simeq 0$ MPa), and this maximum decrease in osmotic potential occurs at pre-dawn leaf water potentials no lower than -1.0 MPa (Jones, 1979). Similarly, Morgan (1977) observed that solute accumulation in fully expanded wheat leaves ceased when leaf water potentials reached -1.3 MPa. Three studies have described an absence of solute accumulation in leaves subjected to water deficits. Fully expanded leaves of several wheat genotypes are unable to respond to declining water potentials at either the boot stage or at mid-grainfilling (Morgan, 1977), and soybean leaves also fail to respond at various developmental stages after flower initiation (Sionit & Kramer, 1977; Turner et al., 1978). Factors which influence the capacity of expanded tissues to accumulate solutes presumably include the concentration or pressure limitation of solute uptake processes (Cram, 1976) and the metabolic limitations on solute synthesis ranging from CO_2 deprivation following stomatal closure to turgor effects on molecular structure and, hence, on biosynthetic pathways.

The rate of dehydration is important in solute accumulation and the maintenance of turgor pressure at moderate leaf water potentials, just as it is in the development of desiccation tolerance. For example, when the pre-dawn leaf water potential of fully expanded sorghum leaves decreased by 1.2 MPa.d^{-1} to -2.5 MPa, no solute accumulation occurred. However, at a stress rate typical of the field situation (0.1 MPa.d^{-1}), an accumulation of solutes resulted in a 0.5 MPa decrease in the osmotic potential at full turgor (Jones & Rawson, 1979). It is likely that many studies of the responses of crop plants have underestimated the capacity for turgor maintenance via solute accumulation, because the rates of stress imposed have been greater than the solute accumulation process can accommodate.

Under field conditions a plant may often experience a series of drying cycles, and it has been proposed that shoots will show an increased capacity for turgor maintenance as water potentials decline if they have been previously subjected to low water potentials (Brown et al., 1976; Cutler & Rains, 1978). An influence of prior solute accumulation on the maintenance of turgor pressure in fully expanded cotton leaves was observed when plants were subjected to a rapid succession of fast drying cycles (Brown et al., 1976). However the effect of a stress history such as this may be less significant to crop plants growing in the field, where there is generally a lag period of several days between recovery from leaf water deficits and the onset of another drying cycle. The question of carry-over of accumulated solutes is obviously a function of the length of the recovery period, as well as the severity of stress. For example, the 0.6 MPa differential between the osmotic potential at full turgor of stressed mature sorghum leaves and controls was reduced to less than 0.1 MPa in an 8 d recovery period (Fig. 3).

In contrast, in the xerophyte *Acacia harpophylla,* which has a naturally low sap osmotic potential, Tunstall and Connor (1975) found that, at the onset of a second drying cycle, an elevated solute concentration in previously stressed phyllodes resulted in the turgor pressures of these phyllodes being up to 1.0 MPa higher than in previously unstressed phyllodes, over a 3.5 MPa range of water potential (Fig. 4). Whether these plants have a greater capacity for additional solute accumulation is not known, and the carry-over of solutes

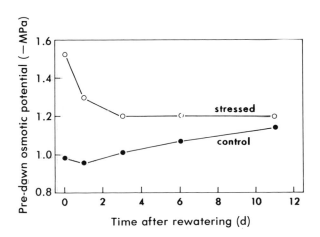

FIG. 3. Pre-dawn osmotic potentials of fully-expanded sorghum leaves of controls (●), or following rewatering of plants stressed so that pre-dawn leaf water potentials declined to −1.5 MPa (○). All values refer to leaves at full turgor (relative water content ≃ 100%; leaf water potential ≃ 0 MPa) applying corrections for an apoplastic water fraction of 0.16. (After Jones and Rawson, 1979.)

accumulated in one drying cycle to the next presumably depends on the nature of the solutes and the metabolic status of the tissue. The difference in responses between the young *Acacia* phyllodes and the mature sorghum leaves may imply that a history of low water potentials has a more significant influence upon responses to subsequent low water potentials if it is experienced by expanding tissues rather than by fully expanded tissues. A reduction in maximum cell volume generally results if expanding tissues experience water deficits (Cutler et al., 1977), and this affects the elastic properties of cells. Cutler and Rains (1978) and Singh et al. (1973) also provide evidence for an increased capacity to accumulate solutes in leaves of cotton and wheat, respectively, following a previous stress period.

Since the magnitude of carbon sources and sinks vary with the stage of development of the plant, and the ion uptake capacities of expanding tissues generally exceed those of fully expanded tissues, it is possible that the ability of leaf tissues to accumulate solutes depends on stage of development. This

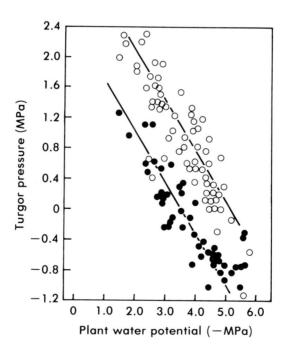

FIG. 4. Relationship between turgor pressure and plant water potential for phyllodes of brigalow (*Acacia harpophylla*) growing in south-eastern Queensland, Australia. Previously undroughted tissue (●), previously droughted tissue (○); values refer to diurnal measurements. (After Tunstall and Connor 1975.)

proposal is supported by a study made by Munns et al. (1979) of the relative capacities of expanding and fully expanded leaves of wheat to maintain turgor pressure by accumulating solutes at low leaf water potentials. Although the two classes of leaves had similar leaf osmotic potentials prior to the onset of stress, zero turgor pressure was reached at a leaf water potential of -2.0 MPa in the fully expanded leaf, whereas the young expanding leaf tissue maintained positive turgor pressure at a leaf water potential of -4.0 MPa.

Studies have been made of the solutes responsible for the decrease in osmotic potential resulting in complete turgor pressure maintenance within the apex and expanding leaves of wheat (Munns et al., 1979), and in partial turgor pressure maintenance within fully expanded sorghum leaves (Jones et al., 1980). Munns et al. (1979) identified the major solutes accumulated within the apex and expanding leaves of wheat as sugars and amino acids (especially proline) which appear to be translocated from other regions of the plant. Although organic acids, potassium and chloride are involved in osmotic adjustments in other systems, they are not accumulated in these regions of the wheat plant. The data in Table IV show that the decreased osmotic potential at full turgor in fully expanded sorghum leaves at mild levels of stress (pre-dawn leaf water potential of -0.85 MPa) is fully accounted for by increases in potassium, chloride, free amino acids and sugars. No significant change occurred in the concentration of either total organic acids or the other

TABLE IV

Contribution of different solutes to the decrease in osmotic potential at full turgor (relative water content = 100% and water potential $\simeq$ 0 MPa) in sorghum leaves at two levels of stress. The osmotic potential due to the accumulation of each solute was calculated from the change in content of solute and the total symplastic water content compared with those in well-watered controls.[a]

		Mild stress	Severe stress
Pre-dawn water potential (MPa)		-0.85	-1.30
Decrease in osmotic potential at full turgor (MPa)		-0.25	-0.49
Osmotic potential (MPa) due to increase in			
sugars	sucrose	-0.04	-0.05
	glucose	-0.04	-0.06
	fructose	-0.02	-0.03
ions	potassium[b]	-0.07	-0.06
	chloride	-0.06	-0.06
	potassium carboxylate[c]	n.s.	-0.08
total free amino acids		-0.02	-0.04
sugar phosphates		n.s.	-0.03
Change in osmotic potential accounted for (%)		100	84

[a]Data from Jones et al. (1980).
[b]Change in potassium, less the equivalent of carboxylic acids.
[c]Calculated for undissociated tribasic acid; the major acids were aconitate and malate.

inorganic cations. The osmotic contribution of total inorganic ions equalled the total of sugars and amino acids, with fructose making only a minor contribution to the sugar component. Almost equal increases occurred in the levels of glucose and sucrose, contrasting with the situation in the apex and expanding leaves of wheat, where non-reducing sugars are the major sugars accumulated (Munns et al., 1979). The concentrations of both chloride and sugars were virtually unaltered by a further 0.45 MPa decline in leaf water potential. Consequently, the contributions of these solutes to the 0.6 MPa decrease in osmotic potential at full turgor at this more severe level of stress were reduced to 12% and 29% respectively. At this more severe stress (pre-dawn leaf water potential of −1.3 MPa), additional solute accumulation was due to carboxylic acids, sugar phosphates and amino acids and, again, potassium was the only inorganic cation whose concentration increased above the level present in well-watered tissue. Potassium salts of carboxylic acids accounted for 16% of the 0.5 MPa decrease in osmotic potential. The solutes responsible for the remaining 16% of osmotic adjustment may include sugar alcohols, betaine or related compounds, which are involved in osmoregulation in other systems.

In these studies, the contribution of individual solutes to the change in osmotic potential was calculated for the tissue as a whole. On this basis, although the concentration of proline increased significantly, its contribution to the total changes in osmotic potential was insignificant. However, it must be pointed out that the analysis ignored the possibility that the osmotic potential of the vacuole and cytoplasm may be regulated by different solutes. If the assumption is made that the proline increase is confined to the cytoplasm (assumed to be 4% of the symplastic water volume; cf. Osmond, 1976), then the level of proline accumulated at a pre-dawn leaf water potential of −1.3 MPa was sufficient to account for all the decrease in osmotic potential. With the same assumptions, the increase in proline concentration in mildly stressed sorghum leaves (pre-dawn leaf water potential of −0.85 MPa) was much less, and would account for less than 35% of the decreased osmotic potential of the cytoplasm. Studies on other plants have suggested that large increases in proline generally occur only at moderate to severe levels of stress (Hanson et al., 1977; McMichael & Elmore, 1977).

2. Tissue elasticity

Noy-Meir and Ginzburg (1969), and Weatherley (1970) have pointed out that, as tissue water content and water potentials decline, tissue with high elasticity has a greater ability to maintain turgor pressure than tissue with low elasticity. However, the value of generalizations about the importance of tissue elasticity is limited by the small number of estimates in the literature of the influence of water deficits upon the bulk elastic modulii of higher plant tissues. Studies on *Vicia faba* (Elston et al., 1976) indicated that in expanding leaf tissues of these two species the bulk elastic modulus decreased (tissue elasticity increased) in response to low leaf water potentials: expanding sunflower leaves, however, showed no such increase (Jones & Turner, 1980). It seems unlikely that fully expanded tissues would increase in elasticity in response to low water potentials. Studies of fully expanded sorghum and sunflower leaves (Jones & Turner, 1978, 1980) and photosynthesizing branches of *Hammada scoparia* (Kappen et al., 1975) showed a decrease or no change in elasticity at low tissue water potentials. Although the elastic properties of the photosynthetic tissues of some species which perform well under water-limiting conditions appear to be unfavourable to the maintenance of positive turgor pressure, they may be important in the survival of these tissues at negative turgor pressures.

3. Water release curves and drought resistance

A relationship between drought resistance and the slope of the water release curve (a plot of relative water content against water potential, see Fig. 5) has been noted for photosynthetic tissues (Weatherley & Slatyer, 1957; Jarvis & Jarvis, 1963; Connor & Tunstall, 1968). A smaller slope of the water release curve (*Acacia harpophylla* in Fig. 5) is usually taken to indicate

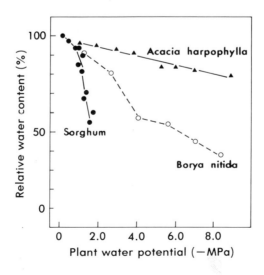

FIG. 5. Water release curves for leaves of three species differing in drought resistance. (Data for sorghum (●) after Jones and Turner, 1978; for *Borya nitida* (○) after Gaff and Churchill, 1976; for *Acacia harpophylla* (▲) after Connor and Tunstall, 1968.)

higher drought resistance, since a larger potential gradient for water uptake results from a given change in the tissue water content. A large value of osmotic potential at full turgor, a high ability to accumulate solutes as tissue water contents decline and a low tissue elasticity each contribute to a small slope of the water release curve. However, the contributions of these variables to the slope of this curve also depend upon the relative distribution of apoplastic and symplastic water. Thus, differences between species in the water release curve may be due to the interactions of these variables.

Despite these difficulties in interpreting water release curves, there is no doubt that the tree, *Acacia harpophylla*, can withstand significantly lower tissue water potentials than the grass, sorghum, and that the superior drought resistance of the former may well be largely due to a lower osmotic potential at full turgor in previously undroughted photosynthetic tissue (2.2 and 1.0 MPa, respectively; see Figs 3 and 4), and to a higher solute-accumulating capacity (Section V.A.1). It may equally well be due to the deep rooting habit of the tree compared with that of the grass. In Figure 5, a representative of the most drought tolerant of species, the resurrection plant, *Borya nitida*, displays an intermediate slope. As discussed below, drought resistance in resurrection plants is probably based on protoplasmic resistance, which involves a complex of different processes. Quite clearly, evaluation of drought resistance on the basis of water release curves is unlikely to be meaningful if different life forms are compared, or if the species compared differ in their mechanisms of drought resistance.

B. PROTOPLASMIC RESISTANCE

Many plants have protoplasm that survives periods at low water content, but the extraordinary properties of desiccation-tolerant plants (poikilohydric, "resurrection" plants) attracted a great deal of attention in the earlier literature. Extrapolation from these plants to others may have led to a possible overemphasis on protoplasmic tolerance as a mechanism of drought resistance. Stocker (1961) suggested that the orderly loss of water from poikilohydric plants is accompanied by dehydration of the cytoplasm in such a way that the metabolic machinery can be reassembled for normal function following rehydration. Figure 1 shows that poikilohydric plants have relatively high osmotic potentials, and Figure 5 shows that the water release characteristics of one of these desiccation-tolerant plants are intermediate between those of sorghum and *Acacia*. These observations suggest that the desiccation tolerance of poikilohydric plants is a special case which may depend on peculiar physical, chemical and structural properties different to those found in other plants.

The most familiar examples of desiccation-tolerant poikilohydric plants are the lichens and mosses which dehydrate within hours and rehydrate within a few minutes (Gwóźdź et al., 1974; Lange et al., 1975; Harris, 1976). Among the vascular plants, more than 100 species of poikilohydric resurrection plants from arid regions of Southern Africa and Australia are now known (Gaff, 1971, 1977; Gaff & Latz, 1978). Most of these plants dehydrate to an air dry condition. In Figure 6, data of Gaff (1977) have been recalculated to show the water potential of viable tissues from about 70 South African resurrection plants collected in the field. In most of these plants the tissue water potentials range between −100 and −200 MPa. Moreover, Gaff (1977) has shown that the poikilohydric plants are able to withstand exposure to very

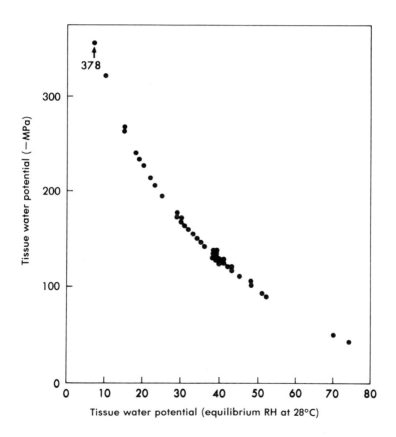

FIG. 6. Water potential of field-dry leaves of poikilohydric vascular plants from southern Africa showing the relationship between water potential expressed as MPa and relative humidity. (Data from Gaff, 1977.)

dry atmospheres for long periods. Plants which had water potentials of −20 to −400 MPa when collected survived storage at zero relative humidity for 6 months. However, survival in a humid atmosphere was remarkably short and, when held at 100% relative humidity, few species survived longer than 9 days.

In spite of the technical difficulties involved, there has been more emphasis on structural changes than on biochemical changes during dehydration and rehydration of resurrection plants and two categories can be distinguished on the basis of the retention or loss of chlorophyll during dehydration (Gaff & Hallam, 1974). In the chlorophyll-retaining species, chloroplast structure appears to be reasonably well preserved after 5 min rehydration of the moss, *Tortula* (Tucker et al., 1975), and 1 h after rehydration of the vascular plant, *Myrothamnus* (Wellburn & Wellburn, 1976). Unusual ultrastructural features recorded in the latter include a peculiar "staircase" arrangement of grana and the presence of "sheaths" around chloroplasts and mitochondria. Wellburn and Wellburn (1976) speculated that the separation of organelles from the cytoplasm by these "sheaths" may be significant in the preservation of function in chloroplasts and mitochondria.

Much more substantial changes are observed in the ultrastructure of desiccation-tolerant plants in which chlorophyll is lost. Chlorophyll loss is associated with disintegration of the chloroplast grana and thylakoids, and the breakdown of double membranes of organelles in *Borya nitida* (Gaff et al., 1976), but not in *Xerophyta villosa* (Hallam & Gaff, 1978). On rehydration, the repair of these outer membranes and the reorganization of grana and thylakoids accompany resynthesis of chlorophyll. No published measurements of the photosynthetic capacity of these plants during dehydration and rehydration are available. Unusual structural changes, such as the apparent increase in the number of mitochondria during desiccation of *B. nitida* and the early reassembly of starch grains in *X. villosa*, may be related to the energy metabolism of these tissues during tolerance induction and membrane reorganization.

Changes in the chemical composition of desiccation-tolerant plants during dehydration and rehydration have not been extensively documented. Disappearance of plastid starch may indicate its hydrolysis to osmotically effective sugars. A similar decrease in the insoluble nitrogen fraction and an increase in the soluble non-protein nitrogen fraction have been generally observed (Gaff & McGregor, 1979), but considerable losses in total nitrogen accompany desiccation of *B. nitida* (Gaff et al., 1976). Proline accumulation, which is specifically implicated in drought tolerance in other plants, was not consistently observed during dehydration of desiccation-tolerant species (Tymms & Gaff, 1979). The significance of the hydrolytic production of soluble compounds from insoluble polymers during dehydration in these plants is uncertain, as such processes may be too slow to contribute to "cryoprotection'' of the cytoplasm of rapidly drying species such as *Tortula ruralis* or in *Polypodium polypodiodes*. The poikilohydric ferns have a high osmotic potential of the sap (Fig. 1), but Stuart (1968) observed that the vacuolar contents suddenly solidified during dehydration. It may be that a special category of ''cryoprotectants'' is present in these plants, members of which interact with membranes and macromolecules to preserve their integrity during rapid dehydration.

VI. IMPLICATIONS OF DIFFERENT DROUGHT RESISTANCE MECHANISMS

This chapter has reviewed, rather briefly, the major categories of plant adaptations and responses which contribute to drought resistance. We have emphasized that the concept of drought resistance is expressed in different terms depending on the viewpoint of the investigator. Drought resistance mechanisms of interest to the agronomist are most often couched with a concern for productivity, whereas those of interest to the ecologist are most often concerned with survival. The metabolic bases of productivity on the one hand and survival on the other are likely to be very different and are often difficult to compare. Many of these processes are discussed in more detail in later chapters of this book, but these differences and difficulties can be illustrated here with some examples which we believe highlight fundamental questions for further study.

Whether one is concerned with productivity or survival in response to drought, the response must depend ultimately on photosynthetic processes. Much attention has been given recently to the role of different photosynthetic carbon fixation pathways in relation to productivity and survival in water-limited environments. Rather less attention has been given to photosynthetic processes in illuminated leaves deprived of external CO_2 due to stomatal closure, the most common of all responses to water stress, and the basis of drought resistance mechanisms related to control of water loss. Midday stomatal closure in crop plants (Turner et al., 1978) limits carbon assimilation, but may optimize carbon assimilation in relation to water use on a daily basis (Cowan & Farquhar, 1977). However, leaves are exposed to peak irradiance without access to external CO_2 at this time, and it is possible that the excess excitation energy absorbed by the photochemical system in these circumstances may result in photodestruction of the light harvesting assemblies in the thylakoids. This problem is much more pronounced in succulent plants (Fig. 2) and in leaves of some evergreen sclerophylls where stomata remain closed during periods of peak irradiance for many weeks at a time. It is possible that internal generation of CO_2 may stabilize the photosynthetic apparatus of those organisms in which drought tolerance is associated with the maintenance of a functional photosynthetic system at high water potential by means of stomatal closure (Osmond et al., 1980).

Osmond and Björkman (1972) proposed that photorespiration generates CO_2 and makes it possible to dissipate photochemical energy without net carbon gain at the CO_2 compensation point. Recent experiments (Powles & Osmond, 1978) established that, if leaves are illuminated in CO_2-free air under conditions which prevent photorespiration, inhibition of photosynthesis is evident following 2 h exposure to normal sunlight. This photoinhibition may be temporary, following midday stomatal closure or, if prolonged, could result in photodestruction and chlorophyll bleaching. In C_4 plants, the C_4-acid decarboxylation systems and metabolite fluxes may play a similar role in maintaining CO_2 supply when stomata close. The reassimilation of respiratory CO_2 during the dark period by succulent plants capable of crassulacean acid metabolism serves as an internal source of CO_2 for at least half the following light period, and photorespiration probably then furnishes internal CO_2 for the remainder of the light period (Osmond, 1978). Presumably, these internal CO_2 sources stabilize the functional photosynthetic system during prolonged isolation from external CO_2 (Osmond et al., 1980).

This discussion draws attention to the implications of the above drought resistance mechanisms for only one complex of biochemical processes. There are likely to be similar consequences at almost all levels of cellular metabolism. However, the discussion also suggests that the central problem of internal generation of CO_2 to maintain photosynthetic integrity when external CO_2 is not available may have been resolved by several different metabolic mechanisms.

Survival of plants during periods of extreme desiccation may be based on functional metabolic systems which are isolated from the environment, as in the case of rhizomes or the leaf and stem succulents. Alternatively, plants may survive as seeds or as dehydrated photosynthetic systems. In other words, there are examples of survival of autotrophic metabolism and of heterotrophic metabolism at low and high water potential. Survival of autotrophic metabolism in succulents or chlorophyll-retaining poikilohydric plants implies that the organism escapes the relatively precarious developmental stages and the transition from heterotrophic metabolism associated with germination and establishment of plants which survive drought in the form of seeds. It is impossible to explore these analogies at length here, or to speculate on the relative adaptive merits of the different strategies. Appreciation of these aspects however, may help preserve relevance in experimental approaches to metabolic aspects of drought resistance.

In the literature dealing with structural and biochemical changes which accompany dehydration and rehydration of desiccation tolerant plants, parallels are almost always sought with changes which follow desiccation of conventional mesophytic plants. It is possible that more might be learned by comparisons with the structural and biochemical changes which accompany the imbibition of water and activation of metabolism during seed germination, or with the germination of resting spores of algae and lower organisms. Plants tolerant to low water potential show remarkable similarities in their metabolic changes. Mitochondria are preserved during dehydration of seeds (Ching, 1972) and, evidently, also in desiccation tolerant *T. ruralis* (Bewley et al., 1974). In both, respiratory CO_2 production is extremely rapid immediately following rehydration. Changes in the ribosome profiles of wheat embryos before and after rehydration (Marcus, 1969) and of *Tortula* before and after rehydration (Gwóźdź et al., 1974) are similar. In both, the polyribosome population is small in the desiccated tissue and rapidly increases during rehydration.

More subtle changes in metabolic systems could be involved in drought resistance of plants exposed to much lower levels of stress. The various forms of solute accumulation outlined above and discussed in more detail in later chapters may reflect either the redirection of metabolic products or major changes in metabolic patterns. For example, sugars may be retained in cells of expanded leaves and accumulated in the vacuole in order to maintain leaf turgor or may be translocated to the root to maintain growth of new roots which may be functional in water uptake, rather than being translocated and used in development of new leaves and production of additional transpiring surface.

Finally, attention is drawn, again, to the data of Walter and Stadelmann (1974) shown in Figure 1 which suggest that desert ephemerals may have a significant capacity for solute accumulation and may show greater physiological and biochemical adaptation to water stress environments than previously recognized. These more subtle mechanisms of drought resistance may be of greater significance for agricultural practice in semi-arid regions where a prime objective must be maximum production under water limited conditions.

CHAPTER 3

Water Collection by Roots

J. B. PASSIOURA

I.	Introduction	39
II.	Factors influencing the rate of water collection	40
	A. Perirhizal flow	41
	B. The interface between root and soil	42
	C. Radial flow across the root	43
	D. Axial flow in the roots	45
	E. Water collection by complete root systems	47
III.	The amount of water collected	47
	A. Maximizing gains of water to the rooting zone	47
	B. Minimizing losses of water from the rooting zone	49
	C. Maximizing the extraction of water from within the rooting zone	50
IV.	The efficiency with which the water is collected	51
V.	The pattern of water collection through time	51
VI.	Conclusions	53

I. INTRODUCTION

Drought resistance is a term appropriate to an ontogenetic time scale. It refers to the ability of a plant to complete its life cycle even though its growth is limited by an inadequate supply of water or by an inability to conduct water to its leaves quickly enough to satisfy a high evaporative demand. This chapter discusses the processes involved in the transport of water from soil to shoot in so far as they influence the growth and particularly the reproduction of plants subject to drought. The processes span a wide range of time scales, from minutes for certain changes in the hydraulic permeability of roots, to months for the slow exploitation of a deep, wet soil by a growing root system. The slow processes can often be directly related to drought resistance as defined above. However, the quick ones cannot, for the complex interactions between them, and with the environment, must first be taken into account.

39

It is common to view the flow of water from soil to shoot as an analogue of the flow of current through a network of resistors (e.g. Weatherley, 1976). Such a view is essentially instantaneous. The more refined treatments add capacitors, and thus extend the analogue to time-dependent phenomena. But even these rely on an instantaneous view of the main structure of the plant, and the phenomena dealt with have time scales no greater than one day. Although these short-term phenomena are fundamental to the water economy of a plant, their connection to drought resistance is obscure, except in the trivial sense that if a plant transports no water to its leaves it does not survive. The connection depends, in subtle ways, on long-term processes occurring both in the plant and in its environment (Passioura, 1976). For example, one cannot say that plants which have roots with a high permeability to water are generally more drought resistant than those that do not. Highly permeable roots may help if a plant is competing for a limited supply of water that must be extracted quickly; they may hinder if the plant has a limited supply of water that must last until the next rain comes.

The long-term phenomena are those associated with changes in the main structure of the plant. They influence a range of interactions between the plant and its environment that have a fairly direct bearing on drought resistance. They are conveniently discussed under three topics: (i) the *amount* of water collected by the roots during the life of the plant; (ii) the *efficiency* with which that water is collected, defined in terms of the amount of assimilate that must be invested in the roots in order to collect the water; and (iii) the *pattern* of the collection over time, which influences the seed production of annuals and the persistence of perennials.

II. FACTORS INFLUENCING THE RATE OF WATER COLLECTION

There have been several recent and excellent reviews that discuss various aspects of the flow of water from soil to shoot through a macroscopically static root system (Greacen et al., 1976; Newman, 1974, 1976; Tinker, 1976). This section draws heavily on these, emphasizing those points that seem relevant to drought resistance.

It is convenient to think of the path of water from soil to shoot as consisting of several sections; (i) pararhizal, from distant soil to soil close to the roots; (ii) perirhizal, through soil adjacent to the roots, i.e. over distances less than about 1 cm; (iii) across the interface between soil and root; (iv) radial, through the cortex and stele to the xylem; and (v) axial, along the xylem. Flow along the path is generally assumed to be passive and driven by gradients in pressure potential, or, where flow across a semi-permeable membrane is involved, total potential. The pararhizal path is important only in wet soil, whose hydraulic conductivity is high. It is unlikely to be important during drought and will not be considered further.

A. PERIRHIZAL FLOW

The geometry of a root system is complicated, but it is useful to idealize it by assuming (i) that water flows radially through the soil to a root, (ii) that the uptake per unit length of active root is uniform, and (iii) that each root has sole access to the water within a hollow cylinder of soil whose inner radius, a, is that of the root and whose outer radius, b, is $(1/\pi L)^{1/2}$ where L is the length of root per unit volume of soil. Given these assumptions, one may derive equations, such as the following (Tinker, 1976), to describe the flow of water through the soil to the root:

$$\Delta\theta = \bar{\theta} - \theta_a \simeq \frac{I}{2\pi D} \cdot \ln \frac{(b)}{(2a)} \tag{1}$$

where $\bar{\theta}$ is the mean volumetric water content of the soil; θ_a is the volumetric water content of the soil at the surface of the root; I is the rate of uptake of water per unit length of root; and D is the diffusivity of water in the soil. D is usually an exponential function of θ, and typically ranges from about 10^{-5} $cm^2.s^{-1}$ in fairly dry soil (at a soil water potential, ψ_{soil}, of about -1.5 MPa) to greater than 10^{-3} $cm^2.s^{-1}$ in moist soil (with ψ_{soil} of about 10 kPa). Equation (1) is derived by assuming that D is constant, but it still works reasonably well when D is not constant, providing a suitable average value is chosen for the particular range of θ, and providing $\Delta\theta$ is not very large. The equation can be used to calculate $\Delta\theta$ which in turn can be used to calculate the water potential at the surface of the root, by making use of the water potential-water content curve for the soil.

The use of this equation has proved controversial, not in principle, because the assumptions on which it is based are reasonable, but in application. The most influential parameters in the equation are I and D, for a and b appear only in a logarithmic term. Although D is difficult to measure, it can be measured, and is not the source of controversy. The problem is with I. Early users of this type of equation (e.g. Gardner, 1960; Cowan, 1965) chose values of I large enough for $\Delta\theta$ to be large even in fairly moist soil. But Newman and others (see Tinker, 1976) have argued that, in real situations, the length of root per unit volume of soil is so large, that I, and hence $\Delta\theta$, is trivially small. It is only when D approaches 10^{-5} $cm^2.s^{-1}$ that the equation becomes relevant, by which time ψ_{soil} is usually less than -0.5 MPa, and little available water remains in the soil. Normally, it is the resistances inside the plant that dominate the distribution of water potential in the system. These arguments are persuasive, but the fact remains that plants do seem to find it more difficult to extract water from soil than from solution unless the soil is quite wet (say, $\psi_{soil} > -50$ kPa) (Faiz & Weatherley, 1977). The reason may be that the proportion of roots that can take up water is much smaller than we think (Caldwell, 1976), or that there is a major interfacial resistance between root and soil, as recent evidence suggests (Weatherley, 1976).

B. THE INTERFACE BETWEEN ROOT AND SOIL

Huck et al. (1970) have shown that cotton roots may contract diurnally by up to 40%. Their work has rekindled interest in the suggestion of Philip (1957) that a vapour gap may form around a root, disrupting the hydraulic continuity between root and soil. The disruption would not be complete, for the root would undoubtedly continue to touch particles of soil at many places. The resulting effect on water uptake would depend, therefore, on whether or not the remaining hydraulic connections were capable of carrying the flow of water without inducing major drops in water potential at the interface. This in turn would be dependent upon the resistances to water flow in both the soil and the root cortex in the region adjacent to the area of contact.

We can get an approximate idea of the resistance in the soil by making use of equation (1). Although this equation was derived by assuming perfect radial flow to the root, it should still apply, albeit only approximately, if the root has a longitudinal stripe of contact with the soil. Water will continue to move more or less radially to the stripe, although the flow lines in the shadow of the root will be rather distorted. The equation will underestimate $\Delta\theta$, but the error is probably small and equivalent to an increase in l of perhaps 30%. The effect on a of the shrinking of the root is much larger. The "radius" of the region of contact may be less than a quarter of that of the root before it shrinks, so that the flux density of water through the region could be many times that through the soil touching an expanded root. Although the effect on a may be large, the effect in the equation need not be, for a is contained in a logarithmic term; even if the "radius" of the region of contact were only a tenth that of the radius of the root, the effect on $\Delta\theta$ would be little more than twofold ($\ln 10 = 2.3$). Thus, the effect of an incomplete vapour gap on the flow of water from soil to root may not be as great as it first appears.

The effect on the radial resistance to flow through the root, however, may be quite large, depending on whether or not the resistance in the cortex is large compared to that in the stele. If the cortical resistance is large, then any channelling of flow through the cortex due to poor contact between epidermis and soil will have a large effect on resistance. On the other hand, if the main radial resistance is in the stele, so that the cortex is by comparison a short circuit, the channelling of flow through the cortex will have little effect. This problem will be discussed more fully in Section II, C, but it is worth recalling Newman's (1974) remarks: unless there is a reasonably large resistance in the cortex, the water potential of the cortex will tend to remain at that of the adjacent soil; if the water potential of the cortex does remain at that of the adjacent soil, it will be unlikely to fluctuate widely enough to bring about the root shrinkage described by Huck et al. (1970).

Thus, the effect of a vapour gap on water flow is unclear, although an intriguing experiment by Faiz (see Weatherley, 1976) strongly suggests that contact between root and soil can pose a problem. Faiz showed that the water content of the leaves of a rapidly transpiring sunflower plant could be suddenly, though transiently, increased by squeezing the soil in which its roots were growing.

There are two complications that can be added to the simple picture of the vapour gap described above. The first is that the flow of water through the soil to the root may not be as easy as we imagine, and root hairs may be needed to help extract the water. The shrinking of a root would disrupt many of the hairs, although, conceivably, the epidermis could grow new ones to bridge the gap.

The second complication is that there may be a major build-up of solutes at the surface of the root, or in the cortex, as a result of the root shrinking. It is not uncommon to find that a substantial proportion of the solutes transported from the soil to the root by convection is rejected by the root (Barber, 1974), and if these solutes flow into the cortex through a bottle-necked junction with the soil, they may be unable to diffuse, through the bottle-neck, back into the soil. They would then manifest themselves as an osmotic potential which would partly counter the pressure gradients across the semi-permeable membranes of the stele. Larger gradients would therefore be needed to maintain the flow of water; that is the permeability of the root would seem to decrease.

The emphasis in the above discussion has been on poor contact between root and soil due to the shrinking of the root. Another, and perhaps more common cause of poor root-soil contact, is that roots frequently grow through large pores or along planes of weakness in soil (Taylor, 1974). In these circumstances, root hairs may play a particularly important role in extracting water from the soil.

C. RADIAL FLOW ACROSS THE ROOT

The largest drop in water potential in the plant usually occurs somewhere between the surface of the root and the xylem (Kramer, 1969). Although it has been studied extensively, the radial flow of water in response to the gradient of water potential still remains mysterious. There are two main problems. The first is that, within certain limits, the gradient remains constant even though the flow rate may vary considerably (Weatherley, 1976). The second is that we do not know by what path the water moves, or where on that path the major resistances lie.

The first problem seems to be associated with well-watered plants transpiring at low to medium rates. It has no apparent connection with drought resistance and will not be considered further.

The second problem has been thoroughly discussed by Newman (1976). He concluded that the most likely path for water was through the symplasm of the cortex to the stele. The rival pathways are (i) through the vacuoles of the cortical cells, and (ii) along the cell walls of the cortex to the endodermis, where the impermeability of the Casparian strip forces the water to pass through the plasmalemma. Newman saw major difficulties with both these pathways: with the first because the water would have to pass so many poorly permeable tonoplasts; with the second because measured permeabilities of cell walls would be much too low. However, he acknowledged that the values he collected for the permeability of cell walls were for flow across the walls rather than along them, and that the longitudinal permeability might be much higher. In fact, there are copious intercellular spaces in the cortex (Esau, 1977), and if there are films of water partly occupying these, the permeability could be very much higher. Simple capillary theory predicts that, at a matric potential of -0.1 MPa, hydrophilic pores of diameter up to 3μm will be filled with water. The intercellular spaces in the cortex of wheat and maize, for example, are $3-10 \mu$m in diameter. They are roughly triangular when viewed in a transverse section, with concave sides, so that there are many grooves between cells that can contain water even if the whole of the intercellular space is not filled. At a matric potential of -0.1 MPa these grooves may be filled to a depth of say 2μm. The intercellular spaces are arranged predominantly in longitudinal columns (O'Brien & McCully, 1969), and radial connections may be rare. It is hard to judge without having good quality tangential sections of the cortex, and they are most difficult to obtain. By making a few simple assumptions, however, a rough estimate can be obtained of the possible effect of radially continuous pores on permeability. If there are 100 pores that radially traverse the cortex per millimetre length of root, and if each has an effective radius of 1μm, then, by assuming that the pores are circular (which enables us to use Poiseuille's equation) and that the cortex is 300μm thick, the calculated permeability is approximately $10^5 \mu$m^2.s^{-1}.MPa^{-1}. This is at least 100 times larger than the value calculated by Newman (1976). Clearly, the assumptions have led to an unrealistically high permeability; the radial paths of the pores may be extremely tortuous —

indeed, they may not be continuous. Alternatively, the plant may have some means of excluding water from the pores. The point remains, however, that flow along the cell walls may be very much easier than flow through them. This is particularly true for longitudinal flow, so that if the hydraulic contact between root and soil is so poor that it is merely a scatter of points, the resulting "point" sources of water at the epidermis would be converted to "line" sources within the cortex, and the radial permeability would thereby be enhanced. Kozinka and Luxova (1971) presented evidence that the longitudinal permeability of the cortex of maize roots may be very large, although it seems likely that their technique may have resulted in the intercellular spaces being artificially saturated with water.

Thus, we do not know whether the cortex is so permeable as to be virtually a short circuit, or so impermeable as to contain the major resistance to the flow of water from the surface of the root to the xylem. The implications of these alternatives are considerable for the extraction of water from soil, as discussed earlier.

Although we are ignorant about the radial path of water in the root, we can measure the overall permeability. Newman (1973) made several such measurements and found permeabilities ranging from 5 to 40 $\mu m^2 . s^{-1} . MPa^{-1}$ for a variety of species. These measurements were for whole root systems. As a root ages the permeability drops, presumably owing to the deposition of suberin; but even in very old roots the permeability may be as much as a tenth of that of young ones (Graham et al., 1974). Newman's (1973) average values for complete root systems probably arose from a mixture of much larger and much smaller values.

D. AXIAL FLOW IN THE ROOTS

Axial flow of water occurs almost entirely in the xylem. In dicots, with their facility for secondary growth, there is abundant xylem, and major axial gradients in water potential would not be expected unless cavitation (Milburn, 1973) emptied many of the vessels. There is no strong evidence showing cavitation in roots. Byrne et al. (1977) observed empty vessels in cotton roots, but their technique of freezing the roots in liquid nitrogen may well have induced cavitation.

In the monocots, where secondary growth is rare, and particularly in the Gramineae, which have no secondary growth, the xylem is not so abundant, and Wind (1955), Passioura (1974), and Greacen et al. (1976) have argued that pressure gradients in the xylem may account for a large proportion of the difference in water potential between shoot and soil. This is particularly true of cereal crops, which frequently have to rely on their seminal roots to extract water from a moist subsoil and to transport it, vertically, through a dry topsoil to the shoot. In a wheat crop, for example, if the environment has not favoured the deep penetration of nodal roots, water collected in the subsoil is carried to the shoot through about three seminal axes per plant. Each axis typically contains only one large xylem vessel, so that if the topsoil is dry, the entire water supply of each plant is carried through the topsoil by only three xylem vessels. The radius of these vessels is usually within the range 25–50 μm. Ponsana (see Greacen et al., 1976) has calculated substantial pressure drops along the axes using data acquired from field observations. The cultivar he used seemed to have particularly large vessels: cultivars with smaller vessels would give even larger pressure drops in the xylem. The flow in the xylem can be described approximately by Poiseuille's equation (Greacen et al., 1976) in which the permeability depends on the fourth power of the radius of the vessel; thus, small changes in the radius can have very large effects on permeability.

There are other examples amongst the monocots in which axial resistance may have a large and even catastrophic effect on the behaviour of the plant. The first concerns wheat seedlings that have been sharply droughted, then rewatered. Frequently, such seedlings never fully recover from the drought and grow poorly even though they are well-watered. Transections of the axes of the affected seedlings (Passioura, unpublished) show that the main xylem vessels have collapsed and, presumably, offer such enormous resistances to axial flow that the plant is forever under water stress. The collapse of the vessels may be due to the suddenness of the drought; without adequate time for hardening, the tissues of the stele are not able to withstand the very large pressure gradients which form.

A second example concerns sorghum plants that have been established initially in moist soil that has subsequently dried out on the surface owing to lack of rain. These plants frequently do not develop nodal roots (R. K. Myers, pers. comm.) and must rely on their single seminal roots to provide water. Their roots, like those of wheat, have only one large xylem vessel, of about 30 μm radius. However, while a wheat crop may have 300 seminal axes.m^{-2} of ground, a sorghum crop, with only one root per plant, and only about 10 plants.m^{-2}, will have only 10 axes.m^{-2}. The axial resistance per unit area of ground will be 30 times that of Ponsana's wheat crop (Greacen et al., 1976) and, presumably, would be too great to enable the leaves to get an adequate water supply. No matter how large a lateral root system each seminal axis develops, it will be unable to overcome the huge axial resistance. Sorghum crops that do not develop nodal roots do, indeed, fail.

A third example is provided by the work of Wilson et al. (1976) who showed that blue grama seedlings grew poorly if drought prevented the development of nodal roots. The resistance to flow through the very small xylem vessels of the single seminal root and the sub-coleoptile internode apparently prevented the leaves from getting an adequate supply of water.

E. WATER COLLECTION BY COMPLETE ROOT SYSTEMS

The previous discussion has been concerned with individual parts of the pathway of water from soil to shoot. A complete root system, growing in the field, integrates all of these parts. The flow of water through it is largely determined by the evaporative demand on the leaves when the soil is wet. During a drought, however, when the soil is drying, the flow becomes a complex function of shoot water potential, the distribution of roots and of soil water, and the properties of the various resistances. There seems to be only one way to handle such a complex system, and that is to make a simulation model of it. Many people have made such models, with varying degrees of success, and at various levels of complexity. Greacen (1977) has recently discussed several of them.

Even if we have a very clear idea of the performance of a given root system, we may still have a poor understanding of the drought resistance of the plant of which it forms a part. The following sections try to provide a context in which the performance of the root system can be judged.

III. THE AMOUNT OF WATER COLLECTED

This section explores the simple proposition that, other things being equal, the more water a plant transpires during its life, the better its performance will be. The mechanisms which maximize the gains of water to the root zone and minimize losses, whilst ensuring, if the plant is an annual, that all available water in the rooting zone is exhausted by maturity, will now be examined.

A. MAXIMIZING GAINS OF WATER TO THE ROOTING ZONE

Apart from the obvious examples of riparian and deep-rooted perennial vegetation which extend their rooting zones to tap water tables, there are two ways in which it is possible for a plant to obtain an increased supply of water from its rooting zone. One is through root extension and tapping water that has accumulated more deeply in the subsoil; the behaviour of lucerne in a Mediterranean climate is a good example. The other is through improvements to the permeability of the soil in its vicinity.

Apart from genetic effects, the most influential factors affecting the exploration of a wet subsoil during a drought are the mechanical resistance of the soil, and nutrition, both organic and inorganic. Soil water potential *per se* seems unlikely to be important, for Newman (1966), working with flax, and Taylor and Ratliff (1969), working with peanuts and cotton, showed that root growth was unaffected unless ψ_{soil} was less than about -0.7 MPa: the roots of flax continued to grow, although very slowly, even at $\psi_{soil} = -2.0$ MPa. Poor aeration, which seriously affects root growth in wet soils, is unlikely to be important during drought, although a shallow root system formed during a wet period may be unable to extract subsoil water during a subsequent drought.

The effects of the mechanical resistance of the soil on root growth have been reviewed by Taylor (1974), Greacen (1977) and Cannell (1977). Many subsoils are very dense and have high mechanical resistance, and there is no doubt that roots have difficulty growing in such soils, particularly at the low temperatures that usually prevail (Greacen & Hignett, 1976).

Subsoils are often poor in nutrients, and those nutrients that travel poorly in the phloem, such as Ca and B, must be locally available so that the roots might grow (Kramer, 1969). Simpson and Lipsett (1973) observed a particularly striking local response by the roots of lucerne to Ca, B and P applied to the subsoil. A common problem in acid subsoils is Al toxicity, which produces stunted roots. However, in an agricultural context, the wide genetic variability in tolerance to Al, both within and between species, suggests that breeding should be able to produce even more tolerant plants than are currently available (Foy, 1974).

The organic nutrition of roots does not suffer greatly during drought and it may even improve, if the size of the root system can be taken as a guide. Drought commonly increases the ratio of root to shoot (Mooney, 1972; Larcher, 1975), and there are several reports of the absolute size of the root system actually increasing during drought (Bennett & Doss, 1960; Doss et al., 1960; Hsaio & Acevedo, 1974; Schultz, 1974). Klepper et al. (1973) found that cotton roots growing in the subsoil of a drying profile grew so much faster than those growing in a well-watered profile, that the total length of the droughted root system was substantially greater than that of the well-watered one. The reasons for the good growth of the roots of droughted plants have been discussed by Hsaio and Acevedo (1974) and Itai and Benzioni (1976). The most likely explanation is that drought affects the growth of the shoot more than it does photosynthesis, so that the amount of assimilate available for root growth is thereby increased.

An increase in the ratio of the root to shoot of a plant during drought has obvious advantages in helping the plant match its water supply to the evaporative demand on its leaves. The differences between species, with respect to the response to drought of their root to shoot ratios, is enormous, with some desert plants having ratios as high as 10:1 (Larcher, 1975). The importance of a large and extensive root system in conferring drought resistance on a plant has often been emphasized (Kramer, 1969; Hurd, 1974). However, the metabolic costs of forming and maintaining such a root system should also be stressed. They are discussed below in Section IV.

In addition to enlarging the rooting zone, plants may obtain an increased water supply by improvements to the permeability of the soil in their vicinity. Slatyer (1962) found that moisture infiltration was substantially faster near the base of an isolated mulga tree than it was some distance away. Moreover, he found that after about 20 min infiltration the rates settled down to fairly steady values that persisted for some hours. This rapid settling down of infiltration rate suggests that the flow of water may have been dominated by the macrostructure of the soil, as discussed by Greacen (1977); that is the water was moving predominantly through large pores and cracks and was not moving as a well-defined wetting front. The distribution of the large pores is presumably influenced by the growth of the roots, particularly with a perennial plant. The flow of water down the stem can be a substantial proportion of the total rainfall for many plants (Saffigna et al., 1976); therefore, having highly permeable soil near the base of the stem would be an advantage, particularly during heavy rain.

B. MINIMIZING LOSSES OF WATER FROM THE ROOTING ZONE

Losses of water from a plant's rooting zone, other than through its own transpiration, are by evaporation from the soil surface, deep drainage beyond the reach of the roots, and uptake by competing plants. During a drought the first and third of these can be major. The second is unlikely to occur except in wet conditions, and if it does then occur, the problem becomes one of the extension of the root system and the tapping of such water if there is a subsequent drought.

The effects of evaporation from the soil are proportionately most severe when the plant is relying on light falls of rain for its main water supply. When the topsoil dries, roots growing in that zone lose most of their ability to take up water (Kramer, 1950; Brix, 1962), and when rain falls, it takes several days before the roots fully recover. During this time a light fall of rain will have largely evaporated. Even a fall as heavy as 10 mm will typically wet no more than the top 5 cm of the soil, unless the soil is very sandy, or unless channelling of rain down the stems of the plants results in deep penetration as discussed earlier. Water within 5 cm of the soil's surface is poorly protected from evaporation, unless the plants have such a large leaf area index that the soil is well shaded. This is unlikely during a drought. Evaporative losses during a growing season frequently exceed 50% of the rainfall when the rain comes in light showers (Fischer & Turner, 1978). Few mechanisms have evolved to reduce this loss. The heavy root suberization that occurs when the soil dries presumably protects the roots from losing water to the soil, but at the same time it largely prevents them from taking up water when the soil is rewetted. As mentioned in Section II, C, suberized roots have been reported to take up water at about 10% of the rate of young roots, but the measurements of permeability were made by immersing the roots in water; much lower values may prevail when the roots are extracting water from soil.

Uptake by the roots of competing plants from a shared supply of water can be lessened by means of allelopathy (Papadakis, 1978) or by extracting the water as fast as possible. Allelopathy is a complex subject that we will not discuss further. Rapid uptake can have disadvantages, and these are discussed below in Sections IV and V. But given that a plant is to take up water quickly, the best means of doing so is to have a large rooting density, that is a large root length per unit volume of soil. A large rooting density ensures that even though the root system as a whole may be taking up water rapidly, the uptake per unit length of root is nevertheless small, and, therefore, so are the drops of water potential across the roots, and the perirhizal soil, as explained in Section II.

C. MAXIMIXING THE EXTRACTION OF WATER FROM WITHIN THE ROOTING ZONE

Plants that grow in drought-prone environments usually survive a ψ_{soil} of less than -2.0 MPa, and some even extract water down to a ψ_{soil} of -10 MPa (Noy-Meir, 1973). The amount of water held by soil between ψ_{soil} of -2.0 MPa and -10 MPa is usually small unless the soil is very heavy, but even a small amount of water may enable a plant to survive a severe drought. The extraction of water at very low ψ_{soil} however, is probably more related to the properties of the leaves than to those of the roots.

Although roots can extract water at quite low values of ψ_{soil}, there are many reports, particularly for crops, of roots failing to extract large amounts of apparently available water from the soil at the bottom of the rooting zone, even though the plants were suffering from drought (Schultz, 1971; Blum, 1974; Hurd, 1974; Walter & Barley, 1974). Greacen (1977) has discussed possible reasons for this behaviour, which could be due to a large axial resistance in the roots (Passioura, 1974; Walter & Barley, 1974), inadequate rooting density, or low permeability of the deep roots.

IV. THE EFFICIENCY WITH WHICH THE WATER IS COLLECTED

A root system grows by using assimilate that could increase the size of the shoot; that is, root growth reduces the potential of the plant for future photosynthesis. But the actual photosynthesis depends in part on the ability of the roots to supply the shoot with water and nutrients. Section III,A emphasized the importance of a large root system in extracting the maximum amount of water from soil. However, if the extra water obtained does no more than allow the shoot to replace the assimilate spent in obtaining it, the process is inefficient. Mooney (1972) discussed the compromises reached by wild plants in their allocation of photosynthate. The cost of growing and maintaining roots may be rather more than the distribution of dry matter within the plant suggests; there is evidence that for roots grown in soil the weight of the root system at harvest may be less than 25% that of the assimilates that have been transported to it (Sauerbeck & Johnen, 1976).

One of the problems faced by wild plants in a drought-prone environment is competition with other plants for a limited supply of water. The compromises that have been evolved presumably take this competition into account. With crop plants, on the other hand, where it is the performance of the community rather than that of the individual that is important, competition for water loses its pertinance (assuming, that is, that weeds are not a major problem). We might expect, therefore, in a given environment, that a crop whose growth is being limited by water would have an optimum ratio of root to shoot growth substantially less than that of similar, but individual, plants that are competing with each other. Whether modern cultivars used in dryland cropping have lower root to shoot ratios than their wild progenitors is hard to say; no relevant data appear to be available. However, it seems that the performance of modern cultivars under drought might be better if their ratio of root to shoot growth was lower. A tremendous concentration of roots in the topsoil (Barley, 1970) seems particularly extravagant in a crop. Admittedly, such roots may lessen evaporative losses from the soil surface, or they may supply nutrients. The latter seems unlikely, however, for there seems to be no problem in mobile nutrients moving by convection to sparse roots and deficient immobile nutrients are frequently placed as fertilizer in a concentrated band close to the seed, and would therefore not need a large root system to exploit them.

V. THE PATTERN OF WATER COLLECTION THROUGH TIME

A plant that has only current rain for its supply of water has its pattern of water use imposed upon it. But one that is living in an environment in which drought is punctuated by long wet spells, which result in substantial amounts of water being stored in the soil, is not so restricted.

There are two contrasting strategies that have been evolved by plants in their use of stored water. The first is the very rapid use of water until there is so little left that it becomes a means of survival rather than of production. This seems an appropriate strategy for plants in a competitive situation, for even though there is the risk of suffering severe water stress, the risk of a competitor capitalizing on the unused water would be even greater. Most wild plants seem to operate in this way (Fischer & Turner, 1978), and so do some crop plants (Ritchie, 1974), even though they are usually not in a very competitive situation. Such behaviour in crop plants may be due to their having been selected, in part, for their ability to compete with weeds. More likely, perhaps, it is due to breeders having been consistently attracted to vigorous looking plants during the early generations of a cross, when the various lines may have been competing with each other for limited resources (Donald, 1968). In terms of the processes discussed in Section II, if a plant is to extract the soil water quickly it is best served by an extensive root system of high rooting density and high permeability. In this way the drop in water potential between soil and shoot remains small until ψ_{soil} is quite low.

The alternative strategy is the conservative use of water, which lessens the risk of running into severe water stress, and, for annual plants in particular, makes it likely that water is available during especially important phases such as flowering and seed filling. This strategy seems appropriate for weed-free crops or for plants growing without competitors. For a crop, drought resistance is usually defined as the ability to yield well when growth is limited by water. The yield of a water-limited crop depends in part on the proportion of its total water supply that is used after flowering (Nix, 1975; Passioura, 1977; Fischer & Turner, 1978): crops that have water for use after flowering are likely to yield better than those that do not.

The type of root system that results in the greatest conservation of water is one that is sparse and poorly permeable, though extensive so that all pockets of available water are explored. Alternatively, it could have a high rooting density, but a slow rate of extension, so that untapped regions of wet soil remain at flowering. One problem with a "conservative" root system is that, although it may improve the drought resistance of a plant, it may also prevent it from responding to good conditions. This problem, at least in principle, can be avoided in the root systems of the temperate cereals because of the high resistance to axial flow in the seminal axes (discussed in Section II, D) and the dual nature of the root systems. The seminal roots (those arising from the seed) are largely responsible for exploiting the subsoil for spring wheat, barley and oats. When the topsoil is dry, a high resistance to axial flow in the seminal roots will ensure that the water in the subsoil is used slowly. But when the topsoil is frequently wet, as it is in a good season, the nodal root system develops well and amply supplies the crop with water; it does not then matter that the resistance in the seminal roots is large.

VI. CONCLUSIONS

The influence of the root system on the drought resistance of a plant has been discussed primarily in terms of its ability to maximize the amount of water it collects, while expending as little assimilate as possible, and while ensuring also that the way in which the water is collected through time is appropriate to the plant's environment. These primary aspects have been discussed against a background of more detailed phenomena that have no obviously direct bearing on drought resistance, such as the factors affecting the rates of transport of water from soil to shoot, and the factors affecting the rate and extent of root growth.

Some of the main points to emerge are:

1. The major loss of potentially useful water is by evaporation from the soil, and there seems to be little that can be done to prevent this.

2. A large ratio of root to shoot growth may be appropriate for drought-affected plants growing amongst competitors, but may be inappropriate for crop plants, which are generally free of major competitors. An excessively large root system uses assimilate that could be better used in the shoot, and it may result in a plant using water too fast in relation to its phenology.

3. In a soil having ψ_{soil} of less than about -0.1 MPa, the major resistance to the flow of water from soil to shoot may be neither in the soil nor in the root, but at the interface between the two. The properties of this interface are, at present, poorly understood.

CHAPTER 4

Water Relations During Drought

MERRILL R. KAUFMANN

I.	Introduction	55
II.	Water transport and redistribution	57
	A. The range of water stress in plants	57
	B. The basic transport process	59
	C. Water relations during drought	61
III.	Water status of plant tissues	67
	A. Water potential components	67
	B. Relative water content	68
	C. Stress hardening	69
	D. Drought avoidance or tolerance	70

I. INTRODUCTION

Explaining, or even defining, drought resistance in plants is a research challenge that is not adequately satisfied with experimental data. While considerable research has been done, two difficulties have prevented a thorough understanding of drought resistance (more accurately, drought tolerance or avoidance). First, the physiology and biochemistry of plant responses to drought have proved to be very complex, involving not one or several physiological processes but rather nearly every major function of plant growth, as illustrated by the inclusive list of topics for this book. Consequently, the study of drought resistance has lacked well-defined hypotheses about the physiology and biochemistry of stressed plants or varieties.

Secondly, research on drought resistance has been limited by the methods available for the examination of the water relations of tissues and cells. Few fields of plant science have undergone the gyrations of methodology experienced in studies of plant-water relations in the past two decades. Out of this activity have come considerably improved and refined methods for many kinds of measurements (see Slavik, 1974), and these methods have permitted

PHYSIOLOGY AND BIOCHEMISTRY
OF DROUGHT RESISTANCE
IN PLANTS

a much better definition of water status in relation to drought response. In concert with improvement of methods has been the extension of water transport theories, many of them based upon principles identified by Stephan Hales 250 years ago. Despite this progress, research remains hindered by inadequate methods for describing the water status of many plant organs, tissues and cells.

Recent trends in research on drought resistance show an intensified interest in the relationship between cellular and subcellular processes and drought responses. Since so much remains to be learned at the cellular and biochemical level, this interest is fully justified. It is also periodically necessary, however, to take an overview. Why can a tomato plant withstand a severe wilt with little subsequent damage? What is it about the ponderosa pine tree that permits it to survive and grow in a dry climatic zone where the Douglas-fir fails? Partial answers come easily, but it is important to recognize that for each plant successfully enduring the conditions at its place of growth there is a system in which structure, physiological processes and environmental conditions are successfully integrated to make survival and growth possible.

Most of the chapters of this volume deal primarily with physiological and biochemical aspects of drought response. This chapter is written to provide more of the whole-plant perspective of water relations during drought. By emphasizing some of the physical and physiological features of water relations of desiccated plants, the interrelationships between environmental conditions, structure and function may become more apparent. Attention is given to studies involving both trees and herbaceous species to emphasize the contrasting behaviour of woody and non-woody plants.

Plants subjected to dry environmental conditions must have certain adaptive features or be able to acclimatize to water stress. Evenari et al. (1975) list the main adaptive features of plants which maintain metabolic activity through drought (Table I). While these features are characteristic of desert plants in particular, those mesophytic plants capable of withstanding some degree of drought appear to have at least some adaptations found in this list. Also, depending upon their stress history, plants within a species or cultivar generally vary in their ability to tolerate water stress conditions. For example, a plant may become acclimatized to a degree by moderate exposure to stress, so that it can withstand harsher conditions than a plant having no history of stress. Consequently, the study of drought response must include a careful analysis, or at least an awareness, of the effects of water stress history.

What is required to characterize the water status of plants in relation to drought? Richter (1976) suggests that a thorough description of plant water status should include the following: (i) information on the numeric value of total water potential at each point in the plant body; (ii) information on the state of the soil-plant-atmosphere continuum resulting in these potentials; and (iii) information on the forces adjusting total potential in different compartments of the plant body. While by these standards a thorough characterization is extremely difficult, if not impossible, the objectives are appropriate and logical. From a drought response standpoint, however, an even more complex requirement must be included, that of characterizing the range of adjustment of these parameters as a function of plant exposure to water stress. Obtaining such information is limited largely by methodology. Nonetheless, the study of various physiological processes in relation to drought may be made more relevant and useful if as much detail as possible can be given about water status. This is particularly important when trying to relate plant response under controlled conditions to response in the natural environment.

II. WATER TRANSPORT AND REDISTRIBUTION

A. THE RANGE OF WATER STRESS IN PLANTS

Leaf water potential varies greatly, depending upon the type of plant and upon environmental conditions. For mesophytic plants (given emphasis in this volume) leaf water potential ranges from nearly 0.0 MPa for well-watered plants having very low transpiration rates to values of −3.0 MPa or lower, when desiccated nearly to the point of death.

TABLE I
Adaptive features of plants active under drought conditions[a]

a.	Tendency to develop xeromorphic structures
b.	High root to shoot ratio
c.	Reduction of metabolically active surface
	1. Small surface in relation to dry weight
	2. Seasonal surface reduction as a function of water stress
	3. Partial death
d.	Capacity to tolerate high soil water stress
	1. Tolerance of high internal water saturation deficits
	2. Capacity to create and tolerate low plant water potentials
	3. Photosynthetic activity even at low osmotic potentials
e.	Reduction of transpiration rate through morphological and anatomical changes
f.	Sensitive stomatal regulation as a function of ambient conditions
	1. Regulation by water stress
	2. Regulation by temperature
	3. Regulation by air humidity
g.	Adaptation of gas exchange mechanisms to high temperatures

[a]From Evenari et al. (1975)

Hsiao et al. (1976) outlined a number of plant responses to water stress which occur well before desiccation becomes lethal. Most responses (e.g. cell growth, wall and protein synthesis, enzyme activities, etc.) are affected by leaf water potential reductions of less than 1.5 MPa. Passive plant control of desiccation itself occurs when stomatal closure results from reduced leaf water potential. Stomatal closure occurs at potentials as high as -0.6 MPa in *Vicia faba* (Kassam, 1975) and -0.7 MPa for lower leaves of wheat (Millar & Denmead, 1976). In contrast, complete stomatal closure may not occur unless leaf water potential is below -2.5 MPa in citrus (Kaufmann & Levy, 1976) and below -3.0 MPa in cotton (Brown et al., 1976). Generally, stomata of herbaceous species close at higher leaf water potentials than those of woody species.

Variation also exists in the lowest leaf water potential at which different plants survive. Sanchez-Diaz and Kramer (1971) observed desiccation injury in corn at a leaf water potential of -1.3 MPa. Occasionally, plants grown under very humid conditions at low radiation are killed by water potentials of -1.0 to -1.5 MPa when exposed suddenly to harsh conditions. A. E. Hall (pers. comm.) observed that cowpea (*Vigna unguiculata*) died at -1.2 to -1.3 MPa even under field conditions. In contrast, Heth and Kramer (1975) found that *Pinus taeda* survived at water potentials of nearly -4.0 MPa. Quiescent plants generally can withstand lower water potentials than actively growing plants. Furthermore, a soil water potential of -1.0 MPa may be considered a mild drought for woody species but a devastating treatment for herbaceous plants.

The greatest temporal and spatial variation of water potential in the plant occurs when well-watered plants are exposed to high radiation and dry air during the day and to cool, humid air at night. Daytime leaf water potentials of -1.5 or -2.0 MPa are not uncommon even when roots are in moist soil and when the water potential of some roots may be near that of the soil. Within the shoot, the water potential of shaded and sunlit foliage may differ by 0.5 MPa or more (Kaufmann, 1975; Richter et al., 1972), and in tall trees gravitational effects alone reduce leaf water potential 0.1 MPa for every 10 m. Plants subjected to a drying cycle typically proceed from having open stomata and high water potentials most of the day, to having stomata open only early in the morning and moderately low water potentials all day, to minimal stomatal opening and seriously low water potentials throughout the day (e.g. Kaufmann, 1977a). Early in the drying cycle root water potential is more similar to that of the soil than that of the leaves, but as drying progresses and stomata restrict water flow, the difference between root and leaf water potential decreases (Kaufmann, 1968).

B. THE BASIC TRANSPORT PROCESS

Evaluation of the relationships between drought resistance and the water status of plants requires some understanding of water movement and redistribution. The 1970s were a period of active study of water transport through plants. In particular, attention centred on describing leaf water potential using Huber's (1924) ''saugkraft'' model or an adaptation of van den Honert's (1948) model of the soil-plant-atmosphere continuum (Elfving et al., 1972; Jarvis, 1976; Kaufmann & Hall, 1974; Oertli, 1976; Richter, 1973). Because of concerns about meeting the requirement of steady state, the soil-plant-atmosphere continuum approach had been considered by many to be more useful as a teaching tool than as a practical solution for studying transport. However, Elfving et al. (1972) collected data showing that a solution of van den Honert's model for leaf water potential (an equation very similar to that of Huber, 1924) was useful for describing how edaphic, atmospheric and plant factors interact to control leaf water potential, even under rapidly changing atmospheric conditions. Perhaps for very large trees a capacitance effect (Waring & Running, 1976; 1978) makes assumptions about steady state questionable, and the treatment of water flux using a single-pathway rather than a branched-pathway model is subject to error (Richter, 1973). Nonetheless, the use of a simple leaf water potential model has provided considerable insight into plant-environment interaction under both field and laboratory conditions, and many of the current problems of interpretation stem not so much from theory of transport as from limited methodology and time for making complete measurements. The following sections on gradients and resistances briefly review water transport when soil water is adequate. Section II, C treats changes in the transport process involving soil water depletion.

1. Gradients

Basic transport law states that movement of a liquid can be described as a function of a gradient and one or more resistances. Water flow in plants is normally described by the ratio of a water potential difference from one point to another and the intervening liquid-phase resistances to flow. The solution of such a transport equation for leaf water potential is useful for examining both gradients for flow and factors affecting leaf water status, since leaf water potential fluctuates with transpiration to establish a satisfactory gradient to move water to the evaporating sites in the leaf (Kaufmann & Hall, 1974). The level of leaf water potential thus reflects the supply potential (ψ_{soil} and $\psi_{gravity}$), the rate of transport (flux), and the liquid-phase resistance ($r_{soil\ to\ leaf}$):

$$\psi_{\text{leaf}} = \psi_{\text{soil}} + \psi_{\text{gravity}} - (\text{flux}) \, (r_{\text{soil to leaf}}) \qquad (1)$$

Drought conditions in the field may affect leaf water potential through changes in both the atmospheric and the edaphic environment. For example, due to their effect on flux, changes in atmospheric conditions (influencing both vapour gradients and stomatal conductance) are chiefly responsible for short-term and diurnal variations in leaf water potential. Depletion of available water in the soil also affects leaf water potential, but the reduction occurs nocturnally as well as diurnally and is typically longer in duration.

Water potential varies spatially as well a temporally. From Equation 1 we can visualize that if flux (transpiration) at the lower leaves is different to that at the upper leaves, or if intervening plant resistances are important, then leaf water potential will differ also. For example, Teare and Kanemasu (1972) reported differences in leaf water potential among levels in the canopy of sorghum and soybean. The patterns varied with time and species, primarily because of differences in transpiration. Variations in water potential within the shoot generally stem from the physiological and microenvironmental effects of sunlight (e.g. Kaufmann, 1975; Richter et al., 1972) and are usually minimal when the entire crown is shaded.

2. Resistance

For a given transpirational flux and supply potential, resistances to movement of liquid water determine how low the leaf water potential must be to accommodate the flow. Consequently, resistances for liquid flow are important in evaluating drought resistance because of their internal effects on plant water deficits. The magnitude of resistances in various portions of the soil-plant pathway has been the subject of considerable speculation. Significant flow resistances are thought to exist both in the root system and in the stems of plants. The importance of resistances external to the root tissue is still a subject of debate (Caldwell, 1976; Denmead & Millar, 1976; Newman, 1974).

Hydraulic resistance to flow is generally determined as the slope of the relationship between the water potential difference (e.g. from soil to leaf) and the flow rate. The large variation in slope suggests that hydraulic resistance under well-watered conditions differs considerably both among and within species (see Kaufmann, 1976a, for a comparison of slopes; Newman, 1974, also compares resistances). Boyer (1971) observed that there was a higher transport resistance in soybean than in either sunflower or bean, and that this was due chiefly to the higher root resistance in soybean. However, Neumann et al. (1974) found as much intraspecific variation in resistance as among species (soybean, sunflower and corn). The cause of contrasting behaviour of a single species between and particularly within experiments is not clear, but it probably involves differences in growing conditions and root development, water stress history, methodology, and effects of coupled solute and water flow (see Kaufmann, 1976a).

Significant flow resistances exist in the xylem of plant shoots, particularly in coniferous species. For example, Hellkvist et al. (1974) observed water potential gradients in Sitka spruce of up to 0.5 MPa.m^{-1} in secondary branches compared with 0.2 MPa.m^{-1} in primary branches and 0.1 MPa.m^{-1} in the trunk. However, based upon path lengths in branches and trunks, plus the volume of flow, they concluded that transport resistances in the trunk were largely responsible for daytime reductions in leaf water potential. Tyree et al. (1975) determined that xylem resistances up to the leaves contributed about two-thirds of the total resistance to flow within the shoots of hemlock *(Tsuga canadensis)*. Data of Waring et al. (1977) which show a high degree of correlation between foliage area and cross-sectional area of stem conducting tissue, suggests a foliar carrying capacity limited by transport capabilities in the stem. Begg and Turner (1970) concluded that petiolar resistance in tobacco was as much as 9 or 10 times higher than stem or root resistance and that stem resistance varied with time of day. Fiscus et al. (1973) cautioned, however, that high lateral transport resistances between flow pathways might alter their interpretation.

Much data indicate that flow resistances are frequently lower at high flow rates; for example, the gradient increases less rapidly than transpiration, so that the relationship between water potential gradient and transpiration is curvilinear. The nature of the apparent change in resistance is not well understood. Regardless of its cause, however, the reduction of resistance to the flow of water to leaves permits a smaller reduction of leaf water potential during periods of peak transpiration. Consequently, if adequate soil water is available, aerial parts of plants may be protected from water stress (Barrs, 1973; Camacho et al., 1974a).

C. WATER RELATIONS DURING DROUGHT

1. Edaphic considerations

Environmental factors and certain plant characteristics figure prominently in the development of water stress in plants. Application of the straightforward concepts outlined in Equation 1 to the study of water relations during drought has resulted in the elaboration of several characteristics of water transport that differ during, or as a result of, drought. For example, reduced soil water potential lowers leaf water potential, both because of supply potential and transport resistance (hydraulic conductivity) effects. It appears, however, that in some (perhaps most) situations soil drying introduces hysteresis into the relationship between leaf water potential and transpiration (Kaufmann, 1977b; Sterne et al., 1977). This is presumably a partial result of acute soil water depletion in the soil adjacent to roots. Furthermore, the progressive development of plant water stress during a soil drying cycle is accompanied not by uniform depletion of soil water but by an integrated depletion based upon remaining soil water, extraction rate and root distribution (Lawlor, 1972). Other evidence indicates that night-time levels of plant water potential reflect the maximum potential in the supply zone, not the integrated or effective supply potential to which plants are exposed during the day when transpiration occurs (Adams et al., 1978; Lawlor, 1972; Sterne et al., 1977).

These observations bear directly on the problem of root distribution and drought resistance and are discussed elsewhere in this book. Plants having a portion of their roots in a remote region of wet soil have the opportunity of maintaining satisfactory plant water status when the bulk of the root zone becomes dry. By exposure to daytime water stress, which results in soil water depletion in much of the profile, the plant attains a balance of shoot and root development appropriate to drought conditions. During this process, the plant retains relatively normal metabolism due to night-time recovery by using water from extremities of the rooting profile. This is possibly ideal from the drought resistance standpoint. Certainly, the classical recommendation to irrigate plants deeply and infrequently has the effect of forcing development of a deeper root system and better shoot to root balance, thereby giving the plant more buffer against rapid depletion of water from a small rooting volume.

2. Hydraulic conductivities

Movement of water through plants is often reduced after the plants have been subjected to a drying cycle. Generally, the reduced flow results from a lower stomatal conductance following water stress (see Hsiao, 1973). However, certain types of experiments have provided information about changes in hydraulic conductivity associated with plant water stress. These experiments have involved the measurement or the control of gradients for liquid-phase flow through either the root system or the entire plant, along with determinations of the amount of flow. For example, Kramer's (1950) classic study of water flow through tomato and sunflower plants demonstrated that water absorption by roots at known gradients was sharply reduced by wilting, and recovery was not immediate.

Camacho et al. (1974b) collected data on the relationship between leaf water potential and transpiration rate for unstressed and pre-stressed citrus seedlings. Exposure of seedlings to several drying cycles resulted in a lower leaf water potential for a given transpiration rate (after re-irrigation), indicating that hydraulic conductivity had decreased. Significantly, the hydraulic conductivity after pre-stressing was similar to that observed under field conditions by Elfving et al. (1972). To avoid any interface geometry effect, Ramos and Kaufmann (1979) evaluated stress effects on the hydraulic conductivity of citrus seedlings by measuring conductivity when the soil was saturated. Their results showed that transport resistance within the root increased as a result of several mild drying cycles (pre-dawn water potentials of −1.1 MPa). Thus stress history appears to have a significant effect, not only on stomatal behaviour, but also on hydraulic flow of liquid water. Such effects place important limitations on the interpretation of water transport data from experiments using potted plants grown without water stress under "optimum" greenhouse or growth chamber conditions.

Questions remain about the role of hydraulic conductivity in various parts of the conducting pathway in relation to drought tolerance or avoidance by plants. For example, what is the significance of contrasting relative conductivities among species? How do leaf area (e.g. demand for water), cross-sectional conducting area, water potential and hydraulic conductivity depend upon each other? Jarvis (1975) noted that in most plants, but not in Sitka spruce, stem resistance to flow is low. The relative conductivity of conifers is about one-fifth that of diffuse-porous deciduous trees and one-tenth that of ring-porous deciduous trees and herbaceous plants. Presumably this is the result of bordered pits in tracheids (Hellkvist et al., 1974). Waring and Running (1978) suggested that the sapwood conductivity of Douglas-fir decreases through the season as water becomes limiting, possibly because water flow is difficult in tracheids cavitated by water stress and having aspirated bordered pits. In red pine, the relative conductivity of roots is high compared with that of stems, and presumably this favours adequate absorption of water when only a fraction of the root system is in moist soil (Stone & Stone, 1975).

The wilting of leafy tissue of herbaceous plants (e.g. tomato) while growing shoot tips remain turgid often has been attributed to differences in osmotic and matric characteristics of the contrasting tissues. Perhaps the relationship between leaf area and hydraulic conductivity should not be dismissed too readily. Hellkvist et al. (1974) repeatedly observed water potentials in the upper portion of the crown of Sitka spruce that were *less* negative than those in the lower crown, but stomatal conductances (and presumably transpiration) were no lower. Zimmerman (1971) showed that the cross-sectional area of xylem tissue per unit foliage mass was considerably higher in the upper portion of an *Abies concolor* shoot than in the lower portion. It is plausible and logical that, both in woody species and in herbaceous plants, the development of conducting tissue outstrips the development of transpiring tissue in the growing portions of the crown of immature plants, and the moderate transpirational demand in relation to conducting capacity favours lower water stress in the immature tissue than in mature leaves.

3. Stomatal control

Perhaps the most critical plant response under drought conditions is stomatal regulation of water loss. The classical control system involves stomatal closure as a result of loss of guard cell turgor at low leaf water potentials. In all species, leaf conductance decreases during an initial drying cycle. However, stomatal response may change within a species as a result of exposure to one or more drying cycles, and differences exist among species in degree of stomatal response to water stress. For example, in sorghum (McCree, 1974) and cotton (Brown et al., 1976; Thomas et al., 1976) repeated drying cycles lowered the leaf water potential, causing stomatal closure. In contrast, the relationship between conductance and leaf water potential of lemon seedlings remained constant during three drying cycles, both at high and low humidities (Kaufmann & Levy, 1976), and in red oak stomata were apparently more responsive to water stress after a drying cycle (Lassoie & Chambers, 1976). Jordan et al. (1975) cautioned that stomatal closure depends not only upon a unique leaf water potential, but also upon age and radiation environment. Also, in Douglas-fir, the maximum conductances observed early in the day depended upon water potential before dawn of that day (Running, 1976). Leaf conductance and transpiration flux density under field conditions are normally lower in tree species than in herbaceous plants and lower in conifers than in hardwoods.

Differences in stomatal response to water stress help determine the relative ability of species to cope with drought conditions. Davies and Kozlowski (1977) observed that stomata of two maple species closed at high water potentials, whereas stomata of black walnut stayed open until lower potentials were reached. Their walnut seedlings underwent senescence when subjected to water stress. The restriction of walnut to moist sites may be related to poor stomatal control of water loss under stress conditions. Pereira and Kozlowski (1977) found that late in the growing season stomata of *Pinus banksiana* closed earlier in the day, and at higher water potentials than *P. resinosa*. Apparently *P. banksiana* was better adapted to avoid drought because of lower transpiration and depletion of soil water. Hall and Yermanos (1975) compared stomatal conductances and leaf water potentials of a number of strains of sesame. Strains having dehiscent seed capsules generally had higher leaf conductances and more negative leaf water potentials. Numerous comparisons have been made of corn and sorghum. Beadle et al. (1973) and Sanchez-Diaz and Kramer (1971) provided representative data indicating that corn stomata closed and wilting occurred as water potential decreased, but at equivalent potentials sorghum stomata closed more slowly, leaves did not wilt and some photosynthesis occurred.

Stomatal response to humidity is one of the more interesting and significant mechanisms by which plants avoid desiccation. In the absence of leaf water deficits, stomata of many species close as the leaf-to-air difference in vapour pressure or humidity increases, perhaps as a result of peristomatal transpiration (Hall et al., 1976; Kaufmann, 1976a; Schulze et al., 1972). Camacho et al. (1974a) and Sheriff and Kaye (1977a) compared the behaviour of contrasting species in their stomatal response to humidity. Camacho et al. suggested that species differ in their strategy: some sharply close their stomata in dry air to conserve water at the expense of photosynthesis; others exhibit only moderate humidity response and maintain high photosynthesis in dry air at the expense of high water use. Stomatal response is not restricted to plants having an adequate soil water supply. Kaufmann (1976b), Schulze et al. (1972), and Sheriff and Kaye (1977b) provided evidence that leaf conductance decreases in dry air even when significant plant water stress exists. Information on the expectation of adequate water supplies, and on the nature of stomatal control of transpiration, could be used to select species for particular agricultural situations.

High evaporative demand is generally accompanied by high transpiration rates, since vapour flux is determined by the product of vapour concentration gradient and leaf conductance. There are notable limitations to this relationship, however, which are relevant to drought resistance. West and Gaff (1976) determined that transpirational flux density of apple leaves increased as the leaf-to-air absolute humidity difference increased to about $15 \mu g.cm^{-3}$, but at higher humidity differences the transpirational flux density decreased. They attributed the lower flux densities at high humidity differences to stomatal closure induced by dry air. Kaufmann and Levy (data published in Kaufmann, 1977c) observed that transpiration rates and xylem pressure potentials of lemon seedlings were similar when vapour pressure deficits were 0.8 and 2.0 kPa, because stomatal conductances were about twice as high at the lower vapour pressure deficit. Hoffmann (1973) provided data showing that low humidity increased transpiration of a number of crop species, but not as much as expected on the basis of vapour pressure differences alone. Transpiration of *Pinus radiata* was only twice as high in a hot, dry environment as in a cool, humid environment (a 5-fold vapour concentration difference), and leaf water stress differed by less than 0.2 MPa (Kaufmann, 1977b). In *Picea engelmanni*, transpiration remained constant over a broad range of humidity difference because of stomatal closure in dry air (Kaufmann, 1979). These experiments challenge the dogma that high evaporative demand, high transpiration rate and high water stress go hand-in-hand.

4. Redistribution within the plant

If transport resistances are not abnormal, water will move most readily to regions of the plant having the lowest water potential. Under normal daytime conditions, this movement will be primarily to the upper leaves of the shoot where transpiration is highest. Some studies suggest that water use in one part of the shoot influences transpiration and leaf water potential in other portions of the shoot (Denmead & Millar, 1976; Hinckley & Ritchie, 1970). However, if significant transport resistances exist after the transport pathway branches, foliage in various parts of the plant may behave nearly independently, as observed by Kaufmann (1975), Sterne et al. (1977) and others. Fiscus et al. (1973) found that the vascular arrangement of tobacco plants made water movement between adjacent leaves more difficult than between phyllotactically related leaves.

In large plants significant amounts of water stored in the plant may be used in transpiration. The shrinkage of non-transpiring plant parts such as the trunk (Running et al., 1975) indicates a depletion of stored water in those parts. In stems, much of the shrinkage may occur in the phloem (Molz & Klepper, 1973; Parlange et al., 1975). Unequal water use in various portions of the shoot and the utilization of water stored within the plant might be expected to alter the diurnal pattern of decline and recovery of leaf water potential, introducing hysteresis into the relationship between water potential and transpiration (Jarvis, 1976). Waring and Running (1978) observed hysteresis in mature Douglas-fir trees when the water content of sapwood was high. However, experiments on well-watered citrus and avocado trees have failed to identify hysteresis (Camacho et al., 1974b; Sterne et al.,1977).

It has been observed frequently that plant water potential recovers rather quickly after rewatering, the rate depending somewhat on the severity of stress (Giles et al., 1976; Kaufmann, 1968; Lassoie & Chambers, 1976). Rapid recovery does not indicate that hydraulic conductivity of the root and stem are high. In fact, it may be lower after water stress than before (see Section II, C, 2). Provided the stress before watering has been great enough, retarded stomatal opening after re-irrigation appears to be universal, and the low transpirational loss of water permits hydraulic recovery regardless of the conductivity of the supply pathway to the shoot.

III. WATER STATUS OF PLANT TISSUES

A. WATER POTENTIAL COMPONENTS

In any tissue or cell, water potential (ψ_w) is the sum of osmotic (ψ_s), pressure (ψ_p), and matric (ψ_m) potentials (neglecting a gravitational effect):

$$\psi_w = \psi_s + \psi_p + \psi_m \qquad (2)$$

Because of methodological difficulties, matric effects are the least well understood. While absolute values may be questionable, it appears reasonable to conclude that matric potential becomes increasingly important as water potential decreases (Boyer, 1967; Roberts & Knoerr, 1977; Shepherd, 1975). Shepherd (1975) suggested that the negative turgor pressures observed in many studies may result from underestimating the importance of matric potential in the measurements. Kyriakopoulos and Richter (1977) and Tyree (1976) also questioned the validity of negative turgor in cells using somewhat different lines of argument. Al-Saadi and Wiebe (1973, 1975) observed variation in matrically-held water among species and tissues, but Tyree cautioned that the methods used by them (and by others) are subject to errors caused by surface tension effects.

Whether or not matric forces are important in the symplast may depend upon the type of tissue. Since matric forces act only over very short distances from solid surfaces, Tyree (1976) contended that matric effects are significant in cell walls but not in the symplast. It seems reasonable to argue, however, that the unvacuolated, immature cells found in meristematic regions may have substantial solid surface areas compared with mature cells occupied primarily by vacuoles, and matric effects may be important both in the symplast and in newly forming walls of young tissues. Al-Saadi and Wiebe (1973) concluded that matrically held water, expressed as a percentage of the original water content, was well correlated with drought tolerance, largely because of species differences in total water content and dry matter fractions. The understanding of matric effects and their role in drought resistance is clearly limited, and much more research is required both on methods of measurement and on the physiological significance of matric forces.

A direct effect of reduced water potential is loss of turgor. Most evidence confirms that the diurnal decrease in leaf water potential of C_3 and C_4 plants is accompanied by a simultaneous decrease in turgor and growth (e.g. Boyer, 1968). In some cases, however, osmotic potential varies substantially during a single day. Hsiao et al. (1976, citing data of Acevedo et al.) reported large decreases in leaf osmotic potential around midday in corn under field conditions with limited soil water. Consequently, turgor pressure decreased only 0.4 MPa during the day (to 0.2 MPa), while leaf water potential varied by about 0.8 MPa. Turner (1974), who also studied water relations under field conditions and drought, observed substantial change in osmotic potential in corn and sorghum, but not in cotton. Meyer and Boyer (1972) found that osmotic adjustment in soybean hypocotyls resulted in constant turgor over a range of water potentials, and significant growth occurred at water potentials low enough to be strongly inhibitory without osmotic adjustment. The ability of plants to accumulate solutes and thereby decrease osmotic potential during daylight hours or periods of water stress has far-reaching implications for plant growth under drought conditions. The capacity for internal osmotic adjustment as a mechanism for maintaining turgor deserves further study, since such a plant feature might be useful in evaluating drought resistance.

Water potential at incipient plasmolysis varies considerably. Elston et al. (1976) found that osmotic potential at incipient plasmolysis decreased through the growing season. While examining wilting patterns in *Vicia faba* under field and laboratory conditions, Kassam (1975) noted that upper leaves consistently had lower osmotic potentials at incipient plasmolysis, indicating that wilting of younger leaves occurred at more negative leaf water potentials. Also, wilting apparently occurred in two stages. Leaves drooped when turgor pressure was 0.2 MPa and buckled when turgor was 0.0 MPa. (No negative turgor was observed). Cutler and Rains (1978) subjected cotton plants to water stress and observed lower osmotic potentials and higher turgor pressures at given relative water contents than in unstressed control plants. Johnson and Brown (1977) concluded that the water potential at zero turgor varied not only among species *(Zea, Bromus* and *Agropyron)*, but also among *Agropyron* hybrids. They noted that field observations of plant performance under water stress conditions agreed with predictions based upon ability to maintain turgor at low water potentials. Turner (1974) demonstrated that osmotic potential differences among leaves resulted in stomatal closure at more negative leaf water potentials in the upper part of the canopy than in the lower part.

B. RELATIVE WATER CONTENT

Plotting the relationship between the inverse of pressure or water potential and relative water content in examining tissue water relations (Boyer, 1969; Richter, 1978; Tyree & Hammel, 1972) has provided considerable evidence regarding the relationship between water potential and relative water content. Various authors have determined that as tissue matures the relative water content becomes higher at given leaf water potentials or at zero turgor (Kassam & Elston, 1974, 1976; Knipling, 1967; Roberts & Knoerr, 1977). In studies on *Vicia faba* (Kassam & Elston, 1974, 1976; and also Elston et al., 1976; Kassam, 1975), the relationship between relative water content and water potential was found to depend upon the osmotic potential and relative water content at zero turgor and a coefficient of enlargement, all of which respond to both age and environmental conditions. Numerous studies indicate that species differences exist, both in the relative water content-water potential curve and in relative water content at zero turgor. Wilted sorghum plants have been found to have a leaf water potential of -1.6 MPa and a relative water content of 55 per cent; values for wilted corn were -1.3 MPa and 71 per cent (Sanchez-Diaz & Kramer, 1971). A dry-site population of *Eucalyptus viminalis* was found to have lower leaf water potentials for equivalent relative water content than a wet-site population (Ladiges, 1975). Levitt and Ben Zaken (1975) made the interesting observation that water stress resulted in a significant reduction in intercellular space in sunflower because leaf area decreased, whereas in citrus intercellular volume remained almost constant because no leaf area change occurred. They suggested that the sclerophyll structure of many species helps maintain adequate oxygen exchange for normal metabolism even when desiccated, whereas in mesophytic species the loss of intercellular space during stress might result in oxygen deficiency.

C. STRESS HARDENING

The diversity of growing conditions to which plants are exposed causes substantial variations in physiology and morphology. Even within plants, leaves produced during periods of stress may be smaller and possess xeromorphic characteristics compared with leaves produced during less harsh periods. Both in terms of water transport characteristics and drought hardiness, plants produced under greenhouse or growth chamber conditions with plentiful water bear little resemblance to plants growing under field conditions. However, Camacho et al. (1974b) and McCree (1974) reported that plants under controlled environment conditions can be made to behave more like field plants by subjecting them to water stress. Effects of water stress on hydraulic flow indicate a greater restriction to flow after water stress than before (see Section II, C, 2).

Kaufmann and Levy (1976) observed that, at given humidities, citrus seedlings preconditioned by water stress had lower conductances than unstressed seedlings, but the slope of the humidity response of stomata was not changed. Consequently, an increase in evaporative demand resulted in greater relative stomatal control in pre-stressed plants than in unstressed plants. This suggests that some species of plants are able to acclimatize when exposed to drought conditions and, by reducing transpiration, are subsequently able to tolerate stress environments better than unhardened plants. This better control of transpiration may result from more sensitive stomatal response, but cuticle development over the epidermis and guard cell structure, and wax deposits in the stoma, may also be significant in many species. However, control of water loss is not the sole factor imparting drought resistance. Ladiges (1974) reported that drought-resistant populations of *Eucalyptus viminalis* had high transpiration rates during the early stages of drought, but apparently owing to the slight physiological effect of desiccation, damage from drought was minimal.

D. DROUGHT AVOIDANCE OR TOLERANCE

It is clear from the preceding sections that the capability of plants to withstand drought conditions depends upon a number of factors. For the most part, avoidance of drought is related to a combination of physical and physiological factors, whereas tolerance of water stress stems largely from physiological and biochemical processes and conditions. Assessment of the drought avoidance capabilities of a plant must include more than a study of the depth and extent of its root systems and the effectiveness of the cuticle and stomata in restricting water loss. A plant successfully avoiding excessive water stress should be viewed as a homeostatic system in which all facets of water absorption, liquid water movement to all parts of the shoot, and transpirational loss are closely linked in a way that the effects of various environmental extremes are minimized. Similarly, a plant capable of withstanding at least moderate amounts of desiccation does so not because of a single type of physiological or biochemical process, but because of beneficial (or at least not highly costly) interactions involving a number of transport, osmotic and metabolic phenomena.

CHAPTER 5

Ion Uptake

M. G. PITMAN

I.   Introduction 71
II. The uptake process 72
III. Interactions of water stress and the uptake process 74
     A. Movement of ions in the soil 74
     B. Interaction of transpiration and ion uptake 79
     C. Ions as osmotica 83
     D. Ion uptake, plant growth and water stress 88
IV. Adaptations 91

I. INTRODUCTION

Plants adapted to arid or semi-arid conditions cover large areas of the world. These plants are less productive than many plants growing in wetter, more favourable conditions, but the biomass is not negligible and the average annual production of new biomass may be appreciable (Table I). Nutrient content of the litter fall provides a minimum estimate of the annual turnover of nutrients, although it is not clear whether tissue levels are the result of uptake under drought conditions or opportune absorption during periods of relative abundance of water. Though there have been extensive studies of water relations of these plants there have been fewer investigations of nutrient uptake.

Part of the ability of a plant to grow in arid conditions is due to an adaptation to water stress. Experimentally, the effect of water stress on nutrient uptake has been studied in various ways. The direct approach of varying the availability of water in the soil has been widely used to investigate the responses of crops to fertilisers and water stress together, and has shown the need to consider movement of ions in the soil as well as properties of the plants in assessing the effects of water flow on nutrient uptake. It also has been convenient to use solutions of high osmotic pressure,

71

avoiding the problems of nutrient transfer in dry soil (though often introducing other difficulties due to the osmotica). Data are available from such experiments to show the effect of low water potentials in the solution on uptake to the roots, transport to the shoot and associated effects on growth. Investigations have also been made of the relations between water flow and ion uptake in different parts of the root.

In this chapter, the effect of water stress at different stages in nutrient uptake by the plant is discussed and considered in relation to adaptation of plants to drought. Nutrient uptake also has an important role in drought tolerance as it helps to maintain adequate osmotic pressures in the leaf cells.

II. THE UPTAKE PROCESS

Studies using plants growing in culture solutions emphasize the efficiency of the processes absorbing ions into the root. Use of flowing culture solutions to maintain nutrient supply at very low concentrations shows that minimum concentrations of the major nutrients needed for plant growth are about 10 μM or less (Asher, 1978). Measurements of rates of uptake at varied external concentrations show that the K_m for uptake (by analogy with Michaelis-Menten enzyme kinetics) ranges from about 5 to 50 μM (Epstein, 1972, 1976). This approach has been used both for excised roots and for whole plants. Investigations of competition between various ions have indicated that there are separate uptake processes or carriers for many of the major nutrients.

Estimation of the electrochemical activity difference for various nutrients between the solution and root cells has shown that most nutrients enter the

TABLE I

Representative figures for biomass and its turnover in different vegetation types[a]

Vegetation	Biomass (t.ha^{-1})	Leaves (t.ha^{-1})	Litter (t.ha^{-1}.yr^{-1})	N	P	K
				Annual turnover of		
				(kg.ha^{-1}.yr^{-1})		
Arid steppe	10	1.5	4.2	45	5	11
Semi-shrub desert	4.3	0.1	1.2	18	1	7
Semi-shrub desert + annuals	12.5	1.8	9.4	108	17	75
Dry Savannah	26.8	2.9	7.2	80	4	11
Acacia harpophylla[b] (shrub brigalow)	160	7.7	1.1	12	0.3	0.8
Subtropical deciduous forest	410	12.0	21.0	226	19	92
Tropical rain forest	500	40.0	25.0	261	15	68

[a]Data from Rodin and Bazilevich (1967) except where shown.
[b]Data from Moore et al. (1967).

root against their electrochemical activity gradient, particularly at low external concentrations. In addition, uptake commonly depends on metabolic energy. It has also been found that root cell membranes contain ATP-ases whose activity in relation to external ionic concentration correlates with the rate of uptake to the roots (Hodges, 1976; Wyn Jones, 1975). Synthesis of these various approaches leads to the hypothesis that ion uptake involves specific carrier molecules which use metabolic energy (as ATP) to transfer ions across the cell membranes.

A more detailed examination of both the electrochemical activity of the transported ions and the energetics of the process suggests that operation of the "carriers" may be more complex than is implicit in an enzyme-substrate model. Uptake of K^+ appears to be coupled with Na^+ efflux in certain roots, and in animal cells the coupling has been shown to involve association of both ions with the transport site. More commonly, influx of K^+ may be coupled with an efflux of H^+, possibly through the electrochemical gradient set up by active H^+ efflux rather than by obligate counter transport of the ions. Anion transport may similarly be coupled with OH^- efflux or H^+ influx. In general, electrogenic potentials set up across the plasmalemma by H^+ or OH^- transport will affect the rate of diffusion of any ions across the cell membranes. The action of the ATP-ases may be more general in transferring charge across the membrane, rather than acting only as specific ion "carriers". Nonetheless, there are differences in transport that show the need for various ion-specific processes. Transport of amino acids and of sugars also has been shown to be coupled with H^+ movement across the membranes.

Diffusive considerations suggest that, at the low external concentrations commonly found in soils, nearly all absorption should occur at the outer boundary of the root rather than at cells throughout the cortex. Once ions have entered the cytoplasm of the outer cells in the root, it is generally considered that movement across the root takes place through the plasmodes-mata which connect the cytoplasms of adjacent cells. This pathway is commonly known as the symplast (see for example Spanswick, 1976; Anderson, 1976). It is generally thought that, while entry to the symplast may involve active transport, movement from cell to cell in the symplast is by diffusion, perhaps facilitated by cytoplasmic circulation.

The cytoplasmic continuum allows movement of nutrients from the cortex into the stele across the endodermis. Within the stele, ions may be released by diffusion into the xylem vessels, or may be actively secreted from xylem parenchyma cells. The relative importance of these processes appears to differ both between species and for different nutrients, but the end result is that ions pass into the xylem where they can be carried to the shoot in transpiration flow. There is some evidence that the amounts released into the xylem are correlated with the demand or growth of the plant; this in turn may also determine the net uptake at the outer boundary of the root. Conversely, uptake into the root may limit the availability of ions for transport to the shoot, and in some cases, therefore, it may also limit plant growth.

This uptake process in the plant has to be considered together with the properties of the soil, as it is the soil that determines the concentration of nutrients available and the actual concentrations presented to the root surface. Supply of ions to the root surface will be determined by the rate of diffusion of nutrients in the soil, which in turn will be related to the cross-section of soil occupied by moisture and the equilibria that occur between the soil solution and the solid phase.

III. INTERACTIONS OF WATER STRESS AND THE UPTAKE PROCESS

Water stress may act on the overall uptake process at various stages, either by the direct action of low water potential on metabolic processes or by an associated effect of low rates of water flow in the system. Movements of ions in the soil, as well as transport in the plant, may be constrained at low water potentials.

A. MOVEMENT OF IONS IN THE SOIL

Many experiments have been carried out with agriculturally important plants to investigate the effects of moisture stress in the soil on growth and nutrient uptake. The subject has been reviewed by Viets (1972), but other useful articles are by Barley (1970), Olsen and Kemper (1968) and papers in Rorison (1969). An excellent discussion is given by Nye and Tinker (1977).

Evidence for reduction of uptake at lowered water potentials comes from experiments in which seedlings are grown in soils of pre-established water content and often for relatively short periods (24 h). For example, Table II shows the reduction of P uptake by maize at lowered water potentials. Phosphate uptake was decreased at all three levels of P in the soil, though the effect was greater at the higher P levels.

The generally accepted explanation of the effect of reduced water content in the soil is that the cross-sectional area of the soil accessible to diffusion is reduced; moreover, the tortuosity of the pathway may increase. Using ^{86}Rb, Danielson and Russell (1957) found that uptake to corn seedlings was proportional to the percentage of moisture in the soil. Place and Barber (1964) measured the self-diffusion co-efficients for ^{86}Rb at varied concentrations and moisture contents and found that uptake was linearly related to the self-diffusion co-efficient, which in turn increased with increasing soil moisture percentage (though not in a simple manner). Olsen et al. (1965) measured self-diffusion coefficients for phosphate in relation to water content, though the values they obtained (0.4 to 6×10^{-11}m^2.s^{-1}) seem large. Lower values (10^{-13} to 10^{-14} m^2.s^{-1}) were obtained by Mahtab et al. (1971), again increasing with water content of the soil used. Further discussion of the relation between diffusion and moisture content is given by Nye and Tinker (1977).

Two processes can contribute to the supply of ions to the root surface. Apart from diffusion from the soil around the root, there could be bulk flow of solution in the soil, in response to transpiration from the plant. This solution will have a composition that matches the properties of the double layers of soil adjacent to the root and will be affected also by processes of exchange or ion absorption by roots and soil. In practice it appears that water flow in the soil is less important than diffusion except in extreme conditions.

Were flow the only process involved, then the flux of ions to the root would be $F = V.C$, where V is velocity of solution flow (generated by transpiration) and C is the concentration in the flowing liquid phase. If diffusion were the only process, then F would be determined by a diffusion equation of the type

$$F \propto D \; \frac{(C_{li} - C_{lr})}{a}$$

where D is a diffusion coefficient, C_{li} and C_{lr} are concentrations in the bulk liquid phase and at the root surface, and a is the diameter at the root.

Although convective flow and diffusion are, in practice, interacting processes, with bulk flow maintaining a supply of ions to the diffusion profile

TABLE II
Uptake of P in 24 h by Maize from soil of varied moisture and P content[a]

Moisture Content (%)	Water potential (MPa)	P uptake[b] (μg.g dry wt^{-1})		
		H	M	L
27.7	−0.033	28.0	12.9	4.5
25.9	−0.05	26.1	8.7	3.9
22.9	−0.1	24.6	7.9	3.7
18.8	−0.3	15.6	4.8	2.7
15.7	−0.9	7.3	4.0	2.1

[a]Data from Olsen et al. (1961).
[b]H, M and L refer to varied phosphate content, being respectively 11, 5 and 3.6 μM phosphate in the soil solution.

and at the same time modifying this profile, the simple addition of these processes appears to describe uptake for most conditions. Passioura (1963) suggested that a suitable form for describing uptake was

$$F = VC_{li} + \frac{(C_i - C_r) Dg}{a} \tag{1}$$

where C_i and C_r are the concentrations in the soil initially and at the surface of the root, D is the diffusion coefficient for the ion in the soil, and g is the function of Dt/a^2 which is usually close to 1.0.

The relative importance of water flow can be more conveniently estimated by transforming Equation 1 so that the diffusion coefficient (D) becomes modified (to D') to allow for the volume of water and the pathway of the ion in the soil. Then we have (Nye & Marriott, 1968; Tinker, 1969):

$$F = C_{li} \left[\frac{V + D'g/a}{1 + D'g/a\alpha} \right] \tag{2}$$

where α is the absorption coefficient defined in $F = \alpha C_{lr}$.

The contribution due to transpiration is then $VC_{li}/(1 + D'g/a\alpha)$, or put another way, the ratio of the flow component to the diffusive component is $Va/D'g$. Under "normal" conditions, with soil water potentials above about $-0.1\,MPa$, these terms are small. For example, Tinker (1969) quotes data for water flow and K^+ flux in roots of single leek plants from which it can be calculated that for relatively high flow rates of about $10\,mm^3.m^{-2}.s^{-1}$, the proportion of K^+ uptake due to water flow was between 2 and 5%.

If we neglect changes in transpiration, then, as the soil dries out, this ratio will change, since D' will decrease and hence V will become more important. In the above example D' was about $10^{-10}m^2.s^{-1}$, compared with a diffusion coefficient of about $10^{-9}m^2.s^{-1}$ in free solution, and implies a relative water content of about 0.3. Reduction of the water content to 0.07, equivalent to a water potential of $-1.5\,MPa$ in a loam, will lead to a diffusion coefficient of about $7 \times 10^{-13}m^2.s^{-1}$ (using values from Nye & Tinker, 1977). As a result of this change $Va/D'g$ will be 4.3, and the flow component of solute uptake will be about 80% of the total. In practice, at such low water contents, transpiration, and hence V, will be reduced too; but this comparison shows the possible trend.

It will be evident also that water flow will be relatively more important for ions such as phosphate which have low diffusion coefficients in the soil.

Reduction in soil moisture also affects the relative concentrations of solutes in the soil. Ions such as Cl^- or nitrate, which are poorly absorbed on soil particles, will increase in concentration, and there will be an equivalent increase in the total concentration of cations, such as K^+, Na^+, Ca^{2+}, Mg^{2+}. Ions that are strongly absorbed or in chemical equilibrium with insoluble salts will tend to increase less in concentration. These changes in concentration may then affect uptake to the plant.

Local concentrations of salts in the soil may also be affected by water flow, and, depending on the relative values of α and V, there may be accumulation or depletion around the root. In general, the rate of convection to the root is VC_{li}, and the uptake is αC_{lr}, so that at steady state, if $V > \alpha$, C_{lr} will be greater than C_{li}, and salt will accumulate around the root. Again, the increase in C_{lr} can be modified by the buffering capacity of the soil for the ion.

The effect of possible increases in salt concentration on uptake to the plant will depend on the relation between α and C_{lr}. For many ions (K^+, phosphate, nitrate) there is a tendency for uptake to become saturated and for α to be proportional to $1/C$, whereas for others (Cl^-, Na^+, Ca^{2+}) uptake may tend to be proportional to concentration. For these latter ions uptake might then increase. This is sometimes the case.

If we consider these effects of drought on ion availability in the soil, it appears that the ability to withstand increased local concentrations of ions might be part of the plant's adaptation to drought. Adaption may be needed to tolerate a larger uptake of ions such as Na^+, Cl^-, Ca^{2+}, Mg^{2+}, or else to show more efficient discrimination. In this respect it is interesting that many arid-adapted plants are halophytes. A large and extensive root system may also reduce convective concentrations of ions by making α (and V) much smaller. This has been found to be the case for many arid species. The common pattern of water uptake, with most transpiration occurring over a short period in the morning and again in the evening, would to some extent help reduce solute build-up around the roots and allow its dissipation. In dry soils, and when plants are under water stress, it is also possible that movement of water and solutes to the root might be blocked by an air gap between root and soil (see Newman, 1974; Nye & Tinker, 1977).

There has been surprisingly little work that analyses the contribution of various soil factors to reduction of uptake of ions at low water potentials, or that allows the effect of low water content of the soil to be separated from effects of low water potentials on the uptake mechanism of the root. Danielson and Russell (1957) tackled this problem by comparing soils with solutions of varied osmotic pressures. Although uptake was inhibited when soil moisture was low, an equivalent osmotic stress (to $-1.2\,\text{MPa}$) in solution had no effect even though the relative water content of the roots was reduced by both treatments. A more detailed analysis was made by Dunham and Nye (1973, 1974, 1976) for uptake of Cl^- and for uptakes of K^+, Ca^{2+}, Mg^{2+} and phosphate (discussed in Nye & Tinker, 1977). Uptake of Cl^- measured at -2.5 MPa was found to be reduced by more than would have been expected from the soil characteristics, implying some reduction in efficiency of absorption. Of the other ions (studied at -0.33 MPa), only phosphate showed any reduction in root absorbing power (Table III).

In general, it appears that influx to root cells is much less sensitive to stress than transport across the root to the xylem. Greenway et al. (1969) measured the effect of culture solutions of varied osmotic pressure (produced by added mannitol) on phosphate (^{32}P) uptake by intact tomato plants. Figure 1 shows that transport to the shoot was much more sensitive to external osmotic pressure than the uptake by the root cells. In the light there was a decrease of 70-75% in water flow in plants at -0.54 MPa, but a similar response to stress was found for plants in the dark (when water flow was very low). Ingelsten (1966) measured sulphate uptake by wheat seedlings in the presence of varied mannitol concentrations and found that transport of sulphate to the shoot was not affected by low external concentrations, with water potential above about -0.63 MPa. At higher concentrations, when the cells were plasmolysed, uptake was inhibited. However, this type of experiment, using non-penetrating osmotic solutions, is not equivalent to the field situation where roots may wilt, not plasmolyse. Using wilted barley seedlings, Pitman et al. (1974) showed that transport of ^{86}Rb and ^{14}C- leucine to the shoot was inhibited when the seedlings were wilted, and it did not recover for about 2 h. However transpiration had recovered within 30 min. Uptake of ^{86}Rb by the roots was increased during this period showing again that uptake into the cells of the root was less affected than transport to the shoot. This type of response resembles the inhibition of ion release to the xylem by abscisic acid and inhibitors of protein synthesis.

It is well known that a decrease in water potential of solution around the

TABLE III

Comparison of root absorbing power for roots in solution and soils of varied water content[a]

Ion absorbed	Final water potential at root surface (MPa)	Root absorbing power $(m.s^{-1} \times 10^8)$	
		Solution	Soil
Chloride	>-0.005	1.0	1.2
	-0.65	7.0	2.0
	-2.5	7.0	1.0
Phosphate	-0.01	>100	20
	-0.33	$>(6)$	0.4

[a]From Nye and Tinker (1977) with one value ( ) inferred.

roots of some plants can reduce the conductivity of the root to water (see, for example, discussion in Newman, 1974). *Atriplex* seedlings, in particular, and tomato and beans show this response. One interpretation of this reduced permeability to water is that the symplast becomes less accessible as a pathway, due to blockage of the plasmodesmata. In this case, movement of ions across the symplast could also be expected to be reduced, as described above. Parallel measurements of ion and water transport under water stress would be particularly useful as a test of this explanation.

B. INTERACTION OF TRANSPIRATION AND ION UPTAKE

Transpiration in plants adapted to drought conditions is often low, even though there may be periodic short periods of high transpiration, particularly at dawn. Water flow can interact with uptake in the plant as well as in the soil, and appears to have less effect on transport of ions in the symplast than outside it.

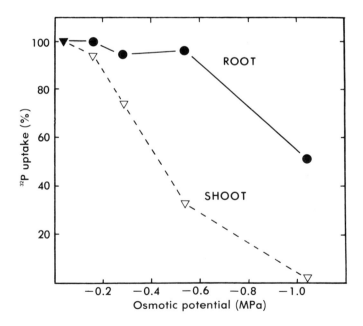

FIG. 1. Effect of decreased osmotic potential (from mannitol) on ^{32}P uptake by tomato plants showing different responses of roots (●) and shoot (▽). Total uptake to the plants decreased with decreasing osmotic potential. (Data from Greenway et al., 1969.)

Clarkson, Robards and colleagues have studied uptake of ions and water into plant roots at varied distances from the apex. This approach compares uptake in the root corresponding to different degrees of differentiation in the endodermis (Fig. 2). When the endodermis differentiates, the casparian strip forms a barrier in the cell wall to diffusion from the cortex to the stele of ions in the apoplast. But ions and water may enter the stele across the membranes of the endodermal cell as well as through its symplastic connections with cortical cells. As the endodermis matures, the inside of the cell becomes lined with suberin and the walls thicken with cellulose so that entry to the stele is only possible through the symplastic connections with cortical cells (Fig. 3). It was found in these experiments that transport of water and of Ca^{2+} across the root to the xylem took place mainly in those parts of the root where the endodermis was in stage I, and there was very little transport of Ca^{2+} across the endodermis when it had become completely suberized. In contrast, transport across the endodermis of K^+ and phosphate was found at all stages of development. It was concluded that K^+ and phosphate moved more easily across the root in the symplast than Ca^{2+}. From observed rates of transfer, Robards and Clarkson (1976) estimated that the flux of phosphate and of K^+

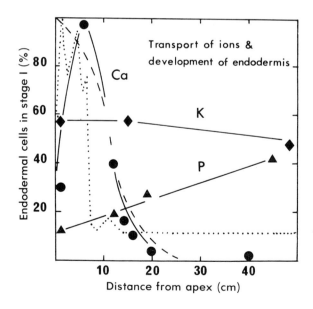

FIG. 2. Transport of ions and water and development of the endodermis. The percentage of endodermis cells in stage I (— — —) is related to water flow (. . . . .) and to Ca^{2+} uptake (●). Uptake of K (◆) and of P (▲) are independent of the development of stage II. (After Clarkson and Robards, 1974; Clarkson et al., 1971.)

through each plasmodesma needed to be about 3.6×10^{-21} and 2.2×10^{-20} mol.s^{-1} respectively in marrow roots when the water flow was 2.4×10^{-20} m^3.s^{-1}. The plasmodesmata are no limitation to ion fluxes of these magnitudes. Concentrations of **K**$^+$ in the cytoplasm are about $60 - 100\,\mu$M, and flow of solution of this concentration in the plasmodesmata would deliver 1.4 to 2.4×10^{-18} mol.s^{-1}, which is about 100 times greater than the observed flux. An alternative way of assessing the efficiency of transport in plasmodesmata is to calculate diffusive fluxes, which, for the size observed through a plasmodesma of length $2\,\mu$m and radius 40 nm (Robards & Clarkson, 1976) would require concentration differences of only $1.0\,\mu$M phosphate or $6\,\mu$M K$^+$. It is pertinent that twofold differences in the dimensions of the plasmodesmata do not appreciably alter the force of the argument.

Many other studies have shown that, in general, uptake of K$^+$, nitrate and phosphate from solutions persists at low rates of water flow, consistent with transport across the root being in the symplast.

Uptake of other ions has been shown to be proportional to external concentration and to rate of transpiration; in particular, Ca^{2+} (Fig. 4) has

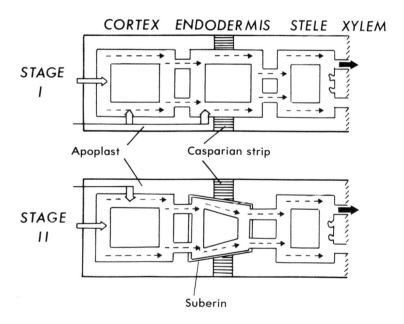

FIG. 3. The casparian strip of the endodermis acts as a barrier in the apoplast between cortex and stele but ions can enter the symplast either at cortical cell boundaries or at endodermal cells. Later, in stage II, the endodermis becomes suberised and then entry to the stele is only possible via plasmodesmata between cortical and endodermal cells.

already been shown to be transported across the root in regions of higher water flow (Fig. 2). For cabbages, Palzkill and Tibbitts (1977) have shown that some degree of water flow (such as guttation) is essential for Ca^{2+} transport into the shoot. Sulphate, too, is taken up by seedlings proportionately to water flow (Table IV), and uptake of silica is also proportional to transpiration (Jones & Handreck, 1965). However, Barber and Koontz (1963) showed that Ca^{2+} uptake to the shoot from 0.5 and 50 mM Ca^{2+} solutions could be inhibited by dinitrophenol, and inhibition has also been reported for sulphate and for silica. An intermediate example is uptake of Cl^- to shoots of barley plants (Greenway, 1965), which increased twofold when water flow increased from 40 to 700 mg.h^{-1}.g^{-1} of shoot, but was inhibited 30-50% in dinitrophenol solution. It appears necessary to postulate that there may be varying degrees of dependence on active transport for entry to the symplast of ions and varying degrees of dependence on water flow either for transport in the symplast or in the apoplast.

The effect of low rates of water uptake, with which we are particularly concerned here, will thus depend on the relative size of symplasmic uptake and the degree to which uptake for the particular ion is coupled with water flow.

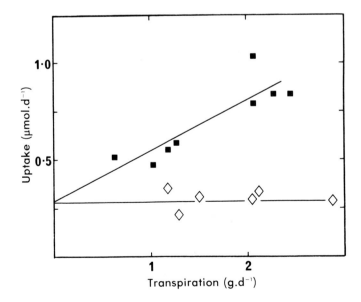

FIG. 4. Relationship between Ca^{2+} uptake and water uptake by barley seedlings growing at two levels of Ca^{2+}, 15 mM (■) and 0.5 mM (◇). There appears to be an uptake which is independent of transpiration (about 0.3 μmol.d^{-1}) and a component proportional to water flow and concentration of Ca^{2+}. (From Lazaroff and Pitman, 1966.)

The significance of these experiments for plants growing in arid conditions is the effectiveness of uptake to the shoot when rates of transpiration are low. In the field, drought may mean a short period of transpiration each day, rather than a continuous, low rate of water loss. A short daily period of transpiration just after dawn would flush out the xylem and remove nutrients that had been transported to the stele by symplasmic transport during the rest of the day. Within the plant it would be expected that transport of K^+, phosphate and nitrate would be less affected by low water flow of a spasmodic nature than uptake of Ca^{2+}, Mg^{2+}, certain trace elements, sulphate and perhaps Cl^- or Na^+. However, an overriding consideration is likely to be the movement of nutrients in dry soil toward the root, as already discussed.

C. IONS AS OSMOTICA

The requirement of plants for nutrients is perhaps better appreciated than their requirement for ions as osmotica. Table V compares levels at which ions are important as osmotica and as nutrients, emphasizing their role as solutes in comparison with their role in specific processes. Only nitrogen has a level in the plant comparable to that of the osmotic ions.

The ability of the plant to extract water from the soil depends on the water potential (ψ_w) that can be generated in the leaves, and this, in turn, is usually limited by the osmotic potential (ψ_s) in the vacuoles of the leaf cells, which is largely due to ions in solution.

Measurements of plant leaves commonly show that ψ_w is at a maximum (less negative) at night and at a minimum during the day. This minimum is often reached within a few hours of the stomata opening. In many plants under low or moderate water stress, ψ_w in the leaves may decrease to about -1.0 MPa or perhaps to -1.5 MPa. In certain plants growing in saline

TABLE IV

Effect of increased water flow on uptake of sulphate by sunflower seedlings from 0.5 μM sulphate, relative to root weight.[a] (Note that the increased uptake with transpiration is due to greater transport from the root to the shoot.)

Transpiration (mg.g fresh wt^{-1}.h^{-1})	Sulphate uptake (nmol.g fresh wt^{-1}.h^{-1})		
	Total	Shoot	Root
85	65	29	
140	78	41	37
225	84	47	37
360	103	66	37
410	140	87	53

[a]Data from Pettersson (1960)

conditions, ψ_w may fall to -4.0 to -6.0 MPa in the leaves (Fig. 5), as found for several mangrove species in North Queensland, Australia (Saddler & Pitman, 1970). Very low water potentials have also been reported for semi-arid vegetation. Brigalow (*Acacia harpophylla*) is the dominant species in several types of forest in the semi-arid parts of eastern Australia. In an extensive survey of water relations Tunstall and Connor (1975) reported a minimum value of ψ_w at -7.2 MPa. The values attained varied with the prevailing water status of the soil.

As $\psi_w = \psi_p + \psi_s$, the value of ψ_s sets limits that ψ_w can attain while retaining positive turgor pressure (ψ_p), or alternatively, while ψ_p is above any "signal" value at which stomata are closed. In the study quoted for brigalow, stomata were found to be open at $\psi_w = -5.5$ MPa, while in mangrove (Fig. 5) they were open at -4.7 MPa, showing the extreme degree of functional adaptation to water stress or drought conditions. The values of ψ_s for brigalow were found to vary between -3.5 and -5.0 MPa under conditions when ψ_w ranged from -3.0 to -5.5 MPa, and there was a small decrease in ψ_s within about 2 h of dawn as water was lost from the plant and ψ_w decreased. Similar responses would be expected for many other species in semi-arid or arid regions.

The relationship between ψ_s and osmolarity is shown in Figure 6, together with the range of values of ψ_w reported for mangroves and for arid vegetation.

TABLE V

Estimated osmotic content of leaves and the amounts of various elements needed to meet nutritional requirements. With the exception of N, the osmotic requirement is much greater than the nutritional requirement.

	Minimum requirement (μmol.g fresh wt^{-1})	Comments
Osmotic		
Total	1160	Assumes ψ_s of -3.0 MPa and fresh wt to dry wt ratio of 6
Cations		
(a) total	580	Assumes osmotica all ionic and cations = anions
(b) part organic	250	Assumes 600 mM organic solutes
Nutritional		
K$^+$	4	Assumes 100 mM K$^+$ in cytoplasm (cytoplasm = 5% of tissue)
Mg^{2+}	10	Assumes 0.2% dry wt (Epstein, 1972)
Ca^{2+}	8	Assumes 0.2% dry wt (Loneragan & Snowball, 1969)
P	4	Uses 20 μmol.g dry wt^{-1} for brigalow (Moore et al. 1967)
N	240	Uses 1.2 mmol. g dry wt^{-1} (Moore et al., 1967)
S	14	Uses N/$_S$ = 17 as ratio in protein

It can be seen that ψ_s of $-4.0\,\text{MPa}$ (i.e. the value for brigalow) requires 1850 mOsm.

R. Storey (pers. comm.) collected sap from a number of species in the semi-arid regions between Hay and Broken Hill in Australia and analysed it to determine the relative contribution of ions and organic solutes to ψ_s. Data are given in Table VI. Cations and their associated anions accounted for approximately 60–70% of the observed osmolarity, and sugars were the next most important component at about 20–30% of the total.

A problem in estimating ψ_s from expressed sap is that the vacuolar concentration may be diluted during expression by water in cell walls or in the xylem vessels so that, in reality, ψ_s may be some 10–20% lower.

Data for brigalow, in which ψ_s appears to be about $-4.0\,\text{MPa}$, are not available, but Moore et al. (1967) found 19.1, 0.7, 15.9 and 36.9 mequiv. $100\,\text{g}$ dry wt^{-1} K^+ Na^+, Mg^{2+} and Ca^{2+} respectively in leaves, which is equivalent to a total cation concentration of 47.2 mmol. $100\,\text{g}$ dry wt^{-1} or about 254 mM tissue water. This leads to the expectation that sugar

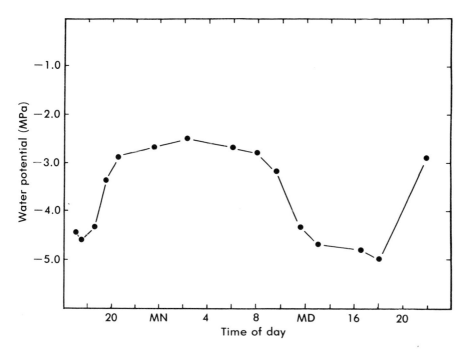

FIG. 5. Diurnal changes in water potential of mangrove shoots (*Avicennia marina*) showing fall from about -2.5 MPa at night to -4.7 MPa during the day. (Data from Saddler and Pitman, 1970.)

levels are high in this plant too, since only 500 of the required 1800 mOsm are accounted for by salts.

Table VII gives estimates of observed ionic concentrations in mangrove leaves and the corresponding ψ_s if all the ions are in solution and balanced by univalent anions. Table VIII gives equivalent data for halophytes. In halophytes the concentration of sugars in the leaf sap is small and the osmotic potential can be accounted for almost entirely by the ionic content (see also data in Waisel, 1972).

Plants thus have two strategies for maintenance of osmotic content: one is to absorb ions from the soil, if possible, and the other is to form organic solutes such as sugars. Halophytes, at one extreme, make efficient use of the

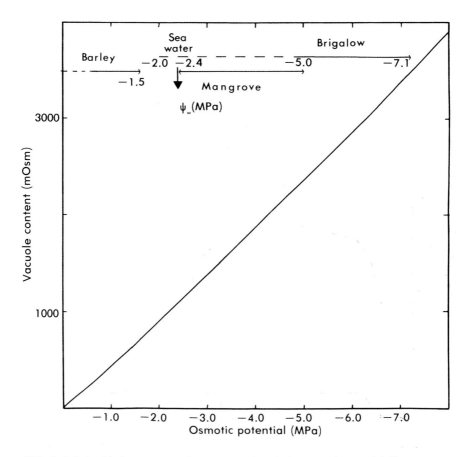

FIG. 6. Relationship between vacuolar content and equivalent osmotic potential (ψ_s). The range of values of water potential (ψ_w in MPa) for different plants is included for comparison.

TABLE VI

Values of osmotic potential for expressed sap and contents of certain ions and organic solutes[a]

Species	Osmotic potential (MPa)	Solutes (mM)					
		K^+	Na^+	Mg^{2+}	Ca^{2+}	Sugars	Other organic compounds
Acacia brachybotrya	−2.4	220	60	60	11	180	40
A. hakeoides	−2.0	200	3	75	30	260	35
Eucalyptus socialis	−3.0	265	0.5	70	20	375	10
E. oleosa	−3.5	110	170	65	25	440	10
Melaleuca uncinata	−2.2	100	115	45	40	200	40
Triodia irritans	−2.4	300	8	30	20	215	140
Pittosporum phillyreoides	−2.2	355	35	100	50	365	15
Vitadinia cuneata	−2.2	315	4	25	40	250	45
Callitris columellaris	−2.2	90	10	80	30	340	5

[a]Data from R. Storey (unpublished).

TABLE VII

Contents of foliage of mangrove species and calculated osmotic potential.

	Ionic contents (mM)					Calculated osmotic potential (MPa)
	K^+	Na^+	Ca^{2+}	Mg^{2+}	Cl^-	
Rhizophora mucronata[a]	110	840	—	—	1020	−3.9
Aegialitis annulata[a]	200	620	—	500	630	−5.5
Avicennia marina[b]	280	1225	95	390	—	−8.2

[a]Atkinson et al. (1967).
[b]Reimold and Queen (1974).

TABLE VIII

Content of foliage of halophyte species. Calculated cationic concentration (assuming fresh wt to dry wt ratio of 10) and osmotic potential.

	Content of foliage (μmol.g dry wt^{-1})					Calculated cation concentration (mM)	Calculated osmotic potential (MPa)
	K^+	Na^+	Ca^{2+}	Mg^{2+}	Cl^-		
Plantago maritima[a]	430	1400	150	120	—	210	−0.93
Triglochin maritima[a]	460	1100	60	100	—	172	−0.76
Suaeda monoica[b]	870	6800	200	—	1910	790	−3.4
Suaeda maritima[c]	440	5100	140	400	—	610	−2.7
Atriplex vesicaria[d]	260	5800	—	—	4100	610	−2.7

[a]Parham (1972)
[b]Waisel (1972)
[c]Yeo (1974)
[d]Black (1960) from Flowers (1975).

ions, while many of the arid species (as shown in Table VI) are able to use organic solutes. The establishment of low osmotic potentials in drought-tolerant plants allows the development of very low water potentials before loss of turgor leads to stomatal closure and, hence, reduced growth.

D. ION UPTAKE, PLANT GROWTH AND WATER STRESS

Many halophytes and mangroves grow poorly in media low in osmoti-cally active ions. This interaction of growth and ionic content was shown convincingly by Gale et al. (1970) who grew seedlings of *Atriplex halimus* in culture solutions with varied concentrations of NaCl at 27% and 65% relative humidity (Fig. 7). At 27% relative humidity the plants showed the charac-teristic response of many halophytes, with increased growth as NaCl increased, followed by a decrease in growth at lower osmotic potentials in the bathing solution. In the more humid environment, the plants on zero NaCl

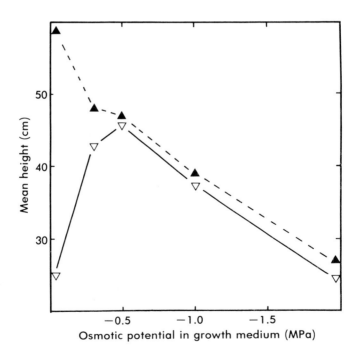

FIG. 7. Effect of varied NaCl concentration on growth of *Atriplex halimus* at 27% ($\triangledown$) and 65% ($\blacktriangle$) relative humidity. (From Gale et al., 1970.)

grew as well as plants at higher NaCl levels. Data from Gale and Poljakoff-Mayber (1970) showed that the osmotic potential of the sap decreased proportionately to NaCl in the solution for plants in the lower humidity, presumably due to increased Na^+ uptake, but no data were given for the sap or tissue content of plants growing in the more humid environment. Unpublished data from R. Storey (Table IX) show that, at very high humidity, uptake of NaCl (and hence decrease in osmotic potential) by *A. spongiosa* is small and appears to be related to rate of transpiration.

It is well known that water availability affects the growth of other plants than halophytes, due to the interaction between stomatal opening and dry matter production. This relation affects the interpretation of field experiments on response of nutrient uptake to water stress since usually (i) the response is to a gradually falling water potential as water is removed from the soil in the vicinity of roots, and (ii) it is difficult to separate effects of water stress on ion uptake on the one hand and dry matter production on the other. For example, in many plants the rate of accumulation of N, P and K^+ is proportional to the rate of growth, so that relative contents tend to be constant. The proportionality in uptake and growth can be attributed variously to increasing root size, to feedback processes in the plant, or to rate of supply of sugars to the root (Pitman & Cram, 1977).

Results from an experiment on interaction of water regime and nitrogen level using *Lolium perenne* are given in Figure 8 (Nielsen, 1963). In this case water was added at varying rates so that the available water differed in 5 treatments and the sward was cut at intervals over a test period of 23 weeks. The average moisture content of the soil was estimated, but unfortunately no data were available for ψ_{soil}. The results shown are for low nitrogen and for high nitrogen levels for the final 11 weeks of the experiment. As the percentage of available water in the soil decreased, there was a strong

TABLE IX

Uptake of Na^+ and Cl^- from culture solutions containing 300 mM NaCl by *A. spongiosa* in 95–100% and 40–45% relative humidities[a]

	Osmotic potential (MPa)	Osmotic concentration (mOsm)	Concentrations (mM)	
			$K^+ + Na^+$	Cl^-
Initial level	−0.96	430	250	7
After 4 days in:				
40–45% R.H.	−1.9	880	470	100
95–100% R.H.	−1.09	490	255	15
Differences:				
40–45% R.H.	−0.94	450	220	93
95–100% R.H.	−0.13	60	5	8

[a]Data from R. Storey (unpublished)

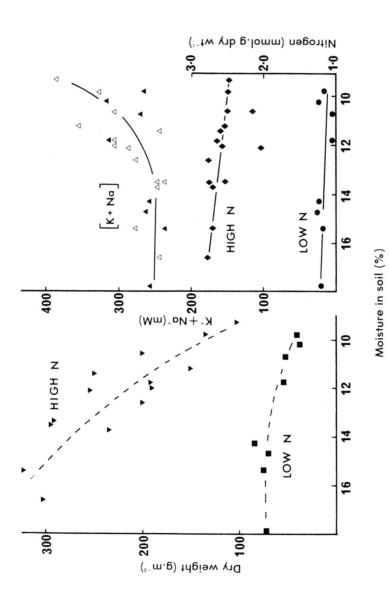

FIG. 8. (a) Effect of average moisture stress on growth at two levels of nitrogen. (b) Relative content of nitrogen from (a) showing little effect of water stress at either level, and the concentration of $(K^+ + Na^+)$ which seems to be unrelated to the N levels in these examples. (Data from Nielsen, 1963.)

decrease in growth at the upper N level due to low water availability, not low nutrient availability (K^+ and P were present to adequate levels in the soil). The relative content of N decreased slightly with reduced growth and possibly reflects an effect of water stress on nitrogen uptake over and above the effect on growth, though no data were available for relative sizes of the root systems. The concentration of ($K^+ + Na^+$) in the cell water increased at the lower water levels, as would be expected if the plants had been adjusting to decreased water potentials in the soil.

Data for a field experiment with maize in which plants were either irrigated or not are shown in Table X. Yield (of grain) of the non-irrigated plants was reduced to 69 from 153 bushels.acre^{-1} and the total dry weight of the plants from 17.6 to 7.4 t.ha^{-1}. Drought effects had clearly set in by August 4, and between then and the final harvest on September 27, it is possible to estimate the growth increments and the relative uptakes of nutrients, that is difference in nutrient content/difference in dry weight. This method of comparison emphasizes that uptake of N and P appears to have been affected by drought as well as by reduced growth. Potassium content of the plants fell over the period, possibly due to senescence of the leaves, but Ca^{2+} and Mg^{2+} increased relatively more in the non-irrigated plants. Continuing transpiration in the non-irrigated plants could explain this greater relative uptake of Ca^{2+} and Mg^{2+} since uptake of these ions can be proportional to water flow in the plant (Fig. 4).

IV. ADAPTATIONS

Average values for annual growth (as in Table I) obscure the true pattern for much arid vegetation which shows short periods of growth, usually following rains, and often with subsequent litter fall. Figure 9 shows the pattern of shoot expansion and litter fall for *Acacia harpophylla*. Tunstall and Connor (1975) stated that, over the period of observation shown in the figure,

TABLE X

Effect of water stress on growth and nutrient uptake by maize in two water regimes. Nutrient increase is calculated as change in nutrient content per increase in weight between 4/8 and 27/9.[a]

	Change in weight (t.ha^{-1})	Nutrient increase (mg.g dry wt^{-1})				
		N	P	K^+	Ca^{2+}	Mg^{2+}
Irrigated	10.4	9.4	1.4	2.2	1.4	1.5
Non-irrigated	2.3	7.0	0.8	−12.0	5.0	3.6

[a]From Jenne et al (1958)

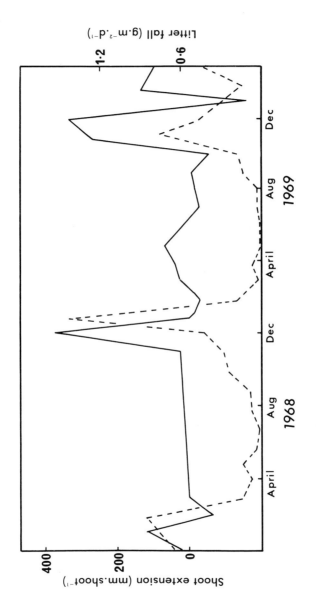

FIG. 9. Shoot extension of brigalow over 2 years (———) and litter fall (— — —). (From Tunstall and Connor, 1975.)

there was a gradual decline in total leaf area until the last few months. The short periods of growth were usually followed by periods of drought in which the new foliage was lost from the trees. At the end of the study, the minimum age of the leaves on the trees was about 2.5 years. The ability of the plants to respond to several growth periods and to survive 2 years without net growth is an adaptation to the vagaries of the arid environment. Unfortunately, there are no data to show if the plant takes up nutrients mainly during the growth period, or whether the level of nutrients in the biomass builds up over the year to meet the sudden demands of a burst of growth.

In a number of arid heath species growing on low-phosphate soils there appears to be the ability to store phosphate as a polyphosphate and to mobilize this in a later period of growth (e.g. Jeffrey, 1968; for *Banksia serrata, Hakea ulicina, Casuarina pusilla*). This, of course, is an adaptation to low nutrient availability.

Many arid plants make efficient use of nutrients by retranslocation to other parts of the plant. Thus, *Eremophila gilesii* extracted 53.3% of the P and 5.4% of the N in its foliage before leaf-fall (Burrows, 1972). *Acacia harpophylla* extracts about 90% of the K^+ from the leaves, about 60% of the P and about 40% of the N (Moore et al., 1967). Specht and Groves (1966) showed that 85–90% of the phosphorus is translocated out of *Eucalyptus baxteri* and *Acacia suaveolens*, and they quote Specht (1953) as showing that 85% of the P content is translocated out of *Banksia ornata* leaves before they fall. It is surprising how much of the total N is retained in the litter of certain species of arid vegetation. This may reflect high microflora development after litter-fall, and in the case of leguminaceous plants, the ability to fix N.

Many arid species have extensive root systems, as shown in Figure 10. Much of the root system was found commonly in the top 20 to 40 cm, though roots were reported (in this case) to have reached 400 cm depth (Jones, 1968). The root biomass was found to fluctuate and was largest in summer (wetter season); the subsequent reduction appeared to be due to the decreased water availability in the upper layers of the soil. Root death occurred in January or February of a year in which little water was available, but, in another year when summer rains occurred, the biomass was high in January and February. Unfortunately, little information is available about the ability of roots to survive in soils of low water potential, or about the reactivation of the root system. This problem also relates to the ionic relations of "resurrection plants" which presumably are able to retain ions in the dessicated material.

Since most of the available nutrients for the plant are in the upper 40 cm of the soil, the ability of the roots to exploit this part of the profile is clearly important, even though the deeper roots may utilize water lower in the soil. Ability of the root biomass to respond to water level in the upper layers of the soil may be an important adaptation of this vegetation to drought conditions.

Charley and Cowling (1968) pointed out that a large proportion of N and P available for a salt bush community on a Solonetzic soil is in the top 10 cm of the soil, and losses of soil by erosion may reduce the level of nutrients available to germinating seedlings. They showed that seedlings became established more readily on bare soil in a dense stand of *Atriplex* than on eroded soil and traced this to low levels of N rather than low water supply.

Plants of arid regions are also adapted to the low water potential of the soil and are often halophytic, able to make use of Na^+, Cl^- or Mg^{2+} as osmotica, or else can store sugars in the vacuoles and other organic solutes in the cytoplasm. The low water potentials of arid zone plants raises the problem of how the plant balances the need for osmotic solutes in the cytoplasm with the inhibitory action of ions such as K^+ or Na^+ on enzyme activity over about 200 mM. Certain plants of the arid regions accumulate proline and/or betaine as

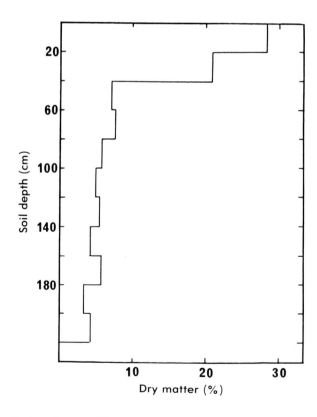

FIG. 10. Distribution of roots of heath vegetation (mainly *Leptospermum* spp) in soil. (From Jones, 1968.)

complementary osmotic solutes (e.g. spinifex grass, *Triodia irritans* and many *Atriplex* spp). Other plants experiencing the same osmotic stress do not accumulate proline or betaine and it is likely that sugars, sugar alcohols or other organic solutes fill the same role in these plants (R. Storey, unpublished data; see also Chapter 6).

The general interactions outlined here have been summarized in Figure 11. Drought can affect ion uptake by reducing soil water, which will limit ion diffusion in the soil and may also lead to local increases in concentrations of certain ions such as Cl^-, Ca^{2+}, Mg^{2+}. The low water potentials in the soil require the plant to have low osmotic potentials in cells of the leaves so that turgor may be maintained and CO_2 fixation continued. Unless adequate osmotica are present, the stomata may close and growth may be reduced, leading to reduced demand for nutrients. In addition, uptake processes may be impaired, either in the roots or associated mycorrhiza. In general, nutrient uptake in drought-adapted species involves opportune exploitation of better

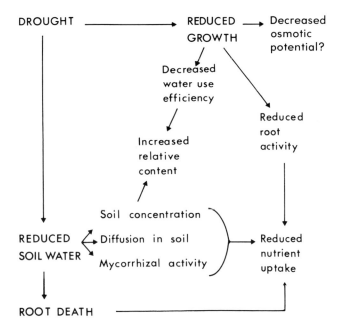

FIG. 11. Interacting effects of drought on plant growth. Drought leads to reduced soil moisture which in turn may lead to root death and also affect nutrient uptake, though increased concentrations may enhance relative uptake of certain ions such as Ca^{2+}, Mg^{2+}. Drought also reduces growth and this too may affect nutrient uptake due to effects on the activity of the roots. Reduced growth may also be related to the osmotic potential of cell contents.

conditions, as well as a certain degree of tolerance of low water potentials. While much is known about the response of agriculturally important plants to water stress, there have been few analyses of the processes involved, and surprisingly little is known about nutrient uptake processes in the real drought-tolerant species indigenous to arid regions of the world.

CHAPTER 6

Solute Accumulation and Regulation of Cell Water Activity

I.	Introduction	97
II.	Terms defined	99
	A. Solvent activity	100
	B. Chemical potential	101
	C. Osmotic pressure	101
	D. Water potential	102
	E. Calculation and use of water activity	103
	F. Comparison of common water stress parameters	103
III.	Physicochemical aspects of solute accumulation	104
	A. Mechanics of accumulating a high concentration of solute	105
	B. Examples of solutes accumulated as regulators of intracellular water activity	111
	C. Solute interaction with enzyme-solvent system	113
	D. Summary of physicochemical properties of water activity-regulating solutes and conclusions	127

I. INTRODUCTION

Cell processes require water: macromolecules must be hydrated to function, and biochemical reactions require water as a direct participant, or as a solvent. Furthermore, the maintenance of structural parameters such as turgor and volume requires water.

Biological membranes are permeable to water. Cells have mechanisms for retaining electrolyte and non-electrolyte solutes within a semi-permeable membrane against a concentration gradient, but water is not retained and tends to move towards regions of low thermodynamic water activity or water potential. This means that, when a cell is water-stressed due to either desiccation or addition of solutes to the surrounding solution (both lower water activity and water potential), net water movement out of the cell is

97

PHYSIOLOGY AND BIOCHEMISTRY
OF DROUGHT RESISTANCE
IN PLANTS

favoured. (For the purposes of this review, "water stress" always refers to a lowering of extracellular water activity or water potential.) Conversely, if the surrounding solution is diluted, water movement into the relatively more solute-rich cell interior is favoured.

In higher plants exposed to the atmosphere, outer surfaces are usually covered by materials of low water conductance such as cutin and suberin, and the exchange of water and CO_2 with the atmosphere is controlled mechanically by means of the stomata. This chapter is concerned with the internal regulation of water activity, and the mechanism to be considered appears to be common to all types of organisms, from the simple prokaryotic bacteria to the complex vascular plants.

This process is traditionally termed osmoregulation, meaning the regulation of osmotic pressure within the cell by addition or removal of solutes from solution until the intracellular osmotic pressure is approximately equal to that of the medium surrounding the cell. I prefer to regard the phenomenon as "water activity regulation", emphasizing regulation of the thermodynamic activity of the solvent rather than solute concentration or osmotic pressure regulation. The concept of water activity also fits rather better into the later discussion on physicochemical aspects of solute-solvent-macromolecule interactions.

However, there is no intrinsic reason to reject the often used term, "osmoregulation", or the term "water potential regulation". For the purposes of this chapter, all of these terms refer to an adjustment in the solute to solvent ratio within the cell to match a similar change in the environment, with the result of preventing net water movement across the plasma membrane of the cell.

In unicellular organisms, the interaction of cell and environment is immediate, and as described above. In multicellular organisms, however, cells not only interact with the external environment, but also with other cells and tissues. For example, cells may respond to changes in the composition of the sap, which reflects indirectly changes in the external environment. The regulation of the intracellular water activity of the individual cells of a multicellular organism, however, is essentially the same as in the unicellular organism.

In most higher plant cells, vacuoles occupy more volume than cytoplasm; a common vacuole to cytoplasm volume ratio is 4 to 1 (Wyn Jones et al., 1976). Many multicelled algae have an even higher vacuole to cytoplasm ratio. Few healthy unicellular algae have large vacuoles, though the giant coenocytic, unicellular green alga, *Valonia*, is a striking exception. The solute composition of the vacuole is different from that of the cytoplasm, and the vacuole plays a role in ionic and volume regulation of the rest of the cell.

However, accumulation of water activity-regulating organic solutes seems to be restricted to the cytoplasm and not the vacuole. Wyn Jones et al. (1976)

proposed that the osmoregulatory solute, betaine, is located in the cytoplasm and not in the vacuole of cells of halophyte plants. This is to be expected as the water-requiring macromolecules and metabolic processes of the cell are located in the cytoplasm or in membrane bound organelles; hence, retention of water through osmoregulation or water activity regulation is important for the cytoplasm and organelles.

All organisms, except the prokaryotic bacteria and cyanobacteria (blue-green algae), have membrane bound organelles, such as nuclei, mitochondria and chloroplasts. These must also "osmoregulate" by maintaining an internal water activity comparable with that of the surrounding cytoplasm to prevent water loss and consequent impairment of their metabolic processes.

In the absence of contrary data, we must assume that chloroplasts, and probably other organelles, employ the same compatible solute(s) as the cytoplasm to maintain comparable water activity. There are reports (Larkum, 1968; Larkum & Bonner, 1972) that chloroplasts from the alga *Tolypella intricata* and pea plants have higher KCl concentrations (around 250 mM) than the surrounding cytoplasm (around 100 mM). These figures may be representative of those plants and algae which osmoregulate merely with K^+ and anion levels of up to several hundred mM. The chloroplast enzymes may be expected to function well in 250 mM KCl, a concentration inhibitory to many cytoplasmic enzymes. The green unicellular alga *Dunaliella* accumulates high concentrations of glycerol in the cytoplasm to balance an environment with low water activity caused by high salt concentrations. In the light, glycerol is produced photosynthetically from CO_2 in the chloroplast and then moves to the cytoplasm (Wegmann, 1971). If an approximate equilibrium of glycerol concentrations is maintained by simple diffusion, the water activity within the chloroplast would automatically follow that of the cytoplasm, and hydration of chloroplast macromolecules and processes would be maintained. If the chloroplast envelope is permeable to glycerol in both directions, a similar equilibrium could be maintained in the dark, when glycerol is synthesized by a catabolic process in the cytoplasm (Borowitzka et al., 1977), not in the chloroplast. It would be very interesting, indeed, to know if glycerol is the major water activity regulator in the chloroplast and in the other organelles of *Dunaliella*. Demonstration of major solutes in the organelles of higher plants and the mechanism for organelle osmoregulation and water activity regulation await elucidation.

II. TERMS DEFINED

During the study of water stress phenomena, several parameters have been defined to measure the effect of increasing the amount of solute or decreasing the amount of water in solution. Nobel (1974) in his excellent book defines the parameters, water activity, water potential and osmotic pressure, whose derivations are listed below. Brown (1976) has reviewed the traditional usage of certain parameters in particular fields. Both Brown and Nobel point out the disagreement on the physical implications of osmotic pressure, but there is no reason why this parameter should not be used where applicable. The three parameters listed above are mathematically related.

A. SOLVENT ACTIVITY

The thermodynamic solvent activity is a "corrected" concentration parameter:

$$a_j = \gamma_j N_j \tag{1}$$

where γ_j is the activity coefficient and N_j is the mole fraction of the solvent. The mole fraction of a species is the ratio of the number of moles of that species to the total number of moles of all species in the system:

$$N_j = \frac{n_j}{n_j + n_i} \tag{2}$$

where n_j = number of moles of solvent and n_i = number of moles of all solutes. γ_j has a value of 1 for an ideal solvent, and less than 1 for real solvents, such as water. Hence the "correction" of the concentration of the solvent gives the more accurate measure of the chemical activity of the amount of solvent.

1. Water activity

Water activity (a_w) is simply the thermodynamic activity of the solvent water. The presence of solutes in an aqueous solution tends to decrease the activity of water (lowers a_w). As a first approximation, the decrease in water activity can be viewed as a dilution effect: as more and more solute is added, the mole fraction of water becomes less as water molecules are displaced by those of the solute. Non-ionizing solutes depress water activity less than ionizing solutes; in Equation 3, n (the number of particles produced by dissolving one molecule of solute) is greater for ionizing solutes (e.g. for KCl, n = 2; for sucrose, n = 1).

$$\ln a_w = \frac{(-18.016).n.m.\phi}{1000} \tag{3}$$

where m = molality of the solute in solution and ϕ = molal osmotic coefficient, to be found in tables given by Robinson and Stokes (1955).

B. CHEMICAL POTENTIAL

The general equation for chemical potential is:

$$\mu_j = \mu_j^* + RT\ln a_j + \overline{V}_jP + z_jFE + m_jgh \tag{4}$$

where μ_j = chemical potential of the substance j, μ_j^* = chemical potential of same substance at standard state (arbitrarily chosen), R is the gas constant (8.31 joules.m^{-1}.°K^{-1}), and T is the temperature in °K. The last three terms in the equation are work terms: the work done to add a mole of species j to the system with pressure change P and volume change $\overline{V}_j$; an electrical work term inapplicable to uncharged water ($z_w = 0$); and a gravitational work term applicable only when large vertical movements of water occur, for example, in trees.

1. Chemical potential of water

In the case of water, the chemical potential simplifies to:

$$\mu_w = \mu_w^* + RT\ln a_w + \overline{V}_wP \tag{5}$$

As activity decreases, the chemical potential of water is lowered, because of a decrease in the term RT ln a_w, representing the thermodynamic concentration of water. The water potential is related to chemical potential and will be discussed later.

C. OSMOTIC PRESSURE

An increase in the concentration of solutes in solution leads to an increase in osmotic pressure (decrease in osmotic potential) of the solution. Osmotic pressure (π) may be simply expressed in terms of total solute concentration in the following equation derived from the van't Hoff relation:

$$\pi = RT\sum_j C_j \tag{6}$$

in which $\sum_j C_j$ is the sum of concentrations of all solutes. The above expression is only justified in the case of ideal solutes. The relation for a dilute solution of real solutes is obtained by replacing the concentration term, C_j, with the activity term, $a_j = \gamma_j C_j$.

A fundamental definition of osmotic pressure (π) is:

$$RT\ln a_w = -\overline{V}_w.\pi \tag{7}$$

As solutes are added, a_w decreases from its value of 1 for pure water, $\ln a_w$ is therefore negative, and π, as defined by the equation, is positive. Substituting the osmotic pressure term, $-\overline{V}_w\pi$ for $RT\ln a_w$ in Equation 5, the following relation between osmotic pressure and chemical potential of water is obtained:

$$\mu_w = \mu_w^* - \overline{V}_w\pi + \overline{V}_w P \tag{8}$$

D. WATER POTENTIAL

The quantity $\mu_w - \mu_w^*$ represents the work involved in moving one mole of water from some point in the system to a pool of pure water at the same temperature and pressure, and with a gravity term of zero. A difference between two locations, in their values for $\mu_w - \mu_w^*$, indicates that water is not at equilibrium; hence there is a tendency of water to flow toward the region where $\mu_w - \mu_w^*$ is lower (i.e. the water flows towards a more concentrated solution).

A quantity proportional to $\mu_w - \mu_w^*$, is the water potential, ψ_w. It is defined as:

$$\psi_w = \frac{\mu_w - \mu_w^*}{\overline{V}_w} = P - \pi + \rho_w gh \tag{9}$$

where ρ_w = density of water, gh is acceleration due to gravity multiplied by height, P = hydrostatic or turgor pressure:

$$\psi_w = \frac{RT\ln a_w}{\overline{V}_w} + P \tag{10}$$

neglecting the gravitational term. Equation (10) relates ψ_w to a_w and shows why these change in the same direction when solutes are added to the solution.

E. CALCULATION AND USE OF WATER ACTIVITY

The effects of both desiccation and increase in the concentration of solutes in the environment, together with the cell's response to them, are conveniently explained in terms of the single parameter, water activity (a_w), and this is the term that will be generally used in this chapter. It should be remembered, however, that water potential responds in the same direction as a_w, and osmotic pressure responds in the opposite direction to both.

Water activity is calculated from the relationship $a_w = \gamma_w N_w$ as defined previously (Equation 1).

Raoult's law may be expressed as:

$$\frac{P}{P_o} = \frac{n_w}{n_w + n_i} \tag{11}$$

where P and P_o are the vapour pressures of the solution, and the pure solvent water, respectively.

Thus, a_w is numerically equal to the activity coefficient of the solution multiplied by the vapour pressure of the solution relative to that of pure water. The activity coefficient is close to 1 for dilute, non-ideal solutions; activity coefficients can vary with temperature (for concentrated non-ideal solutions) and with concentration. They are given in tables in Robinson and Stokes (1949, 1955). However, for easy reference, tables in Robinson and Stokes (1955) give calculated values of a_w for molal solutions of common solutes.

F. COMPARISON OF COMMON WATER STRESS PARAMETERS

Table I gives values for interconversion of each of the commonly used water relations parameters for solutions of NaCl. Molality (moles solute.kg solvent^{-1}) is the correct base expression for calculation of all the parameters in the table. For NaCl concentrations below 1 molal, the terms molarity (moles solute.litre solution^{-1}) and molality are fairly interchangeable, but at higher concentrations the difference becomes important. Osmolality expresses the number of moles of osmotically active (i.e. dissociated and undissociated) particles per kg water. Water potential and osmotic pressure are given in MPa (1 MPa = 0.0987 atmosphere = 0.1 joule.cm^{-3}) and a_w is simply in water activity units. All calculations and values are for 25°C.

Values of a_w relevant to water stress phenomena described in this chapter cover a wide range. Most vascular plants wilt when the environmental water activity is between 1.0 and 0.95. The a_w of seawater is approximately 0.96 (3.5% NaCl is 0.98). Non-halophilic bacteria do not grow below 0.85. Specially tolerant yeasts, fungi, algae and bacteria tolerate 0.75 (with NaCl the solute), the a_w of saturated salt lakes. Some fungi and yeasts (in sugars) tolerate the range 0.75–0.60. At a_w = 0.55, DNA becomes disordered (Brown, 1976).

TABLE I
Water potential, water activity and osmotic pressure of NaCl solutions

Molality NaCl (mol.kg^{-1})	% (w/v) (g.100ml^{-1})	Osmolality (osmol.kg^{-1})	Water potential[a] (MPa)	Water activity[b] (a_w units)	Osmotic pressure[c] (MPa)
0.15	0.87	0.3	− 0.7	0.99	0.74
0.61	3.5	1.2	− 2.8	0.98	2.98
1.2	6.8	2.4	− 5.6	0.96	5.95
2.8	15	5.6	−14.5	0.90	13.8
4.0	19.3	8.0	−21.0	0.85	19.8
5.2	30	10.4	−30.7	0.79	25.8

[a]Water potential is taken from Brock (1975) who calculated values from equations and tables of Lang (1967).
[b]From Robinson and Stokes (1955).
[c]Calculated from $\pi = RT_j C_j$, with RT = 24.8 at 25°C (Nobel, 1974).

III. PHYSICOCHEMICAL ASPECTS OF SOLUTE ACCUMULATION

The activity of intracellular water in different organisms is regulated in response to a variety of different solutes in the surrounding medium. In *Dunaliella*, glycerol regulates internal water activity in response to either NaCl or sucrose levels in the medium (Borowitzka et al., 1977); in the yeast *Saccharomyces rouxii*, the polyol content responds to the glucose, polyethylene glycol or salt concentration of the medium. The type of polyol used to regulate cytoplasmic water activity in the yeast can vary with different solutes in the external medium, but the extent of regulation does not (M. Edgley, pers. comm.). Storey (1976, PhD thesis quoted in Wyn Jones et al., 1976) showed that using either NaCl or polyethylene glycol to vary external solute concentration made no difference to proline and betaine responses in cells of three halophyte plants (*Sueda monoica, Spartina* x *townsendii* and *Atriplex spongiosa*) or in salt resistant and salt sensitive strains of barley. Chu et al. (1976) showed that leaf water potential declined after watering with NaCl, KCl, $CaCl_2$ or Na_2SO_4 solutions, though the decline was less in polyethylene glycol. Proline accumulation, which accounted, at least in part, for the decline in water potential, was slightly lower in the salts than in polyethylene glycol solution of the same osmolarity, though it was highest of all in $MgCl_2$. The authors suggested that the different proline accumulation rates are due to specific ion effects on biochemical pathways of proline biosynthesis and oxidation; the use of permeating solutes complicates the cells' osmoregulatory response. As a generalization, intracellular water activity responds to changes in external water activity caused by evaporation (drought stress) or addition of *non-permeant non-toxic* solutes.

Within the cytosol, changes in water activity can lead to drastic alterations to water structuring and consequent changes in water-macromolecule interactions and solute-water-macromolecule interactions.

A. MECHANICS OF ACCUMULATING A HIGH CONCENTRATION OF SOLUTE

Accumulated solutes may either be transported into the cell from the external medium (the case with ions) or synthesized within the cell (generally the case with organic solutes). Both processes require metabolic energy, complex controls and retention of the solute against a considerable concentration gradient.

Control of the level of a synthesized solute probably involves control of the enzymes involved in synthesis and/or breakdown of the solute. Tables II and III give examples of major water activity-regulating solutes accumulated by different organisms. Most of the accumulated compounds are not components of major biochemical pathways, but rather are synthesized at the end of a small offshoot from a major pathway. For example, glycerol is formed in two steps from the triose phosphate intermediates of the photosynthetic and respiratory pathways. Proline, isofloridoside, mannitol, arabitol, serine and glycine are all synthesized in separate offshoots from major pathways; alanine and glutamate, however, are not. Biochemical proximity to intermediates of major pathways is probably essential for supply of the large amount of substrate which may be suddenly required, or for the rapid removal of the regulating compound if the external water activity rises. It appears that some cells tolerate leakage of the regulating solute as a simple means of adjusting cytoplasmic water activity following dilution of the external medium; for example *Monochrysis lutheri* leaks a specific quantity of cyclohexanetetrol when the growth medium is diluted (Craigie, 1969). This is not the case with *Dunaliella*, which loses no glycerol during moderate decreases in external salinity (Ben-Amotz & Avron, 1973), but rather metabolizes it, ultimately, to a polymer such as starch, which has little influence on water activity, or to CO_2 which is then removed from the cell. The first alternative would require immediate energy input, which could be

TABLE II

Water activity regulating solutes of prokaryotes

Organism	Approximate minimum a_w for growth	Major apparent a_w regulating solutes[a]	Reference
Non-marine bacteria			
Pseudomonas aeruginosa	0.97	glutamate	Gould and Measures (1977)
Salmonella oranienburg	0.95	glutamate + proline	
Clostridium sporogenes	0.945	γ-aminobutyric acid + proline + glutamate	
Streptococcus faecalis	0.94	γ-aminobutyric acid + proline	
Bacillus subtilis	0.90	proline	
Marine bacteria			
marine pseudomonad PL_1	0.95	proline + glutamate	Stanley and Brown (1976)
marine pseudomonad SW_4	0.95	proline + glutamate	Stanley and Brown (1974)
marine pseudomonad MU_3	0.95	glutamate + glutamine	Stanley and Brown (1974)
Beneckea harveyi	0.95	glutamate + threonine	Makemson and Hastings (1979)

	a_w	Major solute[a]	Reference
Halophilic bacteria			
Halobacterium salinarium	0.75 (salt lake)	K^+	Christian and Waltho (1962)
Cyanobacteria (blue-green algae)			
Freshwater isolates:			
Gloeocapsa sp.	0.98	sucrose + trehalose	Mackay, Norton and Borowitzka (unpublished results)
Anabaena cylindrica	0.98	sucrose	Mackay, Norton and Borowitzka (unpublished results)
Marine isolates:			
Synechococcus sp.	0.92	α-glucosylglycerol	Borowitzka et al. (1980)
Members of 7 other genera	0.92	α-glucosylglycerol	Mackay, Norton and Borowitzka (unpublished results)
Salt Lake isolates:			
Aphanothece halophytica	0.75	"free amino acids" + KCl	Tindall et al. (1977)
Aphanothece halophytica (another isolate)	0.90	betaine + glutamate	Mackay, Norton and Borowitzka (unpublished results)
Plectonema tomasinianum	0.91	betaine, trehalose, glucose (+ some amino acids)	Mackay, Norton and Borowitzka (unpublished results)

[a]The major solute is underlined.

TABLE III
Water activity regulating solutes of eukaryotes

Organism	Approximate minimum a_w for growth	Major apparent a_w regulating solutes[a]	Reference
UNICELLS			
Unicellular algae			
Platymonas suecica	0.96 (seawater)	mannitol	Hellebust (1976)
Platymonas subcordiformis	0.96	mannitol	Kirst (1975)
Ochromonas malhamensis	0.96	α-galactosyl glycerol (isofloridoside)	Kauss (1973)
Stichococcus bacillaris	0.96	sorbitol + proline	Brown and Hellebust (1978)
Cyclotella cryptica	0.96	proline	Liu and Hellebust (1976 a, 1976 b, 1976 c)
Cyclotella meneghiniana	0.96	proline	Schobert (1974)
Navicula sp.	0.96	proline	Borowitzka (unpublished results)
Phaeodactylum tricornutum	0.96	proline	Schobert (1979)
Porphyridium purpureum	0.96	proline > glycine > taurine > threonine > glutamate > alanine	Gilles and Pequeux (1977)
Chlorella salina	0.96	proline	Kirst (1977)
Monochrysis lutheri	0.96	cyclohexanetetrol	Craigie (1969)
Dunaliella viridis	0.75 (salt lake)	glycerol	Borowitzka and Brown (1974)
Yeasts[b]			
Debaryomyces hansenii	0.83	glycerol	Gustafsson and Norkrans (1976)
Saccharomyces rouxii	0.83 (salt) 0.60 (sugars)	arabitol and/or glycerol	Edgley and Brown (1978)
unidentified 'YO'	0.83	mannitol	Brown and Simpson (1972)
unidentified 'YE'	0.83[c]	arabitol, glycerol + mannitol	Anand and Brown (1968)
Saccharomyces acidifaciens (and others)	0.83	erythritol and glycerol	Spencer (1968)
Protozoa			
Tetrahymena pyriformis	0.99 (sucrose)	"free amino acids"	Stoner and Dunham (1970)
Miamiensis avidus	0.96	"free amino acids", in particular alanine, glycine and proline	Kaneshiro et al. (1969)

MULTICELLED

Multicelled algae			
Fucus vesiculosus	0.96	"methionine, valine, tryptophan, proline"	Perlyuk et al. (1974)
Fucus vesiculosus (same alga?)	0.96	mannitol + Cl^-	Munda and Kremer (1977)
Fucus serratus	0.96	mannitol + Cl^-	Munda and Kremer (1977)
Porphyra perforata	0.96	floridoside + isofloridoside	Kauss (1969)
Iridophycus flaccidum	0.96	floridoside + isofloridoside	Kauss (1969)
Vascular plants			
Triglochin maritima	0.96	proline	Stewart and Lee (1974)
barley	0.96	proline	Singh et al. (1973)
Sueda monoica + many halophytes	0.96	betaine + proline	Wyn Jones et al. (1976)
Invertebrates			
7 invertebrates, including annelids, shrimp & crayfish	0.96	"free amino acids"	Wilbrandt (1963) (review)
Modiolus demissus demissus (mollusc)	0.96	"free amino acids"; alanine, glycine, taurine & short-term proline peak	Baginski and Pierce (1975)
Mya arenaria (mollusc)	0.96	"free amino acids" including alanine and glycine	Virkar and Webb (1970)
			Du Paul and Webb (1970)
Fish (Marine)	⎫	Urea + methylamine compounds, largely trimethylamine oxide,	
Elasmobranchs	⎬ 0.96	but also betaine, sarcosine,	Yancey and Somero (1979)
Holocephalans	⎭	β-alanine and taurine.	
Coelocanth			

[a] The major solute is underlined.

[b] With many yeasts, type of polyol depends on growth conditions.

[c] Temperature dependent.

largely reclaimed later, on breakdown of the starch; the second would yield immediate reducing equivalents and ATP to the cell. The energy status of the cell at the time may determine the pathway of glycerol removal, though it seems likely that the second route may be often desirable in the osmotically stressed cell.

In addition, fine control of the level of a substance which was a component of a major pathway (e.g. a triose phosphate) would be very difficult; major fluctuations in the level of the regulating substance due to a momentary diversion to another role could be lethal to the cell. Fine control is probably mediated by activation or inhibition of allosteric control enzymes. Induction or repression of enzyme synthesis would take hours to exert any control over solute level, and though that type of control can be useful as a backup or long-term control system, it would not be suitable for quick responses to changes in the external medium. Borowitzka et al. (1977), using the protein synthesis inhibitors chloramphenicol, cycloheximide and rifampicin, have shown that enzyme induction plays little part in regulating the accumulation of glycerol in *Dunaliella* after addition of salt to the growth medium.

Control of solute levels may be maintained by control of rates of one or more key enzyme reactions; for example, in the alga *Dunaliella*, two separate enzyme reactions lead from triose phosphate to glycerol. The last reaction is catalysed by glycerol dehydrogenase, an enzyme which displays cooperative binding kinetics which are characteristic of a control enzyme (Borowitzka & Brown, 1974). A different type of cooperative kinetics applies to the reverse reaction, glycerol to dihydroxyacetone (Borowitzka et al., 1977). A mechanism for homeostatic control of cytoplasmic glycerol levels involving the glycerol dehydrogenase reactions has been proposed (Borowitzka, 1974). Biochemical control of intracellular glycerol levels in *Dunaliella* is discussed in detail by Brown and Borowitzka (1979). Little is known of the control of enzymes en route to betaine and proline in higher plants, although some of the enzymology and effects of salts on some enzymes of proline synthesis are being investigated (e.g. Boggess et al., 1975, and see other chapters).

How the cell senses changes in the extracellular medium is not established. It may detect changes in water or solute concentration at the plasma membrane, or physical changes in cell volume, plasma membrane stretching or net flow of water at the plasma membrane. Furthermore, the mode of transmission of the signal and its action on transport or biosynthetic processes are quite unknown. The signal could be a chemical substance released by the membrane, acting as an allosteric effector on a biosynthetic enzyme or at a transport site. The study of this whole control process warrants highest priority in the field of water stress of organisms. The problem of osmoregulation sensors, signals and controls is outlined admirably in a review by Cram (1976).

There are several physicochemical properties which make certain solutes specially suitable for accumulation to high concentrations:

1. They must be very soluble, as high concentrations are often required by the cell. In general, therefore, low molecular weight substances are favoured. Proline, betaine, polyols and KCl have high solubilities. Glycerol is, in fact, infinitely soluble. Some amino acids, such as glutamate, are rather less soluble and this may be one reason why glutamate accumulation is restricted to bacteria living in relatively dilute environments (see Table II). Phenylalanine and leucine are sparingly soluble in water, hence are unlikely to be important in the regulation of cytoplasmic water activity.

2. They should be uncharged at physiological pH. Accumulation of high concentrations of a charged solute would present an enormous problem for the cell. Charged compounds are accumulated only in small amounts and always with an appropriate concentration of a counterion (e.g. K^+ or possibly Na^+ with glutamate, with oxalate and with malate). The cations are themselves inhibitory to enzyme function at concentrations of several hundred mM and even lower, so the extent of water activity regulation by charged organic solutes and their counterions is restricted by the cation sensitivity of the cell's physiological processes (see later discussion). Both proline and betaine are zwitterions at neutral pH, carrying no net charge, while polyols are never charged.

All of the solutes listed in Tables II and III have these two characteristics, but their physicochemical properties are even more precisely selected to fit the primary need – that of maintaining functional the cell's macromolecules and biochemical reactions in the low water activity-high solute concentration environment within the cell that has adapted to water stress.

B. EXAMPLES OF SOLUTES ACCUMULATED AS REGULATORS OF INTRACELLULAR WATER ACTIVITY

Tables II and III list solutes accumulated by each major group of organisms, with examples from several genera where available. Each group is arranged in approximate order of increasing tolerance to low water activity in the environment.

The need for protection against water loss is perhaps most obvious in unicellular organisms, which are in direct contact with their environment and are therefore very vulnerable to any changes in the composition of their environment.

As far as is known, halophilic bacteria are the only organisms in which massive changes in protein properties with respect to electrolytes has evolved as a mechanism for salinity tolerance. The primary structures of enzyme, membrane and ribosomal proteins of *Halobacterium* are different from those of similar proteins from other sources (Lanyi, 1974), even those from marine bacteria (Tindall et al., 1977). Halophile proteins have an increased number of acidic and neutral amino acid residues with short hydrophobic side chains, and, because of this, cations are *required* to stabilize the tertiary structure of the proteins. This makes the organism an obligate halophile. Apparently halophilic bacteria are the only organisms which depend for survival on a highly saline environment. In other organisms, it appears that synthesis of compatible solutes, rather than specialized protein adaptations, makes growth possible in both dilute and concentrated solutions. Examples of these solutes are shown in Tables II and III. They are generally low molecular weight, neutral organic solutes capable of being accumulated to high concentrations without causing inhibition of cell processes; they fit the definition of "compatible solutes" given by Brown and Simpson (1972).

In any discussion of accumulation of solutes to regulate cytoplasmic water activity, it must be remembered that most organisms maintain a cytoplasmic K^+ concentration of up to about 150 mM. There is evidence that, if the water activity of the medium is sufficiently high (0.98 to 1.0), the intracellular level of K^+ (plus anion, probably not Cl^-) varies in response to changes in the external solution, and there is probably no need for accumulation of an additional compatible type of solute. This has been demonstrated in the unicellular green alga *Platymonas*. When *Platymonas* is grown in salinities below those of seawater, the concentration of intracellular ions, particularly K^+, varies with external solute concentration and maintains the osmotic and, presumably, water activity balance (Kirst, 1977). At higher salinities, mannitol is accumulated as well, its level being dependent on solute concentration in the external medium.

Non-marine and marine bacteria show a progression to more compatible solutes in the species capable of growth in media with low water activities. As increasingly salt-tolerant species are analysed, glutamate gives way to mixtures of compounds, including proline, then finally at $a_w = 0.90$, to proline alone. In all cases, the solute mixture lowers the water activity of the cytoplasm to a level that very closely approximates that of the surrounding medium (Gould & Measures, 1977).

Recent work by Borowitzka, Mackay and Norton, using natural abundance carbon-13 nuclear magnetic resonance spectroscopy, has shown that blue-green algae (cyanobacteria) accumulate different types of organic osmoregulatory compounds, depending on the salinity range tolerated for growth. In eleven freshwater isolates, representing ten diverse genera, the major organic solutes whose concentrations vary with the salinity of the growth medium are sucrose, trehalose and glucose. In a marine *Synechococcus* sp. α-glucosylglycerol is the only major organic osmoregulatory compound (Borowitzka et al., 1980). Eight other marine blue-green algae (from 7 genera) also accumulate α-glucosylglycerol alone as their major organic osmoregulatory solute. Five very salt-tolerant isolates accumulate a quaternary N compound, such as betaine, plus a mixture of simple sugars or amino acids.

Tindall et al. (1977) reported the accumulation of free amino acids plus KCl by *Aphanothece halophytica*; a nuclear magnetic resonance study on an Australian *A. halophytica* has shown that betaine and glutamate are the major organic osmoregulatory compounds, with inorganic ions (probably KCl) also important contributors.

Some of the more complex organisms have additional mechanisms for tolerating low a_w, including removal of cytoplasmic water by contractile vacuoles (protozoa) (Pochmann, 1959) and formation of non-growing seeds and cysts; some bacteria form spores (Gould & Measures, 1977).

C. SOLUTE INTERACTION WITH THE ENZYME-SOLVENT SYSTEM

Solutes dissolved in the water surrounding a macromolecule have two ways of affecting the functioning of that molecule; both involve modifications of the conformation of the macromolecule. They can act: (i) indirectly, by altering the structure of water and hence its interaction with the macromolecule; and/or (ii) by direct site-binding of the solute to the macromolecule.

Neutral salts and their ions may interact with proteins in both ways at once. Two different processes occur when the concentration of an electrolyte in protein solution is increased. First, at low electrolyte concentrations, protein solubility increases; this is "salting-in". Effectiveness in salting-in depends on the ionic strength of the salt. Of course some proteins are soluble in pure water, so salting-in is not observed. Second, after reaching a maximum, protein solubility decreases; this is "salting-out". Salting-out effectiveness is dependent on the types of ions used, and follows the Hofmeister (lyotropic) series for salting-out (examples of the series are given in Section C.2.a.). The situation is not usually clear cut, however. For example, high concentrations of strongly salting-in type ions (e.g. SCN^-, I^-) continue to salt-in individual protein groups even though the overall high salt concentration can lead to denaturing and salting-out of the whole protein.

Organic solutes of the type accumulated do not participate in electrostatic binding; they generally have no aliphatic chain suitable for hydrophobic interaction (although valine, leucine and isoleucine have short chains), so they cannot directly site-bind to the macromolecule. They generally interact with it only indirectly, via the solvent, water.

Proline and betaine have been proposed to act as amphiphiles (Schobert,

1977); that is, to have a polar end capable of hydrogen bonding to water molecules and a non-polar end which can interact directly with non-polar sites on the surface of macromolecules. Presumably, the polar end may also interact with polar groups on the surface of the macromolecule, and the non-polar end with free water, considerably altering the structure of the solvent. The subject of amphiphile binding is discussed later.

The structure of water, the effect of polar and non-polar solutes on it, and solute-solvent-macromolecule interactions are covered in the multi-volumed treatise on water edited by Franks (1972-75), and books by Lewin (1974), Eisenberg and Kauzmann (1969) and Tanford (1973), the latter treating hydrophobic interactions in proteins and solutions. In addition, there is a highly recommended review by von Hippel and Schleich (1969) which covers aspects of neutral salt interactions with solutions of macromolecules, and two further reviews on solvent-macromolecule interactions (Franks & Eagland, 1975; Franks, 1977a). This section (Section C) is a condensed discussion of interactions that are particularly relevant for accumulations of compatible solutes.

1. Structure of water

There are several theories on the structure of liquid water; one that is fairly well accepted and supported by some good evidence is that of the "flickering cluster" of Frank and Wen (1957) and Frank (1958). It is based on the premise that the formation of H-bonds in liquid water is a cooperative process and leads to the formation of regions of local clustering of water molecules. Flickering clusters of short life-times (10^{-10} to 10^{-11} sec) reflect local energy fluctuations. Cooke and Kuntz (1974) favour the existence of a tetrahedral arrangement of four neighbouring water molecules for a similar time interval. The addition of charged ions to the solution seriously perturbs this type of structure; in a 1.0 M solution of a neutral salt (e.g. KCl), no water molecule lies more than 3 molecular diameters from the centre of an ion, and therefore the solution contains essentially no regions of unaffected water structure. The presence of ions disrupts H-bonding and imposes a new order on the structure of the solution. The flickering cluster structure is also altered by the addition of non-polar moieties; in their vicinity, labile "Frank-Evans icebergs" (Frank & Evans, 1945), representing a different type of water structure, are induced. This type of water structure modification is about the only type caused by most non-electrolytes (e.g. alcohols, polyols), as they are generally poorer H-bonders than water. Even charged organic compounds have charge densities much lower than inorganic ions and their charges do not seriously perturb the H-bond based flickering clusters.

In addition to water structure alteration induced by the presence of solute, the presence of hydrophilic (H-bonding) and hydrophobic groups on the surfaces of macromolecules alters the structure of the surrounding water.

2. Effect of solute-structured water on stability and function of macromolecules, particularly proteins

The protein may be regarded as a roughly spherical body, inseparable from water in its native, active state, and dependent, at least in part, on its interactions with the surrounding medium for conformational stability and function (Franks, 1977a). Minor changes in the solution composition (e.g. addition of solute) can cause major upheavals in the protein conformation (Franks, 1977a).

Nuclear magnetic resonance and dielectric dispersion measurements indicate that around a protein molecule there are one or two monolayers of water — "bound water" — whose rotational motions and freezing properties are substantially modified by interaction with protein surface groups. A 20% w/v protein solution has about 10% of the water bound this way. About 0.1% of the total water is very tightly bound to specific sites on the protein for microsecond periods. Most of the water in solution (about 90%) has properties not appreciably altered by the proximity of the protein (Cooke & Kuntz, 1974). Franks (1977b) designated these three regions as B, A and C regions respectively, and states that it is the B region (the region between the tightly bound water of the A region and the bulk water C region) where the influences of temperature and pressure operate on protein stability. It is also the region where the water molecules are involved in hydrophobic interactions with the protein, and in which alteration of solvent structure caused by addition of solute affects the conformation of the nearby protein. The presence of solute in the water will affect the structure of all three types of water, but the effect on the transient, specifically bound water will probably be negligible, and the effect on the bulk water will be of less importance to the protein than the effect on the B region (Cooke & Kuntz, 1974).

Water structure-mediated effects of solutes on protein stability (which, in turn, is correlated with function) are conveniently measured in terms of ability to alter the Tm of the protein. Tm is the transition temperature, the temperature at which the transformation from molecular conformation A to B is 50% complete. If A is the native, active conformation of an enzyme and B is an inactive random coil form, any solute that lowers the Tm has altered the net enthalpy or net entropy change required for the A-B transition, and favours that transition (von Hippel & Schleich, 1969).

Characteristics of water structure-mediated effects of solutes on proteins are:

1. The effect of a particular solute is linear with solute concentration in the range 1–3 molal, but quite insensitive to protein concentration. This is because no direct solute-protein binding is occurring; all solute effects on the protein are due to the solute changing the structure of the water surrounding the protein.

2. Generally, the non-polar residues near the protein surface are involved.

3. The effects of ions follow the Hofmeister (lyotropic) series; the effects for non-polar solutes are dependent on several structural features, such as the length of an unobstructed aliphatic chain.
4. The effects of mixtures of solutes, ionic or non-polar or both, are additive.

a. Salting out by salts

The main solvent-structure-mediated effect of neutral salts and their ions on macromolecules is *salting out*. This stabilizes the native (active) conformation of proteins by tending to salt them out of solution. Salting-out salts encourage intramolecular stabilizing forces (particularly hydrophobic interactions) rather than protein-solvent H-bonding with its concommitant increase in protein solubility and loss of the active conformation (von Hippel & Schleich, 1969). Salting out primarily involves the non-polar residues of the protein; all neutral salts salt out non-polar groups, but they do it with different molar effectiveness. Effectiveness depends strongly on ion type but not on ionic strength; the effectiveness of cations and anions in this type of protein stabilization follows the Hofmeister series (von Hippel & Wong, 1965):

$$\text{For anions: } SO_4^{2-} > Cl^- > Br^- > NO_3^- > ClO_4^- > I^-$$

$$\text{For cations: } K^+ = Na^+ > Li^+ > Ca^{2+} \text{ (for ribonuclease)}$$

Hence, at least at concentrations in the 1–3 molal range, K^+ salts out proteins, so its solutions should tend to stabilize the native, active configurations of proteins by promoting intraprotein interactions rather than protein-solvent interactions. Lanyi and co-workers (reviewed in Lanyi, 1974) proposed that intraprotein hydrophobic interactions, promoted by high concentrations of salting-out salts, are the main barrier to unfolding and denaturing of *Halobacteria* enzymes. The concentrations of K^+ in many cells (from below 100 mM to 200 or 300 mM) are probably too low for K^+ to function generally as a protein stabilizer by salting-out. However, its tendency to salt in (solublize) and destabilize should be less than that of Na^+, which has a higher charge density and therefore salts in proteins more strongly (see Section C.3.a).

b. Solvent-mediated solute effects on enzyme activity

Barring specific ion binding at the active site required for catalytic activity, the order of effectiveness of ions or organic solutes as enzyme inhibitors should follow their order of effectiveness in disrupting enzyme structure. This has been demonstrated with a variety of enzymes by Warren et al. (1966), and von Hippel and Schleich (1969) conclude that the effect of neutral salts on enzyme activity is simply a local (at the active site) manifestation of the general lyotropic structure-disrupting effects of neutral salts. The effect on enzyme activity is probably a more sensitive indicator than the observable protein configuration changes; with myosin ATPase, general enzyme activity was lost at lower salt concentrations than those that caused a visible effect on optical rotary properties of the protein structure (Tonomura et al., 1962).

Recent work by Somero and co-workers suggested that it is apparently not necessary to specify the active site as the site of lyotropic enzyme inhibitory effects. They postulate that amino acid side chains and peptide linkages located all over the surface of the enzyme protein change their exposure to water during conformational changes in catalysis. They further suggest that these protein group transfers to and from water are accompanied by large volume and energy changes which are mainly due to changes in the organization of water around the groups, and that, among other things, the energy changes contribute to catalytic rate enhancement of the reaction. By influencing the degree to which water can organize around transferred protein groups, salts and organic solutes can modify the free energy change leading to rate enhancement (Low & Somero, 1975a, 1975b; Somero & Low, 1977; Somero et al., 1977). They are suggesting, then, that the whole of the enzyme protein participates in the catalytic function; that energy is provided for the reaction from protein-solvent interactions changing during the catalytic step, and the energy derived, and consequent reaction rate, are modified when solute-solvent interactions modify protein-solvent interactions. That changes in hydration of protein residues during ligand binding contribute significantly to conformational change energetics has been demonstrated quite clearly in the case of lysozyme (Banerjee & Rupley, 1973). Using several enzymes from different sources, Somero and co-workers have shown that neutral salts affect reaction rates (and activation volume) in a manner that reflects the salts' position in the Hofmeister series (e.g. Low & Somero, 1975a). This is the expected result for a solvent-mediated solute effect on a protein. A similar series for organic solutes, reflecting their ability to alter water structure, would be expected. This is discussed briefly later.

c. Solvent-mediated effects of organic compounds

Like water structure-mediated effects of salts on protein stability and function, water structure-mediated effects of organic solutes involve mostly the non-polar residues in the protein (von Hippel & Schleich, 1969). The extent of destabilization (measured by Tm depression) and function impairing is largely dependent on the extent of the unobstructed aliphatic character of the solute. For example, Bello et al. (1956) showed that the molar effectiveness ⁿf aliphatic acids as gelatin Tm reducers increases with increasing hydrocarbon chain length. In an alcohol and polyol series, ethylene glycol depresses the Tm of ribonuclease less than methanol (i.e. destabilizes protein structure less), and methanol less than ethanol less than propanol (von Hippel & Wong, 1965). These results, and others, lead to the generalization that methylene groups adjacent to an −OH moiety are ineffective as Tm depressors (protein destabilizers) compared with unobstructed methylene groups. However, if the methylene group is separated from the −OH moiety by another methylene group, the methylene group more distant from the −OH is relatively unaffected by the −OH group; that is, it is "unobstructed", and its aliphatic character is the equivalent of one unobstructed methylene unit of Tm-depressing ability (Schrier & Scheraga, 1962; von Hippel & Schleich, 1969). Hence the increasingly structure-destabilizing and enzyme inhibitory series, methanol < ethanol < propanol, reflects the increasing length of the unobstructed aliphatic chain. Simpson (1976) studied the effects of the position and number of −OH groups in propane and butane diols and butane triol on inhibition of isocitrate dehydrogenase from yeast. Tables IV and V

TABLE IV

Enzyme inhibition by 3C polyhydric compounds in order of increasing inhibition.[a]

Name	Structure	No. of unobstructed methylene units
glycerol	$-\overset{\mid}{\underset{\mid}{C}} - \overset{\mid}{\underset{\mid}{C}} - \overset{\mid}{\underset{\mid}{C}} -$ OH OH OH	0
propane-1,2-diol	$-\overset{\mid}{\underset{\mid}{C}} - \overset{\mid}{\underset{\mid}{C}} - \overset{\mid}{\underset{\mid}{C}} -$ OH OH	1
propane-1,3-diol	$-\overset{\mid}{\underset{\mid}{C}} - \overset{\mid}{\underset{\mid}{C}} - \overset{\mid}{\underset{\mid}{C}} -$ OH OH	1
n-propanol	$-\overset{\mid}{\underset{\mid}{C}} - \overset{\mid}{\underset{\mid}{C}} - \overset{\mid}{\underset{\mid}{C}} -$ OH	2

[a]From Simpson (1976).

show that the enzyme inhibition correlates well with the number of methylene groups unobstructed by the proximity of an −OH group.

The cases of the diols of propane and the butane-2,3 and 1,4-diols indicate that two −OH groups on adjacent C atoms exert more influence on their neighbours than if the hydroxylated C atoms are separated in the chain.

The only compound among those listed in Tables IV and V which has been reported to be accumulated by any organism is glycerol, and it is accumulated to high concentrations by *Dunaliella* and the xerotolerant yeasts. It causes very little inhibition of *Dunaliella* glucose-6-phosphate dehydrogenase, even in a 6 M solution (Borowitzka & Brown, 1974). Other osmoregulatory polyols such as arabitol, erythritol and mannitol share, to some extent, the properties of glycerol (Simpson, 1976); however, enzyme

TABLE V

Enzyme inhibition by 4C polyhydric compounds, in order of increasing inhibition.[a]

Name	Structure	No. of unobstructed methylene units
threitol	$-\overset{\mid}{\underset{\mid}{C}} - \overset{\mid}{\underset{\mid}{C}} - \overset{\mid}{\underset{\mid}{C}} - \overset{\mid}{\underset{\mid}{C}} -$ OH OH OH OH	0
butane-1,2,4-triol	$-\overset{\mid}{\underset{\mid}{C}} - \overset{\mid}{\underset{\mid}{C}} - \overset{\mid}{\underset{\mid}{C}} - \overset{\mid}{\underset{\mid}{C}} -$ OH OH OH	1
butane-2,3-diol	$-\overset{\mid}{\underset{\mid}{C}} - \overset{\mid}{\underset{\mid}{C}} - \overset{\mid}{\underset{\mid}{C}} - \overset{\mid}{\underset{\mid}{C}} -$ OH OH	2
butane-1,3-diol[b]	$-\overset{\mid}{\underset{\mid}{C}} - \overset{\mid}{\underset{\mid}{C}} - \overset{\mid}{\underset{\mid}{C}} - \overset{\mid}{\underset{\mid}{C}} -$ OH OH	2
butane-1,4-diol[b]	$-\overset{\mid}{\underset{\mid}{C}} - \overset{\mid}{\underset{\mid}{C}} - \overset{\mid}{\underset{\mid}{C}} - \overset{\mid}{\underset{\mid}{C}} -$ OH OH	2

[a]From Simpson (1976).

[b]In one out of three experiments butane-1,3-diol was more inhibitory than butane-1,4-diol.

inhibition increases with the chain length of the polyol. This is not a linear correlation; its sigmoidal character led to further investigations to determine additional factors influencing "compatibility" of straight chain polyols.

There was a negative correlation of enzyme inhibition with chromatographic R_f (in butanol:acetic acid:water); R_f was used as a measure of hydrophobic/hydrophilic partition coefficient. Polyols with low R_f values were more inhibitory to yeast isocitrate dehydrogenase than those with high R_f. It was suggested that the polyols with low molecular weights and high R_f have a lower affinity for hydrophobic regions on the protein molecule and a higher affinity for the solvent water (Simpson, 1976). Indeed, as pointed out later, they are particularly water soluble and do not appreciably alter water structure, though these properties diminish as chain length increases. Oddly enough, two short chain polyols, ethylene glycol and threitol (2C and 4C respectively), are missing from the list of polyols known to be accumulated as regulators of water activity.

The generalizations of Simpson cannot be extended to ring-containing sugars. Their stereochemistry seems to dominate their enzyme inhibition efficiency and no correlation with hydrophobic/hydrophilic partition coefficient or molecular weight was found. Sucrose was more inhibitory than the pentose arabinose, which was more inhibitory than the disaccharide maltose. Hexoses were generally less inhibitory than other sugars, the least inhibitory being fructose. The straight chain aldoses, glyceraldehyde and erythrose, caused irreversible enzyme inhibition, implying very tight direct site-binding (probably involving the terminal aldehyde group) to the enzyme (Simpson, 1976).

Cyclohexanetetrol, the α-galactosyl glycerols and α-glucosylglycerol qualify as compatible solutes and are accumulated, probably because of their limited polyhydric character.

Intuitively, it seems that a flexible linear molecule of the polyol type

$$-\overset{\displaystyle |}{\underset{\displaystyle |}{C}}-\overset{\displaystyle |}{\underset{\displaystyle |}{C}}-\overset{\displaystyle |}{\underset{\displaystyle |}{C}}-$$
$$\ \ \ \text{OH}\ \ \text{OH}\ \ \text{OH}$$

could mimic the H$-$OH molecules in structured water fitting into the solution structure rather than altering it. This has been suggested by Schobert (1977) for glycerol, but confirming chemical data are missing. There is some supporting evidence, however. One measure of water-structuring capability of hydrophobic molecules is their ability to reduce surface tension of water. An increasing proportion of $-$OH groups in a solute molecule offsets the water-structuring previously enforced by the hydrophobic groups of the solute.

As a result, 1.0 M solutions of the polyols, sorbitol, erythritol, glycerol and ethylene glycol, and the sugar, D-glucose, have surface tensions very similar to that of pure water. On the other hand, the addition of alcohols, such as ethanol and propanol, to water causes a dramatic reduction in surface tension (Lewin, 1974)

Franks (1977b) has in fact termed solutes which are able to interact with the solvent without major perturbations in the solvent structure as "solvent-compatible" solutes. "Water-compatible" stereochemistry favours hydration interactions; in the case of sugars, those most water-compatible are those with the highest hydration numbers. Sucrose is highest, with 6 mol water. mol sugar^{-1}, followed by maltose, mannose, glucose and ribose (at 5°C). The degree of hydration is dependent on the orientation of $-OH$ groups within the sugar ring and the similarity between the distance apart of the $-OH$ groups to the distance between $-OH$ groups in the water (Franks, 1977b). It is suggested that water structure perturbation beyond the primary hydration sphere of the polyhydric solute would be very limited. This correlates with the proposal that polyhydric compounds cause little perturbation to water because they "fit into it", mimicking water.

Unfortunately, in the case of the monosaccharides and disaccharides, solvent compatibility does not correlate with enzyme compatibility (or lack of enzyme inhibition), using the definition of enzyme-compatible solutes of Brown and Simpson (1972), because it appears that enzyme inhibition caused by the sugars is related to steric hindrance of the enzyme molecule by the sugar rings. However, in the case of polyols, where no such steric hindrance of the protein occurs, and the major effect of the solute on the enzyme is thought to be solvent-mediated, one would expect enzyme-compatible solutes to be also solvent-compatible solutes. Perhaps the high affinity of the compatible solute for water, together with a low affinity for the protein, helps to retain the layer of bound water around the protein, in a form structurally little altered.

There is evidence that the cyclic polyol, myo-inositol, mimics water molecules during dehydration of DNA. During dehydration, myo-inositol maintains bacterial DNA in the B form, the form characteristically found at high relative humidities, when the DNA is maximally hydrated (Webb & Bhorjee, 1968). The authors suggest that the mechanism of protection of the DNA structure involves replacement of the water molecules in contact with the DNA with myo-inositol. This may be the case for DNA and myo-inositol, but, in general, compatible solutes are characterized by their high affinity for water and their comparatively low affinity for macromolecules. This, in part, is what makes them poor enzyme inhibitors and compatible at high concentrations. Rather, it is likely that the myo-inositol, because of its affinity for water and small affinity for DNA, helps retain the monolayers of water around the DNA relatively unaltered, although the bulk water has been removed.

It is suggested that participation in water structure causes little change in enzyme activity, whereas alteration of water structure is inhibitory. This correlates with the respective effects of polyols, which have little effect on stability and function of enzymes, and alcohols, whose aliphatic chains cause formation of the Frank-Evans iceberg type of water structure, and enzyme inhibition.

In an interesting variation from the predicted inhibitory effect of n-propanol on enzyme reactions, Somero et al. (1977) showed that concentrations of up to 1.0 M propanol had no effect on the reaction rate of halibut lactate dehydrogenase. Because n-propanol's major interaction, either through a solvent-mediated effect on the protein or by direct interaction with the protein, must be with non-polar protein groups, the authors suggest that the lack of enzyme rate modification demonstrates a negligible role for hydrophobic group transfers in contributing to the activation free energy of the lactate dehydrogenase reaction.

The presence in a molecule of a charged N atom near an aliphatic chain has an effect similar to the presence of an $-OH$ group. For example, 1.0 M $(CH_3)_4N^+$ (tetramethylammonium ion) has little effect on Tm, but tetraethylammonium ion, $(CH_3CH_2)_4N^+$, has the equivalent of 3 methylene units of Tm-depressing ability (von Hippel & Wong, 1965). Tetramethylammonium oxide and two other methylamine compounds, betaine and sarcosine, have been found to be effective stabilisers of protein structure, and a 1:2 molar concentration ratio of these compounds to urea counteracts perturbations of protein structure by urea. Yancey and Somero (1979) have found combinations of "counteracting solutes" in marine elasmobranch fishes (sharks, skates and rays), holocephans and coelocanths. The presence of a counteracting methylamine solute may explain how the structural and functional properties of proteins of the fish can be maintained in the presence of around 0.4 M urea in intracellular fluids. The N-containing compatible solutes include several neutral amino acids, glycine and alanine, the imino acid proline and the quaternary N compound, betaine. Proline and betaine are both accumulated, to different extents, by halophyte and non-halophyte plants. Proline is also accumulated by bacteria, unicellular algae and other types of cells. The N as part of a heterocyclic ring should have effects on the rest of the compound rather different to what would be expected of N in a straight chain. Schobert (1977) has proposed that the main virtue of the proline structure lies in its amphiphilic character; proline as an amphiphile will be discussed in Section C.3.b.

Betaine is a zwitterion at neutral pH, with the structure

$$CH_3-\underset{\underset{CH_3}{|}}{\overset{\overset{CH_3}{|}}{N^+}}-CH_2-COO^-$$

The proximity of the N^+ to the methyl groups reduces their Tm-depressing ability. Schobert (1977) has further suggested that betaine may also act as an amphiphile, H-bonding water to the protein molecule (see Section C.3.b).

d. Additive effects of mixtures of organic solutes and salts

The effects of salts and organic solutes on solvent structure are additive: there is no interaction between the solutes. The combined effects of salts and organic solutes on several enzymes have been demonstrated to be simply additive (von Hippel & Wong, 1965). Borowitzka (1974) showed that the presence of 3 M glycerol, the compatible solute, had no effect on the activity of glucose-6-phosphate dehydrogenase from *Dunaliella*. When glycerol was added to the enzyme with a mixture of NaCl + KCl, enzyme inhibition was equal to that caused by the salts alone, neither increased nor diminished by the presence of glycerol.

On the other hand, with barley malate dehydrogenase, a small, non-additive, protective effect was found with the combination of betaine and NaCl. Proline also relieved the enzyme inhibition caused by NaCl, though not as effectively as did betaine (Wyn Jones et al., 1976). Relief of salt inhibition may be a consequence of some unknown water-structuring effect of the betaine or the proline, or perhaps of direct binding of the organic solute to the protein, as suggested by Schobert (1977) primarily for proline (but see the discussion of this proposal in Section C.3.b).

Pollard and Wyn Jones (1979) have studied the effects of the series of compounds, betaine, 2-methylglycine, 1-methylglycine (sarcosine) and glycine, on malate dehydrogenase from barley, all in the presence of 300 mM NaCl. Betaine had a protective effect on the enzyme; that is, 300 mM NaCl was not as inhibitory in the presence of betaine as when alone. The protection decreased with the progressive removal of methyl groups from the N. Inhibition of malate dehydrogenase was observed with glycine; in fact, the inhibition caused by glycine with 300 mM NaCl was the same as the sum of the inhibitions caused by each solute separately.

In summarizing solvent-mediated solute-macromolecule interactions, it must be emphasized that changing the solute composition of the solution changes the structure of the water within the solution, and hence its interactions with the nearby macromolecules. Obviously, solutes which change these interactions extensively must be avoided by the cell, so, for water activity regulation, a solute which causes minimum possible alteration to water structure, such as glycerol, is required.

3. Solutes interacting directly with macromolecules

Direct site-binding of the solute to the macromolecule usually involves charged or polar residues at the surface of the macromolecule. Additional properties of direct site-binding (given by von Hippel & Schleich, 1969) are:

    (i)   the solute binds to specific sites on the macromolecule;

   (ii) there are large association (affinity) constants; the binding is usually electrostatic and comparatively strong;

  (iii) there is a demonstrable saturation at low additive concentrations and a dependence on macromolecule concentration (unlike solvent-mediated effects of solutes);

  (iv) solutes interacting this way are generally ions of neutral salts. The extent of their interactions depends on ion type and charge density and does not follow the Hofmeister series.

a. Neutral salts

Salting-in enzyme destabilization. The most usual effect of ion site-binding is salting-in, a destabilizing effect tending to solublize the enzyme by conversion to a form other than its native, active conformation (Dixon & Webb, 1961; von Hippel & Schleich, 1969). Electrostatic interactions between the charged protein groups and the ionic environment lead to a net decrease in the activity coefficient of the protein, reflected in an increase in net solubility. This, in fact, causes unfolding of the native, globular, generally enzymically-active form into the unfolded, random coil type of configuration. Salting-in effectiveness depends only on ion type and ionic strength. Hence $Li^+ > Na^+ > K^+$. K^+, the cation generally accumulated, albeit usually in low concentrations ($\leqslant 150$ mM) in cells, does not effectively salt in and destabilize the native, active structure compared with Na^+ or Li^+. As described in the previous section, its main influence is to salt out, particularly at higher concentrations.

Stabilizing effects of ion binding. In the case of polyelectrolyte macromolecules, such as DNA, and to a lesser extent *Halobacterium* proteins (which have a higher than usual proportion of negative side chains due to aspartate and glutamate residues), cations at low concentrations ($\leqslant 300$ mM) can stabilize the native configuration of the macromolecule by electrostatic binding to negatively charged side chains on the surface of the macromolecule, preventing their mutual repulsion by charge shielding. Lanyi (1974), however, suggests that this is not the most important effect of the high K^+ concentration surrounding *Halobacterium* enzymes (see Section C.2.a on salting out). Nonetheless, K^+ in *Halobacterium* is an example of an ion interacting with a protein, both by direct site-binding and through solvent-mediated solute-macromolecule interaction. Direct ion binding stabilization is unlikely to be important to most enzymes, as few enzymes have an excess of charged side chains. However, the low concentrations of cations found in most cells may play a role in stabilizing DNA and RNA, both of which are polyelectrolytes with negatively charged phosphate moieties in the backbones.

b. Direct binding by organic solutes.

Charged solutes. An amino acid with a net charge at physiological pH would tend to bind electrostatically to charged protein groups, but, because the charge density of the organic solute is much lower than that of an ion, the solubilizing effect is probably minimal. Most water activity-regulating solutes are uncharged; of the others, most are zwitterions with no net charge, so the importance of direct binding to charged protein groups is negligible.

Neutral organic solutes, with non-polar aliphatic chains. Aliphatic chains of a solute may have a small solublizing effect on exposed, non-polar protein groups, but, because of the limited solubility (excluding alcohols) and drastic water structuring properties (including alcohols) of most of the class, they are not accumulated as water activity regulators.

Proline and amphiphile binding. A variation on site binding, specific to proline and possibly betaine, has been proposed by Schobert (1977). Her concept of the action of proline in "water structure regulation" in water-stressed algae and higher plants involves both a type of organic solute site binding and a consequent water structure regulation effect. She proposes that the hydrophobic (heterocyclic ring) moiety of proline is associated with the hydrophobic moieties on the surface of the biopolymer, so that an essentially hydrophilic face, the carboxyl group of the proline, is presented to the surrounding water. She suggests that the resultant H-bonding would tightly bind the surrounding water to the proline and, hence, to the protein, preventing its dehydration in the water stressed cell. Amphiphile binding, then, would lead to considerable changes in water structuring within the cell.

Chemical data showing large-scale close associations of the heterocyclic ring of proline with the surfaces of proteins are obviously required before the proposal can be considered further. In several respects, however, the proposal is at odds with the concepts presented in this review. The extent to which proline would behave as an amphiphile at physiological pH is questionable. Although it is generally listed as an amphiphile (Tanford, 1973), in fact, at its pI it behaves, like other amino and imino acids, as a zwitterion; there is a negative charge on the carboxyl group balanced by a positive charge on the imino N in the heterocyclic ring. The pI of proline is 6.3, which lies within the range generally accepted for cytoplasmic pH (e.g. ^{31}P-NMR indicates a cytoplasmic pH range of 6–8 in *E. coli*, Navon, et al., 1977). The heterocyclic ring would remain charged at pH values below the pI; at pH values above pI the probability of the presence of a positive charge on the ring would decrease (the pK_2 of the imino group is 10.6). Hence, the hydrophobic character of the ring should be greatly reduced around the likely physiological pH because of the presence of a positive charge within it.

The importance of hydrophobic interactions between the protein and proline may be even less, because there may be only a small number of non-polar residues suitably exposed for interaction on the surface of many proteins (von Hippel & Schleich, 1969). Furthermore, site binding by a non-polar moiety to non-polar protein groups, particularly if they are situated within the protein, should tend to alter the conformation of the protein. In fact, Schobert suggests that the combined effect of the hydrophobic proline-protein interactions, and the H-bonding bound-proline-water interaction is to solublize the protein. It is almost axiomatic that a change in conformation, drastic enough to alter solubility of an enzyme, must change the activity of the enzyme. Since the more soluble forms of an enzyme tend to be random coil configurations rather than the specific, active, three-dimensional structure, activity is very likely to decrease with increased solubility (see Section C.2.). A final point is that the properties of most accumulated water activity-regulating solutes seem to be specially adapted to cause the least possible change in normal water structure, yet Schobert's explanation for the efficacy of proline in preserving enzyme activity depends on the formation of highly structured H-bonded water all around the protein.

It is interesting that proline is probably the only amino acid that is suitable for the proposed amphiphile binding role, if, indeed, significant binding does occur. Of all other amino acids with a non-polar end, leucine and phenylalanine are not very soluble, and valine, leucine and isoleucine have aliphatic chains that, as already discussed, have strong water structure-altering tendencies. Tyrosine, γ-aminobutyric acid, the basic, acidic, and S-containing amino acids and hydroxyproline would not suit, though low levels of some of these (usually in combination with others more compatible) are accumulated as water activity regulators by some organisms. Tryptophan, with a different type of heterocyclic ring, may suit the role, but to our knowledge is not accumulated by any organism, nor is it sufficiently soluble.

D. SUMMARY OF PHYSICOCHEMICAL PROPERTIES OF WATER ACTIVITY-REGULATING SOLUTES AND CONCLUSIONS

One purpose of this chapter has been to show that cells regulate the water activity of the cytosol and thus prevent loss of water due to water stress. The answer, then, to Schobert's (1977) question, "Is there an osmoregulatory mechanism in algae and higher plants?", is yes, though the concept of a *water activity*-regulating mechanism is perhaps easier to visualize. Accumulation of solutes regulates the thermodynamic water activity of the cytosol to a level comparable with that of the solution on the other side of the semi-permeable plasma membrane, and thus minimizes net flow of water into or out of the cell.

In addition to the passive role of adjusting water activity, the particular solutes accumulated help to maintain, or at least do not greatly interfere with, water structure. For this reason, the presence of the solutes does not interfere with the solvent-macromolecule interactions necessary for the normal cell metabolism. Because of low affinities for the macromolecules compared with affinities for the solvent, the accumulated compatible solutes interact minimally with the macromolecules and are poor enzyme inhibitors.

Schobert (1977) suggests that "water structure regulation" is the primary role of accumulated solutes. The "water structure regulation" suggested for glycerol involves "fitting into" the water structure and causing minimum perturbation of it, and this is in agreement with the views of this author. Schobert and Tschesche (1978) also suggest that at high proline concentrations (1–6M) the heterocyclic rings in the solution stack in such a way that the solute drastically alters the water structure. The importance to the cell of water structure alteration caused by proline at physiological pH and concentration, and of proline *per se*, is currently being assessed (Paleg et al., 1981; Nash et al., 1981).

However, whatever their effect on water structure, a primary action of accumulated solutes in protecting cells against water stress lies in regulation of intracellular water activity and the minimizing of water loss; this is the process traditionally termed osmoregulation.

Both direct and indirect interactions of inorganic ions with macromolecules have been discussed in this chapter. It was concluded that K^+ was the least inhibitory monovalent cation; it has less affinity than Na^+ or Li^+

or divalent cations for charged or polar residues on the protein surface; hence, its binding to those groups is less "tight" (a feature of a weak enzyme inhibitor) and it has less tendency to alter protein conformation by favouring the more soluble form. In addition, higher concentrations of K^+ effectively stabilize native, active protein conformations by tending to salt them out of solution. In this character it is almost matched by Na^+. Therefore, the order for increasing protein conformation disruption and enzyme inhibition is $K^+ < Na^+ < Li^+ < Mg^{2+} \leqslant Ca^{2+}$. None of the cations at the end of the sequence are accumulated to high concentrations. Of anions, sulphate and Cl^- tend to stabilize native conformations of proteins and should be favoured.

Organic solutes can be divided into several groups: those with long, aliphatic chains; those with polyhydric character, either linear or in rings; those containing charged moieties; and amphiphiles. Those containing long aliphatic chains, either alkanes or alcohols, are extremely inhibitory to enzyme function because of both direct hydrophobic interactions with the protein and their water structure-altering character. Compounds in which the hydrophobic character is diminished by the presence of several $-OH$ or $-N^+$ groups probably bind directly to the protein to a very limited extent; their main influence is through water structure alteration. The polyols and, to a lesser extent, the ring-containing sugars cause relatively little perturbation of water structure and hence are the solutes of choice for accumulation. Tables II and III show that they are indeed accumulated by a wide range of organisms in response to water stress.

The amino acids, glycine, alanine and proline, and the amine, betaine, have no net charge at physiological pH and no aliphatic chain and hence have little affinity for the macromolecule. In addition, their effect on water structure is small. They are commonly accumulated as compatible solutes. The special amphiphilic binding proposed for proline and betaine has been discussed and criticized; chemical data on the binding of these molecules to proteins is required for any further assessment.

The requirements for compatibility in osmoregulatory solutes are summarized below.

1. Requirements for effective function at low water activity:
    (a) They must be very soluble; hence low molecular weight is favoured (e.g. glycerol, mannitol and proline).
    (b) They must carry no net charge at neutral pH (e.g. polyols, proline, betaine and the combinations K^+ malate, K^+ oxalate). The only exception is K^+ in *Halobacteria*.
    (c) They must be retained by the cell's plasma membrane against a large concentration gradient.

2. Requirements for minimal alteration of enzyme structure and inhibition of function:

    (a) They should cause minimal alteration to water structure (e.g. glycerol and betaine are better than K^+ which is better than Na^+ and Li^+).

    (b) When they do alter water structure, they should do so in a way that stabilizes the native, active enzyme conformation, rather than inducing solubility (e.g. K^+ is better than Na^+ and Li^+).

    (c) If they interact directly with the enzyme macromolecule, it is with a low binding affinity and it should tend to stabilize the native, active structure (e.g. K^+ charge-shielding in *Halobacteria* proteins).

3. Biochemical requirements for rapid, fine control by the cell over its compatible solute level:

    (a) For organic solutes they should be separated by several enzyme reaction steps from an intermediate in a major active biochemical pathway. The several steps from the pathway should lead only to the water activity regulating solute and be finely controlled, possibly through activation or inhibition of allosteric enzymes.

    (b) In the case of inorganic solutes (primarily K^+), there must be close metabolic regulation of transport into the cell.

Some solutes, such as ethylene glycol and threitol, satisfy all of these requirements, sometimes, apparently, better than the solutes listed in Tables II and III. However their accumulation as osmoregulators has not been demonstrated. The existence of apparently unexploited compatible solutes emphasizes that there must be further requirements, as yet unknown. Probably the major additional restrictions on type of solute are biochemical and depend on the cell's ability to synthesize the solute, the availability of suitable precursors and energy, and the cell's ability to control the biosynthesis and removal of the solute. Investigation of why some solutes are *not* accumulated could add considerably to our understanding of the biochemistry of compatible solute accumulation.

It is interesting to correlate the type of solute accumulated with the degree of water stress tolerance of each organism. Summarizing Tables II and III, the prokaryote, *Halobacterium*, is tolerant of extremely low water activities, but it must be regarded as an anomaly because of large scale biochemical adaptations of its proteins to the accumulated cation, K^+. The next most tolerant organisms are the unicellular eukaryotes, including yeasts and algae, and all accumulate polyhydric compounds. Less tolerant (about $a_w = 0.96$) organisms include bacteria, algae, protozoa, multicelled algae, invertebrates and vascular plants. Polyols are accumulated by some, but most accumulate combinations of amino acids, in addition to K^+ of course.

This summary reveals two evolutionary trends. The first is that the type of solute accumulated correlates with the degree of water stress tolerance of the organisms. The most compatible solutes, predicted from their physicochemical properties, for example polyols, are accumulated by the organisms most tolerant of low water activity environments. Less compatible solutes, like the neutral amino acids, seem unable to convey tolerance of environmental water activities much lower than 0.90. The second is that the simplest organisms, the unicellular prokaryotes and eukaryotes, have representatives with the greatest tolerance to water stress; multicelled organisms are generally limited to environments with water activities equivalent to seawater (0.96) or higher. It is very likely, also, that solutes accumulated by multicelled, complex organisms have additional, important roles to play, for example as reserves of combined nitrogen, and the solute accumulated represents a compromise between a compatible osmoregulatory solute and other factors. Arguments about evolution of water stress tolerance and selection of the accumulated solute tend to become circular and will be avoided here, but it is certainly a fruitful area for conjecture.

It is clear that regulation of water activity in response to water stress is a widespread phenomenon. Responses of unicells may provide useful, simple models for further investigations of drought stress phenomena in higher plants.

CHAPTER 7

Nitrogen Fixation

JANET I. SPRENT

I.	Introduction	131
II.	Legumes	132
	A. Resistance of rhizobia to dry soil	132
	B. Infection of roots	132
	C. Nodule development and growth	134
	D. Physiology	136
	E. Biochemistry	140
III.	Lichens	142

I. INTRODUCTION

Evidence is accumulating that nitrogen fixation is more sensitive to stress than the uptake of mineral nitrogen (e.g. Williamson & Diatloff, 1975; Habish & Mahdi, 1976). Despite this, the effects of drought on nitrogen fixation have been rather neglected until the past few years. The literature on higher plants, up to 1975, has been reviewed by Sprent (1976). Since then, more information has become available on the effects of soil moisture on survival of *Rhizobium* spp. in soil, infection of legume root hairs, and on various aspects of nitrogen fixation by lichens. None of the published papers considers the mechanisms of resistance of nitrogen fixing systems to drought *per se*. This chapter will thus include speculations on how resistance is, or may be, achieved in the light of the known effects of drought on nitrogen fixation. Only symbiotic systems will be considered: firstly the legume-*Rhizobium* root nodule system and then the nitrogen-fixing lichens.

131

PHYSIOLOGY AND BIOCHEMISTRY
OF DROUGHT RESISTANCE
IN PLANTS

II. LEGUMES

A. RESISTANCE OF RHIZOBIA TO DRY SOIL

The ability of free-living rhizobia to survive and multiply in soil is clearly a prerequisite for nitrogen fixation. The species of *Rhizobium* are frequently classified on the basis of their ability to grow rapidly, or slowly, on yeast extract media. The fast-growing species, which infect peas, beans (*Vicia* and *Phaseolus* types) and clovers, are less able to survive in dry soils than the slow-growing species, which infect soybeans and lupins. In investigating the reasons for this, Bushby and Marshall (1977) could find no differences in water permeability. However, the slow-growing group retained much less water than the susceptible, fast-growing group at equilibrium in dry soil. It was concluded that the fast-growing species have a greater affinity for water than the slow-growing species, as a result of having more energy available for water absorption. Figure 1 shows the calculated energy available at different vapour pressures for several strains of both fast-growing and slow-growing rhizobia, together with an energy curve for montmorillonite clay, which is above that for either group of rhizobia. It was suggested that (i) the equilibrium internal water content of slow-growing rhizobia in dry soil is sufficiently low to enable them to survive desiccation by having a very low metabolic rate, and (ii) fast-growing rhizobia do not have a sufficiently low equilibrium water content and hence are damaged. This concept of stress resistance, resulting from arrested metabolism and aging at low internal water contents, has also been applied to higher plant cells (Ludlow & Ng, 1974).

B. INFECTION OF ROOTS

The most common method of entry by rhizobia into legume roots is via root hairs (Dart, 1975). Both roots and hairs may be covered by a layer of mucigel having pectic components (Greaves & Darbyshire, 1972) and, in the case of soybean root cell cultures, the production of extracellular, pectinaceous filamentous material was stimulated by compatible rhizobia (Reporter et al., 1975). Fisher and Sprent (unpub.) found an abundant production of elastic, thread-like material when *Trifolium glomeratum* seedlings were grown with *Rhizobium trifolii* on vermiculite. Seedlings grown on agar produced much less of this material, which appeared to assist in the adherence of bacteria to root hairs (Fig. 2). Dudman (1977) suggested that extracellular polysaccharides produced by rhizobia could have a protective function by virtue of their hydrophilic properties. Clearly the interface between rhizobia and root hairs is very complex. Moisture stress may result in greater adhesion between root hairs and sand particles (Sprent, 1975), so it is not unreasonable to suggest that it may also affect the physical relationships between bacteria and root hairs. The ability to produce, and the extent of production of extracellular material by one or both partners, could thus be of significance in drought resistance.

Worrall and Roughley (1976) found no effect of moisture stress on the populations of rhizobia in the rhizosphere of inoculated *Trifolium subterraneum* seedlings and concluded that the effects of stress on infection and nodulation were associated with the physiology of the root hair. A decrease in soil moisture from 5.5 to 3.5% resulted in short, fat root hairs rather than the

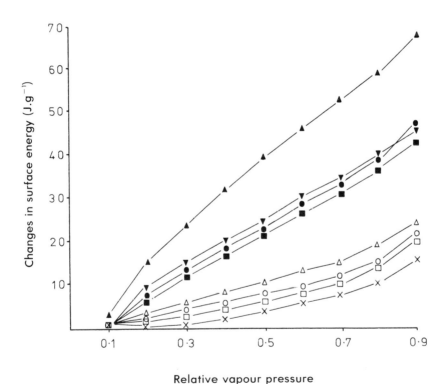

FIG. 1. Changes in surface energy (AΔF).g bacterial dry wt^{-1} or .g Ca-montmorillonite^{-1} with change in relative water vapour pressure. (▲) Ca-montmorillonite; (●) *R. leguminosarum* TA 101; (▼) and (■) *R. trifolii* SU 297/31A (both fast growing species). (△) and (O) *R. lupini* UT 12; (□) *R. japonicum* QA 372 × *R. lupini* UT 2 (all slow growing species). (Reproduced from Bushby and Marshall, 1977, courtesy Cambridge University Press.)

normal long, thin ones. Partially grown hairs resumed growth on rewatering and only normally growing root hairs were capable of being infected with *Rhizobium*. Since the failure to nodulate in dry soil may be a common occurrence (e.g., Habish & Mahdi, 1976), a search for plants which can develop root hairs at low water potentials could be advantageous. This characteristic might also be coupled with a deep rooting habit, an adaptation known in some legumes of arid and semi-arid regions, although such plants are not always found to be naturally well nodulated (e.g. *Trigonella arabica* in Southern Israel: Hely and Ofer, 1972).

C. NODULE DEVELOPMENT AND GROWTH

Following infection by rhizobia, nodules are induced to form in the root cortex. The general pattern appears to be similar in all species studied, but there are differences in detail which may be of significance in drought

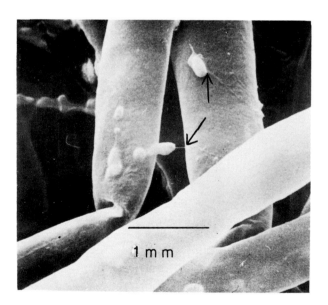

FIG. 2. Scanning electron micrograph of *Trifolium glomeratum* root hairs associated with *R. trifolii*. Note thread-like extracellular products (arrows). × 2340. (Fisher, Sprent and Old, unpublished.)

resistance. These differences relate to root diameter and the position in the cortex (superficial or deep-seated) where meristematic activity begins. Roots of small diameter (about 1 mm or less), as are found in white clover (*Trifolium repens*), and lateral roots of larger-seeded legumes such as *Vicia faba*, have cortices which are only about 6–12 cells wide, whereas young tap roots of *Vicia faba*, for example, are 3–5 mm in diameter and have cortices many cells wide. In *Vicia faba*, nodules arise very close to the endodermis and may not emerge for 2–3 weeks, depending on environmental conditions. Gallacher and Sprent (1978) found that a water-limited environment suppressed the development of *Vicia faba* nodules which had previously been initiated under a plentiful water supply. On return to an adequate water supply, these nodules resumed growth. No corresponding data are available for more superficially formed nodules, but it is possible that nodules of deep-seated origin are better able to resist periods of drought stress.

Nodules fall into two broad groups, indeterminate (sometimes branched) ones, which have a terminal meristem and are usually relatively long-lived (several weeks to perennial), and determinate spherical ones, which have a non-persistent meristem and a relatively short lifespan (a few weeks). *Trifolium* spp. (clover), and *Pisum* (pea) nodules are examples of the first group; *Glycine max* (soybean), *Phaseolus* (bean) and *Vigna unguiculata* (cowpea) are examples of the second. Observations on white clover (*Trifolium repens*, Engin & Sprent, 1973) and *Vicia faba* (Sprent, 1972b) showed that nodules with a persistent meristem can resume growth after relatively severe drought stress, whereas the determinate type (soybean) may be irreversibly damaged by an equivalent stress (Sprent, 1971, 1972a). This resistance may lie in the fact that cells of the meristem are non-vacuolated. Even in susceptible soybean nodules, the last cells to show signs of ultrastructural damage are the non-vacuolated ones. Wahab and Zahran (1979) confirmed these findings and extended them to *Pisum* and *Vigna*.

If nodules of the spherical type are stressed beyond the recovery point, they may wither or be shed; in either case the plant has to produce a new crop of nodules on return to adequate water supplies. This could be an advantage or a disadvantage, depending on the conditions. Renewed root and nodule growth could occur in a different soil layer, which may be less affected by subsequent stress periods. On the other hand, the production of new nodules can put a heavy burden on the plant's resources as has been shown clearly for cowpea during recovery from waterlogging. When the excess water is drained away, so much of the plant's reserves are devoted to nodule production that growth temporarily ceases until the new nodules begin to fix nitrogen (Hong et al., 1977).

D. PHYSIOLOGY

1. Transport into and out of nodules

The requirements of an effective nodule are complex; water is a major one, not only to maintain cell turgidity, but also to transport materials into and out of the nodules. Although much of the water required is obtained directly from the soil, or from the root system via the xylem, a significant amount may arrive with the carbon compounds via the phloem. Minchin and Pate (1973) estimated that of the 0.35 ml water required by pea nodules to export 1 mg of fixed N, almost half may be supplied via the phloem. Thus, any limitation of translocation could affect nodule physiology by reducing essential supplies of both organic compounds and water. Carbon compounds are necessary as recipients of the ammonia produced by nitrogen reduction and also as respiratory substrates in the supply of energy. Efficient gaseous exchange is clearly necessary for respiration as well as nitrogen reduction and, as in any living system, this is inevitably coupled with water loss problems.

Both *Phaseolus* and *Glycine* have determinate nodules, which lack transfer cells. Pate (1976) discussed the problem of making meaningful comparisons between plants whose nodules have transfer cells and those which do not, because of the numerous other differences which also occur. The following proposals, which are amenable to anatomical and physiological experimentation, suggest that the presence or absence of transfer cells may be linked with fundamental differences in the transport systems of determinate and indeterminate nodules. In nodules with apical meristems, growth continues for a considerable time, coupled with the extension of the vascular system which remains discontinuous throughout (Fig. 3A). In a mature determinate nodule, the vascular traces fuse at the apical end (Bieberdorf, 1938; Fraser, 1942). Thus, a closed vascular system is formed which can be considered, at least in cross-section, a branched loop from the stele of the subtending root (Fig. 3B).

In both types of nodule, water may pass through the vascular system along a gradient of water potential established between the multiple sites of junction at which the nodule vascular system joins that of the root. The proportion of the transpirational flow along the root which passes through the nodule will depend on the relative resistances to flow in the root xylem and in the nodule xylem between the sites of entry and egress.

Transpirational flow through the nodule xylem will also be strongly influenced by the direct uptake by, and movement through, the nodule of water from the surrounding soil. The relative importance of this pathway will depend on the amount of moisture in the soil around the nodule, the surface area of the nodule, the permeability of the nodule epidermis, the water potential gradients, and the resistances to flow.

When the soil surrounding the nodule is dry, an intermittent flow of water from the nodule is also possible. During the day, when the plant is transpiring, water will be withdrawn from the nodule and nodule water potential will fall. At night, in the absence of transpiration and with the re-establishment of a water equilibrium in the soil and root system, water will flow back into the nodule and raise the water potential. This model allows flow of a small volume of water once a day, but fluctuations in root pressure or transpiration could result in more frequent intermittent flows.

In each of these possible mechanisms, export via the xylem is mediated by transpirational pull; the evidence considered above is consistent with this. A higher resistance to water movement through the indeterminate nodule could subject the transport system to constraints in both space (within different xylem elements) or time (separation of periods of import and export) or both. These constraints might lead to requirements for (i) a particularly efficient loading-unloading system, necessitating the formation of transfer cells, or (ii) the export of highly soluble products which buffer against fluctuations in the transpiration rate.

At the moment it is not possible to say whether the determinate or indeterminate type of nodule is the more stress resistant. However, it may be of significance that the determinate design is most common in legumes whose origin lies in tropical or sub-tropical regions.

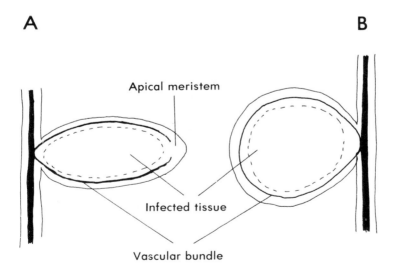

FIG. 3. Discontinuous (A) and continuous (B) vascular systems of indeterminate and determinate spherical nodules respectively.

Pate et al. (1969) reported that *Vicia faba* nodules export asparagine in a highly selective and concentrated manner, near to the limits of its solubility. The key to this efficiency, it was suggested, may lie in the possession of abundant vascular transfer cells. Minchin and Pate (1973), working with *Pisum sativum*, which has nodules generally similar in structure to those of *Vicia faba*, showed that the concentration of nitrogenous materials in nodules was related to the rate of transpiration. When transpiration rates were high, nitrogen compounds were freely transported out of nodules; when they were low, nitrogen compounds accumulated. In a later review, Pate (1976) concluded that nodules normally adjust to wide variations in host plant water balance (transpiration rate) and may also "be able to exhibit even greater adaptability during periods of unusual environmental stress". This adaptability requires the nitrogenous export product from the nodule to be sufficiently soluble for it to remain in solution over wide ranges of concentration. Table I lists the major compounds exported by root nodules, together with their solubilities in water. Asparagine, glutamine and citrulline all fit the solubility criterion and also contain considerable N per unit of C, a factor important for the general carbon economy of the plant. Asparagine is slightly better than glutamine in this respect, but its production incurs the cost of an additional ATP molecule (Scott et al., 1976). Citrulline equals asparagine in its C:N

TABLE I

Properties of some amino acids, amides and ureides exported by root nodules.

Compound	Formula	C:N	Solubility[a] (mol. l^{-1})	Examples of exporting plants
L-asparagine	$COOH.CHNH_2.CH_2.CONH_2$	4:2	0.216(25) 0.125(12.5)	*Lupinus* *Glycine*
L-citrulline	$COOH.CHNH_2(CH_2)_3.NHCONH_2$	6:3	soluble (no value found)	*Albizzia* *Alnus*[b]
L-glutamine	$COOH.CHNH_2(CH_2)_2.CONH_2$	5:2	0.293(25) 0.248(18)	*Pisum* *Coriaria*[b]
allantoin	$OC—CH.NH.CONH_2$ $\quad\ \|\quad\ \|$ $HN—NH$ $\quad\ \backslash\ /$ $\quad\quad C$ $\quad\quad\|$ $\quad\quad O$	4:4	$0.033(20)^c$	*Phaseolus* *Glycine*

[a]Figures in brackets indicate °C at which solubility was calculated. Water is the solvent in all cases.

[b]Nodulated non-legumes.

[c]Largest estimate found.

ratio, and it transports more N per molecule. Citrulline is transported by some tree legumes (such as *Albizzia*) and some non-legumes (such as *Alnus*), but whether it confers any particular advantage is not clear. Its pathway of synthesis in *Alnus* is from ornithine, CO_2 and NH_3, probably using ornithine carbamyl transferase (Gardner & Leaf, 1960), a process which also uses ATP.

Allantoin and allantoic acid are much more economical with respect to carbon than the amides and amino acids but are an order of magnitude less soluble. This could easily impose a transport restriction under conditions of drought stress. These compounds are transported by *Phaseolus* (Pate, 1971) and *Glycine* (Tajima et al., 1977), both of which also transport amides (Antoniw & Sprent, 1978; Pate, 1971). It would be interesting to know whether the balance between the two types of compounds exported varies with drought stress or temperature (the latter itself having major effects on solubility). These aspects are discussed further in Sprent (1980).

2. Photosynthetic supply and nodule respiration

There is much evidence that photosynthetic supplies can limit nodule activity (Hardy & Havelka, 1976). In general, the situation may become much more acute in annual than in perennial species, since the latter tend to have greater reserves of carbohydrate. Soybean appears to be one of the most sensitive species in this regard. Huang et al. (1975a, 1975b) concluded that all of the effects of drought stress on nitrogen fixation in this species could be explained on the basis of reduced carbon fixation, but Tu and Hietkamp (1977) and Sprent and co-workers (e.g. Pankhurst & Sprent, 1975a) considered that direct effects on nodules were also operative. There can be no doubt that sooner or later a reduction in carbon fixation will affect nodule activity. Resistance to short-term drought stress is likely to lie in the storage of photosynthate in the root-nodule system. Even annual species vary considerably in their dependence upon supplies of newly fixed photosynthate, as is evidenced by (i) variations in the extent of diurnal fluctuations in activity, and (ii) variations in the rate at which nodule activity falls off after decapitation or darkening.

Recent work on forage legumes suggests that those generally adapted to dry conditions are likely to show smaller effects of water stress on nitrogen fixation than those less well adapted. For example, the dryland cultivar of *Medicago sativa*, "Tierra de Campos", was able to grow, transpire and fix nitrogen (reduce acetylene) at lower water potentials than the cultivar "Aragon". Recovery from stress was also more rapid in the dryland adapted cultivar (Aparico-Tejo et al., 1980).

Even if a plentiful supply of photosynthate is available, efficient respiratory processes are required in the nodule to generate ATP, reductant and acceptor molecules for the overall process of nitrogen fixation. Sprent (1976) and Pankhurst and Sprent (1975a) discussed the concomitant effects of drought stress on nitrogen fixation and nodule respiration. At least a part of these effects is thought to lie in a drought-increased barrier to oxygen diffusion in nodules. In soybean (Sprent & Gallacher, 1976), but not in *Vicia faba* (Gallacher & Sprent, unpublished), drought stress caused a switch of respiratory pathway to ethanol production.

Another difference between the determinate (soybean) and indeterminate type of nodule (*Vicia*) is that the former has lenticels through which gaseous exchange can take place (Pankhurst & Sprent, 1975b). No such structures have been reported for indeterminate nodules, which may be able to carry out gaseous exchange over all their surfaces (Gallacher & Sprent, 1978). This fact, coupled with a lack of ethanol production and a greater surface to volume ratio of these basically cylindrical structures, appears to offer better prospects for resistance to drought-induced impermeability. Certainly, nodules that were produced on *Vicia* plants under drought stress had the same specific activity (i.e. activity per unit weight of nodule) as those produced under a plentiful water supply (Gallacher & Sprent, 1978). However, they were smaller, with smaller and more dense cells, indicating a degree of adaptation. Cutler et al. (1977) suggested that small cell size may confer drought resistance. Recent evidence derived from soybeans (Criswell et al., 1977) suggested that nodules on intact plants, as opposed to the detached nodules and nodulated root systems principally studied by Sprent and co-workers, might be able to adjust to variations in the supply of oxygen. How this adjustment is effected is not yet clear, but it may enable nodules of the soybean (spherical) type to overcome the drought-imposed barriers to oxygen diffusion.

It is apparent from the above discussions that legume-*Rhizobium* associations have evolved at least two strategies involving basic differences in structure to maximize nitrogen fixation. Non-legume root nodules, which are also sensitive to moisture stress, present yet another set of problems and solutions, since their structure differs from legume nodules in many ways, for example central stele and peripheral infected tissue, different type of endophyte, etc.

E. BIOCHEMISTRY

The actual process of nitrogen reduction takes place in the prokaryotic member of any symbiosis — *Rhizobium* in the case of legume nodules. It requires ATP energy and a supply of low redox potential reductant (about $-430\,mV$).

$$N_2 + 15\,ATP + 6\,e^- + 6\,H^+ + 15\,H_2O \rightarrow 2\,NH_3 + 15\,ADP + 15\,Pi$$

The exact number of ATP molecules consumed is not yet certain. The nitrogenase enzyme has two components, an iron protein and an iron-molybdenum protein. The former reacts with ATP, is reduced by an electron donor such as reduced ferridoxin, and joins with the iron-molybdenum protein binding the nitrogen molecule. Nitrogen reduction is then effected. An aspect of the process which seems inefficient is that a proportion of the electrons flow not to nitrogen, but to H^+, producing hydrogen gas. This diversion occurs after ATP hydrolysis, so that both energy and reducing power are wasted. Schubert and Evans (1976), in studying hydrogen evolution by legume and non-legume root nodules, proposed the term "relative efficiency", defined as

$$1 - \frac{\text{proportion of electrons flowing to } H^+}{\text{total electron flux}}$$

Wide variations in relative efficiency were found, varying from almost one to less than one half. Since then, reports have shown that relative efficiency varies with plant age (Bethlenfalvay & Phillips, 1977), *Rhizobium* strain (Carter et al., 1978), and other factors.

Table II gives data on hydrogen evolution by nodulated root systems of lupins, some of which were drought stressed. It can be seen that drought produced a reversible increase in the rate of hydrogen evolution. It is clearly desirable to minimize the wastage of energy and reducing power, though it is not yet clear whether or not some production of hydrogen is an inevitable consequence of nitrogenase activity. It is known, however, that many nitrogen-fixing organisms, including rhizobia, contain an uptake hydrogenase which can utilize some, or all, of the hydrogen produced by nitrogenase, so that there may be no net hydrogen *evolution* — giving an apparent relative efficiency of one. The report that nodule hydrogenase was located in the *Rhizobium* may explain why relative efficiency varied with the *Rhizobium* strain within a particular host cultivar (Carter et al., 1978). Resistance to hydrogen evolution, therefore, is potentially available by selection or breeding of suitable rhizobia. This would be important, generally, for maximum fixation of nitrogen, but particularly so in a drought situation, because nitrogen fixation is more sensitive to drought stress than the assimilation of combined nitrogen (Williamson & Diatloff, 1975; Minchin & Pate, 1975; Habish & Mahdi, 1976).

TABLE II

Effect of drought stress on hydrogen evolution by nodulated root systems of *Lupinus albus* cv. Neuland. Plants harvested at 60 d when main shoots flowering.[a]

Treatment	H$_2$ evolution[b] (μmol.g dry wt nodule^{-1})
Control	27.96 ± 3.89
Drought stressed for 22 d before sampling	41.01 ± 7.84
Drought stressed for 10 d before sample	50.63 ± 8.40
Drought stressed for 12 d then watered normally for 10 d before sampling	22.42 ± 2.41

[a]Data from Griffiths (unpublished).
[b]Means and standard errors.

III. LICHENS

Lichens colonize a wide variety of habitats, some of which are subject to extremes of moisture content. Many studies have been carried out on the effects of moisture content on lichen photosynthesis (e.g. Harris, 1971; Kershaw, 1972) and it is clear that some species, generally from xeric environments, can photosynthesize at much lower water contents than others. These studies have been principally on two-membered lichens, of which the algal symbiont is a member of the *Chlorophyceae*. In two-membered lichens, which contain a blue-green phycobiont (frequently *Nostoc*), and three-membered lichens, which contain both green and blue-green phycobionts (which may be confined to discrete areas known as cephalodia), the blue-green symbiont fixes nitrogen, and the rate at which it does so is closely related to moisture content (Hitch & Stewart, 1973; Kershaw, 1974; Kershaw & Dzikowski, 1977; and others). (For a general review of nitrogen-fixing lichens see Millbank, 1977.)

Kershaw and Dzikowski (1977) found that the time taken for lichens to recover full nitrogen-fixing activity after drought stress depended on both the length of the drought period and the severity of the stress. Air-dried plants recovered more quickly than those dried in a desiccator over calcium chloride. After 3 d stress (to air dryness), full recovery was achieved 4 h after wetting, and considerable activity was obtained within an hour. It is unlikely that extensive synthesis of new nitrogenase would have occurred in that period, so it must be assumed that the enzyme was not irreversibly damaged. The blue-green symbiont might be protected against excessive desiccation by the fungus, but this seems unlikely in view of the similar drying-wetting responses found by Jones (1977) with free-living blue-green algae in sub-tropical grassland.

The ability of lichens to resume nitrogen fixation rapidly after wetting is considered by Kershaw and co-workers to be a significant feature in their ecology. In an extensive multivariate experiment in which temperature, water content, photon flux density and season of the year were varied, they concluded that, because lichens are frequently dry during the day, a large amount of the nitrogen fixation may take place at night when rehydration occurs. At lower night temperatures, reserves of photosynthate can be utilized to provide energy by respiratory pathways (MacFarlane & Kershaw, 1977; Kershaw et al., 1977). Some interspecific variation in drought sensitivity of *Peltigera* has been found (Kershaw, 1974), but as yet this remains unexplained. In this paper, information was given for the drying cycle, whereas in other papers (Kershaw & Dzikowski, 1977) data was presented for the wetting cycle. The relationship between the percentage of moisture in the thallus and nitrogen-fixing activity in these two cases may not be the same and may depend upon the relative drought sensitivity of associated processes such as respiration.

CHAPTER 8

Nitrate Reductase

S. K. SINHA AND D. J. D. NICHOLAS

I.   Introduction 145
II.   Properties of plant nitrate reductase 146
III. Nitrate reductase, dry matter and yield 148
IV.   Regulation 150
V.   Effect of drought on nitrate reductase 155
VI.   Varietal effects 162
VII. Relative effects of water deficit on nitrate reductase and related enzymes 164
VIII. Evidence for inactivation 165
IX.   Analysis and integration 167
X.   Conclusions 168

I. INTRODUCTION

Water, carbon dioxide and nitrogen, largely in the form of nitrate, are three major inputs in agricultural production. There is almost no human control over the atmospheric carbon dioxide, but the other two inputs are amenable to varying degrees of management. Both water and nitrogen are limiting factors in crop production around the world and limitations in the availability of one can influence utilization of the other. Greenwood (1976) reviewed the topic of nitrogen stress in plants and attempted to develop a method for its quantification. His analysis showed that nitrogen stress was accentuated by water deficit, but that the degree of stress could vary in different plant species. A study of the interaction of water, carbon dioxide and nitrogen in relation to genotypic variability is important, therefore, in developing an understanding of crop productivity in conditions of limited water availability.

Growth and yield are the results of numerous biochemical reactions which are likely to have a high degree of genetic control. Efforts have been made to

PHYSIOLOGY AND BIOCHEMISTRY
OF DROUGHT RESISTANCE
IN PLANTS

understand the biochemical basis of growth and yield in crop plants, with a view to the development of quick, simple and reliable selection criteria (Hageman et al., 1967; Sinha & Khanna, 1975). Among the various biochemical factors limiting growth, Hageman et al. (1967) identified nitrate reductase as a rate-limiting step in nitrate assimilation. Beevers and Hageman (1969) further suggested that nitrate reductase was the logical point to effect regulation of the input of reduced nitrogen by the plant because it is (i) the first enzyme in the pathway; (ii) the rate-limiting step; (iii) substrate-inducible; and (iv) relatively unstable because of its high turnover rate.

The important conclusion that nitrate reductase is the rate-limiting step in nitrate assimilation was based on observations that in conditions influencing growth adversely, such as low light intensity, there was an accumulation of nitrate in the leaves of maize (Hageman et al., 1967). This accumulation of nitrate however, could result from low photosynthetic rates which limited the provision of energy and reducing potential, or from inhibition of the activity of the enzymes associated with the assimilation of nitrate. Since varieties with low nitrate reductase activity accumulated more nitrate, the concept of nitrate reductase as the rate limiting step is reasonable. Additionally, the other enzymes of nitrate assimilation have sufficiently high activity to suggest that they are unlikely to limit the overall response. With this in mind, efforts have been made to determine the relationship between nitrate reductase activity and dry matter production, total reduced nitrogen content, grain protein and yield. It is difficult to establish a cause and effect relationship between growth and nitrate reductase activity, however, although it is generally true that plants showing high growth rates also actively assimilate inorganic nitrogen compounds and often have high nitrate reductase activity.

In water stress, the inhibition of the growth of cells, leaves and the whole plant is accompanied by an accumulation of nitrate in plant tissues, particularly leaves. What then is the relationship between growth and nitrogen assimilation, especially the enzyme nitrate reductase, under such conditions and, in particular, is growth in water-stressed plants inhibited by inadequate assimilation of nitrate?

II. PROPERTIES OF PLANT NITRATE REDUCTASE

The properties of this enzyme have been described in detail by Beevers and Hageman (1969) and Hewitt (1975). These characteristics are reviewed briefly here to serve as a basis for the description of the behaviour of the enzyme during water deficit. Schrader et al. (1968) described this enzyme as a complex molecule which catalysed a three-step electron transfer reaction from NADH to nitrate. The enzyme also utilized reduced flavin mononucleotide as a reductant, had a half-life of about 4 h in maize and could be induced in leaves by light and nitrate. It has also been shown that molybdenum is an integral part of this enzyme (Nicholas & Nason, 1954). The pH optimum is 7.5 with NADH as electron donor, but changes to 6.0–6.25 when NADPH is the electron donor (Jolly et al., 1976). The maximum activity of the enzyme was 250 μmol NO_2^-. g dry wt^{-1}. h^{-1} in the *in vitro* assay; on a protein basis, the maximum activity was between 42 and 36 μmol NO_2^-. mg protein $^{-1}$.h^{-1}. Normally, nitrate reductases from plants utilize NADH only and reports that NADPH may also be a reductant were later shown to be due to a phosphatase converting NADPH to NADH (Hageman & Hucklesby, 1971). In addition, Wray and Filner (1970) showed that barley leaf nitrate reductase also has both NADH-cytochrome *c* reductase and reduced flavin mononucleotide-nitrate reductase activity. Their studies indicated that nitrate induced the development of the activity of all three enzymes. However, NADH-nitrate reductase was more sensitive to p-chloromercuribenzoate than reduced flavin mononucleotide-nitrate reductase activity, and tungstate prevented the activities of NADH-nitrate reductase and reduced flavin mononucleotide-nitrate reductase but caused super-induction of NADH-cytochrome *c* reductase activity. The nitrate reductase enzyme is composed of four cytochrome *c* reductase subunits and a molybdenum cofactor. There is evidence that in both fungi (Nicholas & Nason, 1954; Sorger, 1966; Downey, 1973) and higher plants (Schrader et al., 1968; Wray & Filner, 1970) nitrate reductase is an enzyme complex which can be represented as follows:

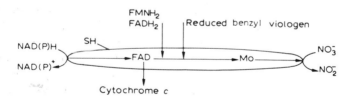

As the activity of nitrate reductase in any assay system is dependent primarily upon the enzyme, the nitrate content and NADH availability, the measured activity could be influenced by variations in any of these. In the *in vitro* assay both nitrate and NADH are in non-limiting quantities, but the extraction procedure and the possible presence of inhibitors and proteases may influence the enzyme (Schrader et al., 1974). Modifications are required to overcome the effects of such interfering factors which may differ for different species and different treatments. For this reason, the *in vitro* method is performed under some limitations and cannot be assumed to represent the physiological performance of the intact plant. It can be argued, however, that this method measures "potential nitrate reductase activity". In contrast, the *in vivo* assay has limitations due to the infiltration of nitrate, the existence of nitrate pools, an anaerobic system, leaching of nitrite, amongst other factors. Despite these limitations, the activity measured *in vivo* is a closer approximation to the physiological activity of the enzyme in the tissue, and we can call it "functional nitrate reductase activity". Since it is likely that one or more factors will be limiting the activity measured by the *in vivo* method, it is not surprising that the *in vivo* assay almost invariably gives a lower estimate than the *in vitro* assay.

It is apparent that the two methods measure different aspects of enzyme activity. Wherever large numbers of samples are to be assessed for "functional nitrate reductase", the *in vivo* assay may be appropriate, whereas the *in vitro* assay will prove more useful in determining the properties of the enzyme and the potential nitrate reductase activity at any given time.

III. NITRATE REDUCTASE, DRY MATTER AND YIELD

If nitrate reductase activity during water deficit is an important determinant of growth, it follows that there should be a close association between these two parameters. Such an association has been claimed for other factors, for instance differences between genotypes (e.g. Deckard et al., 1973; Fig. 1), and it is instructive to examine some of the evidence for this relationship. When growth or yield is compared with nitrate reductase activity per unit plant system (e.g. leaf area), a relationship is frequently found (Abrol & Nair, 1978; Dalling & Loyn, 1977). This relationship, however, may not be close (Dalling & Loyn, 1977) or may not be present at all (Rajagopal et al., 1976; Table I). If growth or yield is compared with total nitrate reductase activity per plant, there is usually a close correlation (Eilrich & Hageman, 1973; Deckard et al., 1973). This is only to be expected as here the correlation is between growth on the one hand, with the resultant product of growth and nitrate reductase activity on a unit basis on the other. The total nitrate reductase activity per plant will be strongly influenced by leaf area, which in turn is dependent on many other factors.

TABLE I

Nitrate reductase activity, biological and grain yield in tall, medium and dwarf wheats.[a]

Variety	Height of main shoot (cm)	Biological yield $(g.m^{-2})$	Grain yield $(g.m^{-2})$	Nitrate reductase activity $(\mu mol.g\ fresh\ wt^{-1}.h^{-1})$
NP 824	101.8	1300	480	4.4
Kalyansona	72.1	1380	560	3.9
Moti	53.5	1190	615	4.6

[a]Data from Sinha (unpublished)

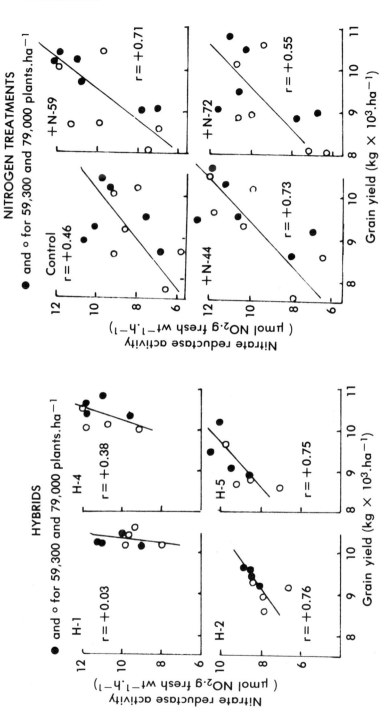

FIG. 1. Relation between nitrate reductase and grain yield in corn (*Zea mays*). (From Deckard et al., 1973.)

Water deficit and revival after a period of stress have marked effects on leaf retention and growth (Begg & Turner, 1976) which will affect the total plant capacity for nitrate reduction. In evaluating the effects of stress on nitrate assimilation we not only have to consider the influence of nitrate reductase activity, but also the variations in leaf area.

IV. REGULATION

Nitrate reductase is regulated both by environmental factors and some endogenous factors, particularly substrates. Amongst the environmental factors, light intensity and spectral distribution, as well as temperature, strongly affect this enzyme (Beevers & Hageman, 1969); in addition, the availability of nitrate and molybdenum controls the synthesis of nitrate reductase. The endogenous concentrations of NADH, amino acids, fructose-1,6-biphosphate, as well as energy charge, influence the activity of this enzyme (Beevers & Hageman, 1969; Sawhney et al., 1978a).

Light plays an important part in the assimilation of nitrate into cell nitrogen compounds in plants. Thus, the enzyme nitrite reductase, which reduces nitrite to ammonia, utilizing reduced ferredoxin as an electron donor, operates in the chloroplasts where light via photosystem I supplies the reducing equivalents. In the absence of light, therefore, nitrite reductase activity is markedly depressed in green leaves (Miflin, 1974). Although nitrate reductase is probably located in the cytoplasm, its activity in green leaves is strictly light-dependent under physiological conditions (Canvin & Atkins, 1974; Atkins & Canvin, 1975).

In isolated leaf discs, however, nitrate is readily reduced to nitrite under anaerobic conditions (Klepper et al., 1971). The results of Sawhney et al. (1978a), as shown in Figures 2 and 3, indicate that the inhibition of electron transfer through the mitochondrial chain to oxygen by anaerobic conditions or by inhibitors triggers off the reduction of nitrate in the dark. It has been proposed that light regulates nitrate reduction in leaves by increasing the cytoplasmic adenylate charge, which on transmission to the mitochondria inhibits the oxidation of NADH via the electron transfer chain to oxygen. Under these conditions, NADH becomes available for the nitrate reductase enzyme located in the cytoplasm (Sawhney et al., 1978a, 1978b). The infiltration of leaf discs of wheat with either ATP or fructose-1,6-biphosphate, resulted in a significant accumulation of nitrite, even in air (see Table II). A smaller stimulation of nitrite accumulation also occurs with ADP, but this could result from the action of adenylate kinase in producing ATP in the leaf discs. Klepper et al. (1971) reported a stimulation of nitrite production in isolated leaf discs by infiltrating with fructose-1,6-biphosphate. They attributed this effect to the production of NADH by glyceraldehyde-3-phosphate

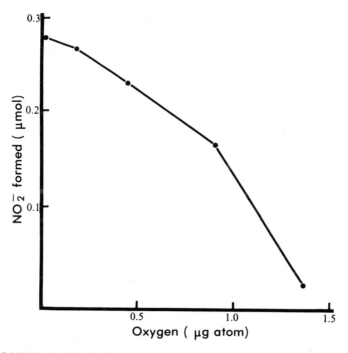

FIG. 2. Inhibition by O_2 of nitrate reduction in intact wheat leaves. (From Sawhney et al., 1978a.)

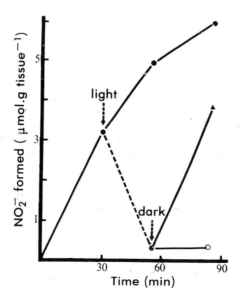

FIG. 3. Reduction of nitrate to nitrite in CO-treated wheat leaves in the dark and its reversal by light. (From Sawhney et al., 1978a.)

dehydrogenase during glycolysis. Sawhney et al. (1978a, 1978b), however, found that when leaf discs were infiltrated with arsenate (which inhibits ATP formation in this enzyme system without affecting the production of NADH), the stimulatory effect of fructose-1,6-biphosphate on nitrate reduction was abolished (see Table III). They concluded that the ATP produced in this reaction stimulates nitrate reduction in air.

Evidence has been obtained that NADH generated via the tricarboxylic acid cycle is primarily involved in nitrate reduction (Sawhney et al., 1978b). Succinate was also found to accumulate in wheat leaves during anaerobic nitrate reduction in the dark, presumably because the respiratory chain was not functioning with oxygen as a receptor (Sawhney et al., 1979). These findings were in the main substantiated by Canvin and Woo (1979) who

TABLE II
Effects of adenine nucleotides and fructose-1, 6-diphosphate on nitrate reduction by wheat leaves in the dark. 300 mg of 0.5 cm diameter leaf discs prepared from leaves of wheat seedlings placed in test tubes and infiltrated with 1.0 ml of either distilled water (control) or with the listed concentrations of the neutralized solutions of metabolites. The tubes were then placed in the dark at 30° C without shaking and after 45 min the nitrite produced was determined.[a]

Additions to infiltration media	Concentration (mM)	Nitrate reduction (μmol NO_2^- . g tissue^{-1}.h^{-1})
None (control)	—	0.70
ATP	5	2.12
ADP	5	1.80
AMP	5	0.72
Fructose-1,6-diphosphate	10	1.46

[a]From Sawhney et al. (1978a).

TABLE III
Effects of arsenate on nitrate reduction in leaf discs of wheat in the presence of fructose-1, 6-diphosphate. Leaf discs (300 mg), placed in Thunberg tubes, were infiltrated with 1 ml of either 10 mM phosphate buffer (pH 7.5) or phosphate buffer containing fructose-1,6-diphosphate (6 mM) and/or arsenate (20 mM). After the final evacuation some tubes were incubated under anaerobic conditions and others in air, all in the dark. Nitrite produced was determined after 30 min at 30°C.[a]

Experimental conditions	Nitrate reduction (μmol NO_2^- . g tissue^{-1}.h^{-1})
Anaerobic	3.60
Anaerobic + arsenate	3.30
Aerobic	0.18
Aerobic + fructose-1,6-diphosphate	0.96
Aerobic + fructose-1,6-diphosphate + arsenate	0.12

[a]From Sawhney et al. (1978a).

proposed that NADH generated outside the mitochondria was used for nitrate reduction in the dark in the absence of air.

Light appears also to control the induced synthesis of nitrate reductase (Hageman & Flesher, 1960; Travis et al., 1970; Travis & Key, 1971; Sawhney & Naik, 1972), although it has been suggested that light is concerned in the maintenance of enzyme activity rather than synthesis (Klepper et al., 1971). It has been proposed that phytochrome is involved in the synthesis of nitrate reductase (Jones & Sheard, 1972), although Nasrulhaq-Boyce and Jones (1977) were unable to confirm this effect.

The regulation of nitrate reductase by nitrate ions and molybdenum is well documented but various aspects of nitrate control need to be considered. The gross nitrate content of the tissue may not in itself regulate enzyme activity due to compartmentation within the cell. It is also known that the nitrate flux to the tissues is important in control.

Many experiments have been done on the effects of heat and moisture stress on the nitrate reductase activity of plants. Thus, Mattas and Pauli (1965) reported that the activity of this enzyme in *Zea mays* decreased sharply with short exposures to stress before changes in water status became evident. Decreased enzyme activity was reflected in accumulation of nitrate. Moisture stress increased the incorporation of reduced nitrogen (soluble non-protein) into non-soluble forms much faster than to soluble protein products. Huffaker et al. (1970) established that water removal decreased nitrate reductase activity at the same time that water potential decreased in the first leaves of barley. Up to 58% of the nitrate reductase activity was lost during the 4 d water stress period. Nitrite reductase activity, however, increased slightly. Bardzik et al. (1971) found that nitrate reductase activity in maize seedlings was decreased markedly with water deficits of 10–20%, but an increase to 50% did not result in an inactive enzyme because a new steady state was reached at around 35%. Partial to complete recovery of enzyme activity occurred 24 h after rehydration of the stressed plants. It was proposed that the level of enzyme activity is a consequence of an equilibrium between the rates of synthesis and degradation and that progressive tissue dehydration reduces both the enzyme synthesis and the enzyme-inactivating systems. Morilla et al. (1973) concluded that nitrate reductase activity was affected primarily by a decrease in the rate of enzyme synthesis in *Zea mays* at low leaf water potentials.

In maize seedlings supplied with adequate water the extractable nitrate reductase is regulated more by the nitrate flux from the roots to shoots than by the nitrate content of the leaves (Shaner & Boyer, 1976a, 1976b). They also concluded that the inhibition of nitrate reductase at low water potential was not controlled by a direct effect of water potential on protein synthesis, nor by alterations in the leaf nitrate content, but rather by a decrease in the nitrate flux that, in turn, regulated the synthesis of the enzyme. In an analysis of factors involved in the *in vitro* stabilization of nitrate reductase in cotton cotyledons, Tischler et al. (1978) showed that an imposition of water stress led to a significant reduction in nitrate reductase activity, but no change in the *in vitro* lability of the enzyme.

Casein hydrolysate and 11 amino acids added individually repressed the synthesis of nitrate reductase in tobacco cell suspensions (Filner, 1966), but arginine and lysine counteracted the repressive action of any of the other amino acids. Proline supplied to an excised shoot stimulated the activity of nitrate reductase within 1 h, both in the light and darkness, in several plant tissues (Fig. 4). Since the leaf was fully turgid in this case, proline may have been oxidized (Boggess et al., 1976), enhancing the availability of NADH which, in turn, stimulated enzyme activity. Although this may indicate that some amino acids regulate nitrate reductase activity through their own metabolism, further work is necessary to establish whether this occurs in intact plants.

An inhibitor of nitrate reductase inactivating system has been identified in the root tips of maize and rice and in suspension culture cells of rice (Kadam

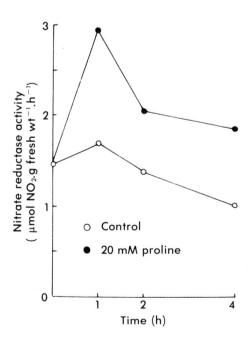

FIG. 4. Effect of 20 mM proline on the stimulation of nitrate reductase activity in wheat. (From Sinha and Rajagopol, unpublished.)

et al., 1974; Wallace, 1974; Yamaya & Ohira, 1976). Nitrate reductase activity precipitated between 0–40% saturation of ammonium sulphate and the inactivating factor precipitated between 40–60% saturation of the salt; the molecular weight of the inactivating protein was found to be 44,000. Wallace (1974) suggested that the NADPH-cytochrome c reductase component of nitrate reductase was the primary site of action of the inactivating enzyme, because there was a much smaller effect on reduced flavin adenine dinucleotide-nitrate reductase activity. Kadam et al. (1974) showed that the inhibitor restricted the activity of nitrate reductase from leaves when either NADH or reduced flavin mononucleotide was used as an electron donor, and its action on the enzyme could be counteracted by NADH.

Shannon and Wallace (1979) isolated a proteinase from maize roots, which had a molecular weight of 54,000 and, based on inhibitor studies, a serine group was identified at its active site. This enzyme readily degraded nitrate reductase prepared from maize roots. In a second group of proteases they identified a macromolecular component which inactivated nitrate reductase, but, unlike the previous proteinase, it was not inhibited by phenylmethylsulphonyl fluoride (a serine inhibitor). However, it was affected by metal chelating agents. The function of these inactivating enzymes *in vivo* is uncertain and it is difficult therefore to assess their physiological significance.

V. EFFECT OF DROUGHT ON NITRATE REDUCTASE

Hanway and Englehorn (1958) provided evidence that nitrate accumulation in plants is due to several factors, among which drought was possibly the most important. In irrigated crops, nitrate accumulation did not occur unless nitrogen application was excessive. In earlier reports it had been shown that accumulated nitrate in various plants could be responsible for nitrate poisoning of stock (Mayo, 1895; see Mattas & Pauli, 1965). This was the concern that prompted the initial investigation of the problem of drought effects on nitrate reductase (Mattas & Pauli, 1965; Younis et al., 1965). Nitrate reductase was also considered important in relation to nitrogen metabolism and plant growth. Hageman and Flesher (1960) and Hageman et al. (1961) demonstrated that light intensity and nitrate availability had a strong effect on this enzyme such that nitrate accumulated in corn grown at low light intensities. The studies of Mattas and Pauli (1965) and Younis et al. (1965) aimed at examining the relationship between nitrate reductase activity and nitrogen metabolism, particularly the free amino acid pool and tissue protein content, under conditions of drought and high temperature. Water stress was achieved by withholding water and the water status of the plants was determined by measurements of water content and relative turgidity. The growth of the seedlings declined on the 4th day of stress when relative turgidity had dropped to 77%. The rate of increase in total nitrogen per plant also fell after the 3rd day and thereafter remained low (Mattas & Pauli, 1965). During these experiments, the nitrate content of the plant increased throughout and nitrate reductase activity declined, even on the 1st day when the relative turgidity had fallen by barely 2%. On the 2nd day of stress, enzyme activity fell to about 25% of the activity on the first day (Fig. 5). In this same period the molybdenum content of the plant increased. It was clear from this investigation that nitrate reductase was extremely sensitive to water stress and was inhibited more rapidly than nitrate uptake. In this experiment, however, the effects of drought and temperature could not be separated.

Younis et al. (1965) attempted to separate the effects of temperature, water stress and light. Increasing the growth temperature of plants from 25/20 to 35/30 caused only a 28% decrease in nitrate content but decreased nitrate reductase activity by 49%. Water stress decreased nitrate content by a maximum of 25%, but nitrate reductase activity was reduced by 48–63% over the range of temperature combinations tested. A high temperature decreased enzyme activity and this effect was accentuated by moisture stress. These studies did not elucidate the reason for the loss of activity, although it appeared to be one of the earliest effects of water stress.

The effects of a mild water stress, ranging from -0.2 to -0.4 MPa leaf water potential, on the activity of nitrate reductase, nitrite reductase, phosphoenolpyruvate carboxylase, ribulose-1,5-biphosphate carboxylase, nitrate content and protein content of barley were examined by Huffaker et al. (1970), who also studied the recovery of these systems following irrigation. Some of these data are presented in Table IV, which demonstrates that nitrate reductase was affected more adversely than was nitrite reductase. Again, the concentration of nitrate in the leaf tissues was less affected than the nitrate reductase activity was. The activities of the two photosynthetic enzymes, phosphoenolpyruvate carboxylase and ribulose-1,5-bisphosphate carboxylase, were also considerably less sensitive to water stress than nitrate reductase. Moreover, the decrease in protein content was also relatively less than the loss of nitrate reductase. In an attempt to interpret the physiological significance of the inhibition of nitrate reductase during water stress, Huffaker et al. (1970) emphasized the importance of the sequence of events in relation to water stress. If processes such as cell division and expansion are the first to be influenced, and reduced growth is the consequence of these events, it then follows that protein requirements of cells would be reduced. Accordingly, the response of nitrate reductase should be considered from this point of view.

In studying the effects of water stress on the activity of various enzymes, Bardzik et al. (1971) chose nitrate reductase, phenylalanine ammonia lyase and

NADH-oxidase. The first two of these enzymes are known to have a relatively short half-life. A water deficit of 10–20% caused 50% reduction in the activities of nitrate reductase and phenylalanine ammonia lyase, but NADH-oxidase activity was unaffected or showed a slight increase. Even at 50% water deficit, however, the nitrate reductase activity was not reduced to zero; activity reached a steady state and when plants were watered there was complete recovery in 24 h. It was postulated that nitrate reductase and phenylalanine ammonia lyase activity, at any given time, is the result of a balance between synthesis and decay. Other studies have shown that the polyribosome level is reduced and protein synthesis is inhibited by water stress (Hsiao, 1970), and this net loss of enzyme activity could be the result of reduced synthesis coupled with enzyme inactivation. However, Bardzik et al. (1971) further suggested that, after a certain degree of water stress,

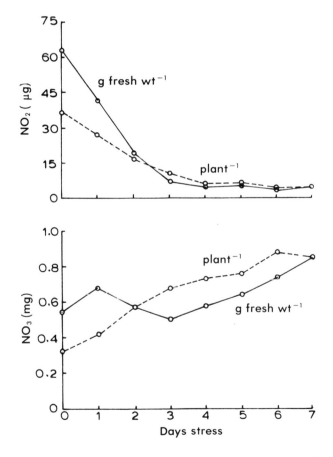

FIG. 5. Changes in nitrate reductase activity (upper) and nitrate content (lower) of corn (*Zea mays*) during heat and moisture stress. (From Mattas and Pauli, 1965.)

TABLE IV

Influence of water stress on nitrate content and nitrate assimilating and carboxylating enzymes in barley.[a]

Time after water with-holding (d)	Treatment	NO_3^- (μg.g fresh wt^{-1})	Nitrate reductase (μmol NO$_2^-$. g fresh wt^{-1}.h^{-1})	Nitrite reductase (μmol NO$_2^-$. g fresh wt^{-1}.h^{-1})	PEP carboxylase (μmol. g fresh wt^{-1}.min^{-1})	RuBP carboxylase (μmol CO$_2$.g fresh wt^{-1}.min^{-1})
2	Control	7,200	15.36	5.33	0.18	2.43
	Stressed	5,700	12.21	5.27	0.16	2.32
	% decrease	20.0	20.5	1.0	8.5	4.5
3	Control	7,500	16.50	10.60	0.21	2.26
	Stressed	5,900	8.24	7.69	0.16	2.38
	% decrease	20.6	50.0	27.50	21.0	0.0
4	Control	7,800	21.55	6.92	0.21	2.62
	Stressed	5,900	9.25	5.76	0.15	2.33
	% decrease	24.6	57.5	17.6	28.0	11.0
5	Control	7,800	16.30		0.21	
	Stressed and rewatered	6,300	16.20		0.19	
	% recovery	18.6	99.4		89.14	

[a]From Huffaker et al. (1970).

even the inactivating system is also inactivated, leading to a steady state. As a further possibility, Bardzik et al. (1971) postulated that the response was due to the existence of two species of nitrate reductase with different behaviour, but this idea has not been supported by subsequent work.

An important aspect of this study was that it demonstrated differential responses of enzymes to water deficit, which could lead to marked effects on metabolism. For instance, the relative stability of NADH-oxidase during water stress could maintain the oxidation of NADH and change the balance of NAD/NADH in the tissue.

Morilla et al. (1973) attempted to relate changes in nitrate reductase to polyribosome content of the tissue since the latter reflects protein synthesis capacity and is decreased by water stress (Hsiao, 1970). Leaf nitrate content and nitrate reductase activity were unrelated in their experiments. It was suggested that the reduction in protein synthesis consequent upon the low level of polyribosomes was responsible for the reduced nitrate reductase activity (Fig. 6). It is questionable whether such a direct relationship between polyribosome content and the activity of a specific enzyme could be supported on the basis of limited data and with the known effects of water stress on several other enzymes. Two further observations from their results are worth mentioning: nitrate reductase activity stabilized after a period of stress, as noted by Bardzik et al. (1971), and the *in vitro* enzyme activity was characterized by a longer half-life in preparations from water-stressed plants compared with those from the controls. This suggests that the enzyme from stressed plants had acquired some property which made it less labile or that the inactivating systems were less pronounced.

In contrast to these suggestions that nitrate reductase activity is reduced in water stress as a consequence of injury to the synthetic system, Shaner and Boyer (1976a, 1976b) suggested that nitrate reductase activity in maize was regulated by nitrate flux which was reduced in water-stressed plants, leading to a lowering of enzyme activity. Various methods were used to reduce transpiration to show that the synthesis of the enzyme was regulated by the consequent change in nitrate flux. Nitrate flux was determined by exposing the root system to pressure to obtain a sample of the transpiration stream. Such a method can be criticized as it might inject ions into the roots that would not be expected in a natural system. Earlier studies had demonstrated that nitrate, as well as total nitrogen, increased per plant as water deficit progressed, whereas a sharp decline was observed in nitrate reductase activity (Mattas & Pauli, 1965). A continuous increase in nitrate content and total nitrogen per plant indicate that the nitrate flux was maintained, although the enzyme activity declined. The experiments of Shaner and Boyer (1976b) are limited by the assumption that nitrate reductase activity could be influenced only by the availability of nitrate or protein synthesis. The fact that both nitrate reduction and protein synthesis involve energy requirements was not considered. Furthermore, in sunflower, when 10μM abscisic acid was applied through the transpiration stream, the leaves had a high stomatal resistance and leaf water potential, with a consequent reduction in transpiration rate and nitrate flux, but this treatment had almost no effect on nitrate reductase activity. It appears, therefore, that the loss of nitrate reductase activity during water stress may, in certain circumstances, flow from a reduction in nitrate flux. A more direct effect of water potential through the impairment of NADH formation has been proposed by Sinha, Aggarwal and Chaturvedi (unpublished).

The response of nitrate reductase to water stress and salt stress was studied by Balusubramanian et al. (1974) to determine the stability of this enzyme in various crops. In the first place, nitrate reductases from wheat, barley, *Brassica* and safflower were found to have a longer half-life than the enzyme of other plant species. In the absence of both nitrate and light, the

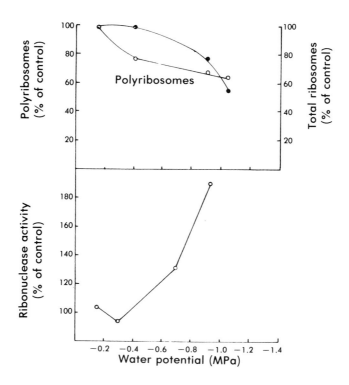

FIG. 6. Effect of decreasing water potential on polyribosomes and RNase activity in maize. (From Morilla et al., 1973.)

half-life ranged from 32.8 h to 66.6 h at 20°C. In barley, a detailed investigation showed that the enzyme in the flag leaf was most susceptible to water stress at the time of anthesis (Fig. 7). A method of comparing flag leaf sensitivity at different stages of growth was developed and designated the sensitivity index. The sensitivity index (SI) was calculated from the following formula:

$$SI = \frac{NRm - NRs}{NRm} \times 100$$

where NRm is the maximum nitrate reductase activity of the sample and NRs is nitrate reductase activity under water stress. Enzyme activity was susceptible to both salt and water stress. *Brassica* and safflower, which are considered relatively more tolerant to water stress than wheat or barley in

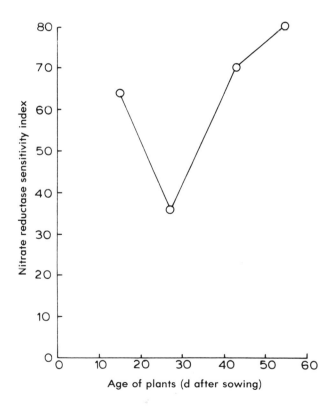

FIG. 7. Sensitivity of nitrate reductase to water deficit at different stages of growth in barley. (From Balasubramanian et al., 1974.)

conditions of dryland agriculture, showed the maximum loss of enzyme activity, although some activity could always be detected. An interesting observation was that enzyme activity increased in some varieties of wheat and barley when the leaves were transferred to a nitrate-free medium. This was subsequently followed by a sharp fall in enzyme activity. In most instances the initial increase was prevented by both salt stress and water stress. This initial rise in activity indicates a mobilization of nitrate from a reserve pool to the metabolic pool, which was prevented by stress in all varieties of wheat except Kalyansona, which is a relatively good yielding variety in dryland conditions. Similarly, most sorghum genotypes and barley cultivars under stress conditions appeared to have the ability to mobilize nitrate from a reserve pool to the metabolic pool.

The response of nitrate reductase to water stress over a 24 h cycle was studied in wheat, along with relative water content, nitrate and leaf proline content. All the variables showed changes over the 24 h cycle, the changes in leaf nitrate content following the changes in relative water content. Moreover, the proline content in the unirrigated plants was maximal when the relative water content was lowest, which coincided with reduced nitrate reductase activity (Rajagopal et al., 1977).

Since proline accumulation is one of the major changes in the nitrogen metabolism of water-stressed plants, the relationship between nitrate reductase and proline accumulation was examined in several crop species (Sinha & Rajagopal, unpublished). There was a sharp decline in enzyme activity in response to water stress in wheat, barley, sorghum, maize, *Brassica* and safflower, and a rapid and considerable simultaneous accumulation of proline in all these species (the values for safflower are presented in Figure 8). Thus it is possible that these two responses are linked. In barley and wheat, when proline was fed to plants stressed with polyethylene glycol, the loss of nitrate reductase activity was reduced (Sinha & Rajagopal, 1975). This suggests that exogenous and, possibly, endogenous proline protects the enzyme from inactivation during water stress. This possibility can only be explored with plant materials which differ in rates of proline accumulation.

VI. VARIETAL EFFECTS

The response of the nitrate reductase activity to water stress for 8 varieties of barley known to accumulate different amounts of proline was studied by Sinha (unpublished). The response was examined at three temperature combinations, and a higher enzyme activity was found in all varieties at 20°/20° than at either 25°/20° or 30°/20°. The decrease in enzyme activity at the highest temperature was considerable. Nitrate reductase activity was decreased within 6 h of imposing water stress and it declined ultimately to about 30% of the initial and control values. In no case did the enzyme activity disappear completely in spite of a

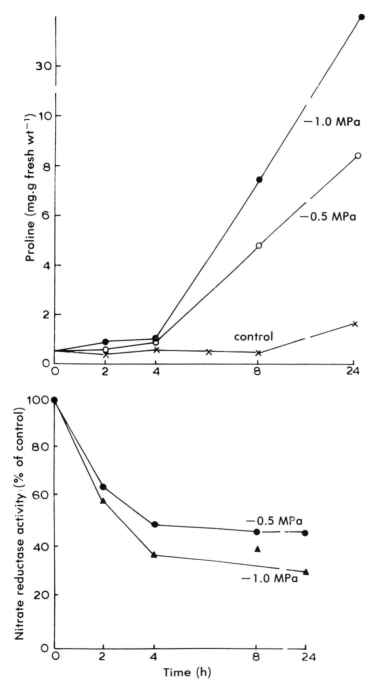

FIG. 8. Effect of −0.5 and −1.0 MPa polyethylene glycol on proline accumulation (upper) and nitrate reductase activity (lower) in safflower. (From Sinha and Rajagopol, unpublished.)

30–40% decrease in relative water content. Similar results were obtained with 4 different varieties of wheat (Sinha, Paleg, Aspinall & Sawhney, unpublished).

Temperature effects on nitrate reductase have also been studied with sorghum and maize (Maranville & Sullivan, 1976; Pal et al., 1976). In maize Pal et al. (1976) considered that the observed effects of high temperature were due to drought because the latter is associated with the former. This assumption is not universal, as water stress develops in several regions of the world when temperatures are low, particularly in temperate crops such as wheat and barley. Pal et al. (1976) concluded that, "While studies involving the use of biochemical selection criteria may provide a better understanding of the complexities of heat [drought] tolerance, pragmatically the difference in plant growth in response to temperature [drought] stress may be the simplest and best selection criterion available." If this conclusion is correct for selection for heat or drought resistance, there is no valid reason why it should not also be so for non-stress conditions. If this is correct, all efforts to seek biochemical selection criteria would appear irrelevant. Pal et al. (1976) were led to this conclusion by the fact that nitrate reductase activity response was not closely correlated with heat tolerance in their studies. Alternatively, the authors' contention that the stability of the enzyme should be related to tolerance may not be correct — this point will be discussed later.

Maranville and Sullivan (1976) have established distinct classes of drought tolerance in sorghum, ranging from tolerant to susceptible types. When they tested the effect of temperature and drought on a range of these genotypes, they observed that the most tolerant types lost nitrate reductase activity to the maximum extent.

VII. RELATIVE EFFECTS OF WATER DEFICIT ON NITRATE REDUCTASE AND RELATED ENZYMES

The loss of nitrate reductase activity in response to water stress is well established (e.g. Anikiev & Kuramagometov, 1975), but the effect of water stress on other enzymes of this pathway is less well understood. In barley, wheat, radish and cucumber, nitrite reductase and glutamine synthetase activities were less affected by drought or high temperature than nitrate reductase activity (Sinha, unpublished). The activities of these two enzymes were always relatively several fold higher than that of nitrate reductase and, when the latter activity was reduced to 30% of the control value by water stress, the activity of nitrite reductase and glutamine synthetase was reduced to only 70%. The results obtained with cucumber nitrate reductase and glutamine synthetase are given in Figure 9. There were clear varietal differences in these responses which were unrelated to drought tolerance (Sinha, unpublished).

These studies demonstrate that all the enzymes of a reaction sequence are not necessarily influenced in the same way and to the same extent by a particular stress. In this case the first enzyme of the reaction sequence is affected most and apparently functions as a regulatory point.

VIII. EVIDENCE FOR INACTIVATION

The sensitivity of nitrate reductase activity to water deficit may be due to a variety of factors, including a possible inactivation of the enzyme (see above). If the enzyme is inactivated by water stress, it may also be possible to reactivate the enzyme in conditions which preclude the synthesis of fresh enzyme. In three varieties of barley, the enzyme activity was reduced in water-stressed plants to about 30% of the control (Table V). When an extract from both

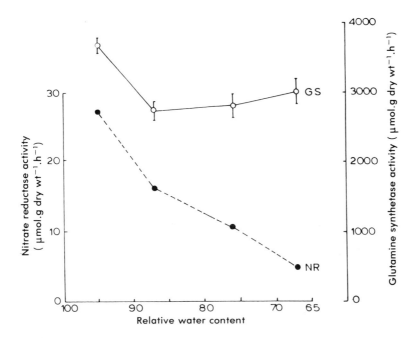

FIG. 9. Effect of water stress on nitrate reductase and glutamine synthetase in cucumber. (From Sinha, unpublished.)

control and water-stressed plants was incubated for an hour with NADH at 4°C before assay, there was almost complete recovery of activity in the extracts from stressed plants to the level found in control plants. There was no increase in the extracts of control plants (Table VI). Activation and inactivation of nitrate reductase in rice by NADH has been reported (Gandhi et al., 1973), and NADH also overcame the effect of a protein inhibitory system (Kadam et al., 1974). In contrast, in *Chorella*, nitrate reductase was inactivated by NADH (Solomonson et al., 1973). In *Aspergillus nidulans*, NADH provided protection from the inactivation of the enzyme (Dunn-Coleman & Pateman, 1975).

If inactivation of nitrate reductase by water deficit and its activation by NADH following relief of stress are possibilities, then it should be feasible to demonstrate this effect *in vivo*. The substantial recovery of nitrate reductase activity, initially reduced by water stress, has been observed in a number of circumstances in which protein synthesis was unlikely, that is in irrigation of plants maintained in darkness (Table VII), in plants in the light maintained on

TABLE V

Effect of water stress on nitrate reductase activity in barley. Reaction mixture contained 0.1 ml of 1 M KNO_3, 0.1 ml of NADH (0.8 μmol), 0.2 ml enzyme extract and 0.6 ml 0.1 M phosphate buffer pH 7.4, incubated at 30°C for 30 min.[a]

Genotype	Treatment	Nitrate reductase activity (μmol NO_2^-.g dry wt^{-1}.h^{-1})	% of control
Arrivat	Control	137.2	—
	Stress	32.1	23
Bankuti Korai	Control	152.8	—
	Stress	48.0	31
Proctor	Control	66.0	—
	Stress	24.6	37

[a]Data from Sinha (unpublished).

TABLE VI

Activation of nitrate reductase from control and water-stressed plants of barley cv. Bankuti Korai. Reaction mixture and incubation as described for Table V.[a]

Treatment		Nitrate reductase activity (μmol NO_2^-.g dry wt^{-1}.h^{-1})	% of control
1.	Control	157.5	—
2.	Control + NADH[b]	180.0	114
3.	Stressed	81.0	51
4.	Stressed + NADH[b]	175.5	111

[a]From Sinha (unpublished).
[b]Treatments 2 and 4 were pre-incubated with NADH for 1 h at 4°C.

a nitrate-free medium, in plants irrigated in the presence of tungstate (an inhibitor of enzyme synthesis), or in plants treated with cycloheximide (Sinha, unpublished data). Though each of these experimental conditions was chosen to minimize possible *de novo* enzyme synthesis, a complete inhibition of synthesis may not have been achieved. The substantial increase in enzyme activity obtained supports the possibility of a regulation of nitrate reductase through the availability of NADH in water-stressed plants, as well as through effects on enzyme synthesis and degradation.

TABLE VII

Effect of water stress and rewatering on nitrate reductase under non-inducible conditions in barley cv. Bankuti Korai. Control and stressed plants were transferred to dark and irrigated and samples for enzyme assay were obtained 8 h later. Reaction was carried out as for Table V.[a]

	Nitrate reductase activity (μmol NO_2^-.g dry $wt^{-1}.h^{-1}$)	% of control
Control	109.3	—
Stressed	31.2	28
Control (8 h dark)	100.6	—
Stressed (8 h dark)	52.5	52

[a]Data from Sinha (unpublished).

IX. ANALYSIS AND INTEGRATION

The evidence available on the responses of nitrate reductase during water deficit and other environmental perturbation indicate that this enzyme functions as a regulatory point in the assimilation of nitrate. The main problem concerning the regulation of this enzyme in water stress is unanswered. Several means of control have been suggested and many are feasible. Thus, the enzyme may be regulated through (i) the availability of nitrate, (ii) an inhibition of protein synthesis consequent upon the reduction in polyribosome level during stress and the inherent high turnover rate of the enzyme, or (iii) a reduction in the availability of NADH through effects on photosynthesis or respiration.

The most likely explanation of the reduction in nitrate reductase activity during water deficit would seem to be that changes in redox potential and energy charge govern the responses of the enzyme. This regulation may be through inactivation or degradation of existing enzyme molecules or inhibition of further synthesis. In consideration of the normal fluctuations of the environment, particularly with respect to diurnal changes, there would seem to be a selective advantage in a rapid recovery of nitrate reductase activity following the advent of rain, even if it occurs in the dark. If there was considerable loss of enzyme through degradation or inhibition of synthesis, the recovery of enzyme activity would be delayed and such a system could not have a metabolic adaptive advantage. Although the inhibition of enzyme synthesis and reduction in enzyme activity during stress are questioned, the retention of some enzyme activity during stress suggests that nitrate reductase is preserved, probably through inactivation. It may be that changes in energy charge consequent upon stress are responsible for regulating the synthesis of the enzyme, whereas changes in the redox potential regulate activation/inactivation of the enzyme. Dehydration has been suggested as a mechanism of enzyme inactivation (Levitt, 1962, 1969), but nitrate reductase activity is reduced at a deficit of -0.2 to -0.4 MPa which would not be a level of dehydration leading directly to the dehydrogenation of macromolecules. Macromolecule dehydrogenation may start at this water potential range through changes in the redox potential, as well as in the $NAD^+/NADH$ or $NADP^+/NADPH$ ratio.

X. CONCLUSIONS

Nitrate reductase is the first enzyme in a sequence of reactions leading to the assimilation of nitrate into amino acids and thence into cell-nitrogen compounds. Thus, it is a suitable system for investigating regulatory mechanisms which are influenced by environmental factors. The present evidence indicates that the activity of this enzyme could be related to reduced nitrogen accumulation and possibly reduced dry matter production during stress, with certain limitations. Although growth is suspended or proceeds at a low rate in water-stressed plants, the primary cause for this appears to be the change in turgor potential. In the absence of active growth, it appears logical to conclude that inhibition or loss of nitrate reductase activity is a regulatory measure which has evolved with the selective advantage of conserving energy when photosynthesis is impaired. The regulation of this enzyme, or any other, could be by inactivation/activation, inhibition of synthesis, degradation, or change of specificity; but since the enzyme is not lost completely, and regulation through inactivation is known to occur, control through the inhibition of synthesis and degradation is not the sole regulation.

There is a considerable body of information concerning the relation between nitrate reductase activity, growth and nitrogen accumulation in normal conditions of water availability. Even here, the data are not unequivocal and several interpretations are possible. There is, however, an almost total lack of definitive information for water-stressed plants. Nonetheless, it would appear reasonable to presume that a cultivar with high nitrate reductase activity shortly after revival from water stress would have an advantage, as it would be able to reduce nitrate more rapidly to support renewed protein synthesis. It is highly likely that the conservation of energy is an essential requirement for survival during stress, so that a rapid loss of nitrate reductase activity would be a metabolic advantage. In fact, definitive experiments have yet to be performed to determine the magnitude of nitrate assimilation during water stress.

CHAPTER 9

Betaines

R. G. WYN JONES AND R. STOREY

I.	Introduction	172
	A. Definitions and nomenclature	172
	B. Naturally occurring betaines	175
II.	Phytotaxonomic distribution of betaines	176
	A. Glycinebetaine	176
	B. Prolinebetaine and hydroxyprolinebetaines	176
	C. β-alaninebetaine	187
	D. Trigonelline and homarine	187
	E. Other betaines	188
	F. Related ammonio compounds	188
	G. Related sulphonio compounds	189
III.	Tissue distribution of betaines	190
	A. Vegetative tissues	190
	B. Non-vegetative tissues	190
IV.	Biosynthetic pathways	191
	A. Glycinebetaine	191
	B. Prolinebetaine	193
	C. β-alaninebetaine	193
V.	Accumulation of betaines in stressed tissues	194
	A. Glycinebetaine	194
	B. Comparison of glycinebetaine and proline accumulation and consumption	196
	C. β-alaninebetaine and prolinebetaine	198
VI.	Possible physiological functions	200
	A. Glycinebetaine as a cytoplasmic osmoticum	200
	B. Other aspects of the physiological chemistry of glycinebetaine	202
	C. Possible function of β-alaninebetaine	203
VII.	Concluding discussion	204

171

PHYSIOLOGY AND BIOCHEMISTRY
OF DROUGHT RESISTANCE
IN PLANTS

I. INTRODUCTION

A. DEFINITIONS AND NOMENCLATURE

In 1953 Wheeland defined *onium* compounds as "substances formed by an addition reaction, in the course of which some atom increases its valency by one unit and in doing so increases its formal charge, algebraically, by one unit". This definition encompasses a very broad group of compounds of which quaternary ammonium and tertiary sulphonium compounds with fixed positive charges on, respectively, the nitrogen and sulphur atoms are probably the more important biologically. These are widely, but apparently erratically, distributed in nature. Cantoni (1960) noted their greater abundance and diversity in marine invertebrates, fish and certain plants compared with micro-organisms and vertebrates. Nevertheless, specific onium compounds, such as acetylcholine, have a fundamental role in vertebrate biochemistry.

In this chapter our major concern will be *ammonio* compounds (the preferred chemical term), particularly that class of fully N-methyl substituted amino acids to which the trivial name *betaines* is applied. Some attention will also be directed to closely related compounds, for example choline-O-sulphate, and to *sulphonio* analogues of the betaines. In plant biochemistry there is some interest in phosphonium compounds in view of their role as plant growth regulators (Cathey, 1964), but they lie outside the scope of this chapter.

The trivial nomenclature in this field is in great disarray and, with the increasing interest in the physiology and biochemistry of these compounds, the establishment of a clear and agreed system assumes some importance. We will adopt the convention of naming individual betaines by reference to their parent amino acid (e.g. N,N'-dimethylproline, often referred to as stachydrine, will be called prolinebetaine by analogy with the well-established practice of calling N,N',N"-trimethylglycine glycinebetaine). A number of betaines found in plants, together with their trivial names, are recorded in Table I. This system of naming will not be applied to the "betaines" produced by the methylation of the ring nitrogen of pyridine as there is no root amino acid; thus the name trigonelline will be retained (Table I). We feel it is important that the use of "betaine" to describe glycinebetaine be discontinued, despite our own use of the term in early papers and its recent use by others (Hall et al., 1978; Hanson & Nelson, 1978). Using the same term for a class of compounds and for a particular member of that class can only lead to confusion. The term, *thetin*, for methyl-substituted sulphonio compounds will be dispensed with as it is not (as used by Challenger, 1959) formally analogous with "betaine"; the recognized chemical terminology, sulphonium (sulphonio), will be employed.

TABLE I

Names and structures of major betaines.

Structures	Preferred trivial names	Other trivial names
	Glycinebetaine	Oxyneurin, Betaine
	β-alaninebetaine	Homobetaine
	2-trimethylamino-6-ketoheptanoate	
	Prolinebetaine	Stachydrine
	Proline	
	(−)4-hydroxyprolinebetaine	Betonicine
	(+)4-hydroxyprolinebetaine	Turicine

Table I continued

Names and Structures of major betaines.

Structures	Preferred trivial names	Other trivial names
	3-hydroxyprolinebetaine	3-oxystachydrine
	Histidinebetaine	Herzynine Ercinine
	Tryptophanbetaine	Hypaphorine
	2-mercaptohistidine- betaine	Ergothioneine
	Pipecolatebetaine	Homostachydrine
	Trigonelline	

B. NATURALLY OCCURRING BETAINES

Of the wide variety of betaines found in plants, glycinebetaine was the first to be isolated and has been subjected to the closest scrutiny. The compound was first isolated by Husemann and Marme in 1863 from the arid zone shrub, *Lycium barbarum,* and was named lycin (see Karrer, 1958). Happily, this and other names found in the early literature (e.g. oxyneurin, glykokollbetaine) have been abandoned. At the turn of the century, the extensive studies of Schulze and Stanek and their colleagues (see Guggenheim, 1958, for references) established that glycinebetaine was found in high concentrations in some plants, particularly *Atriplex* spp. and sugar beet. During this period prolinebetaine and trigonelline were also characterized, as were most of the more obscure betaines noted in Table I. β-alaninebetaine, however, was characterized relatively recently. Interest in sulphonio compounds developed rather later, and the work is described in Challenger's classic book (1959) on organic sulphur chemistry.

Despite the early activity of the German school of natural product organic chemists, little biochemical interest developed in these compounds apart from the recognition of the role of some N-methyl and S-methyl compounds in l-carbon metabolism and methyl donation (Cantoni, 1960). Only recently has an hypothesis been formulated to account for the large quantities of betaines, particularly glycinebetaine, found in certain plants (Storey & Wyn Jones, 1975; Wyn Jones et al., 1977a, 1977b). Glycinebetaine is proposed to be a major cytoplasmic osmoticum in certain higher plant families adapted to salt or water stress. It may be that other betaines and, possibly, methyl sulphonio compounds have a similar function in other species, but in all cases inadequate evidence is available.

In this chapter we will summarize data on the taxonomic and tissue distribution of betaines and will consider their biochemistry and physiology in relation to water and salt stress. It is inevitable that the major emphasis will be on glycinebetaine as less is known about the other compounds. And it is of particular interest to consider whether glycinebetaine accumulation is a positive adaptation to stress or an incidental side reaction. There is extensive literature on betaines and related compounds in invertebrates and, to a lesser extent, marine algae, besides the work of Avi-Dor and his colleagues on a moderately halophilic bacterium.

II. PHYTOTAXONOMIC DISTRIBUTION OF BETAINES

A. GLYCINEBETAINE

Glycinebetaine is structurally the simplest of the betaines; its dipolar structure is given in Table I. Proline is also included in Table I to illustrate the structural similarities of some of the compounds under discussion. As far as is known, glycinebetaine is always present as the free dipole, but this is not the case for some of the other betaines, notably β-alaninebetaine.

In Table II data on the taxonomic distribution of glycinebetaine and some of the other betaines are summarized. Glycinebetaine is widely distributed and often occurs in very large quantities. The data suggest that there is a taxonomic basis to glycinebetaine distribution and almost certainly to its accumulation as a major metabolite. Much more work will be required to establish this firmly and to define which families and species have this capacity.

There are indications in Table II that glycinebetaine accumulation is associated with halophytic and, possibly, xerophytic characteristics and arid and salty habitats. There is, however, a certain distortion inherent in these data. Because glycinebetaine was found in halophytic species, there has been a tendency to concentrate the various surveys on saline and dry habitats, and relatively few glycophytes and mesophytes have been studied. Not all xerophytic or halophytic species accumulate glycinebetaine or other betaines under field conditions, and no salt-sensitive or drought-sensitive plant with a low sap osmotic pressure has been found to accumulate one of these compounds.

Glycinebetaine has also been found in considerable concentrations in the tissues (usually muscle) of marine invertebrates (Beers, 1967; Schoffeniels & Gilles, 1972), in fungi (Ardreeva, 1971), in some marine algae (Takemota & Sai, 1964), and in bacteria (Rafaeli-Eshkol & Avi-Dor, 1968).

B. PROLINEBETAINE AND HYDROXYPROLINEBETAINES

Much attention is focused in this volume on the physiology and biochemistry of proline accumulation in plants subject to water stress. Consequently, it is of particular interest that the betaines of proline and of 3- and 4-hydroxyproline occur in plants (see Table I for nomenclature and structures; see Table II for phytochemical distribution). Of these compounds, prolinebetaine itself appears the most common and is a characteristic product

TABLE II
Distribution of betaines in higher plants

Genus and species	Tissue	DICOTYLEDONS[a]				Assay method and reference
		Division I Lignosae (fundamentally woody)				
		Osmotic potential (10^5 Pa)	Name	Onium compound μmol. g dry wt^{-1} or (.g fresh wt^{-1})	Ecology or habitat of collected species	
Order Capparales						
FAMILY CAPPARACEAE						
36 species	leaves		pb OH-pb	present in 33 species		4 G
Capparis tomentosa	seeds		pb		arid zone	4,5 V
Order Euphorbiales						
FAMILY EUPHORBIACEAE						
Euphorbia paralias	leaves	−8.6	trig		coastal sand dune	1 A
Order Leguminales						
FAMILY LEGUMINOSAE						
Acacia brachybotrya	shoots	−27.0	ND		arid sandy	2 B
Acacia hakeoides	leaves	−22.5	ND		arid sandy	2 B
Acacia lineata	shoots		ND		arid sandy	2 B
Acacia stenophylla	shoots	−24.4			saline	2 B
Acacia triptera	shoots	−25.3	ND		arid sandy	2 B
Cassia artemisioides	shoots	−21.2	trig		arid sandy	2 B
Medicago sativa	shoots	−21.0	pb	(25)	grown in 200 mmol NaCl	1 Z
Phaseolus vulgaris	shoots	−11.3	trig	5	grown in 75 mmol NaCl	1 C,D
Pisum sativum	shoots	−18.2	trig	5	grown in 100 mmol NaCl	1 C,D
Trifolium repens	shoots	−11.3	trig	trace	grown in 75 mmol NaCl	1 C,D
Vicia faba	etiolated shoots		gb	125		3 H

Table II continued

Genus and species	Tissue	Osmotic potential (10^5 Pa)	Name	Onium compound μmol. g dry wt^{-1} or (.g fresh wt^{-1})	Ecology or habitat of collected species	Assay method and reference
Order Malvales						
FAMILY MALVACEAE						
Abutilon albescens	leaves	−1.6	gb		arid coral island	2 D
Abutilon otocarpum	leaves	−36.1	gb		halophyte	2 B
Lavatera plebeja	shoots	−19.8	D+	213	arid sandy	2 B
Order Myrtales						
FAMILY MYRTACEAE						
Melaleuca uncinata	shoots	−25.0	D+		arid sandy	2 B
Order Sapindales						
FAMILY SAPINDACEAE						
Dodonaea attenuata	shoots	−23.9	ND		saline	2 B
Heterodendron oleifolium	shoots	−20.2	trig		arid sandy	2 B
Order Verbenales						
FAMILY VERBENACEAE						
Avicennia marina	leaves	−33.8	gb	265	intertidal mangrove	2 B
DICOTYLEDONS						
Division II Herbaceae (fundamentally herbaceous)						
Order Asterales						
FAMILY ASTERACEAE (Composite)						
Aster tripolium	shoots	−24.9	gb	164	salt marsh	1 A
	shoots		gb,(P)	(29)	coastal	W
Centaurea melitensis	shoots	−15.4	ND		arid sandy	2 B
Chondrilla juncea	shoots	−14.4	ND		arid sandy	2 B
Erigeron bonariensis	shoots	−19.2	gb	68	salt marsh	2 B

Helichrysum apiculatum	shoots	−16.4	ND		arid sandy	2 B
Ixiolaena leptolepis	shoots	−27.2	ND		arid saline	2 B
Matricaria maritima	shoots	−6.4	gb,D+	55	coastal sand dune	i A
Minuria leptophylla	shoots	−50.6	gb	175	halophyte	2 B
Myriocephalus stuartii	shcoots	−10.0	ND		arid sandy	2 B
Pluchea lanceolata			gb		hot regions of India	4 I
Senecio spathulatus	shoots	−15.3	pb		coastal sand dune	2 F
Sonchus oleraceus	shoots	−21.2	ND		dry saline	2 B
Vittadinia cuneata	shoots	−17.2	gb	42	arid sandy	2 B
Waitzia acuminata	shoots	−15.9	ND		dry saline	2 B
Wedelia biflora	leaves	−9.3	dsp		dry coral island	2 E
Order Brassicales						
FAMILY CRUCIFERAE						
Cakile maritima	shoots	−14.9	ND		sand dune	1 A
Cochlearia officinalis	shoots		gb,(P)	trace	coastal	W
Raphanus sativa	shoots		ND		grown in 100 mmol NaCl	2 D
Order Caryphyllales						
FAMILY AIZOACEAE						
Mesembryanthemum crystallinum	shoots	−38.3	ND			2 Z
Psilocaulon (Haw) Schwautes	shoots		2 D+		200 mmol NaCl	2 B
Tetragonia expansa	tops		ND		saline	5 J
FAMILY CAROPHYLLACEAE						
Spergularia marina	shoots		gb,(P)	trace	coastal	W
Spergularia media	shoots		gb,(P)	trace	coastal	W
Order Chenopodiales						
FAMILY CHENOPODIACEAE						
Arthrocnemum halocnemoides	shoots	−59.1	gb	280	halophyte	2 B
Atriplex canescens	leaves		gb	279	halophyte	3 H
	leaves		gb	323	halophyte	5 J
Atriplex halimus	leaves		gb	418	halophyte	3 H
Atriplex hastata	shoots	−18.1	gb	75	halophyte	2 B

Table II continued

Atriplex hortensis	shoots	gb	−34.7	84-107		3 H
Atriplex inflata	leaves	gb	−37.7	223	halophyte	2 B
Atriplex nummularia	leaves	gb		152	halophyte	2 B
Atriplex patula	leaves	gb	−40.2	112-225	halophyte	3 H
Atriplex pseudocampanulata	shoots	gb		236	halophyte	2 B
Atriplex rosea	shoots	gb	−35.6	94		5 J
Atriplex semibaccata	shoots	gb		249	halophyte	2 B
Atriplex spongiosa	leaves	gb	−34.7	340	halophyte — grown in 500 mmol NaCl	2 C,D
Atriplex suberecta	leaves	gb	−13.9	260	saline	2 B
Atriplex vesicaria	shoots	gb	−62.0	251	halophyte	2 B
Atriplex wootinii	leaves	gb		284		5 J
Babbagia acroptera	shoots	gb	−43.6	187	halophyte	2 B
Bassia brachyptera	shoots	gb	−43.2	179	halophyte	2 B
Bassia intricarta	shoots	gb	−48.1	214	halophyte	2 B
Bassia lanicuspus	shoots	gb	−31.2	272	halophyte	2 B
Bassia parviflora	shoots	gb	−27.1	169	halophyte	2 B
Bassia patenticuspis	shoots	gb	−31.3	168	halophyte	2 B
Bassia quinquecuspis	shoots	gb	−32.0	171	halophyte	2 B
Bassia stelligera	shoots	gb	−22.3	193	arid saline	2 B
Bassia tricuspis	shoots	gb	−51.9	205	halophyte	2 B
Beta cycla	leaves	gb		287		5 J
Beta maritima	leaves	gb		195	salt marsh	5 J
Beta trigyna	leaves	gb		179		5 J
Beta vulgaris	leaves	gb		223	salt resistant	5 J
Chenopodium album	leaves	gb		104		5 J
Chenopodium bonus-henricus	leaves	gb		190		3 H
Chenopodium botrys	leaves	gb		129		4 K
Chenopodium foetidum	whole plant	gb		123	sea-shore	5 J
Chenopodium nitrariaceum	shoots	gb	−32.9	173	halophyte	5 J
Chenopodium pseudomicrophyllum	shoots	gb		92	halophyte	2 B
Chenopodium urbicum	shoots	gb	−33.4	37	halophyte	2 B

Species	Part	δ¹³C		No.	Habitat	Ref.
Chenopodium vulvaria	leaves		gb	158		3 H
Corispermum marschellic	whole plant		gb	97		5 J
Corispermum tamnoides	shoots		gb	12		5 J
Enchylaena tomentosa	shoots	−31.0	gb	35	halophyte	5 J
Hablitzia tamnoides	shoots		gb	216		2 B
Halimone portulacoides	whole plant	−20.5	gb	85	frost resistant salt marsh	5 J
Kochia trichophylla	whole plant		gb	238		1 A
Kochia scoparia	whole plant		gb	81		5 J
Maireana sp.	shoots	−28.8	gb	189	halophyte	5 J
Maireana appressa	shoots	−39.4	gb	323	halophyte	2 B
Maireana pyramidata	shoots	−31.8	gb	269	halophyte	2 B
Malacocera tricorne	shoots	−42.7	gb	278	halophyte	2 B
Orbione sibirica	shoots		gb	36	salt marsh	2 B
Pachycornia tenuis	shoots	−59.2	gb	153	halophyte	5 J
Rhagodia spinescens	shoots	−32.3	gb	533	halophyte	2 B
Salicornia quinqueflora	shoots	−30.7	gb	152	halophyte	2 B
Salicornia fructicosa	shoots		gb	181	wet saline	2 B
Salicornia europaea	shoots		gb	174	wet saline	4 L
Salsola kali	shoots		gb	(45)	coastal	W
Salsola kali, tetrandra longifolia and rigida	shoots		gb	81	coastal dunes	5 J
			d	present in all 4		4 M
Spinacia oleracea	leaves		gb	23		3 H
Suaeda maritima	leaves		gb	162	salt resistant	5 J
	shoots		gb	(63)	salt resistant	2 W.X
Suaeda monoica	leaves	−53.1	gb	340	wet saline	2 C.D
Threlkeldia salsuginosa	shoots	−29.7	gb	203	halophyte	2 B
FAMILY AMARANTHACEAE						
Achyranthes aspera	whole plant		gb	22		6 N
Achyranthes aspera	shoots	−7.0	gb			2 E
Amaranthus caudatus	leaves		gb	46	dry coral island	3 H
Amaranthus caudatus	leaves		gb	186		5 J
Amaranthus retroflexus	whole plant		gb	82		5 J

Table II continued

Order Lamiales						
FAMILY LABIATAE						
Ajuga australis	shoots	−14.1	ND		arid sandy	2 B
Eremostachys speciosa			pb	25		O
Lamium album			pb	140		3,4 P
Lagochilus hirtus			pb	57		O
Lagochilus inebrians			pb	36		O
Lagochilus platycalyx			pb	101		O
Lagochilus pubescens			pb	50		O
Lagochilus setulosus			pb	91		O
Leonurus turkestanicus			pb	105		O
Marrubium vulgare			OH-pb	19		6 Q
Marrubium vulgare	shoots	−18.4	D+		arid sandy	2 B
Sideritis montana			pb	57		O
Stachys betonicaeflora			pb	52		O
Stachys hissarica			pb	33		O
FAMILY MYOPORACEAE						
Eremophila mitchelli	shoots	−19.3	D+		arid sandy	2 B
Order Polygonales						
FAMILY POLYGONACEAE						
Muehlenbeckia cunninghamii	shoots	−22.1	trig		arid saline	2 B
Polygonum aviculare	shoots		ND			5 J
Polygonum divaricatum	shoots		ND			5 J
Order Plantaganales						
FAMILY PLANTAGINACEAE						
Plantago coronopus	shoots		ND		coastal	W
Plantago maritima	shoots		ND		coastal	1 A,W
Order Primulales						
FAMILY PLUMBAGINACEAE						
Armeria maritima	shoots	−19.8	β-ab,(P)		salt marsh	1 A,Y

Genus and species	Tissue	Osmotic potential (10^5 Pa)	Onium compound Name	Onium compound μmol. g dry wt^{-1} or (.g fresh wt^{-1})	Ecology or habitat of collected species	Assay method and reference
Limonium vulgare	shoots	−24.7	β-ab,(P)		salt marsh	1 A
Limonium vulgare	shoots		β-ab,(P),tmkh	50	halophyte	4,6 R,S
Plumbago capensis			ND			Y
FAMILY PRIMULACEAE						
Glaux maritima	shoots		gb,(P)	trace	coastal	W
Order Solanales						
FAMILY CONVOLVULACEAE						
Evolvulus alsinoides	whole plant		gb			4,6 T
FAMILY SOLANACEAE						
Cestrum parqui	leaves	−13.3	D+		arid sandy	2 B
Lycium barbarum	whole plant		gb	333		5 J
Lycium chinense	leaves		gb	166		3 H
Lycium ferocissimum	leaves	−24.5	gb	150	saline	2 B
Lycopersicon esculentum	leaves		trig	0.5	100 mmol NaCl	1 C,D
Nicotiana velutina	leaves	−15.3	ND		saline	2 B
Solanum esuriale	shoots	−16.1	trig		arid sandy	2 B
Order Umbellales						
FAMILY UMBELLIFERAE						
Daucus carota	shoots	−18.1	ND		100 mmol NaCl	1 D
Eryngium maritimum	shoots		ND		coastal	W

MONOCOTYLEDONS

Genus and species	Tissue	Osmotic potential (10^5 Pa)	Onium compound Name	Onium compound μmol. g dry wt^{-1} or (.g fresh wt^{-1})	Ecology or habitat of collected species	Assay method and reference
Order Graminales						
FAMILY GRAMINEAE						
Festuceae (Tribe)						
Festuca rubra	shoots		gb,(P)	(19)	coastal	W
Puccinellia distans	shoots		gb,(P)	trace	coastal	W

Table II continued

Puccinellia maritima	young leaves	−22.7	gb,(P)	2.6	salt marsh	1 A,W
Agrosteae						
Agrostis stolonifera	shoots		gb,(P)	(15)	coastal	W
Ammophila arenaria	shoots	−8.1	gb	113,(70)	coastal dunes	1 A,W
Hordeae						
Agropyron junceiforme	shoots		gb	(23)	coastal	W
Agropyron pungens	shoots		gb	(80)	coastal	W
Triticum vulgare	shoots	−18.1	gb	64	grown in 100 mmol NaCl	1 D
Elymus arenaria	shoots		gb	(77)	coastal	W
Hordeum vulgare	shoots	−15 − 17	gb	30 – 80	grown in 150 mmol NaCl	1 D
Aveneae						
Avena sativa	shoots	−17	gb	18	grown in 100 mmol NaCl	1 D
Danthonia caespitosa	shoots	−27	gb		saline	2 B
Chlorideae						
Chloris acicularis	shoots	−37	gb	85	halophyte	2 B
Chloris gayana	shoots		gb	4	grown in 150 mmol NaCl	1 D
Spartina anglica	shoots		gb,dsp,(P)	(120)	coastal	W
Spartina townsendii	shoots	−25	gb,dsp,(P)	258	salt marsh	1 A
Eragrosteae						
Diplachne fusca	shoots	−8.5	gb	40	saline gravel	1 U
Leptureae						
Lepturus repens	shoots		gb		arid coral island	2 E
Sporoboleae						
Sporobolus virginicus	shoots	−20	gb	101	salt marsh	2 B
Paniceae						
Spinifex hirsutus	shoots	−12	gb		coastal sand dune	2 F
Maydeae						
Zea mays	shoots	−13	gb	7	grown in 100 mmol NaCl	1 D
Zoysieae						
Zoysia macrantha	shoots	−15.5	gb	26	salt marsh	2 B
Uncertain						

Species	Tissue	δ	Code		Habitat	Class
Amphipogon caricinus	shoots	−22	gb		saline	2 B
Stenotaphrum secundatum	shoots	−13	gb	75	salt marsh	2 B
Triodia irritans	shoots	−28	gb	61	arid	2 B
Order Liliales						
FAMILY LILIACEAE						
Asphodelus fistulosus	shoots	−14.5	ND		saline	2 B
Dianélla révoluta	shoots	−14	trig		arid sandy	2 B
Order Cyperales						
FAMILY CYPERACEAE						
Carex arenaria	shoots		ND		coastal	W
Scirpus maritimus	shcots		ND		coastal	W
Order Juncales						
FAMILY JUNCACEAE						
Juncus gerardii	shoots		ND		coastal	W
Juncus maritimus	shoots		ND		coastal	W
Order Aponogetonales						
FAMILY ZOSTERACEAE						
Zostera marina	shoots	−26	ND,(P)			2 Z
Order Juncaginales						
FAMILY JUNCAGINACEAE						
Triglochin maritima	shoots	−23	ND,(P)		salt marsh	1 A,W
Posidonia sp	leaves	−26	dsp			2 Z

[a]Classification according to Hutchinson (1973).

Table II continued

Abbreviations

1.	Thin layer photodensitometry	A.	Storey et al. (1977)
2.	Thin layer chromatography and periodide colorimetry	B.	Storey (unpublished data)
3.	Ammonium reineckate or phosphotungstic acid precipitation	C.	Storey (1976)
4.	Chromatography and melting point determination	D.	Storey and Wyn Jones (1977)
5.	Periodide precipitation	E.	Pitman and Storey (unpublished data)
6.	Spectroscopy e.g. UV, IR, NMR or Mass	F.	Condon and Storey (unpublished data)
ND	Not detectable	G.	Delaveau et al. (1973)
gb	Glycinebetaine	H.	Cromwell and Rennie (1953)
trig	Trigonelline	I.	Dasgupta et al. (1968)
D+	Unknown Dragendorff positive	J.	Stanek and Domin (1909)
βab	β-alaninebetaine	K.	Rustembekova et al. (1973)
pb	Prolinebetaine	L.	Susplugas et al. (1969)
OH-pb	Hydroxyprolinebetaine	M.	Karawja et al. (1971)
dsp	Dimethylsulphoniopropionate	N.	Kapoor and Singh (1966).
(P)	Significant proline levels found ($>$15 μmol. g fresh wt^{-1})	O.	Pulatova (1969)
tmkh	2-trimethylamino-6-ketoheptanoate	P.	Proskurnina and Utkin (1960)
		Q.	Paudler and Wagner (1963)
		R.	Larher and Hamelin (1975a)
		S.	Larher and Hamelin (1975b)
		T.	Baveja and Singla (1969)
		U.	Sandhu et al. (1981)
		V.	Cornforth and Henry (1952)
		W.	Stewart et al. (1979)
		X.	Flowers and Hall (1978)
		Y.	Larher (1976)
		Z.	Wyn Jones unpublished data

of at least two families, the Labiatae and the Capparaceae. The hydroxyp-rolinebetaines are also found in these families. Prolinebetaine has also been reported in *Chrysanthemum* (Compositae), various *Citrus* (Rutaceae) and alfalfa *(Medicago sativa,* Leguminosae) (see Guggenheim, 1958, for early references). It is difficult with the evidence available to associate the prolinebetaine-accumulating families with particular ecological habitats. Some members of the Capparidaceae, for example *Capparis* spp., are found in hot arid regions (Walter, 1971) and indeed, Cornforth and Henry (1952) originally investigated *Capparis tomentosa* because of its reputed toxicity to camels! However, this cannot be said for the Labiatae, many of which, for example *Stachys* spp., occur in temperate countries.

The distribution of quaternary ammonium compounds in the Cap-paridaceae (Capparaceae), 39 species from 20 genera, have been studied by McLean (1976), who found prolinebetaine and/or hydroxyprolinebetaine in all but 4 genera. Surprisingly, while 12 genera contained choline salts 5 contained 3-hydroxy-1,1-dimethyl pyrrolidinium salts. Trace quantities of glycinebetaine were found in some species.

C. β-ALANINEBETAINE

Although β-alaninebetaine was originally identified by Engeland (1909), it was only detected in plants in 1973, in the marine alga *Monostroma nitidium* (Abe & Kaneda, 1973). More recently it has been found in a higher plant, *Limonium vulgare* (Larher & Hamelin, 1975a). In this plant β-alaninebetaine is a major nitrogenous component and may exceed $100\,\mu$mol.g dry wt^{-1} (Larher, 1976). A second ammonio compound has been found in *Limonium vulgare* — 2-trimethylamino-6-ketoheptanoate (Table I) (Larher & Hamelin, 1975b). This compound was quantitatively far less important than β-alaninebetaine and occurred exclusively as the choline ester. Larher and Hamelin also reported that, in part, β-alaninebetaine occurs *in vivo* as the choline ester. As such, it would not be dipolar but would be a polycation with fixed positive charges at either end of the carbon ester chain.

So far only xerohalophytic members of the Plumbaginaceae have been reported to accumulate β-alaninebetaine. However, it remains to be seen if this rather specific distribution in higher plants is confirmed.

D. TRIGONELLINE AND HOMARINE

In a study of more than 100 plant species Klein et al. (1931) found trigonelline to be widely distributed in many families, including the Leguminosae, Solanaceae, Cruciferae, Compositae and the Gramineae. In many cases it occurs in the presence of a second, quantitatively more important betaine. However, unlike glycinebetaine, it is not accumulated to high levels in vegetative tissues, although Blaim (1962) found concentrations of greater than 80 μmol.g dry wt^{-1} in the seeds of a number of legumes. The isomer homarine has not been reported in higher plants, although it has been found quite widely in marine invertebrates, particularly the Crustaceae (Beers, 1967).

E. OTHER BETAINES

Tryptophanbetaine (Table I) has been found in the seeds of *Erythrina hypathorus* (Leguminosae), while histidinebetaine has been isolated from the fungi *Agaricus campestris* and *Boletus edulis* (for references see Guggenheim, 1958). Other betaine-like derivatives such as 2-mercaptohistidinebetaine, usually called ergothionein, have been found in fungi (Table I). This is similar to the simpler alkaloids and, indeed, in some texts the betaines are considered as alkaloids. These compounds, including histidinebetaine, etc., have also been reported in marine invertebrates (Ackerman & List, 1958).

F. RELATED AMMONIO COMPOUNDS

Choline, the alcohol related to glycinebetaine, is ubiquitously found in plants (Klein & Zeller, 1930; Toyosawa & Nishimoto, 1967; Storey & Wyn Jones, 1977) because of its role as a precursor of the major membrane constituent, phosphatidylcholine (lecithin). The sulphate and phosphate esters of choline have also been found (Table III). Tolbert and Wiebe (1955) identified choline-O-phosphate as a major phosphatic compound in the sap of tomato and barley, possibly involved in phosphate transport. Later, Nissen and Benson (1961) found that choline-O-sulphate accounted for 5–15% of labelled sulphate in *Zea mays, Hordeum vulgare* and *Helianthus annuus*. More relevant is the observation by Benson and Atkinson (1968) that, of the salt-secreting mangroves, *Avicennia* and *Aegialitis* spp. formed choline-O-sulphate, while *Aegiceras corniculatum* and *Acanthus ilicifolius* formed choline-O-phosphate in large quantities. They suggested that these compounds could be involved in salt transport.

Trimethylamine has been found in flowers, and Cromwell (1950) observed that the surface glands on the stems, leaves and perianth of *Chenopodium vulvaria* produced this amine, which probably arose from choline degradation. The trimethylamine oxide is widely found in fish and marine invertebrates (Prosser, 1973) and is important as an osmoticum.

Structurally related to these compounds is the plant growth regulator chlorocholine chloride (Table III). Various reports have suggested that its application increases the salt (El Damaty et al., 1964) and drought (Halevy & Kessler, 1963; Larter et al., 1965) tolerance of plants, but these have been disputed (cf. Robertson & Greenway, 1973; Imbamba, 1973).

G. RELATED SULPHONIO COMPOUNDS

The sulphonio analogues appear to be less common and less various than their ammonio counterparts; nevertheless, they have rather similar distributions. Challenger and Simpson (1948) isolated β-dimethylsulphoniopropionate from a marine alga and later (see Challenger, 1959) found that this compound occurs quite widely in marine algae, for example, *Polysiphonia* spp., *Enteromorpha* spp., and *Ulva lactuca*. It has also been reported in two fresh water species, *Oedogonium* sp. and *Ulothrix* sp., (Challenger, 1959). Recently it has been reported in a higher plant, *Spartina* sp. (Larher et al., 1977), and we have also found sulphonio compounds in large quantities in a

TABLE III
Name and structures of some methylated sulphonio and other related compounds.

Structures	Trivial names
CH_3—$\overset{+}{S}$—CH_2—CH_2—$C(\!=\!O)$—O^- (with CH_3)	β-dimethylsulphoniopropionate (β-dimethylpropiothetin)
CH_3—$\overset{+}{S}$—CH_2—CH_2—CH_2—CH_2—$C(\!=\!O)$—O^- (with CH_3)	δ-dimethylsulphoniopentanoate
CH_3—$\overset{+}{N}$—CH_2—CH_2—O—$\overset{O}{\underset{O^-}{S}}$=O (with CH_3, CH_3)	Choline-O-sulphate
CH_3—$\overset{+}{N}$—CH_2—CH_2—O—$\overset{O}{\underset{O^-}{P}}$—OH (with CH_3, CH_3)	Choline-O-phosphate (Phosphoryl choline)
CH_3—$\overset{+}{N}$—CH_2—CH_2Cl (with CH_3, CH_3)	Chlorocholine chloride CCC. Cycocel

marine angiosperm, *Posidonia* sp. (Wyn Jones & Hughes, unpublished data) and in *Wedelia biflora* (Gorham & Storey, unpublished data). Other, more complex sulphonio compounds occur in higher plants (the reader is referred to Challenger's book). In addition, Larher and Hamelin (1979) have isolated 5-dimethylsulphoniopentanoate from the flowers of *Diplotaxis tenuifolia* (Cruciferae).

III. TISSUE DISTRIBUTION OF BETAINES

A. VEGETATIVE TISSUES

Only in the case of glycinebetaine is extensive data on tissue distribution available, and most of our comments will be restricted to this compound. Both β-alaninebetaine (Larher, 1976) and glycinebetaine (Storey & Wyn Jones, 1977) are normally found in higher concentrations in shoot than in root tissues of mature plants. Cromwell and Rennie (1953) showed that the glycinebetaine content of *Beta vulgaris* leaves generally increases with age, reaching a maximum at flowering, but the root level declines. Indeed, in the young seedling, the root level exceeds that of the shoot. However, at any particular time the young, actively growing leaves contain much more glycinebetaine than mature, expanded leaves. These trends were confirmed in members of the Chenopodiaceae by Simenauer (1975), and by Stanek's original data (1916). Storey (unpublished data) also found levels of 30 μmol.g fresh wt^{-1} in unstressed *Atriplex spongiosa* apices compared with about 5 μmol.g fresh wt^{-1} in more mature tissue.

Recently, the distribution of glycinebetaine in barley throughout its life cycle has been studied by Ahmad (1978), and a similar pattern emerged. The less mature leaves have higher values, and these decrease as the plant age increases. There is some evidence of transfer from the flag leaf, which has high levels, to the developing grain, which also accumulates glycinebetaine as it matures.

B. NON-VEGETATIVE TISSUES

A number of papers have reported the occurrence of glycinebetaine, prolinebetaine (Cornforth & Henry, 1952) and trigonelline (Blaim, 1962) in seeds. For example, glycinebetaine has been reported in cotton seed (Pollock & Stevens, 1965), in quite remarkable quantity in beet seed (256 μmol.g fresh wt^{-1}), and in *Spartina x townsendii* seed (68 μmol.g fresh wt^{-1}) (Storey, 1976). Chittenden et al. (1978) found very high glycinebetaine concentrations in the mature wheat aleurone and embryo tissues but not in the starchy endosperm. The glycinebetaine content of the aleurone layer is much greater than the total internal amino acid pool. The amount of glycinebetaine did not change significantly during the first days of germination, but both it and the free amino acid pools were dramatically decreased by gibberellic acid treatment after 4 d of germination. Pearce et al. (1976) examined wheat ear tissues and, in Table IV, the glycinebetaine contents, as calculated from their data, are shown. As with the embryo and aleurone, partially dehydrated, but viable tissues, appear to have high levels.

TABLE IV
Glycinebetaine contents of wheat ear tissues.[a]

Tissue	Glycinebetaine (μmol.g dry wt^{-1})
anthers	96
paleas	40
lemmas	27
glumes	19
rachis	14
grain	10
leaves	14

[a]Data calculated from Pearce et al. (1976).

IV. BIOSYNTHETIC PATHWAYS

A. GLYCINEBETAINE

Two pathways for the biosynthesis of glycinebetaine may readily be envisaged (Cromwell & Rennie, 1954a, 1954b; Delwiche & Bregoff, 1957): the sequential methylation of the parent amino acid, glycine, or the oxidation of choline, itself formed by the sequential methylation of ethanolamine. All the recent evidence favours the second pathway, and data showing incorporation of ^{14}C-choline into glycinebetaine have been obtained with wheat (Bowman & Rohringer, 1970), barley (Hanson & Nelson, 1978) and a number of chenopods (Cromwell & Rennie, 1954a; Delwiche & Bregoff, 1957) (Fig. 1). This is also the pathway prevalent in animals (Paxton & Mayr, 1962).

As noted by Hanson and Nelson (1978), the major precursors of glycinebetaine, glycine, serine and formate are all intermediates in the photorespiratory or photo-oxidative carbon cycle. No enzymological data are available for higher plants, and nothing is known of the presumed choline dehydrogenase (choline oxidase) or glycinebetaine-aldehyde dehydrogenase enzymes, despite attempts to isolate them from chenopod tissue (Speed, 1972). Hanson and Nelson (1978) pointed out that, during the sequential methylation steps, there is a net demand for reducing power, which, using formate as the donor, would approximate to an NADPH requirement four times the rate of glycinebetaine accumulation. It should also be noted that there is a net production of a proton per glycinebetaine accumulated (Fig. 1).

The catabolic pathway has not been studied in plants but, by analogy

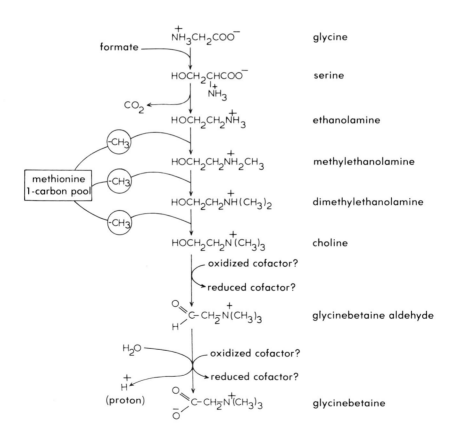

FIG. 1. Probable pathway for glycinebetaine biosynthesis.

with the microbial degradative pathway (Kortstee, 1970; Wyn Jones et al., 1973), the probable path is through the sequential demethylation of glycinebetaine to glycine.

B. PROLINEBETAINE

In their study of prolinebetaine biosynthesis in alfalfa seedlings, Wiehler and Marion (1958) found that 2-week-old plants could convert ornithine and glutamate to proline and, on the further addition of both methionine and folic acid, ^{14}C-methyl label from the methionine was isolated in prolinebetaine. Thus, a pathway involving the sequential methylation of proline was proposed. In a later paper Robertson and Marion (1960), while able to show the conversion of N-methylproline (hygric acid) to prolinebetaine, were unable to show the conversion of proline itself and expressed some reservations whether the simple pathway of sequential methylation was in fact correct.

While prolinebetaine is the major betaine in young alfalfa seedlings, trigonelline and pipecolatebetaine are equally important in seeds. Robertson and Marion (1959) made the interesting suggestion that the biosynthesis of these other betaines may only be initiated after anthesis.

C. β–ALANINEBETAINE

By feeding ^{3}H-β-alanine and ^{14}C-methyl-labelled methionine to *Limonium vulgare* leaves, Larher (1976) found that β-alaninebetaine was probably synthesized by the sequential methylation of the parent amino acid, and that methionine could well be acting as the methyl donor (see Fig. 2). Again the enzymology is unknown. In this context it is interesting to note Challenger's (1959) speculations on the relationship between the presence of dimethylsulphonio propionate and β-alanine in many marine algae (Ericson & Carlson, 1953). He suggested that the decomposition of the sulphonio compounds to dimethylsulphide ($(CH_3)_2S$), acrylic acid ($CH_2{=}CHCOOH$) and a proton (H^+), which has been shown to be enzyme mediated (Cantoni & Anderson, 1956), could initially liberate $^+CH_2CH_2COO^-$, which would yield β-alanine, with ammonia. However, we are aware of no recent biochemical work to confirm this speculative link between β-alanine, or its betaine, and dimethylsulphoniopropionate.

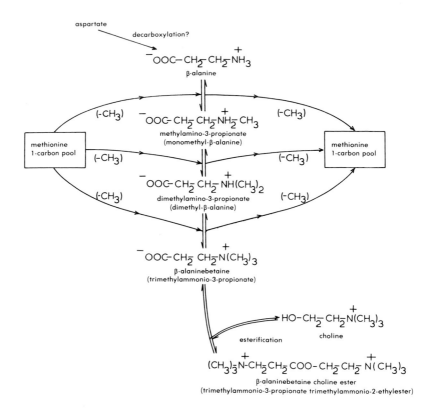

FIG. 2. Possible pathway for β-alaninebetaine biosynthesis.

V. ACCUMULATION OF BETAINES IN STRESSED TISSUES

A. GLYCINEBETAINE

Although there was an intermittent interest in the distribution and biosynthesis of glycinebetaine in higher plants, and a few papers appeared describing the effects of added glycinebetaine on leaf disc and coleoptile expansion (Wheeler, 1963, 1965, 1969), little progress was made in exploring its function. However, this situation is changing rapidly following the key observation that the accumulation of the compound could be induced by salt or water stress (Storey & Wyn Jones, 1975; Storey, 1976). Evidence for progressive glycinebetaine accumulation in plants exposed to increasing external salt (NaCl) concentrations is now available for *Chloris gayana* (Storey & Wyn Jones, 1975), *Hordeum vulgare* cvs. *California Mariout* and *Arimar* (Wyn Jones & Storey, 1978a), *Diplachne fusca* (Sandhu et al., 1981), *Spartina x townsendii* (Storey & Wyn Jones, 1978b), *Atriplex spongiosa* and *Suaeda monoica* (Storey & Wyn Jones, 1979), and *Spinacia oleracea* (Coughlan & Wyn Jones, unpublished data).

Less complete but similar data are available for *Zea mays* var. *WF9 x M14*, *Triticum vulgare* var. *Capelle Desprez, Avena sativa* (Storey & Wyn Jones, 1977) and *Suaeda maritima* (Flowers & Hall, 1978), and there can be little doubt that external NaCl induces glycinebetaine accumulation in many, but perhaps not all members of the Gramineae and Chenopodiaceae (see *Puccinellia maritima* in Table II). However, the amounts accumulated vary from very small, in *Zea mays* ($0.5–2 \, \mu$mol.g fresh wt^{-1}), to very large, in some halophytic species (about $100 \, \mu$mol.g fresh wt^{-1}), some of which have very high basal levels even in the absence of external salinity, for example *Suaeda monoica* with about $50 \, \mu$mol . g fresh wt^{-1} (Storey & Wyn Jones, 1975). In *Atriplex spongiosa* (Storey & Pitman, unpublished data) other salts, such as KCl, Na_2SO_4 and $MgCl_2$, also bring about glycinebetaine accumulation. However, glycinebetaine accumulation does not occur in salt-stressed *Atriplex spongiosa* plants when the relative humidity is maintained at 95–100%; these growth conditions do not result in the net salt accumulation in the leaves observed at lower relative humidities (Storey & Pitman, unpublished data).

There is less evidence to show that water stress brings about an increase in the glycinebetaine content of plants. Nevertheless, polyethylene glycol treatment and water withdrawal induces glycinebetaine accumulation in barley cultivars (Fig. 3; Hanson & Nelson, 1978), and similar observations have been made with *Spinacia oleracea* (Coughlan & Wyn Jones, 1980) and *Atriplex spongiosa* (Storey & Pitman, unpublished data). Thus, it is highly likely that accumulation can be brought about by both salt and water stress, although the former appears to be more effective. This may be due to the substantially greater osmotic pressure change in salt-stressed compared with water-stressed tissue. However, in marked contrast to proline accumulation (cf. Hsiao, 1973), glycinebetaine accumulation cannot be regarded as a general plant response to water stress, as many species, for example *Lycopersicon esculentum, Pisum sativa, Daucus carota* (Storey & Wyn Jones, 1977), do not react in this manner. This difference is underlined by the phytotaxonomic data in Table II; glycinebetaine has not been detected in all plants having high sap osmotic pressures found in saline environments, or xeric environments.

Little is known of the biochemical mechanisms leading to the induction or activation of the glycinebetaine biosynthetic pathway. However it is

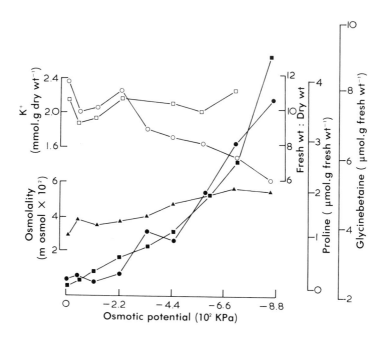

FIG. 3. Influence of water (polyethylene glycol) stress on glycinebetaine and proline levels and related parameters in barley, cv. California Mariout, subjected to a gradual incremental stress. (O) fresh wt: dry wt ratio; (□) K^+; (▲) osmolality; (■) glycinebetaine; (●) proline. (From Wyn Jones and Storey, 1978a.)

interesting to note that Lawlor and Fock (1978) found that the rate of photorespiration relative to photosynthesis increased in maize following water stress. Further, a greater proportion of ^{14}C from labelled CO_2 was found in the amino acids of the photorespiratory pathway, glycine and serine, both probable precursors of glycinebetaine (Fig. 1).

B. COMPARISON OF GLYCINEBETAINE AND PROLINE ACCUMULATION AND CONSUMPTION

The differences and similarities between glycinebetaine and proline accumulation in stressed plant tissues deserve further consideration. Hanson and Nelson (1978) and Wyn Jones and Storey (1978a) noted the close relation between the levels of these two solutes in barley subjected to water or salt stress. However, unstressed glycinebetaine levels are ten-fold higher than those of proline. Since a gradual stress induces a similar rate of glycinebetaine and proline accumulation (about $0.1–0.5\,\mu$mol . g fresh wt^{-1}.d^{-1}.25 mM^{-1} NaCl increment: Wyn Jones & Storey, 1978b), the proportional increase in proline is greater, although the former is still quantitatively more significant. In conditions of salt or osmotic shock such as employed by Hanson and Nelson (1978) and in some experiments by Wyn Jones and Storey (1978a), the proportional increase in proline content is even greater, so that final proline levels exceed those of glycinebetaine. Thus, in barley, there appears to be a relationship between the relative rates of proline and glycinebetaine accumulation and the method of stress application (see also Coughlan & Wyn Jones, 1980).

It is probable that there are differences in the rates of induction of proline and glycinebetaine in that glycinebetaine increases have only been recorded after 24 h whereas proline accumulation has been recorded in tens of minutes (Singh et al., 1973). However, this is not borne out in the data of Hanson and Nelson (1978), and further experimentation is required.

A major difference between the two solutes lies in their rates of degradation. The data of Bowman and Rohringer (1970) on wheat, Storey (1976) on maize, and Hanson and Nelson (1978) on barley indicate that the rate of glycinebetaine degradation in plant tissue is slow in contrast to proline (Singh et al., 1973). A direct comparison is shown in Figure 4 in an experiment in which both NaCl and polyethyleneglycol stress were applied and then withdrawn. While proline levels decreased rapidly after stress withdrawal, particularly in polyethyleneglycol-treated tissues, glycinebetaine remained almost constant. The relative inertness of glycinebetaine led Hanson and Nelson (1978) to suggest that it might be employed as a cumulative index of water stress in barley.

The differences between the patterns of glycinebetaine and proline accumulation are quite pronounced in the salt tolerant chenopods, *Atriplex spongiosa* and *Suaeda monoica* (Storey & Wyn Jones, 1978b). In these species, glycinebetaine increases, particularly on a dry weight basis at low salinities, which stimulate both the growth of the plants and their succulence. Proline accumulation occurs either as a transient response to the initial salt shock of low salinities or as a long-term effect in plants exposed to very high, inhibitory salt levels. Thus, glycinebetaine is strongly correlated with sap osmotic pressure (*A. spongiosa*, R = 0.95, p <0.01; *S. monoica*, r = 0.98; p < 0.01), whereas proline accumulation mirrors the decrease in yield and fall in tissue water content at high salinities. In barley, even fairly low salinities cause some growth inhibition and a decline in fresh weight to dry weight ratio (Storey & Wyn Jones, 1978a). Thus, the differences between the behaviour of glycinebetaine and proline in these species may be due to their different growth and morphological responses to salt (NaCl), and the absence of a significant succulence and growth response in barley.

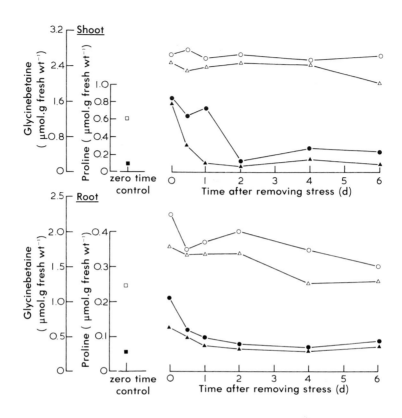

FIG. 4. Comparison of glycinebetaine and proline levels in barley cv. Arimar subject to, and then released from, NaCl and water (polyethylene glycol) stress. Open symbols, glycinebetaine (□, △, ○) subjected to salt (○) and polyethylene glycol (△) stress. Closed symbols, proline (■, ●, ▲), subjected to salt (●) and polyethylene glycol (▲) stress. The final stress, −0.8 MPa, was applied incrementally over 36 h and maintained for 24 h before being removed at day 0. (Ahmad and Wyn Jones, unpublished data.)

C. β-ALANINEBETAINE AND PROLINEBETAINE

In *Limonium vulgare,* Larher (1976) found that the shoot levels of β-alaninebetaine increase with external salinity (Table V) to a final concentration (over 100 μmol . g dry wt^{-1}), fairly similar to the glycinebetaine levels (highest recorded levels over 400 μmol . g dry wt^{-1}). In this species, also, there is a greater proportional increase in proline content although, at the highest salinity, β-alaninebetaine is still, quantitatively, the more important (Table V). Unfortunately, no growth or inorganic ion data were included so that detailed comparisons with the members of the Chenopodiaceae are precluded.

Whilst the presence of prolinebetaine in alfalfa has been known for many years (Steenbock, 1918), only recently (Wyn Jones & Owen, unpublished data) has it been demonstrated that this compound also accumulates under saline conditions (Table VI). In this work, two alfalfa cultivars of very different salt tolerances were compared, and both the basal and the induced levels of prolinebetaine were found to be much higher in the more tolerant cultivar.

TABLE V

Changes in some soluble nitrogen-containing compounds in young *Limonium vulgare* plants grown at different salinities.[a]

Compounds	Control medium[b]	167 mM NaCl	333 mM NaCl
	(μmol.g dry wt^{-1})		
proline	trace	10.7	65.4
α-alanine	17.7	20.0	19.3
glutamate	15.7	7.7	7.7
amides	72.9	24.7	18.7
γ-aminobutyrate	19.0	11.8	10.8
total free amino acids and amides	147	102	141
β-alaninebetaine	46.9	67.1	100.2

[a]Data from Larher (1976).
[b]Plants grown in Hoagland's medium with the addition of NaCl as indicated.

TABLE VI

Effect of salinity on the levels of prolinebetaine and related compounds in the shoots of alfalfa cv 'Hawassi' (2nd cut).[a]

Salinity level[b] (mM NaCl)	Sap osmolality (m osmol)	Proline-betaine	Proline	Choline	Trigonelline	Total onium compounds
			mM in sap			
0	590	12	3.6	1.6	>0.5	18
50	625	15	1.2	2.6	>0.5	18
100	813	17	2.7	2.3	>0.5	19
200	930	18	4.1	0.5	>0.5	23

[a]Unpublished data from Wyn Jones and Owen.
[b]Plants grown in Hoagland's medium with added NaCl as shown.

VI. POSSIBLE PHYSIOLOGICAL FUNCTIONS

A. GLYCINEBETAINE AS A CYTOPLASMIC OSMOTICUM

Early studies (Cromwell & Rennie, 1954a, 1954b; Byerrum et al., 1955) suggested that glycinebetaine might be involved in methyl transfer, but in some cases (Sribney & Kirkwood, 1954) the glycinebetaine methyl group was not transferred readily to a range of acceptors. This work failed to explain the high concentrations found in some plants. However, the close correlation between glycinebetaine concentration and sap osmotic pressure in leaves of various species (Wyn Jones et al., 1977a, 1977b; Storey & Wyn Jones 1978b, 1979) indicated that the compound might have an osmotic role. Evidence of the sensitivity of some cytoplasmic enzymes and organelles from halophytic plants to high concentrations of inorganic ions (Flowers et al., 1977), and increasing evidence of ion compartmentation between cytoplasm and vacuole (see Jeschke, 1979; Wyn Jones et al., 1979), led a number of workers (e.g. Flowers, 1975; Osmond, 1976) to postulate a requirement for cytoplasmic non-toxic osmotica. Wyn Jones and his colleagues (1977a, 1977b) produced evidence that glycinebetaine might fulfil this role in some plants. They also suggested that the cytoplasm would be K^+-specific, with the majority of the Na^+ and Cl^- ions, if present, sequestered in the vacuole. Recently the possible free ion concentrations (activities) in the cytoplasm have been considered in some detail (Wyn Jones et al., 1979), and a unifying hypothesis involving the effects of ions on protein synthesis has been advanced.

If glycinetetaine is utilized as a cytoplasmic osmoticum when the cell sap osmotic pressure exceeds a basal level (about 0.8–1.0 MPa) (Wyn Jones et al., 1977a), then two basic requirements must be met: (i) the solute must be non-toxic to cytoplasmic functions; and (ii) the solute must be preferentially located in the cytoplasm as the concentrations observed can only make a major osmotic contribution if the solute is restricted to a fairly small percentage of the cell volume. (This requirement may also be related to the evidence for the preferential localization of Na^+ and Cl^- in the vacuole: see Jeschke, 1979.)

It may also be suggested that the cytoplasmic osmoticum must be highly water soluble and not carry a net charge which could affect the charge balance of the cytoplasm. Glycinebetaine is dipolar (zwitterionic) and, unlike amino acids, has only one titratable group, the carboxyl, which has a pKa of 1.83 at 25°C, as the cationic charge on the nitrogen is fixed. Thus, over the physiological pH range, glycinebetaine will have no net charge and no buffering capacity. The internal charge compensation is such that it will pass through a mixed bed ion exchange column at neutral pHs (Carruthers et al., 1960). Glycinebetaine is extremely water soluble (157 g.100 ml^{-1} at 19°C), but, effectively, is insoluble in ether (Dawson et al., 1969).

Evidence that glycinebetaine, in concentrations up to $0.5–1.0 \times 10^3$ mM, did not inhibit malate dehydrogenase (decarboxylating) was presented by Wyn Jones et al. (1977b) and confirmed by Flowers et al. (1978). A more detailed study (Pollard & Wyn Jones, 1979) has shown that a number of plant and animal enzymes are not inhibited by glycinebetaine and that the NaCl inhibition of some enzymes is partially relieved by glycinebetaine (200–500 mM). The partial protection probably is not mediated by direct binding of glycinebetaine to the enzyme (cf. Schobert, 1977). We have also found that active intact mitochondria from wheat embryo (Pollard & Wyn Jones, unpublished data), and Type A chloroplasts from spinach leaves (Larkum & Wyn Jones, 1979) may be isolated and studied in glycinebetaine as an alternative osmoticum to sucrose, mannitol or sorbitol. Polysome stability is unimpaired by 500 mM concentrations (Brady & Wyn Jones, unpublished data), while *in vitro* protein synthesis using the wheat embryo system is not significantly inhibited by 250–300 mM glycinebetaine over and above a basal 120 mM potassium acetate medium (Speirs, Brady & Wyn Jones, unpublished data). Thus, the non-toxicity of glycinebetaine is firmly established and the first condition for its role as a cytoplasmic osmoticum has been satisfied.

The second criterion, namely conclusive evidence for a preferential, but not necessarily exclusive, cytoplasmic localization, is more difficult to demonstrate. Nevertheless, three lines of evidence point in this direction.

1. Analyses of tissues of low vacuolation, for example *Atriplex spongiosa* apices, wheat embryo or aleurone, showed very high glycinebetaine concentrations, whereas vacuolated, older tissues have lower levels (see Section III).

2. By a histochemical technique, Hall et al. (1978) showed glycine betaine to be exclusively located in the cytoplasm of *Suaeda maritima* leaf cells.

3. Employing the technique of whole vacuole isolation developed by Leigh and Branton (1976) using red beet storage tissue, Leigh, Ahmad and Wyn Jones (unpublished data; see also Wyn Jones et al., 1977a) found glycinebetaine to be partially excluded from vacuoles.

All the individual techniques may be criticized, but taken together, the results support the original hypothesis and make a strong case for glycinebetaine being largely cytoplasmic. This hypothesis may be applied to halophytes and certain xerophytes, but it is not relevant to ephemeral or succulent xerophytes which maintain low sap osmotic pressure (Walter, 1971). In one sense the concept is more applicable to salt-accumulating halophytes. This is because glycinebetaine, in contrast to proline, is very slowly metabolized in plants and is a semi-permanent end product of metabolism. There is evidence that Na^+ is also held relatively immobile in vacuoles of some plants and is not transported rapidly out of leaves (Yeo,

1976; Jeschke, 1979), so that the accumulation of the metabolically inert glycinebetaine in the cytoplasm may be considered as balancing the absorption of rather immobile Na^+ salts into the vacuoles. In this context, there is unfortunately a lack of good evidence on the distribution of Cl^- (Wyn Jones et al., 1979), but it may also be vacuolar. In the Chenopodiaceae, where this model may be applied best, the major balancing vacuolar anion may be oxalate (Osmond, 1968). Many of these Chenopodiaceae are xerohalophytes and are found in dry, saline habitats. There is a clear relationship in many cases between salt and water stress tolerance.

B. OTHER ASPECTS OF THE PHYSIOLOGICAL CHEMISTRY OF GLYCINEBETAINE

Glycinebetaine has been presented as a solute notable for its lack of toxicity and intracellular metabolic stability. It is, however, rapidly degraded extracellularly by soil micro-organisms (Kortstee, 1970; Wyn Jones et al., 1973). Early work on the addition of glycinebetaine to root media was hampered by microbial interference, but, by using axenic cultures, the positive effects of this compound were demonstrated. Changes in the shoot K^+ and Na^+ contents of treated plants have also been observed (Storey, 1976; Ahmad, 1978). Recently, the possible influence of external glycinebetaine and glycinebetaine loading of tissues on ion fluxes has been studied in greater detail (Ahmad, 1978; Ahmad & Wyn Jones, 1978). Perhaps the most interesting of the phenomena observed was the influence of glycinebetaine loading of barley roots on tonoplast fluxes (Ahmad, Jeschke & Wyn Jones, unpublished data). Using a technique which allowed the separate determination of ^{22}Na efflux and transport in excised barley roots, glycinebetaine loading, or a metabolic consequence thereof, was found to increase Na^+ flux from the cytoplasm to the vacuole and to increase the vacuolar Na^+ concentration. This observation implies a link between the accumulation of the cytoplasmic osmoticum and the partitioning of Na^+ between cytoplasm and vacuole (Table VII). It further suggests, not surprisingly, that the passive model of cytoplasmic osmotic regulation may be superseded by a dynamic model, as various feed-back controls are clearly required between cytoplasm and vacuole to maintain a uniform water potential across the tonoplast. One should also note the structural similarity of glycinebetaine and other *onium* compounds found in nature to compounds well known to modify membrane behaviour (Fluck & Jaffe, 1974; Davidson, 1976).

It is not difficult to relate suggestions that glycinebetaine may have a role in frost resistance (Bokarev & Ivanova, 1971; Sakai & Yoshida, 1968) to the evidence presented above. Similarly, Rafaeli-Eshkol (1968) and Rafaeli-Eshkol and Avi-Dor (1968) originally reported that choline, probably after

TABLE VII

Influence of glycinebetaine loading of excised barley roots on ^{22}Na fluxes. Roots loaded in presence of 1.0 mM glycinebetaine for 24 h.[a]

Tissue	Plasmalemma		Tonoplast influx	Vacuole content
	Influx	Efflux		
	μmol. g fresh wt^{-1}.h^{-1}			μmol. g fresh wt^{-1}
Glycinebetaine				
not loaded	0.65	0.41	0.047	23.0
loaded	0.70	0.47	0.082	30.1

[a]Data from Ahmad, Jeschke and Wyn Jones (unpublished).

conversion to glycinebetaine, increased the salt tolerance of a moderately tolerant bacteria Ba$_1$. More recently, Shkedy-Vinkler and Avi-Dor (1975) have shown the importance of glycinebetaine in protecting a membrane function (respiration) in bacteria exposed to NaCl. They did not stress an osmotic role for glycinebetaine but their data showed a salt-promoted uptake of the solute and an intracellular glycinebetaine concentration of 800 mM under the high salt condition. Thus, it is possible that the solute has an osmotic role as well as a membrane modifying function. These two roles are not necessarily incompatible.

C. POSSIBLE FUNCTION OF β-ALANINEBETAINE

Little is known of the metabolic function of β-alaninebetaine. While the leaf content of β-alaninebetaine increased with external salinity (Larher, 1976), interpretation is complicated by a significant, but ill-defined, proportion being present as the choline ester. As a choline ester this compound, and the 2-trimethylamino-6-ketoheptanoate, would have two fixed cationic charges and would require balancing anions. In contrast to the evidence for glycinebetaine, Larher (1976) observed, by a cytochemical technique, that β-alaninebetaine and/or its choline ester, were sited in the vacuole. If this is confirmed, the rather lower levels found would exclude any simple osmotic role. Drawing an analogy with the structures of acetylcholine antagonists, Larher tentatively suggested that the β-alaninebetaine choline ester may have a role in controlling the permeability of membranes to Na$^+$ and Cl$^-$. Although Larher's work did not include inorganic ion analyses, Mg^{2+} might be added to these ions as other data show the Plumbaginaceae to be very rich in this ion (Storey et al., 1977). A further factor worth considering in future work may be a similarity of these compounds to the polyamines, for example spermidine (Basso & Smith, 1974).

VII. CONCLUDING DISCUSSION

A compound which accumulates in a plant under conditions of water or salt stress may be a by-product, possibly toxic, of that stress, or a possible adaptation to help withstand the effects of the stress. Hanson and Nelson (1978) take the view that the only interpretation of glycinebetaine accumulation justified by the data is the former, and they see both glycinebetaine and proline accumulation as a method for consuming excess reducing power. However, from a consideration of its taxonomic distribution and the glycinebetaine responses of salt tolerant members of the Chenopodiaceae, we take the view that glycinebetaine accumulation is an adaptive response to salt and, possibly, water stress. This view is reinforced by an examination of glycinebetaine distribution in other species, such as marine invertebrates, where the compound appears to be accumulated as an intracellular osmoticum. Further, circumstantial support comes from the comparative data on the effects of inorganic ions and glycinebetaine on enzymes, ribosomes, mitochondria and chloroplasts, which show that glycinebetaine, but not the inorganic ions, is tolerated at high concentrations.

It does not follow from this analysis that the rate or degree of glycinebetaine accumulation is a measure of tolerance (see Wyn Jones & Storey, 1978b). Many physiological and biochemical factors are involved in salt and drought tolerance, and the ability to accumulate glycinebetaine, albeit as an important cytoplasmic osmoticum, may not be limiting. While this solute appears to be the preferred osmoticum in some species, other species have evolved other mechanisms and, in all probability, other cytoplasmic osmotica, of which proline may be an example. There is therefore, *a priori*, no conflict between the hypotheses regarding the two solutes. Nevertheless, some differences exist between the two, particularly in their rapidity of accumulation and metabolic lability, which suggest that proline accumulation could be the major response to a transient stress or shock, and glycinebetaine to a longer, possibly more gradual, stress usually involving net salt accumulation.

We have suggested that the concept of a cytoplasmic non-toxic solute is applicable to seeds and other partially dehydrated tissues such as anthers, as well as xerophytic and halophytic plants. These, indeed, may be examples in which the accumulation of the more metabolically inert solute is favoured. It will be apparent from Section II that a wide range of betaines have been found in seeds. Whether they all fulfil an osmotic-protective role similar to that proposed for glycinebetaine remains to be seen, but their structures and the evidence on the role of β-alanine choline ester makes such a simple explanation unlikely.

CHAPTER 10

Proline Accumulation: Physiological Aspects

D. ASPINALL AND L. G. PALEG

I.	The response	206
	A. Distribution of the response among living organisms	206
	B. Control of accumulation by water potential	206
	C. Variation in proline concentration with time	209
	D. Distribution of accumulated proline	209
	E. Proline loss with relief of water deficit	211
	F. The role of plant hormones	211
	G. Accumulation in response to other environmental stress factors	213
II.	Consequences of proline accumulation	214
	A. Functional aspects of proline accumulation	214
	B. Osmoregulation	215
	C. Hydration characteristics of biopolymers	215
	D. The conservation of energy and amino groups	216
	E. Sink for soluble nitrogen	217
	F. Senescence phenomena	217
III.	Proline accumulation and stress resistance	219
	A. General considerations	219
	B. Hardening	220
	C. Growth retardants	220
	D. Exogenous proline application	221
	E. Comparisons between species	222
	F. Comparisons within species	230
IV.	Selection for proline accumulation	237
	A. Hybrid selection	237
	B. Selection within a cultivar	239
V.	Future prospects	240

PHYSIOLOGY AND BIOCHEMISTRY
OF DROUGHT RESISTANCE
IN PLANTS

I. THE RESPONSE

A. DISTRIBUTION OF THE RESPONSE AMONG LIVING ORGANISMS

At some stage, most living organisms are subjected to a degree of dehydration, which may be due to a water deficit in the environment, as with land plants, or to an increase in the osmotic pressure of an aqueous environment, as with the creatures in a drying salt lake. The metabolic responses to dehydration are diverse and are reflected in changes in the composition of the organism. Certain species, particularly those adapted to extreme environments, show characteristic and, presumably, adaptive changes in composition during dehydration, with the accumulation of substances not normally found in the organism; for example, the accumulation of glycerol by the halophilic alga *Dunaliella* (Borowitzka & Brown, 1974). Many organisms, including species adapted to mesic or arid habitats, accumulate substances which are normal cell constituents, particularly free amino acids, during a period of water deficit. A range of amino acids accumulate to a greater or lesser degree in different organisms, but the most frequent and extensive response is an increase in the concentration of the imino acid, proline. Accumulation of proline upon dehydration due to water deficit or increasing osmotic pressure has been recorded in bacteria (Tempest et al., 1970; Measures, 1975), algae (Besnier et al., 1969; Schobert, 1974, 1977a, 1977b; Brown & Hellebust, 1978), crustaceans (Gilles & Schoffeniels, 1969; Vincent-Marique & Gilles, 1970; Fyhn, 1976) and higher plants (e.g. Palfi et al., 1973). Indeed it has been suggested (Measures, 1975) that proline accumulation is a primitive response of living organisms to increasing osmotic pressure in the environment, which, until the evolution of homeo-osmotic mechanisms in higher animals, was widespread throughout the biological world.

B. CONTROL OF ACCUMULATION BY WATER POTENTIAL

The accumulation of proline in these various organisms is initiated by a reduction in the water potential of the tissues or cells. In barley, accumulation begins rapidly upon exposing the tissues to dehydration, the concentration of free proline in the leaves of the plant at any time being a function of the length of exposure to water deficit, the water potential of the leaves, and the amount transported from the leaves to other tissues (Singh et al., 1973a). In all the available data, the progressive accumulation of proline has been accompanied by a fall in tissue water potential with time (Fig. 1). Unfortunately, however, no experiments have been reported in which intact plants have been maintained at a range of fixed water potentials for a prolonged period, and the rates of proline accumulation recorded. In the absence of such measurements, it is impossible to determine an upper water potential limit for the induction of proline accumulation. It has been suggested that proline accumulation is relatively insensitive to water deficit (Waldren & Teare, 1974; Waldren et al., 1974; McMichael & Elmore, 1977); however, the apparent insensitivity may primarily reflect the time lag between initiation of the response and detection of an increase in free proline concentration. A *lower* limit to the threshold water potential for the response can be calculated from such experiments, however, and for cotton this appears to be -1.2 MPa (McMichael & Elmore, 1977), while for young barley plants it is -0.7 MPa (Fig. 2). This second estimate corresponds reasonably well with the response of detached barley leaves (where water potential can be closely controlled) which accumulate proline at a water potential of -1.0 MPa, but not at -0.5 MPa (Singh et al., 1973b; Aspinall, unpublished). These estimates

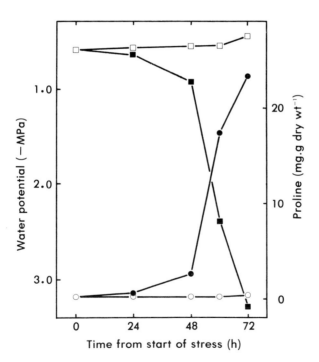

FIG. 1. Relationship between water potential (□, control; ■, stressed) and proline content (○, control; ●, stressed) in 18 d soil-grown radish plants. Control plants were watered daily; stressed plants received no water after 0 h. (After Chu, 1974.)

contrast with values of −2.4 MPa for sorghum (controlled environment) and −1.2 MPa (controlled environment) or −2.0 MPa (field) for soybean (Waldren & Teare, 1974; Waldren et al., 1974). The differences may reflect major species differences but, as the two estimates for soybean suggest, are more likely due to differences in technique.

The initiation of proline accumulation in plant tissues in response to a decrease in tissue water potential could conceivably be due to changes in one of several components of the total potential. Conventionally, the water potential of higher plant tissues has been divided into two or three components, osmotic potential, turgor potential and, in some studies, matric potential. It is not an experimentally easy task to separate unequivocally the effects of changes in these components. Several studies, utilizing solutes of varying tissue penetrance, suggest that changes in turgor potential control biochemical responses of the plant (Greenway & Leahy, 1972). This view has been questioned by Chu et al. (1976a), who reported that accumulation of proline in the barley plant was dependent on changes in osmotic potential rather than on changes in turgor. In any case, a system concerned with osmoregulation (Stewart & Lee, 1974; Savitskaya, 1976; Brown & Hellebust, 1978) could respond to

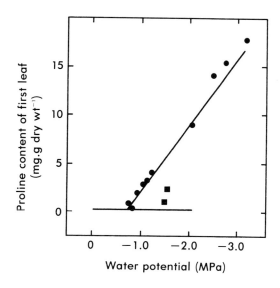

FIG. 2. Relationship between water potential and proline accumulation in the first leaf of 10 d old barley (cv. Prior) plants subjected to −1.0 (●) or −2.0 (■) MPa stress with polyethylene glycol solutions. Regression line (y = −0.6855x−4.704) calculated from all data and indicates that proline increases at water potentials below −0.72 MPa. Horizontal line is level of proline in unstressed plants. (After Singh, 1970.)

turgor, and it is unlikely that gross measurements of tissue turgor and osmotic potential will adequately represent the influence of water deficit at the sub-cellular level of organization where proline accumulation is controlled. The question of the precise control mechanism in proline accumulation has relevance to the role of accumulated proline in the water-stressed plant and this problem will be further developed.

C. VARIATION IN PROLINE CONCENTRATION WITH TIME

Accumulation of proline durine water-deficit continues for at least several days (Singh et al., 1973d), but there has been no report of the concentration ultimately reaching a maximum level in intact higher plants although concentrations as high as 10% of the total leaf dry weight have been recorded (Stewart & Lee, 1974). In diatoms, however, where it is possible to hold cells in a solution of a particular osmotic potential indefinitely, proline concentration rises to a maximum, which varies with the osmotic potential, and then remains at that concentration for a considerable period (Schobert, 1977a). The excised leaves of higher plants do not respond in a manner analogous to unicellular organisms as, in similar experimental circumstances, proline accumulates rapidly at first (24–48 h), but then falls in concentration equally rapidly, presumably due to the metabolic consequences of excision (Kemble & McPherson, 1954; Palfi et al., 1974a; Singh et al., 1973b).

Proline accumulation responds relatively rapidly to changes in leaf water status, and Rajagopal et al., (1977) showed that, in unirrigated field-grown wheat, the proline content reaches a maximum at midday which corresponds closely with the time of minimum relative water content of those leaves. There was a 2.5-fold diurnal range in proline content. Complementing these studies of short-term changes in proline concentration, Stewart and Lee (1974) examined seasonal variation in the proline concentration in the shoot tissues of the halophyte *Triglochin maritima L.* growing in a saline environment. The proline concentration was high throughout the growing season (minimum 50 μmol.g fresh wt^{-1}) and reached a maximum (150 μmol.g fresh wt^{-1}) at the time that the plant was growing most rapidly. Evidently a high tissue concentration of free proline is not incompatible with growth in this species. Similar long-term fluctuations in endogenous proline concentration have been reported in the rose (Decheva et al., 1972) and the peach (Schneider, 1966).

D. DISTRIBUTION OF ACCUMULATED PROLINE

Most studies of proline accumulation in response to water deficit have been concerned with changes in concentration in the shoot or, more specifically, the leaves. However, proline accumulates in all organs of the intact plant during water deficit, although accumulation is most rapid and extensive in the leaves (Chen et al., 1964; Barnett & Naylor, 1965; Singh et al., 1973d). Accumulation in the root occurs both later and less extensively than accumulation in the leaf, following the onset of a water deficit. Excised leaves and stems also accumulate proline when subjected to a water deficit, but, under similar circumstances, excised shoot apices accumulate little proline and excised roots none at all (Stewart et al., 1966; Singh et al., 1973b). However, proline accumulated in excised root tips of *Pisum* and *Tamarix* exposed to salinity stress (Bar-Nun & Poljakoff-Mayber, 1977), and in water-stressed Jerusalem artichoke tubers (Wright et al., 1977). Such findings led to the suggestion that the proline accumulated in the roots of stressed, intact barley plants had been translocated there from the leaves. This was supported by the fact that subjecting the roots of a water-deficient plant to anaerobiosis inhibited proline accumulation in the root but enhanced accumulation in the leaves, the total amount accumulated in the whole plant being unaffected by the treatment (Singh et al., 1973d).

The most obvious difference between the tissues which are capable of accumulating proline when excised and those which are not is the presence of chlorophyll. However, both dark-grown and genetically chlorotic barley leaf tissue is capable of accumulating proline if supplied with precursors and subjected to a water deficit, whereas root tissue is not (Singh et al., 1973b).

Many of the hypotheses which concern the effects of the presence of accumulated proline in the cell hinge upon the assumption that all, or at least most, of the accumulated proline is present in the cytoplasm. To date, this point has not been tested definitively, but the available evidence is consistent with this view. Accumulated proline is not readily washed from tissues; indeed, in some instances it it difficult to ensure that exogenous proline penetrates to the cytoplasm (Boggess et al., 1976a). Evidently the plasmalemma offers a considerable barrier to the passage of proline.

The distribution of accumulated proline in the roots of salinity-stressed corn suggests a cytoplasmic location (Göring et al., 1977). Intact plants were subjected to stress and the roots were then sectioned and analysed for proline. The proline concentration was found to rise towards the root tip, being maximal 1–2 mm from the root tip where the majority of cells lacked vacuoles, and decreasing markedly in segments further from the tip where all cells were highly vacuolated. Accumulation in the vacuole is not excluded by the data presently available, but if it occurs transport across the tonoplast must be rapid and bi-directional since accumulated, labelled proline was rapidly metabolized when water deficit was relieved (Boggess et al., 1976b). Proline did not appear to accumulate in, or be excluded from, chloroplasts, and other organelles in the cell did not occupy a sufficient volume to be considered as a feasible, exclusive location for accumulated proline.

E. PROLINE LOSS WITH RELIEF OF WATER DEFICIT

Proline accumulated during an episode of water deficit is rapidly lost, principally by oxidation to glutamate, once the water deficit is eliminated (Stewart, 1972; Singh et al., 1973d, 1973b; Blum & Ebercon, 1976). A fall in proline concentration is observable within 3–4 h of supplying water, and in barley the proline concentration returns to the control level within 48 h. In sorghum, however, recovery is not as complete, and tissue proline concentration may remain above the non-stressed concentration for several days. Recovery in sunflower is also slow, but this has been attributed to delay in the recovery of leaf water status (Wample & Bewley, 1975). Interestingly, recovery does not begin instantaneously when a salinity stress is relieved, and proline accumulation may continue for 24 h following removal of salt from the rooting medium (Chu et al., 1976a). Eventually, however, the concentration of proline declines rapidly in these circumstances also.

F. THE ROLE OF PLANT HORMONES

The accumulation and subsequent metabolism of proline during an episode of water deficit and recovery may be a consequence of a direct effect of cell water status on proline biosynthesis and oxidation (see following chapter). Alternatively, the response may be mediated through stress effects on one or more effector compounds, and the kinetics of proline accumulation, as presently understood, allow the possibility of an intermediate stage between induction of water deficit and the biochemical events leading to proline accumulation. Plant hormones are candidates for such an intermediary role, and the endogenous concentrations of abscisic acid (Hiron & Wright, 1973), cytokinin (Itai & Vaadia, 1971) and ethylene (El-Beltagy & Hall, 1974) are known to be affected by water deficit.

Applied abscisic acid has been shown to induce proline accumulation in both intact plants and excised leaves of barley (Aspinall et al., 1973). This is unlikely to follow from any effect of abscisic acid on the water status of leaves since stomatal closure following application of abscisic acid would tend to increase leaf water potential, which in turn should inhibit proline accumulation. Similar responses to applied abscisic acid have been found in other plants, including *Lolium temulentum* (Aspinall et al., 1973) and *Pennisetum typhoides* (Huber, 1974; Eder & Huber, 1977), and a rapid accumulation of amino acids in response to abscisic acid has been reported for *Lemna* (Andres & Smith, 1976). The response is not universal, however, since tobacco plants which accumulate both proline (Boggess et al., 1976a) and abscisic acid (Boussiba & Richmond, 1976) as a consequence of water deficit do not accumulate proline in response to applied abscisic acid (Aspinall, unpublished). Sunflowers also lack the ability to accumulate proline when treated with abscisic acid (Wample & Bewley, 1975).

The evidence linking changes in other hormones with the accumulation of proline is even more tenuous. When kinetin or gibberellic acid is supplied to excised barley or radish leaves under conditions in which leaf water potential is unaffected, the accumulation of proline is inhibited (Fig. 3). Cytokinin has also been shown to reduce proline accumulation induced by abscisic acid or salinity (Eder & Huber, 1977), and to reduce the proline content of excised cucumber cotyledons (Udayakumar et al., 1976). The application of gibberellic acid to wheat plants during a period of water deficit may also lead to a decline in leaf proline content (Singh et al., 1973d). Finally, it has been reported that the application of 2-chlorethyl phosphonic acid to *Pennisetum* seedlings, with a presumed increase in endogenous ethylene production, induces proline accumulation (Eder et al., 1977).

Clearly, proline accumulation is modified, and may even be initiated, by changes in hormone concentration in higher plants. However, the relevance of these reported responses to the accumulation of proline during water deficit remains to be established. As proline accumulation is a response to water deficit common to species from different phyla, it would appear intrinsically unlikely that higher plant hormones would play any unique and exclusive role in initiating the response.

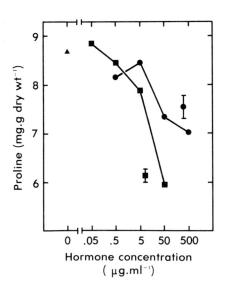

FIG. 3. Proline accumulation by excised, stressed (−2.0 MPa polyethylene glycol solution) barley leaf sections in the absence (▲) or presence ⁻f kinetin (■), or gibberellic acid (●) for 24 h. Vertical bars indicate LSD (P = 0.05). (After Aspinall, unpublished.)

G. ACCUMULATION IN RESPONSE TO OTHER ENVIRONMENTAL STRESS FACTORS

1. High temperature

Proline accumulation is not a response exclusive to situations of plant water deficit. Accumulation has been reported to occur following exposure of plants to high temperature (Chu et al., 1974), salinity stress (Stewart & Lee, 1974; Treichel, 1975), low pH (Anon, 1973), nutrient deficiencies (Savitskaya, 1976) and pathological conditions (Meon et al., 1978). If it may be assumed that proline accumulation is due, in each case, to the same fundamental mechanism, then it is pertinent to enquire about the features which may be common to such apparently disparate stress situations. As an initial hypothesis it was suggested that accumulation in response to low and high temperature (Chu et al., 1974) and to salinity (Chu et al., 1976a) could be due to a disturbance in tissue water status comparable to that observed during simple water deficit. The accumulation in response to high temperature can certainly be explained in this manner. Where barley plants were subjected to a high temperature (35°C) under otherwise normal environmental conditions, they accumulated proline, but this accumulation was accompanied by a fall in leaf water potential. If leaf water potential was prevented from falling by maintaining the plants in a saturated atmosphere, no proline accumulation occurred at this temperature (Chu et al., 1974).

2. Salinity

In the case of salinity stress, a similar explanation of the response is feasible. A parallel has been found between the decrease in leaf water potential and proline accumulation in intact plants subjected to an increasing salinity in the root environment (Chu et al., 1976a). One may question, however, whether absorbed salt itself plays any role in the accumulation mechanism. Both the *in vitro* inhibition of pyrroline-5-carboxylate dehydrogenase activity by a range of inorganic salts (Boggess et al., 1975) and the reported enhancement of pyrroline-5-carboxylate reductase activity *in vitro* by salt (Huber, 1974) suggest that proline accumulation may be specifically promoted by certain inorganic ions. However pyrroline-5-carboxylate reductase activity does not appear to limit proline synthesis *in vivo* (Boggess et al., 1976b), so the significance of this reported promotion by NaCl *in vitro* is questionable. Moreover, with the exception of Mg^{2+} and Ca^{2+} salts, inorganic ions appear to inhibit rather than promote proline accumulation when the response is measured at equivalent leaf water potentials (Chu et al., 1976b). Indeed, proline accumulation is linearly inversely related to tissue Na^+ concentration when excised barley leaves are floated on solutions of NaCl adjusted to the same water potential with polyethylene glycol.

Consistently, however, Mg^{2+} and Ca^{2+} salts promote proline accumulation in both excised leaves and intact plants when compared with plants maintained at an equivalent leaf water potential with a non-absorbable solute (Chu et al., 1976b). Proline accumulation has also been reported to be promoted by K^+ salts (Mukherjee, 1974; Udayakumar et al., 1976; Palfi et al., 1976), although KCl was found to inhibit accumulation in a similar manner to NaCl in both intact plants and excised leaves of barley (Chu et al., 1976b). These various responses of the proline accumulating system to inorganic ions do not suggest that variations in internal ion concentration play any decisive role in initiating proline accumulation, but rather that they modulate the rate of accumulation, possibly through inhibition or promotion of specific enzyme activities concerned in synthesis or oxidation.

3. Low temperature

In contrast to the situations which have been discussed so far, the initiation of proline accumulation in response to low temperature cannot be ascribed to a change in the water potential of the tissue (Chu et al., 1974). It is clear that proline accumulates in barley at temperature below 12°C without any concomitant decrease in the water potential of the leaf tissue (Chu et al., 1974, 1978). This process is completely light dependent, whereas the accumulation induced by water deficit is not. Low temperature-induced accumulation also differs as it is not immediately reversible, since accumulation continues for 24 h when plants are returned to a higher temperature (Chu et al., 1974). Despite these differences, it is possible that a common mechanism for proline accumulation is induced by both low temperatures and water deficit. For example, it is conceivable that the relationship between water and macromolecules or the hydration of membrane surfaces are responsive in a similar manner to both a net reduction in hydration and a lowering of tissue temperature. Such changes may not be observed by measurements of bulk tissue water parameters.

II. CONSEQUENCES OF PROLINE ACCUMULATION

A. FUNCTIONAL ASPECTS OF PROLINE ACCUMULATION

In considering a pronounced metabolic response to stress, it is necessary to ask whether plants possessing such a mechanism have any evolutionary or physiological advantage. This approach draws attention to the possible functional aspects of proline accumulation, rather than treating the accumulation as a consequential and physiologically neutral, or even detrimental effect, of stress. Several possible positive roles for proline accumulation in stress metabolism have been suggested with greater or lesser conviction, and it is worthwhile considering the evidence for these before discussing the more empirical, correlative data linking proline accumulation with stress resistance. The extensive accumulation of proline in plant cells is aided by its outstanding solubility in water; a high concentration (and hence low osmotic potential) of the imino acid in plant tissues is, thereby, possible.

B. OSMOREGULATION

The evidence that accumulated proline acts as a compatible solute regulating and reducing water loss from the cell during episodes of water deficit is compelling and need not be reiterated here. The rapidity of accumulation following the onset of dehydration, coupled with the equally fast decline in concentration upon returning to more favourable conditions, suggests that proline concentration may adjust rapidly to changes in the aqueous environment of the cell. A mechanism such as this can be important in a mesophytic higher plant growing in a field environment where diurnal fluctuations in leaf water potential occur. A different strategy may be involved in habitats where a longer-term or even constant dehydration situation exists; for instance, saline environments. In this case compatible solutes (like the betaines) which undergo less rapid changes in concentration (i.e. have lower adaptability) may be more important (see Chapter 9).

C. HYDRATION CHARACTERISTICS OF BIOPOLYMERS

In higher plants, the phenomenon of accumulation of organic compounds as a response to water stress has been linked primarily to the maintenance of cell turgor (Kauss, 1977). It is apparent that this view is an over-simplification and that the water environment of cell membranes and biologically important macromolecules may be an important consideration. Proline in solution has been shown to affect the solubility of various proteins and to protect bovine albumin from denaturation by $(NH_4)_2SO_4$ or ethanol (Schobert & Tschesche, 1978). It was suggested that this property of proline may be due to an interaction between the proline molecule and hydrophobic surface residues on the proteins, which increases the total hydrophilic area of the associated molecules and hence their stability. If such an interaction occurs in the cytoplasm, at the concentrations of protein and proline which occur in the cell, it will be obviously significant in water deficit situations and will support Schobert's views on the importance of interactions between "biopolymers" and proline in stress responses (Schobert & Tschesche, 1978). This information supports earlier empirical observations of increases in the "bound-water" fraction in cytoplasm in the presence of proline (Palfi et al., 1974b; Savitskaya, 1976) which may be concerned with significant adaptive phenomena (see Chapter 6).

Proline at relatively high concentrations inhibits germination and growth much less than comparable concentrations of glutamine and asparagine (Palfi et al., 1974b), suggesting that free proline does not interfere with plant metabolism at the concentrations accumulated during stress. This was confirmed by the demonstration that the *in vitro* activity of several enzymes from *Triglochin maritima*, a proline accumulating species, is completely unaffected by proline concentrations up to 700 mM (Stewart & Lee, 1974). It has also been suggested that proline may reduce the inhibition of malic dehydrogenase activity caused by 300 mM NaCl, though not itself inhibitory at concentrations up to 500 mM (Wyn Jones, pers. comm.). These observations are in keeping with the hypothesis that the accumulation of proline during periods of stress has definite evolutionary advantage, in that it endows the cells with a measure of resistance, and is not merely a consequence of stress-impaired metabolism.

D. THE CONSERVATION OF ENERGY AND AMINO GROUPS

Our discussion so far has been confined to the possible physical and metabolic consequences of proline accumulation during a period of decreased water potential. However, the presence of a considerable concentration of this readily metabolized substrate will probably have a critical influence on metabolic events in the period immediately following stress relief. Proline is translocated freely within the plant during water stress and accumulates to the highest concentration in younger leaves and shoots (Singh et al., 1973a). The concentration falls rapidly once stress is relieved (Jager & Meyer, 1977) and proline would appear to be a readily utilizable source of energy and amino groups. The significance of the movement of proline within the stressed plant requires further evaluation, however, as it has been calculated that proline constitutes only 13% of the N moved from the barley leaf during stress (Tulley et al., 1979).

Proline is oxidized rapidly to glutamate in turgid tissue (Stewart et al., 1977), but there is no marked increase in glutamate or α-aminobutyrate concentration following stress relief. However, Blum and Ebercon (1976) reported an increase in ammonium concentration after the termination of stress and it can be presumed that, in this case, proline was de-aminated with the carbon skeleton entering the Krebs cycle. This is supported by the rapid evolution of $^{14}CO_2$ following the re-watering of stressed plants previously loaded with ^{14}C-proline (Boggess, pers. comm.). The high concentration of proline accumulated in pollen cells, which is rapidly reduced during pollen tube growth, has also been proposed as a readily accessible energy source (Dashek & Harwood, 1974). A similar suggestion has been made about the proline in the cockroach (Holden, 1973). It is intellectually attractive to consider that the accumulation of proline in stress situations has evolved as a means of conserving both energy and nitrogen in a readily available form which has few physical or metabolic disadvantages.

E. SINK FOR SOLUBLE NITROGEN

A further metabolically useful role which has been suggested for proline during water stress is as a sink for the nitrogen from nitrogenous compounds derived from the net loss of protein (Savitskaya, 1976). Protein synthesis is readily inhibited by water stress, but protein hydrolysis is not inhibited and may even be enhanced (Petrie & Wood, 1958; Shah & Loomis, 1965). Although the uptake of nitrogen from the environment is inhibited by stress, and the activity of enzymes such as nitrate reductase is severely curtailed, the overall result is an accumulation of soluble nitrogen-containing compounds of relatively low molecular weight. Many such compounds are potential inhibitors of cell metabolism. Some, such as the ammonium ion, are toxic in other than low concentrations, while few are as soluble in aqueous solution as proline. While proline synthesis in itself does not appear to be directly involved in ammonia detoxification (Stewart & Hanson, 1980), Yancey and Somero (1979) presented evidence that proline and other, similar solutes can protect enzymes against the deleterious effects of biologically toxic compounds like urea, etc. Thus, in addition to the roles mentioned above, we suggest that the evolution of proline accumulation conferred, on at least some plants, a means of coping with large amounts of soluble nitrogenous compounds which may themselves harm cellular metabolism.

F. SENESCENCE PHENOMENA

Finally, in discussing the consequences of proline accumulation for the metabolism of the water-stressed plant, we have to consider the possibility that there is no adaptive significance to such accumulation, and that it represents merely a manifestation of the damaging effects of stress. The metabolic consequences of water deficit have frequently been compared with those of senescence, and it may be that proline synthesis is such a consequence. Certainly, proline accumulation occurs in detached leaves not subjected to any water stress (Singh et al., 1973b), though not in senescing leaves attached to the plant (Chu et al., 1978). Proline may well be transported away from attached senescing leaves, but this does not necessarily mean that stress-induced proline accumulation is related to senescence. Indeed, leaves which have accumulated large amounts of proline at a low temperature persist on the plant without visible senescence for considerable longer than leaves growing on plants at higher temperatures which accumulate no proline (Chu et al., 1978). In this connection it is interesting that Tyankova (1967b) found that more proline accumulated in green than in yellow wheat leaves during water deficit.

If water stress is sufficiently severe to induce death and desiccation of leaf tissue, accumulated proline may be unable to move from the dead, drying tissue and will be rendered unavailable for further metabolism within the plant

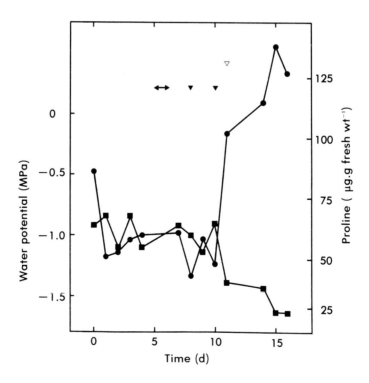

FIG. 4. Variation in water potential (■) and proline content (●) of young leaves of cotton (cv. Deltapine Smooth Leaf) during an extended period of water deficit. Plants grown in glasshouse lysimeters and watered for 12 weeks when watering was discontinued. Proline and water potential measured in leaves 5 and 6 at noon each day. Closed triangles — cloudy days or periods; open triangle — wilting. (After Aspinall, unpublished.)

(Hanson et al., 1977). This may occur if the translocation of proline from the leaf is impaired before its synthesis. In this situation the accumulated proline is of no possible further advantage to the plant and represents a net loss of nitrogen to the plant. In less severe stress, representing the situation of most common interest in the field, proline is likely to accumulate and be re-metabolized, as the water potential of the plant varies with vagaries of the weather and with the diurnal cycle of transpiration (Rajagopal et al., 1977; Fig. 4).

III. PROLINE ACCUMULATION AND STRESS RESISTANCE

A. GENERAL CONSIDERATIONS

If the consequences of proline accumulation in plant tissues during a period of stress are, in aggregate, either beneficial or harmful to the further growth and survival of the plant, one might reasonably expect a correlation, either positive or negative, between proline accumulation potential and stress resistance. Only if, or when, proline accumulation were a neutral attribute in stress resistance (a somewhat unlikely prospect) would no such correlation be apparent. To establish such a correlation, however, numerous pitfalls must be avoided. Firstly, since proline accumulation is a function of tissue water potential and time, care must be taken to ensure that tissue water potential and experimental duration are varied in exactly the same manner in comparisons between species, varieties or treatments. In practice, this is difficult to achieve since variations in stomatal physiology and morphology, plant and leaf size, root attributes, etc. between plants will affect drying rates and the water potential–time relationship. Singh et al. (1972, 1973c) claimed to have achieved parity of tissue water potential treatment within a range of barley cultivars and, thus, to be able to compare proline accumulation in the absence of cultivar differences in water potential. Hanson et al. (1977) could not repeat this using two of the twenty original cultivars of Singh et al. (1973c), but identical methods were not used.

A further problem exists in attempting to derive an effective and readily utilizable measure of stress resistance. In agricultural research the ultimate measure must be the comparative yield in a field stress situation. In surveying the contents of this book it must be apparent that such a measure can only be a function of a multiplicity of resistance characteristics, and it is unlikely that a close relationship can be established between any single character and resistance measured by yield in the field. Nevertheless, such an analysis has been attempted for proline accumulation and stability index (an estimate of the stability of yield in a variety of environments), and a high correlation was reported (Singh et al., 1972). Other measures concerned with individual facets of plant stress resistance are more likely to be correlated with proline accumulation and, arguably, provide a more realistic test of the hypothesis. Both plant growth rate immediately following a period of stress and leaf survival have been found to be correlated with proline accumulation (Singh et al., 1973c) and support the general relationship. It must be understood, however, that each involves a different, although not necessarily exclusive, assumption about the role of proline in stress metabolism.

B. HARDENING

Although the most immediately useful source of variation in stress resistance is genetic, there is ample, if imprecise, evidence of inducible resistance within the same genetic constitution. Resistance can be induced by pre-exposure to water deficit, or by a variety of exogenous substances, notably the growth retardants, and there is some evidence about the effects of these hardening treatments on proline accumulation.

In barley, previous exposure to a water deficit on one or two occasions considerably increased the capacity of the plant to accumulate proline on subsequent exposure to water deficit (no previous exposure 9.0 mg.g dry wt^{-1}; one previous episode 11.7 mg.g dry wt^{-1}; and two previous episodes 14.3 mg.g dry wt^{-1}; Singh et al., 1973c). This increase in proline accumulation was not due to any change in the water status of the leaf in the final exposure to water deficit, nor to any persistence of accumulated proline from previous stress episodes. No growth measurements were made, so the effect of the treatments on stress resistance is difficult to assess, but it is pertinent that the successive cycles of water deficit reduced the loss of chlorophyll which occurred in the final period of water stress.

C. GROWTH RETARDANTS

A similar response was induced by supplying wheat plants with the growth retardant, cycocel (Singh et al., 1973d). Treatment of the plants with the growth retardant for 10 d before the imposition of a sudden, severe stress inhibited growth but had no significant influence on leaf water potential during the period of stress. There was a pronounced enhancement of proline accumulation, however (Fig. 5). The growth retardant treatment was ineffective in modifying plant resistance during stress, as measured by various growth parameters, but may have changed the growth response of the plant during recovery from water stress. This suggestion is consistent with the

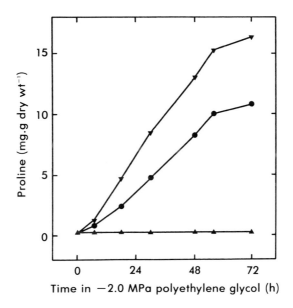

FIG. 5. The effect of a growth retardant ((2-chloroethyl)-trimethylammonium chloride, CCC) on proline accumulation in the second leaf of wheat (cv. Gabo) plants. Wheat seedlings were watered with 8 mg CCC. plant $^{-1}$ 7 d from emergence; 10 d later they were stressed with a −2.0 MPa polyethylene glycol solution. Stressed control (●); stressed and treated with CCC (▼); unstressed with or without CCC (▲). (After Singh et al., 1973d.)

results of Plaut and Halevy (1966) and may be linked with the fact that the accumulated proline was metabolized more rapidly in the retardant-treated plants than in control plants following re-watering.

D. EXOGENOUS PROLINE APPLICATION

Another possible way of assessing the relationship between proline accumulation and stress resistance is to determine the effects of exogenous proline on the response of the plant to stress. This assumes that internal proline concentrations can be significantly elevated by supplying proline and that exogenous proline can reach the same intracellular pools that are available to endogenous proline. During a period of water stress, when proline oxidation is inhibited (Stewart et al., 1977), this is possible, but interpretation is confounded by the necessity to supply proline in aqueous solution with consequent effects on water potential. In watered plants, proline is very rapidly metabolized and it is questionable whether tissue proline levels can be increased significantly by feeding exogenous proline. Reported resistance-inducing effects of such treatment (Tyankova, 1967a; Hubac & Guerrier, 1972; Bal, 1976) may represent responses to an increase in concentration of an energy rich substrate, rather than a specific response to proline. In none of the reported cases was the internal proline concentration measured following application of exogenous proline. Interpretative difficulties of this approach are compounded by the presence of more than one endogenous pool of proline (Boggess et al., 1976a).

E. COMPARISONS BETWEEN SPECIES

The wide, although not universal, occurrence of proline accumulation as a response to water deficit in living organisms has been suggested as evidence that this reaction is a primitive regulatory response (Measures, 1975). If this is so, and proline is unique in this function, one might reasonably expect proline accumulation to be a characteristic of organisms of drier habitats. In higher plants this is clearly not the case, and the occurrence of marked proline accumulation as a response to water deficit is an apparently independent event, possibly as closely associated with species growing in mesic environments as in arid situations (Table I). Two explanations of this distribution are possible: either proline accumulation is a metabolic response of little selective advantage or, more plausibly, proline accumulation is only one of a number of strategies which have conferred advantages on plants in such circumstances. Plants living in saline environments may accumulate proline as a compatible solute (e.g. *Triglochin maritima*, Stewart & Lee, 1974) or may accumulate other organic solutes. This re-enforces the suggestion that, as in the algae, higher plants have evolved a variety of answers to the same basic problem.

Comparisons have been made between pairs of species growing in a similar habitat (Pourrat & Hubac, 1974), and between species apparently adapted to different habitats (Hubac & Guerrier, 1972), with a view to relating proline accumulation to stress resistance. Such comparisons are limited in number but confirm the lack of generality of proline accumulation as a response to water deficit. *Carex pachystylis*, a desert plant, accumulates proline rapidly and extensively during water deficit, but *Artemisia herba-alba*, from the same habitat, does not (Pourrat & Hubac, 1974). On the other hand, in a comparison between two sedge species, it was found that the one adapted to a dry habitat accumulated proline extensively when subjected to a water deficit, while the species from a wetter habitat accumulated proline for a short period in similar circumstances but then metabolized the accumulated proline (Hubac & Guerrier, 1972).

TABLE I
Proline accumulation by different species.

1. Accumulation in response to water deficit.

Species	Control	Stress	Per cent increase	Units of measurement	Conditions and Reference
Order Rosales					
FAMILY ROSACEAE					
Rubus caesius	<0.4	21.8	>5350	mg.g dry wt⁻¹	1 J
Prunus persica	0.1	0.5	400	mg.g dry wt⁻¹	9 B
Order Leguminales					
FAMILY PAPILIONACEAE					
Pisum sativum	<0.4	33.1	>8175	mg.g dry wt⁻¹	1 J
Lens culinaris	<0.4	22.1	>5425	"	1 J
Medicago sativa	<0.4	20.3	>4975	"	1 J
Trifolium repens	<0.4	21.4	>5250	"	1 J
Phaseolus vulgaris	<0.4	8.6	>2050	"	1 J
Vicia faba	1.8	19.5	983	μM.shoot⁻¹	14 G
	0.12	0.54	350	mg.g dry wt⁻¹	9 M
Order Cucurbitales					
FAMILY CUCURBITACEAE					
Cucurbita pepo	<0.4	3.4	>750	mg.g dry wt⁻¹	1 J
Cucumis melo	<0.4	2.9	>625	"	1 J
Colocynthis citrullus	<0.4	3.5	>775	"	1 J
Cucumis sativus	<0.4	3	>650	"	1 J
	0	0.01	—	"	9 M
Order Malvales					
FAMILY MALVACEAE					
Gossypium hirsutum	0	0.19	—	mg.g dry wt⁻¹	9 M

Table I continued

Order Rhamnales						
FAMILY VITACEAE						
Vitis vinifera	<0.4	7.9	>1875	mg.g dry wt^{-1}	1	J
Order Rhoeadales						
FAMILY PAPAVERACEAE						
Papaver somniferum	<0.4	4	>900	mg.g dry wt^{-1}	1	J
Order Brassicales						
FAMILY CRUCIFERAE						
Sinapis alba	<0.4	24.8	>6100	mg.g dry wt^{-1}	1	J
Raphanus sativus	<0.4	26.4	>6500	"	1	J
Brassica napus	<0.4	25.9	>6375	"	1	J
Brassica oleracea	<0.4	43.7	>10825	"	1	J
Brassica oleracea	0.46	50.8	10943	"	1	I
Raphanus sativus	0.4	17.2	4200	"	2	F
Order Polygonales						
FAMILY POLYGONACEAE						
Rumex scatatus	<0.4	3.3	>725	mg.g dry wt^{-1}	1	J
Rheum rhaponticum	0.63	3.1	392	"	17	B
Order Chenopodiales						
FAMILY CHENOPODIACEAE						
Chenopodium album	<0.4	>4.7	1175	mg.g dry wt^{-1}	1	J
Spinacia oleracea	<0.4	>4.2	950	"	1	J
	0.55	3.46	529	"	15	I
	0.4	2.2	450	"	15	I
Beta vulgaris	<0.4	>3.8	850	"	1	J
Order Asterales						
FAMILY ASTERACEAE (Compositae)						
Helianthus annuus	0.2	6.5	3150	mg.g dry wt^{-1}	11	Q

Species			Units			
Maricaria chamomilla	0.2	23.4	µM.g dry wt⁻¹	11600	5	H
Lactuca sativa	<0.4	21.4	"	>5250	1	J
Taraxacum officinalis	<0.4	22.1	"	>5425	1	J
Artemisia vulgaris	<0.4	3	"	>650	1	J
	<0.4	4.2	"	>950	1	J
	<0.4	23.7	"	>5825	1	J
Artemisia absinthium	12	126	"	950	12	L
Artemisia herba-alba	2	10	"	400	13	L
Order Solanales						
FAMILY SOLANACEAE						
Solanum tuberosum	<0.4	29.6	mg.g dry wt⁻¹	>7300	1	J
Capsicum annuum	<0.4	35.2	"	>8700	1	J
Lycopersicon esculentum	<0.4	22.3	"	>5400	1	J
Hyoscyamus niger	<0.4	26.5	"	>6525	1	J
Solanum laciniatum	<0.4	32.6	"	>8050	1	J
	1.5	12.1	"	707	3	B
Nicotiana tabacum	<0.4	28.5	"	>7025	1	J
Order Liliales						
FAMILY LILIACEAE						
Allium cepa	<0.4	4.2	mg.g dry wt⁻¹	>950	1	J
Allium sativum	<0.4	3.6	"	>800	1	J
Order Cyperales						
FAMILY CYPERACEAE						
Carex pachystylis	1	13	µM.g dry wt⁻¹	1200	16	L
Carex setifolia	1	14	"	1300	13	L
Order Graminales						
FAMILY GRAMINEAE						
Triticum aestivum,						
Var 1.	0.28	112	µM.g dry wt⁻¹	39900	4	P
Var 2.	0.86	174	"	20133	4	P

Table I continued

Species	Control	Stress	Per cent increase	Units of measurement	Conditions and Reference
Hordeum vulgare 10 cultivars	0.4	25.7	6325	mg.g dry wt^{-1}	5 H
	0.22–0.32	9.0–24.1	3991–7431	"	6 M
Secale cereale	<0.4	18.6	>4550	"	1 J
Avena sativa	<0.4	17.9	>4375	"	1 J
Oryza sativa	<0.4	21.3	>5225	"	1 J
	0.1–0.2	2–28	1900–13900	"	7 A
Sorghum vulgare	<0.4	20.4	>5000	"	1 J
Cynodon dactylon, Common	<2.7	69.3	>2467	μM.g dry wt^{-1}	8 C
Coastal	<1.1	126	>11355	"	8 C
Festuca pratensis	<0.4	25.7	>6325	mg.g dry wt^{-1}	1 J
Bromus arvensis	<0.4	22.8	>5600	"	1 J
Poa pratensis	<0.4	26.4	>5900	"	1 J
Lolium perenne	<0.4	23.6	>5900	"	1 J
Lolium aristatum	<0.4	31.4	>7750	"	1 J
Lolium temulentum	<0.4	28.5	>7025	"	1 J
Zea mays	0.1	2.1	2100	"	9 M
	<0.4	5.1	1175	"	1 J
	17.8	28.5	60	μM.g fresh wt^{-1}	10 N
	0.13	0.15	15	mg.g dry wt^{-1}	9 M

2. Accumulation in response to salinity stress.

Species	Control	Stress	Per cent increase	Units of measurement	Conditions and Reference
Order Leguminales					
FAMILY PAPILIONACEAE					
Vicia faba	0.41	2.22	441	mg.g dry wt^{-1}	18 E
Pisum sativum	0.19	1.21	537	"	18 E
Phaseolus vulgaris	0.34	1.46	329	"	19 K

Order Cucurbitales						
FAMILY CUCURBITACEAE						
Cucumis sativis	0.2	0.66	230	"	18	E
Order Malvales						
FAMILY MALVACEAE						
Gossypium hirsutum	0.49	0.5	2	"	18	E
Order Brassicales						
FAMILY CRUCIFERAE						
Raphanus raphanis	0.54	3.01	457	"	18	E
Brassica napus	0.73	6.78	829	"	18	E
Order Chenopodiales						
FAMILY CHENOPODIACEAE						
Beta vulgaris	0.46	1.43	211	"	18	E
Order Asterales						
FAMILY ASTERACEAE						
Helianthus annuus	0.42	22.3	5210	"	19	K
Order Solanales						
FAMILY SOLANACEAE						
Lycopersicon esculentum	0.16	0.92	475	"	18	E
Capsicum annuum	0.36	21.7	5928	"	19	K
Order Graminales						
FAMILY GRAMINEAE						
Hordeum vulgare	0.25	4.47	1688	"	18	E
Triticum aestivum	0.45	4.06	802	"	18	E
Avena sativa	0.41	6.54	1495	"	18	E
Zea mays	0.14	0.54	286	"	18	E

Table I continued

Halophytes

Order Primulales						
FAMILY PLUMBAGINACEAE						
Armeria maritima						
Coastal popn.	<5	110	>2100	μM.g fresh wt^{-1}	20	O
Inland popn.	<5	35	>600	"	20	O
Order Juncaginales						
FAMILY JUNCAGINACEAE						
Triglochin maritima	40	360	800	"	20	O
Order Potomogetonales						
FAMILY RUPPIACEAE						
Ruppia maritima	1	4.5	350	"	21	O
Order Graminales						
FAMILY GRAMINEAE						
Phragmites communis	0.13	1.66	1177	mg.g fresh wt^{-1}	22	D

Abbreviations

1. Excised, wilted 4-5 d at 25°C at 60% RH in light.
2. 72 h water loss by intact plants, ψ_{leaf} -3.4 MPa.
3. Excised, floated on -2.0 MPa PEG for 24 h.
4. Plants in soil allowed to dry to permanent wilting.
5. Excised, wilted 3 d.
6. 60 h exposure of intact plants to -2.0 MPa PEG solution.
7. -1.8 MPa soil water stress at vegetative stage.
8. Intact plants, stressed until ψ_{leaf} fell to -3.0 MPa.
9. Excised, floated 24 h on -1.0 MPa PEG solution.
10. Excised leaves, wilted to 65-75% original fresh wt and held for 24 h.
11. Wilted 48 h.
12. Plants deprived of water 8 d.
13. Plants deprived of water 12 d.
14. 10 d stress with -0.6 MPa PEG.
15. "Live wilted".
16. Deprived of water 20 d.
17. Intact plant stressed with -1.0 MPa PEG.
18. Intact plants exposed to -1.0 MPa NaCl for 48 h.
19. Intact plants exposed to 2% Na_2SO_4 for 14 d.
20. 200 mM NaCl for 10 d.
21. 140 mM NaCl for 10 d.
22. 1 M NaCl for 7 d.

A. Anon. (1975).
B. Aspinall, unpubl.
C. Barnett and Naylor (1966).
D. Cho (1977).
E. Chu (1974).
F. Chu et al. (1974).
G. Jager and Meyer (1977).
H. Palfi et al. (1973).
I. Palfi et al. (1974a).
J. Palfi et al. (1974c).
K. Palfi and Juhasz (1970).
L. Pourrat and Hubac (1974).
M. Chu et al. (1978).
N. Stewart et al. (1966).
O. Stewart and Lee (1974).
P. Tyankova (1967b).
Q. Wample and Bewley (1975).

F. COMPARISONS WITHIN SPECIES

1. The extent of intra-specific variation

Variation in a physiological response within a species is likely to be less than that between species, and to be less complicated by major variation in other characters. It can be argued that comparison of genotypes within a species is more likely to lead to an unambiguous assessment of the implications of the response to the physiology of the plant than inter-specific comparison is. There is ample evidence of intra-specific variation in the accumulation of proline in response to water deficit (Barnett & Naylor, 1966; Singh et al., 1972, 1973c; Lewin & Sparrow, 1975; Blum & Ebercon, 1976; Machado et al., 1976; Hanson et al., 1977; Pinter et al., 1977; Anon, 1975; Stewart & Hanson, 1980), and some evidence for intra-specific variation in the absence of any stress (Preil, 1977), in response to low temperature (Benko, 1968; Rochat & Therrien, 1976; Chu et al., 1978), and in response to salinity (Table II). The significance of this intra-specific variation in proline accumulation in relation to drought resistance is disputed, however (Hanson et al., 1977).

The differences in proline accumulation which are likely, of themselves, to be significant are those which occur despite identical plant water potential histories in the compared cultivars. Differences between cultivars are most commonly associated with differences in leaf water status due to the relationship between water potential, time and proline accumulation, but these are of less significance to an assessment of the role of proline accumulation in response to water deficit. Singh et al. (1972, 1973c) found major differences in proline accumulation by different barley cultivars despite identical water

TABLE II

Proline accumulation in response to salinity stress in barley cultivars. Plants for salinity stress were grown for 10 d in water, cultivar then subjected to -1.0 MPa NaCl stress for 2 d.[a]

| Cultivar | Proline content of first leaf (mg.g dry wt^{-1}) | |
	Control	Salinity stress
Excelsior	0.4	15.2
Bankuti Korai	0.3	11.3
Prior A	0.2	9.1
Princess	0.4	7.6
Arivat	0.2	12.3
Velvon II	0.3	6.5
CI 3576	0.3	9.4
BR 1239	0.2	10.3
Maraini	0.4	8.5
Proctor	0.3	14.8

[a]From Chu, Aspinall and Paleg (unpublished).

potential levels. Differences in proline accumulation between cultivars was attributed to factors other than the water potential history of the leaves. In a detailed examination of the responses of two of the cultivars used by Singh et al. (1972, 1973c), Hanson et al. (1977) could not achieve identical rates of water loss in the two cultivars and attributed the differences in proline accumulation which they observed to the difference in water status. The difference in comparative proline accumulation by the two cultivars in the two investigations is presumably also attributable to the differences in water potential history of the tissues. Clearly any investigation in which intact plants are subjected to water deficit by allowing water loss to occur by transpiration, whether the plants are growing in soil or are subjected to an osmotic stress, is liable to pose problems of differences in the rate of water loss by different cultivars (Lewin & Sparrow, 1975). Equally clearly, however, genetic differences in the ability of tissue to accumulate proline in response to a specific water deficit also occur.

Apart from the whole plant studies of Singh et al. (1972, 1973c), unequivocal evidence of intraspecific variation in proline accumulation, unrelated to varietal differences in water potential, is provided by the differences in accumulation recorded for excised leaf material. Those data were obtained by subjecting the leaf material to water deficit by floating on solutions of low osmotic potential. In this technique the tissue water potential equilibrates rapidly with that of the solution, and cultivar differences in water potential are unlikely. Using this approach, differences in proline accumulation have been found between cultivars of barley (Lewin & Sparrow, 1975), bean (Machado et al., 1976) and corn (Pinter et al., 1977).

2. Relationship to stress resistance

Interest in the significance of intra-specific variation in the capacity to accumulate proline during a water deficit was aroused by the claim of Singh et al. (1972) that the variation in barley might be related to the yield capacity of the cultivar during drought in the field. In their experiments, the ability to accumulate a high concentration of proline in the seedling stage in response to water deficit was correlated with the potential of the cultivar to produce a relatively stable yield in environments of varying levels of stress (Fig. 6). This relationship for barley has been questioned (Lewin & Sparrow, 1975) principally because the apparent drought resistance of the barley cultivars used was strongly correlated with their time of maturity in the field. Relatively early-flowering cultivars accumulated most proline and were apparently most drought resistant. This criticism can only be resolved by comparing material of similar maturity but different drought resistance, a task which has not been undertaken as yet.

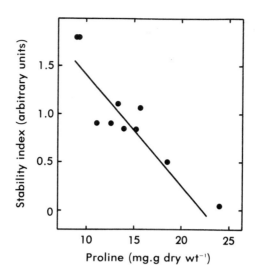

FIG. 6. The relationship between stability index (Finlay & Wilkinson, 1963) and proline accumulation during water deficit in the first leaves of 10 barley cultivars. Correlation co-efficient of two measures equals 0.89. (After Singh et al., 1972.)

   Theoretically, if proline accumulation is a manifestation of stress resistance, there should be a greater possibility of finding correlations between this characteristic and performance during water stress, if assessment is confined to more immediate effects of water deficit than the ultimate grain yield. Any relationship found may also suggest the physiological role of proline in the stressed plant. Singh et al. (1973c) measured several attributes of the growth and metabolism of a group of barley cultivars during and following a severe, relatively brief exposure to water deficit, and compared these responses with proline accumulation. The cultivars included those previously assessed for the relationship between proline accumulation and field performance (Singh et al., 1972). There was no difference between the cultivars in dehydrogenase activity, as measured by the ability of the leaf tissue to reduce triphenyltetrazolium chloride. Dehydrogenase activity declined with the fall in leaf water potential and appeared to be unrelated to proline accumulation. Similarly, leaf chlorophyll content declined by approximately 50% in all cultivars during the course of 60 h exposure to water deficit. There was little recovery in 24 h following relief of the water stress, but by 48 h, leaf chlorophyll content had recovered by 18% in all cultivars. Again, there appeared to be no relationship between this parameter and proline accumulation.

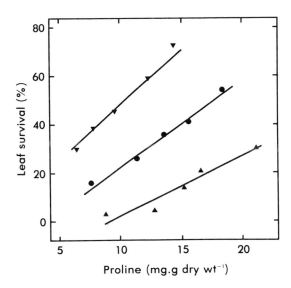

FIG. 7. The relationship between leaf survival (estimated as the percentage of the leaf which remained viable) and leaf proline content in 5 barley cultivars after −2.0 MPa polyethylene glycol water stress of 50 h (▼), 73 h (●), or 97 h (▲). (After Singh et al., 1973c.)

   In contrast to the lack of correlation between proline content and these metabolic effects of water deficit, there was a close relationship between leaf tissue survival and proline accumulation in the 5 cultivars considered (Fig. 7). Barley leaves tend to senesce from the tip to the base under conditions of severe water deficit, and the extent of this senescence was inversely proportional to the amount of proline accumulated by the leaf. An identical relationship for rice has been established with many more cultivars (Anon, 1975). This comparison is complicated by the subsequent observation that free proline may be trapped in the senescing tissues during a water deficit and, consequently, may be unavailable for further metabolism (Hanson et al., 1977). Such trapped proline may well account for the incomplete metabolism of accumulated proline in barley, particularly in the first leaves, following 48 h recovery from water stress, where up to 80% of accumulated proline was still present (Singh et al., 1973c). This consideration does not affect the argument concerning the relationship between proline accumulation and leaf survival, however, as cultivars which accumulated most proline lost least leaf material during the period of water deficit. One may perhaps consider the proline lost to the plant in leaf material dying during drought as part of an incompletely effective defense mechanism.

Once the water deficit was removed from these barley cultivars, the relative growth rate of the plants increased and the accumulated proline disappeared (Singh et al., 1973c). The relative growth rate of the cultivars during this recovery period was related directly to the amount of proline accumulated during the period of water deficit (Fig. 8). The simplest explanation of this relationship is that plants with high proline accumulation also had the most complete leaf survival. Additionally, the rate of consumption of proline during the recovery phase was directly related to the amount available (Fig. 9), and the metabolism of the accumulated proline can reasonably be expected to have participated in the recovery of the plants from the water deficit. This latter potential role of accumulated proline has been suggested for drought resistance of sorghum cultivars (Blum & Ebercon, 1976). Eight cultivars grown in controlled environment were subject to a 5 d water deficit by allowing the young plants to transpire without additional water. It was claimed that this treatment reduced water potential in the leaves of all cultivars to the same level (-2.0 MPa, day 5). The cultivars differed significantly in the amount of proline accumulated during the period of stress, but this variation was not correlated with the desiccation resistance of leaf tissue taken from field-grown plants of the same cultivars. However there was

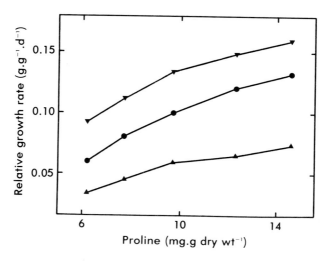

FIG. 8. The relationship between leaf proline content at the end of a -2.0 MPa water (polyethylene glycol) stress, and the daily relative growth rate of barley plants in the periods 0–1 d (▲), 1–2 d (●), 2–3 d (▼) immediately following relief of the stress. (After Singh et al., 1973c.)

a close relationship between proline accumulation and the recovery of the plants from the effects of stress, as measured on an arbitrary scale 24 h after supplying water to the plant, and both recovery and proline content were related to the dark respiration rate during the recovery period. Blum and Ebercon (1976) concluded that, in sorghum, proline accumulation was likely to assist in the recovery of plants from an episode of water deficit but was unlikely to participate in the determination of tissue survival during water deficit. Although their evidence for proline involvement in recovery is persuasive, the assessment of tissue desiccation injury is inadequate to support the second conclusion. The ranking of cultivars for desiccation tolerance was unrelated to their ranking for injury (Table III; Blum & Ebercon, 1976). It may well be that in the sorghum cultivars grown in controlled environment, as for barley, recovery rate was related to leaf tissue survival and both were related to proline accumulation.

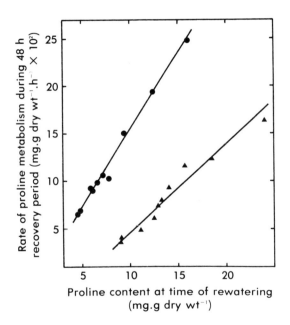

FIG. 9. The relationship between the amount of proline accumulated within a barley leaf during a water deficit and the rate at which the accumulated proline is metabolized following relief of the deficit. Ten cultivars of barley were subjected to a severe water deficit; the proline contents of leaves 1 (▲) and 3 (●) (counting from the base) were measured and the plants were then rewatered. Proline content was remeasured after 48 h recovery. Correlation co-efficient for leaf 1 values is 0.96, and for leaf 2 is 0.99. (After Singh, 1970.)

TABLE III

Results of various tests performed on eight sorghum cultivars at the peak of desiccation (29 d after emergence, DAE) or upon recovery (30 DAE). Water deficit was imposed by terminating irrigation on 24 DAE and was ended by irrigation on 29 DAE.[a]

Cultivar	Water potential (29 DAE) (MPa)	Maximum free proline (29 DAE) (μmol.g fresh wt^{-1})	Recovery rating (30 DAE) (0-5 arbitrary units)	Mean desiccation injury in field (%)
Feterita	−2.11	4.64	4.22	15.9
CK-60	−1.88	3.93	3.50	37.3
Dwarf Yellow Milo	−2.10	3.83	2.43	16.4
Western Blackhull Kafir	−1.87	3.51	3.46	38.6
Manchu Brown Kaoliang	−2.21	3.24	2.90	40.1
Dwarf White Durra	−1.91	2.79	3.76	27.3
Shallu	−2.09	2.70	2.54	44.5
Early Hegari	−1.89	2.26	2.41	9.7
LSD (at P = 0.05)	−0.29	0.94	1.10	24.9

[a]From Blum and Ebercon (1976).

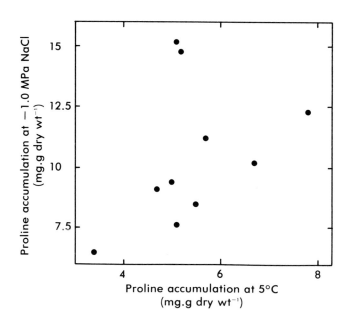

FIG. 10. Proline accumulation in the first leaf of 10 d old barley cultivars in response to low temperature and salinity stress. Seedlings were subjected to low temperature (5°C for 5 d) or salinity stress (−1.0 MPa NaCl for 2 d) before the proline concentration in the first leaves was assessed. (After T. M. Chu, unpublished.)

Intra-specific differences in the accumulation of proline in response to low temperature have been noted, and greater proline accumulation has been associated with frost resistance (Benko, 1968; Rochat & Therrien, 1976). The accumulation of proline at low temperature by a range of 10 barley cultivars was apparently unrelated to the accumulation by the same cultivars in response to salinity stress (Fig. 10), and the range of response was considerably less, lending support to the suggestion that the physiology of the response to the two environmental stress situations differs significantly.

Although there are several points of disagreement between the few reports which have appeared on genetic variation in proline accumulation potential, there is no doubt that considerable variation exists. Some of this variation may be attibuted to cultivar differences in water potential, which is difficult to avoid, but there appears sufficient evidence to conclude that cultivars with identical water potential experiences differ in proline accumulation. The relationship between this innate capacity for proline accumulation and resistance to the effects of water deficit is crucial to the further study of this response and, as with other physiological characters, may best be studied in material which has an otherwise identical genetic complement.

IV. SELECTION FOR PROLINE ACCUMULATION

A. HYBRID SELECTION

The existence of quantitative intra-specific variation in the ability to accumulate proline in response to water deficit suggests that it may be possible to select for this character, particularly in the cereals (Lewin & Sparrow, 1975). Such a selection programme could have three aims: to investigate the inheritance of proline accumulation; to provide more suitable genetic matcrial for an investigation of the relationship between proline accumulation and stress resistance; and, ultimately, to incorporate stress resistance into commercial cultivars.

Lewin and Sparrow (1975) examined an F_2 population from a cross between the barley cultivars Asahi-2, a relatively low proline accumulator, and Clipper, a moderate accumulator. The plants were grown with nutrient solution and subjected to water deficit by flooding the pots with polyethylene glycol (MW 4000, osmotic potential -2.0 MPa) for 3 d. The mean proline concentration induced in Asahi-2 leaves by this treatment was lower than that in Clipper, and the F_2 population mean was intermediate between the two parents (Fig. 11). There was considerable variation between individual plants within both parent cultivars, particularly Clipper. Variation in the F_2 was even greater, and the range extended beyond that of both parents. The results of the cross indicate that the ability to accumulate proline under stress is likely to be a quantitative character. The water potential of the leaves of the seedlings in this investigation was not measured, and it is likely that at least part of the plant to plant variation, and the difference between cultivars, were due to this cause rather than to differences in an innate response of proline accumulation to water potential. Selection for proline accumulation in these circumstances would run the risk of selecting for low water potential in a particular stress situation, as well as for the proline accumulation response. This would not be a particularly progressive process and, as shown by Hanson et al. (1979), would result in selection against water stress resistance rather than towards it. Clearly, it is necessary to differentiate between these two possible reasons for high proline accumulation. The parallel measurement of water potential and proline content is one approach, but it poses problems of scale with the number of water potential measurements required in even a modest selection programme. An alternative is the use of excised leaf material and a regulated water deficit induced by floating the tissue on a solution of known osmotic potential.

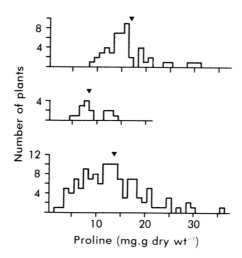

FIG. 11. Distribution of proline-accumulating ability in stressed seedlings of two varieties (Clipper, upper; Asahi 2, middle) of barley and their F_2 population (lower). Triangles indicate mean of each population. (After Lewin and Sparrow, 1975.)

B. SELECTION WITHIN A CULTIVAR

The approach indicated above has been adopted in an investigation of the sources of variation in proline accumulation within a population of one barley cultivar, Clipper (Aspinall & Choi, unpublished). Plants were grown for 10 d in controlled conditions before the first leaf was excised, cut into 1 cm segments and floated on a solution of polyethyleneglycol (MW 4000, osmotic potential -2.0 MPa) for 24 h. As in Lewin and Sparrow's (1975) experiment, considerable intra-cultivar variation was revealed by this procedure (Fig. 12). In this case, presumably, it was not due to variations in leaf water potential during the period of proline accumulation, but it was not solely genetic in

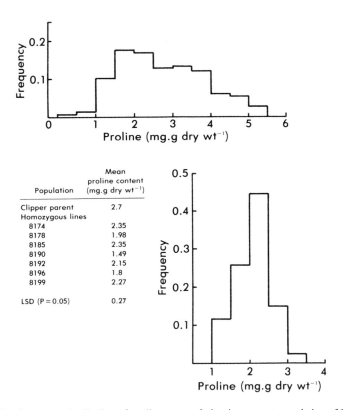

FIG. 12. The frequency distribution of proline accumulation in a parent population of barley, cv. Clipper (upper) compared with that of a number of homozygous lines (8199, 8174, 8185) (lower) derived from the same cultivar. 1 cm sections from the first leaves of 10-d-old plants were floated on polyethylene glycol solution (-1.5 MPa) for 24 h before estimation of proline content. (After Aspinall, unpublished.)

origin either since the mean proline accumulation of leaves excised from plants growing together in a single pot differed significantly at times from that of plants in other pots. This was despite the fact that the plants were grown in a controlled environment, and indicates a significant response to environmental factors other than water. Selection of plants with high or low proline accumulation from this population led to distinct progeny populations when the subsequent generation was tested in the same manner. The mean proline levels accumulated by the two populations were significantly different, although the variation within each population was still considerable. Those data suggest that it is possible to select for proline accumulation within an existing commercial cultivar, since considerable genetic variability for this character remains, despite the glasshouse and field selection to which the cultivar has been subjected.

This view has been reinforced by an examination of 6 homozygous lines from this same barley cultivar, 'Clipper', which were obtained by crossing Clipper with *Hordeum bulbosum* to produce haploids, followed by chromosome doubling (Sparrow, pers. comm.). When these lines were subjected to the same water deficit procedure as described above for the parent 'Clipper' cultivar, the range of plant to plant variation in proline accumulation within each line was considerably less than in the parent heterozygous cultivar (Fig. 12), and, although the mean proline accumulation by several lines was identical, others differed considerably. These data confirm that there is considerable genetic diversity within barley for the characters which determine the rate of proline accumulation under standard conditions of water potential. They also suggest, however, that there is considerable phenotypic variation in this physiological character which is presumably due to unaccounted variations in plant environment even within a controlled environment.

V. FUTURE PROSPECTS

The phenomenon of proline accumulation by plant tissues during water deficit has attracted considerable attention since it was first described, but the precise role of proline in the metabolism of the stressed plant remains to be elucidated. There is considerable evidence, however, from a range of sources which supports the proposition that proline accumulation is positively correlated with drought resistance. The discussion of this correlation is confused by two factors, the lack of a clear, objective measurement of drought resistance and the fact that proline accumulation results from a reduction in plant water potential. The importance of proline accumulation in the complex of factors which determines crop resistance to water deficit in the field must be assessed with this in mind. The relative importance of metabolic factors in the overall plant response, and of factors such as stomatal mechanisms, to the water potential of the plant tissues, has not been assessed; but it is clear that a constantly varying tissue water potential is the normal experience of all crop plants. It is likely that the evolution of land plants has included the acquisition of metabolic adaptations to these fluctuations. It also seems likely that such adaptations ameliorate the effects of even the more extreme variations which we have defined as stress situations.

Further progress in understanding proline accumulation and in its possible utilization in programmes with practical objectives awaits clarification of its role in the metabolism of the plant during water deficit. This objective will be aided by the development of plant strains which differ markedly in proline accumulation but in little else. The selection of such strains may also provide information on the genetics of the response which will be of use in future breeding programmes. It is undoubtedly premature at this juncture to breed varieties with a high proline accumulation potential for use in practical agriculture, if only because the techniques needed have not as yet been formulated. It is reasonable to expect, however, that proline accumulation, together with other objective physiological criteria of plant resistance to water deficit, will complement pragmatic field testing in future cereal breeding programmes.

CHAPTER 11

Proline Accumulation: Biochemical Aspects

CECIL R. STEWART

I.   Introduction 243
II. Proline metabolism 244
     A. Biosynthesis 244
     B. Oxidation 249
     C. Protein synthesis... 253
III. Effects of drought on proline metabolism 254
     A. Effects of drought on proline synthesis.. 255
     B. Effects of drought on proline oxidation 256
     C. Effects of drought on protein synthesis.. 257
IV. Conclusions 258

I. INTRODUCTION

Proline was first noted to accumulate in wilted plant tissue by Kemble and MacPherson (1954) in experiments with excised perennial rye-grass. They observed that proline accumulated in wilted tissue in amounts greater than could be accounted for by proteolysis. In those experiments, plants were continually drying throughout the course of the experiment, and proline only accumulated in wilted plants. Thompson and Morris (1957) confirmed that work by conducting experiments with wilted and turgid excised turnip leaves. In those experiments, wilted leaves were maintained at a constant water content and the accumulated proline disappeared after about 3 d. In 1966, three laboratories reported on the phenomenon of proline accumulation during drought stress (Barnett & Naylor, 1966; Routley, 1966; Stewart et al., 1966; Thompson et al., 1966). At that time, several characteristics of proline accumulation were clear: it accumulated in response to wilting in excised leaves and in intact plants; it accumulated in light or dark, but in darkness there was a requirement for carbohydrates; there was a new synthesis of proline since it accumulated in amounts greater than that released by

243

proteolysis; the new proline was synthesized from glutamic acid; and proline accumulation had been observed in enough species to show that it was apparently a general phenomenon in plants. Now it appears that proline accumulation may be a general response to stress since it also accumulates under salinity and temperature stress (Chu et al., 1974, 1976).

Proline is rather unique among the amino acids in its accumulation during stress. Most amino acids accumulate to an extent (Thompson et al., 1966) and there are some indications that asparagine and perhaps other amino acids, like proline, accumulate in quantities exceeding amounts released by proteolysis. However, only proline accumulates consistently in numerous plant species and under a range of environmental conditions. Certainly, the metabolic effects of wilting (those discussed in this chapter) which lead to proline accumulation have not been observed with any other amino acid.

The results of work prior to 1966 formed the framework within which subsequent investigations into the biochemical mechanisms were conducted. The discovery and characterization of proline accumulation in barley (Singh et al., 1973a, 1973b) led to many studies with barley on which a major part of this chapter is based.

II. PROLINE METABOLISM

This chapter will review the work with plants and refer to the work with other organisms only as it fills in research gaps.

A. BIOSYNTHESIS

1. Pathway

Proline biosynthesis begins with glutamic acid and proceeds via the intermediate Δ^1-pyrroline-5-carboxylic acid, as shown in Figure 1. The γ-carboxyl group of glutamic acid is reduced to an aldehyde in steps 1 and 2. Step 1 would involve the transfer of phosphate from ATP, and step 2 would require an electron donor such as NADH or NADPH. These reactions are shown by dotted lines because no cell-free preparation has been obtained from plants that will catalyse this reduction only. Based on a similar reaction in the conversion of aspartate to aspartic-β-semialdehyde (Black & Wright, 1955) and the reduction of N-acetylglutamic acid to N-acetylglutamic-γ-semialdehyde (Baich & Vogel, 1962), γ-glutamylphosphate is the postulated intermediate. This intermediate has not been isolated and is probably very unstable, but Baich (1969) did find a hydroxamic acid derivative formed from glutamate and ATP in an extract from *Escherichia coli*. Baich (1971) also measured the second enzyme, γ-glutamylphosphate reductase, in extracts of

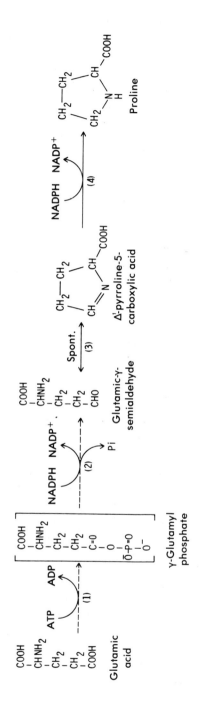

FIG. 1. The proline biosynthetic pathway. Solid arrows represent documented reactions. Dotted arrows refer to postulated reactions.

E. coli. Gamper and Moses (1974) have evidence that steps 1 and 2 are catalysed by an enzyme complex to which the intermediate, γ-glutamyl-phosphate, remains bound.

Morris et al. (1969) demonstrated the conversion of glutamate to proline in extracts from Swiss chard leaves, but intermediates were not identified when glutamate was the substrate. N-acetylglutamate was also converted to proline in those extracts. Step 3 in Figure 1 is a spontaneous cyclization of glutamic-semialdehyde to form Δ^1-pyrroline-5-carboxylic acid. These two compounds are in equilibrium, the cyclic form presumably being the more stable (Strecker, 1960).

The final step in proline synthesis is a reduction of Δ^1-pyrroline-5-carboxylic acid to proline with either NADH or NADPH as the electron donor. The conversion has been shown to occur in plants by the use of radioactive Δ^1-pyrroline-5-carboxylic acid (Thompson et al., 1966; Boggess et al., 1976b), and the enzyme Δ^1-pyrroline-5-carboxylate reductase has been demonstrated in extracts of several plants (Noguchi et al., 1966; Stewart, 1967; Splittstoesser & Splittstoesser, 1973; Rena & Splittstoesser, 1975; Miler & Stewart, 1976).

Arginine and ornithine also can be converted to proline in plant tissue (Mazelis & Fowden, 1969; Splittstoesser, 1969; Stewart, 1974). The possible routes by which this conversion takes place are shown in Figure 2. Arginine is converted to ornithine by hydrolysis catalysed by arginase, producing urea as the other product (step 1, Fig. 2). Ornithine can be converted to proline by two possible routes, both involving transamination of ornithine followed by cyclization and reduction. The difference between the two routes is in which group is transaminated. If the α-amino group of ornithine is transaminated (step 2, Fig. 2), α-keto-δ-aminovaleric acid is produced. It cyclizes to Δ^1-pyrroline-2-carboxylic acid (step 3) which is then reduced to proline (step 4). If, on the other hand, the δ-amino group is transaminated (step 5), glutamine-γ-semialdehyde is produced. Subsequent cyclization (step 6) and reduction (step 7) produces proline via Δ^1-pyrroline-5-carboxylic acid. Much of the literature has assumed that the step 5–7 pathway is the route because those enzymes have been isolated and characterized in plant tissue (Mazelis & Fowden, 1969; Lu & Mazelis, 1975; Splittstoesser & Splittstoesser, 1973; Miler & Stewart, 1976; and others referred to in these papers).

Enzymes which catalyse steps 2 and 4 have not been characterized from plant tissue, but some of the early work indicated they might be present (Meister et al., 1957). In fact, *in vivo* labelling experiments support that pathway. Tissue cultures of Jerusalem artichoke tubers were incubated with ^{15}N-ornithine labelled in the α and δ position. Nitrogen from α-^{15}N-ornithine was not recovered in proline, whereas nitrogen from δ-^{15}N-ornithine was recovered in proline (Duranton & Wurtz, 1964, 1965). Recently, it has been shown that tritium in the 2 position of ornithine was not recovered in proline,

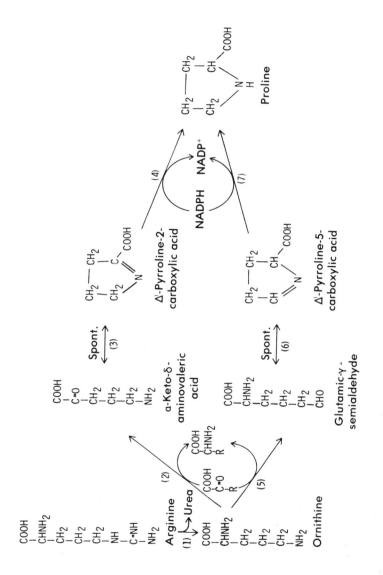

FIG. 2. Pathways of conversion of arginine and ornithine to proline.

whereas tritium in the 5 position of ornithine was recovered in proline (Louis et al., 1979). These tritium experiments with *Nicotiana, Datura* and *Lupinus* spp., along with the ^{15}N experiments using Jerusalem artichoke, constitute strong evidence that the step 2–4 pathway is the one that converts ornithine to proline. These labelling results, however, may still be consistent with an ornithine cyclase such as that purified from *Clostridium sporogenes* (Muth & Costilow, 1974). The ornithine cyclase involves an oxidative deamination of the α-keto-δ-aminovalerate, and the NADH produced is used to reduce Δ^1-pyrroline-2-carboxylate to proline. All intermediates are enzyme bound. It is not clear, however, whether or not tritium would be lost from 2-^3H-ornithine in this reaction, since the enzyme fails to incorporate tritium into proline when the reaction is carried out in T_2O.

The importance of this conversion as a source of proline is unknown. Its significance in wilting-induced proline synthesis is discussed in Section III, A.

2. Control and subcellular localization

The basic mechanism by which amino acids control their own synthesis is through inhibition of the first enzyme in the bio-synthetic pathway by the amino acid itself. Since the first enzyme in proline biosynthesis has not been isolated and characterized, its inhibition by proline has not been investigated. However, there are experiments indicating that proline does control its own synthesis in normal unstressed tissues. Baich and Pierson (1965) found that increasing the concentration of proline in the medium decreased the amount of Δ^1-pyrroline-5-carboxylate excreted by a proline-requiring mutant of *E. coli* which was lacking Δ^1-pyrroline-5-carboxylate reductase. This result was interpreted to indicate that the first step in proline biosynthesis was sensitive to proline. The work with the glutamylkinase in *E. coli* (Baich, 1969) made use of the proline-inhibiting effect in distinguishing between glutamylkinase and other glutamate-dependent ATP hydrolysis reactions.

Several experiments with plants indicate that proline controls its own biosynthesis, but the degree of control is variable. Oaks et al. (1970) found that proline inhibited the incorporation of ^{14}C-acetate into proline in corn roots, and that proline synthesis was more sensitive to proline in root tip segments than it was in more mature segments. They also observed that incorporation of ^{14}C-acetate into protein-proline was more sensitive to proline than incorporation into soluble proline. The interpretation of those results was that only part of proline synthesis in corn roots was sensitive to feedback control and that some control was lost as cells matured. Noguchi et al. (1968) showed that proline inhibited the incorporation of ^{14}C-glutamate into proline in illuminated tobacco leaves, and Boggess et al. (1976a) found that the incorporation of ^{14}C-glutamate into proline was inhibited by proline in turgid barley and tobacco leaves. This inhibition was not observed in wilted leaves.

(The effect of wilting is discussed in Section III, A.) The incorporation of ^{14}C-glutamate into proline was also decreased by feeding unlabelled proline to the diatom *Cyclotella cryptica* (Liu & Hellebust, 1976).

The subcellular location of proline biosynthesis is of interest because the precursor, Δ^1-pyrroline-5-carboxylic acid, is also an intermediate in proline oxidation. Noguchi et al. (1966, 1968) showed that light stimulates proline synthesis from glutamate and that extracts of washed chloroplasts contain Δ^1-pyrroline-5-carboxylate reductase. These observations suggest that there may be proline synthesis in chloroplasts. In addition, Noguchi et al. (1966) found the reductase in the supernatant of chloroplast preparations, indicating that there may also be a cytoplasmic enzyme. The light stimulation of glutamate conversion to proline could be explained by an enhanced supply of NADPH and, perhaps, ATP for the conversion. Stewart and Lai (1974) found Δ^1-pyrroline-5-carboxylate reductase in the supernatant of mitochondrial preparations from etiolated pea seedlings. These results are consistent with proline synthesis occurring in either the chloroplast or cytoplasm or both. Boggess et al. (1976a) demonstrated that, in turgid leaves, the glutamic acid which gives rise to proline is separated from the glutamic acid derived from proline oxidation. Their conclusion was based on the following observations: (i) the concentration-dependence of the feedback control of proline synthesis by proline was very different to the concentration-dependence of proline oxidation; (ii) adding unlabelled proline to leaves supplied with ^{14}C-glutamate did not dilute the radioactivity found in other products of glutamate, such as γ-aminobutyrate and glutamine; (iii) when U-^{14}C-proline and 5-^{3}H-proline were supplied to the same leaf, both ^{14}C and ^{3}H disappeared from proline at the same rate. The latter observation indicates that the glutamate from proline oxidation is separate from the glutamate giving rise to proline, since if it were not, ^{14}C from proline would be converted back to proline via glutamate and the ^{14}C in proline would decrease more slowly than the ^{3}H. Tritium is lost to H_2O from 5-^{3}H-proline during proline oxidation and is not reconverted to proline. Therefore, it appears that proline biosynthesis either occurs in the chloroplast or the cytoplasm, or both, but not in the mitochondria where proline oxidation likely occurs.

B. OXIDATION

1. Pathway

It has been clearly shown that plants have the capability to oxidize proline (Barnard & Oaks, 1970; Oaks et al., 1970; Stewart, 1972a; Wang, 1968; Rena & Splittstoesser, 1974c). The oxidation results in carbon being fed into the Krebs cycle and eventually respired to CO_2 (Stewart, 1972c). The pathway involves the conversion to glutamic acid via the intermediate Δ^1-pyrroline-5-carboxylic acid (Fig. 3).

The conversion of ^{14}C-proline to glutamic acid, organic acids and CO_2 was shown by Barnard and Oaks (1970), Wang (1968), Stewart (1972a), and Rena and Splittstoesser (1974c). Labelled carbon originating from ^{14}C-proline is also found in other amino acids that derive from glutamate, such as γ-aminobutyrate and glutamine, as well as aspartate, which would originate from Krebs cycle intermediates. The order in which glutamate, the intermediates of the Krebs cycle and CO_2 become labelled (Stewart, 1972a) is consistent with the conversion of proline to glutamate and the subsequent metabolism of glutamate by Krebs cycle reactions which release CO_2 as the end product. Evidence for the intermediate, Δ^1-pyrroline-5-carboxylic acid, was provided by recent work with isolated mitochondria (Boggess et al., 1978).

Understanding the first enzymatic step in proline oxidation in plants has been a problem. Mazelis and Fowden (1971) extracted a proline dehydrogenase from peanut seedlings. The reaction was measured at pH 10.3, but they did not identify the product. This enzyme was later found in *Chlorella* (McNamer & Stewart, 1974), pumpkin (Rena & Splittstoesser, 1974a), wheat germ (Mazelis & Creveling, 1974), and fern spores (Gemmrich, 1975). The product of the reaction is Δ^1-pyrroline-5-carboxylate (McNamer & Stewart, 1974; Rena & Splittstoesser, 1974b), but the enzyme reaction cannot be measured at a pH below 10 (R. L. Yang & C. R. Stewart, unpublished data), and the enzyme is apparently a cytoplasmic enzyme (Rena & Splittstoesser, 1974a). There is evidence that the proline dehydrogenase activity is catalysed by the same protein as the Δ^1-pyrroline-5-reductase activity (Rena & Splittstoesser, 1975). The high pH optimum, and the indication discussed in Section II, A, 2, that proline synthesis and oxidation occur in separate compartments, argues against a role for proline dehydrogenase in proline oxidation.

The recent finding that proline supported O_2 uptake in isolated mitochondria from barley, corn, mung bean, soybean and wheat suggests that proline oxidation is a mitochondrial process (Boggess et al., 1978). Proline was metabolized to glutamate, organic acids and CO_2 by those mitochondrial preparations. The conversion of proline to glutamate was inhibited by anaerobiosis, and this inhibition was not reversed by providing NAD^+. This result suggests that plant mitochondria contain a proline oxidase similar to the animal proline oxidase (Strecker, 1971). Such activity has been measured in plant mitochondria using 2,6-dichlorophenol indophenol (Huang & Cavalieri, 1979).

The second step in the proline oxidation pathway is spontaneous, identical to the same reaction in proline biosynthesis (step 3, Fig. 1). The last

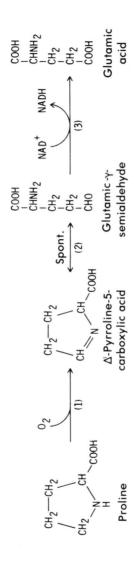

FIG. 3. The pathway of proline oxidation.

step, step 3, is an oxidative one in which Δ^1-pyrroline-5-carboxylate or the open chain form, glutamic-γ-semialdehyde, is oxidized to glutamic acid. The enzyme Δ^1-pyrroline-5-carboxylate dehydrogenase has been measured in mitochondrial preparations from pea, corn, castor bean and pumpkin seedlings (Stewart & Lai, 1974), and barley (Boggess et al., 1975).

Proline oxidase and Δ^1-pyrroline-5-carboxylate dehydrogenase have been further characterized with respect to submitochondrial location and electron transport by Elthon & Stewart (1981). Both enzymes are associated with the inner mitochondrial membrane and are sensitive to rotenone, antimycin A, and azide. Both proline and Δ^1-pyrroline-5-carboxylate yield ADP:O ratios of 1.9 compared to 2.1 for malate plus pyruvate, 1.3 for succinate, and 1.2 for exogenous NADH.

2. Control

In the first experiments in which ^{14}C-proline oxidation was observed, a relatively small proportion of the proline was oxidized compared to the amount incorporated into protein (Wang, 1968; Barnard & Oaks, 1970). It was known, however, that large quantities of proline disappeared from excised leaves after a period of proline accumulation during wilting (Thompson et al., 1966). Stewart (1972a) found that adding proline to bean leaves in quantities sufficient to expand the endogenous pool greatly increased the rate of proline oxidation while not affecting the rate of incorporation into protein. The result was confirmed by Boggess et al. (1976a) and Stewart et al. (1977) in experiments with barley leaves which indicated that the proline oxidation rate increased linearly as the added proline concentration was increased up to 50 mM. This concentration of added proline probably resulted in an endogenous level of 15–20 μmol proline . g fresh wt^{-1} of leaf. Proline oxidation in leaf tissue has not been experimentally saturated with respect to proline concentration. Stewart (1972b) found that proline which had accumulated in bean leaves during wilting was oxidized rapidly upon leaf rehydration. This indicated that the expanded pool of endogenous proline was as susceptible to increased oxidation as exogenous proline. This effect of amino acid concentration on oxidation also has been observed with arginine (Stewart, 1974).

These observations on the effect of proline content on its oxidation suggest a control on the level of proline in an unstressed or stress-relieved leaf. As the level of proline increases, the rate of oxidation increases, tending to lower the level of proline. The rate of incorporation into protein, however, is saturated at normal endogenous levels (0.2 μmol . g fresh wt^{-1}) at which oxidation is relatively slow.

Barnard and Oaks (1970), Oaks et al. (1970) and Stewart (1972a) found that carbohydrates also controlled proline oxidation. This effect was observed by incubating corn roots in the presence and absence of glucose (Barnard & Oaks, 1970; Oaks et al., 1970) and by comparing proline oxidation in bean leaves differing in carbohydrate levels (Stewart, 1972a). Adding sucrose to starved bean leaves inhibited proline oxidation (Stewart, 1972a), and this effect was observed also in rehydration experiments in which the endogenous proline levels were elevated due to wilting (Stewart, 1972b). In barley leaves, proline oxidation is not inhibited by carbohydrates to the extent that it is in bean (Stewart, 1978). Thus some variability among species occurs in the degree of control of proline oxidation by carbohydrate.

Carbohydrates have been found to exhibit an interesting effect on proline oxidation in *Chlorella* (McNamer & Stewart, 1973). In those experiments, there was an apparent glucose or carbohydrate requirement for proline uptake. However, glucose or carbohydrate appeared to inhibit proline oxidation after it was taken up.

This effect of carbohydrate on proline oxidation is an example of the "sparing effect" observed by Yemm (1937). His experiments indicated that, during leaf starvation, protein hydrolysis occurs in the presence of carbohydrate, but subsequent respiration of hydrolysis products is prevented until carbohydrates are depleted, thus conserving the amino acids while carbohydrates are available. This effect of carbohydrates was not observed with arginine catabolism (Stewart, 1974), and was not particularly effective in barley leaves (Stewart, 1978). The fact that arginine catabolism is not inhibited by carbohydrates has been interpreted to indicate that the effect of carbohydrates on proline oxidation is on the first step of the pathway (step 1, Fig. 3) (Stewart, 1974), but this suggestion has not been investigated further.

If proline is to accumulate as it does during stress, its oxidation during accumulation must be minimal. Thus oxidation is likely to be inhibited by carbohydrate concentration or some other effect of stress (see Section III, B).

C. PROTEIN SYNTHESIS

Proline is one of the amino acids found in proteins. In some proteins, after incorporation, some of it is altered by hydroxylation to hydroxyproline (Steward & Durzan, 1964). In tissue having normal levels of proline, incorporation into protein represents its major metabolic fate (Stewart, 1972a; Oaks et al., 1970). This use is controlled by factors which control the general process of protein synthesis, such as modification of tRNA, enzymes forming aminoacyl-tRNA, specificity of factors controlling availability and attachment of mRNA to ribosomes, and the ribosome translational system (Marcus,

1976). Thus, general aspects like carbohydrate level (Stewart, 1972a), growth rate, etc. will influence the incorporation of proline into protein more than they will affect specific aspects of proline metabolism.

III. EFFECTS OF DROUGHT ON PROLINE METABOLISM

Proline accumulation is simply the increase in the level of free proline in the tissue. In the physiology of this effect of stress two points are important. First, proline accumulation occurs under relatively mild water stress (water potentials of -1.0 MPa), and the amount which accumulates is dependent on the severity of the stress (i.e., the lower the leaf water potential, the greater the proline accumulation under otherwise identical conditions). The second point is that proline levels represent a cumulative effect of the tissue being wilted over a period of time. Therefore, the level of proline will be affected very much by the length of time the tissue is under stress. Thus, in assessing the effects of stress on proline metabolism, the rates of synthesis and oxidation in wilted leaves must be compared with rates of these processes in turgid leaves. The effects of altering the rates of various metabolic processes on proline levels is illustrated in Figure 4. Proline accumulation can result from a stimulation of the rate of proline formation or a decrease in the rate of utilization. Proteolysis and synthesis from precursors result in proline formation, while oxidation and protein synthesis result in proline utilization.

It was clear from the first that proline accumulation was not due solely to proteolysis (Kemble & MacPherson, 1954; Thompson et al., 1966). It is possible that wilting stimulates proteolysis, but this is clearly not responsible, by itself, for proline accumulation. Rather, the primary effect of wilting that causes proline to accumulate is the stimulation of proline synthesis from glutamate. Inhibition of proline oxidation and a decrease in the incorporation into protein contribute to proline accumulation but cannot be solely responsible for it.

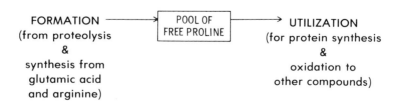

FIG. 4. The contribution of various metabolic processes to the level of free proline.

A. EFFECTS OF DROUGHT ON PROLINE SYNTHESIS

A stimulation of proline synthesis from precursors by drought stress was predicted from the early work showing that proline accumulation exceeded proline released by proteolysis (Kemble & MacPherson, 1954; Thompson et al., 1966). In fact, a wilting-induced stimulation of incorporation of ^{14}C-glutamate into proline was observed by Barnett and Naylor (1966), Morris et al. (1969) and Boggess et al. (1976a). However, it was possible that this apparent stimulation was due to trapping of the label resulting from decreased utilization of proline or synthesis from some other precursor. Boggess et al. (1976b) showed that the amount of ^{14}C in the total proline (free plus protein) from glutamate was stimulated by wilting, and that the specific radioactivity of free proline, as well as the total radioactivity in proline, was increased by wilting. Thus, it is clear that drought stress stimulates proline synthesis from glutamate in barley. The degree of stimulation is over 10 fold and is similar to proline accumulation itself (Boggess et al., 1976b); and it does not occur in starved barley leaves which do not accumulate proline (Stewart, 1978). The incorporation of ornithine (Boggess et al., 1976b) and arginine (Boggess & Stewart, 1976) into proline is also stimulated by drought stress in barley. However, this is observed at times well after proline has begun to accumulate, indicating that it is a result of, rather than a cause of, proline accumulation. The apparent stimulation is due to a trapping of the label in proline as a result of increased synthesis from glutamate, and decreased utilization through oxidation and protein synthesis. Thus, the increased synthesis of proline from glutamate, due to wilting, is apparently an effect on the first step in proline synthesis, the conversion to Δ^1-pyrroline-5-carboxylate (Boggess et al., 1976b). Clearly, there is a loss of feedback control of proline synthesis by proline, because the synthesis is stimulated while proline levels are increasing. Boggess et al. (1976a) experimentally demonstrated the loss of regulation during drought stress in both barley and tobacco leaves.

Huber (1974) observed proline accumulation and higher activities of Δ^1-pyrroline-5-carboxylate reductase in abscisic acid and NaCl treated *Pennisetum typhoides* plants. The greatest stimulation of activity was 3-fold with 8.5 mM NaCl. This treatment also resulted in a 5-fold increase in proline content. Huber suggested that this stimulation may cause proline to accumulate. The experiments discussed above indicate that the first step in proline biosynthesis is the controlling step. Stimulation of the Δ^1-pyrroline-5-carboxylate reductase may occur, but it is not the likely cause of proline synthesis stimulated by drought stress.

Several observations were discussed in Section II, A, 2 indicating that the intermediates in proline synthesis are separated in the cell from intermediates in proline oxidation. When high specific radioactivity proline was given to wilted barley leaves, there was a rapid conversion to glutamate and organic acids (25% of the label recovered in oxidized products after 1.5 h). This label was reconverted to proline in drought-stressed leaves during subsequent incubation (Stewart & Boggess, 1978). This observation indicates that some of the products of proline oxidation are accessible to proline synthesis in the drought-stressed leaves. This result was not observed in turgid leaves. Thus drought stress appears to cause a breakdown in the subcellular compartmentation of proline metabolism.

In bean leaves, the wilting-induced stimulation of proline synthesis from glutamate was more difficult to demonstrate (Stewart & Boggess, 1977) because glutamate was rapidly metabolized to other compounds, and the rate of proline accumulation was much slower than in barley (0.1 compared to $1.0 \, \mu\text{mol.h}^{-1}.\text{g}$ fresh wt^{-1}). The conversion of both ornithine and arginine to proline was stimulated in bean prior to any observed proline accumulation. However, proline accumulated in amounts greater than could be accounted for by the combined loss of arginine and proline from protein. Furthermore, stimulation of the glutamate to proline conversion was observed when large amounts of unlabelled glutamate were added to slow the loss of ^{14}C from glutamate. Thus, drought stress also stimulates proline synthesis from glutamate in bean.

B. EFFECTS OF DROUGHT ON PROLINE OXIDATION

It was suggested in Section II, B, 2 that regulation of the rate of proline oxidation by proline levels could function as a control on the level of proline in normal, unstressed plant tissue. Thus, as proline accumulates due to increased synthesis, the enhancement of proline oxidation will occur and, eventually, proline levels will reach a new steady state. However, during stress proline accumulates to quite high levels, suggesting that wilting also inhibits proline oxidation. Stewart et al. (1977) measured the rate of proline oxidation in turgid barley leaves with proline levels comparable to those in leaves stressed for 1 h (about 20 μg. leaf^{-1}). The rate of proline oxidation was about 4 μg. leaf^{-1}, which was approximately 10% of the rate of proline accumulation in the wilted leaves. They observed a complete inhibition of the conversion of proline to oxidized products in wilted leaves after 2 h wilting. The observation that some of the oxidized products may be reconverted to proline in wilted leaves (Stewart & Boggess, 1978) would still allow for some proline oxidation, but certainly proline oxidation is inhibited by water stress and the rate quite likely approaches zero.

To assess proline oxidation and avoid the reconversion problem, the measurement of tritium recovered in H_2O from 5-^{3}H-proline is useful. Stewart and Boggess (1978) used this method and found that proline oxidation was severely inhibited by stress, and the rate approached zero in wilted leaves after 3 h. It is of interest that the proline oxidation rate increased more than 5-fold as proline concentration increased 10-fold (Stewart et al., 1977). If proline oxidation also increased as it accumulated in wilted leaves, it would reach over 50% of the rate of proline accumulation. Thus, inhibition of proline oxidation alone is not sufficient to cause proline to accumulate, but this effect of stress is necessary to explain the levels which do accumulate.

The inhibition of proline oxidation by water stress was not observed in bean leaves (Stewart, 1972c), and proline only accumulated when sufficiently high levels of carbohydrates were present to inhibit proline oxidation. Wilting did not inhibit proline oxidation in starved bean leaves. This lack of inhibition prevented proline from accumulating in those leaves since stimulation of synthesis from precursors was observed (Stewart, 1972c). This result further indicates that inhibition of proline oxidation is essential for proline to accumulate even though the inhibition alone cannot cause the accumulation.

The effect of wilting on proline oxidation represents an effect on the mitochondria. Sells and Koeppe (1980) have observed a 70% lower proline oxidation rate in mitochondria isolated from water stressed (-1 MPa) corn shoots. This degree of stress resulted in only a slight reduction in oxidation rates of other substrates such as succinate, malate plus pyruvate, and NADH. Mitochondria from stressed shoots gave lower ADP:0 ratios compared to turgid controls for proline but the ratios for other substrates were not affected by stress. Also, the suggestion (Stewart & Boggess, 1978) that wilting causes a loss in compartmentation of proline oxidation products suggests a leakage of oxidation products from the mitochondria to the cytoplasm. Perhaps water stress affects the integrity of the mitochondrial membrane. Effects of stress on mitochondria have been noted from ultra-structural observations (Tucker et al., 1975; Vieira de Silva et al., 1974) and from measurements of enzymatic and oxidative processes (Flowers & Hanson, 1969; Bell et al., 1971).

C. EFFECTS OF DROUGHT ON PROTEIN SYNTHESIS

It is clear that the incorporation of proline into protein is inhibited by water stress (Stewart, 1972c; Stewart et al., 1977). This is due to the influence of tissue dehydration on protein synthesis and has been observed by measuring polyribosome levels (Hsaio, 1970; Morilla et al., 1973), nitrate reductase activity (Morilla et al., 1973) and leucine incorporation (Ben-Zioni et al., 1967). However, recent results indicate that low nitrate reductase levels in leaves under water stress are due to reduced nitrate flux rather than an effect on protein synthesis (Shaner & Boyer, 1976). The mechanism by which stress reduces protein synthesis is not clear but it is readily reversible (Hsiao, 1973).

The possibility that proline accumulation is a consequence of impaired protein synthesis has been examined by Boggess and Stewart (1980). Based on experiments with inhibitors of protein synthesis, they concluded that inhibition of protein synthesis was not sufficient to cause proline to accumulate. However, since protein synthesis accounts for the major part of proline utilization in turgid tissue, its impairment contributes to proline accumulation by slowing the rate of proline utilization (Stewart, 1972c). Using the data and calculation method of Stewart et al. (1977), the rate of proline utilization for protein synthesis was about 6 μg.leaf^{-1} in barley. This rate, compared to the average rate of proline accumulation in the 1–4 h period in the same leaves of 34 μg.leaf^{-1}, constituted less than 20% of the accumulation rate. This calculation means that, if the synthesis and oxidation of proline were unaffected by stress, inhibition of protein synthesis would result in a proline accumulation rate of less than 20% of the observed rate. This amount would be independent of the proline level in the leaf, unlike the situation with proline oxidation. In bean leaves, the rate of proline utilization for protein synthesis was 0.07 μmol.h^{-1}.g fresh wt^{-1} (Stewart, 1972a). Proline accumulated in bean at the rate of about 0.1 μmol.h^{-1}.g fresh wt^{-1} (Stewart, 1972c). Thus, inhibition of protein synthesis, with proline synthesis and oxidation remaining constant, could account for as much as 70% of the rate of proline accumulation. This percentage is greater for bean than barley, but in neither case was incorporation of proline into protein completely inhibited by water stress (Stewart, 1972c; Stewart et al., 1977).

IV. CONCLUSIONS

Even though proline accumulation under drought stress represents an increase in the level of a single, essential metabolite, it is clear that it is a result of several responses to stress. The most important response is the stimulation of proline synthesis from glutamate. This involves a loss of sensitivity to feedback inhibition and a loss of some subcellular compartmentation. The second most important response is the inhibition of proline oxidation because, if it were not inhibited, proline accumulation would be 50% or more, less than the observed rate. This inhibition is probably due to an effect of stress on mitochondrial processes. Finally, the impairment of protein synthesis also contributes to proline accumulation. This effect of stress is due to some influence of dehydration on the process of protein synthesis, perhaps at the translation step.

Thus, the biochemical mechanism of proline accumulation has been described to the extent of being able to ask more specific questions about the effects of drought. What causes a loss in the sensitivity of the first step in proline synthesis to feedback inhibition by proline? What causes that step to be stimulated? What causes altered mitochondrial membrane properties which result in a loss in compartmentation of proline synthesis and oxidation? What causes the decrease in mitochondrial oxidative processes which result in inhibited proline oxidation? What causes the impairment of protein synthesis? These questions can be approached experimentally and of necessity will include basic studies on the enzymatic control of proline biosynthesis and oxidation.

Perhaps one or more of these effects of stress is individually related to drought resistance. For example, a plant in which proline oxidation is less sensitive to drought stress may contain mitochondria which are able to function more effectively under stress. Since the mitochondria are extremely important organelles in energy conservation, this capability may be very advantageous to the plant. Proline oxidation can be assessed with a very simple, rapid and non-destructive method (Mitra et al., 1975). Perhaps the sensitivity of proline oxidation to stress in plant material with varying drought adaptability should be measured. There may be similar ways of approaching the other effects of stress to determine their relation to drought resistance.

CHAPTER 12

Protein Synthesis*

J. DEREK BEWLEY

I.	Introduction	261
II.	Plants with a low tolerance of drought	262
III.	Desiccation-tolerant plants	267
IV.	Tolerance of desiccation by seeds and its loss during seedling growth	275
	A. Seeds	275
	B. Seedlings	279
V.	The relationship between desiccation tolerance, desiccation resistance and protein synthesis	281

I. INTRODUCTION

An essential feature of cellular metabolism is the capacity for protein synthesis, to produce enzymes and structural proteins, and to replace those which have been removed in turnover processes. As a consequence of work carried out over the past decade, it has been recognized that water deficits result in disturbances to the normal pattern of protein synthesis, and that plants with different drought tolerances exhibit different capacities to resume protein synthesis on return to full hydration. For our purposes plants and their parts will be divided into three categories according to their abilities to withstand drought: (1) those plants whose tolerance of drought is low and whose capacity for protein synthesis is markedly affected by mild to moderate water stress; (ii) those plants which can survive extremes of drought (i.e. are tolerant of desiccation) imposed directly by changes in the environment; and (iii) plant parts which are adapted to withstand severe water deficits and for which drying out is an expected or "programmed" event (i.e. seeds).

---

*This work was supported by National Research Council of Canada grant No. A6352.

PHYSIOLOGY AND BIOCHEMISTRY
OF DROUGHT RESISTANCE
IN PLANTS

No account will be given here of the biochemistry of protein synthesis in plants. The reader should consult the reviews of Zalik and Jones (1973), Bray (1976) or Marcus (1976), or any appropriate plant physiology text for details. Experimentally, the ability of a plant to conduct protein synthesis can be determined using three basic techniques. The status of the protein synthesizing complex at any time can be deduced by analysis of the ratio of polysomes (i.e. those ribosomes associated with mRNA) to ribosomes (i.e. those not actively involved in protein synthesis). Most commonly this is achieved by extraction of the total ribosomal pellet, followed by separation into ribosomes and polysomes using sucrose density gradient centrifugation. Alternatively, the activities of the polysomes and ribosomes can be determined using appropriate *in vitro* assays for protein synthesis. The results obtained from these two methods generally are a good indication of the plant's *capacity* for protein synthesis at the time of extraction, rather than an indication of the amount of protein synthesis actually in progress. Instances are known, however, where polysomes were present in plant cells, and were active in *in vitro* assays but were inactive *in vivo* (Malek & Bewley, 1978). The best indication of *in vivo* protein synthesis can be obtained by following the incorporation of amino acids (usually radioactive) into protein over a certain, and usually short, feeding time period. There are drawbacks to this technique (e.g. not all tissues take up amino acids with equal facility), and it is extremely difficult to follow protein synthesis during severe water deficits using a radioactive precursor which itself must be applied in liquid form. In many studies only one technique has been used, and hence there are sometimes limitations to the conclusions which can (or should) be drawn.

II. PLANTS WITH A LOW TOLERANCE OF DROUGHT

The effects of water stress on protein synthesis in plants with low drought tolerance have not received the attention they deserve. The conclusions which can be drawn from the limited number of studies completed to date are that mild to moderate water stress reduces the ability of a plant to synthesize proteins, and that this capacity is regained on subsequent return to full hydration if drought is not too severe. This has been effectively demonstrated by Hsiao (1970) for coleoptilar node segments of corn (*Zea mays*) seedlings grown for 2.75 d. With increasing water stress there is a gradual decline in polysomes (Fig. 1) until at -1.0 to -1.2 MPa stress very few remain. This loss of polysomes is accompanied by an increase in single ribosomes, suggesting that as ribosomes become separated from the messenger RNA they remain intact. On rewetting after 4 h stress at about -1.1 MPa the decrease in water stress is accompanied by an increase in polysomes, until after some 2 h control levels are regained (Fig. 1). Somewhat similar observations have been made on excised aerial portions of corn seedlings 8 and 13 d old (Morilla et al., 1973), although, here, stress of −1.2 to −1.4 MPa for one hour resulted in a decrease in polysomes without a concomitant increase in single ribosomes or ribosomal sub-units. The implication is that not all ribosomes are retained under stress. However, such a loss, and in so short a time, seems unlikely under relatively mild stress conditions, and inadequacies in the extraction and analysis technique (which is not fully quantitative) could account for the observed loss of ribosomes. Changes in ribosomes and polysomes on rehydration after this short-term water stress were not followed. In intact corn seedlings 8 to 13 d old that were stressed slowly to −0.9 MPa over several days, there was a gradual decline in polysomes accompanied by a reduction in the total number of ribosomes. On return to fully hydrated conditions, polysome levels rose to those of well-watered controls within 2 h before declining once more to stressed levels within a further 2 h. Ribosome levels declined continually even on rehydration (Morilla et al., 1973). Thus recovery of polysomes after water stress was demonstrated, but the reason for their subsequent decline, and for the continued decline in ribosomes, is enigmatic. Possibly leaf senescence enhanced by prolonged drought stress was a contributing factor.

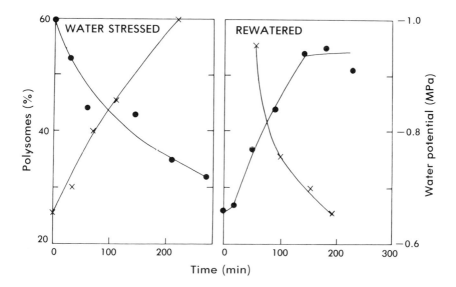

FIG. 1. Effects of water stress (left) and subsequent rewatering (right) on polysomes (●) and water potential (x) in coleoptilar node segments of 2.75-d-old seedlings of corn. Stress was initiated by transferring seedlings to dry paper towels. Rewatering occurred after seedlings had been stressed for 4 h. (After Hsiao, 1970.)

Other higher plant tissues also exhibit a decrease in polysome content under conditions of water stress; for example, immature floral apices of wheat (Barlow et al., 1977), seedlings of black locust (Brandle et al., 1977), pea shoots and pumpkin cotyledons (Rhodes & Matsuda, 1976), corn root tips (Nir et al., 1970), and green and horse bean seedlings (Henckel et al., 1967; Satarova & Tvorus, 1971). In some of these tissues (wheat, pea, pumpkin and green bean) it was observed that the levels of single ribosomes increased as those of polysomes declined. Recovery of polysomes on rehydration was demonstrated in several of the above tissues.

The amount of stress required for polysomes to decrease appears to vary between plants and between plant tissues. The reduction in polysomes in coleoptilar node segments of corn (Hsiao, 1970) appears to be greater than in black locust seedlings (Brandle et al., 1977) or in the aerial parts of corn seedlings 13 d old (Morilla et al., 1973) at certain water deficits. The reason for this is not readily apparent, but it is possible that the ability of plant tissues to conserve polysomes under stress is in some way related to their drought resistance. Hence the more resistant a particular plant (or tissue) is to drought stress, the longer it can continue to synthesize proteins under stress conditions, and consequently its ability to function and grow normally is greater. There is some evidence for differential sensitivity of tissues to water stress. Scott et al. (1979) have shown that large reductions in polysome populations due to mild water stress occur only in growing tissues, due (indirectly) to reductions in growth, and that polysome levels do not decline in mature tissues that have already ceased growing before water stress is imposed. Bewley and Larsen (1980, and unpublished data) found that when rapidly expanding (upper) regions of maize mesocotyls are subjected to stress there is an appreciable loss of polysomes. When the non-growing (lower) regions of the same mesocotyl are subjected to the same stress, protein synthesis ceases without loss of polysomes. Tissues from both regions are able to recommence protein synthesis after stress to -1.0 and -2.0 MPa. Why growing tissues should lose polysomes more readily than non-growing tissues is not known, although our recent observation (Bewley & Larsen, unpublished) that growing maize mesocotyl tissues contain more membrane-bound polysomes than non-growing tissues might indicate an answer. If polysomes associated with membranes are more sensitive to stress than those free in the cytoplasm, then protein synthesis in growing tissues would be expected to be more sensitive to stress than in non-growing ones. This hypothesis remains to be tested adequately.

Henckel, his co-workers and other Russian workers claim that they can increase the drought resistance of several important crop species using a pre-sowing drought hardening treatment (Henckel, 1961; May et al., 1962; Henckel et al., 1964). Furthermore, this treatment, which involves imbibing seeds for one to several days before re-drying and then sowing, is claimed to enhance protein synthesis in hardened plants (Henckel, 1970; Henckel et al., 1972). This has been taken to mean that increased drought resistance due to the hardening treatment enables certain plant species to retain a higher capacity for protein synthesis during times of water deficit, and that this capacity is expressed also on subsequent rehydration. However, the evidence is not unequivocal. In one study (Henckel, 1970) the differences in protein synthetic capacities between hardened and non-hardened plants were small, and they were obtained using a technique which was far from definitive. In a second study (Henckel et al., 1972) protein synthesis by seedlings from hardened and non-hardened seeds was measured by *in vitro* assay, in which extracted polysomes and supernatant fraction activities were measured. Under all test conditions, the components from leaves of hardened wheat seedling catalyzed more protein synthesis than the components from non-hardened seedlings did (Table I). This might be indicative of a higher resistance to drought in the hardened seedlings, but the age of the seedlings might be an important factor here too, for although the comparison was made between non-hardened and hardened seedlings grown for 10 d after sowing, the seeds of the hardened seedlings had previously been soaked for 28–32 h before drying for 48 h. Hence at the time of sowing they were 1–2 d more advanced than the non-hardened control seeds. The observed differences between the two treatments could be simply a consequence of the more advanced state of growth of the hardened seedlings, which had received a more rapid start. The correct comparison would have been between seedlings of a certain age (e.g. 10 d) grown from hardened seeds and those from non-hardened seeds which had been allowed to grow 1–2 d longer. Until this sort of comparison is carried out, the significance of the hardening treatment to protein synthesis must remain in doubt.

TABLE I

The effects of presowing drought hardening treatment and subsequent drought stress on ^{14}C-leucine incorporation into protein using an *in vitro* system containing polysomes and a pH 5 supernatant fraction from leaves of 10-day-old wheat seedlings.[a]

	^{14}C incorporation (nmol .mg rRNA^{-1})	% of hydrated non-hardened seedlings
Non-hardened seedlings		
Hydrated (unstressed controls)	1.69	100
Dry wind for 24 h	1.35	79
With restoration of watering	4.39	259
Hardened seedlings		
Hydrated (unstressed controls)	8.16	482
Dry wind for 24 h	3.04	179
With restoration of watering	7.09	419

[a]Data from Henckel et al. (1972).

Several workers have studied the effects of water stress on protein synthesis by following the incorporation of amino acids into protein. As might be expected, water-stressed tissues invariably incorporate less precursor than well-watered controls, whether or not the stress is imposed by atmospheric drought (Koretskaya & Zholkevich, 1966; Satarova & Tvoris, 1970), osmotica (Ben-Zioni et al., 1967; Dhindsa & Cleland, 1975a), or salinity (Ben-Zioni et al., 1967; Kahane & Poljakoff-Mayber, 1968). However, the changes due to salinity might, in part, be direct salt effects. In *Avena sativa* coleoptiles osmotic stress causes a differential inhibition of protein synthesis, showing that the synthesis of some proteins is affected to a greater extent than others (Dhindsa & Cleland, 1975a). In general, if water stress is not too severe, recovery of protein synthesis can occur on rehydration: excess water loss causes irreversible damage (Fig. 2).

The relationship between RNA synthesis and protein synthesis under water stress conditions has received little attention, and a number of the early studies on RNA changes under stress are suspect (Hsiao, 1973). Reduction in RNA synthesis rates during the imposition of water stress has been reported for corn seedlings (Maranville & Paulsen, 1972) and for the desert plant, *Anastatica hierochuntica*; in the latter, recovery occurred within 12 h of

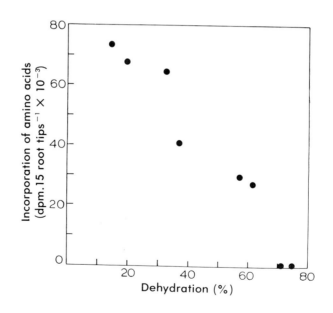

FIG. 2. Incorporation of radioactive amino acids over a one hour period by isolated root tips from 50-h-old corn seedlings during recovery from various degrees of dehydration. (After Nir et al., 1970.)

rewatering after fairly severe stress (Hartung, 1974). Concomitant changes in protein synthesis were not studied, however, and so it is not known in this and other plants if RNA synthesis on rehydration is intimately involved in the recovery of protein synthesis. This subject is worthy of study.

In concluding this section we must consider how and why protein synthesis ceases in tissues under water stress. Nir et al., (1970) proposed that stress-induced changes to cells caused condensation of DNA in the nucleus, thus blocking messenger RNA synthesis, and ultimately protein synthesis as messages became limiting. This possibility has not been tested rigorously, although in corn seedlings, for example, it is questionable if a water potential of -1.2 MPa, which prevents protein synthesis, is sufficiently low to induce chromatin condensation. The fate of messenger RNAs during stress and their status in stressed tissues are also unknown.

There has been considerable argument about whether stress-induced reduction in numbers of polysomes is due to an increase in ribonuclease, an enzyme which can degrade polysomes by cleaving the exposed pieces of messenger RNA between ribosomes. This possibility is favoured by several Russian workers (Henckel et al., 1967; Henckel, 1970; Tvorus, 1970; Satarova & Tvorus, 1971; Henckel et al., 1974; Blekhman & Tvorus, 1974; Blekhman, 1977) who have demonstrated that there is an increase in ribonuclease (and its isoenzymes) in a variety of plants under stress. In no case, however, has a cause-and-effect relationship been demonstrated between an increase in ribonuclease activity and a decline in polysomes. Hsiao (1970, 1973) argued against the involvement of this enzyme in polysome degradation, although his evidence was not conclusive. Better evidence has been provided by Morilla et al. (Fig. 3). They demonstrated that while ribonuclease activity rises in the aerial parts of 8-day-old corn seedlings under stress, it does so only after polysome levels have declined to their minimum value. Here, then, increased ribonuclease activity appears to be unrelated to polysome loss. Similar experiments need to be carried out on other tissues.

Other reasons for the cessation of protein synthesis under stress have been put forward: decline in activity of a supernatant factor (Satarova & Tvorus, 1971); failure of the reinitiation process (Hsiao, 1970); and decrease in membrane-bound polysomes due to membrane changes (Dhindsa & Cleland, 1975b). These and other interesting possibilities remain to be adequately tested.

III. DESICCATION-TOLERANT PLANTS

Our understanding of the effects of desiccation on protein and associated RNA synthesis in desiccation-tolerant plants has come largely from studies on

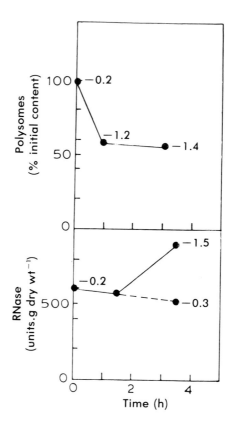

FIG. 3. Levels of polysomes (top) and ribonuclease activity (bottom) in excised aerial parts (mainly leaves) of 8-d-old corn seedlings under water stress (————) and in well-watered controls (— — — —). Numbers at certain points indicate the leaf water potential in MPa. (After Morilla et al., 1973.)

the gametophyte of the moss *Tortula ruralis*. This moss loses water in an apparently uncontrolled manner to drier ambient air and rapidly rehydrates on introduction to liquid water.

The effects of desiccation on polysomes varies with the speed at which water loss takes place. Rapid desiccation occurs within an hour when pieces of the moss gametophyte are placed in an atmosphere of zero relative humidity or are exposed to air on the laboratory bench. Slower desiccation, which takes 3–4 h, is achieved by placing the moss in atmospheres of high relative humidity (Gwóźdź et al., 1974). Moss in the rapidly desiccated state contains about half the polysomes of the undesiccated control, but following slow desiccation polysomes are absent (Fig. 4). There are two possible reasons for this polysome loss during drying: (i) stress-induced production or activation of ribonuclease which degrades polysomes (see previous section); or, (ii) ribosome run-off from mRNA which is coupled with failure to reform an initiation complex under stress conditions. That ribosomes simply become detached from mRNA during water loss is an untenable alternative because some polysomes are retained in rapidly desiccated moss (Fig. 4).

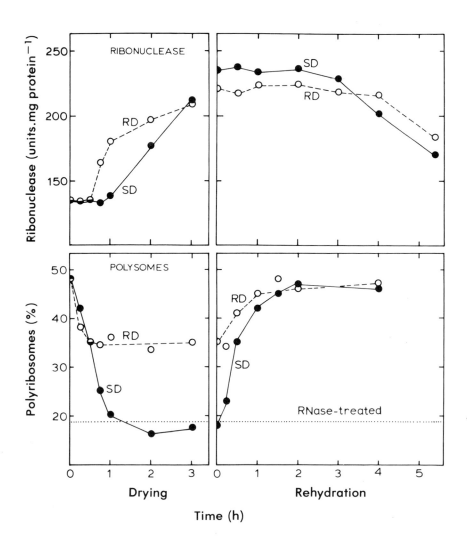

FIG. 4. Changes in ribonuclease (top) and polysomes (bottom) during rapid dessication (RD) and slow dessication (SD) of *Tortula ruralis*, and on subsequent rehydration. (After Bewley and Dhindsa, 1977; Dhindsa and Bewley, 1976a.)

Ribonuclease activity increases during both rapid and slow desiccation (Fig. 4), but as in corn seedlings (Fig. 3) it does so only after polysome levels have declined to their minimum (which also suggests that the enzyme does not arise by *de novo* synthesis). Moreover, while the final ribonuclease level is the same for mosses dried at both speeds, the final polysome level is much higher after rapid desiccation. Thus the lack of both temporal coincidence and quantitative correlation between the increase in enzyme activity and polysome decrease suggests that ribonuclease is not the causative agent. On rehydration after both speeds of desiccation polysome numbers return to control levels within 2 h, but ribonuclease levels do not decline until later (Fig. 4). This again indicates that ribonuclease is not involved in the control of polysome activity.

During desiccation, at both speeds, the ribosomal pellet (containing both polysomes and single ribosomes) decreases in its capacity to effect the formation of peptide bonds, as shown by its increasing inability to utilize puromycin to form peptidyl-puromycin in an *in vitro* assay system (Dhindsa & Bewley, 1976a). This is evidence that as polysomes decline the released ribosomes are not complexed with fragments of messenger RNA, whereas they would be if polysomes were degraded by ribonuclease. Similar results have been obtained using moss maintained under steady-state water stress conditions with polyethylene glycol (Dhindsa & Bewley, 1976b). Hence ribosome run-off from messenger RNA, coupled with failure to reform an initiation complex, appears to be the primary cause of polysome loss during water loss. Presumably, during desiccation at a rapid rate, critical water loss occurs before run-off of ribosomes can be completed. Studies on the factors associated with initiation complex formation have not been carried out, so it is not known if they change or become limiting during desiccation. It appears unlikely that protein synthesis is restricted by declining ATP availability. As with ribonuclease, there is a lack of temporal coincidence and quantitative correlation between levels of ATP and those of polysomes during desiccation (Bewley & Gwóźdź, 1975). During rapid desiccation ATP levels do not decline substantially although those of polysomes do. During slow desiccation polysome levels decline at stress values which have no apparent effects on those of ATP. The status of GTP, another nucleotide intimately involved in protein synthesis, has not been studied.

Since loss of polysomes during desiccation of *T. ruralis* is not due to their degradation by ribonuclease, it is reasonable to expect that in slowly desiccated moss ribosomes exist separated from messenger RNA. This is indeed the case. Both rapidly and slowly desiccated moss contain ribosomes which are active in an *in vitro* protein synthesis assay system using the synthetic messenger RNA, poly-U. As might be expected, slowly desiccated moss contains fewer polysomes and more free ribosomes than rapidly desiccated moss (Table II). Cytoplasmic ribosomal RNA (24S and 17S) and low molecular weight RNA (4-5S) are not degraded during desiccation. This was shown in an experiment in which undesiccated moss was incubated in ^{3}H-uridine for 4 h, washed in unlabelled precursor and then dried and stored for 24 h. RNA was extracted from dry moss and from moss rehydrated for 30, 60 and 120 min before separation by electrophoresis on polyacrylamide gels. The RNA absorbance profiles did not change during the 2 h of rehydration, nor were they substantially different from the RNA profile of the undesiccated moss. Furthermore, the distribution of incorporated ^{3}H-uridine was unchanged during rehydration, an indication of its stability under stress (Tucker & Bewley, 1976).

It appears that messenger RNA also is conserved in the dry moss and is utilized on subsequent rehydration. This can be inferred from the observation that protein synthesis can resume on rehydration of slowly desiccated moss even when most RNA synthesis has been inhibited by cordycepin and actinomycin D (Dhindsa & Bewley, 1978). Other studies on the qualitative aspects of protein synthesis using the double-labelling ratio technique have shown that similar proteins are synthesized before and after desiccation (either rapid or slow) even when RNA synthesis is inhibited on rehydration. This again argues for messenger RNA conservation during desiccation (Dhindsa & Bewley, 1978). Direct and unequivocal evidence for the conservation of messenger RNA in dry *Tortula ruralis* comes from studies in which poly(A)-containing RNA was extracted from rapidly and slowly desiccated moss and then made to catalyze the synthesis of polypeptides *in vitro* (Table III). Extractable poly(A)-messenger RNA activity in slowly desiccated moss was about 80% of that of fully hydrated controls: rapidly desiccated moss contained some 90% messenger RNA activity, although here, presumably,

TABLE II

Effects of rapid and slow desiccation on the *in vitro* activities of polysomes and single ribosomes from the dry mosses *Tortula ruralis* and *Cratoneuron filicinum*.[a]

Desiccation rate	Polysome activity ^{14}C-leucine incorporation (cpm × 10^{-2} .mg rRNA^{-1})	Ribosome activity ^{14}C-phenylalanine incorporation (pmol .mg rRNA^{-1})
Tortula ruralis		
Undesiccated	142	104.5
Rapid	110	119
Slow	13	221.5
Cratoneuron filicinum		
Undesiccated	23	32.4
Rapid	14.5	41.4

[a]After Gwóźdź and Bewley (1975).

TABLE III

Translation *in vitro* of poly(A)-containing messenger RNA from undesiccated and dry gametophytes of *Tortula ruralis*.[a]

RNA source	^{14}C-leucine incorporation (cpm)
Fresh moss	9,175
Rapidly desiccated	7,976
Slowly desiccated	7,185
Deletions:	
No mRNA	693
No S-23	85

[a]After Bewley and Dhindsa (1977); Dhindsa and Bewley (1978).

some was conserved on polysomes. Poly(A)-containing RNA also has been extracted from the hydrated and dry gametophyte of *Polytrichum commune* (Seibert et al., 1976). Air drying (claimed to be slow drying) of *P. commune* did not result in any degradation of total extractable RNA, but whether or not polysomes were present in the dry moss was not indicated. Hence it is not known if the poly(A)-containing RNA is conserved in the free state, or if it is associated with ribosomes in polysomes; nor is it known whether it has messenger RNA-like properties *in vitro*.

Following desiccation *T. ruralis* (Bewley, 1973a; Gwóźdź et al., 1974), *P. commune* (Seibert et al., 1976) and *Neckera crispa* (Henckel et al., 1977) recommence protein synthesis within a few minutes. In *T. ruralis* polysomes are restored to control levels within 2 h (Fig. 4), even after the moss has been stored in the dry state for 10 months (Bewley, 1973b). Protein synthesis resumes at a faster rate after slow desiccation than after rapid desiccation (Fig. 5). However the reason for this is not readily apparent. Polysomes are already present in rapidly desiccated moss (Fig. 4) (and it is known that they resume activity on rehydration: Bewley, 1973a), whereas for slowly desiccated moss to restart protein synthesis the recombination of separated messenger RNA and ribosomes must occur. Nevertheless, studies on other aspects of moss metabolism show rapid desiccation to be harsher than slow desiccation on cellular integrity and metabolism (Bewley & Thorpe, 1974; Dhindsa & Bewley, 1977; Bewley et al., 1978). The reduced rate of initial protein synthesis might be another manifestation of this.

RNA synthesis in *T. ruralis* also recommences rapidly on rehydration after both speeds of desiccation (Gwóźdź et al., 1974; Dhindsa & Bewley, 1978), although the rates of synthesis after these treatments have not been compared. When the fate of newly synthesized RNA is followed in rehydrated moss after slow drying, it is evident that new ribosomal RNA does not become associated with ribosomes until after about 2 h. Even then these

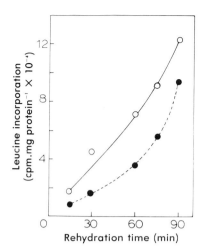

FIG. 5. Protein synthesis by *Tortula ruralis* on rehydration following rapid (●) and slow (○) desiccation. (After Gwóźdź et al., 1974.)

ribosomes are not actively involved in protein synthesis—they are not associated with polysomes (Tucker & Bewley, 1976). Thus the synthesis of neither messenger RNA nor ribosomal RNA appears to be essential for the re-establishment of protein synthesis in *T. ruralis* after desiccation. It has been claimed that RNA synthesis is delayed by some 30–60 min following rehydration of *P. commune* (Seibert et al., 1976), although insensitivity of the experimental technique chosen could contribute to this apparent delay.

For comparative purposes, similar studies have been carried out using mosses which are not normally subjected to desiccation in their natural habitat (i.e. aquatic or semi-aquatic). Preliminary studies on *Bryum pseudotriquetrum* showed that after rapid desiccation this moss does not retain any polysomes, and not only does it not reform any on rehydration, but within 24 h even the ribosomes are degraded (Bewley et al., 1974). Subsequent studies on *Cratoneuron filicinum* (incorrectly identified in some publications as *Hygrohypnum luridum*) have shown that this moss retains a reduced number of polysomes in the dry state after rapid desiccation, compared to undesiccated controls, and retains none following slow desiccation (Malek & Bewley, unpublished): the techniques of sucrose gradient analysis (Bewley, 1974) and *in vitro* assay (Table II) were used. Ribosomes increased as polysomes declined in the dried moss, and they retained their activity *in vitro* (Table II). On rehydration, however, activity of both polysomes and ribosomes decreased precipitously (Gwóźdź & Bewley, 1975). This result suggests that it is rehydration, rather than desiccation, which is lethal. Predictably, after both slow and rapid desiccation, protein synthesis, measured by *in vivo* incorporation of radioactive leucine, failed to resume (Krochko et al., 1978). Even *C. filicinum* is capable of losing a considerable amount of water before its capacity to resume protein synthesis is impaired. Loss of water to about 45% of original fresh weight is possible without a significant deleterious effect on protein synthesis on rehydration (Fig. 6). Moreover, protein synthesis can occur at −4.0 MPa (Fig. 7) and can resume following a 6 h treatment with −6.0 MPa water potential imposed by polyethylene glycol (Dhindsa & Bewley, 1977). Although this moss is not tolerant of desiccation and grows almost entirely immersed in water, it has a tolerance of water stress which is greater than that of many terrestial higher plants (e.g. see Fig. 2).

What is evident from the studies on *Tortula ruralis*, a desiccation tolerant terrestrial moss, is that protein synthesis ceases as water is lost, and it resumes again rapidly on rehydration. Protein synthesis itself is quite sensitive to drought stress, and is reduced by about 50% at −2.0 MPa water potential (Fig. 7), although a low amount occurs even at −6.0 MPa. Hence, protein synthesis may not have a high resistance to drought stress (i.e. it may not continue under severe stress conditions), but it is tolerant of drought, since it can resume even after desiccation. Rapid resumption may be aided by the conservation of the components of the protein synthesizing complex in the dry

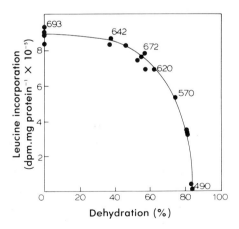

FIG. 6. The loss of capacity for protein synthesis by *Cratoneuron filicinum* at various stages of rapid desiccation. Moss was dried to various percentages of original fresh weight before rehydration. After 2 h of rehydration protein synthesis was monitored for a 1 h period. Figures show protein content (μg.300 mg fresh wt^{-1}) of moss 3 h after rehydration following water loss to the level indicated. (After Krochko et al., 1978.)

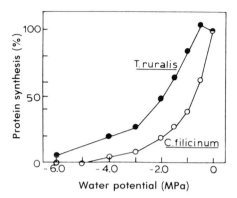

FIG. 7. Inhibition of protein synthesis in *Tortula ruralis* (●) and *Cratoneuron filicinum* (○) by water stress (polyethylene glycol). Moss gametophyte samples were incubated in the appropriate solutions for 1.5 h and protein synthesis was monitored over a further 1 h. Values for 100% control were 680 cpm.μg protein^{-1} and 225 cpm.μg protein^{-1} for *T. ruralis* and *C. filicinum* respectively. (After Dhindsa and Bewley, 1977.)

state. This may be particularly important to those plants receiving only temporary hydration (e.g. by morning dew) and which have but a few hours to continue metabolism before becoming desiccated again. It may be that the components of the synthetic complex itself have an inherent tolerance of desiccation, for even extracted polysomes can be revived from the air-dry state (Gwóźdź & Bewley, 1975). It appears, however, that polysomes and ribosomes from desiccation-intolerant *C. filicinum* also retain their activity in the dry moss, as shown by *in vitro* assay, although they do lose activity rapidly on rehydration. Hence, it is likely that the possession of a stable protein synthesizing complex which can withstand severe drought conditions is an important feature of desiccation-tolerant plants, but other factors are more important in determining the absolute level of tolerance.

IV. TOLERANCE OF DESICCATION BY SEEDS AND ITS LOSS DURING SEEDLING GROWTH

A. SEEDS

Synthesis of proteins is an integral part of development of seed tissues and of germination. Interpolated between these two events in most seeds there is a period of desiccation that occurs irrespective of the ambient humidity. For most seeds desiccation is probably an essential part of normal development, rather than an unpredictable environmental stress which must be tolerated. The fate of the protein synthesizing complex during drying of cereal embryos and axes of dicotyledonous seeds (i.e. those tissues which germinate) has received little attention, although it has been inferred from electron microscope studies that polysomes are lost from lima bean (*Phaseolus lunatus*) axes as they dry out (Klein & Pollock, 1968). This probably is a general phenomenon, for there are a number of reports that dry embryos and axes do not contain polysomes. Whether or not polysome loss is directly related to desiccation or is a programmed event in development remains to be resolved. Nevertheless, as will be discussed in more detail later, dry embryos do conserve ribosomes, messenger and other RNA types, as well as various other factors involved in protein synthesis.

The changes in protein synthesis within storage tissues during the drying phase of maturation have been studied by several workers, particularly in the cotyledons of legumes and the endosperm of castor bean. In the starchy endosperm of cereals and in the endosperm of endospermic legumes, the cytoplasm is occluded by the developing stored reserves, and the mature cells are functionally dead. In early dwarf pea cotyledons, drying is accompanied by a decline in the number of ribosomes associated in polysomes from about 80% to only 20% (Fig. 8), so that at seed maturity most ribosomes are free of messenger RNA. These retain their ability to catalyze protein synthesis, however, for they incorporate phenylalanine when placed in an *in vitro* protein synthesizing system containing poly-U (Beevers & Poulson, 1972). Ribosomes are present also in the dry cotyledons of other legumes and of non-legumes, and generally it has been observed that there is no major decline in total RNA within these storage organs during drying (Millerd & Spencer, 1974; Payne & Boulter, 1969; Smith, 1973). The fate of messenger RNA is unknown, but it is not unreasonable to assume that at least those messages associated with the synthesis of stored reserves are destroyed, for they are not required during germination. Cessation of protein synthesis during the final drying phase in cotyledons of broad bean (*Vicia faba*) is accompanied by a sharp reduction in the number of membrane-bound ribosomes and a concomitant increase in free ribosomes (Payne & Boulter, 1969). Crude preparations of ribosomes extracted from broad bean at this stage appear to have a very limited capacity to catalyse *in vitro* polypeptide synthesis in the presence of poly-U (Payne et al., 1971). Together, these observations suggest that, as free ribosomes are formed during drying, their protein synthetic abilities are lost. This requires confirmation, for it appears to be an exception to the general rule. It has been suggested that it is the supernatant factors that lose their activity during the drying phase of seed maturation in peas (Beevers & Poulson, 1972), but the evidence is not strong. In castor bean endosperm both polysomes and ribosomes decreased while water was lost in the final stages of

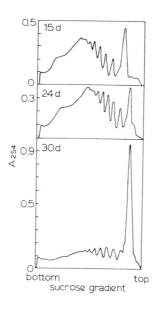

FIG. 8. Polyribosome profiles from peas (*Pisum sativum* cv. Burpeana) at various ages after flowering. The single ribosome peak is towards the top of the gradient, and polysome peaks are lower. (After Beevers and Poulson, 1972.)

maturation, and this was accompanied by a loss of total RNA (Sturani & Cocucci, 1965; Sturani, 1968). Ribosomes, at least on the basis of *in vitro* activity, appeared to be absent from the dry seed. These observations have now been shown to be incorrect (Bewley & Larsen, 1979), and both endosperms and embryos of mature dry castor beans conserve ribosomes, which are active in *in vitro* assay.

There is still a need for more information on the changes the protein synthesizing complex undergoes in both embryos and storage organs during the final stages of maturation. Moreover, we need to know if the changes which occur at this time are due ultimately to water loss from the cells, or if they are a "programmed" part of development and would occur even if the seed were not allowed to dry out. Nevertheless, there is ample evidence that in dry seeds the components of the protein synthesizing complex are maintained in an intact state, and are potentially active. Contained within dry wheat embryos, for example, are ribosomes, messenger and transfer RNAs, and initiation and transfer factors (Giesen et al., 1976; Marcus et al., 1966; Brooker et al., 1978). The presence of active ribosomes and supernatant components has been demonstrated in dry seeds, axes, or embryos of only a few species, e.g. rice, rye, oats, *Pinus* spp., peanuts, peas and lettuce. Other studies have shown that ribosomes are present in dry axes or seeds of radish, cotton and *Phaseolus vulgaris*, although their activity (i.e. ability to catalyse *in vitro* protein synthesis) has not been confirmed (see reviews by Bewley & Black, 1978; Bewley, 1979, for appropriate references). An excellent review by Payne (1976) has assessed the evidence for the presence of conserved (or long-lived) messenger RNA in dry seeds. A poly(A)-containing messenger RNA fraction was extracted from dry peas, rapeseed and rye embryos and its capacity to act as a template for a number of discreet, high-molecular weight proteins has been demonstrated (Gordon & Payne, 1976). Similarly, messenger RNA is conserved in wheat embryos and is utilized for early protein synthesis upon imbibition (Spiegel & Marcus, 1975; Brooker et al., 1978). Studies using inhibitors indicate that protein synthesis can resume without the requirement for new RNA synthesis (Spiegel & Marcus, 1975). RNA with poly(A) sequences has been extracted from mature cotton seeds (but not translated *in vitro* to prove it is mRNA) (Hammett & Katterman, 1975) and, as in dry rapeseeds (Payne et al., 1977) it appeared to be located within the nucleus. This may be a means of protection for conserved messages. As drying occurs, those messages associated with the protein synthesizing complex within the cytoplasm may be destroyed, and only those protected within the cytoplasm (perhaps by being surrounded by protein; Peumans & Carlier, 1977) or away from the cytoplasm (i.e. in the nucleus) are available for germination. It will be interesting to determine the protective mechanism for messenger RNA molecules in dry seeds.

On hydration of a dry seed, protein synthesis can be detected within the first 30–60 min. Some workers failed to detect protein synthesis until after several hours, but invariably this could be attributed to inadequate techniques. In wheat embryos, polysomes are formed within 10–15 min of the start of imbibition, without the requirement for *de novo* synthesized ribosomes or *de novo* synthesized messenger RNA (Marcus et al., 1975). Similarly, in cotton seeds it appears that neither new RNA synthesis, nor processing of conserved mRNA, is essential for initial protein synthesis during imbibition (Hammett & Katterman, 1975). This is not to say, however, that synthesis of RNA does not recommence rapidly following the start of imbibition in wheat embryos (Spiegel et al., 1975); but this is not essential for initial protein synthesis, nor is it known when it is recruited for this process. Early resumption of RNA synthesis occurs in other seeds too; but again it may not be a prerequisite for early protein synthesis.

Little work has been done on the recommencement of RNA and protein synthesis early in rehydration of dry seed storage organs. Thus the involvement of conserved and newly-synthesized RNA in protein synthesis is largely unknown. It is quite possible, however, that RNA and supernatant components are conserved in the dry cotyledons (e.g. in peanut; Jachymczyk & Cherry, 1968) and become reactivated upon rehydration. In the castor bean endosperm, from which there is a marked loss during desiccation, there is a massive synthesis of ribosomal and soluble (transfer) RNA and of new ribosomes on rehydration (Marrè et al., 1965).

On the basis of the above evidence it is apparent that seeds are able to synthesize proteins and all RNA types soon after tissue hydration. The synthesis of RNA is not essential for protein synthesis to commence, and the conservation of RNA and other components of the synthetic complex allows a rapid resumption of cellular activity on exposure of the seed to water. This, presumably, has some importance in accelerating the seed towards completion of those processes essential for germination.

B. SEEDLINGS

Drying of seeds from the early stages of imbibition through to the time of cell division and vacuolation of the developing seedling usually has no permanent deleterious effects on subsequent germination or growth. Hydrated seeds eventually pass through this desiccation-insensitive phase and become sensitive (or intolerant). This occurs in the seedling stage of development at about the time of the duplication of the genome.

Desiccation of oat grains (Akalehiywot & Bewley, unpublished) and wheat embryos during the insensitive stage of development results in a decline in polyribosomes, which reform on subsequent rehydration (Table IV).

TABLE IV

In vitro activity of polysomes and ribosomes of desiccated, rehydrated and undesiccated embryos of wheat. Hydration and rehydration times (in hours) are denoted by the figures without the bar above them, and lengths of desiccation by the barred figures (e.g. $\overline{48}$). Polysomes and ribosomes were extracted at the end of the treatments, and their activity assayed in *in vitro* protein synthesizing systems.[a]

Treatment	Polysome activity (cpm.mg rRNA^{-1})	Ribosome activity (cpm.mg rRNA^{-1} × 10^{-3})
24	4,540	146
24–$\overline{48}$	1,600	145
24–$\overline{48}$–24	3,300	160
72	3,250	32
72–$\overline{48}$	230	31
72–$\overline{48}$–24	405	43

[a]After Chen et al. (1968).

Ribosomes retain their activity in the dry grains, but it is not known if messenger RNA is present. It has been suggested that it is (Chen et al., 1968), but the adequacy of the techniques used to demonstrate the presence or absence of message is questionable. RNA, as well as protein synthesis, resumes rapidly on rehydration of cereal embryos; for example, oats (Akalehiywot & Bewley, unpublished), wheat (Dell'Aquila et al., 1978) and rye (Sen & Osborne, 1974), although the dependency of the protein synthesis on RNA synthesis is not known. Embryos desiccated during their desiccation-sensitive phase irreversibly decline in their capacity to conduct protein (Fig. 2), RNA, or DNA synthesis on rehydration: chromatin remains condensed and DNA may be damaged (Chen et al., 1968; Crèvecour et al., 1976). Both polysomes and ribosomes lose their activity when seedlings are dehydrated (Table IV), and in wheat embryos desiccation in the sensitive phase may result in the destruction of endogenous messenger RNA and of the ability to produce normal intact messages on rehydration (Chen et al., 1968). Unfortunately, however, technical difficulties must be overcome before the experimental evidence can be completely accepted. In the endosperm of germinated castor bean seeds (which does not undergo cell division, and hence probably does not have a desiccation-sensitive phase), water loss results in the loss of polysomes and an increase in single ribosomes, which retain their *in vitro* activity (Table V). In another non-growing, mature seed tissue, the barley aleurone layer, water stress imposed by osmotica reduces protein synthesis, including the production of α-amylase (Armstrong & Jones, 1973; Chrispeels, 1973). Extractable polysome levels decline under stress conditions, but ribosomes maintain their activity. Recovery of α-amylase production commences within an hour of removal of the osmotic stress (Armstrong & Jones, 1973).

TABLE V

The effect of a period of interrupted water supply on the *in vitro* activities of polysomes and ribosomes from endosperm of germinated castor bean seed. Hydration and rehydration times (in hours) are denoted by the figures without the bar above them, and lengths of interrupted water supply by the barred figures (e.g. $\overline{48}$). Polysomes and ribosomes were extracted at the end of the treatments, and their activity assayed in *in vitro* protein synthesizing systems.[a]

Treatment	Polysome activity (cpm.mg rRNA^{-1})	Ribosome activity (cpm.mg rRNA^{-1})
40	498	8800
40–$\overline{48}$	20	6150
40–$\overline{48}$–24	495	7120
64	520	8200

[a]After Sturani et al. (1968).

It is apparent, then, that germinating seeds are more or less insensitive to desiccation stress but, as seedlings develop, their growing tissues, at least, become desiccation-sensitive and irreversible changes occur in their metabolism. This susceptibility might not be due to any inherent changes within the protein synthesizing complex itself, however, as the increased vacuolation which occurs in developing cells is likely to make them more susceptible to severe water loss. Hence, decreased synthetic activity could be but one manifestation of increased cytoplasmic disruption.

V. THE RELATIONSHIP BETWEEN DESICCATION TOLERANCE, DESICCATION RESISTANCE AND PROTEIN SYNTHESIS

There can be little doubt that water stress reduces the capacity of plant tissues to carry out protein synthesis. Some plants are affected by lower water stresses than others, and a feature of drought resistance may be the ability to continue protein synthesis at moderate, or even fairly severe, water deficits. Many plants are resistant to some degree of drought, but cannot tolerate severe drought, or desiccation. In these, protein synthesis does not resume following excessive water loss. However, this may not be due to any direct affect of stress on the protein synthesizing complex itself; but it may be symptomatic of the general cellular disruption which results from severe water loss. Desiccation tolerant plants need not necessarily exhibit a pronounced resistance to water loss (i.e. protein synthesis may cease at lower water deficits than in certain intolerant plants), but they must be able to resume protein synthesis after desiccation. In these tolerant plants all the components of the protein synthesizing complex appear to be conserved in the dried plant, and they become active again on rehydration. It remains to be determined if the individual components of this complex are themselves more tolerant of desiccation than those from intolerant species. They may not be; the cells of tolerant species may simply retain their integrity upon desiccation, thus protecting their components.

Why protein synthesis ceases under stress conditions is not clear. There are indications that stress-induced ribonuclease production or activation is not responsible for the observed reduction of polysomes. A decline in available ATP is also probably not the cause. Structural rearrangements within cells due to declining turgor may play a role, but evidence is lacking—and it may be very difficult to demonstrate. Whatever the reason, it appears to restrict the reinitiation process, thus preventing ribosomes from becoming reattached to messenger RNA. The fate of the components of the protein synthesizing complex in lightly stressed plants with low drought resistance is not clearly understood, although it is likely that at least the ribosomes retain their activity. In the tolerant plants studied to date (i.e. terrestrial mosses and seeds) all components are conserved. This is probably a useful adaptation as far as the mosses are concerned, for their periods of hydration are transitory, and their ability to rapidly resume protein synthesis could be of advantage. The situation in seeds is more complex, because desiccation terminates one phase of development and may trigger another. Seed water loss may be important in inducing the destruction of certain messenger RNA molecules which are no longer required. In addition, germination may be hastened by the rapid resumption of protein synthesis using conserved components. However, the involvement of early RNA synthesis in the resumption of protein synthesis does not appear to be required. In tolerant plants, though, it is apparent that the transcription mechanism is largely unaffected by desiccation. Whether the transcription and translation mechanisms in intolerant species are equally resistant to drought stress has not been determined.

The importance of protein synthesis on our understanding of the mechanisms of drought resistance and drought tolerance is not clear. There is little doubt that the ability of a plant to resume protein synthesis on rewatering after drought stress is a good indication of its ability to have withstood that stress. However, if a plant cannot resume protein synthesis it is unlikely to be because this process alone, or even primarily, has been affected. The changes in protein synthesis induced by stress are only symptomatic of other changes occurring within plant cells, and the elucidation of these latter changes is more likely to lead to an understanding of the mechanisms involved in drought resistance as well as drought and desiccation tolerance.

CHAPTER 13

Photosynthesis

P. E. KRIEDEMANN AND W. J. S. DOWNTON

I.	Introduction	283
II.	Comparative biochemistry and physiology of photosynthesis	284
	A. Biochemical aspects	284
	B. Gas exchange and derivation of diffusive resistances	289
III.	Photosynthetic adjustments to water stress and implications for drought resistance	292
	A. Water use efficiency	292
	B. Stomatal and photosynthetic adjustments	295
	C. Expression of CAM	301
	D. Photochemical and biochemical adjustments to drought	303
IV.	Summary	313

I. INTRODUCTION

Plants have evolved with highly integrated mechanisms whereby radiant energy is captured by pigment assemblies and converted into biologically useful forms which transform CO_2 into carbohydrate. Terrestrial plants have also rationalized the opposed priorities of light interception and CO_2 acquisition against the need to minimize transpiration. This arose because drought constituted an unrelenting selective pressure during the course of evolution and still represents a major environmental constraint. Many terrestrial plants have emerged with adaptations which confer drought resistance, and at least some of these adaptations involve changes in photosynthetic efficiency, either photochemical or biochemical in origin. We will examine the comparative physiology and biochemistry of photosynthetic activity and then analyse photosynthetic processes at different levels of organization from whole plants to organelles. Section II is intended to introduce and analyse those aspects of photosynthesis which are relevant to water stress. The photosynthetic consequences of stress and implications for drought resistance are dealt with in Section III.

283

PHYSIOLOGY AND BIOCHEMISTRY
OF DROUGHT RESISTANCE
IN PLANTS

II. COMPARATIVE BIOCHEMISTRY AND PHYSIOLOGY
OF PHOTOSYNTHESIS

Three distinct modes of CO_2 fixation have been identified in higher plants. For convenience they are referred to as C_3, C_4 and CAM (Crassulacean Acid Metabolism). C_3 plants have a CO_2 assimilation/reduction cycle in which the first stable product from CO_2 fixation is the 3-carbon molecule, 3-phosphoglyceric acid (Calvin & Bassham, 1962). The C_4 and CAM modes utilize additional reactions in which CO_2 is initially fixed into C_4-dicarboxylic acids. In C_4 plants, these acids are immediately translocated to adjacent tissue where decarboxylation occurs providing substrate for the Calvin cycle. During CAM the C_4 acids are synthesized at night and stored until daylight when decarboxylation makes CO_2 available to the Calvin cycle. Regardless of biochemical sequence, all three photosynthetic modes rely on photochemically derived energy for conversion of CO_2 to carbohydrate.

Assimilation of CO_2 by the Calvin cycle requires energy which is provided by 3 molecules of ATP and 2 of $NADPH_2$ for each molecule of CO_2 fixed. Operation of the C_4 pathway is intrinsically less efficient—two additional high-energy phosphate bonds are necessary to regenerate phosphoenolpyruvate from pyruvate so that the initial carboxylation reaction can be sustained (Hatch, 1976). Contrary to expectation, the differing energy requirements of C_3 and C_4 photosynthesis do not necessarily find expression in whole leaves. Ehleringer and Björkman (1977) derived quantum yields of approximately 0.053 (moles of CO_2 fixed per absorbed einstein under limiting light intensity) for both C_3 and C_4 plants in air at 30°C. However, quantum yields from C_3 plants are strongly dependent upon O_2 and CO_2 concentration as well as temperature, and the quantum yield increased to 0.073 in low O_2. Similar quantum yields for C_3 and C_4 plants in air at 30°C represented a balance between decreased quantum yield due to oxygen inhibition of photosynthesis in C_3 plants and the intrinsically lower quantum yield resulting from the additional ATP requirement in C_4 plants. As discussed later, the C_4 pathway of photosynthesis is largely insensitive to O_2.

A. BIOCHEMICAL ASPECTS

1. RuBP carboxylase and photorespiration

Carbohydrate formation in all higher plants, regardless of photosynthetic mode, depends upon the carboxylation of ribulose-1,5-bisphosphate (RuBP). Early investigations revealed an *in vitro* activity for RuBP carboxylase that was difficult to reconcile with measured rates of photosynthesis by intact leaves: the K_m (CO_2) appeared to be an order of magnitude higher than photosynthesis itself (Paulsen & Lane, 1966; Jensen & Bassham, 1966). Subsequent research has resolved the enigma by demonstrating that RuBP carboxylase exhibits different kinetic properties depending upon its degree of activation (Bahr & Jensen, 1974; Andrews et al., 1975). When fully activated by CO_2 and Mg^{2+} prior to assay, RuBP carboxylase has a K_m (CO_2) of 10–20 μM; that is, similar to that for CO_2 fixation by intact chloroplasts (Jensen & Bassham, 1966). The enzyme also exhibits substantial oxygen-fixing (oxygenase) activity (Badger & Andrews, 1974; Bahr & Jensen, 1974; Lorimer et al., 1977). The oxygenase reaction, which in nature normally accompanies carboxylation, results in the formation of phosphoglycolate (Bowes et al., 1971; Lorimer et al., 1973), which then becomes the primary substrate for photorespiration (Tolbert, 1971). This process constitutes an integral part of the C_3 pathway and, as a carbon-oxidation cycle, is responsible for losses of CO_2 just fixed in photosynthesis (Fig. 1). During photorespiration, oxygen is consumed in the conversion of glycolate to glyoxylate in peroxisomes, and CO_2 is released during the subsequent condensation of glycine to serine in mitochondria (Kisaki & Tolbert, 1970; Woo & Osmond, 1976; Chollet, 1977). Serine is further metabolized and can re-enter the Calvin cycle as 3-phosphoglycerate. The net outcome for carbon

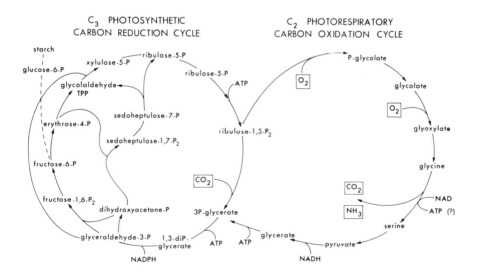

FIG. 1. The integrated C_3 photosynthetic carbon reduction cycle and photorespiratory carbon oxidation cycle, initiated by RuBP carboxylase and linked by conversion of glycolate to 3-phosphoglyceric acid. (From Osmond and Björkman, unpublished.)

balance is that 75% of the carbon channelled into photorespiration is eventually recovered as carbohydrate (Tolbert, 1971). Probably all of the glycolate synthesized in leaves originates from oxygenation of RuBP (Lorimer et al., 1977).

The approximate stoichiometry of photosynthesis and photorespiration at 25°C has been modelled by Laing et al. (1974) and salient points are shown in Figure 2. In this scheme, in which one molecule of O_2 is fixed for every 4 molecules of CO_2, 75% of the carbon entering the glycolate pathway is recovered and photorespiration equals 0.5 C/3.5 C or 14% of the rate of net photosynthesis (as measured by Ludwig & Canvin, 1971). Here 50% of the carbon fixed flows through glycolate (as stated by Zelitch, 1973). In the absence of O_2 (as shown on the left side of Fig. 2) net photosynthesis increases from 3.5 C to 5.0 C fixed (an enhancement of 1.5 C/3.5 C or 43%—a value consistent with many observations). Finally, photorespiratory CO_2 evolution in air accounts for 0.5 C/1.5 C or one-third of the total oxygen inhibition (as noted by Ludwig & Canvin, 1971). The remaining two-thirds arises from direct inhibition of photosynthesis by oxygen (Tregunna et al., 1966; Ludwig & Canvin, 1971; Servaites & Ogren, 1978).

During photosynthesis, CO_2 and O_2 compete for the same site on the active form of RuBP carboxylase; hence their competitive interaction. Significantly, the K_m (CO_2) of the carboxylase is nearly equal to the K_i (CO_2) of the oxygenase; conversely, the K_m (O_2) of the oxygenase is similar to the

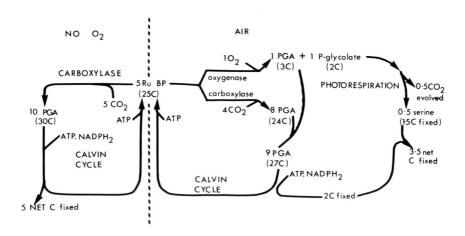

FIG. 2. Approximate stoichiometry of photosynthesis and photorespiration in air (300 μl.l CO_2^{-1}, 21% O_2) and in the absence of O_2 (300 μl.l CO_2^{-1}) at 25°C. (Phosphoglyceric acid — PGA; ribulose-1,5-biphosphate — RuBP.) (After Laing et al., 1974.)

K_i (O_2) of the carboxylase (Badger & Andrews, 1974; Laing et al., 1974). Since the earth's atmosphere contains 0.03% CO_2 and 21% O_2, terrestrial C_3 plants are subject to considerable oxygen inhibition. Net photosynthesis is increased about 45% when a low oxygen (1–2%) gas stream is substituted for normal air (Forrester et al., 1966a, 1966b; Ludwig & Canvin, 1971). Furthermore, the degree of oxygen inhibition of photosynthesis depends upon CO_2 concentration, temperature and leaf moisture status.

2. C_4 photosynthesis

Plants equipped with the classical Calvin cycle or C_3 pathway of photosynthesis rely upon RuBP carboxylase to catalyse the primary step in CO_2 fixation. In C_4 plants, however, the initial fixation is catalysed by phosphoenolpyruvate carboxylase, an enzyme with a higher affinity for CO_2 ($K_m \simeq 7$ μM: Hatch & Osmond, 1976) but devoid of oxygen sensitivity (Bowes & Ogren, 1972). Operation of the C_4 pathway depends upon metabolic cooperation between mesophyll and bundle sheath cells, closely associated cell types of the Kranz complex, which serve to compartment segments of the overall pathway (Hatch & Osmond, 1976; Hattersley, 1976).

Carbon dioxide entering a C_4 leaf is intercepted by phosphoenolpyruvate carboxylase located in mesophyll cells and incorporated into C_4-dicarboxylic acids which are translocated to bundle sheath cells. Here the 4-carbon acids are decarboxylated and the CO_2 released is refixed by RuBP carboxylase into the Calvin cycle. Anatomical separation of the two carboxylase enzymes is essentially absolute (Hatch & Osmond, 1976).

Since atmospheric CO_2 is first fixed, then released in bundle sheath cells, and finally refixed prior to carbohydrate formation, C_4 photosynthesis may seem needlessly repetitive. But this sequence of events serves *inter alia* as a CO_2 concentrating mechanism for RuBP carboxylase. Unlike C_3 plants, where the substomatal liquid phase CO_2 concentration is approximately 6 μM, the level in bundle sheath cells of C_4 plants is an order of magnitude higher (Hatch, 1977) and enough to saturate the catalytic capacity of RuBP carboxylase. Furthermore, the elevated CO_2 concentration within the bundle sheath tissue will favour carboxylation over oxygenation to such an extent that inhibition of the carboxylase by atmospheric levels of O_2 will be abolished; hence the lack of O_2 inhibition and apparent absence of photorespiration in C_4 plants (Forrester et al., 1966b).

3. Crassulacean Acid Metabolism (CAM)

In its original sense, CAM referred to the large diurnal variations in acid titre of assimilatory organs in members of the Crassulaceae. This arises from nocturnal CO_2 assimilation forming organic acids followed by daytime conversion to neutral compounds. Phosphoenolpyruvate carboxylase catalyses primary CO_2 fixation, which results predominantly in the accumulation of malic acid in amounts up to 100–200 μeq.g fresh wt^{-1}. Stored acid is decarboxylated during the subsequent light period, when stomata are closed, and the CO_2 released is refixed via RuBP carboxylase and processed through the Calvin cycle. A parallel is often drawn between C_4 and CAM with respect to CO_2 fixation sequences; their distinction lies in carboxylation events that are spatially separated in C_4 plants, but temporally separated (dark-light) in CAM plants.

Great flexibility exists in the expression of CAM depending upon leaf age and development, species characteristics and environmental conditions; and C_4-like and C_3-like metabolism may be optional photosynthetic processes in CAM plants (Osmond, 1975, 1978). Some of the variations observed in water-stressed plants are detailed in Section III, C.

The general pattern of CO_2 exchange in mature, well-watered CAM plants such as *Agave americana* and *Kalanchoë diagremontiana* (Fig. 3) comprises four phases: CO_2 uptake and acidification during darkness; a burst of CO_2 fixation upon illumination; a subsequent decline in CO_2 uptake to zero during the de-acidification (decarboxylation) phase; and fixation of CO_2 from the atmosphere during the latter part of the light period (Neales et al., 1968; Allaway et al., 1974; Neales, 1975; Osmond, 1978). The diurnal shift in carboxylation sequences from C_4-like to C_3-like is accompanied by fluctua-

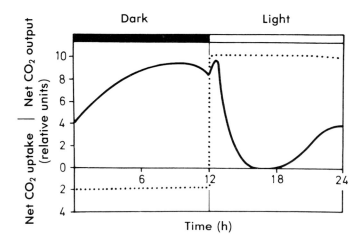

FIG. 3.   Patterns of CO_2 exchange in CAM plants (————) and non-CAM plants
(. . . . .) in a 12 h dark / 12 h light growth cycle. (From Kluge, 1976.)

tions in CO_2 compensation concentration (Jones & Mansfield, 1972) and changes in the O_2 sensitivity of CO_2 fixation (Osmond & Björkman, 1975).

B. GAS EXCHANGE AND DERIVATION OF DIFFUSIVE RESISTANCES

Chloroplasts occupy an aqueous matrix, but in leaves of terrestrial plants their primary substrate, CO_2, is largely derived from relatively drier ambient air. Consequently, transpiration becomes an inevitable corollary to photosynthesis. Mesophytes transpire prodigious quantities of water in comparison to the amount of carbon fixed (Monteith, 1966). With the onset of moisture stress, either biomass is lost due to restrictions on photosynthesis or excessive transpiration results in partial desiccation. The regulatory system, largely stomatal, which has evolved facilitates CO_2 acquisition whilst minimizing dehydration. The operation of the stomata, in association with other gas exchange processes in leaves, can be analysed in terms of gaseous diffusive resistance.

Vapour pressure gradients from leaf to air lead to transpiration, but the flux is controlled by resistances *en route* (summarized diagrammatically in Fig. 4). Renner analysed the situation as early as 1910 and, from physical principles, foreshadowed the importance of boundary layer effects. Empirical analyses were subsequently completed by Raschke (1956) and Gaastra (1959) with respect to both H_2O vapour and CO_2 fluxes from leaves in assimilation chambers. Knowing the concentration of H_2O vapour in the ambient air, and the leaf temperature and transpiration rate, the total diffusive resistance (Σ_r) to H_2O transfer was derived from the expression

$$\Sigma_r \text{ (sec. cm}^{-1}) = \frac{A - B(\mu g. \text{ cm}^{-3})}{\text{transpiration rate } (\mu g. \text{ cm}^{-2}. \text{ s}^{-1})}$$

where B is the moisture content of ambient air and A is the concentration presumed to exist within substomatal cavities. For well-watered mesophytes it is generally assumed that A is equivalent to saturation vapour pressure for that particular leaf temperature. Under steep gradients in H_2O vapour pressure from leaf to air (e.g. arid conditions), the internal vapour pressure could fall as the H_2O meniscii retreat into the walls of cells which form the perimeter of the substomatal cavities. The resultant increase in path length for H_2O vapour diffusion manifests itself as a mesophyll resistance (r_m) to water vapour loss, a component that varies according to species, leaf moisture status and evaporative conditions (e.g. Gale et al., 1967). Mesophyll cell contortion and the reduced air space (hence greater tortuosity) that occurs at low leaf water potential (Levitt & Ben Zaken, 1975) could be an additional contribution to a mesophyll resistance to H_2O vapour diffusion.

Solute accumulation at evaporative sites underneath stomata (Boon-Long, 1941; Whiteman & Koller, 1964) or deposition of wax in stomatal antechambers as described for Sitka spruce by Jeffree et al. (1971) would also contribute to reduced H_2O vapour pressure. The net effect would be restrained transpiration without a commensurate reduction in photosynthesis—an obvious benefit in terms of drought resistance. For present purposes we will simplify the issue and continue with the case of a well-watered mesophyte.

As evident in Figure 4, Σ_r embodies resistances in series, and so Σ_r will be the simple summation of boundary layer resistance (r_a) + stomatal resistance (r_s). Boundary layer resistance is a function of leaf size and shape, and wind speed. It is generally the smallest resistance in the series, about unity or less in assimilation chambers, but it can rise to 4–5 s. cm^{-1} for large leaves under calm conditions in the field (Tinus, 1975). Stomatal resistance is

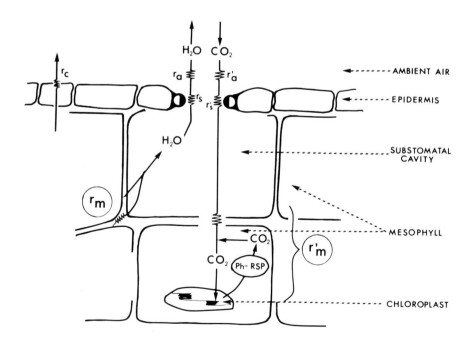

FIG. 4. Diagrammatic summary of gaseous diffusive resistances to CO_2 and H_2O vapour exchange by a leaf. H_2O molecules escaping encounter mesophyll (r_m), stomatal (r_s), and boundary layer (r_a) resistances; CO_2 molecules entering the leaf overcome corresponding resistances designated r'_a, r'_s and r'_m (r'_m being a composite term which embodies physical, biochemical and photochemical limitations). Photorespiratory processes within the mesophyll are abbreviated to Ph-RSP. Cuticular resistance is shown as r_c.

clearly a major control point for both H_2O vapour and CO_2 fluxes. Under the influence of environmental factors or bio-controls (such as hormonal regulation of guard cell turgor, or photosynthetically determined intercellular CO_2 level) it can vary over an order of magnitude for the same leaf. Bulk leaf water potential has an overriding influence and becomes a major factor in photosynthetic responses to moisture stress.

To reach the substomatal cavity, carbon dioxide assimilated by a leaf (Fig. 4) has to negotiate the same pathway as emerging H_2O molecules. It is therefore subject to analogous resistances which are designated r'_a, r'_s and r'_m. They can be derived from concurrent measurements of transpiration and photosynthesis: r_a and r_s are simply adjusted upwards on the basis of relative diffusivities of CO_2 and H_2O molecules. CO_2 is a larger and heavier molecule whose diffusion coefficient is $0.165 \, cm^2.s^{-1}$ compared to $0.258 \, cm^2.s^{-1}$ for H_2O. Accordingly, r'_a and $r'_s = 1.56 \, r_a$ and r_s. However, carbon dioxide molecules are also confronted by additional impedances. At mesophyll cell walls (Fig. 4) the diffusion medium changes from gaseous to aqueous; and diffusive resistance in the cell solution will be of the order of 10^4 times the value within intercellular air spaces (Tinus, 1975). The liquid phase pathway extends from the cell walls to the chloroplasts. Subsequent assimilation by the chloroplast is catalysed by an enzyme of finite capacity and can also be represented as a separate "resistance" together with the diffusive resistance to CO_2 movement within the gaseous and liquid phases of the leaf's mesophyll. Some authors have drawn a distinction between the transport component (sometimes termed r_t) and the quasi-diffusion resistance of carboxylation within the chloroplasts (termed r_x) (e.g. Gifford & Musgrave, 1970). Research from several laboratories has provided some estimates of the relative magnitude of these two components (e.g. Hall & Björkman, 1975; Chartier et al., 1970; and Jones & Slatyer, 1972). In general, $r_x \geqslant r_t$ but measurement techniques and data interpretation become so complex that diffusive resistance analysis has consolidated the use of r'_m as a collective term which embodies physical and biological components. In summary, total diffusive resistance to CO_2 assimilation, termed Σ'_r, can be regarded as the summation of $r'_a + r'_s + r'_m$. To derive Σ'_r it is necessary to know both flux and CO_2 concentration gradient from atmosphere to chloroplast. Flux can be measured but gradient has to be inferred. Atmospheric CO_2 concentration is easily measured, but the estimation of the concentration at sites of fixation presents a problem. Gaastra (1959) assumed that this value must be very low because the enzyme-catalysed assimilation was analogous to an infinite sink. For purposes of calculation he took the value as zero. However, photorespiratory processes have since been recognized (Figs. 1 and 2) and CO_2 generation and consumption are now known to occur concurrently. To minimize this added complication, at least in C_3 plants, it has become common practice to derive diffusive resistances from measurements of H_2O vapour and CO_2 flux in a low O_2 gas stream (1–2%). This approach virtually eliminates photorespiration and at the same time allows full expression of the proficiency of RuBP carboxylase as a carboxylating enzyme unimpeded by its oxygenase capability.

Concurrent measurement of photosynthesis and transpiration in a low O_2 gas stream of known CO_2 concentration can therefore provide a direct measurement of Σ_r, and hence r_a and r_s. Corresponding values for r'_a and r'_s are calculated as described earlier. Σ'_r is derived from the measured flux of CO_2 and the concentration gradient from the external gas stream to the chloroplast, making the assumption that the CO_2 concentration is zero at the site of fixation within the chloroplast. Mesophyll resistance to CO_2 assimilation can then be determined by difference since $\Sigma'_r = r'_a + r'_s + r'_m$.

Mesophyll resistance (r'_m) constitutes an additional and often rate limiting factor for CO_2 uptake compared to H_2O loss, so that changes in stomatal resistance may not affect transpiration and photosynthesis to the same degree. Raschke's (1976) computations of CO_2 and H_2O vapour exchange by leaves of *Xanthium strumarium* as a function of stomatal conductance (reciprocal of resistance) showed that transpiration was almost linearly related to stomatal conductance, whereas photosynthesis approaches an asymptote with increased conductance above about 0.4 cm. s^{-1} (i.e. r_s = 2.5 s. cm^{-1}). At low stomatal resistance it is obvious that photosynthesis should be relatively insensitive to changes in stomatal aperture, but stomatal control over CO_2 fixation does become evident at higher r_s.

III. PHOTOSYNTHETIC ADJUSTMENTS TO WATER STRESS AND IMPLICATIONS FOR DROUGHT RESISTANCE

A. WATER USE EFFICIENCY

Comparisons of photosynthetic rates and water use between species are facilitated by diffusive resistance analysis. A summary of generalized values is given in Table I. More detailed comparisons are provided by Gifford (1974), Zelitch (1971) and Rawson et al. (1977). The potentially higher photosynthetic capacity of C_4 plants puts that group at a distinct advantage in terms of biomass generation and water use efficiency (H_2O/CO_2 fluxes) during the day. For a given stomatal resistance, transpiration from C_3 and C_4 plants will be comparable, but CO_2 assimilation will be potentially greater in the C_4 group because of their greater CO_2 scavenging capacity (evident in Table I as lower r'_m).

At night CAM plants generally show a further improvement on the C_4 situation since dark CO_2 fixation, mediated by phosphoenolpyruvate car-

TABLE I

Gas exchange and minimum diffusive resistance of C_3, C_4 and CAM plants.[a]

	Photosynthesis $(mg\ CO_2.h^{-1}.dm^{-2})$	Stomatal resistance $(s.cm^{-1})$	Mesophyll resistance $(s.cm^{-1})$	Transpiration ratio $(H_2O\downarrow/CO_2\downarrow)$
C_3	20–40	0.5–5.0	3–10	450–600
C_4	30–80	1.0–1.5	1–2	250–350
CAM				
Light	3–20	6.0–10	20–40	150–600
Dark	10–15	2.0–10	1–2	25–150

[a]Adapted from Szarek and Ting (1975).

boxylase, is combined with much reduced transpiration. Accordingly, water use efficiency can improve by almost an order of magnitude (see also Table II).

High cuticular resistance in many CAM plants (r_c in Fig. 4) makes a further contribution to their pattern of water use. When stomata are closed, overall resistance to gas exchange is so high, from 200 s. cm^{-1} (Burrows & Milthorpe, 1976) up to 1000 s. cm^{-1} (Szarek & Ting, 1975), that assimilatory organs become hermetically sealed. In contrast to CAM plants, cuticular resistance in mesophytes generally occurs within the range 19–60 s. cm^{-1} (Cowan & Milthorpe, 1968), and water loss continues despite stomatal closure. Nocturnal transpiration can therefore assume importance for diurnal water use efficiency and appears to be an additional contribution towards the C_4 advantage. For example, in field situations, Rawson et al. (1978) demonstrated lower night-time transpiration in sorghum than soybean, despite lower stomatal density and leaf area index in the C_3 crop. In mesophytes, night-time respiratory output of CO_2 can amount to 40% of gross daytime

TABLE II

Effect of water stress on the gas exchange of *Agave americana* in light and dark periods. The plant roots were deprived of water at the beginning of the dark cycle on day 1.[a]

	Day 1			Day 5		
	Light (16 h)	Dark (8 h)	Whole cycle (24 h)	Light (16 h)	Dark (8 h)	Whole cycle (24 h)
Mean transpiration rate $(mg\ H_2O.dm^{-2}.h^{-1})$	298	199	265	45	166	85
Mean CO_2 influx rate $(mg\ CO_2.dm^{-2}.h^{-1})$	1.71	8.98	4.13	0.18	8.18	2.85
Transpiration ratio	174	22	64	250	20	30

[a]After Neales et al. (1968).

photosynthesis (Gaastra, 1963). CAM plants, on the other hand, have the capacity to recycle respiratory CO_2 and thus minimize such losses. Nocturnal CO_2 uptake therefore confers an additional advantage on CAM plants compared to C_3 or C_4 in terms of maintaining a positive carbon balance under drought.

Estimates of water use efficiency based on the relative magnitudes of photosynthesis and transpiration enable species comparison for a particular set of environmental circumstances and over a given time span. For example, data generated under summer conditions at Akron, Colorado, by Shantz and Piemeisel (1927) clearly distinguish between C_3 plants (e.g. alfalfa, which consumed on average 900 g H_2O.g dry matter produced^{-1}) and the C_4 group (e.g. sorghum, which consumed only 300 g). Such contrast between communities is a direct expression of inherent differences which can also be demonstrated at a whole plant or single leaf level. As summarized by Ludlow (1976), transpiration ratios based on H_2O and CO_2 fluxes by C_4 pasture grasses compared to C_3 legumes (i.e. C_4 v C_3) are as follows: 50 v 115 for leaves; 203 v 374 for whole plants; and 300–340 v 700 for the entire community. Clearly, C_4 plants have maintained their two-fold advantage at all levels of organization.

As anticipated during the previous discussion on diffusive resistances, transpiration will be affected by evaporative conditions to a far greater extent than photosynthesis. Water vapour flux from attached leaves is linearly related to the vapour pressure deficit from leaf to air, whereas CO_2 assimilation is virtually unaffected (Rawson et al., 1977). Valid comparisons of water use efficiency are therefore limited by environmental conditions unless some adjustment is made for the effects of vapour pressure gradient on transpiration. For instance, Rawson et al. (1977) compared the net mass of CO_2 assimilated per unit mass of water transpired per millibar of vapour pressure difference from leaf to air. Their index has dimensions of ng CO_2.ng H_2O^{-1}.mb^{-1} $\times$ 10^3. Comparative values for C_3 and C_4 plants were, on average, 177 and 379 respectively. The two groups comprised (C_3) wheat, sunflower, soybean and jojoba versus (C_4) barnyard grass, sorghum and saltbush. Within each group the desert plants used water most efficiently despite lower photosynthetic capacity: 239 for jojoba and 398 for saltbush.

An alternative index of water use efficiency, based on more fundamental parameters has been pursued by Holmgren et al. (1965). They suggested that the potential of the plant for efficient water use would be an expression of the ratio

$$\frac{r_a + r_s}{r'_a + r'_s + r'_m} \quad \text{i.e.} \quad \frac{\Sigma_r}{\Sigma'_r}$$

The higher the ratio, the greater the potential for efficient use of water; r'_m therefore becomes a crucial factor in this determination, especially at low r_s. These authors derived ratio values of 0.34 for *Quercus robur*, 0.24 for *Helianthus annuus* and 0.21 for *Populus tremula*. The comparison can be extended to include *Zea mays* 0.8–1.5, *Citrus sinensis* 0.2–0.3 and *Persea americana* 0.05–0.11 (Kriedemann & Törökfalvy, unpublished). On this scale, *Zea mays* shows highest water use efficiency (a reflection of C_4 characteristics described previously), whereas perennial evergreen trees of tropical origin are lowest. In addition to such broad scale comparisons, more subtle distinctions are also revealed by this index of Σ_r/Σ'_r. For example, Wuenscher and Kozlowski (1971a, 1971b) were able to relate the gas exchange characteristics of five tree species from southern Wisconsin to the position they occupied on an ecological gradient from xeric to mesic. *Acer saccharum* had the lowest ratio (about 0.1) under all measured conditions and seems to mainly inhabit mesic sites, whereas *Quercus velutina* had a high ratio (0.5 at 35°C) which correlated well with its strong competitive ability in hot dry sites.

Adams et al. (1977) adopted a similar approach in studies on *Simmondsia chinensis* (jojoba) from the Sonoran desert. They took the ratio of conductance to CO_2/conductance to H_2O (in effect the same as Σ_r/Σ'_r) and discovered an increase in ratio from 0.2 to 0.6 as total water potential (ψ_w) fell from −2.7 to −5.0 MPa. The beneficial implications for improved water use efficiency under drought conditions are self-evident.

B. STOMATAL AND PHOTOSYNTHETIC ADJUSTMENTS

During drought stomatal–ψ_w interactions and hormonal systems both relate to drought resistance, either through osmotic adjustment to offset low ψ_w, or via abscisic acid sensitization which lifts the ψ_w threshold for stomatal closure. Drought resistant sorghums, which generate quantities of abscisic acid when under stress illustrate drought resistance via early stomatal closure. Since abscisic acid causes stomatal closure rather than effects on the photosynthetic apparatus *per se*, regulation by this hormone involves additional benefit for drought resistance because r_s will increase without a commensurate increase in r'_m.

Despite these protective measures, the photosynthetic apparatus will ultimately become debilitated if drought intensifies, with the result that photosynthetic recovery will be impaired. Photochemical components seem especially labile or at least more prone to inhibition at low ψ_w than many enzymatic processes.

The extent of stomatal and photosynthetic disruption following drought is a function of both the duration and intensity of the stress. For example, sunflower leaves subjected to only partial desiccation (ψ_w not below -1.2 MPa) show complete recovery in 3–5 h, with r_s controlling gas exchange during both stress and recovery. If ψ_w falls below -1.2 MPa, photosynthetic recovery is incomplete due to increases in both r_s and r'_m; more intense drought (ψ_w -2.0 MPa) is lethal (Boyer, 1971). Spring wheat provides an additional illustration in which the ψ_w threshold for stomatal closure decreases with plant development; *viz.* -1.2 to -1.3 MPa at tillering, -1.6 to -1.8 MPa at heading, and -3.1 MPa during grain filling. The corollary of lower ψ_w for r_s increase is a more protracted photosynthetic recovery; in wheat plants subjected to drought during grain filling, CO_2 assimilation shows no sign of recovery even 48 h after rewatering, despite full and virtually immediate restoration of ψ_w and r_s. Photosynthetic disruption occurs well in advance of general physiological deterioration, because senescence is not accelerated until ψ_w is reduced to -4.4 MPa (Frank et al., 1973).

Although the components of photosynthetic inhibition during drought have been resolved in some cases into diffusive resistances (r_s, r_m and r'_m), photochemical activity and biochemical processes (see Boyer, 1976, and literature cited), the most unequivocal demonstrations of non-stomatal inhibition of photosynthesis occur during recovery. Figure 5 shows a timecourse for ψ_w, stomatal conductance and net photosynthesis (normal air) in the Concord grapevine (*Vitis labruscana*) and provides an example. This mesophytic vine, whose progenitors occur in the cool temperate forests of north-eastern North America, had grown 2 years in an 85 L container under field conditions as part of a larger experiment, and it was irrigated regularly. Stress developed gradually and 14 d elapsed after irrigation ceased before ψ_w fell from -0.6 to -1.6 MPa. Water was withheld for another 3 d and the minimum ψ_w on the vine was -1.8 MPa. Restoration of ψ_w was complete within 2 h of irrigation (Fig. 5), while stomatal recovery was virtually immediate. (The time course was even more compressed when droughted shoots were excised and recut under water.) Nevertheless, photosynthesis in either attached (Fig. 5) or excised shoots showed only slight recovery even after 4 h. Additional photosynthetic recovery occurred over the next 24 h and, at the end of 3 d, light saturated rates exceeded pre-stress levels (22–26 mg CO_2.dm^{-2}.hr^{-1}).

Since photosynthesis and stomatal conductance had shown a parallel decline as vines encountered drought, the question still to be answered is what led to the specific inhibition of photosynthesis during recovery. Accumulation of abscisic acid must be discounted because that inhibitor seems to be r_s specific (Kriedemann et al., 1972), and stomatal recovery was virtually immediate and independent of photosynthesis. Light response curves imply some loss of photochemical efficiency, and suppression by a naturally-occurring inhibitor seems likely. Plant extracts have been shown to cause a specific inhibition of photosynthesis, independent of stomatal closure, with photochemical processes as a possible site of action (Kriedemann et al., 1976, 1980). Decreased photochemical efficiency in other droughted plants (Boyer, 1976) might well depend, in part, on such substances.

Drought resistance in the present context, therefore, can relate to the speed and extent of this post-drought photosynthetic recovery, and especially to the resumption of transpiration relative to CO_2 assimilation. Allaway and Mansfield (1970) view the after-effect of stress on r_s in *Rumex sanguineus* as a fail-safe mechanism to prevent excessive transpiration when soil moisture

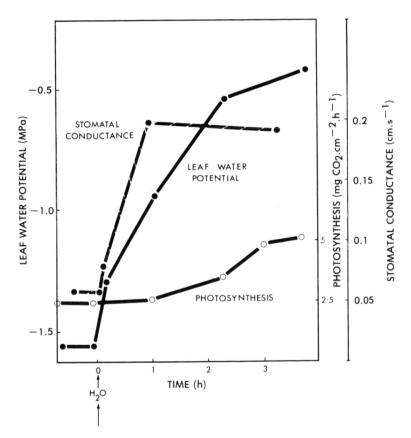

FIG. 5. Time course of recovery in leaf water potential, stomatal conductance and photosynthesis in *Vitis labruscana* following drought. (From Liu, Wenkert and Kriedemann, unpublished data, Cornell Univ., 1973.)

could still be limiting, but really judicious water usage necessitates minimal r'_m compared with r_s, especially after stress. Drought resistant Mitchell grass (*Astrebla lappacea*, C_4) embodies this characteristic, and its leaves combine photosynthetic endurance of low ψ_w (gas exchange ceases around -5.0 MPa) with rapid recovery (Doley & Trivett, 1974). Only 2 h were required for 70% restitution of photosynthesis after intense drought (minimum ψ_w -4.8 MPa) while total recovery was complete in a week. Significantly, transpiration at a given ψ_w was 15% lower after drought than during the drying phase. Such resilience with respect to ψ_w, combined with a photosynthetic optimum in excess of 40°C, makes Mitchell grass ideally suited to summer growth under the sporadic rainfall that typifies its native habitat.

Non-stomatal inhibition of photosynthetic activity as a result of drought is frequently observed as a "hysteresis loop" where net photosynthesis has been plotted as a function of r_s over the full course of a stress-recovery cycle. However, drought resistant plants, are less prone to such secondary inhibition, and this contrast is evident in Hinckley's (1973) comparison of tomato and black locust (Fig. 6). Black locust (*Robinia pseudoacacia*) is a shade intolerant leguminous perennial which is frost and drought resistant, whereas tomato is susceptible to either form of stress. Experimental plants were grown in vermiculite and desiccated to permanent wilting point (5–7 d after withholding irrigation) and then rehydrated. Leaf water potential threshold for stomatal closure was -0.7 MPa in tomato and -1.1 MPa in black locust, but photosynthetic differences were even more definite. Dehydration-rehydration curves for black locust were identical, whereas tomato leaves differed significantly between the two phases (a form of hysteresis as referred to above). The discontinuity in the photosynthetic rate of tomato leaves in the closing stages of dehydration coincided with the appearance of necrotic patches. Although tomato leaves had a greater capacity for gas exchange at high ψ_w, their photosynthetic apparatus was less resilient. Black locust leaves withstood ψ_w down to -2.4 MPa without after-effect, whereas tomato was adversely affected at -1.6 MPa. Photosynthetic endurance of low ψ_w by black locust, combined with immediate recovery upon rehydration, was a feature of the drought resistance of this plant.

Reduction in ψ_w leads to a massive displacement in the processes underlying gas exchange: CO_2 fixation is invariably impaired, whereas the relative rate of CO_2 production can be stimulated. Moreover, increased stomatal resistance can be accompanied by higher r'_m due to the combined influences of greater vapour and liquid phase resistances (Gale et al., 1967; Gaastra, 1959), as well as reduced photochemical (Boyer, 1971; Keck & Boyer, 1974) and carboxylating efficiencies (O'Toole et al., 1977). Regardless of the relative magnitudes in the displacement of carbon assimilation versus dissimilation under stress, an increased CO_2 compensation point at low

ψ_w has been widely reported and carries serious implications for net photosynthesis.

For example, Lawlor (1976a) found that wheat leaf compensation point changed from 60 ppm CO_2 at ψ_w of -0.5 MPa to about 80 ppm at -1.6 MPa and underwent a sharp increase at lower potentials reaching 320 ppm at ψ_w of -2.2 MPa. Leaves in that condition can show CO_2 evolution even when illuminated. Shearman et al. (1972) reported a similar CO_2 efflux for water-stressed sorghum leaves which extended Meidner's earlier observations on corn leaves showing an increase in compensation point from zero to about 26 ppm CO_2 under severe water stress (Meidner, 1967). Clearly, C_4 plants would not necessarily maintain a sustained advantage over C_3 plants under drought as well as they would under water sufficient conditions, if the balance between assimilation and dissimilation was solely responsible for drought resistance. Boyer (1970) provides some support for this view from his comparative studies in which soybean leaves endured a lower ψ_w than corn leaves before photosynthesis was adversely affected. Although corn was capable of faster photosynthesis during initial desiccation (down to about

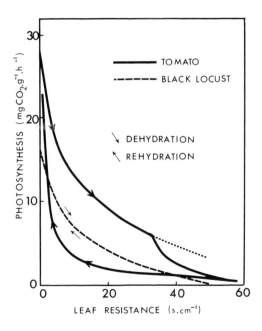

FIG. 6. Photosynthetic response to dehydration and rehydration in tomato (drought sensitive) and black locust (drought resistant). (After Hinckley, 1973.)

−0.8 MPa), stomatal factors supervened by dictating early response patterns to ψ_w. The initial inhibition of net photosynthesis occurred at −0.3 MPa and −1.1 MPa, for corn and soybean respectively, while the corresponding values for ψ_w that coincided with a 50% reduction in photosynthesis were −1.2 MPa and −1.6 MPa. Clearly, soybean was the more resilient (young vegetative plants in both cases) and, in Boyer's comparison, tissue tolerance to desiccation was of more significance for drought resistance than the time course of photosynthetic response. Furthermore, C_3 plants are not as universally disadvantaged by lower rates of photosynthesis as C_4 plants. Mooney et al. (1976) encountered particularly high rates in *Camissonia claviformis*, a winter annual of Death Valley, U.S.A. The desert ecosystem appeared to have selected, in that case, for a C_3 species with high photosynthetic rate.

In summary, the C_4 syndrome cannot be regarded as intrinsically responsible for drought resistance by altering the form of photosynthetic response to stress, or by altering the threshold ψ_w at which stomatal closure is initiated. Variation between plants is more commonly attributable to their environmental history than to their photosynthetic mode (Ludlow, 1976).

If the CO_2 concentration gradient from air to chloroplast remains unchanged despite some reduction in ψ_w, reduced flux become attributable to increased Σ'_r and, depending upon the extent of stomatal control, r'_m can become a key factor. Although derivations of r'_m from gas exchange measurements in normal air carry the disadvantage that photorespiratory factors are not excluded, such data do provide some insight into differences between mesic and xeric plants in their photosynthetic response to moisture stress. Regardless of stomatal factors, maintenance of relatively low r'_m, despite reduced ψ_w, would be advantageous for carbon balance. Data from Bunce (1977) shown in Table III support that inference. From a comparison of gaseous diffusive resistances in mesophytic trees with those of arid zone shrubs, it is obvious that xerophytic shrubs have a photosynthetic advantage at low water potential. The progressive increase in apparent r'_m for the mesophytic group as water potential diminishes might stem from the combined effects of a shallower CO_2 concentration gradient and a higher diffusive resistance *per se*. Unfortunately, Bunce (1977) provides no additional information on the magnitude of low O_2 enhancement or on CO_2 compensation point values at different water potentials, so the issue remains unresolved. Nevertheless, Slatyer (1973) also refers to species differences in r'_m sensitivity to decreased ψ_w that relate to provenance. Drought adapted wheat, millet and saltbush showed a more limited r'_m response to low ψ_w compared to corn and cotton, which were considered to be less drought resistant.

The r'_m sensitivity to ψ_w may also be related to drought resistance (Dubé et al., 1974). These workers compared two lines of corn which differed in

TABLE III
Mesophyll resistance to CO_2 uptake in relation to leaf water potential.[a]

	Leaf water potential (MPa)							
	−0.5	−1.0	−1.5	−2.0	−2.5	−3.0	−3.5	−4.0
	Mesophyll resistance to CO_2							
Mesophytes								
Fraxinus pennsylvanica								
var. *velutina*	5	10	18	25	33	40	50	
Acer saccharum	—	—	60	90	120			
Alnus oblongifolia	4	14	24					
Xerophytes								
Simmondsia chinensis	—	12	14	16	18	20	22	24
Acacia greggii	—	—	—	—	14	19	23	—
Larrea divaricata	—	—	2	6	10	14	18	22
Vauquelinia californica	—	11	12	14	16	18	20	22

[a] After Bunce (1977).

phenotypic response to water stress. One line (Q-188) was a wilting inbred, the other (DR-1) was heat and drought resistant. In both lines, stomatal closure was triggered between −0.85 and −0.95 MPa, and r'_m started to increase within this same narrow range. However, the absolute magnitude and degree of r'_m increase differed substantially. Under adequate moisture (ψ_w −0.2 to −0.8 MPa) r'_m for Q-188 ranged between 1.0 and 1.4 s.cm^{-1}, but increased to a maximum value of 124 s.cm^{-1} at ψ_w −1.1 MPa. By contrast, DR-1 showed r'_m between 0.8 and 1.1 s.cm^{-1} at high ψ_w, with a maximum value of 32 s.cm^{-1} when ψ_w fell to −1.2 MPa.

C. EXPRESSION OF CAM

Crassulacean acid metabolism constitutes a "survival option" for plants exploiting arid environments and is subject to considerable modification during drought (Osmond, 1978). Species such as *Kalanchoë daigremontiana* and *Agave americana*, with a "typical" CAM pattern of gas exchange (Fig. 3), show a progressive decline in daytime assimilation as drought intensifies: nocturnal CO_2 assimilation prevails, and during extreme conditions CAM plants may gain carbon only during the night (Neales et al., 1968; Kluge, 1976; Bartholomew, 1973). Nocturnal gas exchange enables considerable improvement in water use efficiency due to lower evaporative demand (De Luca et al., 1977). Some pertinent data on *Agave americana* are summarized in Table II. In this short-term experiment, transpiration showed an overall reduction to 32% of controls yet assimilation remained at 69%—the ratio of transpiration to photosynthesis was halved (Neales et al.,1968).

Other CAM plants such as *Opuntia basilaris* and *Zygocactus* show little tendency to assimilate CO_2 during the day under well-watered conditions (Szarek et al., 1973; Hanscom & Ting, 1978). During drought, stomatal closure and a virtually impervious cuticle seal the plant hermetically and gas exchange ceases externally, although the daily routine of acidification-deacidification continues internally. *Opuntia bigelovii* maintained such a state over a 3 year period by recycling respiratory CO_2 through fixation pathways. Water conservation was so effective that ψ_w at the apex of excised plants decreased from -0.8 MPa to only -1.3 MPa after 3 years of total drought (Szarek & Ting, 1975). Rehydration of intact plants after rain brings an immediate resumption of night-time and early morning CO_2 uptake.

While drought can reinforce nocturnal fixation in CAM plants, a transition from C_3 to CAM may also occur. *Peperomia obtusifolia* exhibits C_3 tendencies when well watered, in so far as gas exchange patterns indicate only daytime fixation, and titratable acidity shows no clear diurnal fluctuation. However, with the advent of moisture stress, external gas exchange ceases and organic acids then show a large diurnal fluctuation. The plant achieves a form of drought resistance comparable to *Opuntia* or *Zygocactus* (Hanscom & Ting, 1978). However, these presumed changes in photosynthetic mode from C_3 to CAM must remain tentative until supportive biochemical data are available. Nevertheless, the potential exists, as mature leaves of *Mesembryanthemum crystallinum* do in fact change from C_3 photosynthesis to CAM in response to water stress. This alteration in mode has been shown to include a large increase in levels of phosphoenolpyruvate carboxylase (coinciding with the induction of an electrophoretically distinct form of the enzyme), development of an inverted stomatal rhythm, substantial dark CO_2 fixation and diurnal fluctuation in malic acid concentration (Winter, 1974a, 1974b; von Willert et al., 1976; Winter & Lüttge, 1976). Field observations suggest that *Mesembryanthemum* plants develop CAM late in their life cycle, enabling an extension of growth into a period of drought through a more efficient use of water than would be possible in the C_3 mode (Mooney et al., 1974).

In general terms, CAM can be regarded as a survival mechanism which counters extreme aridity by enabling plants to persist with a much reduced growth rate (Ting et al., 1972; Osmond, 1978). Slow growth may derive partly from a limited capacity to store malic acid synthesized at night, while generally high diffusive resistances (Table I) may limit daytime photosynthesis even in well-watered species. Thus, in *Agave deserti* an essentially complete switch from nocturnal CO_2 uptake under drought to C_3-like behaviour following recovery did not result in greater daily carbon gain (Hartsock & Nobel, 1976). Their ecological success is due to the minimization of H_2O lost per CO_2 assimilated and thus is highly dependent upon stomatal behaviour. Furthermore, CAM plants are noted for their low stomatal frequency and high cuticular resistance, which enables moisture retention (Ting et al., 1972). Stomata actually close at higher ψ_w than in crop plants or, most certainly, xerophytes (Osmond, 1978), and the hermetic seal so achieved is crucial to their survival during extended drought. Despite that condition, photosynthetic metabolism is maintained (unlike the suspended animation of resurrection plants), and this internal recycling of assimilation products may well serve to both help dissipate photochemical energy that might otherwise lead to photosynthetic dysfunction and eliminate protracted recovery after moisture stress.

D. PHOTOCHEMICAL AND BIOCHEMICAL ADJUSTMENTS TO DROUGHT

This section explores some of the non-stomatal limitations to CO_2 fixation in droughted plants and examines the consequences of a restricted CO_2 supply following stomatal closure.

1. Light reactions and chloroplast structure

Boyer's studies on desiccating sunflower leaves (Boyer, 1971; Boyer & Bowen, 1970) revealed a close correlation between photosynthesis *in vivo* and photochemical activity *in vitro*. Chloroplasts isolated from leaves at ψ_w below -0.8 MPa showed progressively less ability to evolve O_2 with 2,6-dichloroindophenol as oxidant—an effect that became evident within 5 min of desiccation. Formerly, reductions in photochemical activity had been observed only in tissue subjected to severe or prolonged desiccation; for example, Nir and Poljakoff-Mayber (1967), Santarius (1967) and Santarius and Heber (1967) with various cultivars of *Beta vulgaris*, and Fry (1970) with cotton.

Chloroplasts from fully hydrated leaves show reduced 2,6-dichloroindophenol reduction, ferricyanide reduction and CO_2 fixation when exposed to lower water potential *in vitro*, but transfer to media of higher osmotic potential reverses the effect (Fry, 1972; Plaut & Bravdo, 1973; Potter & Boyer, 1973). Chloroplasts from droughted leaves, on the other hand, do not show this reversal *in vitro* and are considerably more inhibited at a given osmotic potential. The rapidity or technique of leaf desiccation was incidental to the result (Fry, 1972; Potter & Boyer, 1973), and rehydration of the stressed leaf prior to chloroplast isolation leads to the restoration of photochemical activity.

Electron transport through the individual photosystems, and through the combined chain (from H_2O to methyl viologen as acceptor), is progressively inhibited below -1.1 MPa, although a stable residual activity remains below

−1.7 MPa (Keck & Boyer, 1974). Both cyclic and non-cyclic photophos-phorylation are also unaffected to about −1.1 MPa, but then decline to zero at −1.7 MPa. Loss of phosphorylative capacity is associated with a progressive uncoupling of electron transport, and the resulting shortfall in photochemical generation of ATP and $NADPH_2$ probably contributes even further to the decline in photosynthesis in leaves already deprived of CO_2 due to stomatal closure.

Photochemical inhibition due to a decline in ψ_w within the intact leaf is best demonstrated by reduced quantum yield. In sunflower leaves photosyn-thesizing in 2% of O_2, the quantum yield declined from 0.076 in a well-watered plant to 0.020 on the same leaf 3 d later, when ψ_w had fallen to −1.5 MPa. Within 15 h of rewatering, the quantum yield had recovered to 0.060 (Mohanty & Boyer, 1976). *In vitro* measurements of quantum yield, using 2,6-dichloroindophenol as electron acceptor, and chloroplasts from the same well-watered plant, gave values of 0.079 compared to 0.028 for plastids isolated after the leaf had been desiccated to −1.5 MPa. The authors noted that water stress did not alter the chlorophyll content or absorption spectrum of leaves or chloroplasts and suggested that the changes in quantum yield resulted from a fundamental alteration in the thylakoid membranes. The rapidity of quantum yield inhibition during desiccation (5–10 min) and the ease of its reversal *in vivo* (13–15 min) suggests that the changes in membrane conformation may be reversible.

Investigations of ultrastructural alterations in chloroplasts at low water potential (e.g. Alieva et al., 1971; Kurkova & Motorina, 1974; Da Silva et al., 1974; Giles et al., 1974, 1976), with the singular exception of the work by Fellows and Boyer (1976), probably warrant reassessment, because standard fixation procedures were employed. Buffered glutaraldehyde is relatively more hypotonic than most of the desiccated tissue and thus could conceivably lead to osmotic shock and rehydration artifacts during fixation. Fellows and Boyer (1976) guarded against such artifacts by including osmotic support in the fixation medium so that its osmotic potential matched the water potential of the tissue. Under these conditions, in contrast to other ultrastruc-tural studies, there was no loss in the structural integrity of thylakoid membranes. Even in air-dried leaves (ψ_w −12.3 MPa) thylakoid membranes were largely intact.

Despite the overall retention of chloroplast integrity at low ψ_w, there were subtle alterations in structure. Fellows and Boyer (1976) noted a decrease in the thickness of thylakoid lamellae and in the width of the space between thylakoids in grana of sunflower leaves stressed to −2.6 MPa. Differences in thylakoid spacing between well-watered and stressed leaves were lost during chloroplast isolation, but the effect on thickness of thylakoid membranes was preserved. Since thylakoid membranes in control chloroplasts were already in a thinned (energized) state due to pre-illumination prior to fixation (Murakami

& Packer, 1969, 1970a, 1970b), low water potential apparently led to a thinning reaction greater than energization alone. This conformational change could be responsible for photochemical inhibition *in vivo* at low ψ_w, and in chloroplasts isolated from such material, but it remains to be determined if the changes described for chloroplasts at -2.6 MPa are relevant under conditions of less severe stress.

a. Photoinhibition

The observations from Boyer's laboratory accord with the concept of photoinhibition, a phenomenon in which excess excitation energy, rather than being dissipated as heat or fluorescence, is transferred from the light harvesting pigments to the reaction centres of the photosystems. The ensuing inactivation of such reaction centres reduces the quantum yield (Kok, 1956; Jones & Kok, 1966a, 1966b; Björkman, 1968). The fast recovery of photochemical activity and quantum yield in rehydrated leaves (Mohanty & Boyer, 1976) is a likely consequence of the temperature-dependent restoration mechanism which operates in whole cells but not in isolated plastids (Kok, 1956; Jones & Kok, 1966a). While photoinhibition may reduce ATP and $NADPH_2$ generation to match the lower availability of CO_2 during drought, photo-oxidation of light harvesting pigments (bleaching) will probably follow over the longer term since there is decreased opportunity for absorbed light energy to be dissipated in useful chemical work (Jones & Kok, 1966a). Accordingly, Alberte et al. (1977) observed a decline in chlorophyll content of corn leaves (C_4 plant) over 8 d of moisture stress. Most of the chlorophyll lost was from mesophyll cells, and *all* was associated with light harvesting chlorophyll *a/b*-protein. Since this complex is a major intrinsic membrane component accounting for about 50% of the chlorophyll and protein in thylakoids (Thornber, 1975), its loss should have serious consequences for chloroplast structure and function. The reduction in photosynthetic unit size which accompanies the photo-oxidation of chlorophyll (Alberte et al., 1977) will confer some measure of drought resistance, since less radiant energy is trapped and funnelled to the reaction centres. The probability of photoinhibition is thereby reduced, and photochemical conversion of radiant flux slows down to match the availability of CO_2. Corn plants regreened when rewatered, presumably as light harvesting chlorophyll *a/b*-protein was resynthesized and exogenous CO_2 became available once again.

b. Thermostability

Drought is frequently accompanied by high leaf temperature, especially under strong insolation when transpiration is otherwise a significant factor in the foliar heat budget. The increase in leaf temperature due to stomatal closure may result in thermal inactivation of the photosynthetic apparatus if species-specific temperatures are exceeded. For example, light-saturated photosynthesis is inhibited above 37°C in *Atriplex sabulosa*, a C_4 plant native to cool maritime habitats, but above 47°C in *Tidestromia oblongifolia*, a summer-active C_4 plant from the floor of Death Valley (Björkman et al., 1976). Comparison of the quantum yields as a function of temperature shows that the threshold temperature for photosynthetic inhibition is related to the thermal sensitivity of a site in photosystem II, and there are clear species differences in the resistance of photochemical processes to thermal inactivation.

Species differences are also likely to prevail in determining the ψ_w threshold below which a leaf's photosynthetic apparatus becomes subject to photoinhibition or photo-oxidation. Boyer (1970) found that corn showed an r'_m increase below -1.0 MPa, whereas soybean could endure -1.6 MPa before primary processes were adversely affected. Such a distinction may well correlate with species differences in the relationship between r_s and ψ_w and in intracellular CO_2 levels at a given water potential.

Environmental history will also have some bearing on the physiological response of a species due to varying capacity for acclimatization. As demonstrated by Mooney et al. (1977) the quantum yield of *Larrea divaricata* (C_3) grown under laboratory conditions fell at ψ_w below -2.0 MPa, whereas no decrease in quantum yield was reported for plants growing on the floor of Death Valley at ψ_w down to -4.9 MPa. Sorghum (C_4) also appears capable of similar photochemical adjustment (Sullivan & Eastin, 1974). Moreover, field plants of *L. divaricata* have the ability for thermal acclimatization whereby photosynthetic response to temperature changes according to the season (Mooney et al., 1978). During cooler months (January), when mean daily temperature was 20°C, photosynthesis was optimized to this same level and was 60% higher (at 20°C) than in September when prevailing air temperature was 40°C and above. Conversely, in September, the rate at 40°C was about 65% higher than in January. Optimum temperature for net photosynthesis shifted from about 20°C in January to about 32°C in September. Changes in r_s, dark respiration, O_2 inhibition of photosynthesis and r'_m are all involved to some degree in the temperature acclimatization process.

2. Photosynthetic enzymes

Although the carboxylation reaction is recognized as a major rate limiting step in light-saturated CO_2 uptake by C_3 species (Wareing et al., 1968; Björkman, 1971; Neales et al., 1971), RuBP carboxylase does not seem to be much affected by low ψ_w at least in the short term (Huffaker et al., 1970;

Plaut, 1971; Stewart & Lee, 1972; Johnson et al., 1974; Lee et al., 1974; O'Toole et al., 1977). Longer term reductions in RuBP carboxylase probably reflect reduced synthesis and adjustments to a lower level of photosynthetic activity (Björkman, 1968; Björkman et al., 1972; Jones, 1973). RuBP carboxylase activity, though reduced to 20% of control levels when subjected to -1.4 MPa in a pressure membrane apparatus (Darbyshire & Steer, 1973), appears to be protected *in vivo* by chloroplast solutes, such as phosphate, which bind to cationic sites and structure adjacent water (Steer, 1973). Phosphate levels would also tend to rise during water stress as photophosphorylation becomes impaired (Keck & Boyer, 1974).

Other photosynthetic enzymes, such as ribose-5-phosphate isomerase and ribose-5-phosphate kinase in barley and phosphoenolpyruvate carboxylase in sorghum, are also relatively insensitive to water stress (Huffaker et al., 1970; Shearman et al., 1972).

Given the decisive effects of water stress on the light reactions of photosynthesis, greater attention to those photosynthetic enzymes known to be light-activated is probably justified. For example, certain light-activated enzymes in *Atriplex sabulosa* and *Tidestromia oblongifolia* become inactivated at the same temperature at which decreases in photosystem II activity and CO_2 uptake occur. This coincidence suggests that enzyme stability is tied to the maintenance of photochemical function (Björkman et al., 1976; Björkman & Badger, 1977). Moreover, photosynthetic enzymes such as pyruvate, P_i dikinase (Hatch & Slack, 1969), NADP-malate dehydrogenase (Johnson & Hatch, 1970) and NADP-glyceraldehyde phosphate dehydrogenase (Ziegler et al., 1969; Steiger et al., 1971) are sensitive to light intensity and might be expected to lose activity if photochemical efficiency becomes impaired. The light effect is apparently mediated by the reversible oxidation of enzyme sulphydryl groups (Wolosiuk & Buchanan, 1977). Significantly, Stewart and Lee (1972) found NADP-glyceraldehyde phosphate dehydrogenase to be the most sensitive to low ψ_w of ten enzymes investigated in desiccated mosses. The ability to photosynthesize at low ψ_w, especially in the more resistant races, was related to more highly reduced sulphydryl groups on the enzyme.

3. Photorespiration

a. Response to drought

Utilizing a rapid $^{14}CO_2$ feeding technique, Lawlor and Fock (1975) found the specific activity of photorespired CO_2 to be high in well-watered sunflower plants and estimated that photorespiration was 37% of net photosynthesis. However, when ψ_w fell rapidly under laboratory conditions, true photosynthesis, net photosynthesis and photorespiration all declined, although photorespiration *increased as a proportion* of net photosynthesis. Additionally, $^{14}CO_2$ evolved was of lower specific activity, implying an increased use of reserve (non-labelled) material for substrate. TCA-cycle respiration, which is insensitive to O_2 concentrations above 1–2%, increased with stress and accounted for virtually all of the CO_2 produced under illumination by the time ψ_w had fallen to -1.8 MPa. Presumably, the glycolate pathway associated with O_2-sensitive CO_2 evolution was completely inhibited by severe stress. This situation bears some analogy to experiments where 3-(3,4-dichlorophenyl)-1,1-dimethylurea (or DCMU) inhibition of photosynthesis led to CO_2 evolution in light which was O_2-insensitive and which continued at the same rate when light was extinguished (Downton & Tregunna, 1968).

Lawlor and Fock (1975) concluded that desiccation inhibited photosynthesis in sunflower by decreasing stomatal conductance to CO_2 diffusion, thereby changing the balance between CO_2 assimilation and evolution within the leaf. Since rates of photorespiration are supposedly independent of both CO_2 concentration and rate of photosynthesis in well-watered plants (Ludwig & Canvin, 1971), non-stomatal factors must have been responsible to some extent for the decreased rates of photorespiration in stressed plants. Within this context, it is significant that the r'_m and the CO_2 compensation concentration increased in water-stressed wheat leaves (Lawlor, 1976a). In contrast to some earlier reports on tomato and Loblolly pine seedlings (Brix, 1962), dark respiration rates of sunflower, wheat and maize were unaltered by ψ_w.

Leaf water potential also appears to influence substrate partitioning and, in experiments in which $^{14}CO_2$ was fed to plants under stress, a lower total but greater proportion of label accumulated in glycine and serine. Relatively less label was accumulated by organic acids, 3-phosphoglyceric acid, sugar phosphates and sugars (Lawlor, 1976b; Lawlor & Fock, 1977a). Presumably, more carbon flowed to intermediates of the glycolate pathway in response to a limitation on CO_2 supply (higher r_s at lower ψ_w) (Wilson & Calvin, 1955). Measurements of total pool sizes in sunflower leaves indicated the presence of greater quantities of glycine and serine, but lower levels of soluble carbohydrates as ψ_w decreased (Lawlor & Fock, 1977b). In general, the metabolic data are consistent with evidence showing increased relative rates of photorespiration (cf. net photosynthesis) in C_3 plants under moisture stress. In corn, water stress stimulated carbon flux into glycine but photorespiration remained small (Lawlor & Fock, 1978).

These metabolic responses to rapid desiccation can be interpreted (Lawlor, 1978) within the context of RuBP carboxylase kinetics and partitioning of carbon between the Calvin cycle and the glycolate pathway

(Laing et al., 1974). Thus, the major influence of water stress is seen to result in stomatal closure, which restricts exogenous CO_2 supply and thereby changes the balance between carboxylation and oxygenation by RuBP carboxylase. As evident from Figure 7, oxygenation is favoured over carboxylation as intercellular CO_2 concentration decreases. Consequently, the flux of carbon through glycolate, glycine and serine will increase, and photorespiratory CO_2 evolution will be larger relative to CO_2 fixation. Net CO_2 exchange ceases at the CO_2 compensation concentration when oxygenation of RuBP proceeds at twice the rate of carboxylation (Figs. 1 and 8; Osmond & Björkman, 1972). When the ratio exceeds 2, CO_2 is evolved from the leaf and carbon is diverted from storage to maintain the cycle. This response accounts for the reduction in relative specific activities of glycolate pathway intermediates and photorespiratory CO_2 in stressed leaves (Lawlor, 1976b; Lawlor & Fock, 1975, 1977a). Despite the above analysis, the data of Lawlor and Fock indicate that photorespiration and CO_2 flux into the leaf decrease as water stress increases. This is unlike the situation in well-watered plants where intercellular CO_2 concentration does not seem to affect the rate of photorespiration (Ludwig & Canvin, 1971). Clearly, additional factors that lead to suppression of photorespiration as well as photosynthesis are operative during water stress. The reduction in photosynthesis is not simply a

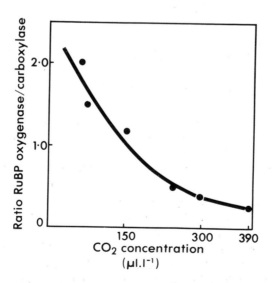

FIG. 7. Ratio of ribulose-1,5-biphosphate oxygenase to ribulose-1,5-bisphosphate carboxylase activity in 21% O_2 and varying CO_2 concentrations at 25°C. (From Lawlor, 1978.)

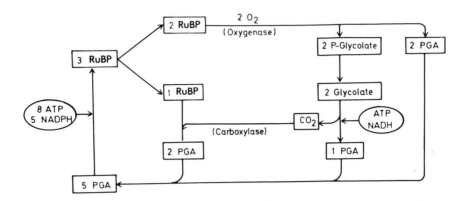

FIG. 8. Balance between oxygenation and carboxylation at the CO_2 compensation point and associated energy requirement. (Phosphoglyceric acid — PGA; ribulose-1,5-bisphosphate — RuBP.) (From Krause and Heber, 1976.)

consequence of greater internal recycling of photorespiratory CO_2 associated with high r_s, because reducing O_2 concentration causes little enhancement of photosynthesis in leaves under severe stress (Lawlor & Fock, 1975; Lawlor, 1976a). Long term responses of photorespiration in plants affected by natural drought remain to be investigated.

Increased leaf temperature, which can accompany stomatal closure in dehydrated plants, especially under strong insolation, will also accelerate photorespiration at the expense of photosynthesis (Jolliffe & Tregunna, 1968, 1973; Jackson & Volk, 1970). This response derives from the interaction of the comparative solubilities of O_2 and CO_2 and the operation of RuBP carboxylase. Temperature has a differential effect on the solubilities of CO_2 and O_2 in water; *viz.* O_2 is relatively more soluble than CO_2 with increasing temperature (Fig. 9), so that O_2 will have a greater competitive advantage over CO_2 on RuBP carboxylase (Badger & Andrews, 1974; Ku & Edwards, 1977). This solubility effect may be further amplified by changes in enzyme kinetics. Badger and Andrews (1974), utilizing crude spinach preparations, noted a higher activation energy for the oxygenase reaction, compared with the carboxylase function, which would favour oxygenation over carboxylation as temperature rises. Moreover, the relative affinities for CO_2 and O_2 may also change disproportionately with temperature—K_m (CO_2) showing a much greater response than K_i (O_2) (Laing et al., 1974; Badger & Collatz, 1977; Servaites & Ogren, 1978). Decreased affinity for CO_2, lower solubility and a shift in activation energy will all contribute to a greater O_2 inhibition of photosynthesis at elevated temperature, but additional research is needed to resolve their relative importance.

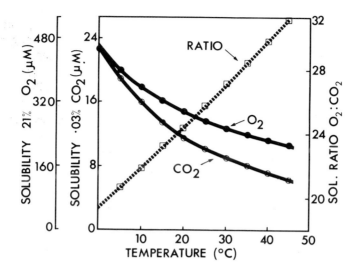

FIG. 9. Solubility of atmospheric O_2 and CO_2, and solubility ratio of O_2 and CO_2 in pure water as a function of temperature. (From Ku and Edwards, 1977.)

b. Function during drought

Photorespiration has been regarded by many investigators as a wasteful, if not useless, process which is responsible for substantial growth decrement in C_3 plants, and its elimination, or at least, attenuation has been a goal for some plant physiologists and breeders. However, seminal comments from Osmond and Björkman (1972), have altered this viewpoint towards a consideration of the energy degrading aspects of the photorespiratory cycle and its possible role in the dissipation of excess excitation energy acquired under CO_2-limiting conditions. Photorespiration would thereby protect the photosynthetic apparatus against damage. For example, when net photosynthesis ceases due to stomatal closure at low ψ_w and a leaf reaches its CO_2 compensation concentration, carboxylation depends upon CO_2 released from photorespiration (Fig. 8). Under these circumstances the amount of ATP and $NADPH_2$ consumed is the same as used by the Calvin cycle. Estimates which take account of reassimilation of the NH_3 released during photorespiration show an even higher energy requirement (Krause et al., 1977).

If photorespiration contributes to the dissipation of excitation energy under low CO_2 (as suggested by Osmond & Björkman, 1972), it should be possible to demonstrate that blockage of photorespiration leads to photochemical lesions. Experiments have been initiated and the data available to date agree with the hypothesis. Studies by Krause et al. (1977) on intact spinach

(C_3) leaves showed that elevated O_2 concentration reduces light scattering. This implies that ATP produced by photophosphorylation is consumed to a greater extent when photorespiration is stimulated. Earlier experiments (Krause & Heber, 1976) showed that isolated spinach chloroplasts, pre-illuminated in the absence of CO_2, become photoinhibited. Presumably, the absence of other organelles, normally juxtaposed in the intact cell, deprive the isolated chloroplasts of any opportunity to dissipate excitation energy, either through CO_2 fixation or via the photorespiratory pathway. Furthermore, leaves exposed to light under low O_2 and CO_2-free conditions lose quantum efficiency (Lorimer et al., 1977), an observation which lends credence to the idea that failure to dissipate excitation energy leads to damage of the photochemical apparatus.

Stomatal closure during water stress reduces intercellular CO_2 concentration thereby limiting both assimilation and the utilization of photochemically derived ATP and $NADPH_2$. At high r_s the leaf is largely isolated from the external atmosphere and soon reaches CO_2 compensation point. Under these conditions, internal recycling of photorespiratory CO_2 may represent the only avenue for dissipation of light energy in C_3 plants. Greater opportunity for energy utilization probably exists in CAM plants, such as *Opuntia basilaris*, which are obliged to recycle endogenously produced CO_2 for a large part of the year (Szarek et al., 1973). This would derive from the daytime reassimilation of respiratory CO_2 trapped as malic acid during the night and CO_2 recycling at the CO_2 compensation point once the malic acid pools become depleted (Jones & Mansfield, 1972; Badger et al., 1974).

The situation for C_4 plants with closed stomata may be even more complex if recycling of CO_2 between bundle sheath cells and mesophyll cells occurs at the CO_2 compensation point, as proposed by Hattersley (1976). He suggested that the CO_2 concentration in bundle sheath cells is likely to be the same as in C_3 cells at the compensation point, due to equilibrium between carboxylation and oxygenation of RuBP. If this is so, a CO_2 diffusion gradient would exist which would permit CO_2 to leak from the bundle sheath to the mesophyll where it would be recaptured by phosphoenolpyruvate carboxylase and sent back through the Calvin cycle as in normal C_4 photosynthesis. The hypothesis is attractive as it provides a means whereby photochemical energy generated in *both* cell types could be degraded under conditions of CO_2 deprivation. It is supported by light scattering studies which show similar energy dissipating mechanisms in both C_4 and C_3 plants (Krause et al., 1977), and also by evidence for photorespiratory capability in C_4 plants (Osmond & Harris, 1971; Chollet & Ogren, 1972; Volk & Jackson, 1972).

Despite the possibility of such protective devices based on different forms of CO_2 recycling in C_3, C_4 and CAM plants, a loss of quantum yield and even bleaching of pigments may occur in chloroplasts during water stress (Mohanty & Boyer, 1976; Alberte et al., 1977). While photorespiration seems to have a stabilizing influence at high ψ_w, its reduction at lower ψ_w (Lawlor & Fock, 1975; Lawlor, 1976a) may eventually limit the plant's ability to deal with surplus energy and the photosynthetic apparatus would become susceptible to photoinhibition and photo-oxidation.

IV. SUMMARY

In photosynthetic terms, drought resistance has been equated with a plant's ability to maintain a positive carbon balance under desiccating conditions, primary components being the capacity to synthesize and utilize photosynthetic products. Synthesis under stress has been achieved by a number of tactics, including biochemical mechanisms which apparently protect the photochemical apparatus against photoinhibition, and physiological modifications (e.g. CAM) which act to disassociate CO_2 assimiliation from adverse conditions. Such basic concepts have been applied in an attempt to identify key factors responsible for drought resistance. Thus, photosynthetic adaptation to drought has been viewed as the expression of a genotype that has survived the environmental pressures encountered during the course of that plant's evolution.

Future research on basic mechanisms needs to be extended well beyond soft laboratory-grown material. It is increasingly apparent that hardened field plants show adaptations at all levels of organization, from photochemical events in relation to ψ_w (Mooney et al., 1977) to stomatal and growth response as a function of plant moisture status (Begg & Turner, 1976). Comprehensive analyses of species' potentials for photosynthetic adjustment to water stress have also begun (Rawson et al., 1978 and associated papers).

Specific areas which require further attention include:

1. Resolution of water stress effects on components of r'_m in material exposed to a progressive, rather than a sudden reduction in ψ_w. The consequences of osmotic adjustment or other forms of adaptation to moisure stress would then be expressed.

2. Identification and characterization of the naturally occurring inhibitors that may be associated with early stomatal closure during drought, and subsequent non-stomatal inhibition of photosynthesis when moisture stress is relieved. Sesquiterpenoids such as abscisic acid or all-*trans* farnesol, or their metabolic derivatives, may hold additional relevance for drought resistance.

3. The interactions of intercellular CO_2 concentrations and endogenous regulators in modulating the ψ_w threshold for stomatal response. Fine control over gas exchange at low r_s appears crucial in maximizing water use efficiency during early drought (Cowan & Farquhar, 1977).

4. The extent to which photorespired CO_2 contributes to consumption of photochemically produced "reducing power", thereby permitting the photosynthetic apparatus to "idle" rather than deteriorate under strong insolation and low ψ_w.

In view of the multifaceted nature of drought resistance in terrestrial plants, and the diversity of environmental situations already occupied by crop plants, the task given to plant breeders of adapting crops to arid environments is an onerous one. Recognition by physiologists and biochemists of the various mechanisms which confer some measure of drought resistance should prove useful to breeders by reducing their dependence upon empiricism.

CHAPTER 14

Stomata and Stomatal Mechanisms

T. A. MANSFIELD AND W. J. DAVIES

I.   Introduction 315
II. First lines of defence 316
     A. Stomatal closure in wind 316
     B. Vapour pressure deficit 322
III. Second lines of defence 328
     A. Stomatal closure stimulated by water stress 328
     B. Control of stomata by endogenous ABA 332
     C. The mechanism of action of ABA on stomata 336
     D. Effects of leaf water potential on the responses of stomata to CO_2 338
IV. Natural and artificial strategies for improving efficiency of water use 341
     A. The after-effects of water stress: an imperfect strategy 341
     B. Artificial control of stomatal behaviour.............................. 344

I. INTRODUCTION

Once a mesophyte leaf has developed fully, its only effective control over the rate of transpiration is through the movements of stomata. Structural modifications can occur in leaves as they develop, but a full-grown leaf cannot change its construction in order to conserve water. The physiological mechanisms by which stomata are controlled therefore play an indispensable part in the mesophyte's survival. The leaf of average thickness has a very low water content compared with the rate at which water can be lost in transpiration. Thus little water is held in reserve, and consequently a leaf which transpires at a rate greater than the replacement of water via the xylem may not survive more than a few minutes. This is shown by the simple, but salutory, experiment depicted in Figure 1. A *Commelina communis* plant was sealed in an inverted beaker to restrict gas exchange with the ambient air and illuminated. Under the conditions of high humidity and low CO_2 concentration

PHYSIOLOGY AND BIOCHEMISTRY
OF DROUGHT RESISTANCE
IN PLANTS

the stomata opened to abnormally wide apertures after 1–2 h. When the beaker was removed and the leaves were exposed to a light wind, they wilted rapidly and parts of the laminae were permanently damaged in consequence. An abrupt change in ambient conditions of this kind could not be tolerated by the leaves because their stomata were unable to close quickly enough to provide protection. Sudden changes like this do not occur in nature, but as a result of more gradual changes the mesophyte leaves are exposed to a wide range of atmospheric conditions. Our simple experiment demonstrates that the precise regulation of stomatal aperture to a level which permits a tolerable amount of transpiration is vital for the survival of the leaf.

Mesophytes avoid the consequences of excessive water loss by some very complex stomatal responses. We still have only a very rudimentary understanding of these processes. There has been a tendency to consider that only those reactions to actual water stress in the plant are significant to its survival under dry conditions. We are going to adopt a different and broader view, that the behaviour of stomata under conditions of high evaporative demand forms only part of an integrated pattern of defensive strategies against water stress. These are more easily described if we categorize them as first and second "lines of defence".

II. FIRST LINES OF DEFENCE

The many responses of stomata to factors of the aerial environment must be regarded as the primary and most commonplace mechanisms of stress avoidance. Figure 1 shows that ordinary atmospheric conditions will lead to severe water stress if the stomata open too widely, even if the soil is moist. Stomata can be looked upon as miniature sense organs, constantly perceiving the environment outside the leaf and adjusting their apertures to achieve the best compromise between the plant's requirement for CO_2 and its need to conserve water.

The most hazardous environmental conditions for the leaf of a mesophyte are wind and a high atmospheric water vapour pressure deficit. The latter is most likely at high ambient temperatures. The reaction of stomata to these factors is therefore the most important first line of defence.

A. STOMATAL CLOSURE IN WIND

1. Effects of carbon dioxide

It has been known for many years that stomata close in response to small increases in CO_2 concentration. Guard cells are able to sense the CO_2

FIG. 1. (a) *Commelina communis* plants potted in moist soil. One plant was sealed in an inverted beaker for 1-2 h to restrict gas exchange with the ambient air. (b) The same plants 5 min after the beaker was removed. The leaves of both plants were exposed to a light wind. (c) Necrotic areas on the leaf of a plant uncovered and subjected to a 5 min wind treatment. The plant was placed in a growth chamber for 4 d after treatment and then photographed.

concentration in the substomatal cavity (Heath, 1948; Scarth & Shaw, 1951), and it has been pointed out that this provides a means of regulating the amount of CO_2 available to the mesophyll from the intercellular air (Raschke, 1975a). Effectively, this is the case, but in sunlight photosynthesis is limited by a shortage of CO_2, even when the stomata are fully open; so there can be no question of an *optimum* level of CO_2 being maintained. It has also been suggested that an outcome of stomatal responses to CO_2 must be at least partial closure in wind (e.g. Heath, 1975). This may be a more realistic assessment of the value to the plant of the effect of CO_2 on stomata. Wind can increase the rate of transpiration by breaking down the resistance to diffusion through the boundary layer adjacent to the leaf surface. Since CO_2 entering the intercellular spaces from the atmosphere follows exactly the same route as water vapour leaving the leaf, it follows that the CO_2 concentration in the substomatal cavity, and the rate of transpiration, must be directly proportional to each other.

The magnitude of the response of stomata to CO_2 varies according to the water status of the plant and the light intensity. There also appear to be wide differences between species. This has led some authors to doubt whether changes in CO_2 concentration inside the leaf play a major part in determining the course of stomatal behaviour under natural conditions (Zelitch, 1969; Hall et al., 1976). However, it seems rather restrictive to suppose that stomata, in their role as sense organs, function in the same way in all species in all situations. Viewed in this context, our knowledge of the responses of stomata to CO_2 is very scanty indeed.

Studies of wheat conducted by Heath and his co-workers nearly 30 years ago established that the magnitude of the response of stomata to CO_2 depends upon light intensity. Since that time no one has achieved such an elaborate evaluation, and some of Heath and Russell's (1954) data still provide the most complete illustration available (Fig. 2). This 3-dimensional presentation of CO_2 response curves for stomata in darkness and three light intensities shows evidence of CO_2 saturation at very low concentrations. The saturation level varies with light intensity, and in darkness it occurs at a CO_2 concentration of only $170 \mu 1.1^{-1}$. However, Raschke (1972) found for maize that there was approximately the same level of saturation in light and darkness, at a CO_2 concentration of more than $1000 \mu 1.1^{-1}$. He was looking at the velocities of stomatal closing induced by CO_2, not apertures at equilibrium as in the work of Heath and Russell, and he found that half-maximal velocity was achieved at approximately $200 \mu 1 \ CO_2.1^{-1}$. The effect of a change in CO_2 concentration was rapid, the average time for a measurable response being 10 s, and the movement was virtually completed within 6–10 min (Fig. 3).

Domes (1971) found marked differences in the responses of stomata in the upper and lower epidermis of maize: those on the lower side of the leaf were much less sensitive to increases in CO_2 concentration. An earlier study

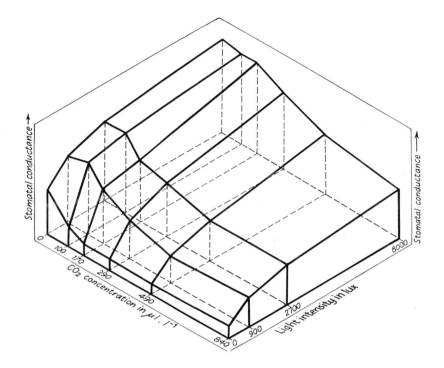

FIG. 2. The effect of CO_2 concentration and light intensity on stomatal aperture in wheat. Determinations were made with a viscous flow porometer. (From data of Heath and Russell, 1954.)

by Domes and Bertsch (1969) had already led to the conclusion that reduced stomatal openings on the upper surface of the maize leaf constituted a drought-avoiding adaptation. These findings strongly support the notion that stomatal responses to CO_2 are significantly related to water conservation.

In a study of the effects of wilting on stomatal behaviour in *Taraxacum officinale*, Heath and Mansfield (1962) discovered an increase in the sensitivity of stomata to CO_2 during the early stages of water stress. This occurred at the time when the leaves were still turgid, but the stomata were beginning to close in response to water shortage. Earlier, Stålfelt (1957, 1959) had obtained evidence that stomatal closing movements in response to water stress ("hydroactive" closure) were greater in higher CO_2 concentrations, and he firmly believed that this was the "CO_2-sensitive phase" of stomatal responses. More recently, Hall and Kaufmann (1975) found that the stomata of *Sesamum indicum* became increasingly sensitive to a raised internal (i.e. intercellular space) CO_2 concentration as the water vapour density gradient between the leaf and the outside air increased (Fig. 4). These observations

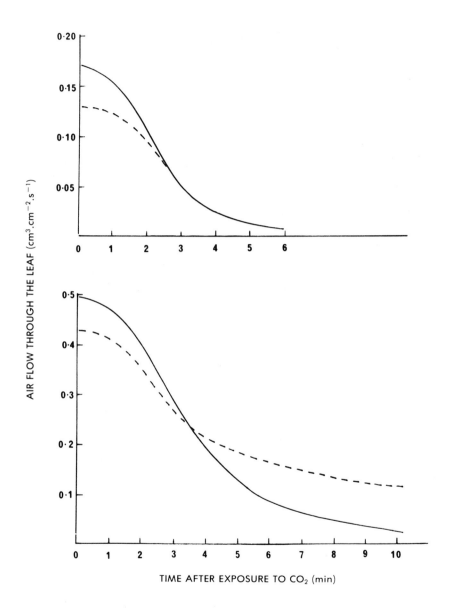

FIG. 3. Examples of porometer records of *Zea mays* stomatal closing in response to CO_2 in light (100 nE.cm^{-2}.s^{-1}) (lower) and dark (upper). At zero time there was a switch from CO_2-free air to 300 μl.l^{-1} (broken line) and 1000 μl.l^{-1} CO_2 (continuous line). (After Raschke, 1972.)

suggest that there could be a link between the water status of a leaf and the extent to which its stomata react to CO_2. This would provide an important mechanism for the regulation of transpiration under conditions of stress. A possible mechanism behind the variable stomatal sensitivity to CO_2 is discussed in Section III, D.

The increase in stomatal sensitivity to CO_2 under low light intensities (see Fig. 2) merits further investigation. Until the recent work of Raschke and Dittrich (1977) it was believed that guard cells were capable of photosynthesis, but these authors could find no evidence that the chloroplasts in guard cells of *Commelina communis* and *Tulipa gesneriana* were able to reduce CO_2 photosynthetically. This finding undermines the generally accepted interpretation that the changing stomatal sensitivity to ambient CO_2 is the result of greater photosynthetic uptake within the guard cells as light intensity increases (Heath & Russell, 1954).

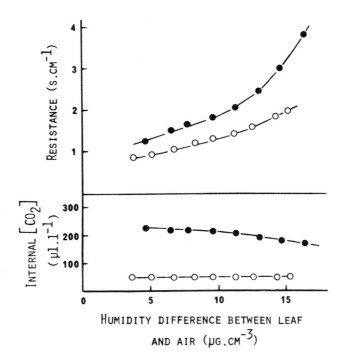

FIG. 4. Leaf resistance to water vapour in *Sesamum indicum* as a function of the humidity difference between leaf and air, at the internal CO_2 concentrations indicated by the equivalent symbols in the lower graph. The data were obtained on consecutive days under the same conditions, viz. a leaf temperature of 25°C and a saturating flux of photosynthetically active quanta of 100 $nE.cm^{-2}.s^{-1}$. (After Hall and Kaufmann, 1975.)

A reduced effect of CO_2 on stomata in higher light intensities might appear to provide an obstacle to our view that this response is important in water conservation. However, much depends on the extent to which effects of water stress can override those of light. In the absence of water stress (i.e. the condition under which Heath and Russell performed their experiments), wider opening of the stomata as light intensity increases is an obvious advantage to the plant. Heath and Russell's experiments were carried out at a time when it was difficult to produce high light intensities in the laboratory. More experiments of this kind must be performed under a wider range of conditions before our understanding can progress.

2. Effects of mechanical stimulation

Stomatal closure following mechanical "shock" was investigated and discussed several decades ago (see Heath, 1959), but there has been little interest in such effects in recent years. Nonetheless, those investigators who use porometers become aware of the necessity to allow a period of several hours' recovery after a leaf has been handled and a porometer cup attached (Fenton et al., 1977). We know that mechanical stimulation has little effect on the stomata of some plants (Davies et al., 1978), but this is clearly worth reinvestigation in the future. This question is significantly related to stomatal mechanisms of water conservation.

3. High evaporative demand in wind

By reducing the aerodynamic resistance to water vapour transfer through the boundary layer, wind can increase the rate of evaporation from leaves. The effect of wind is essentially the same as a fall in the water vapour pressure in the atmosphere, and the latter is known to affect the stomata of some plants directly. We have included this short paragraph to draw attention to the fact that the effects discussed in the section which follows should also be considered in relation to the topic of the present section. When authors discuss the effects of "humidity" on stomata, effects of wind are implicit if not explicit.

B. VAPOUR PRESSURE DEFICIT

During the past 10 years plant physiologists have begun to investigate the stomatal responses of an increasingly wide variety of plants from a large number of different habitats. It is now clear that a stomatal response to variation in humidity is not an uncommon phenomenon. Such a response may be considerably significant for plants in many situations. In a pioneering experiment, Lange and his co-workers (Lange et al., 1971; Lösch, 1977) showed that a stream of dry air directed at the outer side of an epidermal strip taken from the fern *Polypodium vulgare* caused the stomata to close. This movement occurred rapidly and was reversed if the dry air was replaced with moist air. This group of workers (Schulze et al., 1972) were subsequently able to detect changes in stomatal conductance when intact plants of several species growing in the desert were subjected to changes in the water status of the air. An increase in the vapour pressure deficit between the leaf and the air caused a stomatal closing movement; a decrease in the vapour pressure deficit caused stomata to open. Apparent stomatal responses to humidity have now been demonstrated in a number of different species (Hall et al., 1976), although the magnitude of the response varies quite appreciably (Fig. 5).

Although numerous early studies showed changes in leaf conductance following changes in ambient humidity, the work of Schulze et al. (1972) was the first to provide convincing evidence for an effect of humidity that was not due to a negative feedback effect between the bulk leaf water potential and the stomata. An increase in evaporation from the moist cell surfaces of the leaf following an increase in leaf-air vapour pressure deficit will often result in leaf water deficit and stomatal closure. In apricot (*Prunus armeniaca*) Schulze and co-workers observed that an increase in the vapour pressure deficit between the leaf and the air resulted in a *decrease* in leaf conductance but an *increase* in the relative water content of the leaf (Fig. 6). The measurement of bulk leaf water status in this experiment was presumably an approximation of the water status of the mesophyll. One cannot conclude that the stomata of the apricot are able to act independently of the water relations of the leaf, but it does appear that the water relations of the epidermis are, to some extent, independent of those of the mesophyll cells.

Several hypotheses have been proposed to explain the stomatal response to changes in vapour pressure deficit. It has been suggested that the apparent decreases in conductance may not result from a decrease in stomatal aperture but from a reduction in the rate of water loss from the mesophyll cells caused by incipient drying of the cell surfaces (Slatyer, 1966). Using a humidity sensor to detect changes in transpiration rate, such a phenomenon would be indistinguishable from the effects of stomatal closure. Direct observations of stomatal aperture (Lösch, 1977) and measurements made with the viscous flow porometer (Raschke, 1970; Sheriff, 1977a) indicated, however, that changes in stomatal aperture occur when humidity levels are varied. Stomatal responses to a change in humidity must result from the loss of water from either guard cells or adjacent epidermal cells with a close hydraulic connection with the guard cells or from both of them.

Sheriff and Kaye (1977) concluded that the stomatal humidity response is a hydroactive response to water stress within the epidermis. As a result of some simple but extremely informative experiments, Meidner (1975) showed

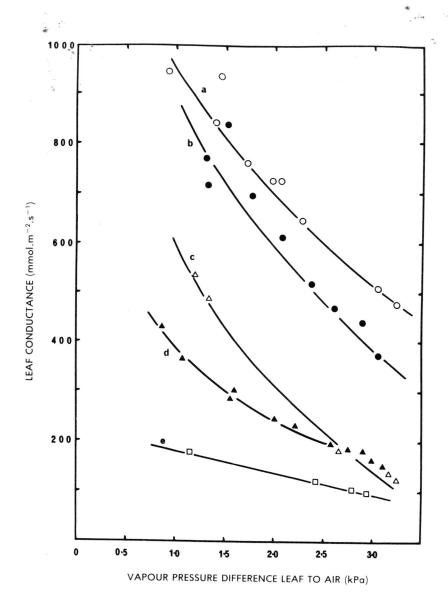

FIG. 5. The influence of vapour pressure difference on leaf conductance of well-watered plants at a leaf temperature of 30°C and at moderate to high irradiances. (a) *Vigna luteola* (○); (b) *Helianthus annuus* (●); (c) *Prunus armeniaca* (△); (d) *Sesamum indicum* (▲); (e) *Hammada scopiaria* (□). (After Hall et al., 1976.)

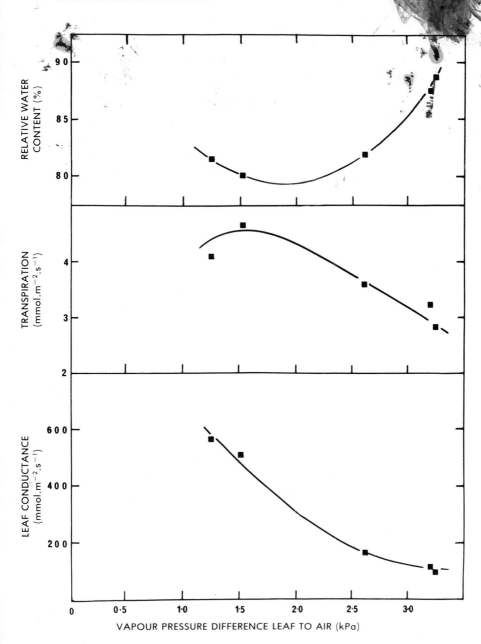

FIG. 6. Steady-state responses by irrigated *Prunus armeniaca* to changes in vapour pressure difference with a constant leaf temperature of 30°C and natural light conditions. (After Hall et al., 1976; data from Schulze et al., 1972.)

that a considerable amount of water may evaporate from the walls of guard cells and adjacent epidermal cells. Water loss from inner and outer epidermal cell walls is approximately equally effective in producing a stomatal response to humidity (Sheriff, 1977b) but water loss from outer walls must occur if transpiration is to remain low when vapour pressure deficit is high (Fig. 6). Lange et al. (1971) proposed that a humidity response results from guard cells losing water directly to the atmosphere via ectodesmata (i.e. peristomatal transpiration). However, ectodesmata are not found in two species which show a definite humidity response (*Avena sativa* and *Triticum aestivum*), and at least one species which has many ectodesmata per stoma (*Clianthus formosus*) does not respond to humidity (Sheriff, 1977a).

As noted above, the reduction of epidermal turgor in plants surrounded by dry air can result in stomatal closure, even though bulk leaf water potential may be high. Such a situation can only arise if an appreciable hydraulic resistance exists between the epidermis and the rest of the leaf (Sheriff & Meidner, 1974). According to Wylie (1952) the epidermis can obtain water directly from bundle sheath extensions and vein extensions, where they exist. It was thought that direct stomatal responses to changes in humidity might be reduced in leaves with this structure. Early evidence suggested that this was the case since stomata of many monocotyledonous species, in which the epidermis has good contact with underlying tissues, seemed insensitive to humidity (Hall et al., 1976). A recent survey of 28 species by Sheriff (1977a) has shown, however, that bundle sheath and vein extensions are equally common in leaves whose stomata respond to humidity and leaves whose stomata do not. In addition, there is no obvious correlation between the capacity of a plant to respond to humidity and the size of the substomatal cavity or depth of the stomatal pore. The latter are two leaf characteristics which might be expected to influence the proportion of transpirational water loss from the cell walls near a stomatal pore. As a result of his survey, Sheriff (1977a) concluded that the presence or absence of a humidity response is not obviously linked to a particular leaf structure and does not depend upon the normal habitat of a plant. Its occurrence however, may be limited to particular generic groups.

The importance of a stomatal response to humidity is amply demonstrated in a series of elegant papers by Schulze and co-workers (1972, 1973, 1974, 1975a, 1975b). Their studies showed that humidity is one of the dominant factors controlling the daily course of stomatal behaviour of the apricot (*Prunus armeniaca*) growing in the Negev Desert. Temperature and plant water deficit also have a controlling influence. Such stomatal regulation by humidity, on a day when the air is dry, leads to a decreased total transpirational water loss (Fig. 7) despite the increase in evaporative demand.

If the stomata respond to both the conditions inside the leaf and the external conditions, a balanced regulation of production and water loss may be possible. A stomatal response to humidity before excessive water loss occurs and before water stress develops in the leaf is a highly efficient strategy for water conservation and water stress avoidance. Such a strategy would enable the plant to maintain a high level of metabolic activity in the mesophyll, so that a considerable CO_2 gain might occur whenever the stomata are open (Schulze et al., 1974), probably in the more humid hours of the morning and evening.

While stomatal closure will result in a decrease in water use by the plant, CO_2 exchange will also be reduced. It may be argued on theoretical grounds that partial stomatal closure will increase the water use efficiency (transpiration/photosynthesis ratio) of a plant (Davies et al., 1978). Some data collated by Mansfield (1976a) show that despite possible complications (Jones, 1976) such an increase in efficiency occurs under some conditions.

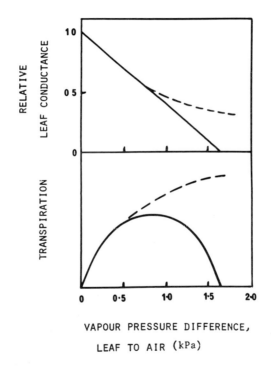

VAPOUR PRESSURE DIFFERENCE,
LEAF TO AIR (kPa)

FIG. 7. The relationship between transpiration and vapour pressure difference as stomata close. Solid line indicates responses of *Prunus armeniaca* (Schulze et al., 1972); dotted line indicates responses of *Citrus sinensis* (Hall et al., 1975); and Sitka spruce (Watts and Neilson, 1978.)

Humidity-induced stomatal closure does appear to increase the transpiration/photosynthesis ratio of some plants substantially (Schulze et al., 1975b) (Fig. 8). In apricot, low transpiration/photosynthesis ratios were recorded in the dry season, at a time when the stomata respond strongly to humidity and the photosynthetic temperature optimum is high. The water use efficiency of apricot compares very favourably with other species. Since the same water use efficiency may occur at both high and low rates of gas exchange, conclusions on adaptive significance are only meaningful if the absolute rates of photosynthesis and water use are known. Nevertheless, the analysis indicates that the stomatal response to humidity has a very beneficial influence on water use by the apricot.

III. SECOND LINES OF DEFENCE

When a fully turgid plant begins to transpire, water is drawn from the capacitance of the plant into the transpiration stream. As a result, plant water potential falls. If osmoregulation occurs, a decline in water potential may not be accompanied by a decline in turgor and growth may continue despite the comparatively low water potential (Osonubi & Davies, 1978). However, if transpiration continues and the soil is not recharged with water, the plant will eventually lose turgor and stop growing despite the capacity of the plant to osmoregulate. In addition, the decrease in water potential will begin to impair cell metabolism (Hsiao, 1973). These events will occur despite the stomatal responses described in the preceding section. As leaf water potential falls, the plant's second lines of defence come into operation.

A. STOMATAL CLOSURE STIMULATED BY WATER STRESS

Closure of stomata is necessary to reduce transpiration, to restore turgor and growth, and to protect the organelles of the leaf that are sensitive to water stress. Water stress has an over-riding influence on the behaviour of stomata, despite the occurrence of some adaptation to stress (Davies, 1977) which is presumably within the stress tolerance of the mesophyll cells of the leaf. Mansfield et al. (1978) suggested that the best way of ensuring that stomata close when protection is necessary would be for a "distress signal" to pass from the water stress sensitive areas to the guard cells. This would impose a ceiling on the extent to which the stomata could open and effectively reduce the amplitude of the opening and closing movements which result from their own sensing of the aerial environment. Some pioneering experiments by Wright (1969) and Wright and Hiron (1969) provided the first clue to the existence of a distress signal. These workers found that, when wheat leaves were water stressed, endogenous levels of the growth regulator abscisic acid (ABA), increased markedly within about 30 min of wilting. Recently, Wright (1977) showed that there is a smooth sigmoid relationship between ABA production and decreasing water potential in wheat. There is a very steep rise in its production as water potential falls from -0.95 to -1.1 MPa (Fig. 9; however see Fig. 8, Ch. 15).

When ABA is applied exogenously to leaves, stomata close and remain closed, in some cases for several days (Mittelheuser & Van Steveninck, 1969;

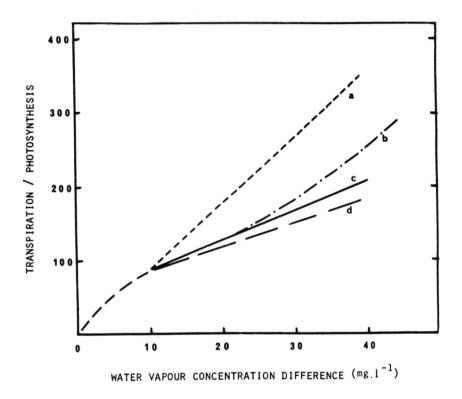

FIG. 8. The transpiration/photosynthesis (T/P) ratio as related to a change in water vapour concentration difference. (Note concurrent increase in leaf temperature from 25°C at 10 mg 40°C at 40 mg $H_2O.1^{-1}$). (a) Simulated T/P response at a constant diffusion resistance for water vapour and at constant photosynthetic activity. (b) Observed values of the T/P ratio. (c) Simulated T/P response calculated under the assumption that the stomata respond both to changing temperature and humidity at a constant photosynthetic activity. (d) Simulated T/P response calculated under the assumption that stomata only respond to changing humidity at a constant photosynthetic activity.

Jones & Mansfield, 1970, 1972). In this respect the after-effect of a single external application of the hormone is similar to the effect of a period of water stress on the plant. A substantial role for ABA in the control of plant water relations was suggested by the discovery that some mutants, which lack the ability to synthesize ABA, wilt easily because they do not close their stomata to reduce water loss (Tal & Imber, 1970). External application of ABA to wilted plants restores their turgor.

It is now generally accepted that, in most plants, an increase in the level of endogenous ABA follows the onset of water stress, induces stomatal closure and so regulates the rate of transpiration in the stressed plant. There is good evidence that the chloroplasts, which are likely to be damaged by water stress (Boyer, 1976), are sites of ABA formation in aerial photosynthetic organs.

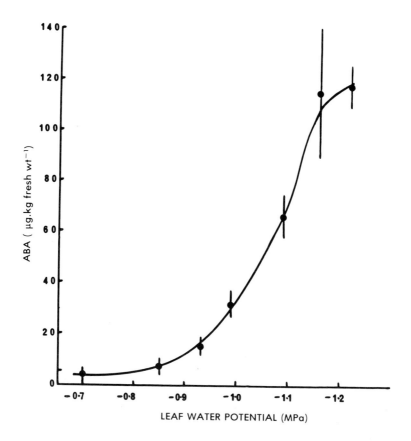

FIG. 9. The effect of leaf water potential on the ABA level in excised wheat leaves. (After Wright, 1977.)

In many plants there is a good correlation between the build up of ABA and the closure of stomata stimulated by water stress. In some cases, however, stomata begin to close before the level of ABA in the plant has risen appreciably (Beardsell & Cohen, 1975; Dörffling et al., 1977) (Fig. 10). This does not necessarily indicate that ABA is not the controlling factor, but it is possible that different distress signals may be produced in different plants. In sorghum, for example, the level of all-*trans* farnesol increases under water stress (Ogunkanmi et al., 1974), and the action of this compound may lead to stomatal closure without the need for synthesis of new ABA (see Section III, B, 2).

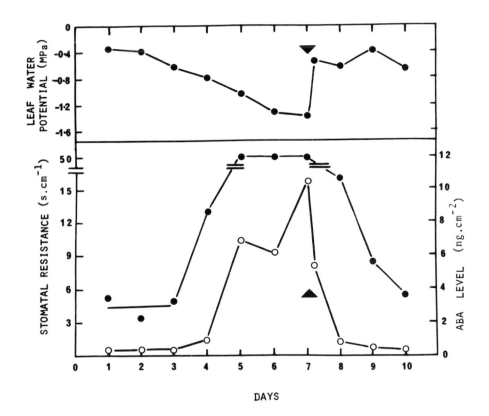

FIG. 10. Changes in leaf water potential, stomatal resistance and ABA content during a stress-rewatering experiment with maize. All measurements were made 2 h after the start of the photoperiod, except those imediately following rewatering, which were made 4 h after the start of the photoperiod. All resistance measurements in excess of 20 s.cm^{-1} are shown as 50 s.cm^{-1}. (After Beardsell and Cohen, 1975.)

Another explanation for the imperfect correlation between ABA production and stomatal closure in some plants should be considered. ABA probably influences guard cells directly, since it affects stomata on isolated epidermis (Tucker & Mansfield, 1971). From this result it can be presumed that the level of the hormone in the guard cells is critical to the functioning of stomata. If this is so, the total amount of ABA in the leaf at any one time may be irrelevant. A correlation between bulk ABA content and stomatal behaviour is usually the best indicator available at present, but it may be unreasonable to expect a perfect correlation if, for example, the first effect of a decrease in water potential is a redistribution of existing ABA within the leaf.

B. CONTROL OF STOMATA BY ENDOGENOUS ABA

1. Intracellular location of ABA synthesis

Milborrow and Robinson (1973) studied the kinetics of ABA formation from a labelled precursor (mevalonic acid), in water-stressed avocado leaves and concluded that the sites of formation might be in the chloroplasts. Milborrow (1974) then showed that only the chloroplast fraction from avocado incorporated labelled mevalonic acid into ABA, and that there was greater incorporation with broken than with intact chloroplasts. (Chloroplast envelopes are known to be relatively impermeable to exogenous mevalonic acid.) For well-watered spinach plants Loveys (1977) found that nearly all the endogenous ABA was located in the chloroplasts. After 4 h of water stress, however, the total level of ABA rose 11 fold while the amount in the chloroplasts only doubled. Thus, it appears that newly formed ABA is rapidly released from the chloroplasts into the cytoplasm.

The guard cells of most species contain chloroplasts, and it might be supposed that the ABA responsible for regulating stomatal aperture could be formed within the guard cells themselves. However, Loveys (1977) provided convincing evidence that the epidermis of *Vicia faba* is unable to synthesize ABA. When isolated epidermis was exposed to an osmotic stress sufficient to induce ABA formation in the intact leaf, there was no detectable increase in its ABA content. Yet epidermis removed from leaves which had been previously stressed contained large and readily measurable quantities of ABA. The implication of these various studies is that stomata are controlled by ABA produced in mesophyll chloroplasts.

2. Release of ABA from mesophyll chloroplasts

The closure of stomata in plants under water stress precedes the formation of new ABA in the tissues (Beardsell & Cohen, 1975) (Fig. 10), and it is possible that the release of ABA already present in the chloroplasts is responsible. This release would depend on a change in the penetrability of the chloroplast envelopes to ABA, and such changes, therefore, may be of the utmost importance in the first manifestation of what we have termed "the second lines of defence".

Comparatively little is known about the penetrability of chloroplast membranes with respect to plant hormones. Wellburn and Hampp (1976) found that the envelope membranes of etioplasts were only modestly penetrated by ABA, but there was a marked increase in penetrability after illumination. This observation is not immediately relevant to the present discussion, but it demonstrates the capacity of the membranes to alter in a manner that would release any stored ABA.

Experiments in our laboratory have shown that a sesquiterpene related to ABA builds up in *Sorghum* during the early stages of water stress (Ogunkanmi et al., 1974; Wellburn et al., 1974). All-*trans* farnesol was found to be capable of inducing reversible stomatal closure when applied to intact leaves of *Sorghum* (Fenton et al., 1977), and observations of its mode of action at the cellular level suggest that it has the ability to cause structural changes in chloroplast envelopes (Fenton et al., 1976). These occur to such a degree with non-physiological amounts of the compound (10^{-4} M and above) that lysis of chloroplasts is observed.

The first interpretation of these findings was that farnesol might have a separate role as an endogenous "anti-transpirant", which is complementary to that of ABA (Wellburn et al., 1974). Further consideration of the data, however, led to the belief that its essential function stems from its ability to alter the permeability of chloroplast membranes, and that the action of farnesol, when applied to leaves of well-watered plants, causes a release of stored ABA from the chloroplasts in the mesophyll. A course of events has been suggested which would link, both metabolically and functionally, the formation of farnesol closely to ABA (Mansfield et al., 1978).

Figure 11 shows part of the biosynthetic pathway in which units of isopentenyl pyrophosphate are successively incorporated into terpenoids of increasing chain length. If the origin of ABA is as suggested by Milborrow's labelling experiments described above, then it will be formed from the same intermediate as farnesol, namely farnesyl pyrophosphate. When the water potential in the leaf falls, it is suggested that a block occurs in the conversion of farnesyl pyrophosphate to geranylgeranyl pyrophosphate within the chloroplast, and the increasing pool of farnesyl pyrophosphate leads to the formation of farnesol. This is then incorporated into the chloroplast envelope membranes where it causes the increase in penetrability necessary for the release of ABA. The production of more ABA under conditions of water stress is stimulated both by the increased pool of its precursor, farnesyl pyrophosphate, and the release of ABA from the chloroplast into the cytoplasm.

This suggested role for farnesol is supported by the specificity of its effects on isolated chloroplasts. Its disruption of membranes inhibits the O_2 evolution stimulated by bicarbonate and phosphoglyceric acid; hence these functions can be used as indicators for assaying the activities of related compounds (Fenton et al., 1976). Other homologous isoprenoid alcohols, such as geraniol and geranylgeraniol, have much reduced activity, and the only one with effects comparable to those of farnesol is its tertiary alcohol isomer, nerolidol.

There is an element of speculation in these suggestions but, nevertheless, they represent a useful working hypothesis, the validity of which can be

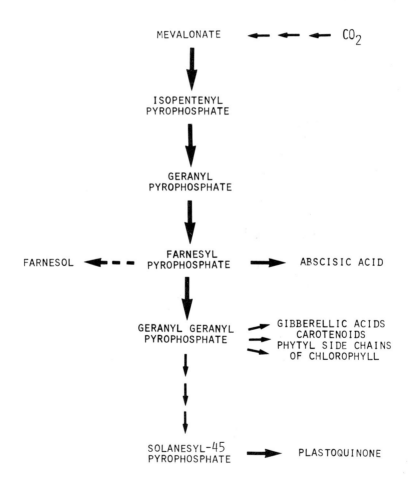

FIG. 11. Pathways of terpenoid biosynthesis in chloroplasts.

explored in future work. A knowledge of the mechanism of the release of ABA from its sites of synthesis is of fundamental importance to our understanding of the way in which this compound functions as a stress hormone.

Studies with pieces of epidermis presented with radioactively labelled ABA have shown that it accumulates quickly and selectively in stomatal guard cells (Itai et al., 1978). This indicates that, if ABA is released from the mesophyll into the epidermal cells, it will travel quickly to its site of action. Unlike many regulatory chemicals in plants, ABA can be fitted into the classical concept of hormonal action, in which the active substance is formed in one location and transported to a target area elsewhere. A possible route for its movement is shown in Figure 12. The distance through which it would have to travel amounts to only a few cells, and thus movement into and out of the vascular system may be unnecessary. The route we suggest would be symplastic, through plasmodesmata, as far as the subsidiary cells, after which it would have to enter the apoplast before reaching guard cells.

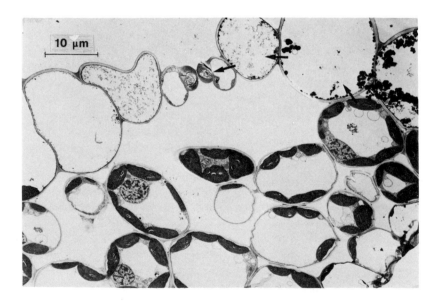

FIG. 12. Postulated route (shown by arrows) for the movement of ABA from the sites of its biosynthesis in chloroplasts to its "target" areas in the epidermis, the guard cells. (Low magnification electron micrograph through leaf of *Phleum bertolonii* used by kind permission of K. Oates and F. I. Woodward, University of Lancaster.)

C. THE MECHANISM OF ACTION OF ABA ON STOMATA

The solute potential in guard cells may be as low as -4.0 MPa when stomata are open, rising to as much as -1.8 MPa during closure (Meidner & Mansfield, 1968). The guard cells themselves can bring about the necessary turgor changes, as shown by studies of isolated stomata (Mouravieff, 1956; Squire & Mansfield, 1972); but the subsidiary and epidermal cells may be important as sources and sinks for solutes entering and leaving the guard cells (Itai et al., 1978). The work of Fujino (1967), Fischer (1968, 1971), and Humble and Raschke (1971) established that potassium ions entering the guard cells play a major part in the changes in solute potential. Electroneutrality in the guard cells is maintained either by the internal generation of malate (Allaway, 1973; Travis & Mansfield, 1977) or by the import of chloride accompanying the potassium coming from surrounding cells (Schnabl & Ziegler, 1977; Vankirk & Raschke, 1978). The much discussed loss of starch from the chloroplasts of guard cells, which normally accompanies stomatal opening (Meidner & Mansfield, 1968), is probably due to its conversion to malate (Willmer & Rutter, 1977).

The regulation of stomata by ABA could be achieved by ABA interfering with these ionic exchanges of guard cells, or with the metabolic events necessary for interconversions between starch and malate. The outcome of the action of ABA is the inhibition of both the uptake of K^+ ions and the disappearance of guard cell starch, under conditions normally conducive to stomatal opening (Mansfield & Jones, 1971). Figure 13 shows how the distribution of potassium in the epidermis of *Commelina communis*, as revealed by a simple histochemical test, is affected by the presence of ABA.

Raschke (1975a) concluded that ABA exerts its effect on an H^+ expulsion mechanism in the plasmalemma of the guard cells. This view is supported by the rapidity of the response to low doses of ABA. Cummins et al. (1971) found that a 10^{-7} M solution of ABA could initiate stomatal closure within 5 min of application. Later, Dittrich and Raschke (1977) showed that ABA could also stimulate the release of malate from the guard cells of isolated pieces of epidermis, into the surrounding medium. A prolonged inhibitory effect of ABA on the stomata of the intact leaf may be exerted if ABA induces a net loss of malate from the guard cells to the neighbouring cells in the intact leaf. Guard cells from unstressed leaves seem to be self-sufficient in the production of malate as its accumulation was not reduced after the isolation of stomata (Travis & Mansfield, 1977). The huge capacity of the chloroplasts in guard cells to store starch is an indication of the importance of a reservoir of carbohydrate from which malate can be produced. A loss of material from this reserve could impair the ability of guard cells to increase their turgor by the amount required for full stomatal opening. The fact that the

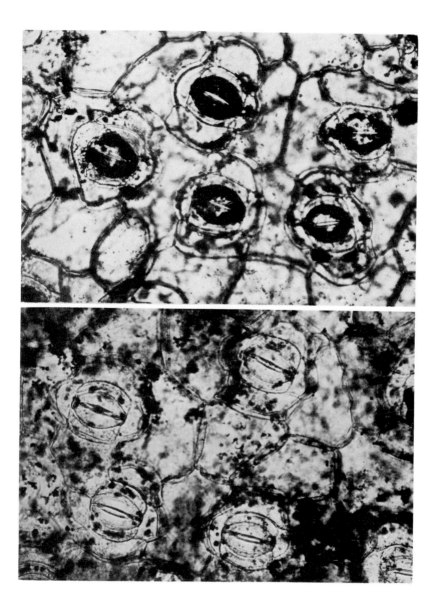

FIG. 13. Effects of 10^{-4}M ABA on the distribution of potassium in the epidermis of *Commelina communis*. Top: control, stomata wide open in light. Bottom: ABA treated, stomata closed in light. Potassium is indicated by the dark stain, the result of the histochemical test using sodium cobaltinitrite. (After Mansfield and Jones, 1971.)

chloroplasts of guard cells are unable to reduce CO_2 photosynthetically (Raschke & Dittrich, 1977) reinforces the view that the retention of carbon skeletons could be important for normal stomatal functioning. We therefore offer the hypothesis that the prolonged effect of ABA on stomatal opening is due to a net loss of osmotically active malate to neighbouring cells, which is then only recovered by the guard cells over a long period of time. This may be as significant to water conservation as the rapid stomatal responses to ABA which have received more attention.

The preceding discussion draws attention to the important influence the neighbouring cells might have in controlling material reaching the guard cells. Another way in which regulation of stomatal opening might be achieved by ABA is in the availability of potassium ions to the guard cells from the adjacent subsidiary cells. Mature guard cells are not connected with their neighbours by plasmodesmata (Allaway & Milthorpe, 1976); all material entering them has to pass through the non-living cell walls, that is through an apoplastic space. It has been shown for *Commelina communis* that a surprisingly high potassium concentration (around 100 mM) is needed around the guard cells for stomatal opening to occur, and it is presumed that this concentration must be achieved in the apoplast when the stomata are functioning normally in an intact leaf (Wilson et al., 1978). Determinations of the amounts of potassium in the various cells in the epidermis of *C. communis* show that there should be no difficulty in maintaining an apoplastic concentration around 100 mM (Penny & Bowling, 1974). However, in the presence of ABA, an even higher concentration of potassium is required to maintain a given degree of stomatal opening (Fig. 14); in other words the inhibitory effect of ABA can be overcome by a greater availability of potassium. Thus, any role of the subsidiary cells in supplying potassium to the guard cells, or withholding it from them, assumes an even greater importance in the presence of ABA.

D. EFFECTS OF LEAF WATER POTENTIAL ON THE RESPONSES OF STOMATA TO CO_2

It was noted earlier (Section II, A, 1) that the sensitivity of stomata to CO_2 increases when leaves are under water stress, or when evaporative demand is high. Raschke (1975b) presented evidence that the stomata of some plant species have a low sensitivity to CO_2 when the leaves have a high water potential because the level of free ABA is then low. Figure 15 shows the effect of an external supply of ABA on the stomata of a leaf from a well-watered plant of *Xanthium strumarium* in CO_2 concentrations from 0–600 μl.l^{-1}. Mansfield (1976b) confirmed that there was an interrelationship between the responses of stomata to CO_2 and ABA, but a factorial experiment

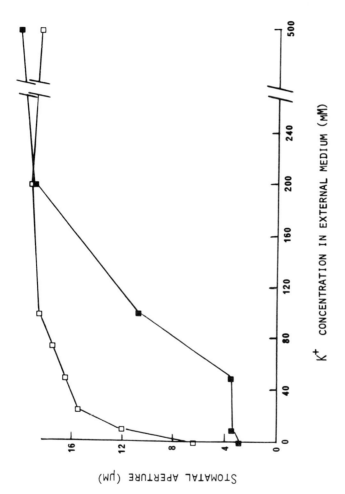

FIG. 14. Apertures of isolated stomata of *Commelina communis* incubated for 150 min in a range of KCl concentrations from 0 to 500 mM with (■) or without (□) 10^{-4} M ABA. Before transfer to the final incubation media stomata were open to 17.0 ± 0.3 μm. Means of 30. (After Wilson et al., 1978.)

with two concentrations of CO_2 in the presence or absence of ABA failed to show any true interaction between the two. It was found, however, that the time-lag in the response to applied ABA was affected by CO_2 concentration, as is also evident in Raschke's data (compare the response times in 150 and 300 μl.l^{-1} CO_2 in Fig. 15).

Raschke (1973, 1975b) succeeded in producing well-watered *Xanthium strumarium* that were virtually insensitive either to CO_2 or to ABA given separately. He found that either an external supply of ABA, or a mild water stress, was able to "sensitize" the stomata to CO_2. Raschke himself doubted the ecological significance of any such interplay between CO_2 and ABA, but when we consider the fact that wind both increases the rate of CO_2 supply to a leaf and its evaporative burden, a stomatal response to CO_2 which is linked, via ABA, to water stress might be considered to be of some value in stress alleviation.

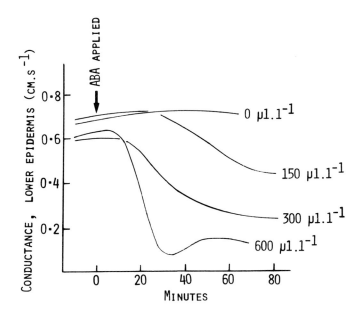

FIG. 15. Stomatal responses to 10^{-5} M ($\pm$)$-$ABA supplied through the petioles of detached and trimmed leaves of *Xanthium strumarium*, in the CO_2 concentrations indicated. Conductance refers to the diffusion of water vapour from the lower epidermis. (After Raschke, 1975b.)

IV. NATURAL AND ARTIFICIAL STRATEGIES FOR IMPROVING EFFICIENCY OF WATER USE

A. THE AFTER-EFFECTS OF WATER STRESS: AN IMPERFECT STRATEGY

Plants do not possess the ability to forecast the weather, and this deficiency prevents them from partially closing their stomata to increase the efficiency of water use in anticipation of the consequences of drought. The response of stomata to humidity may be viewed primarily as a mechanism for avoiding a reduction in mesophyll water potential, which would be an inevitable consequence of increased evaporative demand. This response however, might be looked upon as a crude weather-forecasting mechanism, since severe soil water deficits are usually preceded by periods of low atmospheric humidity.

Stomatal closure in response to low humidity can occur even when leaf water potential is high. Another well-documented example of partial stomatal closure, despite the occurrence of high bulk leaf water potential, is the delayed reopening of stomata following rewatering after water stress. The delay in attaining the capacity to open fully may be a matter of hours or even days after leaf turgor has been re-established (Fig. 16) (Heath & Mansfield, 1962; Allaway & Mansfield, 1970).

At least in some plants it seems likely that the delayed stomatal response to rewatering may be explained by a high residual level of ABA in the plant (Boussiba & Richmond, 1976; Dörffling et al., 1977) (Fig. 17). In other plants, the correlation between the disappearance of ABA and the reopening of stomata is not good (Loveys & Kriedemann, 1973; Beardsell & Cohen, 1975; Dörffling et al., 1977). This is particularly true when stomatal reopening occurs over a number of days. As discussed above, the effective level of ABA in the guard cells may be masked by the changes in ABA levels taking place in the mesophyll cells, which make up the bulk of the leaf. Hiron and Wright (1973) showed that when water stress is removed the level of "free" ABA in the leaf decreases appreciably within a few hours. However, it is possible that a relatively small amount of ABA may remain active in the guard cells for several days. Alternatively, the glucose ester of ABA, the amount of which rises appreciably when turgor is re-established, might act as a source of "free" ABA for several days after rewatering (Mansfield et al., 1978). The dilemma over the effective endogenous levels of ABA will not be resolved until the distribution of different forms of ABA throughout the leaf is determined, both in well-watered and in water-stressed plants. The sensitivity of stomata to ABA seems to depend upon the water status or the water stress history of the plant (Kriedemann et al., 1972; Dörffling et al., 1977; Davies,

1978). Any changes in sensitivity might be expected to influence stomatal behaviour after the relief of water stress.

The delayed stomatal response to rewatering has been considered to be a "safety mechanism", allowing the plant to regain full turgor more rapidly (Dörffling et al., 1977). In many situations this explanation is not entirely convincing, as turgor is often restored several days before stomata exhibit full opening. Mansfield et al. (1978) placed a new interpretation on these observations. Since the first rain after a period of drought will rarely wet the soil thoroughly, an increase in the efficient use of this limited quantity of

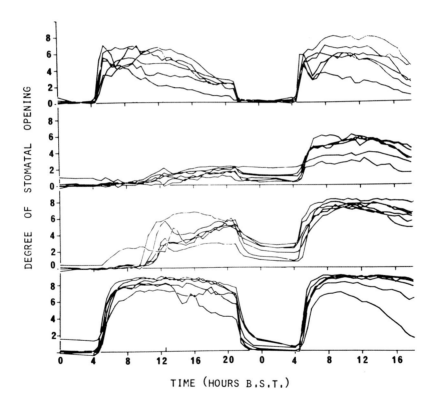

FIG. 16. Viscous flow porometer readings from 6 *Rumex sanguineus* leaves of a single experimental treatment. Plants watered at around 10.00 on day 1. Dark period was from 21.00 to 04.30 British Standard Time each night. Treatments: top — controls, normal air; second — wilted, normal air; third — wilted, CO_2-free air; bottom — controls, CO_2-free air. Water stress treatment involved withholding water for 3 to 6 d until the fourth expanded leaf from the apex had wilted for 2 d. "Degrees of opening" is in the units of the porometer. (After Allaway and Mansfield, 1970.)

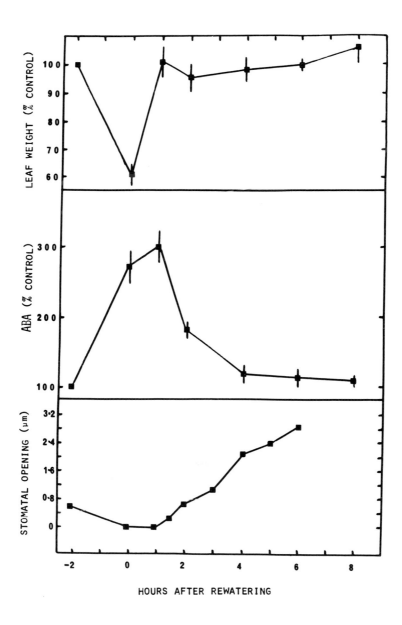

FIG. 17. Changes in leaf weight, ABA content and stomatal opening in *Pisum sativum* during and after a 2 h wilting period. ABA content of controls (unwilted leaves) was 42 mg.100 g fresh wt^{-1}. (After Dörffling et al., 1977.)

water will be of considerable benefit to a plant growing in a natural situation. Such an increase in efficiency is brought about by partial closure of stomata (Mansfield, 1976a). In addition, a reduction in total water use must be an advantage if the renewed water supply is only temporary, for example, after a light rain shower.

B. ARTIFICIAL CONTROL OF STOMATAL BEHAVIOUR

In at least some parts of the world it is possible for man to forecast the development of a drought fairly reliably. In this situation it may be of advantage to control the behaviour of stomata artificially, using an anti-transpirant. This would slow the development of plant water stress or, in the case of a phreatophyte, reduce the use of valuable ground or irrigation water resources.

However, are there real benefits to be obtained by applying an antitranspirant externally? This question may be answered with reference to Figure 18. Coffee plants, last irrigated on day 1, lost a large amount of water for 10 d, until the stomata began to close in response to developing plant water stress. Plants whose leaves were sprayed with the methyl ester of ABA, which causes significant closure of stomata, lost a reduced amount of water for 10 d (Jones & Mansfield, 1971). By this time the effects of the compound had essentially worn off, but after 17 d the treated plants still had enough water to maintain stomatal opening and gas exchange. A further period without water would have had very severe effects on the untreated plants, although it is likely that the treated plants would have survived for many days.

In terms of water conservation the advantages of the treatment applied to the coffee plants are obvious. It is also clear that closure of stomata will inevitably result in a reduction in uptake of CO_2 by the plant. In a non-crop plant this is of little significance; in fact it may be of some advantage to reduce the growth of the plant and, thus, the transpiring area. When a limited quantity of water is available for irrigation, an effective antitranspirant may be one which partially closes stomata, reducing consumption of water, while allowing photosynthesis to continue, albeit at a reduced rate. Partial closure of stomata may result in a reduced amount of water lost per unit of CO_2 fixed, that is, an increase in water use efficiency (Mansfield, 1976a).

Plant water loss may also be reduced by spraying leaves with water-proof films which occlude stomatal pores. Film antitranspirants essentially alter the structure of the leaf, giving the mesophyte the equivalent of some of the physical characteristics of the xeromorph, such as wax occlusions in stomatal pores, which are effective natural antitranspirants found particularly in

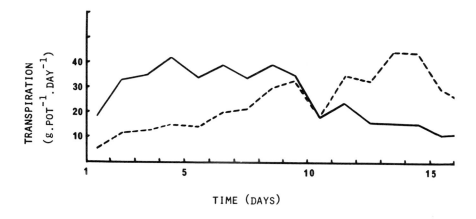

FIG. 18. The influence of the methyl ester of ABA on the water loss of potted coffee plants. Plants not watered after day 1. Solid line, untreated plants; dotted line, treated plants. (After Mansfield et al., 1978.)

conifers (Jeffree et al., 1971). There are a few reports that film antitranspirants can reduce soil water extraction without affecting the amount or quality of the yield (Davenport et al., 1977). Generally, however, the results of such applications tend to be rather unimpressive, with reductions in plant water loss accompanied by large reductions in CO_2 exchange and often by leaf necrosis (Davies & Kozlowski, 1974).

For a stomatal-closing antitranspirant to be of practical interest it should be capable of inducing partial closure without interfering with the capacity of the underlying mesophyll to fix CO_2. Most desirably, a compound should have a specific effect on the guard cells. In the absence of any artificial compound of this nature many general metabolic and growth inhibitors have been screened for antitranspirant activity. In nearly all cases where stomatal closure was induced, the compounds were found to have serious effects on leaf metabolism. One compound, the fungicide phenylmercuric acetate, under some circumstances can produce an increase in water use efficiency when sprayed onto leaves (Zelitch & Waggoner, 1962; Slatyer & Bierhuizen, 1964). Sprayed onto a pine forest, the effects of the compound on stomata were seen as a conservation of soil water, and over one winter this yielded about 25 mm extra water to the ground water (Waggoner & Turner, 1971). Several workers have shown, however, that phenylmercuric acetate can be toxic in a variety of situations (Waisel et al., 1971; Squire & Jones, 1971). In addition, in some circumstances phenylmercuric acetate may prevent stomatal closure with adverse effects on plant water balance (Davenport et al., 1972). Perhaps the greatest drawback, however, is the fact that the compound is an undesirable environmental pollutant.

The discovery that the naturally occurring growth regulator ABA could cause significant stomatal closure when sprayed on leaves gave new impetus to the search for ideal antitranspirants. The hormone has a beneficial effect on water use efficiency (Jones & Mansfield, 1972), is effective in very low concentrations and has only minimal effect elsewhere in the plant (Mizrahi et al., 1974). The most serious drawback to the use of ABA as an antitranspirant is its relatively shortlived effect (Fig. 18).

External application of ABA may have effects other than the closure of stomata, which will tend to restore the turgor of the plant. These are an increase in the permeability of root cell membranes to water (Glinka & Reinhold, 1971, 1972; Glinka, 1977) and the accumulation of sugars in leaves (Malek & Baker, 1978). In addition, Quarrie and Jones (1977) noted that high levels of ABA in a plant can promote the development of xeromorphic leaf characteristics. Therefore repeated ABA applications may have long-term beneficial effects on leaf water potential.

In an attempt to find a compound with more desirable characteristics than ABA, the properties of several analogues of this molecule have been investigated (Jones & Mansfield, 1972; Orton & Mansfield, 1974). Unfortunately, no compounds have been found with longer lasting effects than ABA. To date, however, only a small percentage of the possible variations of the molecule have been tested and it would seem that considerable rewards must lie in this area of research.

CHAPTER 15

Abscisic Acid and Other Hormones

B. V. MILBORROW

I.	Introduction	348
II.	Stress	349
	A. Effects of stress on the content of ABA	349
	B. Adaptation	351
	C. Resistance to unfavourable conditions	352
	D. Ecological aspects	353
III.	Metabolism	354
	A. Biosynthesis	354
	B. Regulation of the concentration of ABA	357
	C. The source of the stress-induced ABA	360
	D. Threshold values of leaf water potential	363
	E. ABA production and leaf age	365
	F. Drought-sensitive and drought-resistant varieties	367
	G. Degradation	368
	H. Xanthoxin	370
	I. Phaseic acid	372
IV.	Solutes and permeability	373
	A. Exudation from roots	373
	B. Uptake of ions	374
	C. Transport in stressed plants	377
	D. Cytokinins and water deficits	379
V.	Effects on stomata	381
	A. Time course	381
	B. Stomatal opening after watering or removal of ABA	384
	C. Metabolism of guard cells	385
	D. Flacca tomatoes	386
VI.	Conclusion	386

PHYSIOLOGY AND BIOCHEMISTRY
OF DROUGHT RESISTANCE
IN PLANTS

I. INTRODUCTION

When leaves wilt there is a sudden increase in their content of abscisic acid (ABA). The rise is often up to 40 times—the most dramatic change in concentration of any hormone in response to an environmental factor and one of the largest alterations of any constituent in response to wilting. This chapter describes the factors that operate in the change, the response of different parts of a plant and some interpretation of the role of the ABA that is synthesized in response to drought.

The effect of a water deficit on the rate of transpiration has been known for several decades. Measurement of water loss by transpiration and the simultaneous measurements of photosynthesis and growth rate have shown that all three parameters decrease as plants suffer a water deficit. The acceptance of an involvement of ABA in regulating these processes is quite a recent development.

The effect of ABA (1)* as an agent that lowered the rate of transpiration of leaves was first noted by Little and Eidt (1968); it was Mittelheuser and Van Steveninck (1969, 1971) and Jones and Mansfield (1970), however, who described how the loss of water was prevented. Both groups found that ABA caused the stomata to close and recognized ABA as the major intrinsic factor involved, one which had eluded identification for many years. At the same time, Wright (1969) found that stressed shoots of wheat *(Triticum aestivum)* increased in their content of a growth-inhibitory material subsequently identified as ABA (Hiron & Wright, 1969). Radiant heat and waterlogging of bean *(Phaseolus vulgaris)*, tomato *(Lycopersicon esculentum)* and wheat plants raised the titre of ABA (Hiron & Wright, 1973), but wilting caused by drought was the most effective treatment.

Investigations of the role played by ABA in the adjustment of plant metabolism to wilting, and the prevention of further water loss, are still at a relatively early stage; there are many gaps in our knowledge of the phenomena and some data are contradictory. In this chapter, in addition to the data that have a direct relationship to the role of ABA in drought-stricken plants, an attempt has been made to explore the biosynthesis and degradation of ABA, what it does, and how its concentrations are affected by the environment. This has been done to provide a background against which new results can be considered. Wherever possible the limitations of present knowledge, and the needs for further experimentation, are also stated.

---

* The numbers in parentheses refer to the structures of ABA and closely related compounds which appear at the end of this chapter.

II. STRESS

A. EFFECTS OF STRESS ON THE CONTENT OF ABA

Wright and Hiron (1969) showed that the increase in ABA occurred within 2 h of the onset of wilting at 20°C. There was no significant increase on raising the temperature to 39°C, and no increase was observed at 2°C. This was taken to indicate that a metabolic process was responsible for the increase. The water potential threshold at which the concentration of ABA increases is described in Section III, D, and it appears that the rise in the amount of ABA generally starts at about the time plants begin to wilt. Hiron and Wright (1973) extended their treatments to include other stress conditions, namely, warm air and waterlogging. Both also caused ABA to increase.

Heat stress applied to mesophytic plants causes a broad spectrum of physiological changes that parallel the changes brought about by wilting (Itai & Ben-Zioni, 1974; Table I). ABA content increases in response to both treatments but the function of the hormone in counteracting the effects of sub-lethal high temperatures is unclear. If heat stress causes incipient wilting

TABLE I

Effects of water and thermal stress on different developmental (1), metabolic (2) and regulatory (3) processes.[a]

Process	Water stress	Heat stress
1. Senescence	Accelerated	Accelerated (Mothes, 1964)
Growth	Reduced	Reduced (Itai et al., 1973)
2. Chlorophyll degradation	Enhanced	Enhanced
Cellulose synthesis	Reduced (Plaut & Ordin, 1964)	Reduced (Itai et al., 1973; Ordin et al., 1974)
Respiration	Enhanced (Nieman, 1962)	Enhanced (Itai & Ben-Zioni, 1973)
Amylolytic activity	Enhanced	Enhanced (Itai & Ben-Zioni, 1973)
CO_2 fixation	Reduced (Plaut, 1971)	Reduced (Ben-Zioni & Itai, 1972)
3. Cytokinin metabolism	Enhanced (Itai & Vaadia, 1971)	Enhanced
Cytokinin activity	Reduced (Itai & Vaadia, 1965)	Reduced
ABA content	Increased	Increased

[a]Data from Itai and Ben-Zioni (1974).

then the effect of heating is not surprising; waterlogging is also known to cause wilting. When bean seedlings were flooded, their content of ABA rose rapidly (Fig. 1) despite the lack of any visible sign of wilting with these or any of the species used by Hiron and Wright (1973). Rice *(Oryza sativa)* seedlings (a species habitually grown on flooded soil) were unaffected by the waterlogging treatment, but when aeration of the roots was prevented by covering the surface of the water with liquid paraffin (nujol), the rice seedlings, as well as those of wheat, tomato and beans, increased their content of ABA. Leaf resistance to transpiration, measured with an Alvim porometer, increased simultaneously, indicating that the stomata were closing. It appears that soil aeration plays an important part in the control of leaf resistance and ABA content (Table II). Whether this control is brought about by an effect on root permeability affecting the supply of water to the leaves, or by some compound released by the roots and carried to the leaves in the sap stream, is not known at present. Ethanol is formed rapidly in roots of plants suddenly waterlogged (Aubertin et al., 1966), but Hiron and Wright (1973) consider an effect on root permeability the more plausible explanation, because the almost immediate rise in ABA content in dwarf bean leaves is difficult to reconcile with the rate of movement of water carrying a compound

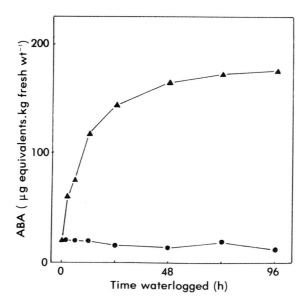

FIG. 1. Concentrations of ABA in waterlogged bean seedling leaves. Roots flooded (▲), control (●). (From Hiron and Wright, 1973.)

from the roots to the leaves. The question could be settled if leaf water potentials were measured but this has not yet been done.

B. ADAPTATION

Hiron and Wright (1973) subjected bean seedlings to a daily wilt–recovery cycle for 7 consecutive days; each morning warm air was blown over the seedlings until they wilted and they were then allowed to recover. ABA was measured in samples taken just prior to the warm air treatment. The endogenous ABA contents never quite returned to the original level after each recovery, and over 7 d rose from about 30 to 70 μg.kg^{-1} ($\pm$)-ABA equivalents (Fig. 2). At the same time it was noticed that with each wilting–recovery cycle the wilting became progressively less severe, as though the plants were becoming adapted to the stress. Similarly, Beardsell and Cohen (1975) found that the fall in ABA concentration became progressively slower following the first 2 h after rewatering wilted maize plants, and that they took up to 3 d to reach the original values. This slow recovery, however, could not account for a progressive rise in the basal recovery level of ABA unless the physiology of the plant had adapted, somewhat, to the changing conditions.

Fischer et al. (1970) measured stomatal aperture directly, as well as indirectly by measuring leaf permeability with a porometer, both measure-

TABLE II

Effects of various waterlogging treatments on the content of ABA in leaves of 4 plant species.[a]

Species	Treatment	($\pm$)-ABA concentration (μg equivalents. kg fresh wt^{-1})
Tomato plants	Control	68
	Waterlogged	524
	Waterlogged and aerated	20
Bean plants	Control	30
	Waterlogged	190
	Waterlogged and aerated	16
Rice seedlings	Control	16
	Waterlogged	5
	Waterlogged with liquid paraffin seal on the water surface	280
Wheat seedlings	Control	31
	Waterlogged	252
	Waterlogged with liquid paraffin seal on the water surface	391

[a]Data from Hiron and Wright (1973).

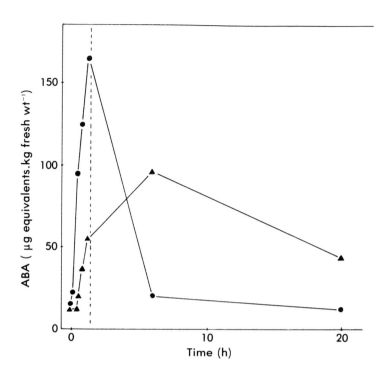

FIG. 2. Concentrations of ABA and ABA conjugate in bean seedling leaves during wilting induced by a warm air treatment, and the subsequent recovery period following removal of the stress. ABA (●), ABA-conjugate (▲). Dotted line marks the end of the period of warm air stress. (From Hiron and Wright, 1973.)

ments clearly demonstrating after-effects of water stress in that stomata opened slowly after turgor was restored. With severe stress the after-effects lasted 2 to 4 d but there was no evidence of permanent damage to the stomata. Stomatal function recovered to pre-stress values when allowance was made for the expected senescence of the leaves during the course of the experiment. This highlights the importance of including untreated controls if evidence of adaptation is to be unambiguous.

C. RESISTANCE TO UNFAVOURABLE CONDITIONS

Gaff and Kriedemann (in press) carried out an experiment with desert plants which were killed if desiccated suddenly while growing, but were able to adjust to extreme drought if dried gradually. An application of ABA to these plants while they were growing enabled them to withstand sudden desiccation. ABA applications have been found to increase drought resistance (Wilson, 1976) and cold hardiness (Rifkin & Richmond, 1976), but whether the former arises from earlier and tighter stomatal closure or from an additional effect of protoplasmic stability is uncertain.

An observation which suggests that ABA does have a direct, stabilizing effect on protoplasm comes from work on oat *(Avena sativa)* mesocotyl sections that had been treated with increasing concentrations of indoleacetic acid (Milborrow, 1966). Supra-optimal solutions of indoleacetic acid (more than $1.0 \text{ mg.} 1^{-1}$) inhibited growth, and above $50 \text{ mg.} 1^{-1}$ the sections became pink and flaccid. However, in the presence of $2 \text{ mg } (\pm)\text{-ABA.} 1^{-1}$, even at 100 mg indoleacetic acid $. 1^{-1}$, the sections appeared healthy and grew at the same rate as controls without indoleacetic acid or ABA. An extension of this protective effect of ABA to other toxic or deleterious inflences on protoplasm has not yet been sought.

D. ECOLOGICAL ASPECTS

One would anticipate that plants would reflect their habitat in their stomatal physiology and regulation of ABA contents. The data are meagre but they seem to follow the expected pattern. Aquatic plants have few or no stomata on their submerged surfaces, and stomatal closure would have little effect on water loss because their cuticles are thin. As predicted, the concentrations of ABA in water plants were low and increased little on wilting (Table III).

TABLE III
Effects of water stress on the content of ABA in aquatic plants.

Species	Treatment	ABA concentration $(\mu g.kg^{-1})$	Wilting-induced increase (%)	Water loss (%)
Water fern[a]				
(*Azolla* sp)	control	4		
	wilted	4	0	17
Hornwort[b]				
(*Ceratophyllum*	control	6.5		
demersum)	wilted	17.7	270	62
Water starwort[b]				
(*Callitriche stagnalis*)				
Aerial rosettes	control	13.4		
	wilted	86.6	650	47
Submerged parts	control	5.0		
	wilted	14.9	300	43

[a]Data from Kriedemann and Loveys (1974).
[b]Data from Milborrow and Robinson (1973).

At the opposite extreme, in ecological terms, is the desert environment where the success of a plant depends on its optimal use of water. Loveys and Kriedemann (1974) discussed the advantage to desert plants of a rapid recovery from drought and, hence, the disadvantage of a massive accumulation of ABA. Some South Australian desert plants showed the expected features; their content of ABA was in the usual range for mesophytes, and during a stress period of 4 h and a 15–30% water loss, their content of ABA increased 2–6 fold (Table IV).

TABLE IV
Effect of water stress on the ABA content of desert plants.[a]

Species	Treatment	ABA concentration (μg. kg^{-1})	Stress-induced increase (%)	Water loss (%)
Encylaena tomentosa				
(Ruby salt bush)	control	21		
	wilted	53	250	15–30
Suaeda australis	control	60		
	wilted	93	150	15–30
Tamarix aphylla				
(Athel tree)	control	56		
	wilted	340	600	15–30
Leea sp.	control	85		
	wilted	355	420	15–30

[a]Data from Kriedemann and Loveys (1974).

III. METABOLISM

A. BIOSYNTHESIS

Like all terpenoids, ABA is synthesized from mevalonic acid, but little is known of the parts of the biosynthetic pathway that are unique to ABA. There is evidence that ABA is synthesized via a series of C_{15} intermediates, but there is also circumstantial evidence that the carotenoid violaxanthin (2) is cleaved photolytically in leaves exposed to sunlight to a number of products of which a minor component is the C_{15} aldehyde xanthoxin (3). The 2-*cis* isomer of this compound has been shown to be converted readily into ABA (Taylor & Burden, 1972, 1973). Carotenoids, of course, are also formed from mevalonic acid so that the incorporation of labelled mevalonate cannot discriminate between the two pathways.

The concentrations of ABA in plants vary considerably from species to species, organ to organ and within the same organ at different ages and physiological conditions. Experiments have shown that the increase in ABA content that occurs on stress is probably regulated in different ways in different tissue. In developing wheat grains the concentration is quite high just after anthesis, falls and then increases to a very high value during maturation (King, 1976) (Fig. 3). The same pattern was observed in cotton bolls (Davis & Addicott, 1972).

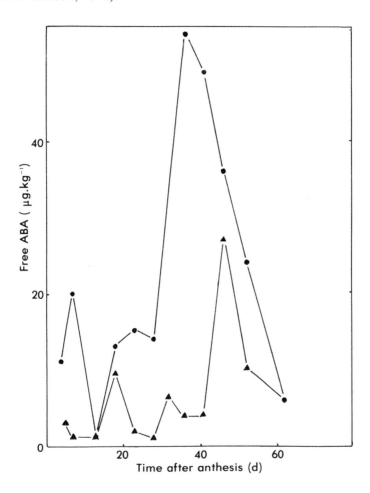

FIG. 3. Changes in (+)-ABA (●) and alkali-hydrolysable ABA (▲) during the maturation of wheat grains. From day 42 the dry wt remained constant while the seeds dried out, losing 34% of their total weight during the next 20 d. N.B. the weights of alkali-hydrolysable ABA are plotted on an expanded scale. (Data from King, 1976, recalculated on a weight basis.)

Daylength (Corgan & Peyton, 1970), quality of illumination, even the time of day (Zeevaart, 1974) under constant illumination can affect the content of ABA. Most experiments, for reasons of convenience, are carried out on herbaceous crop plants such as tomato, wheat, sunflower *(Helianthus annuus)* and spinach *(Spinacea oleracea);* little work has been concerned with xerophytes, halophytes or trees, and nothing is known of the fluctuations in the leaves of natural vegetation. Only one plant, the avocado *(Persea gratissima),* has been dissected and analysed to show where ABA is biosynthesized and which parts respond to stress. Even this work has been done on a semi-tropical tree grown in a glasshouse in England and using imported fruit (Milborrow & Robinson, 1973).

A few water plants growing under natural conditions have been investigated briefly: water starwort *(Callitriche stagnalis)* roots in the bottom of shallow pools and ditches and sends leafy stems to the surface where a floating terminal rosette forms. The floating parts were separated from the proximal, submerged parts and samples of both were wilted or kept moist (Table III). Even when severely wilted the content of ABA was extremely low, and in the submerged parts increased to only 15 μg.kg.$^{-1}$ on wilting; the aerial rosettes increased in content from 13 to 87 μg.kg.$^{-1}$. In the leaves of this water plant the ABA concentration is not only low, but the capacity to form the "extra" ABA on wilting seems to be determined by the environment or physiology of the leaves. Similar experiments with plants from a range of habitats would provide an interesting comparison, but, apart from data presented by Kriedemann and Loveys (1974), these have not been investigated.

Beardsell and Cohen (1975), working with excised maize leaves, found that stomatal resistance increased as soon as the water potential of the excised leaves reached -0.8 MPa, but the rise in the amount of ABA was not detectable for about 50 min. They concluded that stomatal closure does not necessarily involve synthesis of ABA. It is possible that quite a small redistribution of ABA within the leaf tissues could produce an increased concentration in the stomata sufficient to cause closure. It is also possible that such a redistribution could go on simultaneously with a large net synthesis of ABA within the mesophyll. Loveys (1977) could not detect an increase in ABA in isolated broad bean *(Vicia faba)* epidermal strips when they were wilted, so the guard cells of this plant may receive all of their ABA from the mesophyll.

The ABA content in Beardsell and Cohen's (1974) intact, wilted maize plants didn't begin to fall until about 1.5 h after rewatering, at which time the leaf water potential had reached the critical value of -0.8 MPa; thereafter the decrease was more rapid (Fig. 4). The concentration fell to half the maximum wilted value within 2 h but did not regain the pre-stress level for 48 h. Another interesting feature of Beardsell and Cohen's data is that ABA concentrations continued to increase after the stomata were completely closed (Fig. 5). Obviously, there is imperfect correspondence between ABA content and stomatal aperture in severely wilted leaves.

B. REGULATION OF THE CONCENTRATION OF ABA

It has been established that the increase in ABA content that occurs in leaves when they wilt is brought about by biosynthesis, rather than by elaboration of a close precursor, or release from a pool of bound ABA (Milborrow & Noddle, 1970; Milborrow, 1978). In Section III. D, it is shown that the ABA content increases suddenly once a threshold value of water

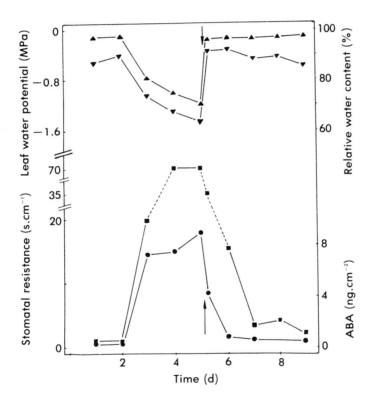

FIG. 4. Changes in leaf water potential (▼) relative water content (▲), ABA content (●) and diffusive resistance of the stomata (■). Arrows indicate time of rewatering. (From Beardsell and Cohen, 1975.)

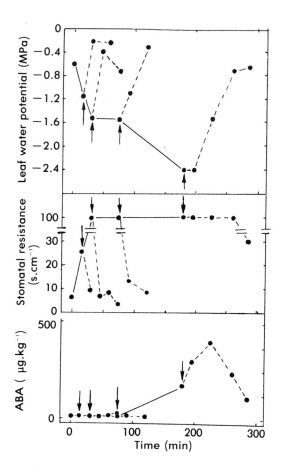

FIG. 5. Non-correspondence between stomatal resistance and ABA concentrations. Excised leaves of maize were given 15, 30, 75 or 120 min water stress and then allowed to recover. Stress periods, solid line; broken lines, recovery. Arrows indicate times of rewatering. (From Beardsell and Cohen, 1975.)

deficit is reached. Once the plants wilt, the content of ABA rises to a new high level, usually within less than 2 h, and then maintains an approximately constant value until the plants regain turgor. After this occurs, the concentration begins to fall to the initial unwilted value, but usually more slowly than it rose (Wright & Hiron, 1972).

Recently, a generalized hypothesis was suggested (Milborrow, in press) in which the ABA content of leaves is regulated through modulation of the permeability of chloroplast membranes. A necessary assumption is that wilting renders the chloroplast membranes permeable to ABA, and that the membrane becomes impermeable to ABA again once turgor has been restored (or once the water potential rises above about -0.9 MPa). This assumption can be justified by Lovey's (1977) results. He found that intact chloroplasts from turgid broad bean *(Vicia faba)* leaves contained 97% of the leaf's content of ABA, while those from wilted leaves contained about 15%. The wilting treatment appeared to have made the chloroplasts permeable to ABA. This is an extremely appealing interpretation but it must be remembered that the physical states of turgid and wilted leaves differ, and it is possible that the mechanical stresses applied to the latter during the isolation procedure could have caused the leakiness. Nevertheless, the assumption is in close accord with the observations.

ABA has been shown to be biosynthesized within plastids in both green and colourless parts of an avocado *(Persea gratissima)* fruit (Milborrow, 1974a), and Gillard and Walton (1976) have shown that ABA is oxidised to phaseic acid (4) by a microsomal fraction from the liquid endosperm of immature wild cucumber *(Echinocystis lobatus)* fruits. Harrison and Walton (1975) clearly demonstrated that ABA turns over rapidly in wilted, detached french bean *(Phaseolus vulgaris)* leaves. The $(+)$-$[2$-$^{14}C]$ABA they supplied was metabolized to phaseic and dihydrophaseic acids (5,6) at a rate greater than $150 \mu g.kg.^{-1}.h^{-1}$ and the true figure, after correction for losses during extraction, was probably close to $300 \mu g.kg^{-1}.h^{-1}$. This occurred while the content of ABA remained constant at $475 \mu g.kg.^{-1}$ over a 20 h period during which the leaves remained wilted.

Harrison and Walton (1975) proposed a model where wilting switches on rapid biosynthesis and, shortly after, once the high concentration of ABA typical of wilted leaves has been reached, the rate of degradation of ABA increases to match the rapid rate of biosynthesis so that the high concentration of ABA is maintained at a constant level. They suggest that there may be a considerable excess of ABA-metabolizing capacity in turgid leaves and that the increased metabolism during a period of wilting is merely the result of substrate availability. These observations can be accommodated by the new hypothesis which suggests that ABA is biosynthesized within the plastids and confined within them by the impermeability of the membranes. The high concentration of ABA within the plastids inhibits its own biosynthesis, so there is little turnover. Once the critical point of water potential deficit has been passed, the chloroplasts (presumably) become permeable to ABA which then leaks out into the cytosol. The concentration of ABA within the chloroplasts falls so that biosynthesis is no longer inhibited and rapid synthesis of ABA occurs. This leads to a net increase in the amount of ABA in the leaf. However, once the ABA passes into the cytosol it can be oxidized and, hence, rapid turnover might be expected during wilting.

When the leaves regain their turgor the chloroplasts are assumed to become impermeable to ABA. Biosynthesis would then continue for a short while until the high intra-chloroplastic concentration was restored. Meanwhile, degradation of the ABA that had leaked into the cytosol would cause the fairly rapid fall in overall content of ABA in the leaf on recovery from wilting.

The rapid biosynthesis of ABA in maturing fruits, and the high concentrations they contain, can now be considered to be the result of the increase in membrane permeability which occurs during the process of ripening. The inhibitory effect of excess ABA on the endogenous biosynthesis of ABA was discovered when a solution of the $(+)$-$[2$-$^{14}C]$diols of ABA was supplied to excised tomato shoots. When the shoots had absorbed the solution, they were wilted and analysed 4 h later (Milborrow, 1972). Most of the diols had been oxidized to ABA, and the specific radioactivity of the ABA showed that virtually no endogenous, unlabelled ABA had been biosynthesized, whereas control shoots supplied with water instead of the diols and wilted similarly formed approximately 360 μg ABA.kg^{-1}. The experiment has been repeated with ABA rather than the diols and gave the same result. The interpretation of this result was that the high concentration of ABA in the leaves operated a negative feedback loop to switch off its own biosynthesis. Another experiment (Milborrow, 1974a), in which $(\pm)$-ABA added to a broken chloroplast preparation apparently stimulated biosynthesis, does not contradict this conclusion. The concentration of ABA added to the chloroplast preparation would still have been less than the concentration within the chloroplasts *in vivo*, and incorporation of radioactivity into ABA was measured rather than net synthesis. The presence of extra, unlabelled ABA would have increased the efficiency of recovery of labelled material, and this, alone, could account for the apparent 100% increase in ^{14}C observed in ABA in the purified samples.

If this new hypothesis is correct, any agent that made chloroplast membranes permeable would cause the release of ABA from the chloroplasts, so that the ABA could move to the stomatal guard cells. At the same time, this would also allow rapid biosynthesis to begin and so raise the overall content of ABA in the leaf. Farnesol and phenylmercuric acetate may act in this way (see Chapter 14) both providing support for the hypothesis and suggesting that the action of the antitranspirants can be interpreted in terms of the ABA synthesis they cause.

C. THE SOURCE OF THE STRESS-INDUCED ABA

An early experiment by Milborrow and Noddle (1970), using wheat leaves, indicated that the "extra" ABA formed in response to wilting was synthesized from mevalonic acid rather than released from pre-existing, partially elaborated precursors. The excised wheat leaves were supplied with a solution of labelled mevalonate and divided into two batches: one was wilted while the other remained turgid. After 6 h the ABA was isolated from each and the sample from the wilted plants contained much more label than that from the turgid ones. The ratio of the counts was 24:1, showing that considerably more mevalonate had been incorporated into ABA in wilted, compared with turgid leaves (Table V). These results could be obtained if either the dilution of label in the precursor pools was different, or if ABA turnover was dissimilar in both sets of plants.

It is known that mevalonate penetrates extremely slowly into chloroplasts, the site of ABA biosynthesis (Milborrow, 1974a). Goodwin (1958) found that very little of the [^{14}C]mevalonate supplied to intact, isolated chloroplasts was incorporated into carotenoids, whereas incorporation occurred readily when the chloroplasts were lysed. Usually, much less than 0.1% of the labelled mevalonate supplied to intact cells is incorporated into ABA. Other experiments with inhibitors (Milborrow, 1974b) have shown that most of the mevalonate entering the cells is converted, probably in the cytosol, into sterols, and only a small proportion reaches and penetrates into the chloroplasts. Consequently, the proportion of mevalonate incorporated into ABA in turgid and wilted leaves cannot be expected to provide a truly comparable measure of the relative rate of biosynthesis under the different conditions. Indeed, the differences in incorporation of label could be attributed to a more rapid and complete uptake of the mevalonate by the water-deficient shoots, or even effects on other metabolic pathways. In avocado stems just such a result was found: although the excised stems merely doubled their content of ABA on wilting, the incorporation of [^{14}C]mevalonate into ABA increased 90 times (Table VI).

In spite of this caveat, the data strongly suggest that a large proportion of the stress-induced ABA is synthesized directly from small molecular weight precursors, and that the existence of a large pool of partially formed precursors is unlikely.

TABLE V

Incorporation of [2-^{3}H$_2$]mevalonate into ABA by wilted or turgid excised wheat shoots.[a]

	Treatment	Radioactivity in ABA (^{3}H dpm)	(+)-ABA concentration (μg.kg^{-1})	Water loss (%)
[^{3}H]mevalonate	turgid	280	15.1	—
	wilted	6771	520	29
Control	turgid	—	19.4	—
	wilted	—	670	29

[a]Data from Milborrow and Noddle (1970).

TABLE VI

Incorporation of $[2\text{-}^{14}C]$mevalonate into ABA by wilted or turgid avocado stem segments. Concentrations of ABA, and dpm are corrected for losses during extraction.[a]

Treatment	(+)−ABA concentration ($\mu g.kg^{-1}$)	Radioactivity in ABA (^{14}C-dpm)	Water loss (%)
Turgid	500	40	—
Wilted	930	3640	30

[a]Data from Milborrow and Robinson (1973).

The other potential source of the accumulated ABA is a bound form in which ABA is either covalently linked with a small molecule such as glucose or bound in some way to a macromolecule. Hydrolyses of plant extracts have shown that the amount of ABA existing in the conjugated fraction is generally about 10% of that present as free acid. In some tissues the bound may exceed the free, and in plants that have undergone a succession of wilting-recovery cycles, the bound ABA is also abundant (Hiron & Wright, 1973). Thus, it is possible that a pool of either protein-bound or covalently-linked ABA could release some of the free acid upon receipt of the wilting stimulus. Zeevaart (1977) considered this to be unlikely as the amount of ABA released by hydrolysis of wilted and turgid spinach leaves was similar. This problem has been investigated by Milborrow (1978) who supplied excised tomato and silverbeet (*Beta vulgaris*) shoots with $(\pm)\text{-}[2\text{-}^{14}C]$ABA and allowed them to metabolize it for a few days. Some of the $(\pm)\text{-}[2\text{-}^{14}C]$ABA was oxidized to phaseic and dihydrophaseic acids while both (+) and (−) enantiomers were converted into an alkali-hydrolysable, conjugated form.

Samples of the plants were then wilted, but there was no decrease in the amount of ^{14}C in the conjugated fraction, nor was there an increase in the $[^{14}C]$ABA in the free acid fraction. Indeed, there was a tendency for the free $[^{14}C]$ABA to fall in the wilted plants, suggesting that the free acid pool was turning over even when the plants were wilted. A similar result was obtained by Harrison and Walton (1975) who followed the degradation of $(+)\text{-}[2\text{-}^{14}C]$ABA to phaseic and dihydrophaseic acids in beans.

Although the experiments which showed that the alkali-hydrolysable conjugate was not hydrolysed were carried out with exogenously applied $(\pm)\text{-}[2\text{-}^{14}C]$ABA, the same conclusion can be drawn from measurements of endogenous, conjugated fractions which remained constant while the amounts of free ABA increased during wilting. As there is no source of ABA-glucose ester (7) other than the pool of free acid (the formation of phaseic acid is irreversible), any net hydrolysis would lead to a fall in the pool of bound ABA. No such fall was observed in spinach (Zeevaart, 1977), bean (Wright, 1977) or tomato (Milborrow, 1978).

D. THRESHOLD VALUES OF LEAF WATER POTENTIAL

Most of the early experiments on the stress-induced rise in ABA concentration were carried out by suddenly subjecting excised plant parts to relatively severe water stress and measuring the rise in ABA. Consequently, there is some confusion, inherent in the method of measurement, between the titre of ABA, duration of the stress and the degree of stress. Zabadal (1974) overcame this by sampling leaves of two species of *Ambrosia* during a 23 h period; after transferring rooted plants to a desiccating environment, he analysed leaves for water potential, fresh weight, dry weight and ABA contents. During the first 8 h the leaf water potential of Roman ragweed (*A. artemisifolia*) remained at −0.9 MPa or decreased from −0.4 to −0.8 MPa when plants of Great ragweed (*A. trifida*) were used. During this time the ABA concentrations remained constant at the initial level (Fig. 6). Once the water potential of the leaves fell below −1.0 MPa the content of ABA suddenly began to increase and, thereafter, the amount of ABA present in the

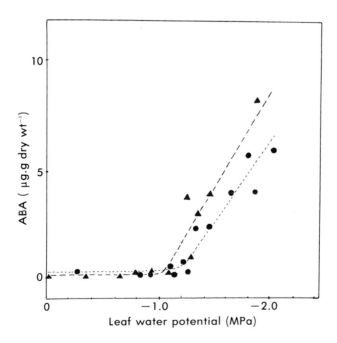

FIG. 6. Relationship between the concentration of ABA and leaf water potential during a period of progressive dehydration. Intact plants of *Ambrosia trifida* (▲) and *A. artemisiifolia* (●) were used. (From Zabadal, 1974.)

leaves was inversely proportional to the water potential. Consequently, it appears that there may be a critical leaf water potential, and once this water deficit is exceeded rapid net synthesis of ABA commences. Beardsell and Cohen (1975) found a similar sudden increase in the content of ABA in maize and sorghum when leaf water potentials reached -0.8 and -0.9 MPa respectively (Fig. 7). The more gradual response to water deficit by sorghum, in comparison with maize, is in accord with sorghum's greater capacity to resist drought.

Wright (1977) has also carried out the same kind of experiment, by inducing a range of leaf water potential deficits in samples of wheat leaf segments. He measured the concentration of ABA after 330 min so the data probably represent equilibrium values, sufficient time having elapsed for the leaves to have synthesized the amount of ABA induced by the conditions (most synthesis occurs during the first hour of wilting, see above) (Fig. 8). The data can be interpreted to show that there is a critical point at -0.9 MPa, and when the leaves are dried beyond this, the amount of "extra" ABA present is directly proportional to the leaf water potential, up to about -0.9 MPa and 110 μg ABA.kg original fresh wt^{-1}.

The question of whether the rate of biosynthesis is also proportional to the water deficit, or whether a uniform rate of synthesis is triggered and

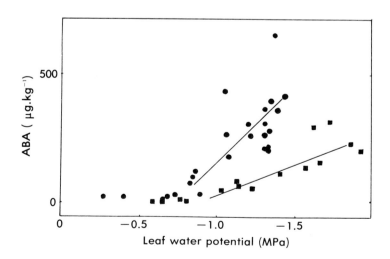

FIG. 7. Relationship between the concentration of ABA and leaf water potential for maize (●) and sorghum (■) leaves. The ordinate values for concentration (μg.kg^{-1}) were calculated from the data for maize. (From Beardsell and Cohen, 1974; 1975.)

ceases at varying times when sufficient ABA has been formed, has not yet been answered, although the latter seems to be more likely from Figure 5.

These experiments can be summarized as follows: leaves of different species have critical water potential values of about −0.8 to −1.0 MPa. When this water deficit has been exceeded, rapid net synthesis of ABA occurs, and the concentration is inversely proportional to the water potential.

E. ABA PRODUCTION AND LEAF AGE

Zeevaart (1977) points out that, although excised young leaves produced considerably more ABA and phaseic acid on wilting than older leaves (Table VII), this does not necessarily mean that young leaves are the site of synthesis of most of the stress-induced ABA in the intact plant. Moreover, older leaves export carbohydrates while young, expanding leaves may show a net import

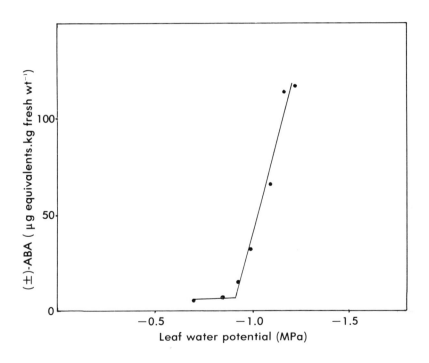

FIG. 8. Relationship between water potential and concentration of ABA in excised wheat leaves. The measurements were made 330 min after commencement of treatment. Early wilting symptoms were observed at −0.92 MPa. (After Wright, 1977.)

of carbohydrate. The transport of other metabolites in the phloem follows the flow of carbohydrates; therefore more ABA would be expected to move out of old leaves than young ones.

Although ABA can be synthesized in leaves, stems, fruit, seed and root tissues, there is a considerable flux between the organs of a plant. Hoad (1973b) found that the high concentration of ABA (6 times normal) in the apices of castor oil (*Ricinus communis*) plants that had been wilted was not present if the apices were excised and then wilted (twice normal) (Table VIII). He suggested that the data lend credence to the idea that the increased amount of ABA in the apices of moisture-stressed plants does not arise *in situ* but is translocated in the phloem from sites of synthesis elsewhere, presumably the leaves. Zeevaart (1977), who also used *Ricinus* (Table IX), determined ABA and its metabolites and found an increase in the concentrations of ABA, phaseic acid and dihydrophaseic acid in the phloem sap of stressed plants.

TABLE VII

Changes in the content of ABA, phaseic and dihydrophaseic acid in *Ricinus* leaves with age.[a]

	ABA concentration (μg.kg^{-1})	Phaseic acid concentration (μg.kg^{-1})	Dihydrophaseic acid concentration (μg.kg^{-1})
Stem tip	80	460	13000
Leaf 1 (youngest)	400	520	4600
2	300	950	2010
3	150	200	560
4	50	150	230
5	60	60	190
Control, detached young leaves	200	1600	8800
Wilted, 8 h.	2500	2600	9100
Control, detached mature leaves	200	200	700
Wilted, 8 h.	300	300	1200

[a]Data from Zeevaart (1977).

TABLE VIII

Concentrations of ABA in apices and leaves of *Ricinus communis*.[a]

	ABA concentration in		
	Apices attached (μg.kg^{-1})	Apices detached prior to wilting (μg.kg^{-1})	Leaves (μg.kg^{-1})
Unwilted	131	197	31
Wilted	830	244	410

[a]Data from Hoad (1973b).

TABLE IX

Concentrations of ABA, phaseic acid and dihydrophaseic acid in the phloem exudate of *Ricinus* plants.[a]

Treatment	Recovery period	ABA concentration $(\mu g.kg^{-1})$	Phaseic acid concentration $(\mu g.kg^{-1})$	Dihydrophaseic acid concentration $(\mu g.kg^{-1})$
Non-stressed	—	1,400	300	400
Stressed	5 h	2,600	700	100
Stressed	30 h	2,200	2,700	2,100

[a]Data from Zeevaart (1977).

F. DROUGHT-SENSITIVE AND DROUGHT-RESISTANT VARIETIES

Larque-Saavedra and Wain (1976) compared the ABA content of a Mexican strain of maize that shows an enhanced ability to withstand drought conditions with two European varieties which had not been selected for their ability to withstand drought. Seedlings of all three were grown under the same conditions of adequate water supply in a growth room. Leaves of seedlings 10 d old were then wilted, losing 10% of their weight. As expected, the content of ABA rose in all three varieties, but the maximum concentrations reached by the drought-tolerant variety, Latente, were over twice that of the normal, drought-sensitive varieties (Table X). The seedlings of Latente contained about 5 times more ABA initially than the European varieties, and the surprising feature of the results is that the drought-sensitive varieties responded to wilting with a 7-fold increase in ABA content, whereas that of Latente increased only 4-fold. It may be too facile to consider that the higher overall concentration would tend to close stomata more thoroughly, because a 7-fold increase in the amount of ABA in the sensitive varieties might do this even better. In fact, Larque-Saavedra and Wain (1974) obtained contradictory results with sorghum strains in that the less drought-resistant Shallu increased its ABA content much less than the more drought-resistant M 35-1 plants. Also, the ABA contents of non-stressed sorghum, a relatively drought-resistant crop, are about 10 times smaller than those of maize.

More information is needed before a genetic basis of drought resistance can be meaningfully attributed to ABA contents. A large (40-fold) increase in ABA concentration in the leaf is frequently encountered with mesophytic plants growing under laboratory conditions, while xerophytic desert plants (Table IV) have neither particularly high ABA contents, nor do these rise much on wilting. Clearly, the significance of the magnitude of the rise in ABA content cannot be defined without taking a host of other factors into consideration. An important step in the breeding of drought-resistant cultivars

TABLE X

Free ABA contents in drought-resistant (Latente) and drought-sensitive (Anjou; L.G.11) strains of maize, and drought-resistant (M35-1) and drought-sensitive (Shallu) strains of sorghum. All data were determined by bioassay.[a]

Variety	$(\pm)$-ABA concentration (μg equivalents. kg fresh wt^{-1})		Wilting-induced loss of weight (%)
	Control	Wilted	
Latente	524	2008	10
Anjou	92	748	10
L.G.11	112	756	10
M35-1	13.2	1149	6
Shallu	13.3	441	6

[a]Data from Larque-Saavedra and Wain (1974, 1976).

may be to dissect out the effects of initial ABA content, chloroplast volume, critical water deficit, magnitude of the rise in ABA and the capacity of the tissue to adapt its ABA physiology to drought. This would then allow the optimum genetic selection of relevant features to be made. While differences between varieties in ABA contents and responses to stress undoubtedly occur, and are genetically determined, their significance is in doubt; in particular, whether they are causes or effects of drought tolerance is uncertain.

G. DEGRADATION

ABA has been shown to be inactivated in plants in two ways: (i) it is esterified with glucose to form 1-abscisyl-β-D-glucopyranoside (Koshimizu et al., 1968; Milborrow, 1970); and (ii) it is hydroxylated on the $6'$-pro-(S) methyl group to form a derivative originally referred to as "Metabolite C" (hydroxymethyl abscisic acid) (8). This compound is unstable and, *in vitro*, rearranges to form phaseic acid (Milborrow, 1969). It is not known whether the rearrangement of hydroxymethyl abscisic acid occurs spontaneously within the cells or if it is catalysed by an enzyme. The isolation of several milligrams of crystalline hydroxymethyl abscisic acid from tomato shoots that had been fed synthetic ABA suggests that no enzyme is involved in the rearrangement and that phaseic acid normally forms spontaneously.

That phaseic acid is a normal intermediate, rather than a rearrangement artefact, is shown by the occurrence in plants of relatively large quantities of its two epimeric reduction products: dihydrophaseic (Tinelli et al., 1973) and *epi*-dihydrophaseic acids (Zeevaart & Milborrow, 1976). These two compounds would not be formed from $4'$-hydroxymethyl abscisic acid, so phaseic acid must be present in the plant. The $6'$-hydroxylating enzyme is highly specific in that it accepts (+)-ABA but not (−)-ABA (Sondheimer et al.,

1971). Gillard and Walton (1976) found that the hydroxylating activity was present in a microsomal preparation while the oxido-reductase was soluble. A conjugate (9) of hydroxymethyl abscisic acid has been isolated from seeds of Black locust (*Robinia pseudacacia*) by Hirai, et al. (1978) in which the 6'-hydroxymethyl group of (8) is esterified with the 5-carboxyl group of 3-hydroxy, 3-methyl glutaric acid (the CoA derivative of this compound is a precursor of mevalonic acid). The esterification of the 6'-hydroxyl group prevents the cyclization of hydroxymethyl abscisic acid to phaseic acid.

Several analyses of the fate of $(\pm)$-[2-^{14}C]ABA metabolized by plants have indicated the presence of labelled material in the final aqueous solution after alkaline hydrolysis and extraction with ethyl acetate. One of these metabolites has been identified as the 1'-glucoside of ABA (10) (Loveys and Milborrow, unpublished). The carboxyl group of ABA, like that of the gibberellins, can be esterified with glucose and the hydroxyl group can be glucosylated.

ABA-glucose ester seems to be formed by a rather unspecific enzyme because both the (+) and the (−) enantiomers are esterified as are 2-*trans*-ABA and 2-*trans*-xanthoxin acid (11). Phaseic acid and both of the epimeric dihydrophaseic acids also occur in an alkali-hydrolysable, bound form which is probably a glucose ester. The specific activity of these compounds, found when plants are fed [^{14}C]ABA, indicates that the conjugates are formed from the respective free acids and not by progressive modification of the acid moiety. The ratios of phaseic and dihydrophaseic acids vary between different plant species, and although dihydrophaseic acid seems not to be the final degradation product of ABA (Martin et al., 1977, have reported the occurrence of hydroxy- and keto-dihydrophaseic acid in pear seeds), it often accumulates to many times the concentration of phaseic acid and ABA. Recent experiments in which $(\pm)$-[2-^{14}C]ABA was incubated with a range of soil microorganisms (Milborrow, Strong and Lee, unpublished results) showed that ABA was degraded to a number of products during 2 or 3 weeks, so it is possible that, in long-term experiments, some of the [^{14}C]ABA supplied is degraded by bacteria. This, of course, in no way excludes the possibility of another metabolic route of deactivation.

The balance between the formation of ABA-glucose ester and phaseic acid has not been investigated. Several experiments that have followed the fall in ABA and the rise in its glucose ester that occurs as leaves recover from wilting have made use of bioassay techniques and so do not detect phaseic or dihydrophaseic acids. The bean seedlings grown by Harrison and Walton (1975) formed little glucose ester from (+)-[2-^{14}C]ABA, whereas the majority of the glucose ester formed from $(\pm)$-[2-^{14}C]ABA was the (−) enantiomer (Milborrow, 1970). In tomato shoots a tendency has been observed for young seedlings to form more phaseic acid rather than glucose ester, while old plants form more glucose ester than phaseic acid. Other than this, nothing is known of how, or if, environmental factors influence the distribution of ABA metabolism between the various pathways.

When plants regain their turgor they rapidly degrade the excess ABA; similarly, unwilted plants can be expected to inactivate excess ABA fed via the sap stream. Harrison and Walton (1975) measured the rate of turnover in unwilted leaves by feeding $(+)$-[2-^{14}C]ABA equivalent to 6 times the endogenous concentration. Consequently their estimates of degradation determined in this way may be considerably faster than the true rate of turnover.

The use of methanol for extractions has recently been shown to be inadvisable if glucose esters are to be determined, because methanol attacks ABA-glucose ester to form methyl-abscisate and releases glucose (Milborrow & Mallaby, 1975). The reaction is particularly rapid in alkaline solutions. Some of the earlier measurements of glucose esters may be underestimates, particularly of ABA; the other acid esters seem less prone to attack (Zeevaart & Milborrow, 1976).

In the graphs published by Hiron and Wright (1973) most of the decrease in the content of free ABA in the attached, primary leaves of bean (*P. vulgaris*, cv. "Canadian Wonder") was balanced by a rise in the bound ABA fraction during recovery from wilting. This acid-hydrolysable fraction, probably 1-abscisyl-β-D-glucopyranoside, exceeded the final ABA content by 100% and the original content by 500%, after 4 or 5 successive wilt–recovery cycles. Harrison and Walton (1975), using detached primary leaves of *P. vulgaris* cv. "Red Kidney", reported that the amount of ^{14}C in the alkali-hydrolysable ABA fraction seldom reached 10% of the free ABA fraction. The cause of this disparity is unknown; the varieties are different and it is also possible that excision of the leaves could alter their metabolic pattern. The similar amounts of glucose ester in wilted and unwilted plants (Zeevaart, 1977), together with the recent findings (Milborrow, 1978) that [^{14}C]ABA-glucose ester in tomato and silver beet plants does not decrease in amount when plants wilt (nor does the ^{14}C in the free ABA fraction rise), are all compatible with the suggestion that the formation of glucose ester is irreversible.

It is interesting to note, in passing, that analysis of the structure:activity relationships of ABA analogues has shown that the free carboxyl group, the 1′-hydroxyl group and the 2′-ring double bond are essential for activity. The degradation pathways of ABA cause the loss of one or other of the features.

H. XANTHOXIN

Simpson and Wain (1961) observed that plants grown in the light contained more of a growth-inhibitory material than those grown in the dark. When the dark-grown plants were transferred into the light, their content of the inhibitor increased. Furthermore, there was a close resemblance between the action spectrum of phototropism and the absorption spectrum of carotenoids. This was taken as an indication of the involvement of carotenoids in light-regulated growth processes. In addition to this, Ohkuma et al. (1965) noted the chemical similarity between the structure of abscisic acid and the terminal rings of some carotenoids.

Taylor and Smith (1967) followed up these observations and exposed a range of carotenoids to light and moisture. One xanthophyll, violaxanthin, gave rise to a powerful inhibitor of seed germination and extension growth of coleoptiles. It was isolated and characterized by Taylor and Burden (1970) as xanthoxin and defined as a mixture of the biologically active 2-*cis*, and inactive 2-*trans*, isomers of a fifteen carbon aldehyde.

When (+)-xanthoxin, labelled with ^{14}C by Taylor and Burden (1973), was fed to excised shoots of beans and tomatoes, some of it was converted into [^{14}C]ABA, in 7 to 11% yield; 4% occurred as conjugated ABA. When [^{14}C]2-*trans*-xanthoxin was supplied, a little free [^{14}C]2-*trans*-ABA was found, but almost all of the 2-*trans*-ABA occurred in the conjugated form. Also 4.4% of the 2-*trans*-xanthoxin was recovered as the partial oxidation product 2-*trans*-xanthoxin acid. Thus, the two geometrical isomers are metabolized differently, both qualitatively and quantitatively.

Zeevaart (1974) investigated the ABA, 2-*cis*, and 2-*trans*-xanthoxin contents of spinach grown under defined daylengths and wilted or kept turgid. The content of ABA in turgid plants was twice as high in long as in short days and increased 8-14 fold as a result of wilting under either daylength condition. 2-*cis*-xanthoxin content, in contrast, increased by half in short days as a result of wilting. Wilting under long days did not induce an increase. The 2-*trans*-xanthoxin content was twice as high in long as in short days and wilting caused almost a doubling of the concentration in short days but decreased it slightly in long days (Table XI).

TABLE XI

Concentrations of ABA, 2-*cis*- and 2-*trans*-xanthoxin in spinach leaves grown under short days (8 h light, SD) or long days (16 h light, LD).[a]

Treatment	ABA concentration (μg.kg^{-1})	2-*cis*-xanthoxin concentration (μg.kg^{-1})	2-*trans*-xanthoxin concentration (μg.kg^{-1})
SD	71	184	393
SD wilted (10%)	1011	277	743
LD	147	248	739
LD wilted (10%)	1208	241	625

[a]Data from Zeevaart (1974).

A precursor of a regulatory compound would not necessarily be expected to increase in concentration while an increased flux of material was passing along the biosynthetic pathway of which it was a constituent. Nevertheless, if wilting produced a large increase in the concentration of ABA via the xanthoxin pathway, then a proportional increase in 2-*trans*-xanthoxin or 2-*trans*-ABA would be expected. No such increase in 2-*trans*-xanthoxin was found by Zeevaart, and the content of 2-*trans*-ABA in the spinach leaves was negligible.

These, and other data in which 2-*trans*-ABA was absent in wilted plants, argue strongly against ABA being formed by the photolytic cleavage of violaxanthin as its major route of biosynthesis. They do not exclude the possibility that xanthoxin is a precursor of ABA by another, less important series of reactions.

The relative amounts of 2-*cis*, 2-*trans*-xanthoxin and associated compounds formed by *in vitro* photolysis of violaxanthin are surprisingly similar to the ratios of the same compounds isolated from leaves (Taylor & Burden, 1972; Firn et al., 1972). 2-*cis*-xanthoxin does occur naturally, and [14C]2-*cis*-xanthoxin applied to leaves is metabolized to [14C]ABA, so it is quite possible that some portion of the ABA in brightly illuminated leaves can be formed from violaxanthin by photolysis. However, the experiments referred to above would indicate that the bulk of the stress-induced "extra" ABA is not made by this means. Experiments with [14C]mevalonic acid supplied to ripening avocado fruit have also shown that [14C]ABA can be biosynthesised as rapidly in darkness as in the light. Firn and Friend (1972) used a model system comprising soybean lipoxygenase and violaxanthin to form the same range of products, including 2-*cis*- and 2-*trans*-xanthoxin, as is formed by photolytic cleavage of the carotenoid. While there is no evidence that this enzyme reaction occurs within normal leaves, the experiment does remove the necessity of light for cleavage. The increase in ABA content, which occurs in stressed bean leaves in darkness (Hiron & Wright, 1973), also eliminates the requirement of light but, by doing this, negates the original correlations on which the hypothesis of photolytic formation of ABA was based.

I. PHASEIC ACID

The ABA content of water-deficient vines increased 44-fold over 6 d (Loveys & Kriedemann, 1973), but, in short-term experiments (1 h), the ABA content of plants kept in a growth chamber rose by 50%; the content of phaseic acid rose from 42 μg.kg original fresh wt^{-1} to 137 μg.kg^{-1}—a rise of 200%. Although phaseic and dihydrophaseic acids have virtually no growth-inhibiting activity (Tinelli et al., 1973), it is possible that both of these acids could exert a slight, modulating influence on other aspects of leaf metabolism. In this regard, Kriedemann et al. (1975) reported that phaseic acid, at 0.07 mM (19 mg.l^{-1}), inhibited photosynthesis, and that, when wilted vine leaves were rewatered, the recovery pattern of CO_2 uptake was well behind that of transpiration. It is possible that the after-effects of wilting may be attributed, in part, to effects of degradation products of ABA which can build up to quite high concentrations (Table IX). At present there is little evidence for this.

IV. SOLUTES AND PERMEABILITY

A. EXUDATION FROM ROOTS

Although exudation by isolated root systems is a well-documented process, the relationship between this phenomenon and the functioning of the whole plant is, as yet, little investigated. Furthermore, the behaviour in isolation of one component of an integrated water-absorbing system does not necessarily give a true measure of the part it plays normally. The volume of sap exuded is considerably less than the volume of water drawn up by transpiration, so the extrapolation of results obtained with exudate to the sap of intact plants may not be entirely justified. For example, irrigating roots of intact plants with ABA might cause a change in their permeability to water, but any response would be rapidly complicated by ABA reaching and closing the stomata. Even the methodology to determine the exudation from "wilted, excised roots" makes use of transient effects, because the excised root systems of wilted seedlings have to be placed in water in order to give any exudate at all. The transient concentrations of ABA are then measured in the earliest samples of exudate. As can be seen elsewhere (Fig. 2) the concentration of ABA in leaves falls rapidly after water is supplied to a stressed plant, and there is no guarantee that the processes that generate xylem sap are not affected by stress and recovery. This problem was overcome, to some extent, by Glinka (1973), who placed excised root systems in mannitol solutions to obtain a measure of the rate of permeation of water into, and out of, the roots. Both rates were affected in the same way as in wilted roots, which gives one some confidence that real effects are measured in the usual excised root experiments.

A solution of ABA (1 μM), bathing the roots of maize, increased the volume of xylem exudate from 1.7 to 2.6 μl.cm^{-2}.h^{-1} after 4 h (Collins & Kerrigan, 1974). The effect began to decrease after about 30 h. Similar results, using tomatoes, have been reported by Tal and Imber (1971) and

Glinka (1973). Kinetin had the opposite action: the flow of exudate was reduced to 0.98 by 4 h with a progressive reduction continuing for a further 24 h. The response occurred with 10 mM kinetin and was detectable at 1.0 nM. The effects of both phytohormones are reversible as the rate of exudation returned to normal about 48 h after the treatments had been stopped.

The amounts of ions in the exudate were also affected: ABA raised the flow rate from maize roots (Collins & Kerrigan, 1974) so that there was a decrease in the concentration of K^+, Ca^{2+} and Cl^-. Kinetin lowered the concentrations of K^+ and Cl^- in spite of decreasing the rate of exudation, but raised the concentration of Ca^{2+} in the exudate.

Mizrahi and Richmond (1972) induced stress in tobacco plants growing in bottles of aerated nutrient solution by stopping the air flow or by replacing the solution with one containing sodium chloride (6 g.1^{-1}) or mannitol (31 g.1^{-1}). They also immersed the roots in ($\pm$)-ABA or kinetin solutions and found that ($\pm$)-ABA at 0.1 mg.1^{-1} reduced the water saturation deficit developed by the plants under stress conditions, while kinetin increased it. However, more seems to be involved than mere stomatal adjustment, because if plants were pretreated with ABA and then placed in a saline solution, they developed greater, rather than the expected lesser, saturation deficits.

The content of endogenous ABA in exudate from tobacco roots was increased by a water deficit and also by osmotic stress, while the effects of both of these treatments on cytokinin activity was to reduce it drastically after 48 h (Itai et al., 1968). If this occurs in intact plants then there would be less competition between the mutually antagonistic effects of ABA and cytokinin in drought-afflicted plants.

B. UPTAKE OF IONS

The uptake of rubidium ions by a tissue, rather than by a root system, was followed by Reed and Bonner (1974). They used ^{86}Rb as a tracer for K^+ on the rationale that one system was responsible for the absorption of K^+ and Rb^+ ions. As has been found with stomatal guard cells, ABA inhibits K^+/Rb^+ uptake. Chloride and two organic compounds, one ionized, the other not (proline and 3-0-methylglucose), were considerably less affected. The experiments of Van Steveninck (1972) show that uptake of Na^+, K^+ and Cl^- are stimulated by ABA (38 μM, i.e. 10 mg.1^{-1}). The author noted that beetroot (*Beta vulgaris*) strains differ widely in their K^+ versus Na^+ selectivity, but the uptake of all three ions appeared to be stimulated to similar extents by ABA. Ion uptake and stomatal mechanisms are discussed in other chapters, but it may be worth noting here that these results, on the effect of ABA on beetroot discs, are not incompatible with work on the ionic content of root exudate, but are difficult to reconcile with the leakage of K^+ during stomatal closure under the influence of ABA (Raschke, 1975; Mansfield & Jones, 1971).

Leaves of tobacco (*Nicotiana rustica*) plants growing in half-strength Hoagland solution were subjected to salinity stress when the nutrient solution was replaced by one to which $6 g.1^{-1}$ NaCl had been added (Mizrahi et al., 1971). The salt solution caused the content of ABA in the leaves to rise, but only under conditions of low humidity (Table XII). The authors conclude that the salt stress causes the ABA content to rise by a direct effect of the salt treatment on the leaves, not by an effect on the roots. The effect on the leaves could be either by some salt reaching the leaves, or possibly by the induction of incipient wilting if the leaves of plants with their roots in saline solution received less water than the controls. The lesser rate of water uptake by plants under low humidity and salt treatments supports this latter view.

Yet another unexpected result was the change in content of ABA under conditions of mineral deprivation (Mizrahi & Richmond, 1972). Transfer from half-strength Hoagland solution to distilled water did not impair the water status of tobacco plants, but the content of ABA in the leaves increased progressively for up to 7 d (Fig. 9). Although the concentration of ABA had doubled by day 2 and quadrupled by day 4, only thereafter did growth rate and leaf chlorophyll decline—both effects could have been caused by ABA or mineral deficiency. This experiment lends strong support to Mizrahi and Richmond's and Hiron and Wright's suggestion that it is unfavourable conditions that cause an increase in ABA content, not solely moisture stress.

Plants that had been subjected to salinity or mineral deprivation showed a greater resistance to the development of a water saturation deficit when the aeration of the solution around their roots was stopped (Mizrahi et al., 1972). The high titre of ABA induced by one unfavourable circumstance may have given the previously stressed leaves an advantage when the plants were subjected to another stress.

Some of the conflicting reports on the effects of ABA and stress on the uptake and exudation of ions can be reconciled in the light of the results

TABLE XII

Contents of (+)-ABA in tobacco leaves, and water uptake. Tobacco leaf dry wt is usually from 8 to 10% of the fresh wt. These data can be made approximately comparable with others in this chapter (where ABA content is given as μg or mg.kg fresh wt^{-1} or $litre^{-1}$) by dividing the figures by 10.[a]

	(+)-ABA concentration (μg.kg leaf dry wt^{-1})		Water uptake (ml. $plant^{-1}$. day^{-1})	
	No salt	Salt treatment	No salt	Salt treatment
High humidity	69	71	95	93
Low humidity	90	573	183	116

[a]Mizrahi et al. (1971).

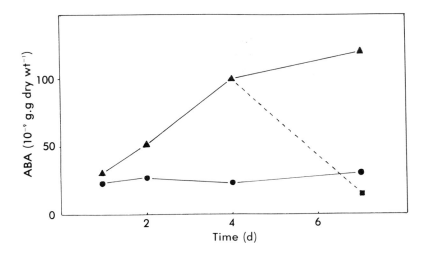

FIG. 9. Changes in the concentration of ABA in tobacco plants transferred from half-strength Hoagland solution to distilled water (▲), returned to half-strength Hoagland solution after 4 d (■) or not transferred (●). The concentrations are expressed per leaf dry wt; to compare them with other data in this chapter they should be divided by approximately 10. (From Mizrahi and Richmond, 1972.)

obtained by Pitman et al. (1974) and Pitman and Wellfare (1978). Water stress affected barley seedling root systems in a remarkably similar fashion to treatment of the roots with ABA. It is probable, therefore, that the increased amounts of ABA formed in response to stress and transported down to the roots produce these effects.

Exposure of excised barley roots to $10 \mu m$ ABA (2.64 mg.1^{-1}) reduced the amount of chloride transported through the roots into the xylem sap, to about 10% of the controls (Fig. 10). The rate of uptake of the ions into the root was unaltered and the chloride that was not transported in the xylem sap accumulated in the root, both in the stele and in the cortex (Pitman et al., 1975).

The flux of water through plant tissues, particularly the root, may also be influenced by ABA, independently of any effects on ion transport (Glinka & Reinhold, 1971; Glinka, 1973). Both the hydraulic conductivity (permeability to water moving along a concentration gradient) and diffusive permeability (permeability to water in the absence of a net flux) of water into or out of carrot discs were increased by the presence of ABA.

The significance of these findings to the whole plant, particularly when under stress, is obscure. While a higher root permeability might allow water

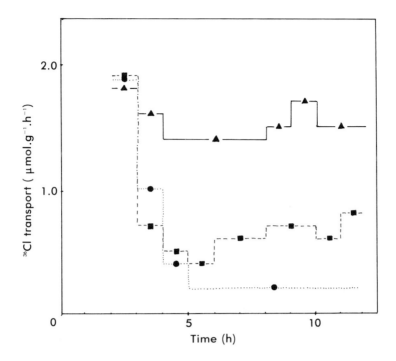

FIG. 10. Effect of (±)-ABA on the transport of Cl⁻ through barley roots at 28°C. (a) Control (▲), (b) 10 μM ABA (2.6 mg.l⁻¹) (●), (c) 10 μM ABA present during the first 2 h and then replaced by water (■). (From Pitman et al., 1974.)

to be absorbed more rapidly from the soil by a stressed plant than one with low concentrations of ABA in its roots, the permeability of the mesophyll cells might also be increased. Mesophyll permeability has not been measured in the presence of ABA. A more permeable mesophyll may not lose any more water than a less permeable one because stomatal resistance is the dominant factor controlling diffusion from the leaf.

C. TRANSPORT IN STRESSED PLANTS

Mild water stress does not appear to reduce the movement of materials in the phloem. The direct treatment of plants with ABA has been tried by Mizrahi et al. (1974), who sprayed seedlings of wheat and barley with (±)-ABA and subjected them to restricted or abundant water supply. The treatment drastically restricted water loss from the plants, so much so that soil water contents were similar to those in pots without plants. The survival of seedlings kept under water-deficient conditions was considerably extended by sprays of ABA every 3 d, and the drought-induced senescence of older leaves was inhibited. The growth of plants with adequate water supplies was reduced by the application of ABA, but, when water became limiting, the ABA-treated plants continued to grow whereas the untreated controls died. Dry matter production by the ABA-treated plants was greater than that by the controls, indicating apparently that ABA had increased the efficiency of water utilization. However, it was observed that the ABA treatments had retarded root growth, irrespective of water regimen, and the ABA-induced increase in dry weight was due entirely to the greater development of the shoot at the expense of the roots. This would seem to be a precarious situation for a plant in a drought-prone environment; and how poor root growth is prevented in plants subjected to intermittent drought (and, presumably, high contents of ABA) is unclear. On the other hand, ABA has been observed on a number of occasions to stimulate root growth (Chin et al., 1969; Collet, 1970; Krelle & Libbert, 1969; Read & Hoysler, 1971). Connor (1975) found that the growth and development of grain yields in wheat crops were strongly influenced by soil water potential. This is not too surprising, but the analysis also showed that under conditions of water stress there was a marked shift in the allocation of growth resources in favour of root growth. This seems to have obvious survival value; but why this shift should occur under field conditions, where ABA concentrations could be expected to be high, when the reverse allocation occurred when plants were treated with ABA, is inexplicable at present.

The results cited above have been obtained with mesophytic crop plants growing under controlled laboratory conditions and then subjected to soil water deficit, high evaporative demand, or a sudden increase in salinity. Short-term changes were measured and the changes in, for example, concentrations of ABA were similar under all conditions. However, the presence of salt in soil water affects long-term growth in a different way from chronic water deficits. The structures of cells and tissues produced under the two circumstances are dissimilar: cell walls formed by plants growing in the presence of excessive salt concentrations are thickened; leaf water deficits cause moderate to severe wilting, whereas the same degree of stress induced by salinity may not cause wilting. Some long-term adjustment of the physiology of the plant takes place, and it may be premature to extrapolate the findings in short-term laboratory experiments described here to field conditions.

D. CYTOKININS AND WATER DEFICITS

The effects of cytokinin and ABA seem, in general, to be mutually antagonistic in that the former stimulates cell division and bud growth, opens stomata and inhibits senescence, while the latter does the reverse. Some of the effects produced by stress may be partly attributable to a lack of cytokinins produced in the roots and transported up to the shoot. During wilting, less sap reaches the shoot, and the concentration of cytokinin, measured immediately after recovery from wilting, is less than in sap of unstressed plants.

Progressive additions of NaCl, up to 0.1 M, and mannitol, up to 0.16 M, to the aerated nutrient solution in which sunflower (*Helianthus annuus*) plants were growing progressively decreased the concentration of cytokinin activity in the xylem exudate when the plants were decapitated (Itai et al., 1968). The normal concentration of cytokinin activity in xylem sap of sunflower plants was restored 2 d after the plants had recovered from wilting. During the period of the wilt, Ben-Zioni et al. (1967) found a decreased incorporation of [^{14}C]leucine into the protein of leaf discs from tobacco leaves. The effect was ameliorated by kinetin.

Shibaoka and Thimann (1970) investigated proteolysis in detached leaves of pea and reported that, while net proteolysis was the dominant reaction during senescence, there was nevertheless a certain amount of protein synthesis occurring, as measured by [^{14}C]leucine incorporation. Kinetin acted not by stimulating protein synthesis but by inhibiting proteolysis.

Senescence of wheat leaves is accompanied by a decline in the incorporation of labelled amino acids into Fraction 1 protein in the chloroplasts. The symptoms of leaf senescence are delayed by applications of kinetin (Tung & Brady, 1972). Applications of ABA cause very similar effects to normal senescence on Fraction 1 protein synthesis; in addition, the proportion of polysomes decreases during senescence and the same feature is observed after applications of ABA or drought. Brady et al. (1974) found that ethylene production also increased under the influence of stress (Fig. 11), but the treatment of detached leaves with ethylene had no detectable effect on the incorporation of [^{3}H]valine into Fraction 1 protein. It appears, therefore, that ethylene plays an insignificant part in the hastening of senescence by stress.

The effects of ABA and senescence on the synthesis of Fraction 1 protein are proportionally greater than they are on the other leaf proteins. Ellis and Hartley (1971) showed that the larger sub-unit, at least of Fraction 1 protein, is assembled on chloroplast ribosomes, so that it would appear that the chloroplast suffers changes at least as great as those in the cytosol during stress.

Waterlogging of sunflower plants (Burrows & Carr, 1969) was found to decrease the cytokinin activity of xylem exudate produced immediately after

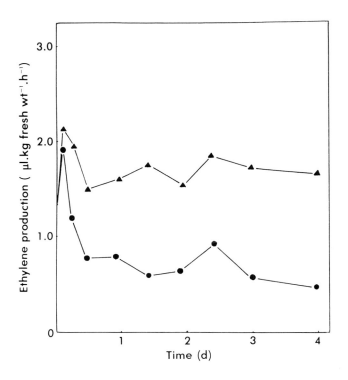

FIG. 11. Effect of water stress on the production of ethylene by wheat seedlings. 13 d old seedlings were placed with their roots in water (●), or in 0.5 M mannitol (▲). (From Brady et al., 1974.)

the roots were re-aerated and the tops removed. There was no decrease in the volume of sap after short periods (less then 3 d) of waterlogging, but this treatment, like wilting, reduced the concentration of cytokinin activity in the sap exuded. The similar effects of these two stress conditions on cytokinin activity in the exudate parallel their effects on ABA metabolism.

The effect of water stress on tobacco shoots was found to be transferred rapidly to the roots (Itai & Vaadia, 1971). A 30 min period of strong evaporative demand caused slight wilting of the shoots, from which they rapidly recovered. After the shoots were cut off, the same volume of exudate could be collected from control root systems of plants whose shoots had been stressed. Nevertheless, the cytokinin activity of the control exudate was twice that of the activity from previously stressed roots. The authors concluded that the influence of stress was transferred to the roots and biosynthesis of cytokins was stopped during the period of wilting. While the observation is interesting, the interpretation of the mechanism by which it was produced is speculative, in the absence of any other evidence.

The effects of water stress on cytokinin concentrations resemble those on ABA in that there appears to be a critical range, if not a critical point, in the region of -0.8 to -1.1 MPa, beyond which plants show a marked decrease in their cytokinin contents (Hsiao, 1973). Itai and Vaadia (1965), studying the effect of water stress on tobacco, found that 30 min wilting caused a detectable fall in the concentration of cytokinin activity in root exudate collected immediately after the plants had been rewatered, and a slight fall in the amount extracted from excised leaves was detectable after only 10 min of wilting. The authors concluded that the rapidity of the change indicated more rapid inactivation in wilted leaves than in turgid ones. In contrast to these results, Mizrahi et al. (1971), working with the same species, at the same institute, could find no difference after intact plants had remained wilted for 24 h.

Kinetin, and more recently other cytokinins and gibberellic acid, have been shown to cause stomatal opening (Livne & Vaadia, 1965; Luke & Freeman, 1968), but the time course of 1–2 h after application suggests that there is no direct antagonism between the action of these two phytohormones and ABA at the site of ABA's rapid action on stomata. A longer-term, indirect antagonism seems more likely. Indirect evidence in support of this can be derived from the results of Pallas and Box (1970). These authors proposed that the opening response of stomata to kinetin was caused by a reduction of the osmotic water potential of the accessory, epidermal and mesophyll cells of oat leaves. The guard cells would then be able to take up water more readily, and thus open. They measured decreases in osmotic potential of an average of -0.22 MPa after treatment with kinetin ($500 \, \mu\text{g.l}^{-1}$, 48 h), in comparison with leaves in distilled water.

Irrespective of the mechanism by which cytokinins act on stomata, the effect of drought in reducing the amount of cytokinin in the xylem sap reaching the shoot would tend to close the stomata and also hasten senescence leading to the shedding of older leaves. All these effects would be accentuated by the high concentrations of ABA formed by stressed plants.

V. EFFECTS ON STOMATA

A. TIME COURSE

The time taken for stomata to respond to ABA is extremely short, of the order of 5 min when synthetic material is supplied to barley (*Hordeum vulgare*) leaves via the sap stream (Cummins et al., 1971), (Fig. 12). This timecourse can be related to the observations of Stålfelt (1929) who could detect stomatal closure about 13 min after subjecting leaves to water stress. If the closure was brought about by ABA synthesized in the leaf, as now seems highly probable, then an increased content of ABA must have been either made in the guard cells or transported to them within about 8 min of the commencement of water stress. A similar time course for the synthesis of ABA has been calculated for bean leaves (Milborrow, 1974b; Wright & Hiron, 1972); the concentration doubled approximately every 7 min.

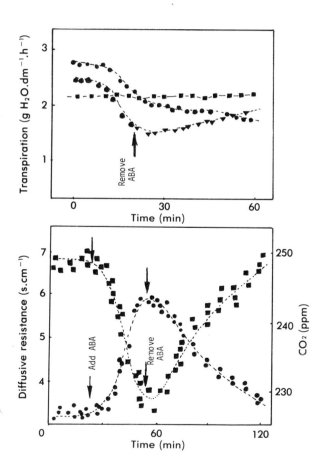

FIG. 12. (a) Changes in diffusive resistance, Σ_r, of barley leaves with time. At time 0, the irrigating distilled water was replaced by 0.1 μM ($\pm$)−ABA (26.4 μg.1^{-1}) (●). H$_2$O (■), ABA removed (▼). (b) Changes in transpiration rates when the water irrigating a barley leaf was replaced by 0.1 μM ($\pm$)−ABA. CO$_2$ (■), Σ_r (●). (From Cummins et al., 1971.)

Stomates are sensitive to modest changes in ABA concentration; in *Commelina communis* the response is linearly proportional to log concentration of supplied ABA, with 50% closure occurring at $0.3 \mu M$ $(80 \mu g.1^{-1})$ (Tucker & Mansfield, 1971). Kriedemann et al. (1972) suggest that a 100% increase in the endogenous ABA content is sufficient to cause a reduction in stomatal aperture in well-watered maize, bean and rose leaves. They assayed the effect of $(\pm)$-ABA supplied via the xylem sap, by monitoring CO_2 and water exchange; stomatal closure was apparent within 3 min of supplying $(\pm)$-$[^{14}C]$ABA. They also determined the endogenous ABA and the amounts of $[^{14}C]$ABA present, and from these measurements were able to compute the amount of endogenous and exogenous ABA in the leaves when the stomata began to close.

If the $(\pm)$-$[^{14}C]$ABA fed to the leaves was distributed in the same way as the endogenous material and could act as effectively, then a doubling of ABA content was sufficient to induce stomatal closure. However, the authors and also Cummins and Sondheimer (1973) found that $(+)$-ABA has twice the activity of synthetic, racemic $(\pm)$-ABA, and it would appear, therefore, that a 50% increase in ABA content is sufficient to initiate stomatal closure.

Using maize, Beardsell and Cohen (1974) found values of 0.5 ng ABA.cm^{-2} (i.e. $31 \mu g.kg^{-1}$) in well-watered leaves and 9 ng.cm^{-2} (i.e. $563 \mu g.kg^{-1}$) in stressed leaves. At the critical leaf water potential of -0.8 MPa, the stomata were closing or closed and the leaf ABA content was 1–2 ng.cm^{-2} (i.e. 60 to $120 \mu g.kg^{-1}$), an increase of 100–300% over the basal value. The concentration of ABA at which stomatal closure occurred is higher than in the experiments described by Kriedemann et al. (1972), but the 2-fold excess over the basal concentration agrees reasonably closely with their findings.

There is usually a close correspondence between stomatal closure and the rise in concentration of ABA brought about by mild water stress; nevertheless, in Beardsell and Cohen's (1975) data, there is a considerable discrepancy between the two. An explanation for this could be that stress can cause ABA to leak out of chloroplasts and bring about stomatal closure even before synthesis begins, and that this redistribution is usually obscured by the rapidity of the rise in the amount of ABA.

Loveys (1977) isolated chloroplasts from spinach leaves and found that a considerable proportion (96.6%) of the ABA in unstressed leaves was in the chloroplasts, while in stressed leaves only 15.2% of the ABA was in the chloroplasts. While this could have arisen because the chloroplasts of wilted leaves are susceptible to damage during isolation, it is more likely to be a true result because the chloroplasts from stressed leaves leaked little ABA on lysis. The ABA appeared to be bound in some way. Similar results have been obtained for gibberellins (Browning & Saunders, 1977) which were extractable from chloroplasts only after detergent treatment, and Wellburn and Hampp

(1976) have found that the membranes of isolated etioplasts were quite impermeable to ABA and gibberellic acid.

B. STOMATAL OPENING AFTER REWATERING OR REMOVAL OF ABA

When Beardsell and Cohen (1974) rewatered their maize plants there appeared to be little change in leaf ABA content during the first 1.5 h, but over the next 30 min the content of ABA fell to 50% of the stressed value. They also measured leaf water potential and ABA during the period after rewatering and found that the critical point of -0.8 MPa was reached after about 1.5 to 2 h. The stomata were slow to re-open completely, diffusive resistance was still 9.8 s.cm^{-1} after 24 h and 7.5 s.cm^{-1} after 48 h, compared with the control value of 1.5 s.cm^{-1}. Some authors have noted that stomatal opening does not occur as rapidly as expected from the falling contents of ABA in leaves recovering from wilting. This could result from a more rapid destruction of ABA in the mesophyll than in the guard cells, but the rapid re-opening of stomata in excised barley leaves, once the supply of ABA solution had been replaced with water, argues that the guard cells can overcome the effect of ABA very quickly.

Cummins (1973) found that the amount of ($\pm$)-[2-^{14}C]ABA applied to barley leaves was not closely related to the degree of opening of the stomata. Uptake of 1.0 μM (264 μg.l^{-1}) ($\pm$)-ABA for 15 min by the excised leaves caused rapid stomatal closure, but after transfer to water the stomata began to re-open after about 35 min. Analysis of the labelled materials showed that at this time about 5% of the ABA had been converted into other products (mostly phaseic acid). The inactivation of this proportion of the [^{14}C]ABA would seem inadequate to account for gradual re-opening, but it must be remembered, firstly, that the analysis includes the whole leaf and the response occurs in a very small part; secondly, 5% of the label in phaseic acid means that 10% of the active ($+$) form has been destroyed because ($-$)-ABA is not oxidized to phaseic acid. Loveys reports that 2.7% of the ABA in a leaf is in the lower epidermis, so it is just possible that the barley stomata can degrade most of their ($+$)-ABA before the destruction of much of the ABA in the mesophyll occurs. An analysis of the label in epidermal strips is required.

The similarity between the time taken for the leaf water potential of maize plants to fall below the critical value of -0.8 MPa, and the time taken before ABA concentrations began to fall in Beardsell and Cohen's experiment, indicates that the same factor that "switches on" rapid biosynthesis of ABA at -0.8 MPa may also regulate its degradation.

When Cummins et al. (1971) replaced solutions of ABA with water, the stomata of barley (*Hordeum vulgare*) leaves rapidly started to open (Fig. 12). This result suggests that ABA acts as a modulator of stomatal behaviour, not as a trigger to initiate irreversible changes. The rapid re-opening of the stomata shows that the effects are not only reversible, but that the guard cells must be able either to deactivate, sequester, or export the ABA very rapidly. In the experiments described here (Beardsell & Cohen, 1974, 1975; Cummins et al., 1971) the amounts of ABA were just sufficient to close the stomata, or the water deficit was close to the critical value (see Section III, D). When ABA was no longer fed, or water was supplied, the stomata began to open almost immediately. This contrasts with other experimental results in which either massive amounts of ABA were applied, or severe wilting caused a rise in ABA concentration far in excess of that necessary to close the stomata. Under these conditions, large amounts of ABA would have to be inactivated or immobilized and the stomata would take a correspondingly long time to adjust.

C. METABOLISM OF GUARD CELLS

Milthorpe et al. (1974) studied the uptake of [^{14}C]CO_2 by stripped *Commelina cyanea* epidermis and mesophyll. The qualitative differences between the products formed in the guard cells and those in the mesophyll tissues, allows the transfer of material between them to be followed. The time taken for the substances to move over these short distances, obviously in the absence of strong permeability barriers, was of the order of 20–30 s (personal communication). Consequently, it is entirely possible that the ABA required to operate stomatal closure could be formed in the mesophyll at the onset of wilting and transferred, actively or by diffusion, to the guard cells. ABA is formed in plastids (Milborrow & Robinson, 1973), so ABA could be formed by chloroplasts in the guard cells. However, Loveys (1977) has found that no ABA was formed when isolated broad bean (*Vicia faba*) epidermis was wilted. Irrespective of whether or not the ABA in the guard cells is made within them or imported from the mesophyll, the interesting question is "What does all the ABA in wilted leaves do?". Only a very minor proportion of the ABA can be present in the guard cells; if all the "extra" ABA in leaves were present in the guard cells it would exceed its solubility limit. This "extra" ABA produced in the mesophyll may also be involved in adaptive responses. It could stabilize the protoplasm of the cells (as suggested in Section II, C) making them better able to withstand physiological stress, or it could move to and adjust the physiology of other parts to drought conditions. Several effects of ABA would appear to be candidates for this: induction of senescence in the older leaves, stimulation of rooting, inhibition of growth, and increasing root permeability.

D. FLACCA TOMATOES

Tal, Imber and co-workers have investigated the physiology of a wilty mutant variety of tomato known as flacca, derived from the cultivar Rheinlands Ruhm. The mutant plants show symptoms reminiscent of excess indoleacetic acid and cytokinin contents, but the wilty characteristics seem to result from lower than normal contents of ABA, and the failure of the stomata to close. Applications of synthetic ABA cause stomatal closure and partially restore the normal appearance (Tal & Imber, 1970, 1971, 1972; Tal et al., 1970; Tal & Nevo, 1973; Tal et al., 1974).

Although the flacca mutant is deficient in ABA it has not completely lost the capacity to synthesize the hormone (Tal & Nevo, 1973). During fruit ripening the content of ABA in flacca fruit reaches only about half the concentration it does in Rheinlands Ruhm. The increase in ABA content in flacca on transfer from very humid to dry conditions (this treatment induced wilting in normal and flacca), was about 30% that in the normal variety treated similarly (Milborrow, unpublished). It appears that the mutation suffered by Rheinlands Ruhm which produced the flacca mutant, has complex effects and is not the mere inability to make ABA, or the failure to respond to its action. The causes of the differences between normal and flacca plants have not been completely defined, so that mutants cannot be used simply as ABA-less plants. The experiments with flacca, in the normal regulation of the stomatal mechanism, do confirm by an independent method that ABA is involved.

VI. CONCLUSION

The changes that occur in the concentrations of ABA in drought-afflicted leaves are well documented, as are its effects on stomata. The movement of ABA to other parts of the plant has been measured and its effect on root permeability and ion uptake seems clear. These phenomena have been known for nearly a decade, yet in the course of reading the literature summarized in this chapter, the overriding impression obtained was of how little had been firmly established. For example, what is the function of all the "extra" ABA in wilted leaves? Why do stomata remain closed when the concentration of ABA in previously stressed leaves falls? Does ABA transport to roots affect water uptake in an intact plant, and does it affect root growth? Does ABA stabilize the cells in unfavourable conditions?

The list of plant species used in stress experiments, and mentioned in this chapter, hardly exceeds a dozen, nearly all of which are mesophytic crop plants of temperate areas. The changes in ABA content that occur in natural plant populations, in halophytes and in xerophytes are virtually unknown. In the remaining years of this century and beyond, mankind will have to grow crops in unproductive, marginal, cold, desert and brackish areas if famine is to be avoided for the increasing world population. Such cultivation will require sure knowledge of the physiology of plants growing under conditions of stress and, consequently, we can anticipate an increasing research interest in the role of ABA in droughted plants.

Structures of ABA and closely related compounds

1. Natural (+)-(S)-abscisic acid
   (revised absolute configuration)

(−)-(R)-abscisic acid

2. violaxanthin

3. 2-cis-xanthoxin

4. phaseic acid

5. dihydrophaseic acid

6. epi-dihydrophaseic acid

Structures of ABA and closely related compounds—*continued*

7. (+)-(S)-1-abscisyl-β-D-glucopyranoside (ABA-glucose ester)

8. 6'-hydroxymethyl abscisic acid
    (Metabolite C)

9. 3-hydroxy-3-methyl-glutaryl-6'-hydroxymethyl abscisic acid

10. 1'-glucoside of abscisic acid

11. 2-*trans*-xanthoxin acid

CHAPTER 16

Ultrastructural Consequences of Drought

ALEXANDRA POLJAKOFF-MAYBER

I. Introduction 389
II. Effect of water stress on the structure and function of the photosynthetic apparatus 390
III. Changes induced by water stress in mitochondrial structure and function 394
IV. Effect of water stress on protein synthesizing apparatus.................................. 397
V. Changes occurring in the nucleus and cytoplasmic membranes due to water stress 399
VI. General discussion.. 401

I. INTRODUCTION

Water plays an important role in all physiological processes in the plant (Crafts, 1968) and water deficit has long been known to affect almost all aspects of plant life and metabolism (Hsiao, 1973). Numerous anatomical and physiological adaptations, enabling the plant to overcome water stress, have been recognised and described as drought-resistance mechanisms (Parker, 1968).

Some of the effects of drought, especially those concerning gas exchange, result from the effect of water stress on stomata (Gaastra, 1963); but photosynthesis may be impaired even when stomata remain open (Slavik, 1963). Results such as these suggest that water stress may impair metabolism through mechanisms other than stomatal aperture, a view reinforced by the demonstration of effects of water stress on enzymatic activity (Todd, 1972).

It was assumed that the association of proteins and lipids in the plasma membranes would be weakened by water stress which would result in visible submicroscopic changes and interference with the activity and turnover of enzymes (Vasileva & Burkina, 1960–61). These ideas reflect, to an extent, the older concepts of "plasmatic drought resistance" in which the development of drought resistance was associated with an eventual strengthening of the bonds (disulphide, hydrogen and others) maintaining structural integrity (Iljin, 1933; Hofler et al., 1941; Stocker, 1956, 1961; Parker, 1968).

389

PHYSIOLOGY AND BIOCHEMISTRY
OF DROUGHT RESISTANCE
IN PLANTS

More recent observations and experimental results enable us to understand more clearly the relationship between structural changes observed at the submicroscopic level and physiological and metabolic responses to water stress. Changes may be observed in the structure and function of the photosynthetic apparatus, the structure and function of mitochondria and the mechanism of protein synthesis. Other changes in the submicroscopic structure of the nucleus and the cellular membranes and their arrangement can also be seen but are as yet unrelated to defined metabolic events.

There is some relationship between the severity of water stress and the extent and reversibility of structural and functional damage (Nir, 1969; Hsiao, 1973; Crevecoeur et al., 1976). As water stress increases, the structural changes become more pronounced and, following extreme loss of the fresh weight in higher plants (usually exceeding 55–60%), the changes are irreversible. Comparisons of the data from different authors are frequently difficult to make, as the various investigators have related the observed changes to different parameters of tissue water status, such as water content (as a percentage of the fresh weight), relative water content and water potential. Furthermore, care was not always taken to adjust the osmotic potential of the fixative solution to match the water potential of the tissue. Therefore, sometimes the observed swelling of organelles (particularly mitochondria and plastids) to assume an "optically empty" appearance and frequently observed vesiculation and breakage of membranes may not faithfully represent the state of the organelles at the time of fixation (Fellows & Boyer, 1976).

There are also exceptions to the general relationship between degree of water stress and extent and reversibility of structural and functional changes. Such exceptions are usually exhibited by lower plants; for example, the terrestrial mosses. Seeds, during development and germination, first undergo severe dehydration followed by rehydration, without damage. Moreover, seed imbibition during germination may be interrupted by dehydration which causes no damage but, on the contrary, apparently induces drought hardiness (Genkel, 1946).

In this chapter the available information on submicroscopic changes induced by water stress will be related to the observed levels of metabolic activity, and a general explanation for their sequence and relationship will be attempted. Not all available information will be cited in this chapter, as the subject has been reviewed relatively recently by Vieira de Silva (1976).

II. EFFECT OF WATER STRESS ON THE STRUCTURE AND FUNCTION OF THE PHOTOSYNTHETIC APPARATUS

A marked reduction in Hill activity and photosynthetic phosphorylation was induced in chloroplasts by water loss exceeding 50% of the fresh weight of the leaves of Swiss chard; at the same time, phosphatase and ATPase activities increased (Nir & Poljakoff-Mayber, 1966, 1967). On EM examination, chloroplasts isolated from such leaves showed distortion of the intergranal lamellae and a generally swollen appearance (Fig. 1); the grana, although slightly swollen, remained intact (Nir, 1965). On rehydration, Hill reaction was restored almost to the level of continuously turgid leaves, although restoration of photophosphorylation was both slower and, at best, partial. No information was given about the reversibility of the changes in chloroplast structure.

Similar results were obtained by Santarius and Ernst (1967) and Santarius and Heber (1967) with spinach and beet chloroplasts. They dehydrated the isolated chloroplasts above $CaCl_2$ at 2°C until the chloroplasts had lost up to 99% of their water content, rehydrated them and tested their ability to carry out Hill reaction and photophosphorylation. Photophosphorylating ability was lost before the ability to carry out Hill reaction. Dehydration apparently caused denaturation of proteins as there was a considerable increase in free SH groups; but

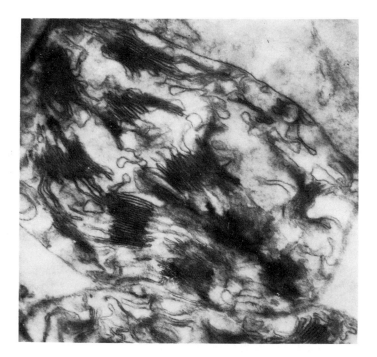

FIG. 1. A chloroplast from a leaf of a swiss chard plant that lost turgor due to cessation of irrigation. × 23,500.

addition of sucrose to the chloroplast suspension gave protection, to some extent, from such protein denaturation. In these studies the critical water loss was found to be between 10 and 15% of chloroplast water content.

Giles et al. (1974) studied ultrastructural changes in the mesophyll and bundle sheath cells of maize leaves in response to water stress. Mesophyll cells were more sensitive to water stress than bundle sheath cells. In the mesophyll cells at a water potential of -1.35 MPa the outer membrane of the chloroplast was swollen and cytoplasmic vesicles appeared, while at -1.9 MPa the chloroplasts were destroyed in 25% of the mesophyll cells, such damage being random and irreversible. In the remaining 75% of the cells, the chloroplasts were swollen and osmiophilic droplets were abundant, but the grana were not displaced. Twenty hours after rewatering, chloroplast structure returned to normal in the viable 75% of the cells. In all bundle sheath cells, however, the damage was much less apparent and completely reversible.

These results may be compared with those of Alberte et al. (1977) showing the loss of chlorophyll from maize leaves upon water stress, which resulted in chlorophyll content falling to almost 60% of control 8 d after irrigation. On rewatering, chlorophyll content began to rise immediately. This loss of chlorophyll occurred mainly from mesophyll cells and could be accounted for by the loss of chloroplast membranes. In cotton, as in Swiss chard, a loss of chloroplast membrane integrity under water stress was correlated with increased phosphatase activity localized on or near the chloroplast membranes (Nir & Poljakoff-Mayber, 1966; Vieira de Silva et al., 1974). Sorghum plants were much less sensitive to water stress than maize (Beardsell & Cohen, 1975; Giles et al., 1976), and reversible swelling of chloroplast membranes occurred only when leaf water potential had fallen to -3.4 MPa.

Wheat chloroplasts also showed swelling when the water potential dropped below -0.9 MPa, but in this case the main damage was not destruction of the chloroplast membranes but extreme vesiculation, the whole chloroplast appearing like a sack with vesicles (Freeman & Duysen, 1975). In contrast, Mitchell grass (*Astrella lappacacea*) showed very high resistance to dehydration; practically no changes were observed in the bundle sheath cells at a water potential of -1.2 MPa, and mesophyll cells were only slightly affected, the changes being completely reversible on return to normal conditions (Mittelheuser, 1977).

Proplastids in maize embryos (Crevecoeur et al., 1976) and roots (Nir et al., 1969) subject to dehydration appeared very swollen and could hardly be distinguished from swollen mitochondria or lysosomes. Proplastid development in leaves of jack bean was inhibited by relatively slight dehydration (Bourque et al., 1975). In plants grown in the dark and then exposed to light in an atmosphere of 85–90% relative humidity, the development of the prolamellar body was well advanced after 2 h; but if the exposure to light was in an atmosphere of only 25% relative humidity, development of the prolamellar body was delayed by at least 24 h. This is indirect evidence of an effect of water stress on membrane formation in the chloroplast.

In summary, the main damage to the chloroplast caused by water stress includes structural changes resulting from excessive swelling, distortion of the lamellae (first intergranal and then granal), vesiculation and the appearance of lipid droplets.

The appearance of osmiophilic droplets in stress-damaged chloroplasts suggests a separation of the lipid and protein phases in the membrane structure. These droplets may function as a possible trigger for further structural and functional changes in the chloroplast, as fatty acids (like linoleic acid, Okamoto & Katoh, 1977; Okamoto et al., 1977) are known to bind to chloroplasts (Cohen et al., 1969) and to damage them (McCarthy & Jagendorff, 1961).

A clear case of extreme drought resistance in chloroplasts occurred in mosses which lost more than 80% of their fresh weight by desiccation, but which returned to normal function after 24 h rehydration (Tucker et al., 1975). On rehydration the chloroplast and general cell structure appeared damaged. The chloroplasts were irregular in shape and swollen, with the outer membrane wrinkled and separated from the thylakoids, which also appeared non-compact, slightly swollen and split in the middle. These changes were considered to be due to the sudden entry of water, but 24 h later the whole structure was repaired and appeared normal. Drought resistance in this case seems due to the ability of the cellular and subcellular membranes to regenerate and undergo self-repair.

Desiccation-tolerant angiosperms are known among the Velloziaceae. They can be dried in the laboratory to 0% relative humidity and on rehydration complete viability is regained. In *Xerophyta villosa* desiccation was accompanied by destruction of the chloroplast's internal structure and loss of chlorophyll. In leaves with 42% relative water content no proper grana could be recognized but stacks of elongated vesicles were observed. On complete desiccation only proplastid-like structures could be identified (Hallam & Luff, 1980a). In *Talbotia elegans*, however, at relative water content of 38%, although granal structure and the thylakoids were completely disorganized, no loss of chlorophyll occurred. Some "staircase stacking" of membranes remained, which probably served as centres of regeneration of chloroplast structure following regeneration. The chloroplast RNA was retained in the dry state, and it seems likely that enzyme synthesis could be resumed on rehydration (Hallam & Gaff, 1978; Hallam & Luff, 1980b). These authors used anhydrous fixatives for electron microscopy.

At least in these two cases it appears as though the maintenance of activity of the photosynthetic apparatus depends on the resistance to dehydration of at least some of the membranal structures, as well as the capability for membrane regeneration and self-repair.

III. CHANGES INDUCED BY WATER STRESS IN MITOCHONDRIAL STRUCTURE AND FUNCTION

Mitochondria isolated from wilted tissue have been found to be uncoupled (Zholkevich & Rogacheva, 1968). Water stress in roots of maize, following equilibration above NaCl or glycerol solutions, caused a reduction in the oxygen consumption of the root tissue. However, the dehydrogenase and cytochrome oxidase activities of mitochondria isolated from such roots was increased (Nir, 1969; Nir et al., 1970b). Loss of 70% of the fresh weight resulted in a 400% increase in the specific activity of the cytochrome oxidase.

In the cells of control roots, mitochondria appeared elongated or ellipsoid (Fig. 2), and in a combined cytochemical-EM investigation at least two types of mitochondria could be distinguished: normal ellipsoid, the cristae of which showed clear cytochrome oxidase activity, and more rounded ones devoid of cytochrome oxidase activity.

In the cells of roots exposed to water stress, mitochondria appeared swollen (rounded rather than ellipsoid) and devoid of cristae (Fig. 3). However, on cytochemical investigation, cristae clearly showing cytochrome oxidase activity, could be observed (Fig. 4). Moreover, the number of active mitochondria per cell increased considerably, confirming the observed increase in cytochrome oxidase activity. It appears, therefore, that severe water stress did not result in destruction of the cristae, but rather induced some change of membrane structure which caused a loss of ability to bind OsO_4. Swollen mitochondria, practically without cristae, were also reported to occur in maize embryos

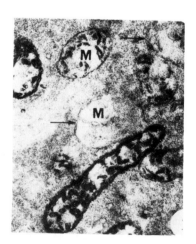

FIG. 2. Mitochondria from a fully turgid maize root tip, treated to show cytochrome oxidase activity. Note the ellipsoid form of the mitochondria. Arrows show more rounded mitochondria that do not show cytochrome oxidase activity. × 17,000. (From Nir et al., 1970b.)

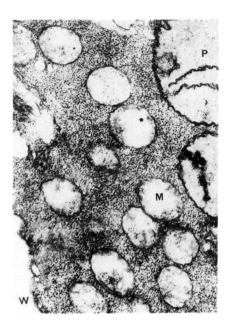

FIG. 3. Mitochondria from maize root tip after exposure to water stress. Tissue lost 11% of its fresh weight. Mitochondria (M) are swollen, rounded and cristae are hardly distinguishable. Between the mitochondria numerous monosomes can be seen. W—cell wall, P—proplastid. × 22,000. (From Nir and Poljakoff-Mayber, unpublished.)

FIG. 4. Mitochondria as in Figure 3, but treated to show cytochrome oxidase activity. × 31,000. (From Nir et al., 1970b.)

allowed to imbibe water and then dehydrated (Crevecoeur et al., 1976) and in the sporangia of certain fungi subjected to water stress (Cohen et al., 1974).

The cristae are considered to consist of structural proteins, enzymes and lipids (Lehninger, 1964), and the appearance of numerous lipid droplets in cells exposed to water stress suggest that some of these cristae lipids are lost to the cytoplasm. This is supported by the observation of a change in their ability to bind osmium (Nir et al., 1969, 1970b). Apparently this change also increased the permeability or induced leakiness of the mitochondrial membrane, resulting in easier access of exogenous cytochrome to the cytochrome oxidase. Some cytochrome oxidase activity also appeared in the supernatant after sedimentation of the mitochondria. Further indirect evidence of membrane changes in mitochondria isolated from water-stressed maize seedlings was deduced by Miller et al. (1971) from measurements of the NADH-dependent swelling-contracting process.

"Cristaeless" mitochondria have also been reported to exist in dry seeds (Sato & Asahi, 1975) but in this tissue it was not a case of the loss of their osmophilic character, as in stressed maize roots. Nawa and Asahi (1973a, 1973b) and Sato and Asahi (1975) showed that in dry pea seeds the existing mitochondria were immature, and upon imbibition there was biogenesis of cristae from protein and phospholipid already existing, apparently in the mitochondria or the cytoplasm. Similar ideas about the reassembly of mitochondrial structure in the cotyledons of pea seeds during germination were advanced by Solomos et al. (1972). This process required no new protein synthesis and was completed apparently during the first 6 h of imbibition (Nawa & Asahi, 1973a, 1973b). If the hydrated seeds were dehydrated once more, malic dehydrogenase and cytochrome oxidase activities were again reduced, only to reappear upon rehydration. NADH-cytochrome C reductase appears to respond in a similar manner (Eldan & Mayer, 1972; see Table I).

These data suggested that the changes induced in mitochondria by initial hydration of seeds were reversible on dehydration. However, it was shown for maize seeds (Crevecoeur et al., 1976) that this dehydration–rehydration process was effective only during the first 36 h of imbibition. If it was applied 72 h after the initiation of imbibition, the embryos could not resume growth on rehydration, although they were able to incorporate amino acids into protein. It seems, therefore, that between 36 h and 72 h after the beginning of growth of the embryo some qualitative, irreversible change occurred later in imbibition, after which the mitochondria appeared to have lost the ability for self-repair or reassembly of membranes. At such a stage of development, dehydration might cause leakiness of the organelle, as occurred in the experiments of Nir et al. (1970b) with maize root tips.

A lack of correlation between oxygen consumption by the tissue, or the mitochondria themselves, and the dehydrogenase or oxidative ability of the

TABLE I

Changes in malic dehydrogenase and cytochrome oxidase activity of mitochondria from cotyledons of pea seeds, and changes in NADH-cytochrome c reductase of lettuce seeds that were subjected to hydration-dehydration-rehydration treatment. Initial weight of pea seeds — 3 g, initial weight of lettuce seeds — 1 g.[a]

	Hydration time (h)	Weight of seeds (g)	Dehydration	Rehydration	Enzyme activity as % of hydrated		
					Malic dehydrogenase	Cytochrome oxidase	Cytochrome c reductase
Pea seeds	6	4.7	−	−	100	100	−
	6	3.6	+	−	47	75	−
	18	5.4	−	−	100	109	−
	18	3.7	+	−	63	47	−
	18	5.6	+	+	116	−	−
Lettuce seeds	0	1.1	−	−	−	100	100
	3	1.6	−	−	−	180	262
	3	1.0	+	−	−	100	100
	3	1.55	+	+	−	−	250

[a]Calculated from data of Nawa and Asahi (1973a) and Eldan and Mayer (1972), for peas and lettuce, respectively.

mitochondria was shown with animal (Raison et al., 1971a, 1971b; Campbell et al., 1975) and plant mitochondria (Campbell et al., 1976) exposed to a high solute concentration. It has been suggested that solutes at high concentration (above 500 mM) interfere with the molecular arrangement of the membrane lipids (Zimmer et al., 1972) and this process may be similar to dehydration. Another reason for such a lack of correlation may be disturbances in protein turnover; thus, treatment of lima bean axes with cycloheximide resulted in decreased oxygen consumption even though the number of mitochondria per cell increased (Klein et al., 1971).

IV. EFFECT OF WATER STRESS ON PROTEIN SYNTHESIZING APPARATUS

Another marked change in plant tissue due to water stress occurs in the protein synthesizing apparatus. In a normal cell, a clear polysomal arrangement can be distinguished (Fig. 5), but dissociation of polysomes and an accumulation of monosomes occurs when tissue is exposed to water stress (Clark et al., 1964; West, 1966; Genkel et al., 1967). In parallel with these changes, the capacity for protein synthesis also decreases considerably in response to water stress (Ben-Zioni et al., 1967; Sturani et al., 1968; Hsiao, 1970). Such changes have been shown to occur in castor bean endosperm, bean cotyledons, tobacco leaves and other plant tissue. Hsiao (1970) reported disintegration of polysomes in maize coleoptile node tissue in response to a water stress of only −0.5 MPa, and a considerable decrease in polysomes could be observed in pumpkin seedlings exposed to a stress of −0.4 MPa for only 10 min (Rhodes & Matsuda, 1976). The meristimatic cells of the wheat apex survived water stress better than the expanded leaves which died when the water potential reached −3.5 MPa; the apex cells survived −6.0 MPa and commenced growth on rehydration. The polysome population in the apical cells was reduced during the stress period from 50% of the total ribosome population to only 10 (Barlow et al., 1977).

With maize root, Nir (1969) and Nir et al. (1970c) showed that, under normal conditions, at least 30% of the ribosomal population was heavier than 77S. In root tips which were allowed to lose 25% of their fresh weight, this fraction of ribosomes (77S+) decreased to less than 20%, and in root tips which had lost 50% or more of their fresh weight the heavier ribosome population was only 8% of the total. In the electron micrograph only monosomes could be observed (Fig. 3), and the ability to incorporate amino acids into protein was practically lost. On rehydration, polysomes were reassembled and protein synthesis restored.

In the desiccation-tolerant *Talbotia elegans* (Hallam & Luff, 1980b), a completely opposite effect was observed. With the decrease in relative water content of the leaves to 50%, the number of polysomes increased as did the ability to incorporate ^{14}C-amino acids into a TCA-insoluble precipitate. It appears, therefore, that the processes in plants with low drought tolerance are not the same as those in desiccation-tolerant plants and in seeds that normally undergo a desiccation–hydration cycle. In the low tolerance plants, the ability

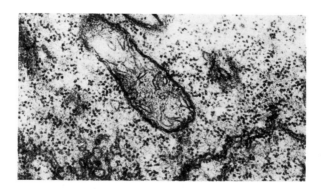

FIG. 5. Normal polysomal arrangement in turgid maize root tip. A normal mitochondrion and a few strands of ER are also visible. × 43,000. (From Nir et al., 1970c.)

to preserve the integrity of polysomes for longer periods may be correlated with their drought tolerance. However, as shown by *Talbotia* (see above) this is not the case for desiccation-tolerant plants, in which other factors besides the preservation of a stable protein synthesizing complex may be more important in determining the level of tolerance.

V. CHANGES OCCURRING IN THE NUCLEUS AND CYTOPLASMIC MEMBRANES DUE TO WATER STRESS

The most significant change that invariably accompanied water stress in the studies by Nir (1969) and Nir et al. (1970a) was in the nucleus. In the normal nucleus chromatin was more or less evenly distributed (Fig. 6), but water stress induced the aggregation of chromatin into big masses around the nucleolus (Fig. 7). This ring of chromatin formed on water stress resembled the arrangement of the chromatin during mitosis, and on severe dehydration this change in arrangement of chromatin was very extensive (Fig. 8). Aggregation was reversed when water stress was relieved. A similar finding was reported by Crevecoeur et al. (1976) and it may be indicative of damage induced by water stress.

In the cytoplasm itself, numerous changes take place in response to water stress. Long units of endoplasmic reticulum (mainly rough ER) were arranged

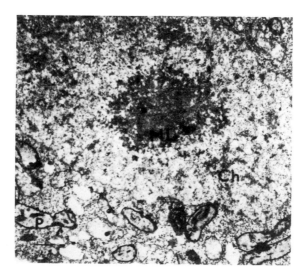

FIG. 6. A normal cell from a turgid maize root. Note dispersed chromatin (Ch) arrangement. NL—nucleolus, P—proplastid. × 9430. (From Nir and Poljakoff-Mayber, unpublished.)

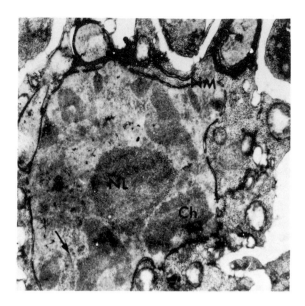

FIG. 7. A cell from a maize root exposed to water stress. Note aggregation of chromatin (Ch). NL—nucleolus, NM—nuclear membrane. × 10,000. (From Nir et al., 1969.)

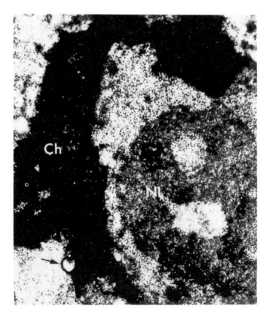

FIG. 8. Severe aggregation of chromatin in a dead maize root cell that lost more than 75% of its fresh weight during dehydration. Ch—chromatin, NL—nucleolus. × 19,800. (From Nir et al., 1969.)

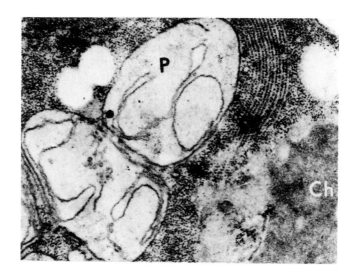

FIG. 9. Strands of rough endoplasmic reticulum (ER) aggregated near a proplastid (P) in a maize root cell that lost 60% of its fresh weight. Ch—chromatin. × 27,500. (From Nir et al., 1969.)

in stacks parallel to each other, in cases of severe dehydration of maize roots (Fig. 9) (Nir, 1969; Nir et al., 1969). When dehydration was mild, such reticular elements did not accumulate but could be found surrounding vacuoles (Fig. 10) (Nir, 1969; Crevecoeur et al., 1976). The endoplasmic reticulum consisted of short, swollen profiles, and the plasmalemma appeared wavy and fragmented and sometimes even formed myelin bodies (Nir, 1969). Osmiophilic lipid droplets became very abundant in the cytoplasm; the tonoplast was severely damaged and, sometimes, under very severe stress, there was a disruption of various organelles (Nir et al., 1970a; Giles et al., 1974; Tucker & Bewley, 1976; Alberte et al., 1977). These changes were generally reversible on rehydration.

VI. GENERAL DISCUSSION

The two main events visible in a cell subjected to water stress are a rearrangement of chromatin and an apparent displacement of lipids from the various cellular membranes to form droplets in the cytoplasm. All other changes and damage induced by water stress could well be consequences of these two central events.

For instance, the condensation of chromatin observed in the nucleus of cells exposed to water stress may repress the transcription of DNA and the

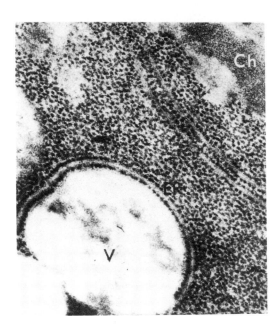

FIG. 10. A vacuole (v) surrounded by a strand of rough endoplasmic reticulum in a maize root cell exposed to water stress; a long strand of ER is also visible. Ch—chromatin. × 54,000. (From Nir and Poljakoff-Mayber, unpublished.)

formation of new mRNA. As a result, polysomes in the protoplasm may be disrupted, protein synthesis inhibited, and enzyme metabolism disturbed. These changes may be reversible if the dehydration of tissue is not too severe, but on severe dehydration they proceed to an irreversible state. It would be of interest to investigate whether these irreversible changes may be accompanied by a more severe degradation of the ribosomal RNA units (18S & 25S) and changes in poly-A-rich RNA, as has been found to occur in seeds during the loss of viability (Osborne, 1977).

    The occurrence of lipid droplets in the cytoplasm on exposure to water stress, and their quick disappearance on rehydration of the tissue, suggests that the lipids are displaced from cellular membranes, and if the dehydration is not severe, they may return to the membranes after rehydration. Loss of water from the cellular membranes may lead to the dissociation of the lipid-protein complexes, and the mitochondrial membranes may become leaky or partially disrupted. Although this change may not cause any direct damage to enzyme protein, it could interfere with the normal oxidation/reduction sequence due to the displacement of the lipid phase necessary for electron transport, and the normal energy generating processes would be interrupted. The energy charge balance is upset and numerous regulatory processes depending on it are disturbed, including polysome assembly and protein synthesis, which, in germinating wheat embryos, depend on the sequential generation of ATP and GTP (Brooker et al., 1977). This is an alternative possibility to account for the polysome disruption observed and, indeed, interference with the energy supply and delay in the normal mRNA turnover, together, are able to bring about many of the secondary features of damage caused to the plant by water stress.

Displacement of the membranal lipids and disruption of the normal ribosomal structure in the chloroplast result in change of the lamellar structure and destruction of the chlorophyll a/b-protein complex (Alberte et al., 1977). As a result, the efficiency of the photosynthetic unit is lowered, the photosynthetic electron transport chain becomes inefficient and photosynthetic energy-yielding processes and the photochemical activity of the chloroplast are inhibited.

In maturing seeds, during desiccation, structural changes were very similar to those occurring in other plant tissue exposed to water stress (e.g., Klein & Pollock, 1968). During germination all structures returned to normal (Klein & Ben-Shaul, 1966) and the seeds became less leaky (Mayer, 1977). Seeds can withstand hydration–dehydration cycles without loss of viability only if the events of germination do not proceed too far. The "point of no return" is apparently associated with onset of DNA synthesis and replication of the genome (Deltour & Jacqmard, 1974), i.e., the *loss* of resistance apparently depends on some change in the DNA-protein (histone?) bonding (Billett & Barry, 1979; Nagl, 1976). Nothing is known, as yet, about the formation of such bonds, or complexes, that confer tolerance to desiccation on the maturing seed.

Desiccation-resistant plants seem able to preserve their membranal structure during desiccation even though the organization of the organelles is sufficiently disturbed to make it impossible to recognize the usual identifying characteristics with the fixatives and stains presently available (Hallam & Luff, 1980a, 1980b).

The sequence of events suggested above, and the possibilities raised for resistance mechanisms in desiccation-tolerant plants are based on facts involved in water stress-induced damage. Some of it is still speculative, however, and it is hoped that at least some of the possibilities will encourage new avenues of investigation and a further elaboration of existing detail.

Appendix

Comparative Systems of Measurement of Water Status

Bars	Atmospheres	cm (Hg)	lb.in^{-2}	Pascals.m^{-2} Newtons.m^{-2}	Joules.kg^{-1}
.2	.20	15.	2.90	.20E+05	20.
.4	.39	30.	5.80	.40E+05	40.
.6	.59	45.	8.70	.60E+05	60.
.8	.79	60.	11.60	.80E+05	80.
1.0	.99	75.	14.50	.10E+06	100.
1.2	1.18	90.	17.40	.12E+06	120.
1.4	1.38	105.	20.30	.14E+06	140.
1.6	1.58	120.	23.20	.16E+06	160.
1.8	1.78	135.	26.10	.18E+06	180.
2.0	1.97	150.	29.00	.20E+06	200.
2.2	2.17	165.	31.90	.22E+06	220.
2.4	2.37	180.	34.80	.24E+06	240.
2.6	2.57	195.	37.70	.26E+06	260.
2.8	2.76	210.	40.60	.28E+06	280.
3.0	2.96	225.	43.50	.30E+06	300.
3.2	3.16	240.	46.40	.32E+06	320.
3.4	3.36	255.	49.30	.34E+06	340.
3.6	3.55	270.	52.20	.36E+06	360.
3.8	3.75	285.	55.10	.38E+06	380.
4.0	3.95	300.	58.00	.40E+06	400.
4.2	4.15	315.	60.90	.42E+06	420.
4.4	4.34	330.	63.80	.44E+06	440.
4.6	4.54	345.	66.70	.46E+06	460.
4.8	4.74	360.	69.60	.48E+06	480.
5.0	4.93	375.	72.50	.50E+06	500.
5.2	5.13	390.	75.40	.52E+06	520.
5.4	5.33	405.	78.30	.54E+06	540.
5.6	5.53	420.	81.20	.56E+06	560.
5.8	5.72	435.	84.10	.58E+06	580.
6.0	5.92	450.	87.00	.60E+06	600.
6.2	6.12	465.	89.90	.62E+06	620.
6.4	6.32	480.	92.80	.64E+06	640.
6.6	6.51	495.	95.70	.66E+06	660.
6.8	6.71	510.	98.60	.68E+06	680.
7.0	6.91	525.	101.50	.70E+06	700.
7.2	7.11	540.	104.40	.72E+06	720.
7.4	7.30	555.	107.30	.74E+06	740.
7.6	7.50	570.	110.20	.76E+06	760.
7.8	7.70	585.	113.10	.78E+06	780.
8.0	7.90	600.	116.00	.80E+06	800.
8.2	8.09	615.	118.90	.82E+06	820.
8.4	8.29	630.	121.80	.84E+06	840.
8.6	8.49	645.	124.70	.86E+06	860.
8.8	8.69	660.	127.60	.88E+06	880.
9.0	8.88	675.	130.50	.90E+06	900.
9.2	9.08	690.	133.40	.92E+06	920.
9.4	9.28	705.	136.30	.94E+06	940.
9.6	9.48	720.	139.20	.96E+06	960.
9.8	9.67	735.	142.10	.98E+06	980.
10.0	9.87	750.	145.00	.10E+07	1000.

Bars	Atmospheres	cm (Hg)	lb.in^{-2}	Pascals.m^{-2} Newtons.m^{-2}	Joules.kg^{-1}
10.2	10.07	765.	147.90	.10E+07	1020.
10.4	10.26	780.	150.80	.10E+07	1040.
10.6	10.46	795.	153.70	.11E+07	1060.
10.8	10.66	810.	156.60	.11E+07	1080.
11.0	10.86	825.	159.50	.11E+07	1100.
11.2	11.05	840.	162.40	.11E+07	1120.
11.4	11.25	855.	165.30	.11E+07	1140.
11.6	11.45	870.	168.20	.12E+07	1160.
11.8	11.65	885.	171.10	.12E+07	1180.
12.0	11.84	900.	174.00	.12E+07	1200.
12.2	12.04	915.	176.90	.12E+07	1220.
12.4	12.24	930.	179.80	.12E+07	1240.
12.6	12.44	945.	182.70	.13E+07	1260.
12.8	12.63	960.	185.60	.13E+07	1280.
13.0	12.83	975.	188.50	.13E+07	1300.
13.2	13.03	990.	191.40	.13E+07	1320.
13.4	13.23	1005.	194.30	.13E+07	1340.
13.6	13.42	1020.	197.20	.14E+07	1360.
13.8	13.62	1035.	200.10	.14E+07	1380.
14.0	13.82	1050.	203.00	.14E+07	1400.
14.2	14.02	1065.	205.90	.14E+07	1420.
14.4	14.21	1080.	208.80	.14E+07	1440.
14.6	14.41	1095.	211.70	.15E+07	1460.
14.8	14.61	1110.	214.60	.15E+07	1480.
15.0	14.81	1125.	217.50	.15E+07	1500.
15.2	15.00	1140.	220.40	.15E+07	1520.
15.4	15.20	1155.	223.30	.15E+07	1540.
15.6	15.40	1170.	226.20	.16E+07	1560.
15.8	15.59	1185.	229.10	.16E+07	1580.
16.0	15.79	1200.	232.00	.16E+07	1600.
16.2	15.99	1215.	234.90	.16E+37	1620.
16.4	16.19	1230.	237.80	.16E+07	1640.
16.6	16.38	1245.	240.70	.17E+07	1660.
16.8	16.58	1260.	243.60	.17E+07	1680.
17.0	16.78	1275.	246.50	.17E+07	1700.
17.2	16.98	1290.	249.40	.17E+07	1720.
17.4	17.17	1305.	252.30	.17E+07	1740.
17.6	17.37	1320.	255.20	.18E+07	1760.
17.8	17.57	1335.	258.10	.18E+07	1780.
18.0	17.77	1350.	261.00	.18E+07	1800.
18.2	17.96	1365.	263.90	.18E+07	1820.
18.4	18.16	1380.	266.80	.18E+07	1840.
18.6	18.36	1395.	269.70	.19E+07	1860.
18.8	18.56	1410.	272.60	.19E+07	1880.
19.0	18.75	1425.	275.50	.19E+07	1900.
19.2	18.95	1440.	278.40	.19E+07	1920.
19.4	19.15	1455.	281.30	.19E+07	1940.
19.6	19.35	1470.	284.20	.20E+07	1960.
19.8	19.54	1485.	287.10	.20E+07	1980.
20.0	19.74	1500.	290.00	.20E+07	2000.

Bars	Atmospheres	cm (Hg)	lb.in^{-2}	Pascals.m^{-2} Newtons.m^{-2}	Joules.kg^{-1}
20.2	19.94	1515.	292.90	.20E+07	2020.
20.4	20.13	1530.	295.80	.20E+07	2040.
20.6	20.33	1545.	298.70	.21E+07	2060.
20.8	20.53	1560.	301.60	.21E+07	2080.
21.0	20.73	1575.	304.50	.21E+07	2100.
21.2	20.92	1590.	307.40	.21E+07	2120.
21.4	21.12	1605.	310.30	.21E+07	2140.
21.6	21.32	1620.	313.20	.22E+07	2160.
21.8	21.52	1635.	316.10	.22E+07	2180.
22.0	21.71	1650.	319.00	.22E+07	2200.
22.2	21.91	1665.	321.90	.22E+07	2220.
22.4	22.11	1680.	324.80	.22E+07	2240.
22.6	22.31	1695.	327.70	.23E+07	2260.
22.8	22.50	1710.	330.60	.23E+07	2280.
23.0	22.70	1725.	333.50	.23E+07	2300.
23.2	22.90	1740.	336.40	.23E+07	2320.
23.4	23.10	1755.	339.30	.23E+07	2340.
23.6	23.29	1770.	342.20	.24E+07	2360.
23.8	23.49	1785.	345.10	.24E+07	2380.
24.0	23.69	1800.	348.00	.24E+07	2400.
24.2	23.89	1815.	350.90	.24E+07	2420.
24.4	24.08	1830.	353.80	.24E+07	2440.
24.6	24.28	1845.	356.70	.25E+07	2460.
24.8	24.48	1860.	359.60	.25E+07	2480.
25.0	24.67	1875.	362.50	.25E+07	2500.
25.2	24.87	1890.	365.40	.25E+07	2520.
25.4	25.07	1905.	368.30	.25E+07	2540.
25.6	25.27	1920.	371.20	.26E+07	2560.
25.8	25.46	1935.	374.10	.26E+07	2580.
26.0	25.66	1950.	377.00	.26E+07	2600.
26.2	25.86	1965.	379.90	.26E+07	2620.
26.4	26.06	1980.	382.80	.26E+07	2640.
26.6	26.25	1995.	385.70	.27E+07	2660.
26.8	26.45	2010.	388.60	.27E+07	2680.
27.0	26.65	2025.	391.50	.27E+07	2700.
27.2	26.85	2040.	394.40	.27E+07	2720.
27.4	27.04	2055.	397.30	.27E+07	2740.
27.6	27.24	2070.	400.20	.28E+07	2760.
27.8	27.44	2085.	403.10	.28E+07	2780.
28.0	27.64	2100.	406.00	.28E+07	2800.
28.2	27.83	2115.	408.90	.28E+07	2820.
28.4	28.03	2130.	411.80	.28E+07	2840.
28.6	28.23	2145.	414.70	.29E+07	2860.
28.8	28.43	2160.	417.60	.29E+07	2880.
29.0	28.62	2175.	420.50	.29E+07	2900.
29.2	28.82	2190.	423.40	.29E+07	2920.
29.4	29.02	2205.	426.30	.29E+07	2940.
29.6	29.22	2220.	429.20	.30E+07	2960.
29.8	29.41	2235.	432.10	.30E+07	2980.
30.0	29.61	2250.	435.00	.30E+07	3000.

Bars	Atmospheres	cm (Hg)	lb.in^{-2}	Pascals.m^{-2} Newtons.m^{-2}	Joules.kg^{-1}
30.2	29.81	2265.	437.90	.30E+07	3020.
30.4	30.00	2280.	440.80	.30E+07	3040.
30.6	30.20	2295.	443.70	.31E+07	3060.
30.8	30.40	2310.	446.60	.31E+07	3080.
31.0	30.60	2325.	449.50	.31E+07	3100.
31.2	30.79	2340.	452.40	.31E+07	3120.
31.4	30.99	2355.	455.30	.31E+07	3140.
31.6	31.19	2370.	458.20	.32E+07	3160.
31.8	31.39	2385.	461.10	.32E+07	3180.
32.0	31.58	2400.	464.00	.32E+07	3200.
32.2	31.78	2415.	466.90	.32E+07	3220.
32.4	31.98	2430.	469.80	.32E+07	3240.
32.6	32.18	2445.	472.70	.33E+07	3260.
32.8	32.37	2460.	475.60	.33E+07	3280.
33.0	32.57	2475.	478.50	.33E+07	3300.
33.2	32.77	2490.	481.40	.33E+07	3320.
33.4	32.97	2505.	484.30	.33E+07	3340.
33.6	33.16	2520.	487.20	.34E+07	3360.
33.8	33.36	2535.	490.10	.34E+07	3380.
34.0	33.56	2550.	493.00	.34E+07	3400.
34.2	33.76	2565.	495.90	.34E+07	3420.
34.4	33.95	2580.	498.80	.34E+07	3440.
34.6	34.15	2595.	501.70	.35E+07	3460.
34.8	34.35	2610.	504.60	.35E+07	3480.
35.0	34.54	2625.	507.50	.35E+07	3500.
35.2	34.74	2640.	510.40	.35E+07	3520.
35.4	34.94	2655.	513.30	.35E+07	3540.
35.6	35.14	2670.	516.20	.36E+07	3560.
35.8	35.33	2685.	519.10	.36E+07	3580.
36.0	35.53	2700.	522.00	.36E+07	3600.
36.2	35.73	2715.	524.90	.36E+07	3620.
36.4	35.93	2730.	527.80	.36E+07	3640.
36.6	36.12	2745.	530.70	.37E+07	3660.
36.8	36.32	2760.	533.60	.37E+07	3680.
37.0	36.52	2775.	536.50	.37E+07	3700.
37.2	36.72	2790.	539.40	.37E+07	3720.
37.4	36.91	2805.	542.30	.37E+07	3740.
37.6	37.11	2820.	545.20	.38E+07	3760.
37.8	37.31	2835.	548.10	.38E+07	3780.
38.0	37.51	2850.	551.00	.38E+07	3800.
38.2	37.70	2865.	553.90	.38E+07	3820.
38.4	37.90	2880.	556.80	.38E+07	3840.
38.6	38.10	2895.	559.70	.39E+07	3860.
38.8	38.30	2910.	562.60	.39E+07	3880.
39.0	38.49	2925.	565.50	.39E+07	3900.
39.2	38.69	2940.	568.40	.39E+07	3920.
39.4	38.89	2955.	571.30	.39E+07	3940.
39.6	39.09	2970.	574.20	.40E+07	3960.
39.8	39.28	2985.	577.10	.40E+07	3980.
40.0	39.48	3000.	580.00	.40E+07	4000.

References

Abe, S., and Kaneda, T. (1973). Studies on the effect of marine products on cholesterol metabolism in rats VIII. The isolation of a hypocholesterolemic substance from green layer. *Bull. Jpn. Soc. Sci. Fish.* **39**, 383–389.

Abrol, Y. P., and Nair, T. V. R. (1978). *In* "Nitrogen Assimilation and Crop Productivity" (S. P. Sen, Y. P. Abrol and S. K. Sinha, eds.), Assoc. Publishing Comp., New Delhi.

Ackerman, D., and List, P. H. (1958). The occurrence of herzynine, ergothionine, homarine, trigonelline, glycinebetaine, choline, trimethylamine, adenine and of almost all amino acids of proteins in King Crab (*Limulus polyphemus*). *Z. Physiol. Chem.* **313**, 30–36.

Adams, J. A., Johnson, H. B., Bingham, F. T., and Yermanos, D. M. (1977). Gaseous exchange of *Simmondsia chinensis* (Jojoba) measured with a double isotope porometer and related to water stress, salt stress, and nitrogen deficiency. *Crop Sci.* **17**, 11–15.

Adams, J. A., Bingham, F. T., Kaufmann, M. R., Hoffman, G. J., and Yermanos, D. M. (1978). Response of stomata and water, osmotic, and turgor potentials of jojoba to water and salt stress. *Agron. J.* **70**, 381–387.

Ahmad, N. (1978). Aspects of glycinebetaine phytochemistry and metabolic functions in plants. Ph.D. Thesis, Univ. of Wales, Cardiff.

Ahmad, N., and Wyn Jones, R. G. (1978). Influence of glycinebetaine on Na fluxes in barley seedlings. *Proc. Fed. Europ. Plant Physiol. Soc.* p. 190.

AICRPDA (All-India Coordinated Research Project for Dryland Agriculture), (1979). "Improved Agronomic Practices for Dryland Crops in India." Director of Extension, Ministry of Agric. and Irrig., New Delhi.

Alberte, R. S., Thornber, J. P., and Fiscus, E. L. (1977). Water stress effects on the content and organisation of chlorophyll in mesophyll and bundle sheath chloroplasts of maize. *Plant Physiol.* **59**, 351–353.

Alieva, S. A., Tageeva, B. V., Tairbekov, M. G., Kasatkina, V. S., and Vagabova, M. E. (1971). Structural and functional condition of the chloroplasts as a function of the water regime. *Sov. Plant Physiol.* **18**, 416–422.

Allaway, W. G. (1973). Accumulation of malate in guard cells of *Vicia faba* during stomatal opening. *Planta* **110**, 63–70.

Allaway, W. G., and Mansfield, T. A. (1970). Experiments and observations on the after-effect of wilting on stomata of *Rumex sanguineus*. *Can. J. Bot.* **48**, 513–521.

Allaway, W. G., and Milthorpe, F. L. (1976). Structure and functioning of stomata. *In* "Water Deficits and Plant Growth" (T. T. Kozlowski, ed.) Vol. 4, pp. 57–102, Academic Press, New York.

Allaway, W. G., Austin, B., and Slatyer, R. O. (1974). Carbon dioxide and water vapour exchange parameters of photosynthesis in a Crassulacean plant: *Kalanchoë diagremontiana*. *Aust. J. Plant Physiol.* **1**, 397–405.

Al-Saadi, H., and Wiebe, H. H. (1973). Survey of the matric water potential of various plant groups. *Plant Soil* **39**, 253–261.

Al-Saadi, H., and Wiebe, H. H. (1975). The influence of maturity, season and part of plant on matric bound water. *Plant Soil* **43**, 371–376.

Anand, J. C., and Brown, A. D. (1968). Growth rate patterns of the so-called osmophilic and non-osmophilic yeasts in solutions of polyethylene glycol. *J. Gen. Microbiol.* **52**, 205–212.

411

Anderson, W. P. (1976). Transport through roots. *In* "Encycl. Plant Physiol." New Ser. IIB (U. Lüttge and M. G. Pitman, eds) pp. 129–156. Springer-Verlag, Berlin.

Andres, J., and Smith, H. (1976). Evidence for a rapid effect of abscisic acid on amino acid metabolism in *Lemna*. *Plant Sci. Lett.* **6**, 315–318.

Andrews, T. J., Badger, M. R., and Lorimer, G. H. (1975). Factors affecting interconversion between kinetic forms of ribulose diphosphate carboxylase–oxygenase from spinach. *Arch. Biochem. Biophys.* **171**, 93–103.

Anikiev, V. V., and Kuramagomedov, M. K. (1975). Activity of nitrate reductase in leaves of barley shoots at different levels of soil moisture. *Sov. Plant Physiol.* **22**, 293–297.

Anon. (1973). Proline as an index of stress. *Int. Rice Res. Inst. (Los Baños) Annu. Rep.* 1973, pp. 103–104.

Anon. (1975). Proline assay, leaf desiccation. *Int. Rice Res. Inst. (Los Baños) Annu. Rep.* 1975, pp. 154–156.

Antoniw, L. D., and Sprent, J. I. (1978). Metabolites of *Phaseolus vulgaris* nodules. *Phytochemistry* **17**, 675–678.

Aparico-Tejo, P. M., Sánchez-Díaz, M. F., and Peña, J. I. (1980). Nitrogen fixation, stomatal response and transpiration in *Medicago sativa, Trifolium repens* and *T. subterraneum* under water stress and recovery. *Physiol. Plant.* **48**, 1–4.

Ardreeva, S. M. (1971). Betaine content in mushrooms of the order, Agariales. *Mikol. Fitopatol.* **5**, 29–32 (C.A.75 1061032).

Armstrong, J. E., and Jones, R. L. (1973). Osmotic regulation of α-amylase synthesis and polyribosome formation in aleurone cells of barley. *J. Cell Biol.* **59**, 444–455.

Arnon, I. (1975). Physiological principals of dryland crop production. *In* "Physiological Aspects of Dryland Farming" (U.S. Gupta, ed.), pp. 3–145. Oxford Press, New Delhi.

Asher, C. J. (1978). *In* "CRC Handbook in Nutrition and Food" (M. Rechcigl, ed.) Section G, Vol. III, pp. 575–609, CRC Press, Cleveland.

Aspinall, D., Singh, T. N., and Paleg, L. G. (1973). Stress metabolism V. Abscisic acid and nitrogen metabolism in barley and *Lolium temulentum L. Aust. J. Biol. Sci.* **26**, 319–327.

Atkins, C. A., and Canvin, D. T. (1975). Nitrate, nitrite and ammonia assimilation by leaves: effects of inhibitors. *Planta* **123**, 41–51.

Atkinson, M. R., Findlay, G. P., Hope, A. B., Pitman, M. G., Saddler, H. D. W., and West, K. R. (1967). Salt regulation in mangroves *Rhizophora mucronata* Lam. and *Aegialitis annulata* R.Br. *Aust. J. Biol. Sci.* **20**, 589–599.

Aubertin, G. M., Rickman, R. W., and Letey, J. (1966). Plant ethanol content as an index of the soil-oxygen status. *Agron. J.* **58**, 305–307.

Badger, M. R., and Andrews, T. J. (1974). Effects of CO_2, O_2 and temperature on a high-affinity form of ribulose diphosphate carboxylase–oxygenase from spinach. *Biochem. Biophys. Res. Commun.* **60**, 204–210.

Badger, M. R., and Collatz, G. J. (1977). Studies on the kinetic mechanism of ribulose-1, 5-bisphosphate carboxylase and oxygenase reactions, with particular reference to the effect of temperature on kinetic parameters. *Carnegie Inst. Washington Yearb.* **76**, 355–361.

Badger, M. R., Andrews, T. J., and Osmond, C. B. (1974). Detection in C_3, C_4 and CAM plant leaves of a low-K_m (CO_2) form of RuDP carboxylase having high RuDP oxygenase activity at physiological pH. *In* "Proceedings of Third International Congress on Photosynthesis" (M. Avron, ed.), pp. 1421–1429. Elsevier, Amsterdam.

Baginski, R. M., and Pierce, Jr., S. K. (1975). Anaerobiosis: a possible source of osmotic solute for high salinity acclimation in marine molluscs. *J. Exp. Biol.* **62**, 589–598.

Bahr, J. T., and Jensen, R. G. (1974). Ribulose diphosphate carboxylase from freshly ruptured spinach chloroplasts having an *in vivo* K_m (CO_2). *Plant Physiol.* **53**, 39–44.

Baich, A. (1969). Proline synthesis in *Escherichia coli*. A proline inhibitable glutamic acid kinase. *Biochim. Biophys. Acta* **192**, 462–467.

Baich, A. (1971). The biosynthesis of proline in *Escherichia coli*. Phosphate dependent glutamate-γ-semialdehyde dehydrogenase (NADP), the second enzyme in the pathway. *Biochim. Biophys. Acta* **244**, 129–134.

Baich, A., and Pierson, D. J. (1965). Control of proline synthesis in *Escherichia coli*. *Biochim. Biophys. Acta* **104**, 397–404.

Baich, A., and Vogel, H. J. (1962). N-acetyl-γ-glutamokinase and N-acetyl-glutamic-γ-semialdehyde dehydrogenase: Repressible enzymes of arginine synthesis in *Escherichia coli*. *Biochem. Biophys. Res. Comm.* **7**, 491–496.

Bal, A. R. (1976). Salinity tolerance through seed treatment with proline. *Biol. Plant.* (Praha) **18**, 227–229.

Balasubramanian, V., Rajagopal, V., and Sinha, S. K. (1974). Stability of nitrate reductase under moisture and salt stress in some crops. Breeding Researches In Asia and Oceania, *Indian J. Genet.* **34A**, 1055–1061.

Banerjee, S. K., and Rupley, J. A. (1973). Temperature and pH dependence of the binding of oligosaccharides to lysozyme. *J. Biol. Chem.* **248**, 2117–2124.

Barber, D. A. and Koontz, H. V. (1963). Uptake of dinitrophenol and its effect on transpiration and calcium accumulation in barley seedlings. *Plant Physiol.* **38**, 60–66.

Barber, S. A. (1974). Influence of the plant root on ion movement in soil. *In* "The Plant Root and its Environment" (E. W. Carson, ed.), pp. 525–564. Univ. Virginia Press, Charlottesville.

Bardzik, J. M., Marsh, H. V. J., and Havis, J. R. (1971). Effects of water stress on the activities of three enzymes in maize seedlings. *Plant Physiol.* **47**, 828–831.

Barley, K. P. (1970). The configuration of the root system in relation to nutrient uptake. *Adv. Agron.* **22**, 159–201.

Barlow, E. W. R., Munns, R., Scott, N. S., and Reisner, A. H. (1977). Water potential, growth, and polyribosome content of the stressed wheat apex. *J. Exp. Bot.* **28**, 909–916.

Barnard, R. A., and Oaks, A. (1970). Metabolism of proline in maize root tips. *Can. J. Bot.* **48**, 1155–1158.

Barnett, N. M., and Naylor, A. W. (1965). Amino acid and protein synthesis in Bermuda grass during water stress. *Plant Physiol.* **40**, vi.

Barnett, N. M., and Naylor, A. W. (1966). Amino acid and protein metabolism in Bermuda grass during water stress. *Plant Physiol.* **41**, 1222–1230.

Bar-Nun, N. and Poljakoff-Mayber, A. (1977). Salinity stress and the content of proline in roots of *Pisum sativum* and *Tamarix tetragyna*. *Ann. Bot.* **41**, 173–179.

Barrs, H. D. (1973). Controlled environment studies of the effects of variable atmospheric water stress on photosynthesis, transpiration and water status of *Zea mays* L. and other species. *In* "Plant Response to Climatic Factors". Proc. Uppsala Symp., UNESCO, pp. 249–258.

Bartholomew, B. (1973). Drought response in the gas exchange of *Dudleya farinosa* (Crassulaceae) grown under natural conditions. *Photosynthetica* **7**, 114–120.

Basso, L. C., and Smith, T. C. (1974). Effect of mineral deficiency on amine formation in higher plants. *Phytochemistry* **13**, 875–883.

Baveja, S. K., and Singla, R. D. (1969). Investigation of *Evolvulus alsinoides* Linn. (Shankhpushpi). *Indian J. Pharm.* **31**, 108–110.

Beadle, C. L., Stevenson, K. R., Neumann, H. H., Thurtell, G. W., and King, K. M. (1973). Diffusive resistance, transpiration, and photosynthesis in single leaves of corn and sorghum in relation to leaf water potential. *Can. J. Plant Sci.* **53**, 537–544.

Beardsell, M. F., and Cohen, D. (1974). Endogenous abscisic acid–plant water stress relationships under controlled environmental conditions. *In* "Mechanisms of Regulation of Plant Growth" (R. L. Bieleski, A. R. Ferguson, and M. M. Cresswell, eds.), *Roy. Soc. N.Z. Bull.* **12**, pp. 411–415.

Beardsell, M. F., and Cohen, D. (1975). Relationship between leaf water status, abscisic acid levels, and stomatal resistance in maize and sorghum. *Plant Physiol.* **56**, 207–212.

Beers, J. R. (1967). The species distribution of some naturally occurring quaternary ammonium compounds. *Comp. Biochem. Physiol.* **21**, 11–21.

Beevers, L., and Hageman, R. H. (1969). Nitrate reduction in higher plants. *Annu. Rev. Plant Physiol.* **20**, 495–522.

Beevers, L., and Poulson, R. (1972). Protein synthesis in cotyledons of *Pisum sativum* L. I. Changes in cell-free amino acid incorporating capacity during seed development and maturation. *Plant Physiol.* **49**, 476–481.

Begg, J. E., and Torsell, B. W. R. (1974). Diaphotonastic and parahelionastic leaf movements in *Stylosanthes humilis* H. B. K. (Townsville stylo). *In* "Mechanisms of Regulation of Plant Growth" (R. L. Bieleski, A. R. Ferguson, and M. M. Cresswell, eds.), *R. Soc. N.Z., Bull.* **12**, 277–283.

Begg, J. E., and Turner, N. C. (1970). Water potential gradients in field tobacco. *Plant Physiol.* **46**. 343–346.

Begg, J. E., and Turner, N. C. (1976). Crop water deficits. *Advan. Agron.* **28**, 161–217.

Bell, D. T. , Koeppe, D. E., and Miller, R. J. (1971). The effects of drought stress on respiration of isolated corn mitochondria. *Plant Physiol.* **48**, 413–415.

Bello, J., Reise, H. C. A., Vinograd, J. R. (1956). Mechanism of gelation of gelatin. Influence of certain electrolytes on the melting points of gels of gelatin and chemically modified gelatins. *J. Phys. Chem.* **60**, 1299–1306.

Ben-Amotz, A., and Avron, M. (1973). The role of glycerol in the osmotic regulation of the halophilic alga *Dunaliella parva*. *Plant Physiol.* **51**, 875–878.

Benko, B. (1968). The content of some amino-acids in young apple shoots in relation to frost resistance. *Biol. Plant.* **11**, 334–337.

Bennett, O. L., and Doss, B. D. (1960). Effect of soil moisture level on root distribution of cool-season forage species. *Agron. J.* **52**, 204–207.

Benson, A. A., and Atkinson, M. R. (1967). Choline sulphate and phosphate in salt excreting plants. *Fed. Proc.* **26**, 394.

Ben-Zioni, A., and Itai, C. (1972). Short and long-term effects of high temperature (47–49°C) on tobacco leaves. I. Photosynthesis. *Physiol. Plant.* **27**, 216–219.

Ben-Zioni, A., Itai, C., and Vaadia, Y. (1967). Water and salt stress, kinetin and protein synthesis in tobacco leaves. *Plant Physiol.* **42**, 361–365.

Besnier, V., Bazin, M., Marchelidon, J., and Genevot, M. (1969). Étude de la variation du pool intracellulaire des acides aminés libre d'une diatomée marine en fonction de la saltinité. *Bull. Soc. Chim. Biol.* **51**, 1255-1262.

Bethlenfalvay, G. J., and Phillips, D. A. (1977). Ontogenetic interactions between photosynthesis and symbiotic nitrogen fixation in legumes. *Plant Physiol.* **60**, 419–421.

Bewley, J. D. (1973a). Polyribosomes conserved during desiccation of the moss *Tortula ruralis* are active. *Plant Physiol.* **51**, 285–288.

Bewley, J. D. (1973b). Dessication and protein synthesis in the moss *Tortula ruralis*. *Can. J. Bot.* **51**, 203–206.

Bewley, J. D. (1974). Protein synthesis and polyribosome stability upon desiccation of the aquatic moss *Hygrohypnum luridum*. *Can. J. Bot.* **52**, 423–427.

Bewley, J. D. (1979). Physiological aspects of desiccation-tolerance. *Annu. Rev. Plant Physiol.* **30**, 195–238.

Bewley, J. D., and Black, M. (1978). "Physiology and Biochemistry of Seeds in Relation to Germination. 1. Development, Germination and Growth." Springer-Verlag, Berlin. 306 pp.

Bewley, J. D., and Dhindsa, R. S. (1977). Stability of components of the protein synthesizing complex of a plant during desiccation. *In* "Translation of Natural and Synthetic Polynucleotides". (A. B. Legocki, ed.), pp. 386–391. Publishers of Poznań Agricultural University, Poznań.

Bewley, J. D., and Gwóźdź, E. A. (1975). Plant desiccation and protein synthesis. II. On the relationship between endogenous ATP levels and protein synthesizing capacity. *Plant Physiol.* **55**, 1110–1114.

Bewley, J. D., and Larsen, K. (1979). Endosperms and embryos of mature dry castor bean seeds contain active ribosomes. *Phytochemistry* **18**, 1617–1619.

Bewley, J. D., and Larsen, K. (1980). Cessation of protein synthesis in water-stressed pea roots and maize mesocotyls without loss of polyribosomes. Effects of lethal and non-lethal water stress. *J. Exp. Bot.* **31**, 1245–1256.

Bewley, J. D., and Thorpe, T. A. (1974). On the metabolism of *Tortula ruralis* following desiccation and freezing: Respiration and carbohydrate oxidation. *Physiol. Plant.* **32**, 147–153.

Bewley, J. D., Tucker, E. B., and Gwóźdź, E. A. (1974). The effects of stress on the metabolism of *Tortula ruralis*. *In* "Mechanisms of Regulation of Plant Growth" (R. L. Bieleski, A. R. Ferguson, and M. M. Cresswell, eds.), *R. Soc. N.Z., Bull.* **12**, 395–402.

Bewley, J. D., Halmer, P., Krochko, J. E., and Winner, W. E. (1978). Metabolism of a drought-tolerant and a drought-sensitive moss. Respiration, ATP synthesis and carbohydrate status. *In* "Dried Biological Systems" (J. H. Crowe and J. S. Clegg, eds.), Academic Press, New York.

Bieberdorf, P. W. (1938). The cytology and histology of the root nodules of some leguminosae. *J. Am. Soc. Agron.* **30**, 375–389.

Billett, M. A., and Barry, J. M. (1974). Role of histones in chromatin condensation. *Eur. J. Bioch.* **49**, 477–484.

Biscoe, P. V. (1972). The diffusion resistance and water status of leaves of *Beta vulgaris. J. Exp. Bot.* **23**, 930–940.

Björkman, O. (1968). Further studies on differentiation of photosynthetic properties in sun and shade ecotypes of *Solidago virgaurea. Physiol. Plant.* **21**, 84–99.

Björkman, O. (1971). Comparative photosynthetic CO_2 exchange in higher plants. *In* "Photosynthesis and Photorespiration" (M. D. Hatch, C. B. Osmond and R. O. Slatyer, eds.), pp. 18–32. Wiley Interscience, Sydney.

Björkman, O., and Badger, M. (1977). Thermal stability of photosynthetic enzymes in heat- and cool-adapted C_4 species. *Carnegie Inst. Washington Yearb.* **76**, 346–354.

Björkman, O., Boardman, N. K., Anderson, J. M., Thorne, S. W., Goodchild, D. J., and Pyliotis, N. A. (1972). Effect of light intensity during growth of *Atriplex patula* on the capacity of photosynthetic reactions, chloroplast components and structure. *Carnegie Inst. Washington Yearb.* **71**, 115–135.

Björkman, O., Boynton, J., and Berry, J. (1976). Comparison of the heat stability of photosynthesis, chloroplast membrane reactions, photosynthetic enzymes, and soluble protein in leaves of heat-adapted and cold-adapted C_4 species. *Carnegie Inst. Washington Yearb.* **75**, 400–407.

Black, R. F. (1960). Effects of NaCl on the ion uptake and growth of *Atriplex vesicaria* Howard. *Aust. J. Biol. Sci.* **13**, 249–66.

Black, S., and Wright, N. G. (1955). β-aspartokinase and β-aspartyl phosphate. *J. Biol. Chem.* **213**, 27–38.

Blaim, K. (1962). O Wystepowaniu betain I choliny w nasionach. *Rocz. Nauk. Roln.* **86**, 527–531.

Blekhman, G. I. (1977). A possible mechanism behind changes of cytoplasmic ribonuclease activity in leaves of wheat seedlings during dehydration and rehydration. *Sov. Plant Physiol.* **24**, 407–411.

Blekhman, G. I., and Tvorus, E. K. (1974). Intracellular distribution of ribonuclease activity in leaves of wheat seedlings and certain factors behind its increase in the cytoplasmic fraction under the influence of drought. *Sov. Plant Physiol.* **21**, 961–966.

Blum, A. (1974). Genotypic responses in sorghum to drought stress. I. Response to soil moisture stress. *Crop Sci.* **14**, 361–364.

Blum, A. (1975). Infrared photography for selection of dehydration-avoidant *Sorghum* genotypes. *Z. Pflanzenkf. Pflanzenshutz.* **75**, 339–445.

Blum, A., and Ebercon, A. (1976). Genotypic responses in sorghum to drought stress. III. Free proline accumulation and drought resistance. *Crop Sci.* **16**, 428–431.

Blum, A., Schertz, K. F., Toler, R. W., Welch, R. I., Rosenow, D. T., Johnson, J. W., and Clark, L. E. (1978). Selection for drought avoidance in sorghum using aerial infrared photography. *Agron. J.* **70**, 472–477.

Boggess, S. F., and Stewart, C. R. (1976). Contribution of arginine to proline accumulation in water stressed barley leaves. *Plant Physiol.* **58**, 796–797.

Boggess, S. F., and Stewart, C. R. (1980). The relationship between water stress induced proline accumulation and inhibition of protein synthesis in tobacco leaves. *Plant Sci. Lett.* **17**, 245–252.

Boggess, S. F., Paleg, L. G., and Aspinall, D. (1975). Δ^1-pyrroline-5-carboxylic acid dehydrogenase in barley, a proline-accumulating species. *Plant Physiol.* **56**, 259–262.

Boggess, S. F., Aspinall, D., and Paleg, L. G. (1976a). Stress metabolism, IX. The significance of end-product inhibition of proline biosynthesis and of compartmentation in relation to stress-induced proline accumulation. *Aust. J. Plant Physiol.* **3**, 513–525.

Boggess, S. F., Stewart, C. R., Aspinall, D., and Paleg, L. G. (1976b). Effect of water stress on proline synthesis from radioactive precursors. *Plant Physiol.* **58**, 398–401.

Boggess, S. F., Stewart, C. R., and Koeppe, D. E. (1977). Metabolism of proline by wheat mitochondria. *Plant Physiol.* **60**, S–386.

Bokarev, K. S., and Ivanova, R. P. (1971). The effect of certain derivatives and analogs of choline and betaine on content of free amino acids in leaves of two species of potato differing with respect to frost resistance. *Sov. Plant Physiol.* **18**, 302–5.

Boon-Long, T. S. (1941). Transpiration as influenced by osmotic concentration and cell permeability. *Am. J. Bot.* **28**, 333–343.

Borowitzka, L. J. (1974). Physiological aspects of salt tolerance in the unicellular green alga, *Dunaliella*. Ph.D. Thesis, Univ. New South Wales, Australia.

Borowitzka, L. J., and Brown, A. D. (1974). The salt relations of marine and halophilic species of the unicellular green alga, *Dunaliella*. The role of glycerol as a compatible solute. *Arch. Microbiol.* **96**, 37–52.

Borowitzka, L. J., Kessly, D. S., and Brown, A. D. (1977). The salt relations of *Dunaliella*. Further observations on glycerol production and its regulation. *Arch. Microbiol.* **113**, 131–138.

Borowitzka, L. J., Demmerle, S., Mackay, M. A., and Norton, R. S. (1980). Carbon-13 nuclear magnetic resonance study of osmoregulation in a blue-green alga. *Science* **210**, 650–651.

Bourque, D. P., McMillan, P. M., Clingenpeel, W. J., and Naylor, A. W. (1975). Ultrastructural effects of water stress on chloroplast development in Jack beans (*Cavanalia ensiformis* L.D.C.). *Plant Physiol.* **56**, 160–163.

Boussiba, S., and Richmond, A. E. (1976). Abscisic acid and the after-effect of stress in tobacco plants. *Planta* **129**, 217–219.

Boutrais, J. (1977). Une conséquence de la sécheresse: les migrations d'eleveurs vers les Plateaux Camerounais. *In* "Drought in Africa. 2" (D. Dalby, R. J. Harrison Church and F. Bezzaz, eds.), pp. 127–39. International African Institute, London.

Bowes, G., and Ogren, W. L. (1972). Oxygen inhibition and other properties of soybean ribulose 1,5-diphosphate carboxylase. *J. Biol. Chem.* **247**, 2171–2176.

Bowes, G., Ogren, W. L., and Hageman, R. H. (1971). Phosphoglycolate production catalyzed by ribulose diphosphate carboxylase. *Biochem. Biophys. Res. Commun.* **45**, 716–722.

Bowman, M. S., and Rohringer, R. (1970). Formate metabolism and betain formation in healthy and rust infected wheat. *Can. J. Bot.* **48**, 803–811.

Boyer, J. S. (1967). Matric potentials of leaves. *Plant Physiol.* **42**, 213–217.

Boyer, J. S. (1968). Relationship of water potential to growth of leaves. *Plant Physiol.* **43**, 1056–1062.

Boyer, J. S. (1969). Measurement of the water status of plants. *Annu. Rev. Plant Physiol.* **20**, 351–364.

Boyer, J. S. (1970). Differing sensitivity of photosynthesis to low leaf water potentials in corn and soybeans. *Plant Physiol.* **46**, 236–239.

Boyer, J. S. (1971a). Recovery of photosynthesis in sunflower after a period of low leaf water potential. *Plant Physiol.* **47**. 816-820.

Boyer, J. S. (1971b). Resistances to water transport in soybean, bean and sunflower. *Crop Sci.* **11**, 403-407.

Boyer, J. S. (1974). Water transport in plants: mechanisms of apparent changes in resistance during absorption. *Planta* **117**, 187–207.

Boyer, J. S. (1976a). Photosynthesis at low water potentials. *Philos. Trans. R. Soc. London* Ser. B. **273**, 501–512.

Boyer, J. S. (1976b). Water deficits and photosynthesis. *In* "Water Deficits and Plant Growth" (T. T. Kozlowski, ed.), Vol. 4, pp. 153–190. Academic Press, New York.

Boyer, J. S., and Bowen, B. (1970). Inhibition of oxygen evolution in chloroplasts isolated from leaves with low water potentials. *Plant Physiol.* **45**, 612–615.

Brady, C. J., Scott, N. S., and Munns, R. (1974). The interaction of water stress with the senescence pattern of leaves. *In* "Mechanisms of Regulation of Plant Growth" (R. L. Bieleski, A. R. Ferguson, and M. M. Cresswell, eds.), *Roy. Soc. N.Z. Bull.* **12**, p. 403–409.

Brandle, J. R., Hinckley, T. M., and Brown, G. N. (1977). The effects of dehydration–rehydration cycles on protein synthesis of black locust seedlings. *Physiol. Plant.* **40**, 1–5.

Bray, C. M. (1976). Protein synthesis. *In* "Molecular Aspects of Gene Expression in Plants" (J. A. Bryant, ed.), pp. 109–138, Academic Press, London.

Brix, H. (1962). The effect of water stress on the rates of photosynthesis and respiration in tomato plants and loblolly pine seedlings. *Physiol. Plant.* **15**, 10–20.

Brock, T. D. (1975). Salinity and the ecology of *Dunaliella* from Great Salt Lake. *J. Gen. Microbiol.* **89**, 285–292.

Brooker, J. D., Cheung, C. P., and Marcus, A. (1977). Protein synthesis and seed germination. *In* "Physiology and Biochemistry of Seed Dormancy and Germination" (A. A. Kahn, ed.), pp. 347–356. North-Holland, Amsterdam.

Brooker, J. D., Tomaszewski, M., and Marcus, A. (1978). Preformed messenger RNAs and early wheat embryo germination. *Plant Physiol.* **61**, 145–149.

Brown, A. D. (1976). Microbial water stress. *Bacteriol. Rev.* **40**, 803–846.

Brown, A. D., and Borowitzka, L. J. (1979). Halotolerance of *Dunaliella*. *In* "Biochemistry and Physiology of Protozoa" (M. Levandowsky and S. H. Hutner, eds.), Vol. 1, pp. 139–190, Academic Press, New York.

Brown, A. D., and Simpson, J. R. (1972). Water relations of sugar-tolerant yeasts: the role of intracellular poyols. *J. Gen. Microbiol.* **72**, 589–591.

Brown, K. W., Jordan, W. R., and Thomas, J. C. (1976). Water stress induced alterations of the stomatal response to decreases in leaf water potential. *Physiol. Plant.* **37**, 1–5.

Brown, L. M., and Hellebust, J. A. (1978). Sorbitol and proline as intracellular osmotic solutes in the green alga, *Stichococcus bacillaris*. *Can. J. Bot.* **56**, 676–679.

Browning, G., and Saunders, P. F. (1977). Membrane localised gibberellins A$_9$ and A$_4$ in wheat chloroplasts. *Nature* (London) **265**, 375–377.

Bunce, J. A. (1977). Nonstomatal inhibition of photosynthesis at low water potentials in intact leaves of species from a variety of habitats. *Plant Physiol.* **59**, 348–350.

Bunting, A. H., Dennett, M. D., Elston, J., and Milford, J. R. (1976). Rainfall trends in the West African Sahel. *Q.J.R. Meteorol. Soc.* **102**, 59–64.

Burrows, F. J., and Milthorpe, F. L. (1976). Stomatal conductance in the control of gas exchange. *In* "Water Deficits and Plant Growth" (T. T. Kozlowski, ed.), Vol. IV, pp. 103–152. Academic Press, New York.

Burrows, W. (1972). Productivity of an arid zone shrub (*Eremophila gilesii*) community in south-western Queensland. *Aust. J. Bot.* **20**, 317–329.

Burrows, W., and Carr, D. J. (1969). Effect of flooding the root system of sunflower plants on the cytokinin content of xylem sap. *Physiol. Plant.* **22**, 1105–1112.

Bushby, H. V. A., and Marshall, K. C. (1977). Water status of rhizobia in relation to their susceptibility to desiccation and to their protection by montmorillonite. *J. Gen. Microbiol.* **99**, 19–27.

Byerrum, R. U., Ringler, R. L., Hamill, R. L., and Ball, C. D. (1955). Serine and formaldehyde as metabolic precursors for the nicotine N-methyl group. *J. Biol. Chem.* **216**, 371–378.

Byrne, G. F., Begg, J. E., and Hansen, G. K. (1977). Cavitation and resistance to water flow in plant roots. *Agric. Meteorol.* **18**, 21-25.

Caldwell, J. C. (1977). Demographic aspects of drought: an examination of the African drought of 1970-74. *In* "Drought in Africa. 2" (D. Dalby, R. J. Harrison Church, and F. Bezzaz, eds.), pp. 93–100. International African Institute, London.

Caldwell, M. M. (1976). Root extension and water absorption. *In* "Water and Plant Life: Problems and Modern Approaches" (O. L. Lange, L. Kappen and E.-D. Schulze, eds.), pp. 63–85. Springer, Berlin.

Caldwell, M. M., White, R. S., Moore, R. T., and Camp, L. B. (1977). Carbon balance, productivity and water use of cold-winter desert shrub communities dominated by C_3 and C_4 species. *Oecologia* **29**, 275–300.

Calvin, M., and Bassham, J. A. (1962). "The Photosynthesis of Carbon Compounds". W. A. Benjamin, Inc., New York.

Camacho-B., S. E., Hall, A. E., and Kaufmann, M. R. (1974a). Efficiency and regulation of water transport in some woody and herbaceous species. *Plant Physiol.* **54**, 169–172.

Camacho-B., S. E., Kaufmann, M. R., and Hall, A. E. (1974b). Leaf water potential response to transpiration by citrus. *Physiol. Plant.* **31**, 101–105.

Campbell, L. C., Raison J. K., and Brady, C. J. (1975). Factors limiting mitochondrial respiration in media of high solute content. *J. Bioenerg.* **7**, 189–200.

Campbell, L. C., Raison, J. K., and Brady, C. J. (1976). The response of plant mitochondria to media of high solute content. *J. Bioenerg. Biomembr.* **8**, 121-129.

Cannell, R. Q. (1977). Soil aeration and compaction in relation to root growth and soil management. *Appl. Biol.* **2**, 1–86.

Cantoni, G. L. (1960). Onium compounds and their biological significance. *In* "Comparative Biochemistry" (M. Florkin and H. S. Mason, eds.), Vol. 1, pp 181–241. Academic Press, New York.

Cantoni, G. L., and Anderson, D. G. (1956). Enzymatic cleavage of dimethylpropiothetin by *Polysiphonia lanosa*. *J. Biol. Chem.* **222**, 171–177.

Canvin, D. T., and Atkins, C. A. (1974). Nitrate, nitrite and ammonia assimilation by leaves: effect of light, carbon dioxide and oxygen. *Planta* **116**, 207-224.

Canvin, D. T., and Woo, K. C. (1979). The regulation of nitrate reduction in spinach leaves. *Can. J. Bot.* **57**, 1155-1160.

Carruthers, A., Oldfield, J. F. T., and Teague, H. J. (1960). The removal of interfering ions in the determination of betaine in sugar-beet and plant material. *Analyst* (London) **85**, 272–275.

Carter, K. R., Jennings, N. T., Hanus, J., and Evans, H. J. (1978). Hydrogen evolution and uptake by nodules of soybeans inoculated with different strains of *Rhizobium japonicum*. *Can. J. Microbiol.* **24**, 307–311.

Cathey, H. M. (1964). Physiology of growth retarding chemicals. *Annu. Rev. Plant Physiol.* **15**, 271–302.

Challenger, F. (1959). "Aspects of the Organic Chemistry of Sulphur", pp. 32–72. Butterworth, London.

Challenger, F. and Simpson, M. I. (1948). Studies on biological methylation XII. A precursor of the dimethyl sulphide evolved by *Polysiphonia fastigiata.* Dimethyl-2-carboxyethylsulphonium hydroxide and its salts. *J. Chem. Soc.* 1591-1597.

Charley, J. L., and Cowling, S. W. (1968). Changes in soil nutrient status resulting from overgrazing and their consequences in plant communities of semi-arid areas. *Proc. Ecol. Soc. Aust.* **3**, 28–38.

Charreau, C., and Nicou, R. (1971a). L'amelioration du profil cultural dans les sols sableux et sablo-argileux de la zone tropicale seche ouest-africaine et ses incidences agronomiques. *Agron. Trop.* **26**, 209–255.

Charreau, C., and Nicou, R. (1971b), L'amelioration du profil cultural dans les sols sableux et sablo-argileux de la zone tropicale seche ouest-africaine et ses incidences agronomiques. *Agron. Trop.* **26**, 565–631.

Charreau, C., and Nicou, R. (1971c). L'amelioration du profil cultural dans les sols sableux et sablo-argileux de la zone tropicale seche ouest-africaine et ses incidences agronomiques. *Agron. Trop.* **26**, 903–978.

Chartier, P., Chartier, M., and Cátský, J. (1970). Resistances for carbon dioxide diffusion and for carboxylation as factors in bean leaf photosynthesis. *Photosynthetica* **4**, 48–57.

Chatterton, N. J., Hanna, W. W., Powell, J. B., and Lee, D. R. (1975). Photosynthesis and transpiration of bloom and bloomless sorghum. *Can. J. Plant Sci.* **55**, 641–643.

Chen, D., Kessler, B., and Monselise, S. P. (1964). Studies on water regime and nitrogen metabolism of citrus seedlings grown under water stress. *Plant Physiol.* **39**, 379–386.

Chen, D., Sarid, S., and Katchalski, E. (1968). The role of water stress in the inactivation of messenger RNA of germinating wheat embryos. *Proc. Nat. Acad. Sci. USA* **61**, 1378–1383.

Chin, T. Y., Meyer, M. M. Beevers, L. (1969). Abscisic acid-stimulated rootings of stem cuttings. *Planta* **88**, 192–196.

Ching, T. M. (1972). Metabolism of germinating seeds. *In* "Seed Biology" (T. T. Kozlowski, ed.), Vol. II, pp. 103–218. Academic Press, New York.

Chinoy, J. J. (1960). Physiology of drought resistance in wheat. I. Effect of wilting at different stages of growth on survival values of eight varieties of wheat belonging to seven species. *Phyton (Buenos Aires).* **14**, 147–157.

Chittenden, C. G., Laidman, D. L., Ahmad, N., and Wyn Jones, R. G. (1978). Amino acid and quaternary nitrogen compounds in the germinating wheat grain. *Phytochemistry* **17**, 1209–1216.

Cho, I. H. (1977). Studies of the salient metabolites of plant tissues. I. Nitrogen metabolism and proline accumulation in halophytes. *Hanguk Nonghwa Hakhoe Chi* **20**, 221–227.

Chollet, R. (1977). The biochemistry of photorespiration. *Trends Biochem. Sci.* **2**, 155–159.

Chollet, R., and Ogren, W. L. (1972). Oxygen inhibits maize bundle sheath photosynthesis. *Biochem. Biophys. Res. Commun.* **46**, 2062–2066.

Chrispeels, M. J. (1973). Mechanism of osmotic regulation of hydrolase synthesis in aleurone cells of barley: inhibition of protein synthesis. *Biochem. Biophys. Res. Commun.* **53**, 99–104.

Christian, J. H. B., and Waltho, J. A. (1962). Solute concentrations within cells of halophilic and non-halophilic bacteria. *Biochim. Biophys. Acta* **65**, 506–508.

Chu, T. M. (1974). The effect of environmental stress on proline accumulation in barley and radish. Ph.D. thesis. Univ. of Adelaide, South Australia.

Chu, T. M., Aspinall, D., and Paleg, L. G. (1974). Stress metabolism. VI. Temperature stress and the accumulation of proline in barley and radish. *Aust. J. Plant Physiol.* **1**, 87–97.

Chu, T. M., Aspinall, D., and Paleg, L. G. (1976a). Stress metabolism. VII. Salinity and proline accumulation in barley. *Aust. J. Plant Physiol.* **3**, 219–228.

Chu, T. M., Aspinall, D., and Paleg, L. G. (1976b). Stress metabolism. VIII. Specific ion effects on proline accumulation in barley. *Aust. J. Plant Physiol.* **3**, 503–511.

Chu, T. M., Jusaitis, M., Aspinall, D., and Paleg, L. G. (1978). Accumulation of free proline at low temperatures. *Physiol. Plant.* **43**, 254–260.

Clark, M. F., Mathews, R. E. F., and Ralph, R. K. (1964). Ribosomes and polyribosomes in *Brassica pekinensis. Biochim. Biophys. Acta* **91**, 289–304.

Clarkson, D. T., and Robards, A. W., (1974). The endodermis, its structural development and physiological role. *In* "Root Structure and Function" (J. Torrey and D. T. Clarkson, eds.), pp. 415–436. Academic Press, London.

Clarkson, D. T., Robards, A. W., and Sanderson, J. (1971). The tertiary endodermis of barley roots; fine structure in relation to radial transport of ions and water. *Planta* **96**, 292–305.

Cohen, W. S., Nathenson, B., White, J. E., and Brady, M. (1969). Fatty acids as model systems for the action of Ricinus leaf extract on higher plant chloroplasts and algae. *Arch. Biochem. Biophys.* **135**, 21–27.

Cohen, Y., Perl, M., Rotem, J., Eyal, H., and Cohen, J. (1974). Ultrastructural and physiological changes in sporangia of *Pseudoperonospora cubensis* and *Phytophthora infestans* exposed to water stress. *Can. J. Bot.* **52**, 447–450.

Collet, C. F. (1970). Action de l'acide abscissique sur la rhizogenese. *C. R. Hebd. Seances Acad. Sci.* Ser. D. **271**, 667–670.

Collins, J. C., and Kerrigan, A. P. (1974). The effect of kinetin and abscisic acid on water and ion transport in isolated maize roots. *New Phytol.* **73**, 309–314.

Connor, D. J. (1975). Growth, water relations and yield of wheat. *Aust. J. Plant Physiol.* **2**, 353–366.

Connor, D. J., and Tunstall, B. R. (1968). Tissue water relations for brigalow and mulga. *Aust. J. Bot.* **16**, 487–490.

Constable, G. A., and Hearn, A. B. (1978). Agronomic and physiological responses of soybean and sorghum crops to water deficits. I. Growth, development and yield. *Aust. J. Plant Physiol.* **5**, 159–167.

Cooke, R., and Kuntz, I. D. (1974). The properties of water in biological systems. *Annu. Rev. Biophys. Bioeng.* **3**, 95–126.

Corgan, J. N., and Peyton, C. (1970). Abscisic acid levels in dormant peach flower buds. *J. Am. Soc. Hortic. Sci.* **95**, 770–774.

Cornforth, J. W., and Henry, A. J. (1952). The isolation of L-stachydrine from the fruit of *Capparis tomentosa. J. Chem. Soc.* 601–603.

Coughlan, S., and Wyn Jones, R. G. (1980). Some responses of *Spinacea oleracea* to salt stress. *J. Exp. Bot.* **31**, 883–893.

Cowan, I. R. (1965). Transport of water in the soil–plant–atmosphere system. *J. Appl. Ecol.* **2**, 221–239.

Cowan, I. R. (1977). Stomatal behaviour and environment. *Adv. Bot. Res.* **4**, 117–228.

Cowan, I. R., and Farquhar, G. D. (1977). Stomatal function in relation to leaf metabolism and environment. *In* "Integration of Activity in the Higher Plant" (D. H. Jennings, ed.), Vol. 31, pp. 471–505. Symp. Soc. Exp. Biol., Cambridge Univ. Press, London.

Cowan, I. R., and Milthorpe, F. L. (1968). Plant factors influencing the water status of plant tissues. *In* "Water Deficits and Plant Growth" (T. T. Kozlowski, ed.), Vol. I. pp. 137–193. Academic Press, New York.

Crafts, A. S. (1968). Water deficits and physiological processes. *In* "Water Deficit and Plant Growth" (T. T. Kozlowsky, ed.), Vol. II. pp. 85–134. Academic Press, New York.

Craigie, J. S. (1969). Some salinity-induced changes in growth, pigments and cyclohexanetetrol content of *Monochrysis lutheri. J. Fish. Res. Board Can.* **26**, 2959–2967.

Cram, W. J. (1976). Negative feedback regulation of transport in cells. The maintenance of turgor, volume and nutrient supply. *In* "Encycl. Plant Physiol." New Ser. IIA. (U. Lüttge and M. G. Pitman, eds.), pp. 284–316. Springer-Verlag, Berlin.

Crèvecoeur, M., Deltour, R., and Brouchart, R. (1976). Cytological study on water stress during germination of *Zea mays*. *Planta* **132**, 31–41.

Criswell, J. G., Havelka, U. D., Quebedaux, B., and Hardy, R. W. F. (1977). Effect of rhizosphere pO_2 on nitrogen fixation by excised and intact nodulated soybean roots. *Crop Sci.* **17**, 34–44.

Cromwell, B. T. (1950). The micro-estimation and origin of trimethylamine in *Chenopodium vulvaria*. L. *Biochem. J.* **46**, 578–582.

Cromwell, B. T., and Rennie, S. D. (1953). The biosynthesis and metabolism of betaines in plants. I. The estimation and distribution of glycinebetaine in *Beta vulgaris* L. and other plants. *Biochem. J.* **55**, 189–192.

Cromwell, B. T., and Rennie, S. D. (1954a). The biosynthesis and metabolism of betaines in plants. II. The biosynthesis of glycinebetaine in higher plants. *Biochem. J.* **58**, 318–322.

Cromwell, B. T., and Rennie, S. D. (1954b). The biosynthesis and metabolism of betaines in plants. III. Studies on the biosynthesis of precursors of glycinebetaine in seedlings of wheat (*Triticum vulgare*). *Biochem. J.* **58**, 322–326.

Cummins, W. R. (1973). The metabolism of abscisic acid in relation to its reversible action on stomata in leaves of *Hordeum vulgare* L. *Planta* **114**, 159–167.

Cummins, W. R., and Sondheimer, E. (1973). Activity of the asymmetric isomers of abscisic acid in a rapid bioassay. *Planta* **111**, 365–369.

Cummins, W. R., Kende, H., and Raschke, K. (1971). Specificity and reversibility of the rapid stomatal response to abscisic acid. *Planta* **99**, 347–351.

Cutler, J. M., and Rains, D. W. (1978). Effects of water stress and hardening on the internal water relations and osmotic constituents of cotton leaves. *Physiol. Plant.* **42**, 261–268.

Cutler, J. M., Rains, D. W., and Loomis, R. S. (1977). The importance of cell size in the water relations of plants. *Physiol. Plant.* **40**, 255–260.

Dalling, M. J., and Loyn, R. H. (1977). Level of activity of nitrate reductase at the seedling stage, as a predictor of grain nitrogen yield in wheat (*Triticum aestivum* L.). *Aust. J. Agric. Res.* **28**, 1–4.

Danielson, R. E., and Russell, M. B. (1957). Ion absorption by corn roots as influenced by moisture and aeration. *Soil Sci. Soc. Am. Proc.* **21**, 3–6.

Darbyshire, B., and Steer, B. T. (1973). Dehydration of macromolecules. I. Effect of dehydration on indoleacetic acid oxidase, ribonuclease, ribulosediphosphate carboxylase, and ketose-1-phosphate adolase. *Aust. J. Biol. Sci.* **26**, 591–604.

Dart, P. J. (1975). Legume root nodule initiation and development. *In* "The Development and Function of Roots." (J. G. Torrey and D. T. Clarkson, eds.), pp. 467–506. Academic Press, London.

Dasgupta, B., Basu, K., and Dasgupta, S. (1968). Chemical investigation of *Pluchea lanceolata*. II. Identity of pluchine with betaine hydrochloride. *Experientia* **24**, 882.

Dashek, W. V., and Harwood, H. I. (1974). Proline, hydroxyproline and lily pollen tube elongation. *Ann. Bot.* **38**, 947–959.

Da Silva, J. V., Naylor, A. W., and Kramer, P. J. (1974). Some ultrastructural and enzymatic effects of water stress in cotton (*Gossypium hirsutum* L.) leaves. *Proc. Nat. Acad. Sci. U.S.A.* **71**, 3243–3247.

Davenport, D. C., Fisher, M. A., and Hagan, R. M. (1972). Some counteractive effects of antitranspirants. *Plant Physiol.* **49**, 722–724.

Davenport, D. C., Hagan, R. M., and Uriu, K. (1977). Reducing transpiration to conserve water in soil and plants. *Calif. Agric.* **31**, 40–41.

Davidson, N. (1976). "Neurotransmitter Amino Acids". Academic Press, New York.

Davies, W. J. (1977). Stomatal responses to water stress and light in plants grown in controlled environments and in the field. *Crop Sci.* **17**, 735–740.

Davies, W. J. (1978). Some effects of abscisic acid and water stress on stomata of *Vicia faba* L. *J. Exp. Bot.* **29**, 175–182.

Davies, W. J., and Kozlowski, T. T. (1974). Short- and long-term effects of antitranspirants on water relations and photosynthesis of woody plants. *J. Am. Soc. Hortic. Sci.* **99**, 297-304.

Davies, W. J., and Kozlowski, T. T. (1977). Variations among woody plants in stomatal conductance and photosynthesis during and after drought. *Plant Soil* **46**, 435–444.

Davies, W. J., Gill, K., and Halliday, G. (1978). The influence of wind on the behaviour of stomata of photosynthetic stems of *Cytisus scoparius* (L.) Link. *Ann. Bot.* **42**, 1149–1154.

Davis, L. A., and Addicott, F. T. (1972). Abscisic acid: correlations with abscission and with development in cotton fruit. *Plant Physiol.* **49**, 644–648.

Dawson, R. W. C., Elliot, D. C., Elliot, W. H., and Jones, K. M. (1969). "Data for Biochemical Research," 2nd Edition. p. 12. Clarendon Press, Oxford.

Decheva, R., Koseva, D., and Nelchinov, I. (1972). Dynamics of free proline accumulation in *Rosa damascara, Rosa alba* and hybrid *27/51* during an all-year period of development. *Rastenievud, Nauki* **9**, 11–18.

Deckard, E. L., Lambert, R. J., and Hageman, R. H. (1973). Nitrate reductase activity in corn leaves as related to yields of grain and grain protein. *Crop Sci.* **13**, 343–350.

Delaveau, P., Koudogbo, B., and Pousset, J. L. (1973). Alkaloids of capparidaceae. *Phytochemistry* **12**, 2893–2895.

Dell'Aquila, A., Savino, G., and De Leo, P. (1978). Metabolic changes induced by hydration–dehydration treatments in wheat embryos. *Plant Cell Physiol.* **19**, 349–354.

Deltour, R. and Jacqmard, A. (1974). Relation between water stress and DNA synthesis during germination of *Zea mays* L. *Ann. Bot.* **38**, 524–534.

De Luca, P., Alfani, A., and Virzo De Santo, A. (1977). CAM, transpiration and adaptive mechanisms to xeric environments in the succulent Cucurbitaceae, *Bot. Gaz.* (Chicago) **138**, 474–478.

Delwiche, C. C., and Bregoff, H. M. (1957). Pathway of betaine and choline synthesis in *Beta vulgaris. J. Biol. Chem.* **233**, 430–433.

Denmead, O. T., and Millar, B. D. (1976). Water transport in wheat plants in the field. *Agron. J.* **68**, 297–303.

Derera, N. F., Marshall, D. R., and Balaam, L. N. (1969). Genetic variability in root development in relation to drought tolerance in spring wheats. *Exp. Agric.* **5**, 327–337.

Dhindsa, R. S., and Bewley, J. D. (1976a). Plant desiccation: polyribosome loss not due to ribonuclease. *Science* **191**, 181–182.

Dhindsa, R. S., and Bewley, J. D. (1976b). Water stress and protein synthesis. IV. Responses of a drought-tolerant plant. *J. Exp. Bot.* **27**, 513–523.

Dhindsa, R. S., and Bewley, J. D. (1977). Water stress and protein synthesis. V. Protein synthesis, protein stability and membrane permeability in a drought-sensitive and a drought-tolerant moss. *Plant Physiol.* **59**, 295-300.

Dhindsa, R. S., and Bewley, J. D. (1978). Messenger RNA is conserved during drying of drought-tolerant *Tortula ruralis. Proc. Nat. Acad. Sci. U.S.A.* **75**, 842–846.

Dhindsa, R. S., and Cleland, R. E. (1975a). Water stress and protein synthesis. I. Differential inhibition of protein synthesis. *Plant Physiol.* **55**, 778–781.

Dhindsa, R. S., and Cleland, R. E. (1975b). Water stress and protein synthesis. II. Interaction between water stress, hydrostatic pressure, and abscisic acid on the pattern of protein synthesis in *Avena* coleoptiles. *Plant Physiol.* **55**, 782–785.

Dimond, A. E. (1966). Pressure and flow relations in vascular bundles of the tomato plant. *Plant Physiol.* **41**, 119–131.

Dittrich, P., and Raschke, K. (1977). Malate metabolism in isolated epidermis of *Commelina communis* L. in relation to stomatal functioning. *Planta* **134**, 77–81.

Dixon, M., and Webb, E. C. (1961). Enzyme fractionation by salting-out: a theoretical note. *Adv. Protein Chem.* **16**, 197–219.

Doley, D., and Trivett, N. B. A. (1974). Effects of low water potentials on transpiration and photosynthesis in Mitchell grass (*Astrebla lappacea*). *Aust. J. Plant Physiol.* **1**, 539–550.

Domes, W. (1971). Different CO_2-sensitivities of the gas exchange of the two leaf surfaces of *Zea mays*. *Planta* **89**, 47-55.

Domes, W., and Bertsch, A. (1969). CO_2-gaswechsel amphistomatisher blätter. *Planta* **86**, 84-91.

Donald, C. M. (1968). The breeding of crop ideotypes. *Euphytica* **17**, 385–403.

Dörffling, K., Streich, J., Kruse, W., and Muxfeldt, B. (1977). Abscisic acid and the after-effect of water stress on stomatal opening potential. *Z. Pflanzenphysiol.* **81**, 43–56.

Doss, B. D., Ashley, D. A., and Bennett, O. L. (1960). Effect of soil moisture regime on root distribution of warm-season forage species. *Agron. J.* **52**, 569–572.

Downey, R. J. (1973). The multimeric nature of NADPH-nitrate reductase from *Aspergillus nidulans*. *Microbios* **7**, 53–60.

Downton, W. J. S., and Tregunna, E. B. (1968). Photorespiration and glycolate metabolism: a re-examination and correlation of some previous studies. *Plant Physiol.* **43**, 923–929.

Dubé, P. A., Stevenson, K. R., and Thurtell, G. W. (1974). Comparison between two inbred corn lines for diffusive resistances, photosynthesis and transpiration as a function of leaf water potential. *Can. J. Plant Sci.* **54**, 765–770.

Dudman, W. F. (1977). The role of surface polysaccharides in natural environments. *In* "Surface Polysaccharides of the Prokaryotic Cell." (I. W. Sutherland, ed.), pp. 357–414. Academic Press, London.

Dunham, R. J., and Nye, P. H. (1973). The influence of soil water content on the uptake of ions by roots. I. Soil water content gradients near a plane of onion roots. *J. Appl. Ecol.* **10**, 585–598.

Dunham, R. J., and Nye, P. H. (1974). The influence of soil water content on the uptake of ions by roots. II. Chloride uptake and concentration gradients in soil. *J. Appl. Ecol.* **11**, 581–596.

Dunham, R. J., and Nye, P. H. (1976). The influence of soil water content on the uptake of ions by roots. III. Phosphate, potassium, calcium and magnesium uptake and concentration gradients in soil. *J. Appl. Ecol.* **13**, 967–984.

Dunn-Coleman, N. S., and Pateman, J. A. (1975). The regulation of nitrate reductase in the fungus *Aspergillus nidulans*. *Biochem. Soc. 556th Meet.*, London, No. **3**, Pt. I, p. 531.

Du Paul, W. D., and Webb, K. L. (1970). The effect of temperature on salinity induced changes in the free amino acid pool of *Mya arenaria*. *Comp. Biochem. Physiol.* **32**, 785–801.

Duranton, H., and Wurtz, R. (1964). Conversion de l'ornithine en proline dans les tissus de Topinambour cultives *in vitro*. *C. R. Hebd. Seances Acad. Sci. Ser. D.* **259**, 2506–2508.

Duranton, H., and Wurtz, R. (1965). Conversion de l'ornithine en proline dans les tissus de Topinambour. *Physiol. Veg.* **3**, 7–22.

Eder, A., and Huber, W. (1977). About the effect of abscisic acid and kinetin on biochemical changes in *Pennisetum typhoides* during stress conditions. *Z. Pflanzenphysiol.* **84**, 303–311.

Eder, A., Huber, W., and Sankhla, N. (1977). Interaction between salinity and ethylene in nitrogen metabolism of *Pennisetum typhoides* seedlings. *Biochem. Physiol. Pflanz.* **171**, 93–100.

Edgley, M., and Brown, A. D. (1978). Response of xerotolerant and non-tolerant yeasts to water stress. *Gen. Microbiol.* **104**, 343–345.

Ehleringer, J. R. (1976). Leaf absorptance and photosynthesis as affected by pubescence in genus *Encelia*. *Carnegie Inst. Washington Yearb.* **75**, 413–418.

Ehleringer, J. R. (1977). Adaptive value of leaf hairs in *Encelia farinosa*. *Carnegie Inst. Washington Yearb.* **76**, 367–369.

Ehleringer, J., and Björkman, O. (1977). Quantum yields for CO_2 uptake in C_3 and C_4 plants. *Plant Physiol.* **59**, 86–90.

Eilrich, G. L., and Hageman, R. H. (1973). Nitrate reductase activity and its relationship to accumulation of vegetative grain nitrogen in wheat (*Triticum aestivum* L.). *Crop Sci.* **13**, 59–66.

Eisenberg, D., and Kauzmann, W. (1969) "The Structure and Properties of Water". Clarendon Press, Oxford.

El-Beltagy, A. S., and Hall, M. A. (1974). Effect of water stress upon endogenous ethylene levels in *Vicia faba. New Phytol.* **73**, 47–60.

El Damaty, A. H., Kuhn, A. M., and Linser, M. (1964). A preliminary investigation on increasing salt tolerance of plants by application of (2-chlorethyl)-trimethyl ammonium chloride. *Agrochimica* **8**, 129–138.

Eldan, M. and Mayer, A. M. (1972). Evidence for the activation of NADH-cytochrome c reductase during germination of lettuce. *Physiol. Plant.* **26**, 67–72.

Elfving, D. C., Kaufmann, M. R., and Hall, A. E. (1972). Interpreting leaf water potential measurements with a model of the soil–plant–atmosphere continuum. *Physiol. Plant.* **27**, 161–168.

Ellis, R. J., and Hartley, M. R. (1971). Sites of synthesis of chloroplast proteins. *Nature* (London) **233**, 193–196.

Elston, J., Karamanos, A. J., Kassam, A. H., and Wadsworth, R. M. (1976). The water relations of the field bean crop. *Philos. Trans. R. Soc. London* Ser. B. **273**, 581–591.

Elthon, T. E., and Stewart, C. R. (1981). Submitochondrial location and electron transport characteristics of enzymes involved in proline oxidation. *Plant Physiol.* **67**, (in press).

Engeland, R. (1909). Zur kenntris der bestandteile des fleischextraktes. *Ber. Dtsch. Chem. Ges.* **42**, 2457–2462.

Engin, M., and Sprent, J. I. (1973). Effects of water stress on growth and nitrogen fixing activity of *Trifolium repens. New Phytol.* **72**, 117–126.

Epstein, E. (1972). "Mineral Nutrition of Plants: Principles and Perspectives." Wiley, New York.

Epstein, E. (1976). Kinetics of ion transport and the carrier concept. *In* "Encycl. Plant Physiol." New Ser. IIB (U. Lüttge and M. G. Pitman, eds.), pp. 70–94. Springer-Verlag, Berlin.

Ericson, L. E., and Carlson, B. (1953). Occurrence of amino acids, niacin and pantothenic acid in marine algae. *Ark. Kemi* **6**, 511–522.

Esau, K. (1977). "Anatomy of Seed Plants". Wiley, New York.

Evenari, M., Shanan, L., and Tadmor, N. (1971). "The Negev: The Challenge of a Desert". Harvard Univ. Press, Cambridge, Massachusetts.

Evanari, M., Schulze, E.-D., Kappen, L., Buschbom, U., and Lange, O. L. (1975). Adaptive mechanisms in desert plants. *In* "Physiological Adaptation to the Environment" (F. J. Vernberg, ed.), pp. 111–129. Intext Educ. Publishers, New York.

Faiz, S. M. A., and Weatherley, P. E. (1977). The location of the resistance to water movement in the soil supplying the roots of transpiring plants. *New Phytol.* **78**, 337–347.

Faulkingham, R. H. (1977). Ecologic constraints and subsistence strategies: the impact of drought in a Hausa village, a case study from Niger. *In* "Drought in Africa. 2". (D. Dalby, R. J. Harrison Church and F. Bezzaz, eds.), pp. 148–158. International African Institute, London.

Faulkingham, R. H., and Thorbahn, P. F. (1975). Population dynamics and drought: a village in Niger. *Popul. Stud.* **29**, 463–477.

Fellows, R. J., and Boyer, J. S. (1976). Structure and activity of chloroplasts of sunflower leaves having various water potentials. *Planta* **132**, 229–239.

Fenton, R., Mansfield, T. A., and Wellburn, A. R. (1976). Effects of isoprenoid alcohols on oxygen exchange of isolated chloroplasts in relation to their possible physiological effects on stomata. *J. Exp. Bot.* **27**, 1206–1214.

Fenton, R., Davies, W. J., and Mansfield, T. A. (1977). The role of farnesol as a regulator of stomatal opening in *Sorghum. J. Exp. Bot.* **28**, 1043-1053.

Fernandez, O. A., and Caldwell, M. M. (1975). Phenology and dynamics of root growth of three cool semi-desert shrubs under field conditions. *J. Ecol.* **63**, 703–714.

Filner, P. (1966). Regulation of nitrate reductase in cultured tobacco cells. *Biochem. Biophys. Acta* **118**, 299–310.

Finlay, K., and Wilkinson, G. (1963). The analysis of adaptation in a plant breeding programme. *Aust. J. Agr. Res.* **14**, 742–754.

Firn, R. D., and Friend, J. (1972). Enzymatic production of the plant growth inhibitor, xanthoxin. *Planta* **103**, 263–266.

Firn, R. D., Burden, R. S., and Taylor, H. F. (1972). Detection and estimation of the growth inhibitor xanthoxin in plants. *Planta* **102**, 115–126.

Fischer, R. A. (1968). Stomatal opening in isolated epidermal strips of *Vicia faba*. I. Response to light and CO_2-free air. *Plant Physiol.* **43**, 1947–1952.

Fischer, R. A. (1971). Role of potassium in stomatal opening in the leaf of *Vicia faba. Plant Physiol.* **47**, 555–558.

Fischer, R. A., and Maurer, R. (1978). Drought resistance in spring wheat cultivars. 1. Grain yield responses. *Aust. J. Agric. Res.* **29**, 897–912.

Fischer, R. A., and Turner, N. C. (1978). Plant productivity in the arid and semiarid zones. *Annu. Rev. Plant Physiol.* **29**, 277–317.

Fischer, R. A., Hsiao, T. C., and Hagan, R. M. (1970). After effect of water stress on stomatal opening potential. *J. Exp. Bot.* **21**, 371–385.

Fischer, R. A., Sanchez, M., and Syme, J. R. (1977). Pressure chamber and air flow porometer for rapid indication of water status and stomatal condition in wheat. *Exp. Agric.* **13**, 341–351.

Fiscus, E. L., Parsons, L. R., and Alberte, R. S. (1973). Phyllotaxy and water relations in tobacco. *Planta* **112**, 285–292.

Flowers, T. J. (1975). Halophytes. *In* "Ion Transport in Plant Cells and Tissues" (D. A. Baker and J. L. Hall, eds.), pp. 309–334. North-Holland, Amsterdam.

Flowers, T. J., and Hall, J. L. (1978). Salt tolerance in the halophyte, *Suaeda maritima* (L) Dum: The influence of salinity of the culture solution on the content of various organic compounds. *Ann. Bot.* **42**, 1057–1063.

Flowers, T. J., and Hanson, J. B. (1969). The effect of reduced water potential on soybean mitochondria. *Plant Physiol.* **44**, 939–945.

Flowers, T. J., Troke, P. F., and Yeo, A. R. (1977). The mechanism of salt tolerance in halophytes. *Annu. Rev. Plant Physiol.* **28**, 89–121.

Flowers, T. J., Hall, J. L., and Ward, M. E. (1978). Salt tolerance in the halophyte, *Suaeda maritima* (L) Dum: Properties of malic enzyme and PEP carboxylase. *Ann. Bot.* **42**, 1065–1074.

Forrester, M. L., Krotkov, G., and Nelson, C. D. (1966a). Effect of oxygen on photosynthesis, photorespiration and respiration in detached leaves. I. Soybean. *Plant Physiol.* **41**, 422–427.

Forrester, M. L., Krotkov, G., and Nelson, C. D. (1966b). Effect of oxygen on photosynthesis, photorespiration and respiration in detached leaves. II. Corn and other monocotyledons. *Plant Physiol.* **41**, 428–431.

Foy, C. D. (1974). Effects of aluminium on plant growth. *In* "The Plant Root and its Environment". (E. W. Carson, ed.), pp. 601–642. Univ. Virginia Press, Charlottesville.

Frank, A. B., Power, J. F., and Willis, W. O. (1973). Effect of temperature and plant water stress on photosynthesis, diffusion resistance, and leaf water potential in spring wheat. *Agron. J.* **65**, 777–780.

Franks, F. (ed.) (1972-1975). "Water — a Comprehensive Treatise". Vol. 1 (1972), Vol. 2 (1973), Vol. 3 (1973), Vol. 4 (1975), Vol. 5 (1975). Plenum Press, New York.

Franks, F. (1977a). Solvation and conformational effects in aqueous solutions of biopolymer analogues. *Philos. Trans. R. Soc. London,* Ser. B. **278**, 33–56.

Franks, F. (1977b). Solvation interactions of proteins in solution. *Philos. Trans. R. Soc. London,* Ser. B. **278**, 89–95.

Franks, F, and Eagland, D. (1975). The role of solvent interactions in protein conformation. *Crit. Rev. Biochem.* **3**, 165–217.

Frank, H. S. (1958). Covalency in the hydrogen bond and the properties of water and ice. *Proc. R. Soc. London,* Ser. A. **247**, 481–492.

Frank, H. S., and Evans, M. W. (1945). Entropy in binary liquid mixtures; partial molal entropy in dilute solutions; structure and thermodynamics in aqueous solutions. *Chem. Phys.* **13**, 507–532.

Frank, H. S., and Wen, W.-T. (1957). Structural aspects of ion solvent interaction in aqueous solutions — water structure. *Faraday Discuss. Chem. Soc.* **24**, 133–140.

Fraser, H. L. (1942). The occurrence of endodermis in leguminous root nodules and its effect upon nodule function. *Proc. R. Soc. Edinburgh Sect. B.* **61**, 328–343.

Freeman, T. P., and Duysen, M. E. (1975). The effect of imposed water stress on the development and ultrastructure of wheat chloroplasts. *Protoplasma* **83**, 131–145.

Fry, K. E. (1970). Some factors affecting the Hill reaction activity in cotton chloroplasts. *Plant Physiol.* **45**, 465–469.

Fry, K. E. (1972). Inhibition of ferricyanide reduction in chloroplasts prepared from water stressed cotton leaves. *Crop Sci.* **12**, 698–701.

Fujino, M. (1967). Role of adenosinetriphosphate and adenosinetriphosphatase in stomatal movement. *Sci. Bull. Fac. Educ. Nagasaki Univ.* **18**, 1–47.

Fyhn, H. J. (1976). Holeuryhalinity and its mechanism in a cirripid crustacean *Balanus improvisus*. *Comp. Biochem. Physiol.* **53**, 19–30.

Gaastra, P. (1959). Photosynthesis of crop plants as influenced by light, CO_2, temperature and stomatal diffusion resistances. *Meded. Landbouwhogesch. Wageningen* **13**, 1–68.

Gaastra, P. (1963). Climatic control of photosynthesis and respiration. *In* "Environmental Control of Plant Growth" (L. T. Evans, ed.), pp. 113–140. Academic Press, New York.

Gaff, D. F. (1971). Desiccation tolerant flowering plants in Southern Africa. *Science* **174**, 1033–1034.

Gaff, D. F. (1977). Desiccation tolerant vascular plants of Southern Africa. *Oecologia* **31**, 95–109.

Gaff, D. F., and Churchill, D. M. (1976). *Borya nitida* Labill. — an Australian species in the Liliaceae with desiccation-tolerant leaves. *Aust. J. Bot.* **24**, 209–224.

Gaff, D. F., and Hallam, N. D. (1974). Resurrecting desiccated plants. *In* "Mechanisms of Regulation of Plant Growth". (R. L. Bieleski, A. R. Ferguson and M. M. Cresswell, eds.), *R. Soc. N.Z. Bull.* **12**, 389–393.

Gaff, D. F., and Latz, P. K. (1978). The occurrence of resurrection plants in the Australian flora. *Aust. J. Bot.* **26**, 485–492.

Gaff, D. F., and McGregor, G. R. (1979). The effect of dehydration and rehydration on the nitrogen content of various fractions from resurrection plants. *Biol. Plant.* **21**, 92–99.

Gaff, D. F., Zee, S.-Y., and O'Brien, T. P. (1976). The fine structure of dehydrated and reviving leaves of *Borya nitida* Labill. — a desiccation-tolerant plant. *Aust. J. Bot.* **24**, 225–236.

Gale, J., and Poljakoff-Mayber, A. (1970). Interrelations between growth and photosynthesis of salt bush (*Atriplex halimus* L.) grown in saline media. *Aust. J. Biol. Sci.* **23**, 937–945.

Gale, J., Poljakoff-Mayber, A., and Kahane, I. (1967). The gas diffusion porometer technique and its application to the measurement of leaf mesophyll resistance. *Isr. J. Bot.* **16**, 187–204.

Gale, J., Naaman, R., and Poljakoff-Mayber, A. (1970). Growth of *Atriplex halimus* L. in sodium chloride salinated culture solutions as affected by the relative humidity of the air. *Aust. J. Biol. Sci.* **23**, 947–952.

Gallacher, A. E., and Sprent, J. I. (1978). The effect of different water regimes on growth and nodule development of greenhouse-grown *Vicia faba*. *J. Exp. Bot.* **29**, 413–423.

Gamper, H., and Moses, V. (1974). Enzyme organization in the proline biosynthetic pathway of *Escherichia coli*. *Biochim. Biophys. Acta* **354**, 75–87.

Gandhi, A. P., Sawhney, S. K., and Naik, M. S. (1973). Activation of nitrate reductase from rice seedlings by NADH. *Biochem. Biophys. Res. Commun.* **55**, 291–296.

Gardner, I. C., and Leaf, G. (1960). Translocation of citrulline in *Alnus glutinosa*. *Plant Physiol.* **35**, 948–950.

Gardner, W. R. (1960). Water availability to plants. *Soil Sci.* **89**, 63–73.

Gavande, S. A., and Taylor, S. A. (1967). Influence of soil water potential and atmospheric evaporative demand on transpiration and the energy status of water in plants. *Agron. J.* **59**, 4–7.

Gemmrich, A. R. (1975). Prolinedehydrogenase aus Keimenden Farnsporen. *Phytochemistry* **14**, 353–357.

Genkel, P. A. (1946). Resistance of plants to drought and ways to increase it. (In Russian). *Tr. Inst. Fiziol. Rast.* (Moscow) **5**, 1.

Genkel, P. A., Satarova, N. A., and Tvorus, E. K. (1967). Effect of drought on protein synthesis and the state of ribosomes in plants. (In Russian with English summary.) *Fiziol. Rast.* **14**, 898–907.

George, C. J., Ramasastri, K. S., and Rentala, G. S. (1973). "Incidence of droughts in India". *Meteorological Monograph Agrimet* **5**. India Meteorological Dept, Poona.

Giesen, M., Roman, R., Seal, S. N., and Marcus, A. (1976). Formation of an 80S methionyl-tRNA initiation complex with soluble factors from wheat germ. *J. Biol. Chem.* **251**, 6075–6081.

Gifford, R. M. (1974). A comparison of potential photosynthesis, productivity and yield of plant species with differing photosynthetic metabolism. *Aust. J. Plant Physiol.* **1**, 107–111.

Gifford, R. M., and Musgrave, R. B. (1970). Diffusion and quasi-diffusion resistances in relation to the carboxylation kinetics of maize leaves. *Physiol. Plant.* **23**, 1048–1056.

Giles, K. L., Beardsell, M. F., and Cohen, D. (1974). Cellular and ultrastructural changes in mesophyll and bundle sheath cells of maize in response to water stress. *Plant Physiol.* **54**, 208–212.

Giles, K. L., Cohen, D., and Beardsell, M. F. (1976). Effects of water stress on the ultrastructure of leaf cells of *Sorghum bicolor*. *Plant Physiol.* **57**, 11–14.

Gillard, D. F., and Walton, D. C. (1976). Abscisic acid metabolism by a cell-free preparation from *Echinocystis lobatus* liquid endosperm. *Plant Physiol.* **58**, 790–795.

Gilles, R., and Pequeux, A. (1977). Effect of salinity on the free amino acids pool of the red alga *Porphyridium purpureum* (= *P. cruentum*). *Comp. Biochem. Physiol.* **57A**, 183–185.

Gilles, R., and Schoffeniels, E. (1969). Isosmotic regulation in isolated surviving nerves of *Eriochein sinensis* Milne Edwards. *Comp. Biochem. Physiol.* **31**, 927–939.

Glinka, Z. (1973). Abscisic acid effect on root exudation related to increased permeability to water. *Plant Physiol.* **51**, 217–219.

Glinka, Z. (1977). Effects of abscisic acid and hydrostatic pressure gradient on water movement through excised sunflower roots. *Plant Physiol.* **59**, 933–935.

Glinka, Z., and Reinhold, L. (1971). Abscisic acid raises the permeability of plant cells to water. *Plant Physiol.* **48**, 103–105.

Glinka, Z., and Reinhold, L. (1972). Induced changes in permeability of plant cell membranes to water. *Plant Physiol.* **49**, 602–606.

Goode, J. E., and Higgs, K. H. (1973). Water, osmotic and pressure potential relationships in apple leaves. *J. Hortic. Sci.* **48**, 203–215.

Goodwin, T. W. (1958). Studies in carotenogenesis. 25. The incorporation of $^{14}CO_2$,

$[2\text{-}^{14}C]$acetate and $[2\text{-}^{14}C]$ mevalonate into β-carotene by illuminated etiolated maize seedlings. *Biochem. J.* **70**, 612–617.

Gordon, M. E., and Payne, P. I. (1976). *In vitro* translation of the long-lived messenger ribonucleic acid of dry seeds. *Planta* **130**, 269–273.

Göring, Von H., Dreier, W., and Heinke, F. (1977). Zytoplasmatische Osmoregulation durch Prolin bei Wuyeln von Zea Mays L. *Biol. Rundsch.* **15**, 377–380.

Gould, G. W., and Measures, J. C. (1977). Water relations in single cells. *Philos. Trans. R. Soc. London,* Ser. B. **278**, 151–165.

Graham, J., Clarkson, D. T., and Sanderson, J. (1974). Water uptake by the roots of marrow and barley plants. *Annu. Rep. Agric. Res. Counc. Letcombe Lab. 1973,* 9–11.

Greacen, E. L. (1977). Mechanisms and models of water transfer. *In* "Soil Factors in Crop Production in a Semi-arid Environment". (J. S. Russell and E. L. Greacen, eds.), pp. 163–196. Univ. Queensland Press, St. Lucia.

Greacen, E. L., and Hignett, C. T. (1976). A water balance model and supply index for wheat in South Australia. Div. Soils Tech. Paper No. 27, CSIRO (Australia).

Greacen, E. L. and Oh, J. S. (1972). Physics of root growth. *Nature* (London) **235**, 24–25.

Greacen, E. L., Ponsana, P., and Barley, K. P. (1976). Resistance to water flow in the roots of cereals. *In* "Water & Plant Life". (O. L. Lange, L. Kappen and E.-D. Schulze, eds.), pp. 86–100. Springer, Berlin.

Greaves, M. P., and Darbyshire, J. F. (1972). The ultrastructure of mucilaginous layers on plant roots. *Soil Biol. Biochem.* **4**, 443–449.

Greenway, H. (1965). Plant responses to saline substrates IV. Chloride uptake by *Hordeum vulgare* as affected by inhibitors, transpiration, and nutrients in the medium. *Aust. J. Biol. Sci.* **18**, 249–268.

Greenway, H., and Leahy, M. (1972). Effects of rapidly and slowly permeating osmotica on macromolecule and sucrose synthesis. *J. Exp. Bot.* **23**, 459–468.

Greenway, H., Hughes, P. G., and Klepper, B. (1969). Effects of water deficit on phosphorus nutrition of tomato plants. *Physiol. Plant.* **22**, 199–207.

Greenwood, E. A. N. (1976). Nitrogen stress in plants. *Adv. Agron.* **28**, 1–35.

Guggenheim, M. (1958). Die biogenen amine in der pflanzenwelt. *In* "Encycl. Plant Physiol." VIII (W. Ruhland, ed.), pp. 919–927. Springer-Verlag, Berlin.

Gustafsson, L., and Norkrans, B. (1976). On the mechanism of salt tolerance. Production of glycerol and heat during growth of *Debaryomyces hansenii. Arch. Microbiol.* **110**, 177–183.

Gwóźdź, E. A., and Bewley, J. D. (1975). Plant desiccation and protein synthesis. An *in vitro* system from dry and hydrated mosses using endogenous and synthetic messenger RNA. *Plant Physiol.* **55**, 340–345.

Gwóźdź, E. A., Bewley, J. D., and Tucker, E. B. (1974). Studies on protein synthesis in *Tortula ruralis:* polyribosome reformation following desiccation. *J. Exp. Bot.* **25**, 599–608.

Habish, H. A., and Mahdi, A. A. (1976). Effects of soil moisture on nodulation of cowpea and hyacinth bean. *J. Agric. Sci.* **86**, 553–560.

Hageman, R. H., and Flesher, D. (1960). Nitrate reductase activity in corn seedlings as affected by light and nitrate content of nutrient media. *Plant Physiol.* **35**, 700–708.

Hageman, R. H., and Hucklesby, D. P. (1971). Nitrate reductase from higher plants. *Methods in Enzymology* **23**, 491–503.

Hageman, R. H., Flesher, D., and Gitter, A. (1961). Diurnal variation and other light effects influencing the activity of nitrate reductase and nitrogen metabolism in corn. *Crop Sci.* **1**, 201–204.

Hageman, R. H., Leng, E. R., and Dudley, J. W. (1967). A biochemical approach to corn breeding. *Adv. Agron.* **19**, 45–86.

Halevy, A. H., and Kessler, B. (1963). Increased tolerance of bean plants to soil drought by means of growth retarding substances. *Nature* (London) **197**, 310–311.

Hall, A. E., and Björkman, O. (1975). Model of leaf photosynthesis and respiration. *In* "Ecological Studies". Vol. 12. Perspectives of Biophysical Ecology (D. M. Gates and R. B. Schmerl, eds.), pp. 55–72. Springer-Verlag, Berlin.

Hall, A. E., and Kaufmann, M. R. (1975). Stomatal response to environment with *Sesamum indicum* L. *Plant Physiol.* **55**, 455–459.

Hall, A. E., and Yermanos, D. M. (1975). Leaf conductance and leaf water status of sesame strains in hot, dry climates. *Crop Sci.* **15**, 789–793.

Hall, A. E., Camacho-B, S. E., and Kaufmann, M. R. (1975). Regulation of water loss by citrus leaves. *Physiol. Plant.* **33**, 62–65.

Hall, A. E., Schulze, E.-D., and Lange, O. L. (1976). Current perspectives of steady-state stomatal responses to environment. *In* "Water and Plant Life" (O. L. Lange, L. Kappen, and E.-D. Schulze, eds.), *Ecol. Stud.* **19**, 169–188. Springer-Verlag, New York.

Hall, J. L., Harvey, D. M. R., and Flowers, T. J. (1978). Evidence for the cytoplasmic localization of betaine in leaf cells of *Suaeda maritima. Planta,* **140**, 59–62.

Hallam, N. D., and Gaff, D. F. (1978). Reorganisation of fine structure during rehydration of desiccated leaves of *Xerophyta villosa. New Phytol.* **81**, 349-355.

Hallam, N. D., and Luff, S. E. (1980a). Fine structural changes in the mesophyll tissue of the leaves of *Xerophyta villosa* during desiccation. *Bot. Gaz.* **141**, 173–179.

Hallam, N. D., and Luff, S. E. (1980b). Fine structural changes in the leaves of the desiccation-tolerant plant *Talbotia elegans* during extreme water stress. *Bot. Gaz.* **141**, 180–187.

Hammett, J. R., and Katterman, F. R. (1975). Storage and metabolism of poly(adenylic acid)-mRNA in germinating cotton seeds. *Biochemistry* **14**, 4375–4379.

Hanscom, Z., and Ting, I. P. (1978). Responses of succulents to plant water stress. *Plant Physiol.* **61**, 327-330.

Hanson, A. D., and Nelsen, C. E. (1978). Betaine accumulation and ^{14}C-formate metabolism in water stressed barley leaves. *Plant Physiol.* **62**, 305–312.

Hanson, A. D., Nelsen, C. E., and Everson, E. H. (1977). Evaluation of free proline accumulation as an index of drought resistance using two contrasting barley cultivars. *Crop Sci.* **17**, 720–726.

Hanson, A. D., Nelsen, C. E., Pedersen, A. R., and Everson, E. H. (1979). Capacity for proline accumulation during water stress in barley and its implications for drought-resistance. *Crop. Sci.* **19**, 489–493.

Hanway, J. J., and Englehorn, A. J. (1958). Nitrate accumulation in some Iowa crop plants. *Agron, J.* **50**, 331–334.

Hardy, R. W. F., and Havelka, U. D. (1976). Photosynthate as a major factor limiting nitrogen fixation by field-grown legumes with emphasis on soybeans. *In* "Symbiotic nitrogen fixation in plants" (P. S. Nutman, ed.), IBP synthesis Vol. 7, 421–439. Cambridge University Press, London.

Harris, G. P. (1971). The ecology of corticolous lichens. II. The relationship between physiology and the environment. *J. Ecol.* **59**, 441–452.

Harris, G. P. (1976). Water content and productivity of lichens. *In* "Water and Plant Life" (O. L. Lange, L. Kappen and E.-D. Schulze, eds.), *Ecol. Stud.* **19**, pp. 454–468. Springer, Heidelberg.

Harrison, M. A., and Walton, D. C. (1975). Abscisic acid metabolism in water-stressed bean leaves. *Plant Physiol.* **56**, 250-254.

Hartsock, T. L., and Nobel, P. S. (1976). Watering converts a CAM plant to daytime CO_2 uptake. *Nature* (London) **262**, 574–576.

Hartung, W. (1974). The effect of water stress on the nucleic acid content in *Anastatica hierochuntica* L. *Flora* (Jena), **163**, 156–162.

Hatch, M. D. (1976). Photosynthesis: The path of carbon. *In* "Plant Biochemistry" (J. Bonner and J. E. Varner, eds.), pp. 797–844. Academic Press, London.

Hatch, M. D. (1977). C_4 pathway photosynthesis: mechanism and physiological function. *Trends Biochem. Sci.* **2**, 199–202.

Hatch, M. D., and Osmond, C. B. (1976). Compartmentation and transport in C_4 photosynthesis. *In* "Encycl. Plant Physiol". New Ser., Vol. III. (C. R. Stocking and U. Heber, eds.), pp. 144–184. Springer-Verlag, Berlin.

Hatch, M. D., and Slack, C. R. (1969). Studies on the mechanism of activation and inactivation of pyruvate, phosphate dikinase — a possible regulatory role for the enzyme in the C_4-dicarboxylic acid pathway of photosynthesis. *Biochem. J.* **112**, 549–558.

Hattersley, P. W. (1976). Specification and functional significance of the leaf anatomy of C_4 plants. Ph.D. Dissertation, Australian National Univ., Canberra.

Heath, O. V. S. (1948). Control of stomatal movement by a reduction in the normal carbon dioxide content of the air. *Nature* (London) **161**, 179–181.

Heath, O. V. S. (1959). The water relations of stomatal cells and the mechanism of stomatal movement. *In* "Plant Physiology", Vol. II, (F. C. Steward, ed.), pp. 193–250. Academic Press, New York.

Heath, O. V. S. (1975). "Stomata". Oxford Univ. Press, London.

Heath, O. V. S., and Mansfield, T. A. (1962). A recording porometer with detachable cups operating on four separate leaves. *Proc. R. Soc. London.* Ser. B. **156**, 1–13.

Heath, O. V. S., and Russell, J. (1954). An investigation of the light responses of wheat stomata with the attempted elimination of control by the mesophyll. Part I. Effects of light independent of carbon dioxide. *J. Exp. Bot.* **5**, 1–15.

Hellebust, J. A. (1976). Effect of salinity on photosynthesis and mannitol synthesis in the green flagellate *Platymonas suecica. Can J. Bot.* **54**, 1735–1741.

Hellkvist, J., Richards, G. P. and Jarvis, P. G. (1974). Vertical gradients of water potential and tissue water relations in Sitka spruce trees measured with the pressure chamber. *J. Appl. Ecol.* **11**, 637–667.

Hely, F. W., and Ofer, I. (1972). Nodulation and frequencies of wild leguminous species in the Northern Negev region of Israel. *Aust. J. Agric. Res.* **23**, 267–284.

Henckel, P. A. (1961). Drought resistance in plants: methods of recognition and intensification. *In* "Plant-Water Relationships in Arid and Semi-Arid Conditions". *Proc. Madrid Symp.* **16**, 167–174.

Henckel, P. A. (1970). Role of protein synthesis in drought resistance. *Can. J. Bot.* **48**, 1235–1241.

Henckel, P. A., Martyanova, K. L., and Zubova, L. S. (1964). Production experiments on pre-sowing drought hardening of plants. *Sov. Plant Physiol.* **11**, 457–461.

Henckel, P. A., Satarova, N. A., and Tvorus, E. K. (1967). Effect of drought on protein synthesis and the state of ribosomes in plants. *Sov. Plant Physiol.* **14**, 754–762.

Henckel, P. A., Satarova, N. A., and Tvorus, E. K. (1972). Functional activity of ribosomes in plants adapted to drought. *Sov. Plant Physiol.* **19**, 888–893.

Henckel, P. A., Satarova, N. A., Blekhman, G. I., and Tvorus, E. K. (1974). Effect of a water deficit on the functional activity of cytoplasmic ribosomes in wheat leaves and the isoenzyme spectrum of cytoplasmic ribonuclease. *Sov. Plant Physiol.* **21**, 91–96.

Henckel, P. A., Satarova, N. A., and Shaposhnikova, S. V. (1977). Protein synthesis in poikiloxerophytes and wheat embryos during the initial period of swelling. *Sov. Plant Physiol.* **24**, 737–741.

Heth, D., and Kramer, P. J. (1975). Drought tolerance of pine seedlings under various climatic conditions. *For. Sci.* **21**, 72–82.

Hewitt, E. J. (1975). Assimilatory nitrate-nitrite reduction. *Annu. Rev. Plant Physiol.* **26**, 73–100.

Hinckley, T. M. (1973). Responses of black locust and tomato plants after water stress. *Hort. Science* **8**, 405–407.

Hinckley, T. M., and Ritchie, G. A. (1970). Within-in crown patterns of transpiration, water stress, and stomatal activity in *Abies amabilis*. *For. Sci.* **16**, 490–492.

Hirai, N., Fukui, H., and Koshimizu, K. (1978). A novel abscisic acid metabolite from seeds of *Robinia pseudacacia. Phytochemistry* **17**, 1625–1628.

Hiron, R. W. P., and Wright, S. T. C. (1973). The role of endogenous abscisic acid in the response of plants to stress. *J. Exp. Bot.* **24**, 769–781.

Hitch, C. J. B., and Stewart, W. D. P. (1973). Nitrogen fixation by lichens in Scotland. *New Phytol.* **72**, 509–524.

Hoad, G. V. (1973). Effect of moisture stress on abscisic acid levels in *Ricinus communis* L. with particular reference to phloem exudate. *Planta* **113**, 367–372.

Hodges, T. K. (1976). *In* ''Encycl. Plant Physiol'', New Ser. Vol. IIA, (U. Lüttge and M. G. Pitman, eds.), pp. 260–283. Springer-Verlag, Berlin.

Hoffman, G. J. (1973). Humidity effects on yield and water relations of nine crops. *Trans. A.S.A.E.* **16**, 164–167.

Hofler, K., Migsoh, H., and Rottenberg, W. (1941). Uber die Austrocknungs-resistenz landwirtschaftlicher Kulturpflanzen. *Forschungsdienst* **12**, 50–61.

Holden, J. S. (1973). Free amino acid levels in the cockroach, *Peripleneta americana. J. Physiol.* **232**, 61P–62P.

Holmgren, P., Jarvis, P. G., and Jarvis, M. S., (1965). Resistances to carbon dioxide and water vapour in leaves of different species. *Physiol. Plant.* **18**, 557–573.

Honert, T. H. van den. (1948). Water transport in plants as a catenary process. *Discuss. Faraday Soc.* **3**, 146–153.

Hong, T. D., Minchin, F. R. and Summerfield, R. J. (1977). Recovery of nodulated cowpea plants (*Vigna unguiculata* (L.) Walp) from waterlogging during vegetative growth. *Plant Soil* **48**, 661–672.

Hsiao, T. C. (1970). Rapid changes in levels of polyribosomes in *Zea mays* in response to water stress. *Plant Physiol.* **46**, 281–285.

Hsiao, T. C. (1973). Plant responses to water stress. *Annu. Rev. Plant Physiol.* **24**, 519–570.

Hsiao, T. C., and Acevedo, E. (1974). Plant responses to water deficits, water-use efficiency, and drought resistance. *Agric. Meteorol.* **14**, 59–84.

Hsiao, T. C., Acevedo, E., Fereres, E., and Henderson, D. W. (1976). Stress metabolism: water stress, growth, and osmotic adjustment. *Philos. Trans. R. Soc. London,* Ser. B. **273**, 479–500.

Huang, A. H. C., and Cavalieri, A. J. (1979). Proline oxidase and water stress-induced proline accumulation in spinach leaves. *Plant Physiol.* **63**, 531–535.

Huang, C.-Y., Boyer, J. S., and Vanderhoef, L. N. (1975a). Acetylene reduction (nitrogen fixation) and metabolic activities of soybean having various leaf and nodule water potentials. *Plant Physiol.* **56**, 222–227.

Huang, C.-Y., Boyer, J. S., and Vanderhoef, L. N. (1975b). Limitation of acetylene reduction (nitrogen fixation) by photosynthesis in soybean having low water potentials. *Plant Physiol.* **56**, 228–232.

Hubac, C., and Guerrier, D. (1972). Étude de la composition en acides aminés de deux Carex: Le *Carex stenophylla* Wahl. f. *pachystylis* (J. Gay) Asch. et Graebn., très résistant a la sécheresse, et le *Carex setifolia* Godron non Kunye, peu résistant. Effet d'un apport de Proline exogène. *Oecol. Plant.* **7**, 147–165.

Huber, B. (1924). Die Beurteilung des Wasserhaushaltes der Pflanze. Ein Beitrag zur Vergleichenden Physiologie. *Jahrb. Wiss. Bot.* **64**, 1–120.

Huber, W. (1974). Influence of NaCl and abscisic acid treatment on protein metabolism and some further enzymes of amino acid metabolism in seedlings of *Pennisetum typhoides, Planta* **121**, 225–235.

Huck, M. G., Klepper, B., and Taylor, H. M. (1970). Diurnal variations in root diameter. *Plant Physiol.* **45**, 529–530.

Huffaker, R. C., Radin, T., Kleinkopf, G. E., and Cox, E. L. (1970). Effects of mild water stress on enzymes of nitrate assimilation and of the carboxylative phase of photosynthesis in barley. *Crop Sci.* **10**, 471–474.

Humble, G. D, and Raschke, K. (1971). Stomatal opening quantitatively related to potassium transport. *Plant Physiol.* **48**, 447–458.

Hurd, E. A. (1974). Phenotype and drought tolerance in wheat. *Agric. Meteorol.* **14**, 39–55.

Hutchinson, J. (1973). "The Families of Flowering Plants". Clarendon Press, Oxford.

ICAR (Indian Council of Agricultural Research) (1972). Proc. National Seminar on Integrated Dryland Research and Development Projects, Sept. 1972, New Delhi, India.

ICRISAT (International Crops Research Institute for the Semi-Arid Tropics) (1974). Proc. International Workshop on Farming Systems, Nov. 1974, Hyderabad, India.

ICRISAT (International Crops Research Institute for the Semi-Arid Tropics) (1979). Proc. International Workshop on Socio-Economic Constraints to Development of Semi-Arid Tropical Agriculture, Feb. 1979, Hyderabad, India.

Iljin, W. A. (1933). Uber Absterben der Pflanzengewebe durch Austrocknung und uber ehre Bewahrung vor dem Trockentode. *Protoplasma* **19**, 414–442.

Imbamba, S. K. (1973). Response of cowpeas to salinity and (2-Chloroethyl) trimethyl-ammonium chloride, C.C.C. *Physiol. Plant.* **28**, 346–349.

Ingelsten, B. (1966). Absorption and transport of sulfate by wheat at varying mannitol concentration in the medium. *Physiol. Plant.* **19**, 563–579.

Itai, C., and Ben-Zioni, A. (1973). Short and long-term effects of high temperature (47–49°C) on tobacco leaves. II. O_2 uptake and amylolytic activity. *Physiol. Plant.* **28**, 490–492.

Itai, C., and Ben-Zioni, A. (1974). Regulation of plant response to high temperature. *In* "Mechanisms of Regulation of Plant Growth" (R. L. Bieleski, A. R. Ferguson and M. M. Cresswell, eds.), *Roy. Soc. N.Z. Bull.* **12**, pp. 477–482.

Itai, C., and Ben-Zioni, A. (1976). Water stress and hormonal response. *In* "Water & Plant Life" (O. L. Lange, L. Kappen, and E.-D. Schulze, eds.), pp. 225–242. Springer, Berlin.

Itai, C., and Vaadia, Y. (1965). Kinetin-like activity in root exudate of water-stressed sunflower plants. *Physiol. Plant.* **18**, 941–944.

Itai, C., and Vaadia, Y. (1971). Cytokinin activity in water-stressed shoots. *Plant Physiol.* **47**, 87–90.

Itai, C., Richmond, A., and Vaadia, Y. (1968). The role of root cytokinins during water and salinity stress. *Isr. J. Bot.* **17**, 187-195.

Itai, C., Ben-Zioni, A., and Ordin, L. (1973). Correlative changes in endogenous hormone levels and shoot growth induced by short heat treatments to the root. *Physiol. Plant.* **29**, 355–360.

Itai, C., Weyers, J. D. B., Hillman, J. R., Meidner, H., and Willmer, C. M. (1978). Abscisic acid and guard cells of *Commelina communis* L. *Nature.* (London) **271**, 652–654.

Jachymczyk, W. J., and Chery, J. H. (1968). Studies on messenger RNA from peanut plants: *in vitro* polyribosome formation and protein synthesis. *Biochim. Biophys. Acta* **157**, 368–377.

Jackson, W. A., and Volk, R. J. (1970). Photorespiration. *Annu. Rev. Plant Physiol.* **21**, 385–432.

Jager, H.-J., and Meyer, H. R. (1977). Effect of water stress on growth and proline metabolism of *Phaseolus vulgaris* L. *Oecologia* **30**, 83–96.

Jarvis, P. G. (1975). Water transfer in plants. *In* "Heat and Mass Transfer in the Biosphere. I. Transfer Processes in the Plant Environment (D. A. de Vries and N. H. Agfan, eds.), pp. 369–394. Scripta Washington, D. C.

Jarvis, P. G. (1976). The interpretation of the variations in leaf water potential and stomatal conductance found in canopies in the field. *Philos. Trans. R. Soc. London, Ser, B.* **273**, 593–610.

Jarvis, P. G., and Jarvis, M. S. (1963). The water relations of tree seedlings. IV. Some aspects of the tissue water relations and drought resistance. *Physiol. Plant.* **16**, 501–516.

Jeffree, C. E., Johnson, R. P. C., and Jarvis, P. G. (1971). Epicuticular wax in the stomatal antechamber of Sitka spruce and its effects on the diffusion of water vapour and carbon dioxide. *Planta* **98**, 1–10.

Jeffrey, D. W. (1968). Phosphate nutrition of Australian heath plants II. The formation of polyphosphate by five heath species. *Aust. J. Bot.* **16**, 603–613.

Jenne, E. A., Rhoades, H. F., Yien, C. H., and Howe, O. W. (1958). Change in nutrient element accumulation by corn with depletion of soil moisture. *Agric. J.* **50**, 71–74.

Jensen, R. G., and Bassham, J. A. (1966). Photosynthesis by isolated chloroplasts. *Proc. Nat. Acad. Sci. U.S.A.* **56**, 1095–1101.

Jeschke, W. D. (1979). Univalent cation selectivity and compartmentation in cereals. *In* "Recent Advances in the Biochemistry of Cereals" (D. L. Laidman and R. G. Wyn Jones, eds.), Academic Press, London.

Jodha, N. S. (1975). Famine and famine policies: some empirical evidence. *Economic and Political Weekly* **10**(41), 1609–1623.

Jodha, N. S. (1978). Effectiveness of farmers' adjustments to risk. *Economic and Political Weekly* **13**(25), A38–A48.

Johnson, D. A., and Brown, R. W. (1977). Psychrometric analysis of turgor pressure response: a possible technique for evaluating plant water stress resistance. *Crop Sci.* **17**, 507–510.

Johnson, H. S., and Hatch, M. D. (1970). Properties and regulation of leaf nicotinamide-adenine dinucleotide phosphate-malate dehydrogenase and 'malic' enzyme in plants with the C_4-dicarboxylic acid pathway of photosynthesis. *Biochem. J.* **119**, 273–280.

Johnson, R. R., Frey, N. M., and Moss, D. N. (1974). Effect of water stress on photosynthesis and transpiration of flag leaves and spikes of barley and wheat. *Crop. Sci.* **14**, 728–731.

Jolliffe, P. A., and Tregunna, E. B. (1968). Effect of temperature, CO_2 concentration and light intensity on oxygen inhibition of photosynthesis in wheat leaves. *Plant Physiol.* **43**, 902–906.

Jolliffe, P. A., and Tregunna, E. B. (1973). Environmental regulation of the oxygen effect on apparent photosynthesis in wheat. *Can. J. Bot.* **51**, 841–853.

Jolly, S. O., Campbell, W., and Tolbert, N. E. (1976). NADPH- and NADH-nitrate reductases from soybean leaves. *Arch. Biochem. Biophys.* **174**, 431–439.

Jones, H. G. (1973). Moderate-term water stresses and associated changes in some photosynthetic parameters in cotton. *New Phytol.* **72**, 1095–1105.

Jones, H. G. (1976). Crop characteristics and the ratio between assimilation and transpiration. *J. Appl. Ecol.* **13**, 605–622.

Jones, H. G. (1978). Stomatal behaviour and breeding for drought resistance. *In* "Stress Physiology of Crop Plants" (H. Mussell and R. C. Staples, eds.), Wiley Interscience, New York.

Jones, H. G. and Slatyer, R. O. (1972). Estimation of the transport and carboxylation components of the intracellular limitation to leaf photosynthesis. *Plant Physiol.* **50**, 283–288.

Jones, K. (1977). The effects of moisture on acetylene reduction by mats of blue-green algae in sub-tropical grassland. *Ann. Bot.* (London) **41**, 801–806.

Jones, L. H. P., and Handreck, K. A. (1965). Studies of silica in the oat plant. III. Uptake of silica from soils by the plant. *Plant Soil* **23**, 79–96.

Jones, L. W., and Kok, B. (1966a). Photoinhibition of chloroplast reactions. I. Kinetics and action spectra. *Plant Physiol.* **41**, 1037–1043.

Jones, L. W., and Kok, B. (1966b). Photoinhibition of chloroplast reactions. II. Multiple effects.

Plant Physiol. **41**, 1044–1049.

Jones, M. B., and Mansfield, T. A. (1972). A circadian rhythm in the level of carbon dioxide compensation in *Bryophyllum fedtschenkoi* with zero values during the transient. *Planta* **103**, 134–146.

Jones, M. M. (1979). Physiological responses of sorghum and sunflower to leaf water deficits. Ph.D. Thesis, Australian Natl. Univ., Canberra.

Jones, M. M. and Rawson, H. M. (1979). Influence of rate of development of leaf water deficits upon photosynthesis, leaf conductance, water use efficiency, and osmotic potential in sorghum. *Physiol. Plant.* **45**, 103–111.

Jones, M. M., and Turner, N. C. (1978). Osmotic adjustment in leaves of sorghum in response to water deficits. *Plant Physiol.* **61**, 122–126.

Jones, M. M., and Turner, N. C. (1980). Osmotic adjustment in expanding and fully expanded leaves of sunflower in response to water deficits. *Aust. J. Plant Physiol.* **7**, 181–192.

Jones, M. M., Osmond, C. B., and Turner, N. C. (1980). Accumulation of solutes in leaves of sorghum and sunflower in response to water deficits. *Aust. J. Plant Physiol.* **7**, 193–205.

Jones, R. (1968). Estimating productivity and apparent photosynthesis from the differences in consecutive measurements of total living plant parts of an Australian heathland. *Aust. J. Bot.* **16**, 589–602.

Jones, R. J., and Mansfield, T. A. (1970). Suppression of stomatal opening in leaves treated with abscisic acid. *J. Exp. Bot.* **21**, 714–719.

Jones, R. J., and Mansfield, T. A. (1971). Antitranspirant activity of the methyl and phenyl esters of abscisic acid. *Nature* (London) **231**, 331–332.

Jones, R. J., and Mansfield, T. A. (1972). Effects of abscisic acid and its esters on stomatal aperture and the transpiration ratio. *Physiol. Plant.* **26**, 321–327.

Jones, R. W., and Sheard, R. W. (1972). Nitrate reductase activity: phytochrome mediation of induction in etiolated peas. *Nature* (London) **238**, 221–222.

Jordan, W. R., Brown, K. W., and Thomas, J. C. (1975). Leaf age as a determinant in stomatal control of water loss from cotton during water stress. *Plant Physiol.* **56**, 595–599.

Kadam, S. S., Gandhi, A. P., Sawhney, S. K., and Naik, M. S. (1974). Inhibitor of nitrate reductase in the roots of rice seedlings and its effect on the enzyme activity in the presence of NADH. *Biochem. Biophys. Acta* **350**, 162–170.

Kahane, I., and Polkajoff-Mayber, A. (1968). Effect of substrate salinity on the ability for protein synthesis in pea roots. *Plant Physiol.* **43**, 1115–1119.

Kampen, J., and Krantz, B. A. (1977). Soil and water management in semi-arid India. *Ekistics* **43**, 283–287.

Kaneshiro, E. S., Holz, Jr., G. G., and Dunham, P. B. (1969). Osmoregulation in a marine ciliate, *Miamiensis avidus*. II. Regulation of intracellular free amino acids. *Biol. Bull.* (Woods Hole, Mass.) **137**, 161–169.

Kapoor, V. K., and Singh, H. (1966). Isolation of betaine from *Achyranthes aspera*, Linn. *Indian J. Chem.* **4**, 461.

Kappen, L., Lange, O. L., Schulze, E.-D., Evenari, M., and Buschbom, U. (1972). Extreme water stress and photosynthetic activity of the desert plant *Artemisia herba-alba* Asso. *Oecologia* **10**, 177–182.

Kappen, L., Oertli, J. J., Lange, O. L., Schulze, E.-D., Evenari, M., and Buschbom, U. (1975). Seasonal and diurnal courses of water relations of the arido-active plant *Mammada scoparia* in the Negev Desert. *Oecologia* **21**, 175–192.

Karawja, M. S., Wassel, G. M., Ruecker, S., Baghdadi, H. H., and Ahmed, Z. F. (1971). Isolation of triacetonamine from *Salsola tetrandra*. *Phytochemistry* **10**, 3303–3304.

Karrer, W. (1958). "Konstitution und Vorksmmen der Organischen Pflanzentoffe", pp. 993–994. Birkhaeuser Verlag, Basel.

Kassam, A. H. (1975). Wilting in leaves of *Vicia faba* L. *Ann. Bot.* **39**, 265–271.

Kassam, A. H., and Elston, J. F. (1974). Seasonal changes in the status of water and tissue characteristics of leaves of *Vicia faba* L. *Ann. Bot.* **38**, 419–429.

Kassam, A. H., and Elston, J. F. (1976). Changes with age in the status of water and tissue characteristics in individual leaves of *Vicia faba* L. *Ann. Bot.* **40**, 669–679.

Katz, R. W., and Glantz, M. H. (1977). Rainfall statistics, droughts and desertification in the Sahel. *In* "Desertification", (M. H. Glantz, ed.), pp. 81–102. Westview Press, Boulder, Col.

Kaufmann, M. R. (1968). Water relations of pine seedlings in relation to root and shoot growth. *Plant Physiol.* **43**, 281–288.

Kaufmann, M. R. (1975). Leaf water stress in Engelmann spruce; influence of the root and shoot environments. *Plant Physiol.* **56**, 841–844.

Kaufmann, M. R. (1976a). Water transport through plants: current perspective. *In* "Transport and Transfer Processes in Plants" (I. F. Wardlaw and J. B. Passioura, eds.), pp. 313–327. Academic Press. New York.

Kaufmann, M. R. (1976b). Stomatal response of Engelmann spruce to humidity, light, and water stress. *Plant Physiol.* **57**, 898–901.

Kaufmann, M. R. (1977a). Soil temperature and drought effects on growth of Monterey pine. *For. Sci.* **23**, 317–325.

Kaufmann, M. R. (1977b). Soil temperature and drying cycle effects on water relations of *Pinus radiata. Can J. Bot.* **55**, 2413–2418.

Kaufmann, M. R. (1977c). Citrus — a case study of environmental effects on plant water relations. *Proc. Int. Soc. Citri.* **1**, 57–62.

Kaufmann, M. R. (1979). Stomatal control and the development of water deficit in Engelmann spruce seedlings during drought. *Can. J. For. Res.* **9**, 297–304.

Kaufmann, M. R., and Hall, A. E. (1974). Plant water balance — its relationship to atmospheric and edaphic conditions *Agric. Meteorol.* **14**, 85–98.

Kaufmann, M. R., and Levy, Y. (1976). Stomatal response of *Citrus jambhiri* to water stress and humidity. *Physiol. Plant.* **38**, 105–108.

Kauss, H. (1969). Osmoregulation mit α-Galaktosylglyzeriden bei *Ochromonas* und Rotalgen. *Ber. Dtsch. Bot. Ges.* **82**, 115–125.

Kauss, H. (1973). Turnover of galactosyl glycerol and osmotic balance in *Ochromonas. Plant Physiol.* **52**, 613–615.

Kauss, H. (1977). Biochemistry of osmotic regulation. *In* "International Review of Biochemistry, Plant Biochemistry II", (D. H. Northcote, ed.), **13**, 119–139.

Keck, R. W., and Boyer, J. S. (1974). Chloroplast response to low leaf water potentials. III. Differing inhibition of electron transport and photophosphorylation. *Plant Physiol.* **53**, 474–479.

Kemble, A. R. and MacPherson, H. T. (1954). Liberation of amino acids in perennial rye grass during wilting. *Biochem. J.* **58**, 46–49.

Kershaw, K. A. (1972). The relationship between moisture content and net assimilation rate of lichen thalli and its ecological significance. *Can. J. Bot.* **50**, 543–555.

Kershaw, K. A. (1974). Dependence of the level of nitrogenase activity on the water content of the thallus in *Peltigera canina, P. evansiana* and *P. praetexta. Can. J. Bot.* **52**, 1423–1427.

Kershaw, K. A., and Dzikowski, P. A. (1977). Physiological-environmental interactions in lichens VI. Nitrogenase activity in *Peltigera polydactyla* after a period of desiccation. *New Phytol.* **79**, 417–421.

Kershaw, K. A, MacFarlane, J. D., and Tysiaczny, M. J. (1977). Physiological-environmental interactions in lichens V. The interaction of temperature with nitrogenase activity in the dark. *New Phytol.* **79**, 409–416.

King, R. W. (1976). Abscisic acid in developing wheat grains and its relationship to grain growth and maturation. *Planta* **132**, 43–51.

Kirst, G. O. (1975). Beziehungen zwischen Mannitkonzentration und osmotischer Belastung bei der Brackwasseralge *Platymonas subcordiformis* (Hazen). *Z. Pflanzenphysiol.* **76**, 316–325.

Kirst, G. O. (1977). Ion composition of unicellular marine and freshwater algae, with special reference to *Platymonas subcordiformis* cultivated in media with different osmotic strengths. *Oecologia* **28**, 177–189.

Kisaki, T., and Tolbert, N. E. (1970). Glycine as a substrate for photorespiration. *Plant Cell Physiol.* **11**, 247–258.

Klein, G., and Zeller, A. (1930). Detection of choline in plants. *Ostr. Bot. Zeitschrift* **79**, 40–57.

Klein, G., Kirsch, M,. Pollauf, G., and Soos, G. (1931). Glykokollbetain, Stachydrin und Trigonellin (gleichzeitig ein Beitrag zum Nachweis von Cholin und Nikotinsäure). *Ostr. Bot. Zeitschrift* **80**, 273–307.

Klein, S., and Ben-Shaul, Y. (1966). Changes in cell fine structure of lima bean axes during early germination. *Can J. Bot.* **44**, 331–340.

Klein, S., and Pollock, B. M. (1968). Cell fine structure of developing lima bean seeds related to seed desiccation. *Am. J. Bot.* **55**, 658–672.

Klein, S., Bernholz, H., and Budnik, A. (1971). The initiation of growth in isolated lima bean axes. Physiological and fine structural effects of actinomycin D, cycloheximide and chloramphenicol. *Plant Cell Physiol.* **12**, 47–60.

Klepper, B., Taylor, H. M., Huck, M. G., and Fiscus, E. L. (1973). Water relations and growth of cotton in drying soil. *Agron. J.* **65**, 307–310.

Klepper, L., Flesher, D., and Hageman, R. H. (1971). Generation of reduced nicotinamide adenine dinucleotide for nitrate reduction in green leaves. *Plant Physiol.* **48**, 580–590.

Kloth, T. I. (1974). *In* "Sahel Nutrition Survey, 1974". U.S. Public Health Serv. Center for Disease Control, Atlanta, Ga., USA.

Kluge, M. (1976). Crassulacean acid metabolism (CAM): CO_2 and water economy. *In* "Ecological Studies" Vol. 19. Water and Plant Life. (O. L. Lange, L. Kappen, and E.-D. Schulze, eds.), pp. 313–322. Springer-Verlag, Berlin

Knipling, E. B. (1967). Effect of leaf aging on water deficit–water potential relationships of dogwood leaves growing in two environments. *Physiol. Plant.* **20**, 65–72.

Kok, B. (1956). On the inhibition of photosynthesis by intense light. *Biochim. Biophys. Acta* **21**, 234–244.

Koretskaya, T. F., and Zholkevich, V. N. (1966). Restoration of proteins during plant wilting. *Sov. Plant Physiol.* **13**, 873–879.

Kortstee, G. J. J. (1970). The aerobic decomposition of choline by microorganisms. *Arch. Microbiol.* **71**, 235–244.

Koshimizu, K., Fukui, H., Mitsui, T., and Ogawa, Y. (1968). Isolation of (−)-abscisyl-β-D-glucopyranoside from immature fruit of *Lupinus luteus*. *Agric. Biol. Chem.* **32**, 789–791.

Kozinka, V., and Luxova, M. (1971). Specific conductivity of conducting and non-conducting *Zea mays* root. *Biol. Plant.* **13**, 257–266.

Kozlowski, T. T. (1976). Water supply and leaf shedding. *In* "Water Deficits and Plant Growth" (T. T. Kozlowski, ed.). Vol. 4, pp. 191–231. Academic Press, New York.

Kramer. P. J. (1950). Effects of wilting on the subsequent intake of water by plants. *Am. J. Bot.* **37**, 280–284.

Kramer, P. J. (1969). "Plant and Soil Water Relationships: a Modern Synthesis". McGraw-Hill, New York.

Krause, G. H., and Heber, U. (1976). Energetics of intact chloroplasts. *In* "The Intact Chloroplast" (J. Barber, ed.), pp. 171–214. Elsevier, North-Holland. Amsterdam.

Krause, G. H., Lorimer, G. H. Heber, U., and Kirk, M. R. (1977). Photorespiratory energy dissipation in leaves and chloroplast. *In* "Proceedings of the Fourth International Congress on Photosynthesis" (D. O. Hall, ed.), pp. 299–310. Biochem. Soc. London.

Krelle, E., and Libbert, E. (1969). Interactions between abscisic acid and gibberellic acid regarding root formation. *Flora* (Jena) Abt. A, **160**, 299–300.

Kriedemann, P. E., and Loveys, B. R. (1974). Hormonal mediation of plant responses to environmental stress. *In* "Mechanisms of Regulation of Plant Growth" (R. L. Bieleski, A. R. Ferguson and M. M. Cresswell, eds.), *Roy. Soc. N.Z. Bull.* **12**, pp. 461–465.

Kriedemann, P. E., Loveys, B. R. Fuller, G. L., and Leopold, A. C. (1972). Abscisic acid and stomatal regulation. *Plant Physiol.* **49**, 842–847.

Kriedemann, P. E., Loveys, B. R., and Downton, W. J. S. (1975). Internal control of stomatal physiology and photosynthesis. II. Photosynthetic responses to phaseic acid. *Aust. J. Plant Physiol.* **2**, 553–567.

Kriedemann, P. E., Loveys, B. R., Possingham, J. V., and Satoh, M. (1976). Sink effects on stomatal physiology and photosynthesis. *In* "Transport and Transfer Processes in Plants" (I. F. Wardlaw and J. B. Passioura, eds.), pp. 401–414. Academic Press, New York.

Kriedemann, P. E., Loveys, B. R. and van Dijk, H. M. (1980). Photosynthetic inhibitor from *Capsicum annuum* L.: extraction and bioassay. *Aust. J. Plant Physiol.* **7**, 629–633.

Krochko, J. E., Bewley, J. D., and Pacey, J. (1978). The effects of rapid and very slow speeds of drying on the ultrastructure and metabolism of the desiccation-sensitive moss *Cratoneuron filicinum. J. Exp. Bot.* **29**, 905–917.

Ku, S. B., and Edwards, G. E. (1977). Oxygen inhibition of photosynthesis. I. Temperature dependence and relation to O_2/CO_2 solubility ratio. *Plant Physiol.* **59**, 986–990.

Kurkova, E. B., and Motorina, M. V. (1974). Chloroplast ultrastructure and photosynthesis at different rates of dehydration. *Sov. Plant Physiol.* **21**, 28–31.

Kyriakopoulos. E., and Richter, H. (1977). A comparison of methods for the determination of water status in *Quercus ilex* L. *Z. Pflanzenphysiol.* **82**, 14–27.

Ladiges, P. Y. (1974). Variation in drought tolerance in *Eucalyptus viminalis* Labill. *Aust. J. Bot.* **22**, 489–500.

Ladiges, P. Y. (1975). Some aspects of tissue water relations in three populations of *Eucalyptus viminalis* Labill. *New Phytol.* **75**, 53–62.

Laing, D. R., and Fischer, R. A. (1977). Adaptation of semi-dwarf wheat cultivars to rainfed conditions. *Euphytica* **26**, 129–139.

Laing, W. A., Ogren, W. L., and Hageman, R. H. (1974). Regulation of soybean net photosynthetic CO_2 fixation by the interaction of CO_2, O_2 and ribulose-1,5-diphosphate carboxylase. *Plant Physiol.* **54**, 678–685.

Lang, A. R. G. (1967). Osmotic coefficients and water potentials of sodium chloride solutions from 0 to 40°C. *Aust. J. Chem.* **20**, 2017–2023.

Lange, O., Lösch, R., Schulze, E.-D., and Kappen, L. (1971). Responses of stomata to changes in humidity. *Planta* **100**, 76–86.

Lange, O., Schulze, E.-D., Kappen, L., Buschbom, U., and Evenari, M. (1975). Adaptations of desert lichens to drought and extreme temperatures. *In* "Environmental Physiology of Desert Organisms". (N. F. Hadley, ed.), pp. 20–37. Dowden, Hutchinson and Ross Inc., Stroudsburg, Pennsylvania.

Lanyi, J. K. (1974). Salt-dependent properties of proteins from extremely halophitic bacteria. *Bacteriol. Rev.* **38**, 272–290.

Larcher, W. (1975). "Physiological Plant Ecology". Springer, Berlin.

Larher, F. (1976). "Sur quelques particularites due metabolisme azote d'une halophyte: *Limonium vulgare*" Thèse Doct. Sc. Nat., Rennes.

Larher, F., and Hamelin, J. (1975a). L'acide β-trimethylaminopropionique des rameaux de *Limonium vulgare* Mill. *Phytochemistry* **14**, 205–207.

Larher, F., and Hamelin, J. (1975b). Mise en evidence de l'acide 2-trimethylamino-6-ketoheptanoique dans les rameaux de *Limonium vulgare. Phytochemistry* **14**, 1789–1791.

Larher, F. and Hamelin, J. (1979). L'acide dimethylsulfonium-5-pentanoique de *Diplotaxis tenuifolia. Phytochemistry* **18**, 1396–1397.

Larher, F., Hamelin, J., and Stewart, G. P. (1977). L'acide dimethylsulfonium-3-propanoique de *Spartina anglica. Phytochemistry* **16**, 2019.

Larkum, A. W. D. (1968). Ionic relations of chloroplasts *in vivo. Nature* (London) **218**, 447–449.

Larkum, A. W. D., and Bonner, W. D. (1972). Light-induced oxidation of cytochrome *f* in isolated chloroplasts of *Pisum sativum. Biochim. Biophys. Acta* **256**, 385–395.

Larkum, A. W. D., and Wyn Jones, R. G. (1979). Carbon dioxide fixation by chloroplasts isolated in glycinebetaine: a putative cytoplasmic osmoticum. *Planta* **145**, 393–394.

Larque-Saavedra, A., and Wain, R. L. (1974). Abscisic acid levels in relation to drought tolerance in varieties of *Zea mays* L. *Nature* (London) **251**, 716–717.

Larque-Saavedra, A., and Wain, R. L. (1976). Studies on plant growth-regulating substances. XLII. Abscisic acid as a genetic character related to drought tolerance. *Ann. Appl. Biol.* **83**, 291–297.

Larter, E. N., Samh, M., and Sosulski, F. W. (1965). The morphological and physiological effects of C.C.C. on barley. *Can. J. Plant. Sci.* **45**, 419–427.

Lassoie, J. P., and Chambers, J. L. (1976). The effects of an extreme drought on tree water status and net assimilation rates of a transplanted northern red oak under greenhouse conditions. *In* "Central Hardwood Forest Conference" (J. S. Fralish, G. T. Weaver, and R. C. Schlesinger, eds.), Proc. First Meeting at South. Ill. Univ., pp. 269–283.

Lawlor, D. W. (1972). Growth and water use of *Lolium perenne*. I. Water transport. *J. Appl. Ecol.* **9**, 79–98.

Lawlor, D. W. (1976a). Water stress induced changes in photosynthesis, photorespiration, respiration and CO_2 compensation concentration of wheat. *Photosynthetica* **10**, 378–387.

Lawlor, D. W. (1976b). Assimilation of carbon into photosynthetic intermediates of water-stressed wheat. *Photosynthetica* **10**, 431–439.

Lawlor, D. W. (1978). Effects of water and heat stress on carbon metabolism of plants with C_3 and C_4 photosynthesis. *In* "Stress Physiology of Crop Plants" (H. Mansell and R. C. Staples, eds.), Wiley Interscience, New York.

Lawlor, D. W., and Fock, H. (1975). Photosynthesis and photorespiratory CO_2 evolution of water-stressed sunflower leaves. *Planta* **126**, 247–258.

Lawlor, D. W. and Fock, H. (1977a). Photosynthetic assimilation of $^{14}CO_2$ by water-stressed sunflower leaves at two O_2 concentrations and the specific activity of products. *J. Exp. Bot.* **28**, 320–328.

Lawlor, D. W. and Fock, H. (1977b). Water stress induced changes in the amounts of some photosynthetic assimilation products and respiratory metabolites of sunflower leaves. *J. Exp. Bot.* **28**, 329–337.

Lawlor, D. W., and Fock, H. (1978). Photosynthesis, respiration and carbon assimilation in water-stressed maize at two oxygen concentrations. *J. Exp. Bot.* **29**, 579–593.

Lazaroff, N., and Pitman, M. G. (1966). Calcium and magnesium uptake by barley seedlings. *Aust. J. Biol. Sci.* **19**, 991–1005.

Lee, K. C., Campbell. R. W., and Paulsen, G. M. (1974). Effects of drought stress and succinic acid-2,2-dimethylhydrazide treatment on water relations and photosynthesis in pea seedlings. *Crop Sci.* **14**, 279–282.

Lehninger, A. L. (1964). "The Mitochondrion: Molecular Basis of Structure and Function." W. A. Benjamin, New York.

Leigh, R. A., and Brandon, D. (1976). Isolation of vacuoles from root storage tissue of *Beta vulgaris* L. *Plant Physiol.* **58**, 656–662.

Levitt, J. (1962). A sulphydryl-disulphide hypothesis of frost injury and resistance in plants. *J. Theor. Biol.* **3**, 355–391.

Levitt, J. (1969). Growth and survival of plants at extremes of temperature — a unified concept. *Symp. Soc. Exp. Biol.* **23**, 395–448.

Levitt, J. (1972). "Responses of Plants to Environmental Stresses". Academic Press, New York.

Levitt, J., and Ben Zaken, R. (1975). Effects of small water stress on cell turgor and intercellular space. *Physiol. Plant.* **34**, 273–279.

Levitt, J., Sullivan, C. Y. and Krull, E. (1960). Some problems in drought resistance. *Bull. Res. Counc. Isr.* Sect. 8D, 173–180

Lewin, L. G., and Sparrow, D. H. (1975). The genetics and physiology of resistance to stress. *Barley Genetics III, Proc. 3rd Int. Barley Genetic. Symp., Garching 1975*, pp. 486–501.

Lewin, S. (1974). "Displacement of Water and its Control of Biochemical Reactions". Academic Press, London.

Linsley, R. K., Kohler, M. A., and Paulhus, J. L. H. (1959). "Applied Hydrology". McGraw-Hill, New York.

Little, C. H. A. and Eidt, D. C. (1968). Effect of abscisic acid on bud break and transpiration in a woody species. *Nature* (London) **220**, 498–499.

Lui, M. S., and Hellebust, J. A. (1976a). Effects of salinity changes on growth and metabolism of the marine centric diatom *Cyclotella cryptica*. *Can. J. Bot.* **54**, 930–937.

Lui, M. S., and Hellebust, J. A. (1976b). Effects of salinity and osmolarity of the medium on amino acid metabolism in *Cyclotella cryptica*. *Can. J. Bot.* **54**, 938–948.

Liu, M. S., and Hellebust, J. A. (1976c). Regulation of proline metabolism in the marine centric diatom *Cyclotella cryptica*. *Can J. Bot.* **54**, 949–959.

Livne, A., and Vaadia, Y. (1965). Stimulation of transpiration rate in barley leaves by kinetin and gibberellic acid. *Physiol. Plant.* **18**, 658–664.

Loneragan, J. F., and Snowball, K. (1969). Calcium requirements of plants. *Aust. J. Plant Physiol.* **20**, 465–478.

Lorimer, G. H., Andrews, T. J., and Tolbert, N. E. (1973). Ribulose diphosphate oxygenase. II. Further proof of reaction products and mechanism of action. *Biochemistry* **12**, 18–23.

Lorimer, G. H., Woo, K. C., Berry, J. A., and Osmond, C. B. (1977). The C_2 photorespiratory carbon oxidation cycle in leaves of higher plants: pathway and consequences. *In* "Proceedings of the Fourth International Congress on Photosynthesis" (D. O. Hall, ed.), pp. 311–322. Biochem. Soc., London.

Lösch, R. (1977). Responses of stomata to environmental factors — experiments with isolated epidermal strips of *Polypodium vulgare*. I. Temperature and humidity. *Oecologia* **29**, 85–97.

Louis, J., Mestichelli, R. N. G., and Spenser, I. D. (1979). The biosynthetic route from ornithine to proline. *J. Biol. Chem.* **254**, 640–647.

Loveys, B. R. (1977). The intracellular location of abscisic acid in stressed and non-stressed leaf tissues. *Physiol. Plant.* **40**, 6–10.

Loveys, B. R., and Kriedemann, P. E. (1973). Rapid changes in abscisic acid-like inhibitors following alterations in vine leaf water potential. *Physiol. Plant.* **28**, 476–479.

Loveys, B. R., and Kriedemann, P. E. (1974). Internal control of stomatal physiology and photosynthesis. 1, Stomatal regulation and associated changes in endogenous levels of abscisic and phaseic acid. *Aust. J. Plant Physiol.* **1**, 407–415.

Low. P. S., and Somero, G. N. (1975a). Activation volumes in enzymic catalysis: their sources and modification by low-molecular-weight solutes. *Proc. Nat. Acad. Sci. U.S.A.* **72**, 3014–3018.

Low, P. S., and Somero, G. N. (1975b). Protein hydration changes during catalysis: a new mechanism of enzymic rate enhancement and ion activation/inhibition of catalysis. *Proc. Nat. Acad. Sci. U.S.A.* **72**, 3305–3309.

Lu, T., and Mazelis, M. (1975). L-Ornithine: 2-oxoacid aminotransferase from squash *(Curcurbita pepo,* L) cotyledons. *Plant Physiol.* **55**, 502–506.

Ludlow, M. M. (1976). Ecophysiology of C_4 grasses. *In* "Ecological Studies" Vol 19. Water and

Plant Life. (O. L. Lange, L. Kappen and E.-D. Schulze, eds.), pp. 364–386. Springer-Verlag. Berlin.

Ludlow, M. M, and Ng, T. T. (1974). Water stress suspends leaf aging. *Plant Sci. Lett.* **3**, 235–240.

Ludwig, L. J., and Canvin, D. T. (1971). The rate of photorespiration during photosynthesis and the relationship of the substrate of light respiration to the products of photosynthesis in sunflower leaves. *Plant Physiol.* **48**, 712–719.

Luke, H. H., and Freeman, T. E. (1968). Stimulation of transpiration by cytokinins. *Nature* (London) **217**, 873–874.

McCarthy, R. E., and Jagendorff, A. T. (1961). Chloroplast damage due to enzymatic hydrolysis of endogenous lipids. *Plant Physiol.* **40**, 725–730.

McCree, K. J. (1974). Changes in the stomatal response characteristics of grain sorghum produced by water stress during growth. *Crop. Sci.* **14**, 273–278.

MacFarlane, J. D., and Kershaw, K. A. (1977). Physiological-environmental interactions in lichens IV. Seasonal changes in nitrogenase activity in *Peltigera canina* (L.) Willd var. *praetextata* (Floerke in Somm.) Hue and *P. canina* (L.) Willd var. *rufescens* (Weiss) Mudd. *New Phytol.* **79**, 403–408.

Machado, R. C. R., Bragarena, A., and Vieira, C. (1976). Effect of osmotic dehydration on free proline accumulation in leaf disks of twenty bean *(Phaseolus vulgaris* L.) cultivars. *Rev. Ceres.* **23**, 302–309.

McLean, W. F. H. (1976). Ph. D. Thesis, School of Pharmacy, Portsmouth Polytechnic, U.K.

McMichael, B. L., and Elmore, C. D. (1977). Proline accumulation in water stressed cotton leaves. *Crop Sci.* **17**, 905–908.

McMichael, B. L., Jordan, W. R., and Powell, R. D. (1973). Abscission processes in cotton: induction by plant water deficit. *Agron. J.* **65**, 202–204.

McNamer, A. D., and Stewart, C. R. (1973). Proline uptake and utilization by *Chlorella pyrenoidosa*. *Plant Physiol.* **52**, 561–564.

McNamer, A. D., and Stewart, C. R. (1974). Nicotinamide adenine dinucleotide-dependent proline dehydrogenase in *Chlorella*. *Plant Physiol.* **53**, 440–444.

Mahtab, S. K., Godfrey, C. L., Swoboda, A. R., and Thomas, G. W. (1971). Phosphorus diffusion in soils I. The effect of applied P, clay content and water content. *Soil Sci. Soc. Am. Proc.* **35**, 393–397.

Makemson, J. C., and Hastings, J. W. (1979). Glutamate functions in osmoregulation in a marine bacterium. *Appl. Microbiol.* **38**, 178–180.

Malek, F., and Baker, D. A. (1978). Effect of fusicoccin on proton co-transport of sugars in phloem loading of *Ricinus communis* L. *Plant Sci. Lett.* **11**, 233–239.

Malek, L., and Bewley, J. D. (1978). Effects of various rates of freezing on the metabolism of a drought-tolerant plant, the moss *Tortula ruralis*. *Plant Physiol.* **61**, 334–338.

Mansfield, T. A. (1976a). Chemical control of stomatal movements. *Philos. Trans. R. Soc. London* Ser. B. **273**, 541–550.

Mansfield, T. A. (1976b). Delay in the response of stomata to abscisic acid in CO_2-free air. *J. Exp. Bot.* **27**, 559–564.

Mansfield, T. A., and Jones, R. J. (1971). Effects of abscisic acid on potassium uptake and starch content of stomatal guard cells. *Planta* **101**, 147–158.

Mansfield, T. A., Wellburn, A. R., and Moreira, T. J. S. (1978). The role of abscisic acid and farnesol in the alleviation of water stress. *Philos. Trans. R. Soc. London* Ser. B. **284**, 471–482.

Maranville, J. W., and Paulsen, G. M. (1972). Alteration of protein composition of corn *(Zea mays* L.) seedlings during moisture stress. *Crop Sci.* **12**, 660–663.

Maranville, J. W., and Sullivan, C. Y. (1976). *In* "The physiology of yield and management of sorghum in relation to genetic improvement''. University of Nebraska Press, Lincoln, Nebraska.

Marcus, A. (1969). Seed germination and the capacity for protein synthesis. *In* "Dormancy and Survival''. (H. W. Woolhouse, ed.) *Symp. Soc. Exp. Biol.* **23**, pp. 143–160. Cambridge Univ. Press, London.

Marcus, A. (1976), Protein Biosynthesis. *In* "Plant Biochemistry'' (J. Bonner and J. E. Varner, eds.), 3rd edn, pp. 507–524. Academic Press, New York.

Marcus, A., Feeley, J., and Volcani, T. (1966). Protein synthesis in imbibed seeds. III. Kinetics of amino acid incorporation, ribosome activation, and polysome formation. *Plant Physiol* **41**, 1167–1172.

Marcus, A., Spiegel, S., and Brooker, J. D. (1975). Preformed mRNA and the programming of early embryo development. *In* "Control Mechanisms in Development''. (R. H. Meints and E. Davies, eds.), pp 1–19, Plenum, New York.

Marrè, E., Cocucci, S., and Sturani, E. (1965). On the development of the ribosomal system in the endosperm of germinating castor bean seeds. *Plant Physiol.* **40**, 1162–1170.

Martin, G. C., Dennis, F. G., MacMillan, J., and Gaskin, P. (1977). Hormones in pear seeds. I. Levels of gibberellins, abscisic acid, phaseic acid, dihydrophaseic acid, and two metabolites of dihydrophaseic acid in immature seeds of *Pyrus communis* L. *J. Am. Soc. Hortic. Sci.* **102**, 16–18.

Mattas, R. E., and Pauli, A. W. (1965). Trends in nitrate reduction and nitrogen fractions in young corn *(Zea mays* L.) plants during heat and moisture stress. *Crop Sci.* **5**, 181–184.

May, L. H., and Milthorpe, F. L. (1962). Drought resistance of crop plants, *Field Crop Abstr.* **15**, 171–179.

May, L. H., Milthorpe, E. J., and Milthorpe, F. L. (1962). Pre-sowing hardening of plants to drought. An appraisal of the contributions of P. A. Henckel. *Field Crop Abstr.* **15**, 93–98.

Mayer, A. M. (1977). Metabolic control of germination. *In* "The Physiology and Biochemistry of Seed Dormancy and Germination''. (A. A. Kahn, ed.), pp. 357–384. North-Holland, Amsterdam.

Mayer, A. M., and Shain, Y. (1974). Control of seed germination. *Annu. Rev. Plant Physiol.* **25**, 167–193.

Mayo, N. S. (1895). Cattle poisoning by potassium nitrate. Mastitis. *Kans. Agric. Exp. Stn. Bull.* No. **49**.

Mazelis, M., and Creveling, R. K. (1974). L-proline dehydrogenase of *Triticum vulgare* germ: Purification, properties and cofactor interactions. *Phytochemistry* **13**, 559–565.

Mazelis, M., and Fowden, L. (1969). Conversion of ornithine into proline by enzymes from germinating peanut cotyledons. *Phytochemistry* **8**, 801–809.

Mazelis, M., and Fowden, L. (1971). The metabolism of proline in higher plants. II. L-proline dehydrogenase from cotyledons of germinating peanut (*Arachis hypogea* L.) seedlings. *J. Exp. Bot.* **22**, 137–145.

Measures, J. C. (1975). Role of amino acids in osmoregulation of non-halophilic bacteria. *Nature* (London) **257**, 398–400.

Meidner, H. (1967). Further observations on the minimum inter-cellular space carbon-dioxide concentration (Γ) of maize leaves and the postulated roles of "photo-respiration'' and glycollate metabolism. *J. Exp. Bot.* **18**, 177–185.

Meidner, H. (1975). Water supply, evaporation, and vapour diffusion in leaves. *J. Exp. Bot.* **26**, 666–673.

Meidner, H., and Mansfield, T. A. (1968). "Physiology of Stomata''. McGraw-Hill, London.

Meister, A., Radhakrishnan, A. N., and Buckley, S. D. (1957). Enzymatic synthesis of L-pipecolic acid and proline. *J. Biol. Chem.* **229**, 789–800.

Meon, S., Fisher, J. M., and Wallace, H. R. (1978). Changes in free proline following infection of plants with either *Meloidogyne javanica* or *Agrobacterium tumefaciens*. *Physiol. Plant Pathol.* **12**, 251–256.

Meyer, R. F., and Boyer, J. S. (1972). Sensitivity of cell division and cell elongation to low water potentials in soybean hypocotyls. *Planta* **108**, 77–87.

Miflin, B. J. (1974). Nitrite reduction in leaves: studies on isolated chloroplasts. *Planta* **116**, 187–196.

Milborrow, B. V. (1966). The effects of synthetic *dl*-dormin (abscisin II) on the growth of the oat mesocotyl. *Planta* **70**, 155–171.

Milborrow, B. V. (1969). Identification of "Metabolite C" from abscisic acid and a new structure for phaseic acid. *J. Chem. Soc. D* **17**, (supersedes *Chem. Comm.*), 966–967.

Milborrow, B. V. (1970). The metabolism of abscisic acid. *J. Exp. Bot.* **21**, 17–29.

Milborrow, B. V. (1972). The biosynthesis and degradation of abscisic acid. *In* "Plant Growth Subst. Proc. Int. Conf. 7th, 1970". (D. J. Carr, ed.). pp. 281–290, Springer-Verlag, Berlin.

Milborrow, B. V. (1974a). Biosynthesis of abscisic acid by a cell-free system. *Phytochemistry* **13**, 131–136.

Milborrow, B. V. (1974b). The chemistry and physiology of abscisic acid. *Annu. Rev. Plant Physiol.* **25**, 259–307.

Milborrow, B. V. (1978). The stability of conjugated abscisic acid during wilting. *J. Exp. Bot.* **29**, 1059–1066.

Milborrow, B. V., and Mallaby, R. (1975). Occurrence of methyl (+)-abscisate as an artefact of extraction *J. Exp. Bot.* **26**, 741–748.

Milborrow, B. V., and Noddle, R. C. (1970). Conversion of 5-(1,2-epoxy-2,6,6-trimethylcyclohexyl)-3-methylpenta-*cis*-2-*trans*-4-dienoic acid into abscisic acid in plants. *Biochem. J.* **119**, 727–734.

Milborrow, B. V., and Robinson, D. R. (1973). Factors affecting the biosynthesis of abscisic acid. *J. Exp. Bot.* **24**, 537–548.

Milburn, J. A. (1973). Cavitation in *Ricinus* by acoustic detection: induction in excised leaves by various factors. *Planta* **110**, 253–265.

Miler, P. M., and Stewart, C. R. (1976). Pyrroline-5-carboxylic acid reductase from soybean leaves. *Phytochemistry* **15**, 1855–1857.

Millar, B. D., and Denmead, O. T. (1976). Water relations of wheat leaves in the field. *Agron. J.* **68**, 303–307.

Millbank, J. W. (1977). Lower plant associations. *In* "A treatise on dinitrogen fixation. III Biology". (R. W. F. Hardy and W. S. Silver, eds.), pp. 125–151, John Wiley and Sons, N.Y.

Miller, R. J., Bell, D. T., and Kaeppe, D. E. (1971). The effect of water stress on some membrane characteristics of corn mitochondria. *Plant Physiol.* **48**, 229–231.

Millerd, A., and Spencer, D. (1974). Changes in RNA-synthesizing activity and template activity in nuclei from cotyledons of developing pea seeds. *Aust. J. Plant Physiol.* **1**, 331–341.

Milthorpe, F. L., Pearson, C. J., and Thrower, S. (1974). The metabolism of guard cells. *In* "Mechanisms of Regulation of Plant Growth". (R. L. Bieleski, A. R. Ferguson and M. M. Cresswell, eds.), *Roy. Soc. N.Z. Bull.* **12**, p. 439–443.

Minchin, F. R., and Pate, J. S. (1973). The carbon balance of a legume and the functional economy of its root nodule. *J. Exp. Bot.* **24**, 259–271.

Minchin, F. R., and Pate, J. S. (1975). Effects of water, aeration and salt regime on nitrogen fixation in a nodulated legume — definition of an optimum root environment. *J. Exp. Bot.* **26**, 60–69.

Mitra, R., Gross, R. D., and Varner, J. E. (1975). An intact tissue assay for enzymes that labilize C-H bonds. *Anal. Biochem.* **64**, 102–109.

Mittelheuser, C. J. (1977). Rapid ultrastructural recovery of water stressed leaf tissue. *Z. Pflanzenphysiol.* **82**, 458–461.

Mittelheuser, C. J., and Van Steveninck, R. F. M. (1969). Stomatal closure and inhibition of transpiration induced by (RS)-abscisic acid. *Nature* (London) **221**, 281–282.

Mittelheuser, C. J., and Van Steveninck, R. F. M. (1971). Rapid action of abscisic acid on photosynthesis and stomatal resistance. *Planta* **97**, 83–86.

Mizrahi, Y., and Richmond, A. E. (1972). Abscisic acid in relation to mineral deprivation. *Plant Physiol.* **50**, 667–670.

Mizrahi, Y., Blumenfeld, A., Bittner, S., and Richmond, A. E. (1971). Abscisic acid and cytokinin contents of leaves in relation to salinity and relative humidity. *Plant Physiol.* **48**, 752–755.

Mizrahi, Y., Blumenfeld, A., and Richmond, A. E. (1972). The role of abscisic acid and salination in the adaptive response of plants to reduced aeration. *Plant Cell Physiol.* **13**, 15–21.

Mizrahi, Y., Scherings, S. G., Arad, S. M., and Richmond, A. E. (1974). Aspects of the effect of ABA on the water status of barley and wheat seedlings. *Physiol. Plant.* **31**, 44–50.

Mohanty, P., and Boyer, J. S. (1976). Chloroplast response at low leaf water potentials. IV. Quantum yield is reduced. *Plant Physiol.* **57**, 704–709.

Molz. F. J., and Klepper, B. (1973). On the mechanism of water-stress-induced stem deformation. *Agron. J.* **65**, 304–306.

Monteith, J. L. (1966). The photosynthesis and transpiration of crops. *Exp. Agric.* **2**, 1–14.

Mooney, H. A. (1972). The carbon balance of plants. *Annu. Rev. Ecol. Syst.* **3**, 315–346.

Mooney, H. A. Troughton, J. H., and Berry, J. A. (1974). Arid climates and photosynthetic systems. *Carnegie Inst. Washington Yearb.* **73**, 793–805.

Mooney, H. A., Ehleringer, J., and Berry, J. A. (1976). High photosynthetic capacity of a winter annual in Death Valley. *Science* **194**, 322–324.

Mooney, H. A., Björkman, O., and Collatz, G. J. (1977). Photosynthetic acclimation to temperature and water stress in the desert shrub *Larrea divaricata*. *Carnegie Inst. Washington Yearb.* **76**, 328–335.

Mooney, H. A., Ehleringer, J., and Björkman, O. (1977). The energy balance of leaves of the evergreen desert shrub *Atriplex hymenelytra*. *Oecologia* **29**, 301–310.

Mooney, H. A., Björkman, O., and Collatz, G. J. (1978). Photosynthetic acclimation to temperature in the desert shrub, *Larrea divaricata*. *Plant Physiol.* **61**, 406–410.

Moore, A. W., Russell, J. S., and Coaldrake, J. E. (1967). Dry matter and nutrient content of a subtropical sem-arid forest of *Acacia harpophylla* F. Muell. (brigalow). *Aust. J. Bot.* **15**, 11–24.

Morgan, J. M. (1977). Differences in osmoregulation between wheat genotypes. *Nature* (London) **270**, 234–235.

Morilla, C. A., Boyer, J. S., and Hageman, R. H. (1973). Nitrate reductase activity and polyribosomal content of corn (*Zea mays* L.) having low leaf water potentials. *Plant Physiol.* **51**, 817–824.

Morris, C. J., Thompson, J. F., and Johnson, C. M. (1969). Metabolism of glutamic acid and N-acetylglutamic acid in leaf discs and cell free extracts of higher plants. *Plant Physiol.* **44**, 1023–1026.

Morris, M. D. (1974). What is a famine? *Economic and Political Weekly.* **9**(44), 1855–1864.

Moss, D. N., Wolley, J. T., and Stone, J. F. (1974). Plant modification for more efficient water use: the challenge. *Agric. Meteorol.* **14**, 311–320.

Mothes, K. (1964). The role of kinetin in plant regulation, *In* "Int. Conf. Plant Growth Substances, Proc. 5th". CNRS, Paris, **123**, 131–140.

Mouravieff, I. (1956). Action du gaz carbonique et de la lumière sur l'appareil stomatique isolé. *C. R. Hebd. Seances Acad. Sci.* Ser. D. **242**, 926–927.

Mukherjee, I. (1974). Effect of potassium on proline accumulation in maize during wilting. *Physiol. Plant.* **31**, 288–291.

Mulroy, T. W., and Rundel, P. W. (1977). Annual plants: adaptation to desert environment. *BioScience* **27**, 109–114.

Munda, I. M., and Kremer, B. P. (1977). Chemical composition and physiological properties of fucoids under conditions of reduced salinity. *Mar. Biol.* **42**, 9–15.

Munns, R., Brady, C. J., and Barlow, E. W. R. (1979). Solute accumulation in the apex and leaves of wheat during water stress. *Aust. J. Plant Physiol.* **6**, 379–389.

Murakami, S., and Packer, L. (1969). Reversible changes in the conformation of thylakoid membranes acompanying chloroplast contraction or expansion. *Biochim. Biophys. Acta* **180**, 420–423.

Murakami, S., and Packer, L. (1970a). Light-induced changes in the conformation and configuration of the thylakoid membrane of *Ulva* and *Porphyra* chloroplasts *in vivo*. *Plant Physiol.* **45**, 289–299.

Murakami, S., and Packer, L. (1970b). Protonation and chloroplast membrane structure. *J. Cell Biol.* **47**, 332–351.

Muth, W. L., and Costilow, R. N. (1974). Ornithine cyclase (deaminating). III. Mechanism of the conversion of ornithine to proline. *J. Biol. Chem.* **249**, 7463–7467.

Nagl, W. (1976). Nuclear organization. *Ann. Rev. Plant Physiol.* **27**, 39–69.

Nash, D., Paleg, L., and Wiskich, J. T. (1981). Effect of proline and betaine on the heat stability of some mitochondrial enzymes. *Aust. J. Plant Physio.* **8**.

Nasrulhaq-Boyce, A., and Jones, O. T. G. (1977). The light-induced development of nitrate reductase in etiolated barley shoots: an inhibitory effect of laevulinic acid. *Planta* **137**, 77–84.

Navon, G., Ogawa, S., Shulman, R. G., and Yamane, T. (1977). High resolution ^{31}P nuclear magnetic resonance studies of metabolism in aerobic *Escherichia coli* cells. *Proc. Nat. Acad. Sci. U.S.A.* **74**, 888–891.

Nawa, Y., and Asahi, T. (1973a). Relationship between the water content of pea cotyledons and mitochondrial development during the early stages of germination. *Plant Cell Physiol.* **14**, 607–610.

Nawa, Y., and Asahi, T. (1973b). Biochemical studies on development of mitochondria in pea cotyledons during the early stages of germination: effect of antibiotics on the development. *Plant Physiol.* **51**, 833–838.

Neales, T. F. (1975). The gas exchange patterns of CAM plants. *In* "Environmental and Biological Control of Photosynthesis" (R. Marcelle, ed.), pp. 299–310. Dr. W. Junk, The Hague.

Neales, T. F., Patterson, A. A., and Hartney, V. J. (1968). Physiological adaptation to drought in the carbon assimilation and water loss of xerophytes. *Nature* (London) **219**, 469–472.

Neales, T. F., Treharne, K. J., and Wareing, P. F. (1971). A relationship between net photosynthesis, diffusive resistance and carboxylating enzyme activity in bean leaves. *In* "Photosynthesis and Photorespiration" (M. D. Hatch, C. B. Osmond and R. O. Slatyer, eds.), pp. 89–96. Wiley Interscience, Sydney.

Neumann, H. H., Thurtell, G. W., and Stevenson, K. R. (1974). *In situ* measurements of leaf water potential and resistance to water flow in corn, soybean, and sunflower at several transpiration rates. *Can. J. Plant Sci.* **54**, 175–184.

Newman, E. I. (1966). Relationship between root growth of flax (*Linum usitatissimum*) and soil water potential. *New Phytol.* **65**, 273–283.

Newman, E. I. (1973). Permeability to water of the roots of five herbaceous species. *New Phytol.* **72**, 547–555.

Newman, E. I. (1974). Root and soil water relations. *In* "The Plant Root and its Environment".

(E. W. Carson, ed.), pp. 363–440. Univ. Virginia Press, Charlottesville.

Newman, E. I. (1976). Water movement through root systems. *Philos. Trans. R. Soc. London.* Ser. B. **273**, 463–478.

Nicholas, D. J. D., and Nason, A. (1954). Molybdenum and nitrate reductase. II. Molybdenum as a constituent of nitrate reductase. *J. Biol. Chem.* **207**, 353–360.

Nielsen, B. F. (1963). "Plant Production, Transpiration Ratio and Nutrient Ratios as Influenced by Interactions between Water and Nitrogen." Ph.D. Thesis, Univ. of Copenhagen.

Nieman, R. H. (1962). Some effects of sodium chloride on growth, photosynthesis and respiration of twelve crop plants. *Bot. Gaz.* **123**, 279–285.

Nir, I. (1965). Effect of Drought on Photochemical and Enzymic Activity of Chloroplasts. M.Sc. Thesis, Hebrew Univ., Jerusalem (in Hebrew).

Nir, I. (1969). Changes in Ultrastructure and Biochemical Activity Which Occur in Plant Tissues as a Result of Dehydration. Ph.D. Thesis, Hebrew Univ., Jerusalem (in Hebrew).

Nir, I., and Poljakoff-Mayber, A. (1966). The effect of water stress on the activity of phosphatases from Swiss chard chloroplasts. *Isr. J. Bot.* **15**, 12–16.

Nir, I., and Poljakoff-Mayber, A. (1967). Effect of water stress on the photochemical activity of chloroplasts. *Nature* (London) **213**, 418–419.

Nir, I., Poljakoff-Mayber, A., and Klein, S. (1969). Effect of moisture stress on submicroscopic structure of maize roots. *Aust. J. Biol. Sci.* **22**, 17–33.

Nir, I., Klein, S., and Poljakoff-Mayber, A. (1970a). Changes in fine structure of root cells from maize seedlings exposed to water stress. *Aust. J. Biol. Sci.* **23**, 489–491.

Nir, I., Poljakoff-Mayber, A., and Klein, S. (1970b). The effect of water stress on mitochondria of root cells. *Plant Physiol.* **45**, 173–177.

Nir, I., Poljakoff-Mayber, A., and Klein, S. (1970c). The effect of water stress on polysome population and the ability to incorporate amino acids in maize root tips. *Isr. J. Bot.* **19**, 451–452.

Nissen, P., and Benson, A. A. (1961). Active transport of choline sulphate by barley roots. *Plant Physiol.* **39**, 586–589.

Nix, H. A. (1976). The Australian climate and its effect on grain yield and quality, *In* "Australian Field Crops. I. Wheat and Other Temperate Cereals". (A. Lazenby and E. M. Matherson, eds.), pp. 183–266. Angus and Robertson, Sydney.

Nobel, P. S. (1974). "Introduction to Biophysical Plant Physiology". W. H. Freeman and Co., San Francisco.

Nobel, P. S. (1977). Water relations and photosynthesis of a barrel cactus, *Ferocactus acanthodes*, in the Colorado Desert. *Oecologia* **27**, 117–133.

Noguchi, M., Kowai, A., Yokoyama, M., and Tamaki, E. (1968). Studies on nitrogen metabolism in tobacco plants. IX. Effect of various compounds on proline biosynthesis in the green leaves. *Plant Cell Physiol.* **9**, 35–47.

Noguchi, M., Kowai, A., and Tamaki, E. (1966). Studies on nitrogen metabolism in tobacco plants. *Agric. Biol. Chem.* **30**, 452–456.

Noy-Meir, I. (1973). Desert ecosystems: environment and producers. *Annu. Rev. Ecol. Syst.* **4**, 25–51.

Noy-Meir, I., and Ginzburg, B. Z. (1969). An analysis of the water potential isotherm in plant tissue. II. Comparative studies on leaves of different types. *Aust. J. Biol. Sci.* **22**, 35–52.

Nye, P. H., and Marriott, F. H. C. (1968). The importance of mass flow in the uptake of ions by roots from soil. *Trans. Int. Congr. Soil Sci. Soc.* 9th, 1968, **1**, 127–134.

Nye, P. H., and Tinker, P. B. (1977). "Solute Movement in the Soil-Root System". Blackwell, Oxford.

Oaks, A., Mitchell, D. J., Barnard, R. A., and Johnson, F. J. (1970). The regulation of proline biosynthesis in maize roots. *Can. J. Bot.* **48**, 2249–2258.

O'Brien, T. P., and McCully, M. E. (1969). "Plant Structure and Development". Macmillan, London.

OECD (Organisation for Economic Co-operation and Development) (1976). "Analysis and Synthesis of Long Term Development Strategies for the Sahel". OECD Development Center, Paris.

Oertli, J. J. (1976). The soil–plant–atmosphere continuum. *In* "Water and Plant Life" (O. L. Lange, L. Kappen, and E.-D. Schulze, eds.), *Ecol. Stud.* **19**, 32–41. Springer-Verlag, New York.

Ogunkanmi, A. B., Wellburn, A. R., and Mansfield, T. A. (1974). Detection and preliminary identification of endogenous antitranspirants in water-stressed *Sorghum* plants. *Planta* **117**, 293–302.

Oguntoyinbo, J. S., and Richards, P. (1977). The extent and intensity of the 1969-73 drought in Nigeria: a provisional analysis. *In* "Drought in Africa. 2" (D. Dalby, R. J. Harrison Church and F. Bezzaz, eds.), pp. 114–126. International African Institute, London.

Ohkuma, K., Addicott, F. T., Smith, O. E., and Thiessen, W. E. (1965). The structure of abscisin II. *Tetrahedron Lett.* **29**, 2529–2535.

Okamoto, T., and Katoh, S. (1977). Linolenic acid binding by chloroplasts. *Plant Cell Physiol.* **18**, 539–550.

Okamoto, T., Katoh, S., and Marakami, S. (1977). Effect of linolenic acid on spinach chloroplast structure. *Plant Cell Physiol.* **18**, 551–560.

Olsen, S. R., and Kemper, W. D. (1968). Movement of nutrients to plant roots. *Advan. Agron.* **20**, 91–151.

Olsen, S. R., Watanabe, F. S., and Danielson, R. E. (1961). Phosphorus absorption by corn roots as affected by moisture and phosphorus concentration. *Soil Sci. Soc. Am. Proc.* **25**, 289–294.

Olsen, S. R., Kemper, W. D., and van Schaik, J. C. (1965). Self-diffusion coefficients of phosphorus in soil measured by transient and steady-state methods. *Soil Sci. Soc. Am. Proc.* **29**, 154–158.

Ordin, L., Itai, C., Ben-Zioni, A., Musolan, C., and Kindinger, D. I. (1974). Effect of heat shock in plant growth and on lipid and glucan synthetases. *Plant Physiol.* **53**, 118–121.

Orshan, G. (1963). Seasonal dimorphism of desert and Mediterranean chamaephytes and its significance as a factor in their water economy. *In* "The Water Relations of Plants" (A. J. Rutter and F. H. Whitehead, eds.), pp. 206–222. Blackwell, London.

Orton, P. J., and Mansfield, T. A. (1972). The activity of abscisic acid analogues as inhibitors of stomatal opening. *Planta* **121**, 263–272.

Osborne, D. J. (1977). Nucleic acids and seed germination. *In* "Physiology and Biochemistry of Seed Dormancy and Germination". (A. A. Kahn, ed.), pp. 319–333. North-Holland, Amsterdam.

Osmond, C. B. (1968). Ion absorption in *Atriplex* leaf tissue. 1. Absorption by mesophyll cells. *Aust. J. Biol. Sci.* **21**, 1119–1130.

Osmond, C. B. (1975). Environmental control of photosynthetic options in crassulacean plants. *In* "Environmental and Biological Control of Photosynthesis". (R. Marcelle, ed.), pp. 311–321. Dr. W. Junk, The Hague.

Osmond, C. B. (1976). Ion absorption and carbon metabolism in cells of higher plants. *In* "Encycl. Plant Physiol." New Ser. IIA, (U. Lüttge and M. G. Pitman, eds.), pp. 347–372. Springer-Verlag, Berlin.

Osmond, C. B. (1978). Crassulacean acid metabolism: a curiosity in context. *Annu. Rev. Plant Physiol.* **29**, 379–414.

Osmond, C. B., and Björkman, O. (1972). Simultaneous measurements of oxygen effects on net photosynthesis and glycolate metabolism in C_3 and C_4 species of *Atriplex*. *Carnegie Inst. Wahsington Yearb.* **71**, 141–148.

Osmond, C. B., and Björkman, O. (1975). Pathways of CO_2 fixation in the CAM plant *Kalanchoe diagremontiana*. II. Effects of O_2 and CO_2 concentration on light and dark CO_2 fixation. *Aust. J. Plant Physiol.* **2**, 155–162.

Osmond, C. B., and Harris, B. (1971). Photorespiration during C_4 photosynthesis. *Biochim. Biophys. Acta* **234**, 270–282.

Osmond, C. B., Winter, K., and Powles, S. B. (1980). Adaptive significance of carbon dioxide cycling during photosynthesis in water-stressed plants. *In* "Adaptation of Plants to Water and High Temperature Stress". (N. C. Turner and P. J. Kramer, eds.), pp. 139–154, Wiley-Interscience, New York.

Osonubi, O., and Davies, W. J. (1978). Solute accumulation in leaves and roots of woody plants subjected to water stress. *Oecologia* **32**, 323–332.

O'Toole, J. C., and Chang, T. T. (1979). Drought resistance in cereals: rice a case study. *In* "Stress Physiology of Crop Plants". (H. Mussell and R. C. Staples, eds.), pp. 373-405, Wiley-Interscience, New York.

O'Toole, J. C., and Moya, T. B. (1978). Genotypic variation in maintenance of leaf water potential in rice. *Crop Sci.* **18**, 873–76.

O'Toole, J. C., Ozbun, J. L., and Wallace, D. H. (1977). Photosynthetic response to water stress in *Phaseolus vulgaris*. *Physiol Plant.* **40**, 111–114.

Pal, U. R., Johnson, R. R., and Hageman, R. H. (1976). Nitrate reductase activity in heat (drought) tolerant and intolerant maize genotypes. *Crop Sci.* **16**, 775–779.

Paleg, L. G., Douglas, T. J., van Daal, A., and Keech, D. B. (1981). Proline and betaine protect enzymes against heat inactivation. *Aust. J. Plant Physiol.* **8**, 107–114.

Palfi, G., and Juhasz, J. (1970). Increase of the free proline level in water deficient leaves as a reaction to saline of cold root media. *Acta Agron Acad. Sci. Hung.* **19**, 79–88.

Palfi, G., Bito, M., and Palfi, Z. (1973). Free proline and water deficit in plant tissues. *Fiziol. Rast.* **20**, 233–238.

Palfi, G., Bito, M., Nehez, R., and Sebestyen, R. (1974a). A rapid production of protein-forming amino acids with the aid of water stress and photosynthesis. 1. The "proline pathway" of amino acid metabolism. *Acta Biol.* (Szeged) **20**, 95–106.

Palfi, G., Köves, E., Bito, M. and Sebestyen, R. (1974b). The role of amino acids during water-stress in species accumulating proline. *Phyton* **32**, 121–127.

Palfi, G., Köves, E., and Nehez, R. (1974c). Main types of amino acid regulation in cultivars with deficient water supply and their practical application in agriculture. *Noventermeles* **23**, 219–228.

Palfi, G., Nehez, R., and K'Drev, R. (1976). The effect of some growth substances and KCl on proline and free amino acid content during water stress. *Fiziol. Rast.* **2**, 10–18.

Pallas, J. E., and Box, J. E. (1970). Explanation for the stomatal response of excised leaves to kinetin. *Nature* (London) **227**, 87–88.

Palmer, W. C. (1964). "Meteorological Drought", U.S. Weather Bureau, Dept. Commer. Res. Paper 45. U.S. Government Printing Office, Washington, D.C.

Palzkill, D. A., and Tibbitts, T. W. (1977). Evidence that root pressure flow is required for calcium transport to head leaves of cabbage. *Plant Physiol.* **60**, 854–856.

Pankhurst, C. E., and Sprent, J. I. (1975a). Effects of water stress on the respiratory and nitrogen-fixing activity of soybean root nodules. *J. Exp. Bot.* **26**, 287–304.

Pankhurst, C. E., and Sprent, J. I. (1975b). Surface features of soybean root nodules. *Protoplasma* **85**, 85–98.

Papadakis, J. (1978). Root toxins and crop growth: allelopathy. *In* "Crop Physiology". (U. S. Gupta, ed.), pp. 202–237. Oxford and IBH, New Delhi.

Parham, M. R. (1972). A comparative study of the mineral nutrition of selected halophytes. Ph.D. Thesis. Univ. East Anglia.

Parker, J. (1968). Drought resistance mechanism. *In* "Water Deficit and Plant Growth". (T. T. Kozlowski, ed.), Vol. I. pp. 195–234. Academic Press, New York.

Parlange, J.-Y., Turner, N. C., and Waggoner, P. E. (1975). Water uptake, diameter change, and non-linear diffusion in tree stems. *Plant Physiol.* **55**, 247–250.

Passioura, J. B. (1963). A mathematical model for the uptake of ions from the soil solution. *Plant Soil* **18**, 225–238.

Passioura, J. B. (1972). Effect of root geometry on the yield of wheat growing on stored water. *Aust. J. Agric. Res.* **23**, 745–752.

Passioura, J. B. (1974). The effect of root geometry on the water relations of temperate cereals (wheat, barley, oats). *In* "Structure and Function of Primary Root Tissues" (J. Kolek, ed.), pp. 357–363. Veda, Bratislava.

Passioura, J. B. (1976). The control of water movement through plants. *In* "Transport and Transfer Processes in Plants" (I. F. Wardlaw and J. B. Passioura, eds.), pp. 373–380. Academic Press, New York.

Passioura, J. B. (1977). Grain yield, harvest index, and water use of wheat. *J. Aust. Inst. Agric. Sci.* **43**, 117–121.

Pate, J. S. (1971). Movement of nitrogenous solutes in plants. *In* "N-15 in soil-plant studies". pp. 165–187. I.A.E.A., Vienna.

Pate, J. S. (1976). Transport in symbiotic systems fixing nitrogen. *In* 'Transport in Plants II B." Encycl. Plant Physiol. New Ser. (U. Lüttge and M. G. Pitman, eds.), **2**, 278–303. Springer-Verlag, Berlin.

Pate, J. S., Gunning, B. E. S., and Briarty, L. G. (1969). Ultrastructure and functioning of the transport system of the leguminous root nodule. *Planta* **85**, 11–34.

Paudler, W. W., and Wagner, S. (1963). Major alkaloid of *Marrubium vulgare*. *Chem. Ind.* **43**, 1693–1694.

Paulsen, J. M., and Lane, M. D. (1966). Spinach ribulose diphosphate carboxylase. I. Purification and properties of the enzyme. *Biochemistry* **5**, 2350–2357.

Paxton, R. G., and Mayr, H. H. (1962). Untersuchingen uber das Naturliche Vorkommen Quarternarer Ammoniumbasen in *Lycopersicon esculentum*. *Planta* **59**, 165–174.

Payne, E. S., Brownrigg, A., Yarwood, A., and Boulter, D. (1971). Changing protein synthetic machinery during development of seeds of *Vicia faba*. *Phytochemistry* **10**, 2299–2303.

Payne, P. I. (1976). The long-lived messenger ribonucleic acid of flowering plant seeds. *Biol. Rev.* **51**, 329–363.

Payne, P. I., and Boulter, D. (1969). Free and membrane bound ribosomes of the cotyledons of *Vicia faba* (L.). *Planta* **84**, 263–71.

Payne, P. I., Gordon, M. E., Barlow, P. W., and Parker, M. L. (1977). The subcellular location of the long-lived messenger RNA of rape seed. *In* "Translation of Natural and Synthetic Polynucleotides". (A. B. Legocki, ed.), pp. 224–227. Publishers of Poznań Agricultural University, Poznań.

Pearce, R. B., Strange, R. N., and Smith, H. (1976). Glycinebetaine and choline in wheat: distribution and relation to infection by *Fusarium graminearum*. *Phytochemistry* **15**, 953–956.

Penny, M. G., and Bowling, D. J. F. (1974). A study of potassium gradients in the epidermis of intact leaves of *Commelina communis* L. in relation to stomatal opening. *Planta* **119**, 17–25.

Pereira, J. B., and Kozlowski, T. T. (1977). Water relations and drought resistance of young *Pinus banksiana* and *P. resinosa* plantation trees. *Can. J. For. Res.* **7**, 132-137.

Perlyuk, M. F., Zlobin, V. S., and Orlova, T. A. (1974). Variability of amino acid composition of algae inhabiting zone of variable salinity. *Gidrobiol. Zh.* **10**, 53–58.

Petrie, A. K. H., and Wood, J. G. (1958). Studies on the nitrogen metabolism of plants. III. On the effect of water content on the relationship between proteins and amino acids. *Ann. Bot.* **33**, 887–898.

Pettersson, S. (1960). Ion absorption in young sunflower plants. I. Uptake and transport mechanisms for sulphate. *Physiol. Plant.* **13**, 133–147.

Peumans, W. J., and Carlier, A. R. (1977). Messenger ribonucleoprotein particles in dry wheat and rye embryos. *In vitro* translation and size distribution. *Planta* **136**, 195–201.

Philip, J. R. (1957). The physical principles of soil water movement during the irrigation cycle. *Proc. Int. Congr. Irrig. Drain.* **8**, 125–154.

Pinter, L., Kalman, L., Nemeth, J., and Palfi, G. (1977). Study of proline, total free amino acid and soluble total protein content of isolated plant parts in two maize hybrids of different water demand. *Novenytemales* **26**, 253–263.

Pitman, M. G., and Cram, W. J. (1977). Regulation of ion content in whole plants. *In* "Integration of Activity in the Higher Plant". (D. H. Jennings, ed.), pp. 391–424, Cambridge Univ. Press, London.

Pitman, M. G., and Wellfare, D. (1978). Inhibition of ion transport in excised barley roots by abscisic acid; relation to water permeability of the roots. *J. Exp. Bot.* **29**, 1125–1138.

Pitman, M. G., Lüttge, U., Lauchli, A., and Ball, E. (1974). Effect of previous water stress on ion uptake and transport in barley seedlings. *Aust. J. Plant Physiol.* **1**, 377–385.

Pitman, M. G., Schaeffer, N., and Wildes, R. A. (1975). Effects of abscisic acid on fluxes of ions in barley roots. *In* "Membrane Transport in Plants and Plant Organelles" (U. Zimmerman and J. Dainty, eds.), pp. 391–396. Springer-Verlag, Berlin.

Place, G. A., and Barber, S. A. (1964). The effect of soil moisture and rubidium concentration on diffusion and uptake of rubidium-86. *Soil Sci. Soc. Am. Proc.* **28**, 239–243.

Plaut, Z. (1971). Inhibition of photosynthetic carbon dioxide fixation in isolated spinach chloroplasts exposed to reduced osmotic potentials. *Plant Physiol.* **48**, 591–595.

Plaut, Z., and Bravdo, B. (1973). Response of carbon dioxide fixation to water stress. Parallel measurements on isolated chloroplasts and intact spinach leaves. *Plant Physiol.* **52**, 28–32.

Plaut, Z., and Halevy, A. H. (1966). Regeneration after wilting, growth and yield of wheat plants, as affected by two growth-retarding compounds. *Physiol. Plant.* **19**, 1064–1072.

Plaut, Z., and Ordin, L. (1964). The effect of moisture tension and nitrogen supply on cell wall metabolism of sunflower leaves. *Physiol. Plant.* **17**, 279–286.

Pochmann, A. (1959). Über die Tätigkeit der nichtkontraktilen Importvakuole und den Modus der Osmoregulation bei dem Salzflagellaten *Choanogaster* nebst Bemerkungen über die Funktion der Pusulen. *Ber. Dtsch. Bot. Ges.* **72**, 99–108.

Pollard, A., and Wyn Jones, R. G. (1979). Enzyme activities in concentrated solutions of glycinebetaine and other solutes. *Planta* **144**, 291–298.

Pollock, J. R. A., and Stevens R. (1965). "Dictionary of Organic Compounds", 4th edn. Eyre and Spottiswoode, London.

Potter, J. R., and Boyer, J. S. (1973). Chloroplast response to low leaf water potentials. II. Role of osmotic potential. *Plant Physiol.* **51**, 993–997.

Pourrat, Y., and Hubac, C. (1974). Comparaison des mécanismes de la résistance à la sécheresse chez deux plantes désertiques: *Artemisia herba alba* Asso et *Carex pachystylis* (J. Gay) Asch. et Graebn. *Physiol. Veg.* **12**, 135–147.

Powles, S. B., and Osmond, C. B. (1978). Inhibition of the capacity and efficiency of photosynthesis in bean leaflets illuminated in CO_2-free atmosphere at low oxygen: a possible role for photorespiration. *Aust. J. Plant Physiol.* **5**, 619–629.

Preil, W. (1977). Early selection of winter grown tomatoes. Relations between free proline in the leaves of seedlings and yield. *Z. Pflanzenzuecht* **79**, 224–237.

Proskurnina N. F., and Utkin, L. M. (1960). DL-Stachydrine in *Logochilus*. *Med. Promst. S.S.R.* **14**, 30–31.

Prosser, C. L. (1973). "Comparative Animal Physiology". Saunders, Philadelphia.

Pulatova, T. P. (1969). Presence of alkaloids in some plants of the family Labiatae. *Khim. Prir. Soedin* **5**, 62–63 (CA 71:10282).

Quarrie, S. A., and Jones, H. G. (1977). Effects of abscisic acid and water stress on development and morphology of wheat. *J. Exp. Bot.* **28**, 192–203.

Rafaeli-Eshkol, D. (1968). Studies on halotolerance in a moderately halophilic bacterium. Effect of growth conditions on salt resistance of the respiratory system. *Biochem. J.* **109**, 679–688.

Rafaeli-Eshkol, D., and Avi-Dor, Y. (1968). Studies on halotolerance in a moderately halophilic bacterium. Effect of betaine on salt resistance of the respiratory system. *Biochem. J.* **109**, 687–691.

Raison, J. K., Lyons, J. M., and Thomson, W. W. (1971a). The influence of membranes on the temperature-induced changes in the kinetics of some respiratory enzymes of mitochondria. *Arch. Biochem. Biophys.* **142**, 83–90.

Raison, J. K., Lyons, J. M., Welhorn, R. J., and Keith, A. D. (1971b). Temperature-induced phase changes in mitochondrial membranes detected by spin labeling. *J. Biol. Chem.* **246**, 4036–4040.

Rajagopal, V., Rao, N. G. P., and Sinha, S. K. (1976). Nitrate reductase in sorghum. I. Variation in cultivars during growth and development. *Indian J. Genet.* **36**, 156–161.

Rajagopal, V., Balasubramanian, V., and Sinha, S. K. (1977). Diurnal fluctuations in relative water content, nitrate reductase and proline content in water-stressed and non-stressed wheat. *Physiol. Plant.* **40**, 69–71.

Ramos, C., and Kaufmann, M. R. (1978). Hydraulic resistance of rough lemon roots. *Physiol. Plant.* **45**, 311–314.

Raschke, K. (1956). Über die physikalischen Beziehungen zwischen Wärmeübergangszahl, Strahlungsaustausch, Temperatur und Transpiration eines Blattes. *Planta* **48**, 200–238.

Raschke, K. (1970). Stomatal responses to pressure changes and interruptions in the water supply of detached leaves of *Zea mays* L. *Plant Physiol.* **45**, 415–423.

Raschke, K. (1972). Saturation kinetics of the velocity of stomatal closing in response to CO_2. *Plant Physiol.* **49**, 229–234.

Raschke, K. (1973). Abscisic acid sensitizes stomata to CO_2 in leaves of *Xanthium strumarium* L. *Plant Growth Subst. Proc. Int. Conf. VIII*, Tokyo.

Raschke, K. (1975a). Stomatal action. *Annu. Rev. Plant Physiol.* **26**, 309–340.

Raschke, K. (1975b). Simultaneous requirement of carbon dioxide and abscisic acid for stomatal closing in *Xanthium strumarium* L. *Planta* **125**, 243–259.

Raschke, K. (1976). How stomata resolve the dilemma of opposing priorities. *Philos. Trans. R. Soc. London* Ser. B. **273**, 551–560.

Raschke, K., and Dittrich, P. (1977). [14C]-carbon dioxide fixation by isolated leaf epidermis with stomata closed or open. *Planta* **134**, 69–75.

Rawson, H. M., Begg, J. E., and Woodward, R. G. (1977). The effect of atmospheric humidity on photosynthesis, transpiration and water use efficiency of leaves of several plant species. *Planta* **134**, 5–10.

Rawson, H. M., Turner, N. C., and Begg, J. E. (1978). Agronomic and physiological response of soybean and sorghum crops to water deficits IV. Photosynthesis, transpiration and water use efficiency of leaves. *Aust. J. Plant Physiol.* **5**, 195–209.

Read, P. E., and Hoysler, V. (1971). Improving rooting of carnation and poinsettia cuttings with succinic acid-2,3-dimethylhydrazide. *HortScience.* **6**, 350–351.

Reed, N. R., and Bonner, B. A. (1974). The effect of abscisic acid on the uptake of potassium and chloride into *Avena* coleoptile sections. *Planta* **116**, 173–185.

Reimold, R. J., and Queen, W. H. (1974). "Ecology of Halophytes". Academic Press, New York.

Rena, A. B., and Splittstoesser, W. E. (1974a). Proline dehydrogenase from pumpkin (*Cucurbita moschata*) cotyledons. *Physiol. Plant.* **32**, 177–181.

Rena, A. B., and Splittstoesser, W. E. (1974b). Δ¹-pyrroline-5-carboxylate: The product of proline dehydrogenase from *Cucurbita moschata* cotyledons. *Phytochemistry* **13**, 2081–2084.

Rena, A. B., and Splittstoesser, W. E. (1974c). The metabolism of proline in cotyledons of pumpkin (*Cucurbita moschata*). *Plant Cell Physiol.* **15**, 681–686.

Rena, A. B., and Splittstoesser, W. E. (1975). Proline dehydrogenase and pyrroline-5-carboxylate reductase from pumpkin cotyledons. *Phytochemistry* **14**, 657–661.

Renner, O. (1910). Beitrage zur Physik der Transpiration. *Flora* (Jena) **100**, 451–547.

Reporter, M., Raveed, D., and Norris, G. (1975). Binding of *Rhizobium japonicum* to cultured soybean root cells: morphological evidence. *Plant Sci. Lett.* **5**, 73–76.

Rhodes, P. R., and Matsuda, K. (1976). Water stress, rapid polyribosome reductions and growth. *Plant Physiol.* **58**, 631-635.

Richter, H. (1973). Frictional potential losses and total water potential in plants: a re-evaluation. *J. Exp. Bot.* **24**, 983–994.

Richter, H. (1976). The water status in the plant: experimental evidence. *In* "Water and Plant Life". (O. L. Lange, L. Kappen, and E.-D. Schulze, eds.), *Ecol. Stud.* **19**, 42–58. Springer-Verlag, New York.

Richter, H. (1978). Water relations of single drying leaves: evaluation with a dewpoint hygrometer. *J. Exp. Bot.* **29**, 277–280.

Richter, H., Halbwachs, G., and Holzner, W. (1972). Saugspannungsmessungen in der Krone eines Mammutbaumes (*Sequoiadendron giganeum*). *Flora* (Jena) Abt. A. **161**, 401–420.

Rifkin, A., and Richmond, A. E. (1976). Amelioration of chilling injuries in cucumber seedlings by abscisic acid. *Physiol. Plant.* **38**, 95–97.

Ritchie, J. T. (1974). Atmospheric and soil water influences on the plant water balance. *Agric. Meteorol.* **14**, 183–198.

Robards, A. W., and Clarkson, D. T. (1976). The role of plasmodesmata in the transport of water and nutrients across roots. *In* "Intercellular Communication in Plants: Studies on Plasmodesmata". (B. E. S. Gunning and A. W. Robards, eds.), pp. 107–120. Springer-Verlag, Berlin.

Roberts, S. W., and Knoerr, K. R. (1977). Components of water potential estimated from xylem pressure measurements in five tree species. *Oecologia* **28**, 191–202.

Robertson, A. V., and Marion L. (1959). The biogenesis of alkaloids XXI. The biogenesis of (−)homostachydrine and the occurrence of trigonelline in alfalfa. *Can. J. Chem.* **37**, 1043–1047.

Roberston, A. V., and Marion, L. (1960). The biogenesis of alkaloids XXV. The role of hygric acid in the biogenesis of stachydrine. *Can. J. Chem.* **38**, 396–398.

Robertson, G. A., and Greenway, H. (1973). Effects of C.C.C. on drought resistance of *Triticum aestivum* L and *Zea mays,* L. *Ann. Bot.* **37**, 929–934.

Robinson, R. A., and Stokes, R. H. (1949). Tables of osmotic and activity coefficient of electrolytes in aqueous solution at 25°. *Trans. Faraday Soc.* **45**, 612–624.

Robinson, R. A., and Stokes, R. H. (1955). "Electrolyte Solutions". Butterworth, London.

Rochat, E., and Therrien, K. P. (1976). Study of amino acids in relation to resistance to cold in Kharkov and Kent winter wheats. *Nat. Can. (Que.)* **103**, 517–525.

Rodin, L. E., and Bazilevich, N. I. (1967). "Production and Mineral Cycling in Terrestrial Vegetation." Oliver and Boyd, Edinburgh.

Rorison, I. H. (ed.) (1969). "Ecological Aspects of the Mineral Nutrition of Plants". Blackwell, Oxford.

Routley, D. G. (1966). Proline accumulation in wilted ladino clover leaves. *Crop Sci.* **6**, 358–361.

Running, S. W. (1976). Environmental control of leaf water conductance in conifers. *Can. J. For. Res.* **6**, 104–112.

Running, S. W., Waring, R. H., and Rydell, R. A. (1975). Physiological control of water flux in conifers. *Oecologica* **18**, 1–16.

Rustembokova, G. B., Goryaev, M. I., and Gladyshev, P. P. (1973). Isolation of betaine from *Chenopodium botrys*. *Khim. Prir. Soedin.* **9**, 569(CA 80:63782).

Ryan, J. G. (1974). "Socio-economic aspects of agricultural development in the semi-arid tropics". Occasional Paper 6. ICRISAT, Patancheru, A. P., India.

Saddler, H. D. W., and Pitman, M. G. (1970). An apparatus for the measurement of sap flow in unexcised leafy shoots. *J. Exp. Bot.* **21**, 1048–1059.

Saffigna, P. G., Tanner, C. B., and Keeney, D. R. (1976). Non-uniform infiltration under potato canopies caused by interception, stemflow, and hilling. *Agron. J.* **68**, 337–342.

Sakai, A., and Yoshida, S. (1968). Protective action of various compounds against freezing injury in plant cells. *Teion Kagaku, Seibutsu-Hen.* **26**, 13–21. (CA 71:934y).

Salter, P. J., and Goode, J. E. (1967). Crop responses to water at different stages of growth. *Commonw. Bur. Anim. Health Rev. Ser.*

Sanchez-Diaz. M. F., and Kramer, P. J. (1971). Behaviour of corn and sorghum under water stress and during recovery. *Plant Physiol.* **48**, 613–616.

Sandhu, G. R., Aslam, Z., Salim, M. Sattar, A., Qureshi, R. H., Ahmad, N., and Wyn Jones, R. G. (1981). Effect of root zone salinity on the yield and quality of Kallar grass (*Diplachne fusca*). *Plant Cell & Environ.* (in press).

Santarius, K. A. (1967). Das Verhalten von CO_2-Assimilation, NADP- und PGS-Reduktion und ATP-Synthese intakter Blattzellen in Abhängigkeit vom Wassergehalt. *Planta* **73**, 228–242.

Santarius, K. A., and Ernst, R. (1967). Das Verhalten von Hill-Reaktion und Photophosphorylierung isolierter Chloroplasten in Abhängigkeit vom Wassergehalt. I. Wasserentzug mittels Konzentrierter losungen. *Planta* **73**, 91–108.

Santarius, K. A., and Heber, U. (1967). Das Verhalten von Hill-Reaktion und Photophosphorylierung isolierter Chloroplasten in Abhängigkeit vom Wassergehalt. II. Wasserentzug uber $CaCl_2$. *Planta* **73**, 109–137.

Satarova, N. A., and Tvorus, E. K. (1970). Changes in protein synthesis and state of the ribosomes during drought. *Fiziol. Biokhim. Kul'.t Rast.* **2**, 349–353.

Satarova, N. A., and Tvorus, E. K. (1971). Changes in *in vitro* functional activity of ribosomes from bean seedlings exposed to drying. *Sov. Plant Physiol.* **18**, 448–453.

Sato, S., and Asahi, T. (1975). Biochemical properties of mitochondrial membrane from dry pea seeds and changes in the properties during inhibition. *Plant Physiol.* **56**, 816–820.

Sauerbeck, D., and Johnen, B. (1976). Der Umsatz von Pflanzenwurzeln im Laufe der Vegetationsperiode und dessen Beitrag zur "Bodenatmung". *Z. Pflanzenern aehr. Bodenkd.* **3**, 315–328.

Savitskaya, N. N. (1976). On the physiological role of proline in plants. *Biol. Nauki* (Moscow) **19**, 49–61.

Sawhney, S. K., and Naik, M. S. (1972). Role of light in the synthesis of nitrate reductase and nitrite reductase in rice seedlings. *Biochem. J.* **130**, 475–485.

Sawhney, S. K., Naik, M. S., and Nicholas, D. J. D. (1978a). Regulation of nitrate reduction by light, ATP and mitochondrial respiration in wheat leaves. *Nature* (London) **272**, 647–648.

Sawhney, S. K., Naik, M. S., and Nicholas, D. J. D. (1978b). Regulation of NADH supply for nitrate reduction in green plants via photosynthesis and mitochondrial respiration. *Biochem. Biophys. Res. Commun.* **81**, 1209–1216.

Sawhney, S. K., Nicholas, D. J. D., and Naik, M. S. (1979). Accumulation of succinate in wheat leaves during anaerobic nitrate reduction in the dark. *Indian J. Biochem. Biophys.* **16**, 37–38.

Scarth, G. W., and Shaw, M. (1951). Stomatal movements and photosynthesis in *Pelargonium*. I. Effects of light and CO_2. *Plant Physiol.* **26**, 207–225.

Schnabl, H., and Ziegler, H. (1977). The mechanism of stomatal movement in *Allium cepa* L. *Planta* **136**, 37–43.

Schneider, A. (1966). Les variations de la proline chez le pêcher. *C. R. Hebd. Seances Acad. Sci.* Ser. D. **262**, 2726–2729.

Schobert, B. (1974). The influence of water stress on the metabolism of diatoms. 1. Osmotic resistance and proline accumulation in *Cyclotella meneghiniana. Z. Pflanzenphysiol.* **74**, 106–120.

Schobert, B. (1977). Is there an osmotic regulatory mechanism in algae and higher plants? *J. Theor. Biol.* **68**, 17-26.

Schobert, B. (1979). Die Akkumulierung von Prolin in *Phaeodactylum tricornutum* und die Funktion der "compatible solutes" in Pflanzenzellen unter Wasserstress. *Ber. Deutsch. Bot. Ges.* **92**, 23–30.

Schobert, B., and Tschesche, H. (1978). Unusual solution properties of proline and its interaction with proteins. *Biochim. Biophys. Acta* **541**, 270–277.

Schoffeniels, E., and Gilles, R. (1972). Ionoregulation and osmoregulation in mollusca. *In* "Chemical Zoology". (M. Florkin and B. T. Scheer, eds.), Vol. VIII. pp. 393–420. Academic Press, New York.

Schrader, L. E., Ritenour, G. L., Eilrich, G. L., and Hageman, R. H. (1968). Some characteristics of nitrate reductase from higher plants. *Plant Physiol.* **43**, 930–40.

Schrader, L. E., Cataldo, D. A., and Peterson, D. M. (1974). Use of protein in extraction and stabilization of nitrate reductase. *Plant Physiol.* **53**, 688–690.

Schrier, E. E., and Scheraga, H. A. (1962). The effect of aqueous alcohol solutions on the thermal transition of ribonuclease. *Biochim. Biophys. Acta* **64**, 406–408.

Schubert, K. R., and Evans, H. J. (1976). Hydrogen evolution: a major factor affecting the efficiency of nitrogen fixation in nodulated symbionts. *Proc. Nat. Acad. Sci. U.S.A.* **73**, 1207–1211.

Schultz, J. E. (1971). Soil water changes under fallow-crop treatments in relation to soil type, rainfall and yield of wheat. *Aust. J. Exp. Agric. Anim. Husb.* **11**, 236–242.

Schultz, J. E. (1974). Root development of wheat at the flowering stage under different cultural practices. *Agric. Record* **1**, 12–17.

Schulze, E.-D., Lange, O. L., Buschbom, U., Kappen, L., and Evenari, M. (1972). Stomatal responses to changes in humidity in plants growing in the desert. *Planta* **108**, 259–270.

Schulze, E.-D., Lange, O. L., Kappen, L., Buschbom, U., and Evenari, M. (1973). Stomatal responses to changes in temperature at increasing water stress. *Planta* **110**, 29–42.

Schulze, E.-D., Lange, O. L., Evenari, M., Kappen, L., and Buschbom, U. (1974). The role of air humidity and temperature in controlling stomatal resistance of *Prunus armeniaca* L. under desert conditions. I. A simulation of the daily course of stomatal resistance. *Oecologia* **17**, 159–170.

Schulze, E.-D., Lange, O. L., Kappen, L. Evenari, M., and Buschbom, U. (1975a). The role of air humidity and leaf temperature in controlling stomatal resistance of *Prunus armeniaca* L. under desert conditions. II. The significance of leaf water status and internal carbon dioxide concentration. *Oecologia* **18**, 219–233.

Schulze, E.-D., Lange, O. L., Evenari, M., Kappen, L., and Buschbom, U. (1975b). The role of air humidity and temperature in controlling stomatal resistance of *Prunus armeniaca* L. under desert conditions. III. The effect on water use efficiency. *Oecologia* **19**, 303–314.

Scott, D. B., Farnden, K. J. F., and Robertson, J. G. (1976). Ammonia assimilation in lupin nodules. *Nature* (London) **263**, 705–707.

Scott, N. S., Munns, R., and Barlow, E. W. R. (1979). Polyribosome content in young and aged wheat leaves subjected to drought. *J. Exp. Bot.* **30**, 905–911.

Seaman, J., Holt, J., and Rivers, J. (1974). "Hararghe under Drought: A Survey on the Effects of Drought upon Human Nutrition in Hararghe Province": Ethiop. Gov. Relief and Rehabil. Commission, Addis Ababa.

Seibert, G., Loris, K., Zollner, J., Frenzel, B., and Zahn, R. K. (1976). The conservation of poly-A-containing RNA during the dormant state of the moss *Polytrichum commune*. *Nucleic Acids Res. Spec. Publ.* **3**, 1997–2003.

Sells, G. D., and Koeppe, D. E. (1980). Proline oxidation by water-stressed corn shoot mitochondria. *Plant Physiol.* **65**, 25–31.

Sen, S., and Osborne, D. J. (1974). Germination of rye embryos following hydration-dehydration treatments: enhancement of protein and RNA synthesis and earlier induction of DNA replication. *J. Exp. Bot.* **25**, 1010–1019.

Servaites, J. C., and Ogren, W. L. (1978). Oxygen inhibition of photosynthesis and stimulation of photorespiration in soybean leaf cells. *Plant Physiol.* **61**, 62–67.

Shah, C. B., and Loomis, R. S. (1965). Ribonucleic acid and protein metabolism in sugar beet during drought. *Physiol. Plant.* **18**, 240–254.

Shaner, D. L., and Boyer, J. S. (1976a). Nitrate reductase activity in maize (*Zea mays* L.) leaves. I. Regulation by nitrate flux. *Plant Physiol.* **58**, 499–504.

Shaner, D. L., and Boyer, J. S. (1976b). Nitrate reductase activity in maize (*Zea mays* L.) leaves. II. Regulation by nitrate flux at low leaf water potential. *Plant Physiol.* **58**, 505–509.

Shannon, J. D., and Wallace, W. (1979). Isolation and characterisation of peptide hydrolases from the maize root. *Eur. J. Biochem.* **102**, 399–408.

Shantz, H. L., and Piemeisel, L. N. (1927). The water requirement of plants at Akron, Colorado, *J. Agric. Res.* **34**, 1093–1189.

Shearman, L. L., Eastin, J. D., Sullivan, C. Y., and Kinbacher, E. J. (1972). Carbon dioxide exchange in water stressed sorghum. *Crop Sci.* **12**, 406–409.

Shepherd, W. (1975). Matric water potential of leaf tissue — measurement and significance. *J. Exp. Bot.* **26**, 465–468.

Sheriff, D. W. (1977a). The effect of humidity on water uptake by, and viscous flow resistance of, excised leaves of a number of species: physiological and anatomical observations. *J. Exp. Bot.* **28**, 1399–1407.

Sheriff, D. W. (1977b). Where is humidity sensed when stomata respond to it directly? *Ann. Bot.* **41**, 1083–1084.

Sheriff, D. W., and Kaye, P. E. (1977a). Responses of diffusive conductance to humidity in a drought avoiding and a drought resistant (in terms of stomata response) legume. *Ann. Bot.* **41**, 653–655.

Sheriff, D. W., and Kaye, P. E. (1977b). The response of diffusive conductance in wilted and unwilted *Atriplex hastata* L. leaves to humidity. *Z. Pflanzenphysiol.* **83**, 463–466.

Sheriff, D. W., and Meidner, H. (1974). Water pathways in leaves of *Hedera helix* L. and *Tradescantia virginiana* L. *J. Exp. Bot.* **25**, 1147–1156.

Shibaoka, H., and Thimann, K. V. (1970). Antagonisms between kinetin and amino acids. Experiment on the mode of action of cytokinins. *Plant Physiol.* **46**, 212–220.

Shkedy-Vinkler, C., and Avi-Dor, Y. (1975). Betaine-induced stimulation of respiration at high osmolarities in a halotolerant bacterium. *Biochem. J.* **150**, 219–226.

Simenauer, A. (1975). Biochemistry of choline and its derivatives XXXVII. Betaine and choline in *Beta vulgaris. Bull. Soc. Chim. Biol.* **39**, 1429–1439. (CA.52 : 18688)

Simpson, G. M., and Wain, R. L. (1961). A relationship between gibberellic acid and light in the control of internode extension of dwarf peas *(Pisum sativum). J. Exp. Bot.,* **12**, 207–216.

Simpson, J. R. (1976). Water relations of the sugar tolerant yeast, *Saccharomyces rouxii*. Ph.D. Thesis Univ. New South Wales. Australia.

Simpson, J. R., and Lipsett, J. (1973). Effects of surface moisture supply on the subsoil nutritional requirements of lucerne. *(Medicago sativa* L.). *Aust. J. Agric. Res.* **24**, 199–209.

Singh, T. N. (1970). Water stress and amino acid metabolism in cereals. Ph. D. thesis, Univ. of Adelaide.

Singh, T. N., Aspinall, D., and Paleg, L. G. (1972). Proline accumulation and varietal adaptability to drought in barley: a potential metabolic measure of drought resistance. *Nature,* (London) **236**, 188–190.

Singh, T. N., Paleg, L. G., and Aspinall, D. (1973a). Stress metabolism. I. Nitrogen metabolism and growth in the barley plant during water stress. *Aust. J. Biol. Sci.* **26**, 45–56.

Singh, T. N. Aspinall, D., Paleg, L. G. and Boggess, S. F. (1973b). Stress metabolism. II. Changes in proline concentration in excised plant tissues. *Aust. J. Biol. Sci.* **26**, 57–63.

Singh, T. N., Paleg, L. G., and Aspinall, D. (1973c). Stress metabolism. III. Variations in response to water deficit in the barley plant. *Aust. J. Biol. Sci.* **26**, 65–76.

Singh, T. N., Aspinall, D., and Paleg, L. G. (1973d). Stress metabolism. IV. The influence of (2-chloroethyl)-trimethylammonium chloride and gibberellic acid on the growth and proline accumulation of wheat plants during water stress. *Aust. J. Biol. Sci.* **26**, 77–86.

Sinha, S. K., and Khanna, R. (1975). Physiological, biochemical and genetic basis of heterosis. *Adv. Agron.* **27**, 123–174.

Sinha, S. K., and Rajagopal, V. (1975). Proline slows down the loss of nitrate reductase in moisture stressed plants. *Plant Physiol. (Suppl.)* **56**, No. 2, 22.

Sionit, N., and Kramer, P. J. (1977). Effect of water stress during different stages of growth of soybean. *Agron. J.* **69**, 274–278.

Slatyer, R. O. (1962). Methodology of a water balance study conducted on a desert woodland *Acacia aneura* F. Muell.) community in central Australia. *Arid Zone Res.* **16**, 15–26.

Slatyer, R. O. (1966). Some physical aspects of the control of leaf transpiration. *Agric. Meteorol.* **3**, 281–292.

Slatyer, R. O. (1973). The effect of internal water status on plant growth, development and yield. *In* "Plant Response to Climatic Factors". (R. O. Slatyer, ed.), pp. 171–191. Uppsala Symp. UNESCO, Paris.

Slatyer, R. O., and Bierhuizen, J. F. (1964). The effect of several foliar sprays on transpiration and water use efficiency of cotton plants. *Agric. Meteorol.* **1**, 42–53.

Slavik, B. (1963). On the problem of the relationship between hydration of leaf tissue and intensity of photosynthesis and respiration. *In* "The Water Relations of Plants". (V. S. Rutter and F. H. Whitehead, eds.), pp. 225–234, Blackwell, Oxford.

Slavik, B. (1974). "Methods of Studying Plant Water Relations". Springer-Verlag, New York.

Smith, D. L. (1973). Nucleic acid, protein, and starch synthesis in developing cotyledons of *Pisum arvense* L. *Ann. Bot.* (London) **37**, 795–804.

Solomonson, L. P., Jetschmann, K., and Vennesland, B. (1973). Reversible inactivation of the nitrate reductase of *Chlorella vulgaris Beijerinck*. *Biochem. Biophys. Acta* **309**, 32–43.

Solomos, T., Malhotra, S. S., Prasad, S., Malhotra, S. K., and Spencer, M. (1972). Biochemical and structural changes in mitochondria and other cellular components of pea cotyledons during germination. *Can. J. Biochem.* **50**, 725–737.

Somero, G. N., and Low, P. S. (1977). Enzyme hydration may explain catalytic efficiency differences among lactate dehydrogenase homologues. *Nature* (London) **266**, 276–278.

Somero, G. N., Neubauer, M., and Low, P. S. (1977). Neutral salt effects on the velocity and activation volume of the lactate dehydrogenase reaction: evidence for enzyme hydration changes during catalysis. *Arch. Biochem. Biophys.* **181**, 438–446.

Sondheimer, E., Galston, E. C., Chang, Y. P., and Walton, D. C. (1971). Asymmetry, its importance to the action and metabolism of abscisic acid. *Science* **174**, 829–831.

Sorger, G. J. (1966). Nitrate reductase electron transport systems in mutant and in wild-type strains of *Neurospora*. *Biochim. Biophys. Acta* **118**, 484–494.

Spanswick, R. M. (1976). Symplasmic transport in tissues. *In* "Encycl. Plant Physiol." New Ser. Vol. IIB (U. Lüttge and M. G. Pitman, eds.), pp. 35–53. Springer-Verlag, Berlin.

Specht, R. L. (1953). The ecology of the heath vegetation in the upper south-east of South

Australia. Ph.D. thesis, Univ. of Adelaide.

Specht, R. L., and Groves, R. H. (1966). A comparison of the phosphorus nutrition of Australian heath plants and introduced economic plants. *Aust. J. Bot.* **14**, 201–221.

Speed, D. J. (1972). The biosynthesis of betaine and related compounds in higher plants and fungi. Ph.D. thesis. Univ. of Durham.

Spencer, J. F. T. (1968). Production of polyhydric alcohols by yeasts. *In* "Progress in Industrial Microbiology". (D. J. D. Hockenhull, ed.), Vol. 7, pp. 1–42. J. and A. Churchill Ltd. London.

Spiegel, S., and Marcus, A. (1975). Polyribosome formation in early wheat embryo germination independent of either transcription or polyadenylation. *Nature* (London) **256**, 228–230.

Spiegel, S., Obendorf, R. L., and Marcus, A. (1975). Transcription of ribosomal and messenger RNAs in early wheat embryo germination. *Plant Physiol.* **56**, 502–507.

Splittstoesser, S. A., and Splittstoesser, W. E. (1973). Pyrroline-5-carboxylate reductase from *Cucurbita* cotyledons. *Phytochemistry* **12**, 1565–1568.

Splittstoesser, W. E. (1969). Metabolism of arginine by aging and 7 day old pumpkin seedlings. *Plant Physiol.* **44**, 361–369.

Sprent, J. I. (1971). The effects of water stress on nitrogen fixing root nodules. I. Effects on the physiology of detached soybean nodules. *New Phytol.* **70**, 9–17.

Sprent, J. I. (1972a). The effects of water stress on nitrogen fixing root nodules. II. Effects on the fine structure of detached soybean nodules. *New Phytol.* **71**, 443–450.

Sprent, J. I. (1972b). The effects of water stress on nitrogen fixing root nodules. IV. Effects on whole plants of *Vicia faba* and *Glycine max. New Phytol.* **71**, 603–611.

Sprent, J. I. (1975). Adherence of sand particles to soybean roots under water stress. *New Phytol.* **74**, 461–463.

Sprent, J. I. (1976). Water deficits and nitrogen fixing root nodules. *In* "Water Deficits and Plant Growth". (T. T. Kozlowski, ed.), Vol. IV, pp. 291–315. Academic Press. New York.

Sprent, J. I. (1980). Root nodule anatomy, type of export product and evolutionary origin in some leguminosae. *Plant Cell & Envir.* **3**, 35–43.

Sprent, J. I., and Gallacher, A. (1976). Anaerobiosis in soybean root nodules under water stress. *Soil Biol. Biochem.* **8**, 317–320.

Squire, G. R., and Jones, M. B. (1971). Studies on the mechanism of action of the antitranspirant, phenylmercuric acetate, and its penetration into the mesophyll. *J. Exp. Bot.* **22**, 980–991.

Squire, G. R., and Mansfield, T. A. (1972). A simple method of isolating stomata on detached epidermis by low pH treatment : observations of the importance of the subsidiary cells. *New Phytol.* **71**, 1033–1043.

Sribney, M., and Kirkwood, S. (1954). The role of betaine in plant methylations. *Can. J. Chem.* **32**, 918–920.

Stålfelt, M. G. (1929). Die Abhängigkeit der Spaltöffnungsreaktionen von der Wasserbilanz. *Planta* **8**, 287–340.

Stålfelt, M. G. (1957). The water output of the guard cells of the stomata. *Physiol. Plant.* **10**, 752–773.

Stålfelt, M. G. (1959). The effect of carbon dioxide on hydroactive closure of the stomatal cells. *Physiol. Plant.* **12**, 691–705.

Stanek, V. (1916). Migration of betaine in plants. *Z. Zuckerindus Böhmen* **40**, 300–308.

Stanek, V., and Domin, K. (1909). Uber die lokalisation von betainen in pflanzen. *Z. Zuckerindus Böhmen* **34**, 297–304.

Stanley, S. O., and Brown, C. M. (1974). Influence of temperature and salinity on the amino acid pools of some marine pseudomonads. *In* "Effects of the Ocean Environment on Microbial Activities" (R. R. Colwell and R. Y. Morita, eds.), pp. 92–103. University Park Press. Baltimore.

Stanley, S. O., and Brown, C. M. (1976). Inorganic nitrogen metabolism in marine bacteria: the intracellular free amino acid pools of a marine pseudomonad. *Mar. Biol.* **38**, 101–109.

Steenbock, H. (1918). Isolation and identification of stachydrin from alfalfa hay. *J. Biol. Chem.* **35**, 1–13.

Steer, B. T. (1973). Dehydration of macromolecules. II. Protective effects of certain anions on ribulosediphosphate carboxylase subjected to low water potentials *in vitro. Aust. J. Biol. Sci.* **26**, 1435–1442.

Steiger, E., Ziegler, I., and Ziegler, H. (1971). Unterschiede in der Lichtaktivierung der NADP-abhangigen Glycerinaldehyd-3-phosphat-Dehydrogenase und der Ribulose-5-phosphat-Kinase bei Pflanzen des Calvin-und des C_4-Dicarbonsaure-Fixierungtypus. *Planta* **96**, 109–118.

Sterne, R. E., Kaufmann, M. R., and Zentmyer, G. A. (1977). Environmental effects on transpiration and leaf water potential in avocado. *Physiol. Plant.* **41**, 1–6.

Steward, F. C., and Durzan, D. J. (1964). Metabolism of nitrogenous compounds. *In* "Plant Physiology, A Treatise" (F. C. Steward, ed.), Vol. IVA, pp. 493–497.

Stewart, C. R. (1967). The effects of water and oxygen content on changes in amino acid content of excised leaves and studies on proline metabolism in wilted and unwilted leaves. Ph.D. Thesis. Cornell Univ.

Stewart, C. R. (1972a). Effects of proline and carbohydrates on the metabolism of exogenous proline by excised bean leaves in the dark. *Plant Physiol.* **50**, 551–555.

Stewart, C. R. (1972b). Proline content and metabolism during rehydration of wilted excised leaves in the dark. *Plant Physiol.* **50**, 679–681.

Stewart, C. R. (1972c). The effect of wilting on proline metabolism in excised bean leaves in the dark. *Plant Physiol.* **51**, 508–511.

Stewart, C. R. (1974). The effect of carbohydrates and arginine on arginine metabolism by excised bean leaves in the dark. *Plant Physiol.* **55**, 741–744.

Stewart, C. R. (1978). The role of carbohydrates in proline accumulation in wilted barley leaves. *Plant Physiol.* **61**, 775-778.

Stewart, C. R., and Boggess, S. F. (1977). The effect of wilting on the conversion of arginine, ornithine, and glutamate to proline in bean leaves. *Plant Sci. Lett.* **8**, 147–153.

Stewart, C. R., and Boggess, S. F. (1978). Metabolism of [5-^{3}H]- proline by barley leaves and its use in measuring the effects of water stress on proline oxidation. *Plant Physiol.* **61**, 654–657.

Stewart, C. R., and Hanson, A. D. (1980). Proline accumulation as a metabolic response to water stress. *In* "Adaptation of Plants to Water and High Temperature Stress" (N. C. Turner and P. J. Kramer, eds.), John Wiley and Sons Inc., New York.

Stewart, C. R., and Lai, E. Y. (1974). Δ^1-pyrroline-5-carboxylic acid dehydrogenase in mitochondrial preparations from plant seedlings. *Plant Sci. Lett.* **3**, 173–181.

Stewart, C. R., Morris C. J., and Thompson, J. F. (1966). Changes in amino acid content of excised leaves during incubation. II. Role of sugar in the accumulation of proline in wilted leaves. *Plant Physiol.* **41**, 1585–1590.

Stewart, C. R., Boggess, S. F., Aspinall, D., and Paleg, L. G. (1977). Inhibition of proline oxidation by water stress. *Plant Physiol.* **59**, 930–932.

Stewart, G. R., and Lee, J. A. (1972). Desiccation injury in mosses. II. The effect of moisture stress on enzyme levels. *New Phytol.* **71**, 461–466.

Stewart, G. R., and Lee, J. A. (1974). The role of proline accumulation in halophytes. *Planta* **120**, 279–289.

Stewart, G. R., Larher, F., Ahmad, I., and Lee, J. A. (1979). Nitrogen metabolism and salt tolerance in higher plant halophytes. *In* "Ecological Processes in Coastal Environments" (R. L. Jefferies and A. J. Davy, eds.), Blackwell Scientific Publications, Oxford.

Stocker, O. (1956). Die Abhängigkeit der Transpiration von den Umweltfaktoren. *In* "Handbuch der Pflanzenphysiologie" (W. Ruhland, ed.), Vol. 3, pp. 639–654, Springer, Berlin.

Stocker, O. (1961). Contribution to the problem of drought resistance of plants. *Indian J. Plant Physiol.* **4**, 87–102.

Stone, J. E., and Stone, E. L. (1975). Water conduction in lateral roots of red pine. *For. Sci.* **21**, 53–60.

Stoner, L. C., and Dunham, P. B. (1970). Regulation of cellular osmolarity and volume in *Tetrahymena*. *J. Exp. Biol.* **53**, 391–399.

Storey, R. (1976). Salt resistance and quaternary ammonium compounds in plants. Ph.D. Thesis, Univ. of Wales, Cardiff.

Storey, R., Ahmad, N., and Wyn Jones, R. G. (1977). Taxonomic and ecological aspects of the distribution of glycinebetaine and related compounds in plants. *Oecologia* **27**, 319–332.

Storey, R., and Wyn Jones, R. G. (1975). Betaine and choline levels in plants and their relationship to NaCl stress. *Plant. Sci. Lett.* **4**, 161–168.

Storey, R., and Wyn Jones, R. G. (1977). Quaternary ammonium compounds in plants in relation to salt resistance. *Phytochemistry* **16**, 447–453.

Storey, R., and Wyn Jones, R. G. (1978a). Salt stress and comparative physiology in the Gramineae. I. Ion relations in two salt and water-stressed barley cultivars, California Mariout and Arivar. *Aust. J. Plant Physiol.* **5**, 801–816.

Storey, R., and Wyn Jones, R. G. (1978b). Salt stress and comparative physiology in the Gramineae. III. The effect of salinity upon the ion relations and glycinebetaine and proline levels in *Spartina x townsendii*. *Aust. J. Plant Physiol.* **5**, 831–838.

Storey, R., and Wyn Jones, R. G. (1979). Responses of *Atriplex spongiosa* and *Suaeda monoica* to salinity. *Plant Physiol.* **63**, 156–162.

Strecker, H. J. (1960). The interconversion of glutamic acid and proline II. The preparation and properties of Δ^1-pyrroline-5-carboxylic acid. *J. Biol. Chem.* **235**, 2045–2050.

Strecker, H. J. (1971). The preparation of animal proline oxidase (rat liver), and its use for the preparation of Δ^1-pyrroline-5-carboxylate. *Methods Enzymol.* **17b**, 251–263.

Stuart, T. S. (1968). Revival of respiration and photosynthesis in dried leaves of *Polypodium polypodioides*. *Planta* **83**, 185–206.

Sturani, E. (1968). Protein synthesis activity of ribosomes from developing castor bean endosperm. *Life Sci.* **7**, 527–537.

Sturani, E., and Cocucci, S. (1965). Changes of the RNA system in the endosperm of ripening castor bean seeds. *Life Sci.* **4**, 1937–1944.

Sturani, E., Cocucci, S., and Marrè, E. (1968). Hydration dependent polysome-monosome interconversion in the germinating castor bean endosperm. *Plant Cell Physiol.* **9**, 783–795.

Subramanian, V. (1975). "Parched Earth: The Maharashtra Drought 1970-73." Orient Longman, Bombay.

Sullivan, C. Y., and Eastin, J. D. (1974). Plant physiological responses to water stress. *Agric. Meteorol.* **14**, 59–84.

Sullivan, C. Y., and Ross, W. M. (1978) "Screening for drought and heat resistance in grain sorghum". *In* "Stress Physiology of Crop Plants". (H. Mussell and R. C. Staples, eds.), Wiley Interscience, New York.

Susplugas, J., Privat C., Pellecer, J. and Llopis, J. (1969). Constituents of *Salicornia fructicosa*. *Trav. Soc. Pharm. Montpellier,* **29**, 129–132. (CA 72:63644).

Szarek, S. R. and Ting, I. P. (1974). Seasonal patterns of acid metabolism and gas exchange in *Opuntia basilaris*. *Plant Physiol.* **54**, 76–81.

Szarek, S. R., and Ting, I. P. (1975). Photosynthetic efficiency of CAM plants in relation to C_3 and C_4 plants. *In* "Environmental and Biological Control of Photosynthesis". (R. Marcelle, ed.), pp. 289–297. Dr. W. Junk, The Hague.

Szarek, S. R., Johnson, H. B., and Ting, I. P. (1973). Drought adaptation in *Opuntia basilaris*. *Plant Physiol*. **52**, 539–541.

Tajima, S., Yatazawa, M., and Yamamoto, Y. (1977). Allantoin production and its utilization in relation to nodule formation in soybeans. *Soil Sci. Plant Nut*. (Tokyo) **23**, 225–235.

Takemota, T., and Sai, T. (1974). Constituents of *Ceratodictyon spongiosum*. *Yakugaku Zasshi* **84**, 1224-1227. (CA 62:8121e).

Tal, M. and Imber, D. (1970). Abnormal stomatal behaviour and hormonal imbalance in *flacca*, a wilty mutant of tomato. II. Auxin and abscisic acid-like activity. *Plant Physiol*. **46**, 373–376.

Tal, M., and Imber, D. (1971). Abnormal stomatal behaviour and hormonal imbalance in *flacca*, a wilty mutant of tomato. III. Hormonal effects on the water status in the plant. *Plant Physiol*. **47**, 849–850.

Tal, M., and Imber, D. (1972). The effect of abscisic acid on stomatal behaviour in *flacca*, a wilty mutant of tomato in darkness. *New Phytol*. **71**, 81–84.

Tal, M., Imber, D., and Itai, C. (1970). Abnormal stomatal behaviour and hormonal imbalance in *flacca*, a wilty mutant of tomato. I. Root effect and kinetin-like activity. *Plant Physiol*. **46**, 367–372.

Tal, M., and Nevo, Y. (1973). Abnormal stomatal behaviour and root resistance, and hormonal imbalance in three wilty mutants of tomato. *Biochem. Genet*. **8**, 291–300.

Tal, M., Imber, D., and Gardi, I. (1974). Abnormal stomatal behaviour and hormonal imbalance in *flacca*, a wilty mutant of tomato. *J. Exp. Bot*. **25**, 51–60.

Tanford, C. (1973). "The Hydrophobic Effect: Formation of Micelles and Biological Membranes". Wiley-Interscience, New York.

Taylor, H. F., and Burden, R. S. (1970). Identification of plant growth inhibitors produced by photolysis of violaxanthin. *Phytochemistry* **9**, 2217–2223.

Taylor, H. F., and Burden, R. S. (1972). Xanthoxin, a recently discovered plant growth inhibitor. *Proc. R. Soc. London* Ser. B. **180**, 317–346.

Taylor, H. F., and Burden, R. S. (1973). Preparation and metabolism of 2-[14C]-*cis, trans*-xanthoxin. *J. Exp. Bot*. **24**, 873-880.

Taylor, H. F., and Smith, T. A. (1967). Production of plant growth inhibitors from xanthophylls: a possible source of dormin. *Nature* (London) **215**, 1513–1514.

Taylor, H. M. (1974). Root behaviour as affected by soil structure and strength. *In* "The Plant Root and its Environment". (E. W. Carson, ed.), pp. 271–291. Univ. Virginia Press, Charlottesville.

Taylor, H. M., and Ratliff, L. F. (1969). Root elongation rates of cotton and peanuts as a function of soil strength and soil water content. *Soil Sci*. **108**, 113–119.

Teare, I. D., and Kanemasu, E. T. (1972). Stomatal-diffusion resistance and water potential of soybean and sorghum leaves. *New Phytol*. **71**, 805–810.

Tempest, D. W., Meers, J. L., and Brown, C. M. (1970). Influence of environment on the content and composition of microbial free amino acid pools. *J. Gen. Microbiol*. **64**, 171–185.

Thomas, J. C., Brown, K. W., and Jordan W. R. (1976). Stomatal response to leaf water potential as affected by pre-conditioning water stress in the field. *Agron. J*. **68**, 706–708.

Thompson J. F., and Morris, C. J. (1957). Changes in nitrogen compounds under wilting conditions. *Plant Physiol*. **32**, XXIV.

Thompson, J. F., Stewart, C. R., and Morris, C. J. (1966). Changes in amino acid content of excised leaves during incubation I. The effect of water content of leaves and atmospheric oxygen levels. *Plant Physiol*. **41**, 1578–1584.

Thornber, J. P. (1975). Chlorophyll-proteins: light-harvesting and reaction centre components of plants. *Annu. Rev. Plant Physiol*. **26**, 127–158.

Thornthwaite, C. W. (1941). Climate and settlement in the Great Plains. *In* "Climate and Man",

(U.S. Dep. Agric., ed.), pp. 177–187. U.S. Government Printing Office, Washington D.C.

Tindall, D. R., Yopp, J. H., Schmid, W. E., and Miller, D. M. (1977). Protein and amino acid composition of the obligate halophile *Aphanothece halophytica* (Cyanophyta). *J. Phycol.* **13**, 127–133.

Tinelli, E. T., Sondheimer, E., Walton, D. C., Gaskin, P., and MacMillan, J. (1973). Metabolites of 2-[^{14}C]-abscisic acid. *Tetrahedron Lett.* No. 2, 139–140.

Ting, I. P., Johnson, H. B., and Szarek, S. R. (1972). Net CO_2 fixation in crassulacean acid metabolism plants. *In* "Net Carbon Assimilation in Higher Plants". (C. C. Black, ed.), pp. 26–53. South. Sect. Am. Soc. Plant Physiol./Cotton Inc., Mobile, Alabama.

Tinker, P. B. (1969). The transport of ions in the soil around plant roots. *In* "Ecological Aspects of the Mineral Nutrition of Plants" (I. H. Rorison, ed.), pp. 135–147, Blackwell, Oxford.

Tinker, P. B. (1976). Transport of water to plant roots in soil. *Philos. Trans. R. Soc. London* Ser. B. **273**, 445–461.

Tinus, R. W. (1975). Impact of the CO_2 requirement on plant water use. *Agric. Meteorol.* **14**, 99–112.

Tischler, C. R., Purvis, A. C., and Jordan, W. R. (1978). Factors involved in *in vitro* stabilization of nitrate reductase from cotton (*Gossypium hirsutum* L.) cotyledons. *Plant Physiol.* **61**, 714–717.

Todd, G. W. (1972). Water deficit and enzymatic activity. *In* "Water Deficit and Plant Growth". (T. T. Kozlowski, ed.), Vol. III. pp. 177–216. Academic Press, New York.

Tolbert, N. E. (1971). Microbodies — peroxisomes and glyoxysomes. *Annu. Rev. Plant Physiol.* **22**, 45–74.

Tolbert, N. E., and Wiebe, H. (1955). Phosphorus and sulphur compounds in plant xylem sap. *Plant Physiol.* **30**, 499–504.

Tonomura, Y., Sekiya, K., and Imamura, K. (1962). The optical rotatory dispersion of myosin A. 1. Effect of inorganic salt. *J. Biol. Chem.* **237**, 3110–3115.

Toupet, C. (1977). La grande sécheresse en Mauritanie. *In* "Drought in Africa. 2". (D. Dalby, R. J. Harrison Church and F. Bezzaz, eds.), pp. 109–113. International African Institute London.

Toynbee, A. J. (1946). "A Study of History". (abridgement of volumes 1–7 by D. C. Somerwell). Oxford Univ. Press, New York.

Toyosowa, I., and Nishimoto, U. (1967). Systematic determination of various forms of choline in plants. *Agr. Biol. Chem.* **31**, 275–283.

Travis, A. J., and Mansfield, T. A. (1977). Studies of malate formation in isolated guard cells. *New Phytol.* **78**, 541–546.

Travis, R. L., and Key, J. L. (1971). Correlation between polyribosome level and the ability to induce nitrate reductase in dark-grown corn seedlings. *Plant Physiol.* **48**, 617–620.

Travis, R. L., Huffaker, R. C., and Key, J. L. (1970). Light-induced development of polyribosomes and the induction of nitrate reductase in corn leaves. *Plant Physiol.* **46**, 800–805.

Tregunna, E. B., Krotkov, G., and Nelson, C. D. (1966). Effect of oxygen on the rate of photorespiration in detached tobacco leaves. *Physiol. Plant.* **19**, 723–733.

Treichel, S. (1975). Effect of NaCl on concentration of proline in different halophytes. *Z. Pflanzenphysiol.* **76**, 56–68.

Tu, C. M., and Hietkamp, G. (1977). Effect of moisture on acetylene reduction (symbiotic nitrogen fixation) by *Rhizobium japonicum* and soybean root nodules in silica sand. *Commun. Soil Sci. Plant Anal.* **8**, 81–86.

Tucker, D. J., and Mansfield, T. A. (1971). A simple bioassay for detecting "antitranspirant" activity of naturally occurring compounds such as abscisic acid. *Planta* **98**, 157–163.

Tucker, E. B., and Bewley, J. D. (1976). Plant desiccation and protein synthesis. III. Stability of cytoplasmic RNA during dehydration and its synthesis on rehydration of the moss *Tortula ruralis*. *Plant Physiol.* **57**, 564–567.

Tucker, E. B., Costerton, J. W., and Bewley, J. D. (1975). The ultrastructure of the moss *Tortula ruralis* on recovery from desiccation. *Can. J. Bot.* **53**, 94–101.

Tully, R. E., Hanson, A. D., and Nelsen, C. E. (1979). Proline accumulation in water-stressed barley leaves in relation to translocation and the nitrogen budget. *Plant Physiol.* **63**, 518–523.

Tung, H. F., and Brady, C. J. (1972). Kinetin treatment and protein synthesis in detached wheat leaves. *In* "Plant Growth Subst. Proc. Int. Conf. 7th, 1970". (D. J. Carr, ed.), pp. 589–597. Springer-Verlag, Berlin.

Tunstall, B. R., and Connor, D. J. (1975). Internal water balance of brigalow (*Acacia harpophylla* F. Muell.) under natural conditions. *Aust. J. Plant Physiol.* **2**, 489–499.

Turner, N. C. (1974). Stomatal behaviour and water status of maize, sorghum, and tobacco under field conditions. *Plant Physiol.* **53**, 360–365.

Turner, N. C. (1975). Concurrent comparisons of stomatal behaviour, water status, and evaporation of maize in soil at high or low water potential. *Plant Physiol.* **55**, 932–936.

Turner, N. C. (1979). Drought resistance and adaptation to water deficits in crop plants. *In* "Stress Physiology in Crop Plants". (H. Mussell and R. C. Staples, eds.), pp. 343–372. Wiley-Interscience, New York.

Turner, N. C. (1981). Designing crops for dryland Australia: can the deserts help us? *J. Aust. Inst. Agric. Sci.* **47**, (in press).

Turner, N. C., and Begg, J. E. (1973). Stomatal behaviour and water status of maize, sorghum, and tobacco under field conditions. I. At high soil water potential. *Plant Physiol.* **51**, 31–36.

Turner, N. C., and Begg, J. E. (1978). Responses of pasture plants to water deficits. *In* "Plant Relations in Pastures" (J. R. Wilson, ed.), pp. 50–66. CSIRO, Melbourne.

Turner, N. C., and Jones, M. M. (1980). Turgor maintenance by osmotic adjustment: a review and evaluation. *In* "Adaptation of Plants to Water and High Temperature Stress" (N. C. Turner and P. J. Kramer, eds.), pp. 89–103. Wiley Interscience, New York.

Turner, N. C., Begg, J. E., Rawson, H. M., English, S. D., and Hearn, A. B. (1978). Agronomic and physiological responses of soybean and sorghum crops to water deficits. III. Components of leaf water potential, leaf conductance, $^{14}CO_2$ photosynthesis, and adaptation to water deficits. *Aust. J. Plant Physiol.* **5**, 179–194.

Tvorus, E. K. (1970). Effect of drought and temperature increase on ribonuclease activity in plants. *Sov. Plant Physiol.* **17**, 658–664.

Tyankova, L. A. (1966). Influence of proline on the resistivity of wheat plants to drought. *C. R. Acad. Bulg. Sci.* **19**, 847–850.

Tyankova, L. A. (1967). Distribution of the free and bound proline and of the free hydroxyproline in the separate organs of wheat plants during drought. *C. R. Acad. Bulg. Sci.* **20**, 583–586.

Tymms, M. J., and Gaff, D. F. (1979). Proline accumulation during water stress in resurrection plants. *J. Exp. Bot.* **30**, 165–168.

Tyree, M. T. (1976). Negative turgor pressure in plant cells: fact or fallacy? *Can. J. Bot.* **54**, 2738–2746.

Tyree, M. T., and Hammel, H. T. (1972). The measurement of the turgor pressure and the water relations of plants by the pressure-bomb technique. *J. Exp. Bot.* **23**, 267–282.

Tyree, M. T.; Caldwell, C., and Dainty, J. (1975). The water relations of hemlock (*Tsuga canadensis*). V. The localization of resistances to bulk water flow. *Can. J. Bot.* **53**, 1078–1084.

Udayakumar, M., Rama Rao, S., Prasad, T. G., and Krishna Sastry, K.S. (1976). Effect of potassium on proline accumulation in cucumber cotyledons. *New Phytol.* **77**, 593–598.

Vankirk, C. A., and Raschke, K. (1978). Presence of chloride reduces malate production in epidermis during stomatal opening. *Plant Physiol.* **61**, 361–364.

Van Steveninck, R. F. M. (1972). Abscisic acid stimulation of ion transport and alteration in K+/Na+ selectivity. *Z. Pflanzenphysiol.* **67**, 282–286.

Vasileva, N. G. and Burkina, Z. S. (1960). Water conditions in cell organelles (in Russian with English summary). *Fiziol. Rast.* **7**, 401–406.

Vieira de Silva, J. (1976). Water stress, ultrastructure and enzymatic activity. *In* "Water and Plant Life" (O. L. Lange, L. Kappen and E.-D. Schulze, eds.). *Ecol. Stud.* **19**, pp. 207–224, Springer-Verlag, Berlin.

Vieira de Silva, J., Naylor, A. W., and Kramer, P. J. (1974). Some ultrastructural and enzymatic effects of water stress in cotton (*Gossypium hirsutum* L.). *Proc. Nat. Acad. Sci. USA* **71**, 3243–3247.

Viets, F. G. Jr. (1972). Water deficits and nutrient availability. *In* "Water Deficits and Plant Growth" (T. T. Kozlowski, ed.), Vol. III, pp. 217–239, Academic Press, New York.

Vincent-Marique, C., and Gilles, R. (1970). Modification of the amino acid pool in blood and muscle of *Eriocheir sinensis* during osmotic stress. *Comp. Biochem. Physiol.* **35**, 479–485.

Virkar, R. A., and Webb, K. L. (1970). Free amino acid composition of the soft-shell clam, *Mya arenaria* in relation to salinity of the medium. *Comp. Biochem. Physiol.* **32**, 775–783.

Volk, R. J., and Jackson, W. A. (1972). Photorespiratory phenomena in maize. O_2 uptake, isotope discrimination and CO_2 efflux. *Plant Physiol.* **49**, 218–223.

von Hippel, P. H., and Schleich, T. (1969). The effects of neutral salts on the structure and conformational stability of macromolecules in solution. *In* "Structure and Stability of Biological Macromolecules" (S. N. Timasheff and G. D. Fasman, eds.), pp. 417–574. Marcel Dekker, Inc., New York.

von Hippel, P. H., and Wong, K.-Y. (1965). On the conformational stability of globular proteins. The effects of various electrolytes and nonelectrolytes on the thermal ribonuclease transition. *J. Biol. Chem.* **240**, 3909–3923.

von Willert, D. J., Treichel, S., Kirst, G. O., and Curdts, E. (1976). Environmentally controlled changes of phosphoenolpyruvate carboxylases in *Mesembryanthemum*. *Phytochemistry* **15**, 1435–1436.

Waggoner, P. E., and Turner, N. C. (1971). Transpiration and its control by stomata in a pine forest. *Conn. Agric. Exp. Stn.* New Haven, Bull. **726**, 1–87.

Wahab, A. M. A., and Zahran, H. H. (1979). The effect of water stress on N_2 (C_2H_2) — fixation and growth of four legumes. *Agricultura* (Heverlee) **28**, 383–400.

Waisel, Y. (1972). "Biology of Halophytes". Academic Press, New York.

Waisel, Y., Borger, G. A., and Kozlowski, T. T. (1971). Effects of phenylmercuric acetate on stomatal movement and transpiration of excised *Betula papyrifera* March leaves. *Plant Physiol.* **44**, 685–690.

Waldren, R. P., and Teare, I. D. (1974). Free proline accumulation in drought-stressed plants under laboratory conditions. *Plant Soil* **40**, 689–692.

Waldren, R. P., Teare, I. D., and Ehler, S. W. (1974). Changes in free proline concentration in sorghum and soybean plants under field conditions. *Crop Sci.* **14**, 447–450.

Wallace, W. (1974). Purification and properties of a nitrate-reductase inactivating enzyme. *Biochim. Biophys. Acta* **341**, 265–276.

Walter, C. J., and Barley, K. P. (1974). The depletion of soil water by wheat at low, intermediate and high rates of seeding. *Proc. 10th Int. Congr. Sov. Soil Sci.* **1**, 150–158.

Walter, H. (1971). "Ecology of Tropical and Subtropical Vegetation". Oliver & Boyd, Edinburgh.

Walter, H., and Stadelmann, E. (1974). A new approach to the water relations of desert plants. *In* "Desert Biology". (G. W. Brown, Jr., ed.), Vol. 2, pp. 213–310. Academic Press, New York.

Wample, R. L., and Bewley, J. D. (1975). Proline accumulation in flooded and wilted sunflower and the effects of benzyladenine and abscisic acid. *Can. J. Bot.* **53**, 2893–2896.

Wang, D. (1968). Metabolism of ^{14}C-labeled proline in higher plants. *Contrib. Boyce Thompson Inst.* **24**, 117–122.

Wareing, P. F., Khalifa, M. M., and Treharne, K. J. (1968). Rate-limiting processes in photosynthesis at saturated light intensities. *Nature* (London) **220**, 453–457.

Waring, R. H., and Running, S. W. (1976). Water uptake, storage and transpiration by conifers: a physiological model. *In* "Water and Plant Life". (O. L. Lange, L. Kappen, and E.-D. Schulze, eds.), *Ecol. Stud.* **19**, 189–202.

Waring, R. H., and Running, S. W. (1978). Sapwood water storage: its contribution to transpiration and effect upon water conductance through the stems of old-growth Douglas-fir. *Plant, Cell and Envir.* **1**, 131–140.

Waring, R. H., Gholz, H. L., Grier, C. C., and Plummer, M. L. (1977). Evaluating stem conducting tissue as an estimator of leaf area in four woody angiosperms. *Can. J. Bot.* **55**, 1474–1477.

Warren, J. C., Stowring, L., and Morales, M. F. (1966). The effect of structure-disrupting ions on the activity of myosin and other enzymes. *J. Biol. Chem.* **241**, 309–316.

Watts, W. R., and Neilson, R. E. (1978). Photosynthesis in Sitka spruce (*Picea sitchensis* (Bong.) Carr.). VIII. Measurements of stomatal conductance and $^{14}CO_2$ uptake in controlled environments. *J. Appl. Ecol.* **15**, 245–255.

Weatherley, P. E. (1970). Some aspects of water relations. *Adv. Bot. Res.* **3**, 171–206.

Weatherley, P. E. (1976). Introduction: water movement through plants. *Philos. Trans. R. Soc. London. Ser. B.* **273**, 435–444.

Weatherley, P. E., and Slatyer, R. O. (1957). Relationship between relative turgidity and diffusion pressure deficit in leaves. *Nature* (London) **179**, 1085–1086.

Webb, S. J., and Bhorjee, J. S. (1968). Infrared studies of DNA, water and inositol associations. *Can. J. Biochem.* **46**, 691–695.

Wegmann, K. (1971). Osmotic regulation of photosynthetic glycerol production in *Dunaliella*. *Biochim. Biophys. Acta* **234**, 317–323.

Wellburn, A. R., and Hampp, R. (1976). Fluxes of gibberellic and abscisic acids, together with that of adenosine–3',5'-cyclic phosphate, across plastid envelopes during development. *Plant* **131**, 95–96.

Wellburn, A. R., Ogunkanmi, A. B., Fenton, R., and Mansfield, T. A. (1974). All-*trans*-farnesol: a naturally occurring anti-transpirant? *Planta* **120**, 255–263.

Wellburn, F. A. M., and Wellburn, A. R. (1976). Novel chloroplasts and unusual cellular ultrastructure in the "resurrection" plant *Myrothamnus flabellifolia* Welw. (Myrothem-naceae) *Bot. J. Linn. Soc.* **72**, 51–54.

West, D. W., and Gaff, D. F. (1976). The effect of leaf water potential, leaf temperature and light intensity on leaf diffusion resistance and the transpiration of leaves of *Malus sylvestris*. *Physiol. Plant.* **38**, 98–104.

West, S. H. (1966). Sub-cellular physiology as affected by drought. *Proc. Int. Grassl. Congr.* X. pp. 91–94.

Wheeland, G. W. (1953). "Advanced Organic Chemistry". 2nd Edn. Wiley, New York.

Wheeler, A. W. (1963). Betaine: a plant growth substance from sugar-beet (*Beta vulgaris*). *J. Exp. Bot.* **14**, 265–271.

Wheeler, A. W. (1969). Effects of C.C.C. and glycinebetaine on growth and growth substance content of primary leaves of dwarf French beans. *Ann. Appl. Biol.* **63**, 127–133.

Whiteman, P. C., and Koller, D. (1964). Environmental control of photosynthesis and transpiration in *Pinus halepensis*. *Isr. J. Bot.* **13**, 166–176.

Wiehler, G., and Marion, L. (1958). The biogenesis of alkaloids. XX. The induced biogenesis of stachydrine. *J. Biol. Chem.* **231**, 799–805.

Wilbrandt, W. (1963). Transport through biological membranes. *Annu. Rev. Physiol.* **25**, 601–630.

Williamson, A. J. P., and Diatloff, A. (1975). Effect of supplementary nitrogen fertilizer on nodulation, yield and seed characteristics of soybean (*Glycine max*) on the Darling Downs. *Aust. J. Exp. Agric. Anim. Husb.* **15**, 694–699.

Willmer, C. M., and Rutter, J. C. (1977). Guard cell malic acid metabolism during stomatal movements. *Nature,* (London) **269**, 327–328.

Wilson, A. M., Hyder, D. N., and Briske, D. D. (1976). Drought resistance characteristics of blue grama seedlings. *Agron. J.* **68**, 479–484.

Wilson, A. T., and Calvin, M. (1955). The photosynthetic cycle. CO_2 dependent transients. *J. Am. Chem. Soc.* **77**, 5948–5957.

Wilson, J. A., Ogunkanmi, A. B., and Mansfield, T. A. (1978). External buffering of ABA-induced K^+ leakage from isolated stomata of *Commelina communis.* *Plant Cell Environ.* **1**, 199–201.

Wilson, J. M. (1976). The mechanisms of chill- and drought-hardening of *Phaseolus vulgaris* leaves. *New Phytol.* **76**, 257–270.

Wind, G. P. (1955). Flow of water through plant roots. *Neth. J. Agric. Sci.* **3**, 259–264.

Winter, K. (1974a). Evidence for the significance of crassulacean acid metabolism as an adaptive mechanism to water stress. *Plant Sci. Lett.* **3**, 279–281.

Winter, K. (1974b). Einfluss von Wasserstress auf die Aktivität der Phosphoenolpyruvat-Carboxylase bei Mesembryanthemum crystallinum. *Planta* **121**, 147–153.

Winter, K., and Lüttge, U. (1976). Balance between C_3 and CAM pathway of photosynthesis. *In* "Ecological Studies", Vol. 19. Water and Plant Life. (O. L. Lange, L. Kappen and E.-D. Schulze, eds.), pp. 323–334. Springer-Verlag, Berlin.

Wolosiuk, R. A., and Buchanan, B. B. (1977). Thioredoxin and glutathione regulate photosynthesis in chloroplasts. *Nature* (London) **266**, 565–567.

Woo, K. C., and Osmond, C. B. (1976). Glycine decarboxylation in mitochondria isolated from spinach leaves. *Aust. J. Plant Physiol.* **3**, 771–785.

Wood, C. A. (1977). A preliminary chronology of Ethiopian droughts. *In* "Drought in Africa. 2". (D. Dalby, R. J. Harrison Church and F. Bezzaz, eds.), pp. 68–73. International African Institute, London.

Worrall, V. S., and Roughley, R. J. (1976). The effect of moisture stress on infection of *Trifolium subterraneum* L. by *Rhizobium trifolii. J. Exp. Bot.* **27**, 1233–1241.

Wray, J. L., and Filner, P. (1970). Structural and functional relationships of enzyme activities induced by nitrate in barley. *Biochem, J.* **119**, 715–725.

Wright, L., Wrench, P., Hinde, R. W., and Brady, C. J. (1977). Proline accumulation in tubers of Jerusalem artichoke. *Aust. J. Plant Physiol.* **4**, 51–60.

Wright, S. T. C. (1969). An increase in the "inhibitor β" content of detached wheat leaves following a period of wilting. *Planta* **86**, 10–20.

Wright, S. T. C. (1977). The relationship between leaf water potential (Ψ leaf) and the levels of abscisic acid and ethylene in excised wheat leaves. *Planta* **134**, 183–189.

Wright, S. T. C., and Hiron, R. W. P. (1969). (+)-Abscisic acid, the growth inhibitor induced in detached wheat leaves by a period of wilting. *Nature* (London) **224**, 719–720.

Wright, S. T. C., and Hiron, R. W. P. (1972). The accumulation of abscisic acid in plants during wilting and under other stress conditions. *In* "Plant Growth Subst. Proc. Int. Conf. 7th, 1970". (D. J. Carr, ed.), pp. 291–298, Springer-Verlag, Berlin.

Wuenscher, J. E., and Kozlowski, T. T. (1971a). The response of transpiration resistance to leaf temperature as a desiccation resistance mechanism in tree seedlings. *Physiol. Plant.* **24**, 254–259.

Wuenscher, J. E., and Kozlowski, T. T. (1971b). Relationship of gas exchange resistance to tree-seedling ecology. *Ecology* **52**, 1016–1023.

Wylie, R. B. (1952). The bundle sheath extension in leaves of dicotyledons. *Am. J. Bot.* **39**, 645–651.

Wyn Jones, R. G. (1972). A possible new method for improving plant growth in saline and calcareous environments. *In* "Isotopes and Radiation in Soil-Plant Relationships including Forestry". pp. 109–122, I.A.E.A., Vienna.

Wyn Jones, R. G. (1975). *In* "Ion Transport in Plant Cells and Tissues". (D. A. Baker and J. L. Hall, eds.), pp. 193–230, North-Holland, Amsterdam.

Wyn Jones, R. G., and Storey, R. (1978a). Salt stress and comparative physiology in the Gramineae. II. Glycinebetaine and proline accumulation in two salt and water stressed barley cultivars. *Aust. J. Plant Physiol.* **5**, 817–829.

Wyn Jones, R. G., and Storey, R. (1978b). Salt stress and comparative physiology in the Gramineae. IV. Comparison of salt stress in *Spartina x townsendii* and three barley cultivars. *Aust. J. Plant Physiol.* **5**, 839–850.

Wyn Jones, R. G., Rippin, A. J., and Storey, R. (1973). Metabolism of choline in the rhizosphere and its possible influence on plant growth. *Pestic. Sci.* **4**, 375–383.

Wyn Jones, R. G., Storey, R., and Pollard, A. (1976). Ionic and osmotic regulation in plants particularly halophytes. *In* "Transmembrane Ionic Exchanges in Plants". (J. Dainty and M. Thellier, eds.), Colloq. Int. C.N.R.S., Paris.

Wyn Jones, R. G., Storey, R., Leigh, R. A., Ahmad, N., and Pollard, A. (1977a). A hypothesis on cytoplasmic osmoregulation. *In* "Regulation of Cell Membrane Activities in Plants". (E. Marrè and O. Ciferri, eds.), pp. 121–136. North Holland, Amsterdam.

Wyn Jones, R. G., Storey, R., and Pollard, A. (1977b). Ionic and osmotic regulation in plants, particularly halophytes. *In* "Transmembrane Ionic Exchanges in Plants". (M. Thellier, A. Monnier, M. Demarty and J. Dainty, eds.), pp. 537–544. C.N.R.S., Paris.

Wyn Jones, R. G., Brady, C. J., and Spiers, J. (1979). Ionic and osmotic regulation in plants. *In* "Recent Advances in the Biochemistry of Cereals. 1979". (D. L. Laidman and R. G. Wyn Jones, eds.), Academic Press, London.

Yamaya, T., and Ohira, K. (1976). Nitrate reductase inactivating factor from rice cells in suspension culture. *Plant Cell Physiol.* **17**, 633–641.

Yancey, P. H., and Somero, G. N. (1979). Counteraction of urea destabilization of protein structure by methylamine osmoregulatory compounds of elasmobranch fishes. *Biochem. J.* **183**, 317–323.

Yemm, E. W. (1937). Respiration of barley plants. III. Protein catabolism in starving leaves. *Proc. R. Soc. London.* Ser. B. **123**, 243–273.

Yeo, A. R. (1974). Salt tolerance in *Suaeda maritima* L. Dum. Ph.D. Thesis. Univ. Sussex, England.

Younis, M. A., Pauli, A. W., Mitchell, H. L., and Stickler, F. C. (1965). Temperature and its interaction with light and moisture in nitrogen metabolism of corn. (*Zea mays* L.) seedlings. *Crop Sci.* **5**, 321–326.

Zabadal, T. J. (1974). A water potential threshold for the increase of abscisic acid in leaves. *Plant Physiol.* **53**, 125–127.

Zalik, S., and Jones, B. L. (1973). Protein biosynthesis. *Annu. Rev. Plant Physiol.* **24**, 47–68.

Zeevaart, J. A. D. (1974). Levels of (±)-abscisic acid and xanthoxin in spinach under different environmental conditions. *Plant Physiol.* **53**, 644–648.

Zeevaart, J. A. D. (1977). Sites of abscisic acid synthesis and metabolism in *Ricinus communis* L. *Plant Physiol.* **59**, 788–791.

Zeevaart, J. A. D., and Milborrow, B. V. (1976). Metabolism of abscisic acid and the occurrence of *epi*-dihydrophaseic acid in *Phaseolus vulgaris. Phytochemistry* **15**, 493–500.

Zelitch, I. (1969). Stomatal control. *Annu. Rev. Plant Physiol.* **20**, 329–350.

Zelitch, I. (1971). "Photosynthesis, Photorespiration and Plant Productivity". Academic Press, New York.

Zelitch, I. (1973). Plant productivity and the control of photorespiration. *Proc. Nat. Acad. Sci. U.S.A.* **70**, 579–584.

Zelitch, I., and Waggoner, P. E. (1962). Effect of chemical control of stomata on transpiration and photosynthesis. *Proc. Nat. Acad. Sci. U.S.A.* **48**, 1101–1108.

Zholkevich, V. N., and Rogacheva, A. Y. (1968). P/O ratio in mitochondria isolated from wilting plant tissue. (in Russian with English summary). *Fiziol. Rast.* **15**, 537–545.

Ziegler, H., Ziegler, I., Muller, B., and Dorr, I. (1969). Activation of NADP+-dependent glyceraldehyde-3-phosphate dehydrogenase in relation to photosynthetic electron transport. *In* "Progress in Photosynthesis Research". (H. Metzner, ed.), pp. 1636–1645. I.U.B.S., Tübingen.

Zimmer, G., Keith, A. D., and Packer, L. (1972). Effect of sucrose and uncouplers on lipid spin labeling of mitochondria. *Arch. Biochem. Biophys.* **152**, 105–113.

Zimmerman, M. H. (1971). Transport in the Xylem. *In* "Trees, Structure and Function" (M. H. Zimmerman and C. L. Brown, eds.), pp. 169–220. Springer-Verlag, New York.

Author Index

A

Abe, S., 187
Abrol, Y. P., 148
Acevedo, E., 24, 25, 48, 58, 67
Ackerman, D., 188
Adams, J. A., 62, 295
Addicott, F. T., 355, 371.
Ahmad, I., 186
Ahmad, N., 175, 186, 190, 191, 195, 200, 201, 202, 203
Ahmed, Z. F., 186
AICRPDA, 8
Alberte, R. S., 61, 66, 305, 312, 392, 401, 403
Alfani, A., 301
Alieva, S. A., 304
Allaway, W. G., 288, 297, 336, 338, 341, 342
Al-Saadi, H., 67
Anand, J. C., 108
Anderson, D. G., 193
Anderson, J. M., 307
Anderson, W. P., 73
Andres, J., 211
Andrews, T. J., 285, 287, 310, 312
Anikiev, V. V., 164
Anon, 213, 229, 230, 233
Antoniw, L. D., 139
Aparico-Tejo, P. M., 139
Arad, S. M., 377
Ardreeva, S. M., 176
Armstrong, J. E., 280
Arnon, I., 16
Asahi, T., 396, 397
Ashley, D. A., 48
Asher, C. J., 72
Aslam, Z., 186, 195
Aspinall, D., 11, 28, 104, 109, 110, 154, 197, 206, 207, 208, 209, 210, 211, 212, 213, 214, 216, 217, 218, 219, 220, 221, 222, 229, 230, 231, 232, 233, 234, 244, 246, 248, 249, 252, 254, 255, 256, 257, 258
Atkins, C. A., 150
Atkinson, M. R., 87, 188
Aubertin, G. M., 350
Austin, B., 288

Avi-Dor, Y., 176, 202, 203
Avron, M., 105

B

Badger, M. R., 285, 287, 307, 310, 312
Baghdadi, H. H., 186
Baginski, R. M., 109
Bahr, J. T., 285
Baich, A., 244, 248
Baker, D. A., 346
Balaam, L. N., 19
Balasubramanian, V., 160, 161, 162, 209, 219
Bal, A. R., 222
Ball, C. D., 202
Ball, E., 78, 376, 377
Banerjee, S. K., 117
Barber, D. A., 82
Barber, S. A., 43, 74
Bardzik, J. M., 153, 156, 157, 159
Barley, K. P., 40, 45, 46, 50, 51, 74
Barlow, E. W. R., 25, 29, 30, 264, 398
Barlow, P. W., 278
Barnard, R. A., 248, 249, 250, 252, 253
Barnett, N. M., 210, 229, 230, 243, 255
Bar-Nun, N., 210
Barrs, H. D., 61
Barry, J. M., 403
Bartholomew, B., 301
Bassham, J. A., 284, 285
Basso, L. C., 203
Basu, K., 186
Baveja, S. K., 186
Bazilevich, N. 1., 72
Bazin, M., 206
Beadle, C. L., 65
Beardsell, M. F., 76, 304, 331, 332, 341, 351, 356, 357, 358, 364, 383, 384, 385, 392, 401
Beers, J. R., 176, 188
Beevers, L., 146, 150, 276, 277, 378
Begg, J. E., 11, 17, 21, 22, 23, 35, 45, 61, 150, 292, 293, 294, 313
Bell, D. T., 257, 396
Bello, J., 117
Ben-Amotz A., 105
Benko, B., 230, 237
Bennett, O. L., 48

Ben-Shaul, Y., 403
Benson, A. A., 188
Ben Zaken, R., 69, 289
Ben-Zioni, A., 48, 257, 266, 349, 379, 397
Bernholz, H., 397
Berry, J., 285, 286, 300, 302, 306, 307, 312
Bertsch, A., 319
Besnier, V., 206
Bethlenfalvay, G. J., 114
Bewley, J. D., 33, 34, 37, 211, 212, 229,
    257, 262, 264, 268, 269, 270, 271, 272,
    273, 274, 275, 277, 278, 393, 401
Bhorjee, J. S., 121
Bieberdorf, F. W., 136
Bierhuizen, J. F., 345
Billett, M. A., 403
Bingham, F. T., 62, 295
Biscoe, P. V., 25
Bito, M., 206, 209, 216, 229
Bittner, S., 375, 381
Björkman, O., 23, 24, 36, 284, 289, 291,
    305, 306, 307, 309, 311, 313
Black, M., 278
Black, R. F., 87
Black, S., 244
Blaim, K., 188, 190
Blekhman, G. I., 267
Blum, A., 11, 12, 50, 211, 216, 230, 234,
    235, 236
Blumenfeld, A., 375, 381
Boardman, N. K., 307
Boggess, S. F., 110, 154, 207, 209, 210, 211,
    213, 216, 217, 221, 222, 244, 246, 248,
    249, 250, 252, 255, 256, 257, 258
Bokarev, K. S., 202
Bonner, B. A., 374
Bonner, W. D., 99
Boon-Long, T. S., 290
Borger, G. A., 345
Borowitzka, L. J., 99, 104, 107, 108, 110,
    113, 119, 123, 206
Bouchart, R., 390, 392, 396, 399, 401
Boulter, D., 276
Bourque, D. P., 392
Boussiba, S., 211, 341
Boutrais, J., 2
Bowen, B., 303
Bowes, G., 285, 287
Bowling, D. J. F., 338
Bowman, M. S., 191, 197
Box, J. E., 381
Boyer, J. S., 21, 25, 60, 67, 68, 139, 153,
    159, 160, 257, 263, 264, 267, 268, 296,
    297, 298, 299, 303, 304, 305, 306, 307,
    312, 330, 390
Boynton, J., 306, 307

Brady, C. J., 25, 29, 30, 200, 202, 210, 379,
    380, 397
Brady, M., 393
Bragarena, A., 230, 231
Brandle, J. R., 264
Brandon, D., 201
Bravdo, B., 303
Bray, C. M., 262
Bregoff, H. M., 191
Briarty, L. G., 138
Briske, D. D., 46
Brix, H., 49, 308
Brock, T. D., 104
Brooker, J. D., 277, 278, 403
Brouchart, R., 280
Brown, A. D., 99, 100, 104, 107, 108, 110,
    112, 119, 121, 206
Brown, C. M., 106, 206
Brown, G. N., 264
Brown, K. W., 27, 58, 64
Brown, L. M., 108, 206, 209
Brown, R. W., 68
Browning, G., 383
Brownrigg, A., 276
Buchanan, B. B., 307
Buckley, S. D., 246
Budnik, A., 397
Bunce, J. A., 300, 301
Bunting, A. H., 2
Burden, R. S., 354, 371, 372
Burkina, Z. S., 389
Burrows, F. J., 293
Burrows, W. H., 93
Burrows, W. J., 379
Buschbom, U., 18, 22, 31, 33, 56, 57, 65,
    323, 325, 326, 327, 328
Bushby, H. V. A., 132, 133
Byerrum, R. U., 200
Byrne, G. F., 45

C

Caldwell, C., 61
Caldwell, J. C., 2
Caldwell, M. M., 20, 21, 42, 60
Calvin, M., 284, 308
Camacho-B, S. E., 61, 62, 65, 66, 69, 327
Camp, L. B., 20, 21
Campbell, L. C., 397
Campbell, R. W., 307
Campbell, W., 147
Cannell, R. Q., 48
Cantoni, G. L., 172, 175, 193
Canvin, D. T., 150, 152, 286, 287, 308, 309
Carlier, A. R., 278
Carlson, B., 193
Carr, D. J., 379

Carruthers, A., 200
Carter, K. R., 141
Cataldo, D. A., 147
Cathey, H. M., 172
Catsky, J., 291
Cavalieri, A. J., 250
Challenger, F., 172, 175, 189, 193
Chambers, J. L., 64, 66
Chang, T. T., 10, 16, 19
Chang, Y. P., 368
Charley, J. L., 94
Charreau, C., 9
Chartier, M., 291
Chartier, P., 291
Chatterton, N. J., 24
Chen, D., 210, 279, 280
Cherry, J. H., 279
Cheung, C. P., 403
Chin, T. Y., 378
Ching, T. M., 37
Chinoy, J. J., 19
Chittenden, C. G., 191
Cho, I. H., 229
Chollet, R., 285, 312
Chrispeels, M. J., 280
Christian, J. H. B., 107
Chu, T. M., 104, 207, 208, 213, 214, 218, 229, 230, 244
Churchill, D. M., 31
Clark, L. E., 12
Clark, M. F., 397
Clarkson, D. T., 45, 80, 81
Cleland, R. E., 266, 267
Clingenpeel, W. J., 392
Coaldrake, J. E., 72, 84, 85, 93
Cocucci, S., 277, 279, 280, 397
Cohen, D., 76, 304, 331, 332, 341, 351, 356, 357, 358, 364, 383, 384, 385, 392, 401
Cohen, J., 396
Cohen, W. S., 393
Cohen, Y., 396
Collatz, G. J., 306, 310, 313
Collet, C. F., 378
Collins, J. C., 373, 374
Connor, D. J., 27, 28, 31, 84, 91, 92, 378
Constable, G. A., 24
Cooke, R., 114, 115
Corgan, J. N., 356
Cornforth, J. W., 186, 187, 190
Costerton, J. W., 34, 257, 393
Costilow, R. N., 248
Coughlan, S., 195, 197
Cowan, I. R., 21, 35, 41, 293, 313
Cowling, S. W., 94
Cox, E. L., 153, 156, 158, 306, 307
Crafts, A. S., 389

Craigie, J. S., 105, 108
Cram, W. J., 26, 89, 110
Crèvecoeur, M., 280, 390, 392, 396, 399, 401
Creveling, R. K., 250
Criswell, J. G., 140
Cromwell, B. T., 186, 188, 190, 191, 200
Cummins, W. R., 336, 382, 383, 384, 385
Curdts, E., 302
Cutler, J. M., 25, 27, 28, 68, 140

D

Dainty, J., 61
Dalling, M. J., 148
Danielson, R. E., 74, 75, 77
Darbyshire, B., 307
Darbyshire, J. F., 132
Dart, P. J., 132
Dasgupta, B., 186
Dasgupta, S., 186
Dashek, W. V., 217
Da Silva, J. V., 304
Davenport, D. C., 345, 346
Davidson, N., 202
Davies, W. J., 64, 322, 327, 328, 333, 341, 345
Davis, L. A., 355
Dawson, R. W. C., 200
Decheva, R., 209
Deckard, E. L., 148, 149
Delaveau, P., 186
De Leo, P. 280
dell'Aquila, A., 280
Deltour, R., 280, 390, 392, 396, 399, 401, 403
De Luca, P., 301
Delwiche, C. C., 191
Demmerle, S., 113
Denmead, O. T., 58, 60, 66
Dennet, M. D., 2
Dennis, F. G., 369
Derera, N. F., 19
Dhindsa, R. S., 266, 267, 269, 270, 271, 272, 274, 275
Diatloff, A., 131, 141
Dimond, A. E., 21
Dittrich, P., 321, 336, 338
Dixon, M., 124
Doley, D., 298
Domes, W., 318, 319
Domin, K., 186
Donald, C. M., 52
Dörffling, K., 331, 341, 342, 343
Dorr, I., 307
Doss, B. D., 48
Douglas, T. J., 127
Downey, R. J., 147

Downton, W. J. S., 308, 373
Dreier, W., 210
Dubé, P. A., 300
Dudley, J. W., 146
Dudman, W. F., 132
Dunham, P. B., 108
Dunham, R. J., 77
Dunn-Coleman, N. S., 166
Du Paul, W. D., 109
Duranton, H., 246
Durzan, D. J., 253
Duysen, M. E., 392
Dzikowski, P. A., 142, 143

E
Eagland, D., 114
Eastin, J. D., 299, 306, 307
Ebercon, A., 211, 216, 230, 234, 235, 236
Eder, A., 211, 212
Edgley, M., 108
Edwards, G. E., 310, 311
Ehler, S. W., 207, 208
Ehleringer, J., 23, 24, 284, 300
Eidt, D. C., 348
Eilrich, G. L., 146, 147, 148
Eisenberg, D., 114
El-Beltagy, A. S., 211
El Damaty, A. H., 189
Eldan, M., 396, 397
Elfving, D. C., 59, 63
Elliot, D. C., 200
Elliot, W. H., 200
Ellis, R. J., 379
Elmore, C. D., 30, 207
Elston, J., 2, 31, 68, 69
Elthon, T. E., 252
Engeland, R., 187
Engin, M., 135
Englehorn, A. J., 155
English, S. D., 22, 35
Epstein, E., 72, 84
Erickson, L. E., 193
Ernst, R., 391
Esau, K., 44
Evans, H. J., 141
Evans, M. W., 114
Evenari, M., 18, 22, 24, 31, 33, 56, 57, 65,
　　323, 325, 326, 327, 328
Everson, E. H., 30, 219, 230, 231, 233, 238
Eyal, H., 396

F
Faiz, S. M. A., 42
Farnden, K. J. F., 138
Farquhar, G. D., 21, 35, 313
Faulkingham, R. H., 2, 7

Feeley, J., 277
Fellows, R. J., 304, 390
Fenton, R., 322, 333, 334
Fereres, E., 24, 25, 58, 67
Fernandez, O. A., 21
Filner, P., 147, 154
Findlay, G. P., 87
Finlay, K., 232
Firn, R. D., 372
Fischer, R. A., 10, 11, 12, 17, 19, 20, 50,
　　52, 336, 351
Fiscus, E. L., 48, 61, 62, 305, 312, 392, 401,
　　403
Fisher, J. M., 213
Fisher, M. A., 346
Flesher, D., 150, 153, 155
Flowers, T. J., 87, 172, 186, 195, 200, 201,
　　257
Fock, H., 196, 307, 308, 309, 310, 313
Forrester, M. L., 287
Fowden, L., 246, 250
Foy, C. D., 48
Frank, A. B., 296
Frank, H. S., 114
Franks, F., 114, 115, 121
Fraser, H. L., 136
Freeman, T. E., 381
Freeman, T. P., 392
Frenzel, B., 272, 273
Frey, N. M., 307
Friend, J., 372
Fry, K. E., 303
Fujino, M., 336
Fukui, H., 368, 369
Fuller, G. L., 296, 341, 383
Fyhn, H. J., 206

G
Gaastra, P., 289, 291, 294, 298, 389
Gaff, D. F., 31, 33, 34, 65, 393
Gale, J., 88, 89, 289, 298
Gallacher, A. E., 135, 140
Galston, E. C., 368
Gamper, H., 246
Gandhi, A. P., 154, 155, 166
Gardi, I., 386
Gardner, I. C., 139
Gardner, W. R., 41
Gaskin, P., 368, 369, 372
Gavande, S. A., 25
Gemmrich, A. R., 250
Genevot, M., 206
Genkel, P. A., 390, 397
George, C. J., 4
Gholz, H. L., 61

Giesen, M., 277
Gifford, R. M., 291, 292
Giles, K. L., 76, 304, 392, 401
Gill, K., 322, 327
Gillard, D. F., 359, 369
Gilles, R., 108, 176, 206
Ginzburg, B. Z., 30
Gitter, A., 155
Gladyshev, P. P., 186
Glantz, M. H., 3
Glinka, Z., 346, 373, 374, 376
Godfrey, C. L., 75
Goodchild, D. J., 307
Goode, J. E., 19, 25
Goodwin, T. W., 361
Gordon, M. E., 278
Göring, H. Von, 210
Goryaev, M. I., 186
Gould, G. W., 106, 112, 113
Graham, J., 45
Greacen, E. L., 25, 40, 45, 46, 47, 48, 49, 50
Greaves, M. P., 132
Greenway, H., 78, 79, 82, 189, 208
Greenwood, E. A. N., 145
Grier, C. C., 61
Gross, R. D., 259
Groves, R. H., 93
Guerrier, D., 222
Guggenheim, M., 175, 187, 188
Gunning, B. E. S., 138
Gustafsson, L., 108
Gwóźdź, E. A., 33, 37, 268, 270, 271, 272, 273, 275

H

Habish, H. A., 131, 134, 141
Hagan, R. M., 345, 346, 351
Hageman, R. H., 146, 147, 148, 149, 150, 153, 155, 159, 160, 164, 257, 263, 264, 267, 268, 285, 286, 287, 309, 310
Halbwachs, G., 58, 60
Halevy, A. H., 189, 221
Hall, A. E., 59, 61, 62, 63, 64, 65, 66, 69, 291, 318, 319, 321, 323, 324, 325, 326, 327
Hall, J. L., 172, 186, 195, 201
Hall, M. A., 211
Hallam, N. D., 34, 393, 398, 403
Halliday, G., 322, 327
Halmer, P., 272
Hamelin, J., 186, 187, 189, 190
Hamill, R. L., 200
Hammel, H. T., 68
Hammett, J. R., 278
Hampp, R., 333, 383
Handreck, K. A., 82

Hanna, W. W., 24
Hanscom, Z., 302
Hansen, G. K., 45
Hanson, A. D., 30, 172, 191, 192, 195, 196, 197, 204, 216, 217, 219, 230, 231, 233, 238
Hanson, J. B., 257
Hanus, J., 141
Hanway, J. J., 155
Hardy, R. W. F., 139, 140
Harris, B., 312
Harris, G. P., 33, 142
Harrison, M. A., 359, 362, 369, 370
Hartley, M. R., 379
Hartney, V. J., 288, 293, 301
Hartsock, T. L., 302
Hartung, W., 267
Harvey, D. M. R., 172, 201
Harwood, H. I., 217
Hastings, J. W., 106
Hatch, M. D., 284, 287, 307
Hattersley, P. W., 287, 312
Havelka, U. D., 139, 140
Havis, J. R., 153, 156, 157, 159
Hearn, A. B., 22, 24, 35
Heath, O. V. S., 318, 319, 321, 322, 341
Heber, U., 303, 310, 311, 312, 391
Heinke, F., 210
Hellebust, J. A., 108, 206, 209, 249
Hellkvist, J., 21, 61, 63
Hely, F. W., 134
Henckel, P. A., 264, 265, 267, 272
Henderson, D. W., 24, 25, 58, 67
Henry, A. J., 186, 187, 190
Heth, D., 58
Hewitt, E. J., 146
Hietkamp, G., 139
Higgs, K. H., 25
Hignett, C. T., 48
Hillman, J. R., 335, 336
Hinckley, T. M., 66, 264, 298, 299
Hinde, R. W., 210
Hirai, N., 369
Hiron, R. W. P., 211, 328, 341, 348, 349, 350, 351, 352, 358, 362, 370, 372, 382
Hitch, C. J. B., 142
Hoad, G. V., 366
Hodges, T. K., 73
Hoffman, G. J., 62, 65
Hofler, K., 389
Holden, J. S., 217
Holmgren, P., 294
Holt, J., 2
Holz, Jr., G. G., 108
Holzner, W., 58, 60
Honert, T. H. van den, 59

Hong, T. D., 135
Hope, A. B., 87
Howe, O. W., 91
Hoysler, V., 378
Hsiao, T. C., 11, 24, 25, 48, 58, 62, 67, 157, 159, 195, 257, 258, 262, 263, 264, 266, 267, 328, 351, 381, 389, 390, 397, 398
Huang, A. H. C., 250
Huang, C.-Y., 139
Hubac, C., 222, 229
Huber, B., 59
Huber, W., 211, 212, 213, 255
Huck, M. G., 42, 43, 48
Hucklesby, D. P., 147
Huffaker, R. C., 153, 156, 158, 306, 307
Hughes, P. G., 78, 79
Humble, G. D., 336
Hurd, E. A., 11, 49, 50
Hutchinson, J., 185
Hyder, D. N., 46

I

ICAR, 9
ICRISAT, 9
Iljin, W. A., 389
Imamura, K., 117
Imbamba, S. K., 189
Imber, D., 330, 373, 386
Inglesten, B., 78
Itai, C., 48, 211, 257, 266, 335, 336, 349, 374, 379, 380, 381, 386, 397
Ivanova, R. P., 202

J

Jachymczyk, W. J., 279
Jackson, W. A., 310, 312
Jacqmard, A., 403
Jagendorff, A. T., 393
Jager, H. J., 216, 229
Jarvis, M. S., 31, 294
Jarvis, P. G., 21, 31, 59, 61, 63, 66, 290, 294, 345
Jeffree, C. E., 290, 345
Jeffrey, D. W., 93
Jenne, E. A., 91
Jennings, N. T., 141
Jensen, R. G., 285
Jeschke, W. D., 200, 202
Jetschmann, K., 166
Jodha, N. S., 5, 6, 7
Johnen, B., 51
Johnson, C. M., 246, 255
Johnson, D. A., 68
Johnson, F. J., 248, 249, 253
Johnson, H. B., 295, 302, 303, 312
Johnson, H. S., 307

Johnson, J. W., 12
Johnson, R. P. C., 290, 345
Johnson, R. R., 164, 307
Jolliffe, P. A., 310
Jolly, S. O., 147
Jones, B. L., 262
Jones, H. G., 11, 24, 291, 307, 327, 346
Jones, K., 142
Jones, K. M., 200
Jones, L. H. P., 82
Jones, L. W., 305
Jones, M. B., 289, 312, 345
Jones, M. M., 25, 26, 29, 31
Jones, O. T. G., 153
Jones, R., 93, 94
Jones, R. J., 330, 336, 337, 344, 346, 348, 375
Jones, R. L., 280
Jones, R. W., 153
Jordan, W. R., 24, 27, 58, 64, 154
Jusaitis, M., 214, 218, 229, 230
Juhasz, J., 229

K

Kadam, S. S., 154, 155, 156
Kaeppe, D. E., 396
Kahane, I., 266, 289, 298
Kalman, L., 230, 231
Kampen, J., 8
Kaneda, T., 187
Kanemasu, E. T., 60
Kaneshiro, E. S., 108
Kapoor, V. K., 186
Kappen, L., 18, 22, 31, 33, 56, 57, 65, 323, 325, 326, 327, 328
Karamanos, A. J., 31, 68, 69
Karawja, M. S., 186
Karrer, W., 175
Kasatkina, V. S., 304
Kassam, A. H., 31, 58, 68, 69
Katchalski, E., 279, 280
Katoh, S., 393
Katterman, F. R., 278
Katz, R. W., 3
Kaufmann, M. R., 58, 59, 60, 61, 62, 63, 64, 65, 66, 67, 69
Kauss, H., 108, 109, 215
Kauzmann, W., 114
Kaye, P. E., 65, 323
K'Drev, R., 241
Keck, R. W., 298, 304, 307
Keech, D. B., 127
Keeney, D. R., 49
Keith, A. D., 397
Kemble, A. R., 209, 243, 254, 255
Kemper, W. D., 74, 75

Kende, H., 336, 382, 384, 385
Kerrigan, A. P., 373, 374
Kershaw, K. A., 142, 143
Kessler, B., 189, 210
Kessly, D. S., 99, 104, 107, 110
Key, J. L., 153
Khalifa, M. M., 306
Khanna, R., 146
Kinbacher, E. J., 299, 307
Kindinger, D. I., 349
King, K. M, 65
King, R. W., 355
Kirk, M. R., 311, 312
Kirkwood, S., 200
Kirsch, M., 187
Kirst, G. O., 108, 112, 302
Kisaki, T., 285
Klein, G., 187, 188
Klein, S., 264, 266, 267, 276, 392, 394, 395, 396, 397, 398, 399, 400, 401, 403
Kleinkopf, G. E., 153, 156, 158, 306, 307
Klepper, B., 42, 43, 48, 66, 78, 79
Klepper, L., 150, 153
Kloth, T. I., 7
Kluge, M., 288, 301
Knipling, E. B., 68
Knoerr, K. R., 67, 68
Koeppe, D. E., 250, 257
Kohler, M. A., 2
Kok, B., 305
Koller, D., 290
Koontz, H. V., 82
Koretskaya, T. F., 266
Kortstee, G. J. J., 193, 202
Koseva, D., 209
Koshimizu, K., 368, 369
Koudogbo, B., 186
Köves, E., 216, 229
Kowai, A., 246, 248, 249
Kozinka, V., 45
Kozlowski, T. T., 24, 64, 295, 345
Kramer, P. J., 21, 26, 43, 48, 49, 58, 62, 65, 69, 257, 304, 392
Krantz, B. A., 8
Krause, G. H., 310, 311, 312
Krelle, E., 378
Kremer, B. P., 109
Kriedemann, P. E., 296, 297, 341, 353, 354, 356, 372, 373, 383
Krishna Sastry, K. S., 212, 214
Krochko, J. E., 272, 274
Krotkov, G., 286, 287
Krull, E., 17
Kruse, W., 331, 341, 342, 343
Ku, S. B., 310, 311
Kuhn, A. M., 189

Kuntz, I. D., 114, 115
Kuramagomedov, N. K., 164
Kurkova, E. B., 304
Kyriakopoulos, E., 67

L
Ladiges, P. Y., 69, 70
Lai, E. Y., 249, 252
Laidman, D. L., 191
Laing, D. R., 10
Laing, W. A., 286, 287, 309, 310
Lambert, R. J., 148, 149
Lane, M. D., 285
Lang, A. R. G., 104
Lange, O. L., 18, 22, 31, 33, 56, 57, 65, 318, 323, 324, 325, 326, 327, 328
Lanyi, J. K., 112, 116, 125
Larcher, W., 48, 49
Larher, F., 186, 187, 189, 190, 193, 198, 199, 203
Larkum, A. W. D., 99, 201
Larque-Saavedra, A., 367, 368
Larsen, K., 264, 277
Larter, E. N., 189
Lassoie, J. P., 64, 66
Latz, P. K., 33
Läuchli, A., 78, 376, 377
Lawlor, D. W., 62, 196, 299, 307, 308, 309, 310, 313
Lazaroff, N., 82
Leaf, G., 139
Leahy, M., 208
Lee, D. R., 24
Lee, J. A., 109, 186, 208, 209, 213, 216, 222, 229, 307
Lee, K. C., 307
Lehninger, A. L., 396
Leigh, R. A., 175, 200, 201
Leng, E. R., 146
Leopold, A. C., 296, 341, 383
Letey, J., 350
Levitt, J., 16, 17, 69, 168, 289
Levy, Y., 58, 64, 69
Lewin, L. G., 230, 231, 237, 238, 239
Lewin, S., 114, 121
Libbert, E., 378
Linser, M., 189
Linsley, R. K., 2
Lipsett, J., 48
List, P. H., 188
Little, C. H. A., 348
Liu, M. S., 108, 249
Livne, A., 381
Llopis, J., 186
Loneragan, J. F., 84
Loomis, R. S., 28, 140, 217

Lorimer, G. H., 285, 286, 311, 312
Loris, K., 272, 273
Lösch, R., 323, 326
Louis, J., 248
Loveys, B. R., 296, 297, 332, 341, 353, 354, 356, 359, 372, 373, 383, 385
Low, P. S., 117, 122
Loyn, R. H., 148
Lu, T., 246
Ludlow, M. M., 132, 294, 300
Ludwig, L. J., 286, 287, 308, 309
Luff, S. E., 393, 398, 403
Luke, H. H., 381
Lüttge, U., 78, 302, 376, 377
Luxova, M., 45
Lyons, J. M., 397

M

MacFarlane, J. D., 143
Machado, R. C. R., 230, 231
Mackay, M. A., 113
MacMillan, J., 368, 369, 372
MacPherson, H. T., 209, 243, 254, 255
Mahdi, A. A., 131, 134, 141
Mahtab, S. K., 75
Makemson, J. C., 106
Malek, F., 346
Malek, L., 262
Malhotra, S. K., 396
Malhotra, S. S., 396
Malis Arad, S., 346
Mallaby, R., 370
Mansfield, T. A., 289, 297, 312, 319, 321, 322, 327, 328, 330, 331, 332, 333, 334, 336, 337, 338, 339, 341, 342, 344, 345, 346, 348, 375, 383
Marakami, S., 393
Maranville, J. W., 164, 266
Marchelidon, J., 206
Marcus, A., 37, 253, 262, 277, 278, 403
Marion, L., 193
Marrè, E., 279, 280, 397
Marriott, F. H. C., 76
Marsh, H. V. J., 153, 156, 157, 159
Marshall, D. R., 19
Marshall, K. C., 132, 133
Martin, G. C., 369
Martyanova, K. L., 264
Mathews, R. E. F., 397
Matsuda, K., 264, 398
Mattas, R. E., 153, 155, 156, 157, 159
Maurer, R., 10, 19
May, L. H., 16, 19, 264
Mayer, A. M., 396, 397, 403
Mayo, N. S., 155
Mayr, H. H., 191

Mazelis, M., 246, 250
McCarthy, R. E., 393
McCree, K. J., 64, 69
McCully, M. E., 44
McGregor, G. R., 34
McLean, W. F. H., 187
McMichael, B. L., 24, 30, 207
McMillan, P. M., 392
McNamer, A. D., 250, 253
Measures, J. C., 106, 112, 113, 206, 222
Meers, J. L., 206
Meidner, H., 21, 299, 323, 326, 335, 336
Meister, A., 246
Meon, S., 213
Mestichelli, R. N. G., 248
Meyer, H. R., 216, 229
Meyer, M. M., 378
Meyer, R. F., 25, 68
Miflin, B. J., 150
Migsoh, H., 389
Milborrow, B. V., 332, 353, 356, 357, 359, 360, 361, 362, 368, 369, 370, 382, 385
Milburn, J. A., 45
Miler, P. M., 246
Milford, J. R., 2
Millar, B. D., 58, 60, 66
Millbank, J. W., 142
Miller, D. M., 107, 112, 113
Miller, R. J., 257, 396
Millerd, A., 276
Milthorpe, E. J., 264
Milthorpe, F. L., 16, 19, 264, 293, 338, 385
Minchin, F. R., 135, 136, 138, 141
Mitchell, D. J., 248, 249, 253
Mitchell, H. L., 155, 156
Mitra, R., 259
Mitsui, T., 368
Mittelheuser, C. J., 329, 348, 392
Mizrahi, T., 346
Mizrahi, Y., 374, 375, 376, 377, 381
Mohanty, P., 304, 305, 312
Molz, F. J., 66
Monselise, S. P., 210
Monteith, J. L., 289
Mooney, H. A., 23, 24, 48, 51, 300, 302, 306
Moore, A. W., 72, 84, 85, 93
Moore, R. T., 20, 21
Morales, M. F., 116
Moreira, T. J. S., 328, 333, 341, 342, 345
Morgan, J. M., 25, 26
Morilla, C. A., 153, 159, 160, 257, 263, 264, 267, 268
Morris, C. J., 210, 229, 243, 244, 246, 252, 254, 255
Morris, M. D., 3, 4

Moses, V., 246
Moss, D. N., 9, 11, 307
Mothes, K., 349
Motorina, M. V., 304
Mouravieff, I., 336
Moya, T. B., 11, 12
Mukherjee, I., 214
Muller, B., 307
Mulroy, T. W., 18, 19
Munda, I. M., 109
Munns, R., 25, 29, 30, 264, 379, 380, 398
Murakami, S., 304, 305
Musgrave, R. B., 291
Musolan, C., 349
Muth, W. L., 248
Muxfeldt, B., 331, 341, 342, 343

N
Naaman, R., 88
Nagl, W., 403
Naik, M. S., 150, 151, 152, 153, 154, 155, 166
Nair, T. V. R., 148
Nash, D., 127
Nason, A., 147
Nasrulhaq-Boyce, A., 153
Nathenson, B., 393
Navon, G., 126
Nawa, Y., 396, 397
Naylor, A. W., 210, 229, 230, 243, 255, 257, 304, 392
Neales, T. F., 288, 293, 301, 306
Nehez, R., 209, 214, 229
Neilson, R. E., 327
Nelchinov, I., 209
Nelsen, C. E., 30, 172, 191, 192, 195, 196, 197, 204, 216, 219, 230, 231, 233, 238
Nelson, C. D., 286, 287
Nemeth, J., 230, 231
Neubauer, M., 117, 122
Neumann, H. H., 60, 65
Nevo, Y., 386
Newman, E. I., 40, 43, 44, 45, 48, 60, 77, 79
Ng, T. T., 132
Nicholas, D. J. D., 147, 150, 151, 152
Nicou, R., 9
Nielsen, B. F., 89, 90
Nieman, R. H., 349
Nir, I., 264, 266, 267, 303, 390, 391, 392, 394, 395, 396, 398, 399, 400, 401
Nishimoto, U., 188
Nissen, P., 188
Nix, H. A., 52
Nobel, P. S., 22, 99, 104, 302
Noddle, R. C., 357, 360, 361
Noguchi, M., 246, 248, 249

Norkrans, B., 108
Norris, G., 132
Norton, R. S., 113
Noy-Meir, I., 30, 50
Nye, P. H., 74, 75, 76, 77, 78

O
Oaks, A., 248, 249, 250, 252, 253
Obendorf, R. L., 278
O'Brien, T. P., 34, 44
OECD, 2
Oertli, J. J., 31, 59
Ofer, I., 134
Ogawa, S., 126
Ogawa, Y., 368
Ogren, W. L., 285, 286, 287, 309, 310, 312
Ogunkanmi, A. B., 331, 333, 338, 339
Oguntoyinbo, J. S., 2
Oh, J. S., 25
Ohira, K., 155
Ohkuma, K., 371
Okamoto, T., 393
Oldfield, J. F. T., 200
Olsen, S. R., 74, 75
Ordin, L., 349
Orlova, T. A., 109
Orshan, G., 24
Orton, P. J., 346
Osborne, D. J., 280, 402
Osmond, C. B., 29, 30, 36, 200, 202, 285, 286, 287, 288, 289, 301, 302, 303, 309, 311, 312
Osonubi, O., 328
O'Toole, J. C., 10, 11, 12, 16, 19, 298, 307
Ozbun, J. L., 298, 307

P
Pacey, J., 274
Packer, L., 304, 305, 397
Pal, U. R., 164
Paleg, L. G., 11, 28, 104, 109, 110, 127, 154, 197, 206, 207, 208, 209, 210, 211, 212, 213, 214, 217, 218, 219, 220, 221, 222, 229, 230, 231, 232, 233, 234, 235, 244, 248, 249, 252, 254, 255, 256, 257, 258
Palfi, G., 206, 209, 214, 216, 229, 230, 231
Palfi, Z., 206, 229
Pallas, J. E., 381
Palmer, W. C., 3
Palzkill, D. A., 82
Pankhurst, C. E., 139, 140
Papadakis, J., 50
Parham, M. R., 87
Parker, J., 389
Parker, M. L., 278

Parlange, J. Y., 66
Parsons, L. R., 61, 66
Passioura, J. B., 11, 40, 45, 50, 52, 76
Pate, J. S., 136, 138, 139, 141
Pateman, J. A., 166
Patterson, A. A., 288, 293, 301
Paudler, W. W., 186
Paulhus, J. L. H., 2
Pauli, A. W., 153, 155, 156, 157, 159
Paulsen, G. M., 266, 307
Paulsen, J. M., 285
Paxton, R. G., 191
Payne, E. S., 276, 278
Payne, P. I., 278
Pearce, R. B., 191
Pearson, C. J., 385
Pedersen, A. R., 238
Pellecer, J., 186
Peña, J. I., 139
Penny, M. G., 338
Pequeux, A., 108
Pereira, J. B., 64
Perl, M., 396
Perlyuk, M. F., 109
Peterson, D. M., 147
Petrie, A. K. H., 217
Pettersson, S., 83
Peumans, W. J., 278
Peyton, C., 356
Philip, J. R., 42
Phillips, D. A., 141
Piemeisel, L. N., 294
Pierce, Jr., S. K., 109
Pierson, D. J., 248
Pinter, L., 230, 231
Pitman, M. G., 78, 82, 84, 85, 87, 89, 376, 377
Place, G. A., 74
Plaut, Z., 221, 303, 307, 349
Plummer, M. L., 61
Pochmann, A., 113
Poljakoff-Mayber, A., 88, 89, 210, 264, 266, 267, 289, 298, 303, 391, 392, 394, 395, 396, 398, 399, 400, 401
Pollard, A., 98, 104, 109, 123, 175, 200, 201
Pollauf, G., 187
Pollock, B. M., 276
Pollock, J. R. A., 190
Pollock, M., 403
Ponsana, P., 40, 45, 46
Possingham, J. V., 297
Potter, J. R., 303
Poulson, R., 276, 277
Pourrat, Y., 222, 229
Pousset, J. L., 186
Powell, J. B., 24

Powell, R. D., 24
Power, J. F., 296
Powles, S. B., 36
Prasad, S., 396
Prasad, T. G., 212, 214
Preil, W., 230
Privat, C., 186
Proskurnina, N. F., 186
Prosser, C. L., 188
Pulatova, T. P., 186
Purvis, A. C., 154
Pyliotis, N. A., 307

Q

Quarrie, S. A., 11, 24, 346
Quebedaux, B., 140
Queen, W. H., 87
Qureshi, R. H., 186, 195

R

Radhakrishnan, A. N., 246
Radin, T., 153, 156, 158, 306, 307
Rafaeli-Eshkol, D., 176, 202
Rains, D. W., 25, 27, 28, 68, 140
Raison, J. K., 397
Rajagopal, V., 148, 160, 161, 162, 209, 219
Ralph, R. K., 397
Rama Rao, S., 212, 214
Ramasastri, K. S., 4
Ramos, C., 63
Rao, N. G. P., 148
Raschke, K., 289, 292, 318, 320, 321, 323, 336, 338, 340, 375, 382, 384, 385
Ratliff, L. F., 48
Raveed, D., 132
Rawson, H. M., 22, 26, 35, 292, 293, 294, 313
Read, P. E., 378
Reed, N. R., 374
Reimold, R. J., 87
Reinhold, L., 346, 376
Reise, H. C. A., 117
Reisner, A. H., 264, 398
Rena, A. B., 246, 249, 250
Renner, O., 289
Rennie, S. D., 186, 190, 191, 200
Rentala, G. S., 4
Reporter, M., 132
Rhoades, H. F., 91
Rhodes, P. R., 264, 398
Richards, G. P., 21, 61, 63
Richards, P., 2
Richmond, A. E., 211, 341, 346, 353, 374, 375, 376, 377, 379, 381
Richter, H., 56, 58, 59, 60, 67, 68
Rickman, R. W., 350

Rifkin, A., 353
Ringler, R. L., 200
Rippin, A. J., 193, 202
Ritchie, G. A., 66
Ritchie, J. T., 52
Ritenour, G. L., 146, 147
Rivers, J., 2
Robards, A. W., 80, 81
Roberts, S. W., 67, 68
Robertson, A. V., 193
Robertson, G. A., 189
Robertson, J. G., 138
Robinson, D. R., 332, 353, 356, 362, 385
Robinson, R. A., 101, 103, 104
Rochat, E., 230, 237
Rodin, L. E., 72
Rogacheva, A. Y., 394
Rohringer, R., 191, 197
Roman, R., 277
Rorison, I. H., 74
Rosenow, D. T., 12
Ross, W. M., 11
Rotem, J., 396
Rottenberg, W., 389
Roughley, R. J., 133
Routley, D. G., 243
Ruecker, S., 186
Rundle, P. W., 18, 19
Running, S. W., 59, 63, 64, 66
Rupley, J. A., 117
Russell, J. S., 72, 84, 85, 93, 318, 319, 321
Russell, M. B., 74, 77
Rustembokova, G. B., 186
Rutter, J. C., 336
Ryan, J. G., 4, 5
Rydell, R. A., 66

S
Saddler, H. D. W., 84, 85, 87
Saffigna, P. G., 49
Sai, T., 176
Sakai, A., 202
Salim, M., 186, 195
Salter, P. J., 19
Samh, M., 189
Sanchez, M., 12
Sánchez-Díaz, M. F., 58, 65, 69, 139
Sanderson, J., 45, 80
Sandhu, G. R., 186, 195
Sankhla, N., 212
Santarius, K. A., 303, 391
Sarid, S., 279, 280
Satarova, N. A., 264, 265, 266, 267, 272, 397
Sato, S., 396

Satoh, M., 297
Sattar, A., 186, 195
Sauerbeck, D., 51
Saunders, P. F., 383
Savino, G., 280
Savitskaya, N. N., 208, 213, 216, 217
Sawhney, S. K., 150, 151, 152, 153, 154, 155, 166
Scarth, G. W., 318
Schaeffer, N., 376
Scheraga, H. A., 118
Scherings, S. G., 346, 377
Schertz, K. F., 12
Schleich, T., 114, 115, 116, 117, 118, 124, 126
Schmid, W. E., 107, 112, 113
Schnabl, H., 336
Schneider, A., 209
Schobert, B., 108, 113, 120, 122, 123, 125, 127, 201, 206, 209, 215
Schoffeniels, E., 176, 206
Schrader, L. E., 146, 147
Schrier, E. E., 118
Schubert, K. R., 141
Schultz, J. E., 48, 50
Schulze, E.-D., 18, 22, 31, 33, 56, 57, 65, 318, 323, 324, 325, 326, 327, 328
Scott, D. B., 138
Scott, N. S., 264, 379, 380, 398
Seal, S. N., 277
Seaman, J., 2
Sebestyen, R., 209, 216, 229
Seibert, G., 272, 273
Sekiya, K., 117
Sells, G. D., 257
Sen, S., 280
Servaites, J. C., 286, 310
Shah, C. B., 217
Shanan, L., 24
Shaner, D. L., 153, 159, 257
Shannon, J. D., 155
Shantz, H. L., 294
Shaposhnikova, S. V., 272
Shaw, M., 318
Sheard, R. W., 153
Shearman, L. L., 299, 307
Shepherd, W., 67
Sheriff, D. W., 21, 65, 323, 326
Shibaoka, H., 379
Shkedy-Vinkler, C., 203
Shulman, R. G., 126
Simenauer, A., 190
Simpson, G. M., 370
Simpson, J. R., 48, 108, 112, 118, 119, 120, 121
Simpson, M. I., 189

Singh, H., 186
Singh, T. N., 11, 28, 109, 197, 206, 207, 208, 209, 210, 211, 212, 217, 219, 220, 221, 230, 231, 232, 233, 234, 235, 244
Singla, R. D., 186
Sinha, S. K., 146, 148, 160, 161, 162, 209, 219
Sionit, N., 26
Slack, C. R., 307
Slatyer, R. O., 31, 49, 288, 291, 300, 323, 345
Slavik, B., 55, 389
Smith, D. L., 276
Smith, H., 191, 211
Smith, O. E., 371
Smith, T. A., 371
Smith, T. C., 203
Snowball, K., 84
Solomonson, L. P., 166
Solomos, T., 396
Somero, G. N., 109, 117, 122, 217
Sondheimer, E., 368, 372, 383
Soos, G., 187
Sorger, G. J., 147
Sosulski, F. W., 189
Spanswick, R. M., 73
Sparrow, D. H., 230, 231, 237, 238, 239
Specht, R. L., 93
Speed, D. J., 192
Spencer, D., 276
Spencer, J. F. T., 108
Spencer, M., 396
Spenser, I. D., 248
Spiegel, S., 278
Spiers, J., 200, 202
Splittstoesser, S. A., 246
Splittstoesser, W. E., 246, 249, 250
Sprent, J. I., 131, 133, 135, 139, 140
Squire, G. R., 336, 345
Sribney, M., 200
Stadelmann, E., 18, 25, 37
Stålfelt, M. G., 319, 382
Stanek, V., 186, 190
Stanley, S. O., 106
Steenbock, H., 199
Steer, B. T., 307
Steiger, E., 307
Sterne, R. E., 62, 66, 67
Stevens, R., 190
Stevenson, K. R., 60, 65, 300
Steward, F. C., 253
Stewart, C. R., 154, 210, 211, 213, 216, 217, 221, 229, 230, 243, 244, 246, 249, 250, 252, 253, 254, 255, 256, 257, 258
Stewart, G. P., 189
Stewart, G. R., 109, 186, 208, 209, 213, 216, 222, 229, 307

Stewart, W. D. P., 142
Stickler, F. C., 155, 156
Stocker, O., 32, 389
Stokes, R. H., 101, 103, 104
Stone, E. L., 63
Stone, J. E., 63
Stone, J. F., 9, 11
Stoner, L. C., 108
Storey, R., 98, 104, 109, 123, 175, 186, 188, 190, 191, 193, 194, 195, 196, 197, 200, 201, 202, 203, 204
Stowring, L., 116
Strange, R. N., 191
Strecker, H. J., 246, 250
Streich, J., 331, 341, 342, 343
Stuart, T. S., 35
Sturani, E., 277, 279, 280, 397
Subramanian, V., 1, 3, 5
Sullivan, C. Y., 11, 17, 164, 299, 306, 307
Summerfield, R. J., 135
Susplugas, J., 186
Swoboda, A. R., 75
Syme, J. R., 12
Szarek, S. R., 22, 293, 302, 303, 312

T
Tadmor, N., 24
Tageeva, B. V., 304
Tairbekov, M. G., 304
Tajima, S., 139
Takemota, T., 176
Tal, M., 330, 373, 386
Tamaki, E., 246, 248, 249
Tanford, C, 114, 126
Tanner, C. B., 49
Taylor, H. F., 354, 371, 372
Taylor, H. M., 42, 43, 48
Taylor, S. A., 25
Teague, H. J., 200
Teare, I. D., 60, 207, 208
Tempest, D. W., 206
Therrien, K. P., 230, 237
Thiessen, W. E., 371
Thimann, K. V., 379
Thomas, G. W., 75
Thomas, J. C., 27, 58, 64
Thompson, J. F., 210, 229, 243, 244, 246, 252, 254, 255
Thomson, W. W., 397
Thorbahn, P. F., 7
Thornber, J. P., 305, 312, 392, 401, 403
Thorne, S. W., 307
Thornthwaite, C. W., 6
Thorpe, T. A., 272
Thrower, S., 385
Thurtell, G. W., 60, 65, 300
Tibbitts, T. W., 82

Tindall, D. R., 107, 112, 113
Tinelli, E. T., 368, 372
Ting, I. P., 22, 293, 302, 303, 312
Tinker, P. B., 40, 41, 74, 75, 76, 77, 78
Tinus, R. W., 290, 291
Tischler, C. R., 154
Todd, G. W., 389
Tolbert, N. E., 147, 188, 285, 286
Toler, R. W., 12
Tomaszewski, M., 277, 278
Tonomura, Y., 117
Torssell, B. W. R., 23
Toupet, C., 2
Toynbee, A. J., 4
Toyosowa, I. 188
Travis, A. J., 336
Travis, R. L., 153
Tregunna, E. B., 286, 308, 310
Treharne, K. J., 306
Treichel, S., 213, 302
Trivett, N. B. A., 298
Troke, P. F., 200
Troughton, J. H., 302
Tschesche, H., 127, 215
Tu, C. M., 139
Tucker, D. J., 332, 383
Tucker, E. B., 33, 34, 37, 257, 268, 271, 272, 273, 393, 401
Tully, R. E., 216
Tung, H. F., 379
Tunstall, B. R., 27, 28, 31, 84, 91, 92
Turner, N. C., 11, 16, 17, 19, 20, 21, 22, 24, 25, 26, 29, 31, 35, 50, 52, 61, 66, 68, 150, 293, 313, 345
Tvorus, E. K., 264, 265, 266, 267, 397
Tyankova, L. A., 218, 222, 229
Tymms, M. J., 34
Tyree, M. T., 61, 67, 68
Tysiaczny, M. J., 143

U

Udayakumar, M., 212, 214
Uriu, K., 345
Utkin, L. M., 186

V

Vaadia, Y., 211, 257, 266, 349, 374, 379, 380, 381, 397
van Daal, A., 127
Vanderhoef, L. N., 139
van Dijk, H. M., 297
Vankirk, C. A., 336
van Schaik, J. C., 75
van Steveninck, R. F. M., 329, 348, 374
Varner, J. E., 259
Vasileva, N. G., 389
Vennesland, B., 166

Vieira, C., 230, 231
Vieira de Silva, J., 257, 390, 392
Viets, F. G., Jr., 74
Vincent-Marique, C., 206
Vinograd, J. R., 117
Virkar, R. A., 109
Virzo de Santo, A., 301
Vogel, H. J., 244
Volcani, T., 277
Volk, R. J., 310, 312
von Hippel, P. H., 114, 115, 116, 117, 118, 122, 123, 124, 126
von Willert, D. J., 302

W

Wadsworth, R. M., 31, 68, 69
Waggoner, P. E., 66, 345
Wagner, S., 186
Wahab, A. M. A., 135
Wain, R. L., 367, 368, 370
Waisel, Y., 86, 87, 345
Waldren, R. P., 207, 208
Wallace, D. H., 298, 307
Wallace, H. R., 213
Wallace, W., 155
Walter, C. J., 50
Walter, H., 18, 25, 37, 187, 201
Waltho, J. A., 107
Walton, D. C., 359, 362, 368, 369, 370, 372
Wample, R. L., 211, 212, 229
Wang, D., 249, 250, 252
Ward, M. E., 201
Wareing, P. F., 306
Waring, R. H., 59, 61, 63, 66
Warren, J. C., 116
Wassel, G. M., 186
Watanabe, F. S., 75
Watts, W. R., 327
Weatherley, P. E., 30, 31, 40, 42, 43, 44
Webb, E. C., 124
Webb, K. L., 109
Webb, S. J., 121
Wegmann, K., 99
Welch, R. I., 12
Welhorn, R. J., 397
Wellburn, A. R., 34, 328, 331, 333, 334, 341, 342, 345, 383
Wellburn, F. A. M., 34
Wellfare, D., 376
Wen, W.-T., 114
West, D. W., 65
West, K. R., 87
West, S. H., 397
Weyers, J. D. B., 335, 336
Wheeland, G. W., 172
Wheeler, A. W., 194
White, J. E., 393

White, R. S., 20, 21
Whiteman, P. C., 290
Wiebe, H. H., 67, 188
Wiehler, G., 193
Wilbrandt, W., 109
Wildes, R. A., 376
Wilkinson, G., 232
Williamson, A. J. P., 131, 141
Willis, W. O., 296
Willmer, C. M., 335, 336
Wilson, A. M., 46
Wilson, A. T., 308
Wilson, J. A., 338, 339
Wilson, J. M., 353
Wind, G. P., 45
Winner, W. E., 272
Winter, K., 36, 302
Wiskich, J. T., 127
Wolley, J. T., 9, 11,
Wolosiuk, R. A, 307
Wong, K.-Y., 116, 118, 122, 123
Woo, K. C., 152, 285, 286, 312
Wood, C. A., 2
Wood, J. G., 217
Woodward, R. G., 292, 294
Worrall, V. S., 133
Wray, J. L., 147
Wrench, P., 210
Wright, L., 210
Wright, N. G., 244
Wright, S. T. C., 211, 328, 329, 330, 341,
    348, 349, 350, 351, 352, 358, 362, 364,
    365, 370, 372, 382
Wuenscher, J. E., 295
Wurtz, R., 246
Wylie, R. B., 326
Wyn Jones, R. G., 73, 98, 104, 109, 123,
    175, 186, 188, 190, 191, 193, 194, 195,
    196, 197, 200, 201, 202, 203, 204

Y

Yamamoto, Y., 139
Yamane, T., 126
Yamaya, T., 155
Yancey, P. H., 109, 122, 217
Yarwood, A., 276
Yatazawa, M., 139
Yemm, E. W., 253
Yeo, A. R., 87, 200, 201
Yermanos, D. M., 62, 64, 295
Yien, C. H., 91
Yokoyama, M., 248, 249
Yopp, J. H., 107, 112, 113
Yoshida, S., 202
Younis, M. A., 155, 156

Z

Zabadal, T. J., 363
Zahn, R. K., 272, 273
Zahran, H. H., 135
Zalik, S., 262
Zee, S.-Y., 34
Zeevaart, J. A. D., 356, 362, 365, 366, 367,
    368, 370, 371
Zelitch, I., 286, 292, 318, 345
Zeller, A., 188
Zentmyer, G. A., 62, 66, 67
Zholkevich, V. N., 266, 394
Ziegler, H., 307, 336
Ziegler, I., 307
Zimmer, G., 397
Zimmerman, M. H., 63
Zlobin, V. S., 109
Zollner, J., 272, 273
Zubova, L. S., 264

Biological Index

A

Abies concolor, 63
Acacia brachybotrya, 87
  greggii, 301
  hakeoides, 87
  haropohylla, 27, 28, 31, 32, 72, 84, 91, 93
  suavelens, 93
Acanthus ilicifolius, 188
Acer saccharum, 295, 301
Aegialitis, 188
  annulata, 87
Aegiceras carniculatum, 188
Agaricus campestris, 188
Agave americana, 288, 293, 301
  deserti, 302
Agropyron, 68
Albizzia, 138, 139
Alfalfa, 187, 193, 199, 294
Alnus, 138, 139
  oblongifolia, 301
Ambrosia, 363
  artemisifolia, 363
  trifida, 363
Anabaena cylindrica, 107
Anastatica hierochuntica, 266
Aphanothece halophytica, 107, 113
Apple, 65
Apricot, 323, 328
Artemisia herba-alba, 222
Aspergillus nidulans, 166
Astrebla lappacea, 298, 392
Athel tree, 354
Atriplex, 79, 94, 95, 175
  halimus, 88
  hymenelytra, 23, 24
  sabulosa, 306, 307
  spongiosa, 89, 104, 190, 195, 197, 201
  vesicaria, 87
Avena sativa, 195, 266, 326, 353
Avicennia, 188
  marina, 85, 87
Avocado, 66, 332, 356, 359, 361, 362, 372
Azolla, 353

B

Bacillus subtilis, 106
Banksia ornata, 93

  serrata, 93
Barley, 19, 52, 78, 82, 104, 109, 123, 147, 153, 156, 158, 160–167, 188–191, 195–198, 202, 206–214, 219, 220, 230–240, 244, 248, 250, 252–258, 280, 307, 376, 377, 381, 382, 384
Barnyard grass, 294
Bean, 79, 231, 252, 253, 256, 257, 258, 348–352, 362, 369–372, 382, 383, 398
  Broad, 276, 356, 359, 385
  Castor, *see* Castor bean
  French, 359
  Green, 264
  Horse, 264
  Jack, 392
  Lima, 276
  Mung, 250
Beet, 190, 374, 391
  Red, 201
  Silverbeet, 362, 370
  Sugar, 25, 175
  Swiss chard, 246, 391
Beneckea harveyi, 106
Beta vulgaris, 190, 303, 362, 374
Black locust, 264, 298, 299, 369
Blue grama, 46
Boletus edulis, 188
Borya nitida, 31, 32, 34
Brassica, 160, 161, 162
Brigalow, 84, 85, 92
Bromus, 68
Bryum pseudotriquetrum, 273

C

Cabbage, 82
Callitriche stagnalis, 353, 356
Callitris columellaris, 87
Camissonia claviformis, 300
Capparaceae, 176
Capparis, 187
  tomentosa, 187
Carex pachystylis, 222
Carrot, 376
Castor bean, 8, 252, 276, 277, 279, 280, 366, 398
Casuarina pusilla, 93
Ceratophyllum demersum, 353
Chenopodiaceae, 190, 202, 204

481

Chenopodium vulvaria, 188
Chlorella, 166, 250, 253
  salina, 108
Chloris gayana, 195
Chlorophyceae, 142
Chrysanthemum, 187
Citris sinensis, 295, 327
Clianthus formosus, 326
Clostridium sporogenes, 106, 248
Clover, white, 135
Coffee, 344, 345
Commelina communis, 315, 317, 321,
  336–339, 383
  cyanea, 385
Coriaria, 138
Corn, 60, 65–69, 74, 155, 210, 231, 248, 250,
  252, 253, 257, 263–268, 270, 299, 300, 305,
  306
Cotton, 27, 28, 42, 45, 48, 49, 58, 64, 68, 154,
  190, 207, 218, 278, 300, 303, 355, 392
Cowpea, 8, 58, 135
Cratoneuron filicinum, 271, 274, 275
Cucumber, 164, 165, 359
  wild, 359
Cyanobacteria, 112
Cyclotella cryptica, 108, 249
  meneghiniana, 108

D
Datura, 248
Daucus carota, 195
Debaryomyces hansenii, 108
Diplachne fusca, 195
Diplotaxis tenuifolia, 190
Douglas-fir, 63, 64, 66
Dunaliella, 99, 104, 105, 110, 119, 123, 206
  viridis, 108

E
Echinocystis lobatus, 359
Enclyaena tomentosa, 354
Enteromorpha, 189
Eromophila gilesii, 93
Erythrina hypathorus, 188
Escherichia coli, 126, 244, 246, 248
Eucalyptus baxteri, 93
  oleosa, 87
  socialis, 87
  viminalis, 69, 70
Eucelia farinosa, 24

F
Ferocactus acanthodes, 22
Finger millet, 8

Flax, 48
Fraxinus pennsylvanica, 301
Fucus serratus, 109
  vesiculosus, 109

G
Gloeocapsa, 107
Glycine, 136
  max, 135
Gramineae, 45
Grape, Concord, 296

H
Hakea ulicina, 93
Halobacteria, 112, 116, 124, 125, 128, 129
Halobacterium salinarium, 107
Hammada scoparia, 31, 324
Helianthus annuus, 188, 295, 324, 356, 379
Hemlock, 61
Hordeum bulbosum, 240
  vulgare, 188, 195, 381, 384
Hornwort, 353
Horsegram, 8
Hygrohypnum luridum, 273

I
Iridophycus flaccidum, 109

J
Jerusalem artichoke, 210, 246, 248
Jojoba, 294

K
Kalanchoë diagremontiana, 288, 301

L
Labiatae, 187
Larrea divaricata, 301, 306
Leea, 354
Leek, 76
Lemna, 211
Lemon, 64, 65
Leptospermum, 94
Lettuce, 278, 397
Limonium vulgare, 187, 193, 198, 199
Lolium perenne, 89
  temulentum, 211
Lucerne, 47, 48
Lupinus, 132, 138, 248
  albus, 142
Lycium barbarum, 175

Lycopersicon esculentum, 195, 348

M

Maize, 8, 44, 45, 74, 75, 91, 146, 153, 154, 155, 159, 160, 162, 164, 196, 197, 264, 308, 318, 319, 331, 351, 356, 358, 364, 367, 368, 373, 374, 383, 384, 392, 394-402
Mangrove, 84, 85, 86, 88
Maple, 64
Marrow, 81
Medicago sativa, 139, 187
Melaleuca uncinata, 87
Mesembryanthemum crystallinum, 302
Miamiensis avidus, 108
Millet, 2, 300
 finger, *see* Finger millet
 pearl, 8
Mitchell grass, 298, 392
Modiolus demissus demissus, 109
Monochrysis lutheri, 105, 108
Monostrema nitidium, 187
Mulga, 49
Mya avenaria, 109
Myrothamnus, 34

N

Navicula, 108
Neckera crispa, 272
Nicotiana, 248
 rustica, 375
Nostoc, 142

O

Oats, 52, 278, 279, 280, 353
Ochromonas malhamensis, 108
Oedogonium, 189
Opuntia, 302
 basilaris, 22, 302, 312
 bigelovii, 302
Oryza sativa, 350

P

Pea, 99, 252, 264, 276, 277, 278, 379, 396, 397
 cowpea, *see* Cowpea
 pigeon, 8
Peach, 209
Peanut, 48, 278, 279
Peltigera, 143
Pennisetum, 212
 typhoides, 211, 255
Peperomia obtusifolia, 302
Persea americana, 295
 gratissima, 356, 359

Phaeodactylum tricornutum, 108
Phaseolus, 132, 135, 136, 138, 139
 lunatus, 276
 vulgaris, 278, 348, 359, 370
Phleum bertelonii, 335
Picea engelmanni, 65
Pine, loblolly, 308
 red, 63
Pinus, 278
 banksiana, 64
 radiata, 65
 resinosa, 64
 taeda, 58
Pisum, 135, 138, 210
 sativum, 138, 195, 277, 343
Pittosporum phillyreoides, 87
Plantago maritima, 87
Platymonas, 112
 subcordiformis, 108
 sulcica, 108
Plectonema tomasinianum, 107
Plumbaginaceae, 203
Polypodium polypodioides, 35
 vulgare, 323
Polysiphonia, 189
Polytrichum commune, 272, 273
Populus tremula, 295
Porphyra perforata, 109
Porphyridium purpureum, 108
Posidonia, 190
Prunus armeniaca, 323, 326-327
Pseudomonas aeruginosa, 106
Puccinellia maritima, 195
Pumpkin, 250, 252, 264, 398

Q

Quercus robur, 295
 velutina, 295

R

Radish, 164, 207, 212, 278
Ragweed, Great, 363
 Roman, 363
Rape, 278
Rhizobium, 131, 132, 134, 140, 141
 japonicum, 133
 leguminosarum, 133
 lupini, 133
 trifolii, 132, 133, 134
Rhizophora mucronata, 87
Rice, 2, 3, 154, 166, 233, 278, 350, 351
Ricinus, 367
 communis, 366
Robinia pseudoacacia, 298, 369
Rose, 209, 383

Rumex sanguineus, 297
Rye, 278, 280

S

Saccharomyces acidifaciens, 108
   rouxii, 104, 108
Safflower, 160–163
Salmonella oranienburg, 106
Saltbush, 294, 300
   ruby, 354
Sedge, 222
Sesame, 64
Sesamum indicum, 321, 324
Simmondsia chinensis, 295, 301
Sitka spruce, 61, 63, 290, 327
Sorghum, 2, 8, 25–32, 46, 60, 64, 65, 68, 69,
   162, 164, 208, 211, 234, 235, 293, 294, 295,
   299, 306, 307, 331, 333, 364, 367, 368, 392
Soybean, 26, 60, 68, 132, 135, 139, 140, 208,
   250, 293, 294, 299, 300, 306, 372
Spartina, 189
   x *townsendii*, 104, 191, 195
Spinach, 201, 310, 311, 312, 332, 356, 362, 371,
   372, 383, 391
Spinacia oleracea, 195, 356
Spinefex grass, 95
Stachys, 187
Stichococcus bacillaris, 108
Streptococcus faecalis, 106
Stylosanthes humilis, 23
Suaeda australis, 354
   maritima, 87, 195, 201
   monoica, 87, 104, 109, 195, 197
Sunflower, 24, 31, 43, 60, 62, 69, 160, 211, 212,
   294, 296, 303, 304, 307, 308, 356, 379
Synechoccus, 107, 112

T

Tabotia elegans, 393, 398, 399
Tamarix, 210
   aphylla, 354
Taraxacum officinale, 319
Tetrahymena pyriformis, 108
Tidestromia oblongifolia, 306, 307
Tobacco, 61, 66, 154, 211, 248, 255, 374–376,
   379, 380, 381, 398
Tolypella intricata, 99
Tomato, 62, 63, 78, 79, 188, 298, 299, 308, 348,
   350, 351, 356, 360, 362, 369, 370, 371, 373
   flacca, 386
Tortula, 34

ruralis, 35, 37, 268–275
Trifolium, 135
   glomeratum, 132, 134
   repens, 135
   subterraneum, 133
Triglochin maritima, 87, 109, 209, 216, 222
Trigonella arabica, 134
Triodia irritans, 87, 95
Triticum aestivum, 326, 348
   vulgare, 195
Tsuga canadensis, 61
Tulipa gesneriana, 321
Turnip, 243

U

Ulothrix, 189
Ulva lactuca, 189

V

Valonia, 98
Vauquelinia californica, 301
Vicia, 132
   faba, 31, 58, 68, 69, 135, 138, 140, 276, 332,
   356, 359, 385
Vigna, 135
   luteola, 324
   unguiculata, 58, 135
Vitadinia cuneata, 87
Vitis lubruscana, 296, 297

W

Walnut, black, 64
Water starwort, 353, 356
Wedelia biflora, 190
Wheat, 2, 3, 19, 24–30, 37, 44, 46, 52, 58, 78,
   148, 150, 151, 152, 154, 160, 161, 162, 164,
   191, 197, 201, 209, 212, 218, 220, 250, 264,
   265, 277–280, 294, 296, 299, 300, 308, 318,
   319, 329, 330, 348, 350, 351, 355, 356, 360,
   361, 364, 365, 377–380, 392, 398, 403

X

Xanthium strumarium, 292, 338, 340
Xerophyta villosa, 34, 393

Z

Zea mays, 68, 153, 188, 195, 262, 295, 320
Zygocactus, 302

Subject Index

A

Abscisic acid, 78, 160, 295, 335, 348
  accumulation, in guard cells, 335
  accumulation, water potential threshold, 363, 364, 365
  action on stomata, 329, 336
  application, 344
  bound form, 362
  chloride transport, 377
  chloroplasts as sites of formation, 330
  concentration increase with heat stress, 349
  concentration increase with water deficit, 329, 349, 332, 357
  concentration in plant, 355, 356, 366, 384
  control of plant water relations, 330
  degradation, 368, 369
  endogenous concentration, 330, 341
  endogenous location, 332
  glucose ester, 362, 369
  intracellular location of synthesis, 332
  lack of synthesis in epidermis, 332
  leaf chlorophyll, 375
  mutants lacking ability to synthesize, 330
  oxidation, 359
  penetration of chloroplast envelope, 333
  potassium distribution, 337
  potassium uptake, 374
  proline accumulation, 211
  redistribution, 356
  release from chloroplast, 332, 333
  residual level, 341
  root growth, 378
  seedling survival in water deficit, 378
  stomatal response, 332, 336, 338, 341, 383, 384
  symplastic movement, 335
  synthesis, 354, 359, 360, 361, 362, 366, 386
  translocation, 366
  waterlogging, 350, 351
  xylem exudate, 373
1-abscisyl-β-D-glucopyranoside, 368, 370
Alanine, 105, 109
β-alaninebetaine, 173, 175, 176, 187, 193, 194, 198, 203
Allantoin, 138, 139
Allelopathy, 50
Amino acids, role as osmoregulants, 109
α-aminobutyrate, 216

γ-aminobutyrate, 106, 250
Ammonia, detoxification, 217
Amphiphile binding, 114, 125
Amphiphiles, 113
α-amylase, 280
Anti-transpirant, 333, 344, 345, 346
Apoplastic water, 32
Arabinose, 120
Arabitol, 105, 108, 119
Arginase, 246
Arginine, 246, 252, 253, 255
Asparagine, 138, 216, 244
Aspartate, 250

B

Betaine, 99, 104, 110, 111, 113, 122, 123, 125, 128, 129
  accumulation, 30, 94, 95
  as osmoregulant, 107, 109
  protein stabilization, 122
  structure, 123
Betaines, 172
  distribution in higher plants, 177–186
Blue-green algae, 113
Boundary layer resistance, 289, 290, 291, 318, 322
Bound water, 115, 216
Bulk elastic modulus, 30, 31
Bundle sheath cells, 287, 312, 392

C

C_3 pathway, 18, 21, 284
C_3 to CAM transition, 302
C_4 pathway, 18, 21, 36, 284, 287, 312
Calcium transport, 82
Calvin cycle, 284, see also C_3 pathway
Carbon balance in drought, 294
Carbon dioxide
  compensation point, 298, 299
  exchange, 327, 345
Carboxylic acids, accumulation, 30
Casparian strip, 44, 80
Cavitation in xylem, 45
Chemical potential
  definition, 101
  of water, 101

485

Chlorocholine chloride, structure, 189
Chlorophyll
  bleaching, 36
  content of leaf, 232
  loss on water deficit, 392
  synthesis on rehydration, 34
Chloroplast membranes
  loss during water deficit, 392
  permeability to abscisic acid, 358
Chloroplasts
  abscisic acid synthesis, 361, 383
  effect of water deficit on structure, 304, 391,
    392
  structure following rehydration, 34
  vesiculation, 392
Choline, 188
Choline-O-phosphate, 188, 189
Choline-O-sulphate, 172, 189
Chromatin, aggregation, 267, 399, 400
Citrulline, 138, 139
Citrus, 58, 63, 66, 69, 187,
    see also Biological Index
Clovers, 132,
    see also Biological Index
Coelocanth, 109
Cold hardiness, exogenous abscisic acid, 353
Compatible solute, 99, 112, 120–124, 127–130,
    215
Competition, for water, 51, 52
Conservation, of water, 52
Cortex, root, 73
Crassulacean acid metabolism (CAM), 36,
    284, 287, 288, 292, 301, 302, 312
Cristaea, biogenesis, 396
Crop management, 9
Cropping systems, 9
Cuticle, 22, 70
Cuticular resistance to water loss, 293, 303
Cutin, 98
Cyclohexanetetrol, 105, 108, 120
Cycocel, 220
Cytochrome oxidase, 396
Cytokinin, 379
  effect of water deficit on concentration, 381
  xylem sap, 374, 379

D

Dark respiration, 235
Dehydrogenase activity, 232
Desert ephemerals, 19, 37
Desert perennials, 20
Desert plants, 49, 56
Desiccation injury, 235
Desiccation tolerance, 11, 267, 281, 300
Desiccation-tolerant plants, 32, 34, 36
Developmental plasticity, 19

Diffusive permeability, effect of abscisic acid,
    376
Dihydrophaseic acid, 362, 366, 372
5-dimethylsulphoniopentanoate, 190
β-dimethylsulphoniopropionate, 189
DNA, condensation with water deficit, 267
Drought
  social and economic consequences, 2–8, 15
  susceptible regions, 1–9, 13, 23, 24, 326
Drought avoidance, 16, 70
Drought escape, 16, 17, 19, 20
Drought resistance, 11, 18, 19, 23, 24, 25, 37,
    55, 56, 281, 283, 295, 302
  abscisic acid, 353, 367
  adaptations, 57
  breeding, 9–12, 19
  definition, 52
  natural communities, 17
  mechanisms, 10, 17, 35
  photosynthesis, 313
  plant water status, 31, 59
  productivity, 35
  protoplasmic, 32
  root system, 49, 62
  selection for, 10, 12
  survival, 35
  time scale, 39
  types, 16
Drought tolerance, 16, 17, 20, 24, 67

E

Elasmobranchs, 109
Elasticity of cells, 28, 31
Electrostatic binding, 125
Endodermis, 44, 73, 135
  ion diffusion, 80
Enzyme activity, solute effect, 116, 121
Ephemerals, 17, 18, 26
Epidermal cells, source of solutes, 336
Epidermal strip, stomatal response, 323
Epidermis, resistance, 21, 23, 318
Erythritol, 108, 119
Ethylene, production during water deficit, 379,
    380
Ethylene glycol, 120, 129
Evaporation from soil, 49, 50, 53
Evaporative surface area, 24
Evapo-transpiration demand, 4, 322
Evergreen sclerophylls, 35
Excitation energy, dissipation, 311

F

Famine, 2
Farnesol, 331, 333, 334, 360
Farnesyl pyrophosphate, 333

Fish, 109
Flag leaf, nitrate reductase activity, 161
Floridoside, 109
Food preference, 2
Fructose, 30, 120
Fungi, 396,
   see also Biological Index

G

α-galactosyl glycerol, 120, *see also*
   Isofloridoside
Gaseous diffusion resistance, 289, 290, 291,
   300
Geraniol, 334
Geranylgeraniol, 334
Gibberellic acid, 212
Glucose, 30, 107
Glucose-6-phosphate dehydrogenase, 119, 123
α-glucosylglycerol, 107, 112, 120
Glutamatic acid, 105, 106, 111, 216, 244, 246,
   249, 250, 255
Glutamic semialdehyde, 246, 252
Glutamine, 106, 138, 216, 250
Glutamine-γ-semialdehyde, 246
Glutamine synthetase, 164, 165
Glutamylkinase, 248
γ-glutamylphosphate, 244
γ-glutamylphosphate reductase, 244
Glycerol, 105, 110, 111, 118, 119, 120, 123, 127,
   129
   accumulation, 99
   breakdown, 110
   metabolism, 105
   osmoregulation, 104, 108
Glycine, 105, 138, 139, 285, 308
Glycinebetaine, 175, 176, 190, 191, 193, 200
   accumulation, 175, 194–197
   biosynthesis, 191, 192
   degradation, 197, 198
   enzyme function, 201
   halophytes, 176
   location in cell, 201, 202
   role, 200, 202, 203, 204
   structure, 173
Grana, effect of water deficit, 391
Guard cells, 316, 321, 328, 336

H

Halophytes, 26, 86, 88
Heat tolerance, 11
Herzynine, 174, *see also* Histidinebetaine
Hill activity, loss in water deficit, 390
Histidinebetaine, 174, 188
Holocephalans, 109

Homobetaine, 173, *see also*
   β-alaninebetaine
Homostachydrine, 174, *see also*
   Pipecolatebetaine
Humidity, stomatal response, 322, 323, 326
Hydraulic conductivity, 21, 62, 63, 66, 376
Hydraulic resistance, 60
Hydrogen evolution by nodules, 142
Hydrophobic interactions in proteins, 114, 116
Hydroxymethyl abscisic acid, 368, 369
Hydroxyproline, 253
Hydroxyprolinebetaine, 174, 176
Hypaphorine, 174, *see also*
   Tryptophanbetaine

I

Incipient drying of cell surfaces, 323
Indeterminate growth habit, 19
Infra-red photography, 12
Inorganic ions, accumulation, 30, 84, 85
Intercellular spaces in root cortex, 44
Ions
   availability in soil, 77
   effect on water structure, 114
   flux to root surface, 75
   movement in root, 73, 78, 80, 81, 83
   role in osmoregulation, 112
   uptake from soil, 71–74, 76, 77, 79, 82, 89, 95
Isofloridoside, 105, 108, 109, *see also*
   α-galactosyl glycerol
Isopentenyl pyrophosphate, 333

K

α-keto-δ-aminovaleric acid, 246, 248
Kranz anatomy, 18, 287

L

Land-water management, 9
Leaf conductance, 64, 65, 323, 324, 325
Leaf rolling, 12
Leaf survival, relationship to proline
   accumulation, 233
Leaf temperature, 23, 24
   effect on photorespiration, 310
Leaf water potential, 57, 58, 59, 66
   critical level for abscisic acid synthesis, 363,
      364, 365
   lower limit for survival, 58
Lenticels, 140
Lichens, 33, 142, 143
   recovery from drought, 142
Light intensity, stomatal response, 318, 321
Lipid droplets, 396, 401
Liquid-phase resistances to water flow, 59

M

Malic acid, 288, 302, 312
Malic dehydrogenase, 201, 216, 396
Maltose, 120
Mannitol, 105, 112, 119
    role as osmoregulant, 108, 109
Matric potential, 67
Mechanical resistance of soil, 48
Membranes, regeneration following water deficit, 393
Mesophyll cells, response to water deficit, 392
Mesophyll resistance to CO_2 uptake, 289–301
Mesophytic plants, 56
Messenger RNA, 271, 280
Methyl-abscisate, 370
Methylamine compounds, as osmoregulants, 109
Mevalonic acid, 332, 354, 361, 372
Mineral nutrients,
    movement to root surface, 74
    root growth, 48
Mitochondria, 395, 396
    effect of water deficit, 394
    enzyme activity, 394, 397
    structure after rehydration, 34, 396
    uncoupling due to water deficit, 394
Molybdenum, 147, 150, 156
Mosses, 33, 390, 393,
    see also Biological Index
Myo-inositol, 121

N

NADH-oxidase, 157, 159
NADP-glyceraldehyde phosphate dehydrogenase, 307
NADP-malate dehydrogenase, 307
Nerolidol, 334
Nitrate
    accumulation, 146, 155
    assimilation, 146, 150, 167
    content, 156, 159, 162
    flux, 160
    mobilization, 162
    reduction, 152
    see also Nitrate reductase
Nitrate reductase, 146, 147, 156, 168, 217
    activation, 166
    degradation, 155
    enzyme structure, 147
    half-life, 160
    inactivation, 154, 166
    in vitro assay, 147
    in vivo assay, 147
    properties, 146, 155
    regulation, 150, 153
    synthesis, 153

Nitrate reductase activity, 147, 148, 153, 155, 163, 167
    effect of nitrate flux, 153, 159
    effect of proline, 162
    effect of temperature, 156, 164
    effect of water deficit, 148, 153–157, 160, 161, 162, 164–167
    inhibition, 155
    potential, 147
    recovery on rehydration, 153
    relationship to growth, 146, 148
    relationship with polyribosome content, 159
    role of light, 150
    stability after a period of stress, 159
Nitrite reductase, 150, 156, 164
Nitrogen
    accumulation, 153, 168
    assimilation, 156
    fixation, 131, 132, 140
        by lichens, 143
    stress, 145
Nitrogenase, 141, 142
Nodulation, failure in dry soil, 134
Nodules,
    determinate, 135
    development, 134
    effect of photosynthesis on activity, 139
    gaseous diffusion, 140
    hydrogen evolution, 141
    indeterminate, 135
    production following stress, 135
    shedding during water deficit, 135
    transport, 136
    types, 135
    water status, 136, 137
    vascular system, 136, 137
Nucleus, changes with water deficit, 399

O

Obligate halophiles, 112
Organelles, effect of water deficit, 390
Organic acids, accumulation, 30
Organic solutes, 117, 118, 128
Osmiophilic droplets, 393, see also Lipid droplets
Osmolality, definition, 103
Osmolarity, relationship to osmotic potential, 84
Osmoregulation, 30, 98, 99, 127, 208, 215, 328
    control, 105, 110
    in organelles, 99
    properties of suitable solutes, 111
Osmotic adjustment, 26–30, 68, 295, see also Osmoregulation
Osmotic potential, 18, 67
    expressed sap, 87

leaf, 95
relationship to vacuole osmolarity, 86
role in stomatal opening, 84
Osmotic pressure, 67
definition, 101, 102
Osmotica, role of ions, 83
Ornithine, 246, 255
Ornithine cyclase, 248
Oxygenase activity, 285
Oxyneurin, *see* Glycinebetaine
3-oxystachydrine, *see* 3-hydroxyproline
betaine

P

Pararhizal water flow, 40
Perirhizal water flow, 40, 41
Peristomal transpiration, 65, 326
Permeability
of root cell walls to water, 44, 45
of the soil, 49
Phaseic acid, 362, 366, 368, 369, 372, 384
Phenylalanine ammonia lyase, 157
Phenylmercuric acetate, 345, 360
Phosphatase activity, 392
Phosphate uptake from soil, 75
Phosphoenolpyruvate, 284
Phosphoenolpyruvate carboxylase, 156, 287,
288, 302, 307, 312
3-phosphoglyceric acid, 284, 285, 308
Phosphoglycolate, 285
Phosphorylation, in chloroplast, 390
Photochemical activity, 303
Photochemical efficiency, 296
Photochemical inhibition at low water
potential, 305
Photodestruction of chlorophyll, 35
Photoinhibition of photosynthesis, 36, 305
Photo-oxidation, 305
Photophosphorylation, 304
Photorespiration, 285, 287, 307, 308, 309, 311,
312
dissipation of photochemical energy, 36
recycling of CO_2, 312
stoichiometry, 286
Photosynthesis, 23, 24
inhibition by endogenous compounds, 297
inhibition by O_2, 286, 287
recovery after water deficit, 296, 297
response to water deficit, 296, 299
stoichiometry, 286
thermal inactivation, 306
water potential, 291, 298
Photosynthetic efficiency, 283
Photosynthetic enzymes, light-activated, 307
Pipecolatebetaine, 174, 193
Plant persistence, 16

Plasmalemma, 44, 401
Plasmodesmata, ion movement, 73
Poikilohydric plants, 20, 32, 33, 35, 36
Pollen, 217
Polyols, 111, 129
enzyme inhibition, 120
osmoregulation, 119
variation with environment, 104
Polypeptide synthesis, decline during seed
drying, 276
Polyribosome content, decline with water
deficit, 157, 279, *see also* Polysomes
Polysomes, 262, 272, 281
activity, 280
decline during seed drying, 276
loss in water deficit, 262, 264, 269, 273, 276,
397, 398
population in shoot apex, 398
reassembly following stress, 275, 398
Porometer, 12, 322, 323
Potassium
accumulation, 30
concentration and stomatal opening, 338
protein stability, 128
Pre-sowing drought hardening, 264
Pressure chamber, 12
Productivity, 8, 16
Proline, 29, 104, 110–113, 122–128, 154, 162,
163, 173, 176
abscisic acid and accumulation, 211
accumulation, 30, 34, 94, 95, 105, 196, 197,
206, 209, 213, 219, 232, 254, 258
and frost resistance, 237
and senescence, 217, 218
with time, 209
amphiphilic character, 122
biosynthesis, 244–249, 254, 255, 256
compartmentation, 210, 256
concentration in roots, 210
cycocel and accumulation, 220, 221
cytokinin and accumulation, 212
dehydrogenase, 250
distribution in plant, 209, 210
diurnal variation in concentration, 209
effect of relief of water deficit, 198, 211
effect of specific ions on accumulation, 213
effect on enzyme activity, 216
effect on nitrate reductase, 162
exogenous application, 221, 222
high temperature and accumulation, 213
incorporation into protein, 253
interaction with protein, 126, 215
leaf survival and accumulation, 234
low temperature and accumulation, 214, 236
metabolism after stress, 235
oxidation, 216, 249–257
oxidase, 250

Proline—continued
relationship with stress resistance, 219, 220, 230, 231, 234, 235
role as osmoregulant, 106, 108, 109
role of accumulation, 214
salinity and accumulation, 213, 214, 226–230, 236
seasonal variation in content, 209
selection for accumulation, 238, 240
translocation, 216
variation in accumulation between species, 222–226
variation in accumulation within species, 230, 231, 236, 237, 239
water potential and accumulation, 206, 207, 208
Prolinebetaine, 172, 173, 176, 190, 193, 199
n-propanol, 118
Proplastid development and water deficit, 392
Protein
conformation, 115
denaturation with dehydration, 391
destabilization by organic solutes, 115, 118
salting-in, 113, 116, 124
salting-out, 113
solubility, effect of ions, 113
Protein-solvent interactions, 117
Protein synthesis, 261, 264, 278, 281
complex-fate during drying, 276, 277, 281
decrease with water deficit, 257, 258, 262, 266, 270, 397
and drought resistance, 282
hardening during water deficit, 265
relationship with proline accumulation, 258
resumption after water deficit, 272, 274, 278, 280
tolerance to water deficit, 274
Protoplasmic tolerance of desiccation, 25, 32
Δ'-pyrroline-2-carboxylic acid, 246, 248
Δ'-pyrroline-5-carboxylate dehydrogenase, 213, 252
Δ'-pyrroline-5-carboxylate reductase, 213, 246, 248, 249, 250, 255
Δ'-pyrroline-5-carboxylic acid, 244, 246, 248–252, 255
Pyruvate, 284
Pyruvate, P_i dikinase, 307

Q

Quantum yield of photosynthesis, 284, 304, 305, 306
Quasi-diffusion resistance of carboxylation, 291
Quaternary ammonium compounds, 172

R

Radial flow of water across root, 43, 44, 45
Radiation absorption, 23
Rainfall deficit, 15, 16
Ratoon crop, 7
Reflectance characteristics of leaves, 23, 24
Relative water content, 68, 69
Reproductive efficiency, 16
Resistance to flow of water, 21, 60, 61
Resurrection plants, 25, 32, 33, 93
Rhizobium
infection of roots, 132
rhizosphere populations, 133
survival in dry soil, 132
Ribonuclease, 267, 268, 270
Ribose-5-phosphate isomerase, 307
Ribose-5-phosphate kinase, 307
Ribosomes, fate during water deficit, 263, 270
Ribulose-1,5-bisphosphate, 284
Ribulose-1,5-bisphosphate carboxylase
see RuBP carboxylase
RNA synthesis, 266, 272, 278
Root absorbing power, 78
Root
cortex, 42, 43, 135
death, 93
density, 20, 50
distribution, 62, 94
growth, 48
growth, ratio to shoot growth, 20, 48, 49, 51, 53
hairs, 43, 134
resistance to water flow, 11, 21, 40, 42, 44, 45, 50, 52, 60, 79
shrinkage, 42, 43
suberization, 19, 50
system, 41, 47, 48, 51, 93
water potential, 58
water uptake, 41, 42
Rooting patterns, 11, 20
Rooting zone, 50
RuBP carboxylase, 156, 284, 286, 287, 292, 306, 307, 308, 310

S

Salt crystallization, effect on leaf reflectance, 24
Salting-out of macromolecules, 113, 116
Screening for drought resistance, 10, 12
Seeds, effects of water deficit on ultrastructure, 390, 396
Seminal roots, 45, 46, 47, 52
Serine, 105, 285, 308
Sodium chloride, effect on growth, 88
Soil water deficit, 15, 61

Solute accumulation, 25–30, *see also* Osmoregulation
Solute–macromolecule interactions, 125
Solute potential in guard cells, 336, *see also* Osmotic potential
Solutes, root surface, 43, 76
Solution flow in soil, 75
Solvent activity, 100
Sorbitol, 108
Stability index, 219, 232
Stachydrine, *see* Prolinebetaine
Starch granules, reassembly after rehydration, 34
Stele, 42, 43, 46, 73
Stomata, wax deposits, 70
Stomatal closure, 19, 22, 58, 316
    abscisic acid, 329, 332, 382
    carbon dioxide, 316, 320
    effect on chlorophyll stability, 35
    farnesol, 331
    in wind, 318
    mechanical stimulation, 322
    partial, 327
    water deficit, 296, 326, 328
Stomatal conductance to CO_2, 69, 308
Stomatal control of water loss, 11, 21, 64
Stomatal opening, relationship with abscisic acid concentration, 384
Stomatal resistance, 290, 291
Stomatal response
    effect of KCl, 339
    effect of re-watering, 341, 342, 351
    to abscisic acid, 338, 340, 356, 358, 381
    to CO_2, 318, 319, 321, 338
    to humidity, 65, 322, 323, 326
    to water deficit, species differences, 64
    to wilting, 319
Stored water, 52
Stress avoidance, 316
Stress hardening, 69
Stress resistance, 220
Stress tolerance, 328
Structural integrity, role of disulphide bonds, 389
Suberin, 45, 80, 98
Submicroscopic structure, effects of water deficit, 390, 392
Subsidiary cells, 336
Substomatal cavity, CO_2 concentration, 318
Succulent plants, 19, 22, 35, 36
Sucrose
    as osmoregulant, 107
    enzyme inhibition, 120
Sucrose accumulation, 30
Sugar phosphates, 308
Sugars

accumulation in water deficit, 29
    water-compatability, 121
Sulphonium compounds, 172
Surface wax, effect on reflectance, 23
Symplastic ion transport, 73, 81
Symplastic water, 32

T
Terpenoid biosynthesis, 334
Threitol, 129
Threonine, 106
Thylakoid membranes, 304, *see also* Chloroplast membranes
Tissue elasticity, 25, 30
Tonoplast, 44, 401
Transfer cells, 136, 138
Transpiration, 65, 315, 326, 329, 348
Trehalose, 107
Trigonelline, 172, 174, 187, 190, 193
Trimethylamine, 188
Tryptophanbetaine, 174, 188
Turgor
    diurnal variation, 67
    pressure, 24, 67
    maintenance, 24, 25, 26, 29, 30
    see also Osmoregulation

U
Urea, role as osmoregulant, 109

V
Vacuole, volume ratio to cytoplasm, 98
Vapour gap between soil and root, 42, 43
Vapour pressure deficit, stomatal response, 322, 323, *see also* Stomatal response to humidity
Vines, 372
Violaxanthin, 93, 371, 372

W
Water activity, 98, 100, 103, 127
Water conservation, 319, 322, 327, 344
Water deficit
    after effects, 341
    interaction with nitrogen supply, 90, 91
Water extraction by plants, 50
Water flow, 59
    across root, 42, 44
    along cell walls, 45
    effect on sulphate movement, 82
    from soil to shoot, 40
    transport equation, 59

Water infiltration, 49
Water potential
  bulk leaf, 323
  components, 67, 83
  definition, 102
  incipient plasmolysis, 68
  plant, 22
  in semi-arid plants, 84
  variations, 60, 61, 85
Water release curve, 31, 32
Water stored in plant, 66
Water structure, 114, 120, 122, 127
Water uptake by root, 41, 42
Water use efficiency, 19, 23, 24, 292, 294, 295,
    301, 327, 328, 329, 342–346

Wax in stomata, 70
Wilting, 63
  effect on radiation absorption, 23
  stomatal response, 319
Wind, stomatal closure, 318

X
Xanthoxin, 354, 370
Xeromorphic plants, 26, 69
Xylem vessels in roots, 45, 46

Y
Yield stability, 10

1 2 3 4 5 6 7 8 9 0
A B C D E F G H I J